THE COLLECTED WORKS OF

ABRAHAM LINCOLN

THE COLLECTED WORKS OF

ABRAHAM LINCOLN

THE ABRAHAM LINCOLN ASSOCIATION

SPRINGFIELD, ILLINOIS

V

ROY P. BASLER, *EDITOR*

MARION DOLORES PRATT AND LLOYD A. DUNLAP
ASSISTANT EDITORS

RUTGERS UNIVERSITY PRESS

NEW BRUNSWICK, NEW JERSEY

SOURCES
AND LOCATION SYMBOLS

DESCRIPTION OF SOURCES

THE following symbols provide a description of sources as cited at the beginning of the first footnote to each item. In addition to the customary symbols for describing manuscripts, the editors have employed symbols or single words to identify other sources which have been cited repeatedly in the first footnote.

AD	Autograph Document
ADS	Autograph Document Signed
ADf	Autograph Draft
ADfS	Autograph Draft Signed
AE	Autograph Endorsement
AES	Autograph Endorsement Signed
AL	Autograph Letter
ALS	Autograph Letter Signed
ALS copy	Autograph Letter Signed, copied by Lincoln and preserved in his papers
Copy	Copy not by Lincoln
D	Document
DS	Document Signed
Df	Draft
DfS	Draft Signed
ES	Endorsement Signed
F	Facsimile—following any of the preceding symbols
LS	Letter Signed
P	Photostat—following any of the preceding symbols

Angle	*New Letters and Papers of Lincoln.* Compiled by Paul M. Angle. Boston and New York: Houghton Mifflin Company, 1930.
Herndon	*Herndon's Lincoln: The True Story of a Great Life.* By William H. Herndon and Jesse W. Weik. 3 volumes. Chicago, New York, and San Francisco: Belford, Clarke & Company, [1889].
Hertz	*Abraham Lincoln: A New Portrait.* By Emanuel Hertz. 2 volumes. New York: Horace Liveright, Inc., 1931.
Lapsley	*The Writings of Abraham Lincoln.* Edited by Arthur Brooks Lapsley. 8 volumes. New York: P. F. Collier and Son, 1905.

SOURCES

NH   *Complete Works of Abraham Lincoln.* Edited by John G. Nicolay and John Hay. 12 volumes. New York: Francis D. Tandy Company, 1905.

OR   *The War of the Rebellion: A Compilation of the Official Records of the Union and Confederate Armies.* 4 series; 70 "volumes"; 128 books. Washington: Government Printing Office, 1880-1901. Roman numerals are used for Series, Volume, and Part (if any); pages are in arabic.

Tarbell   *The Life of Abraham Lincoln. . . .* By Ida M. Tarbell. 2 volumes. New York: The Doubleday & McClure Company, 1900.

Tracy   *Uncollected Letters of Abraham Lincoln.* Edited by Gilbert A. Tracy. Boston and New York: Houghton Mifflin Company, 1917.

Wilson   *Uncollected Works of Abraham Lincoln.* Edited by Rufus Rockwell Wilson. 2 volumes. Elmira, New York: Primavera Press, 1947-1948.

LOCATION SYMBOLS

CCamStJ   St. John's Seminary Library, Camarillo, Calif.

CLCM   Los Angeles County Museum Library, Los Angeles, Calif.

CSmH   Henry E. Huntington Library, San Marino, Calif.

CoHi   State Historical Society of Colorado, Denver, Colo.

CoU   University of Colorado Library, Boulder, Colo.

Ct   Connecticut State Library, Hartford, Conn.

CtHi   Connecticut Historical Society, Hartford, Conn.

CtLHi   Litchfield Historical Society, Litchfield, Conn.

CtSoP   Pequot Library, Southport, Conn.

CtWat   Watertown Library Association, Watertown, Conn.

CtY   Yale University Library, New Haven, Conn.

DLC   Library of Congress, Washington, D. C.

DLC-HW   Herndon-Weik Collection, Library of Congress

DLC-RTL   The Robert Todd Lincoln Collection of the Papers of Abraham Lincoln, Library of Congress

DLM   Lincoln Museum, Ford's Theatre, National Park Service, Washington, D. C.

DNA   National Archives, Washington, D. C. All additional abbreviations and numbers given with this symbol are those employed by the National Archives at the time the manuscript was located.

DNM   National Museum Library, Washington, D. C.

DeHi	Historical Society of Delaware Library, Wilmington, Del.
DeWI	Wilmington Institute Free Library, Wilmington, Del.
I-Ar	Archives Division, Illinois State Library, Springfield, Ill.
IBloHi	McLean County Historical Society, Bloomington, Ill.
ICHi	Chicago Historical Society, Chicago, Ill.
ICU	University of Chicago Library, Chicago, Ill.
IDecJ	James Millikin University Library, Decatur, Ill.
IFre	Freeport Public Library, Freeport, Ill.
IHi	Illinois State Historical Library, Springfield, Ill.
IJI	Illinois College Library, Jacksonville, Ill.
ISLA	The Abraham Lincoln Association, Springfield, Ill.
IU	University of Illinois Library, Urbana, Ill.
IaCrM	Iowa Masonic Library, Cedar Rapids, Iowa
IaDaM	Davenport Public Museum, Davenport, Iowa
IaHA	Iowa State Department of History and Archives, Des Moines, Iowa
In	Indiana State Library, Indianapolis, Ind.
InFtwL	Lincoln National Life Foundation, Fort Wayne, Ind.
InHi	Indiana Historical Society, Indianapolis, Ind.
InLTHi	Tippecanoe County Historical Association, Lafayette, Ind.
InU	Indiana University Library, Bloomington, Ind.
KyBC	Berea College Library, Berea, Ky.
KyU	University of Kentucky Library, Lexington, Ky.
LU	Louisiana State University Library, Baton Rouge, La.
MB	Boston Public Library, Boston, Mass.
MCon	Free Public Library, Concord, Mass.
MFai	Millicent Library, Fairhaven, Mass.
MH	Harvard University Library, Cambridge, Mass.
MHi	Massachusetts Historical Society, Boston, Mass.
MS	Springfield Library Association, Springfield, Mass.
MSHi	Connecticut Valley Historical Society, Springfield, Mass.
MdAA	Hall of Records, State of Maryland, Annapolis, Md.
MdHi	Maryland Historical Society, Baltimore, Md.
MeHi	Maine Historical Society, Portland, Me.
MiD	Detroit Public Library, Detroit, Mich.
MiK-M	Kalamazoo Public Library Museum, Kalamazoo, Mich.
MiU-C	William L. Clements Library, University of Michigan, Ann Arbor, Mich.

MiU-Hi	Michigan Historical Collection, University of Michigan, Ann Arbor, Mich.
MnHi	Minnesota Historical Society, St. Paul, Minn.
MnSM	Macalester College Library, St. Paul, Minn.
MoHi	State Historical Society of Missouri, Columbia, Mo.
MoSHi	Missouri Historical Society, St. Louis, Mo.
N	New York State Library, Albany, N. Y.
NAuE	Fred L. Emerson Foundation, Auburn, N. Y.
NBLiHi	Long Island Historical Society, Brooklyn, N. Y.
NBuG	Grosvenor Library, Buffalo, New York
NBuHi	Buffalo Historical Society, Buffalo, N. Y.
NDry	Southworth Library, Dryden, N. Y.
NHi	New-York Historical Society, New York City
NIC	Cornell University Library, Ithaca, N. Y.
NN	New York Public Library, New York City
NNC	Columbia University Library, New York City
NNP	Pierpont Morgan Library, New York City
NRU	University of Rochester Library, Rochester, N. Y.
NSh	John Jermain Memorial Library, Sag Harbor, N. Y.
NSk	Skaneateles Library Association, Skaneateles, N. Y.
NWM	U. S. Military Academy Library, West Point, N. Y.
NbO	Omaha Public Library, Omaha, Nebr.
NcGu	Guilford College Library, Guilford, N. C.
NhExP	Phillips Exeter Academy, Exeter, N. H.
NjP	Princeton University Library, Princeton, N. J.
OCHP	Historical and Philosophical Society of Ohio, Cincinnati, Ohio
OCICS	Case Institute of Technology, Cleveland, Ohio
OClWHi	Western Reserve Historical Society, Cleveland, Ohio
OFH	Hayes Memorial Library, Fremont, Ohio
OMC	Marietta College Library, Marietta, Ohio
ORB	Oliver R. Barrett Collection, Chicago, Ill.*
OSHi	Clark County Historical Society, Springfield, Ohio
OrHi	Oregon Historical Society, Portland, Ore.
PHC	Haverford College Library, Haverford, Pa.
PHi	Historical Society of Pennsylvania, Philadelphia, Pa.

* After the *Collected Works* was in press, the collection of the late Oliver R. Barrett was sold at auction by Parke-Bernet Galleries (Catalog 1315) on February 19-20, 1952. It has been impossible to trace all new owners of the more than two hundred items, and impracticable to change the source citations for those which are known, but many of the more important items went to such well-known collections as those in the Library of Congress (Debates Scrapbook, purchased for the Alfred Whital Stern Collection) and Illinois State Historical Library (letters to Joshua F. Speed, etc.).

PMA	Allegheny College Library, Meadville, Pa.
PP	Free Library of Philadelphia, Philadelphia, Pa.
PPDrop	Dropsie College Library, Philadelphia, Pa.
PSt	Pennsylvania State College Library, State College, Pa.
PU	University of Pennsylvania Library, Philadelphia, Pa.
RPAB	Annmary Brown Memorial Library, Providence, R. I.
RPB	Brown University Library, Providence, R. I.
THaroL	Lincoln Memorial University, Harrogate, Tenn.
THi	Tennessee Historical Society, Nashville, Tenn.
ViU	University of Virginia Library, Charlottesville, Va.
VtU	University of Vermont Library, Burlington, Vt.
WBeloHi	Beloit Historical Society, Beloit, Wis.
WHi	State Historical Society of Wisconsin, Madison, Wis.
WvU	West Virginia University Library, Morgantown, W. Va.

FEBRUARY 23, 1861
By Mathew B. Brady

THE COLLECTED WORKS OF
ABRAHAM LINCOLN

THE COLLECTED WORKS OF
ABRAHAM LINCOLN

———— ◄◄◆►► ————

To David Hunter[1]

Washington, Oct. 24, 1861

Sir: The command of the Department of the West having devolved upon you, I propose to offer you a few *suggestions,* knowing how hazzardous it is to bind down a distant commander in the field to specific lines and operations, as so much always depends on a knowledge of localities & passing events. It is intended therefore, to leave a considerable margin for the exercise of your judgment & discretion.

The main rebel army (Prices)[2] west of the Mississippi, is believed to have passed Dade county, in full retreat upon North-Western Arkansas, leaving Missouri almost freed from the enemy, excepting in the South-East of the State. Assuming this basis of fact, it seems desireable, as you are not likely to overtake Price, and are in danger of making too long a line from your own base of supplies and reinforcements, that you should give up the pursuit, halt your main army, divide it into two corps of observation, one occupying Sedalia, and the other Rolla, the present *termini* of Railroads; then recruit the condition of both corps, by re-establishing, and improving, their discipline and instruction; perfecting their clothing and equipments, and providing less uncomfortable quarters. Of course both Railroads must be guarded, and kept open, judiciously employing just so much force as is necessary for this. From these two points, Sedalia and Rolla, and especially in judicious co-operation with Lane on the Kansas border, it would be so easy to concentrate, and repel any army of the enemy returning on Missouri from the South-West, that it is not probable any such attempt to return will be made before, or during, the approaching cold weather. Before spring the people of Missouri will be in no favorable mood to renew, for next year, the troubles which have so much afflicted, and impoverished them during this.

If you adopt this line of policy, and if, as I anticipate, you will see no enemy in great force approaching, you will have a surplus of force, which you can withdraw from these points and direct to others, as may be needed, the railroads furnishing ready means of re-inforcing these main points, if occasion requires. Doubtless local uprisings, for a time, will continue to occur; but these can be met by detachments, and local forces of our own, and will, ere long, tire out of themselves.

While, as stated at the beginning of this letter, a large discretion must be, and is, left with yourself, I feel sure that an indefinite pursuit of Price, or an attempt, by this long and circuitous route, to reach Memphis, will be exhaustive beyond endurance, and will end in the loss of the whole force engaged in it. Your Obt. Servt.

A. LINCOLN.

To the Commander of the Department of the West.

¹ ALS, CSmH; ADf (fragment), DLC-RTL. The fragment in the Lincoln Papers is a portion of Lincoln's first draft beginning "on the Kansas border" and ending with the last words ("tire out of themselves") in the next to last paragraph. Although Lincoln's letter to Curtis (*supra*) indicates that this letter to Hunter, as well as *General Orders No. 18*, was to be enclosed, it seems evident that Lincoln decided to withhold it a few days, and in fact enclosed it in another letter to Curtis on October 28 (q.v. *infra*). Lincoln's suggestions to Hunter originated in the War Department. A preliminary draft (DNA WR RG 94, Adjutant General, Letters Received, P 943) bearing Winfield Scott's endorsement ("It is hoped the President will modify freely the within. W.S.") is as follows:

"To Major Genl. Hunter, U.S. Volunteers.   Washington, Oct. 24, 1861.

"Sir: The command of the Department of the West, having, for a time, devolved upon you, I propose to offer you a few *suggestions*, knowing how hazardous it is to bind down a distant commander in the field to specific lines & operations, as so much always depends on a knowledge of localities & of passing events. It is intended, therefore, to leave a considerable margin for the exercise of your judgement & discretion.

"The main rebel army (Price's) west of the Mississippi, is believed to have passed Cedar county, in full retreat upon Southern Kansas & the Indian country, leaving Missouri almost freed from the enemy, excepting in the South-East of the State. Assuming this basis, it seems desirable, as you are not likely to overtake Price, that you should give up the pursuit, halt your main army; divide it into two corps of observation, one occupying Sedalia & the other Rolla, the termini of rail roads; then recruit both corps, & re-establish their discipline & instruction. As you will probably, have a surplus of force after guarding those important points, that surplus would be disposable for other points—say the South Eastern part of the State &c. &c.

"It is particularly expected of you to look into the many reported extravagancies & abuses, in public money & property, in your Department, to arrest any officer on evidence of probable guilt, & to dismiss other faulty agents."

² Major General Sterling Price, ex-governor of Missouri (1853-1857).

To Caleb B. Smith¹

October 24, 1861

The within letter of the Secretary of the Navy, is written concerning the proposed contract with my indorsement thereon which is herewith inclosed. After it was written a promise was obtained from me that I would submit it to the Secretary of the Interior, asking him, if he could spare the time, to form a definite opinion whether such a contract can legally, and ought to be made.

Oct. 24. 1861.   A. LINCOLN

¹ AES, DNA FI RG 56, General Records, Treasury Department, Series AB, 1861, Letters from Executive Officers, II, 5a. Lincoln's endorsement is written on the back of a letter from Gideon Welles, August 29, 1861, in which the secretary states he has not "the time necessary to investigate the subject of the proposed Chiriqui contract . . . . if any contract is to be made, it should be by some other officer than myself. . . ." The presence of this letter among the records of the Treasury Department arises from the fact of its later referral there. Chase wrote Lincoln on November 12, "I have given the Chiriqui business all the consideration I could today; and am much impressed by the prospects it offers. . . . At present I am not prepared for a conclusion; but as soon as I return from New York I will give it special attention. . . ." (DLC-RTL). Francis P. Blair, Sr., seems also to have been called upon for an opinion, for in a lengthy and favorable report Blair recommended that Henry T. Blow, U.S. minister to Venezuela, be sent to Chiriqui to examine the premises for the government (F. P. Blair, Sr., to Lincoln, November 16, 1861, ibid.). Although the Blairs went so far as to prepare an order assigning Captain Ambrose Thompson (son of Ambrose W. Thompson, who headed the Chiriqui Improvement Company) as military escort for Henry T. Blow and an order detaching a vessel from the fleet for the purpose of conveying him (Francis P. Blair, Jr., to Montgomery Blair [December, 1861?] ibid.), Lincoln seems not to have followed their recommendations. The Chiriqui project was held in abeyance until April, 1862.

To Simon Cameron¹

October 25, 1861

I have no doubt that the gentlemen named within, are true and faithful; and that their mission of charity is most worthy, and praiseworthy.   A. LINCOLN

Oct. 25. 1861.

¹ AES, IHi. Lincoln's endorsement is written on a letter from General John E. Wool, October 23, 1861, introducing Reverend Marble N. Taylor and Chaplain T. W. Conway "on an errand of charity and humanity." Below Lincoln's endorsement Cameron wrote "I heartily approve the mission of these gentlemen. SIMON CAMERON." There is no further record of the mission, but Chaplain Conway and Reverend Taylor (a Methodist minister and Virginian by birth, who was declared provisional governor of North Carolina by the Hatteras Convention on November 18, 1861) were active in organizing Unionists in North Carolina. See Lincoln to George Bancroft, November 18, infra.

Memorandum: Letter of Samuel T. Glover¹

I have not had time to read this. Please read & return it.

Oct. 25. 1861   A. LINCOLN

¹ AES, DLC-RTL. Lincoln's endorsement is written on the back of an eight-page letter from Samuel T. Glover, October 19, 1861, giving advice on problems confronting the government. To whom Lincoln referred the letter is not known.

Recommendation for a Pass[1]

October 25, 1861

The loyalty of Mr. Larrabee, as seen within, is vouched by Gov. Hicks. He wishes a pass for himself and driver, to cross and recross the Potomac, taking oysters to our camps. I think he should have the pass.   A. LINCOLN

Oct. 25. 1861.

[1] AES, owned by Lemuel A. Welles, New York City. Mr. Larrabee has not been identified.

To Simon Cameron[1]

October 26, 1861

Mr. Brown, named within, says a Mr. Hill[2] of Toledo Ohio, was appointed a *Major* in one of the new regular regiments, & resigned, thus making a vacancy, which is not yet filled. He wishes the place, & I have no objection, believing him to be a worthy gentleman.   A. LINCOLN

Oct. 26. 1861

[1] AES, owned by C. Norton Owen, Chicago, Illinois. Lincoln's endorsement is written on the back of a letter from Representative James M. Ashley of Ohio, asking that Samuel E. Brown, appointed captain in the Seventeenth Infantry, Regular Army, be given a majority. An endorsement by Benjamin F. Wade concurs in Ashley's request. There is no record of Samuel E. Brown's appointment as major.
[2] Charles W. Hill, who declined appointment in the Regular Army, but served as colonel of the One Hundred Twenty-eighth Ohio Infantry.

To Simon Cameron[1]

Sec. of War, please see the bearer, nephew of Hon. John M. Botts.

Oct. 26. 1861.   A. LINCOLN

[1] ALS, DLC-Cameron Papers. The nephew has not been positively identified but may have been Randolph Botts of New York, appointed captain and quartermaster of Volunteers July 17, 1862.

To George B. McClellan[1]

Major. Gen. McClellan   Executive Mansion
My dear Sir   Oct. 26. 1861

A battery of repeating guns, on wheels, can be seen at the Arsenal any hour to-day. Could you, without inconvenience, see them at 3. or 4. o clock—please answer. Yours   A. LINCOLN

[4]

¹ ALS, PP. McClellan's reply dated "Saturday Morning" expressed his regrets that it would scarcely be possible for him to return from the review of General Fitz-John Porter's division, scheduled at 11 A.M., in time to keep the appointment (DLC-RTL).

To William H. Seward¹

Hon. Sec. of State   Executive Mansion
My dear Sir   Oct. 26. 1861.
    This will introduce Judge A. D. Russell, of New-York, who comes to me with a very kind letter of introduction from Mr. Bennett of the Herald.
    Please give him a kind reception. Yours truly   A. LINCOLN

¹ ALS, NAuE. James Gordon Bennett's letter of October 22, introduced Russell as ". . . a most worthy and competent man for any species of public service. . . ." (DLC-RTL). Abraham D. Russell was a municipal judge of New York City.

Authorization for the *Pembroke*¹

[October 28, 1861]

Abraham Lincoln,
President of the United States of America

To all whom these presents may concern
Greeting:
    Know Ye, that, whereas, by the first section of the Act of Congress approved the 5th. of August last, entitled "An Act supplementary, to an Act entitled 'An act to protect the commerce of the United States, and Punish the Crime of Piracy,'" it is enacted "That any vessel or boat which shall be built, purchased, fitted out in whole or in part, or held for the purpose of being employed in the commission of any piratical aggression, search, restraint, depredation, or seizure, or in the commission of any other act of piracy, as defined by the law of nations, shall be liable to be captured and brought into any port of the United States if found upon the high seas, or to be seized if found in any port or place within the United States, whether the same shall have actually sailed upon any piratical expedition or not, and whether any act of piracy shall have been committed or attempted upon or from such vessel or boat or not; and any such vessel or boat may be adjudged and condemned, if captured by a vessel authorized as herein after mentioned, to the use of the United States and to that of the captors, and if seized by a collector, surveyor, or marshal, then to the use of the United States, after due process and trial, in like manner

as is provided in section four of the act to which this act is supplementary, which section is hereby made in all respects applicable to cases arising under this act."

And whereas by the second section of the same Act, the President of the United States is authorized to instruct the commander of any suitable vessel to subdue, seize, take, and, if on the high seas, to send into any port of the United States any vessel or boat, built, purchased, fitted out or held as in the said first section mentioned:

Now, therefore, I, Abraham Lincoln, President of the United States, in pursuance of the authority thus in me vested, do hereby authorize the propeller Pembroke, owned by R. B. Forbes of Boston and commanded by   to take any vessel or boat, built, purchased or fitted out as aforesaid, and for so doing, this shall be his warrant.

Given under my hand and the seal of the United States at Washington this twenty-eighth day of October, in the year of our Lord one thousand eight hundred [L.S.] and sixty one, and of the Independence of the United States the eighty-sixth.

By the President: ABRAHAM LINCOLN.

WILLIAM H. SEWARD, Secretary of State.

[1] Copy, DNA WR NB RG 45, Executive Letters, No. 96a.

To Simon Cameron[1]

Executive Mansion, Oct. 28, 1861.

I have not sufficient time to study and mature an opinion on this plan. If the Secretary of War has confidence in it, and is satisfied to adopt it, I have no objections.   A. LINCOLN.

[1] William R. Plum, *The Military Telegraph During the Civil War* . . . . (1882), I, 129. According to Plum's account, Lincoln's endorsement was written on a letter from Thomas A. Scott, October 28, 1861, referring to the president Anson Stager, general superintendent of Western Union at Cleveland, Ohio, with a plan for managing the military telegraph. Cameron approved the plan, and Stager was commissioned captain and assigned to duty in the War Department, where he served as chief of U.S. Military Telegraph with rank of colonel from February 26, 1862.

To Simon Cameron[1]

Wampole.

Will Gen. Cameron please find something for Col. Wampole? The within papers are ample & excellent.   A. LINCOLN

Oct. 28. 1861

[1] AES, DNA FS RG 59, Appointments, Box 398. Lincoln's endorsement is written on an envelope containing recommendations of Elias Wampole of Pennsylvania. There is no record of Wampole's appointment to a War Department post, but he was nominated consul at Laguayra, Venezuela, on February 10, and confirmed March 6, 1862.

To Samuel R. Curtis[1]

Executive Mansion,

Brigadier General S. R. Curtis.　　Washington, Oct. 28. 1861.

My dear Sir. Herewith is a document, half letter, half order, which, wishing you to *see*, but not to make *public* I send unsealed. Please read it, and then inclose it to the officer who may be in command of the Department of the West, at the time it reaches him. I can not *now* know whether Fremont, or Hunter will *then* be in command. Yours truly　　　　　　　　　　　　A. LINCOLN

[1] ALS, IHi. This letter appears in the *Official Records* (I, III, 555) under date of October 24 with a note appended as follows: "No inclosure found, but see Lincoln to Commander of Department of the West, October 24, p. 553." The editors' belief is that Lincoln held the letter to the Commander of the Department of the West until October 28 in order to give his letter to Curtis enclosing *General Orders No. 18*, time to be put in force. See Lincoln to Curtis, October 24, *supra*.

Memorandum:
Resolutions of United Presbyterian Synod[1]

To be presented to the Cabinet next Tuesday. Pres. Genl. Ass. Oct. 28, 1861.

[1] AE, DLC-RTL. Lincoln's endorsement is written on a communication from the United Presbyterian Synod of New York and New Jersey sending resolutions passed by the assembly concerning slavery and the war. Secretary Seward acknowledged the resolutions and expressed the president's thanks for the invocations and support of the Synod, November 27, 1861.

To Simon Cameron[1]

October 29, 1861

I wish a point strained to have Hon. Daniel S. Dickinson obliged by the appointment of James L. *Cramer* to a Paymastership. Although Mr. Cramer's name is not in this letter, it nevertheless, was given Mr. Paine, to procure Mr. Cramer's appointment.

Oct. 29. 1861　　　　　　　　　　　　　　　A. LINCOLN

[1] AES, IHi. Lincoln's endorsement is written on a letter from Daniel S. Dickinson introducing "my good friend Col. N. E. Paine of Western N. Y." James L. Cramer was not appointed additional paymaster of Volunteers until January 23,

1863. His appointment was confirmed by the Senate February 19, recalled February 21, and returned by the president to the Senate February 24, 1863. Cramer's service record shows him to have served, however, until February 15, 1866.

To Simon Cameron[1]

Sec. of War, please see Mr. King & Mr. Paine.
Oct. 29, 1861   A. LINCOLN

[1] ALS, DLC-Cameron Papers. Senator Preston King and N. E. Paine of Rochester, New York, probably called on Cameron about the appointment of James L. Cramer, *supra*.

To William H. Seward[1]

October 29, 1861

If the Consul at Jerusalem has resigned (as I believe he has) let Hon. Mr. Dunn of Indiana, be obliged by the appointment of Josiah S. Weyer, of Ia. to the the [*sic*] place.   A. LINCOLN
Oct 29. 1861.

[1] AES, NAuE. Lincoln's endorsement is written on a letter from Representative William M. Dunn, October 29, 1861, requesting appointment of Josiah S. Weyer of Indiana, to the consulship of Jerusalem. There is no record of Weyer's appointment.

To William H. Seward[1]

Sec. of State, please see this lady. She wishes the bond may be several & not joint. I think it might be so.   A. LINCOLN
Oct. 29, 1861.

[1] Parke-Bernet Catalog 73, December 6, 1938, No. 133. According to the catalog description, Lincoln's note concerned the case of John Williams, arrested as a spy. Mrs. Cecilia Williams, wife of John Williams, Jr., Norfolk, Virginia, who had been arrested in Boston on orders of General Benjamin F. Butler, arranged for her husband's release on oath and $10,000 bond. Seward to John A. Dix, October 31, 1861, "In answer to your note of the 29th . . . handed to me by Mrs. Williams . . . the U.S. district attorney . . . has been authorized to accept the sureties . . . severally instead of jointly. . . ." (OR, II, II, 461).

To F. M. Magrath[1]

Executive Mansion
Rev. F. M. Magrath   Washington, D.C. October 30, 1861.
Sir: Having been solicited by Christian Ministers, and other pious people, to appoint suitable persons to act as Chaplains at the hospitals for our sick and wounded soldiers, and feeling the intrinsic propriety of having such persons to so act, and yet believing there is no law conferring the power upon me to appoint them, I

think fit to say that if you will voluntarily enter upon, and perform the appropriate duties of such position, I will recommend that Congress make compensation therefor at the same rate as Chaplains in the army are compensated.   A. LINCOLN

1 Tracy, p. 196. See Lincoln to John J. Hughes, October 21, *supra*, and Form Letter to Chaplains, December 3, 1861, *infra*. Although Lincoln sent this letter to at least seven chaplains, none of the originals have been located by the editors.

Memorandum: Answer to Ebenezer White[1]

[c. October 30, 1861]

I am to examine this & have Mr. Hay write the writer.

1 AE, DLC-RTL. Lincoln's endorsement is written on a letter from Ebenezer White to Lyman Trumbull, October 30, 1861, asking assistance in getting authorization for recruiting "a Company of Mounted Sappers, Miners, & Engineers" for General Lane's Kansas Brigade. John Hay's notation follows Lincoln's endorsement, "Answered November 6, 1861."

To George D. Ramsay[1]

If the gentlemen bearing this are, as they say, workmen in the line of work at the Arsenal, I think Major Ramsay better employ them.
Oct. 31. 1861   A. LINCOLN

1 ALS-P, ISLA.

Memorandum:
Appointment of Daniel P. Abercrombie[1]

[November, 1861?]

Very high recommendations for Daniel P. Abercrombie to be a Cadet. Mr. Train[2] of Mass. introduces the boy & mother, the latter being very anxious for the appointment.

1 AE, DNA WR RG 94, U.S. Military Academy, 1862, No. 4, Box 80. There is no record of Abercrombie's appointment. Lincoln's endorsement is written on an undated envelope, but the recommendations indicate November, 1861, as probable date of the endorsement.   2 Charles R. Train.

To George B. McClellan[1]

Private.

Major General Geo. B. McClellan   Executive Mansion
My dear Sir   Nov. 1. 1861

Lieut. Genl. Scott having been, upon his own application, placed on the list of retired officers, with his advice, and the concurrence of the entire cabinet, I have designated you to command the whole

Army. You will, therefore, assume this enlarged duty at once, conferring with me so far as necessary. Yours truly A. LINCOLN

P.S. For the present, let Gen. Wool's command be excepted[2]

A L

[1] ALS, DLC-McClellan Papers. See Lincoln's order retiring General Scott, *infra*.

[2] Lincoln's exception of General Wool may be explained by the fact that the elderly general had let it be known that he would resign if any younger officer were appointed commander-in-chief (Ira Harris to Lincoln, November 1, and John Jay to Lincoln, November 2, 1861, DLC-RTL).

Order Retiring Winfield Scott from Command[1]

Executive Mansion, Washington, November 1, 1861.

On the 1st day of November, A.D. 1861, upon his own application to the President of the United States, Brevet Lieutenant General Winfield Scott is ordered to be placed, and hereby is placed, upon the list of retired officers of the Army of the United States, without reduction in his current pay, subsistence, or allowances.

The American people will hear with sadness and deep emotion that General Scott has withdrawn from the active control of the army, while the President and a unanimous Cabinet express their own and the nation's sympathy in his personal affliction and their profound sense of the important public services rendered by him to his country during his long and brilliant career, among which will ever be gratefully distinguished his faithful devotion to the Constitution, the Union, and the Flag, when assailed by parricidal rebellion.[2] ABRAHAM LINCOLN.

[1] AGO *General Orders No. 94*, November 1, 1861. General Scott's retirement had been delayed since August 9, by the president's request. Although Scott's physical infirmity was the reason given the public for his retirement, McClellan had long been in disagreement with his superior, and on August 8 wrote him a letter which Scott deemed an insult. Scott's letter to Cameron of August 9, indicated the nub of dissension as follows: "McClellan has propagated, in high quarters, the idea expressed in the letter before me, that Washington was not only 'insecure,' but in 'imminent danger' . . . . I am confident in the opposite opinion. . . . Accordingly I must beg the President . . . to allow me to be placed on the *officers' retired list*. . . ." (DLC-RTL). On August 10, Lincoln asked McClellan to withdraw his critical letter and requested Scott to withdraw his resignation. Scott wrote to Cameron, August 12, that he still wished to resign because of his conviction that McClellan intended to maintain an attitude of insubordination: "The original offence given to me by . . . McClellan . . . seems to have been the result of deliberation between him & some of the members of the cabinet, by whom all the greater war questions are to be settled—without report to, or consultation with, me. . . ." (DLC-RTL).

[2] A preliminary draft of this paragraph, in the handwriting of Salmon P. Chase, is as follows:

"The President avails himself of this occasion to express to Lieutenant General

Scott his profound sense of the important services rendered by him to his country during his long and brilliant career; among which a grateful people will ever especially distinguish his faithful devotion to the Constitution, the Union & the Flag, when assailed by parricidal rebellion." (DLC-RTL).

Remarks to Winfield Scott[1]

November 1, 1861

GENERAL: You will naturally feel solicitude about the gentlemen of your staff, who have rendered you and their country such faithful service. I have taken that subject into consideration. I understand that they go with you to New-York. I shall desire them at their earliest convenience, after their return, to make their wishes known to me. I desire you now, however, to be satisfied that, except the unavoidable privation of your counsel, and society, which they have so long enjoyed, the provision which will be made for them will be such as to render their situation hereafter as agreeable as it has been heretofore.

[1] New York *Tribune*, November 2, 1861. Following the cabinet meeting at which Scott's resignation was accepted and McClellan's appointment decided upon, the president and cabinet members called at Scott's residence. Lincoln read the order of retirement, to which General Scott replied in a simple and moving speech, after which Lincoln's brief remarks were made.

To Simon Cameron[1]

November 2, 1861

I think any officer who has been dismissed on suspicion of disloyalty, but does not go over to the enemy, continuing to protest his loyalty, entitles himself to a hearing, and I hope this case will be enquired into.   A. LINCOLN

Nov. 2, 1861.

[1] Copy, ISLA. Lincoln's endorsement is on a letter from First Lieutenant George T. Balch, November 2, 1861, requesting a court of inquiry for Captain John McNab (see Lincoln to Cameron, August 10, *supra*).

To Simon Cameron[1]

If the within request can be consistently granted, I shall be very glad for it to be done.   A. LINCOLN

Nov. 2. 1861

[1] AES, IHi. Lincoln's endorsement is written on the back of a letter from Colonel James S. Jackson of the Third Kentucky Cavalry, October 28, 1861, asking that Captain William B. Lane lately resigned from the Third U.S. Cavalry in New Mexico, be permitted to withdraw his resignation and ". . . take

the place in my Regiment vacated by the appointment of R[ichard] W Johnson Brigadier General." A further endorsement by the adjutant general's office, November 5, 1861, declares that permission had already been given to Lane to withdraw his resignation.

To Simon Cameron[1]

November 2, 1861

If the appointment within recommended, can be made, without interfering, with the appointment of Buchanan, already recommended by Gen'l Scott, let it be done.

[1] American Art Association Anderson Galleries Catalog 4325, April 29-30, 1937, No. 322. According to the catalog description, Lincoln's endorsement is written on the back of a letter from George B. McClellan, recommending Major John Oakes for inspector general. There is, however, no record of John Oakes. Major James Oakes of the Fifth Cavalry, who was later made inspector of cavalry, may have been the man McClellan recommended, and Lieutenant Colonel Robert C. Buchanan may have been the officer recommended by Scott, but neither is listed in the inspector general's office by the *U.S. Official Register*.

Memorandum[1]

[November 2, 1861?]

Moving the guns—Sickles—
New-Department, Lane.
Missouri—Strong
Missouri—Gamble.
Harbor defences.

[1] AD, DLC-RTL. Lincoln's memorandum is on a small card. The bracketed date is that assigned to the document as cataloged in the Lincoln Papers. Presumably the memorandum was jotted down as a reminder of problems currently pressing for solution. See Lincoln to Strong, November 3, to Cameron, November 4, and the order approving Governor Gamble's plan, November 6, *infra*. Recommendations for formation of a new military department west of Missouri were currently under consideration, and a letter from Benjamin F. Wade, Zachariah Chandler, and David Kilgore, November 1, 1861, recommended the appointment of General James Lane as commander of the proposed department (*ibid.*).

To William H. Seward[1]

November 2, 1861

As this recommendation is made by Bishops Janes & Simpson, I am anxious an appointment to a Consulship shall be made accordingly, if one can be found.   A. LINCOLN

Nov. 2, 1861

[1] Stan. V. Henkels Catalog 1154, December 8, 1915, No. 179A. According to the catalog description, Lincoln's endorsement is written on a letter from Methodist Bishops Edmund S. Janes and Matthew Simpson, but the name of the person recommended is not given.

To Joseph G. Totten[1]

November 2, 1861

If Genl Totten & myself are both alive, and in place in June 1862, & he Genl T. will remind me of it, I then wish to give a Cadetship to a son of Professor Mahan.   A LINCOLN

Nov 2. 1861

[1] Copy, DNA WR RG 94, U.S. Military Academy, 1861, Box 79, No. 558. Frederick A. Mahan, son of Dennis H. Mahan, professor of civil and military engineering at West Point, was not appointed until July 1, 1863.

To Gideon Welles[1]

November 2, 1861

This will be handed to you by the daughter of Major Marston of the Marine Corps. She desires to have her father placed on active duty. I shall be glad for her to be obliged if it can consistently be done.

[1] American Art Association Catalog, January 21-22, 1926, No. 335. According to the catalog description, this communication is an ALS. The *U.S. Official Register* for 1863, lists Lieutenant Colonel Ward Marston, commanding Marine Barracks, Portsmouth, New Hampshire.

To William K. Strong[1]

(Copy of Ans' sent Nov. 3. 1861)

Gen. McClellan is in command of substantially the whole Army, including the Department of the West   A LINCOLN

[1] ALS copy, DLC-RTL. Lincoln's copy of his reply (probably by telegram) to General Strong is written on the back of a telegram received from Strong, St. Louis, November 2, 1861, "Do you let us know I beg of you who is in command of this department. The suspense we are in working most disastrously I fear all will be lost unless there is some power established by you at once that will be respected & obeyed." (DLC-RTL).

To Simon Cameron[1]

November 4, 1861

Respectfully submitted to the Secretary of War, with the suggestion that it be laid before the Engineer and Ordnance bureaus, respectively, for examination and report.   A. LINCOLN.

November 4, 1861

[1] Thirty-seventh Congress, Second Session, *House of Representatives Executive Document No. 14*, p. 6. Lincoln's endorsement is on a letter from Governor Israel Washburn, Jr., of Maine, October 23, 1861, concerning coastal defenses of his state. *House Document No. 14* prints numerous communications concerned with preparation of plans for construction of fortifications to be financed by the federal government.

To Oliver P. Morton[1]

With the consent of Gov. Morton I concur with the suggestion of the Sec. of War.   A. LINCOLN

Nov. 4. 1861

[1] AES, CSmH-Eldridge Collection. Lincoln's endorsement is written on a letter from Schuyler Colfax to Cameron, October 24, 1861, requesting appointment of ex-Senator Graham N. Fitch (1857-1861) as brigadier general. Lincoln's endorsement follows that of Cameron recommending the appointment on condition that Fitch ". . . raise three more regiments, independently of those being organized by the Governor." Fitch was appointed colonel of the Forty-sixth Indiana Infantry, November 1, 1861, and served until August 2, 1862.

To Samuel R. Curtis[1]

November 5, 1861

What has been done in the matter sent you by Mr. Swett?

[1] Metropolitan Art Association Catalog, January 14, 1914, No. 494. According to the catalog description, this communication is an autograph dispatch. Leonard Swett did not report on his mission until November 9 (see Lincoln to Curtis, October 24, *supra*, and note), but Curtis replied by telegraph, November 6, "Your orders were sent and delivered at Genl Fremonts Head Quarters November second. . . ." (DLC-RTL).

To James Guthrie, George D. Prentice, and James Speed[1]

James Guthrie   Head-Quarters,
G. D. Prentice & James Speed.   Army of the Potomac,
Jeffersonville, Indiana.   Washington, Nov. 5. 1861.

       How near to Louisville is Buckner? Is he moving towards Louisville? Has he crossed Green River? Is the bridge over Green River repaired? Can he cross Green River in face of Mc-Cook? If he were on the North side of Green River, how long could McCook hold him out of Louisville, holding the railroad with power to destroy it inch by inch?   A. LINCOLN

[1] ALS, DLC-McClellan Papers. Lincoln's communication was prompted by a telegram of the same date from the men whom he addressed, reading as follows: "If Sherman is not promptly reinforced he may meet fate of Lyon in Missouri.

The consequences of such a result you can see." (DLC-RTL). A longer telegram received the same day from George D. Prentice estimated Buckner's force as "four (4) probably six (6) or seven (7) times" Sherman's. No reply to Lincoln's specific queries is in the Lincoln Papers.

Memorandum: Appointment of Charles Devens[1]

November 5, 1861

To-day, Nov. 5, 1861, Mr. James Lawrence, Dr. Russell, and Attorney General, Foster, call, and two of them recommend that Col. Charles Devens be made a Brigadier General.

[1] AD, IHi. Of several persons bearing the name, this James Lawrence has not been positively identified, but Dr. Ira Russell was surgeon in the Eleventh Massachusetts Infantry, and Dwight Foster was attorney general of Massachusetts. Colonel Charles Devens of the Fifteenth Massachusetts Infantry was made brigadier general of Volunteers, April 15, 1862.

Endorsement: Petition for Formation of a District of Columbia Regiment[1]

I join Gen. McClellan in the above recommendation.
Nov. 6, 1861   A. LINCOLN

[1] Copy, DNA WR RG 153, Judge Advocate General, KK 438. Lincoln's endorsement is preserved in an attested copy of the petition signed by Isaac A. Peck and others, October 28, 1861, for formation of a District of Columbia regiment, filed with the court-martial record of Charles McHannon, private Company G, Second Regiment, District of Columbia Volunteers, pardoned January 23, 1865, for desertion (q.v. infra).

Order Approving the Plan of Governor Gamble of Missouri[1]

November 6, 1861

This plan, approved with the modification that the Governor stipulates that when he commissions a major-general of militia it shall be the same person at the time in command of the United States Department of the West, and in case the United States shall change such commander of the department, he, the Governor, will revoke the State commission given to the person relieved, and give one to the person substituted to the United States command of said department.   A. LINCOLN.

[1] OR, I, VIII, 456. Hamilton R. Gamble, under direction of resolutions passed by a Missouri convention on October 31, 1861, went to Washington to present his plan of co-operation between state and federal authority in Missouri. Al-

though dated at the Executive Mansion, November 5, presumably the draft of Gamble's plan had been previously prepared. The text of the plan approved is as follows:

"Executive Mansion, Washington, November 5, 1861.

"The Governor of the State of Missouri, acting under the direction of the Convention of that State, proposes to the Government of the United States that he will raise a military force, to serve within the State as State militia during the war there, to co-operate with the troops in the service of the United States in repelling the invasion of the State and suppressing rebellion therein; the said State Militia to be embodied and to be held in the camp and in the field, drilled, disciplined, and governed according to the Army Regulations and subject to the Articles of War; the said State militia not to be ordered out of the State except for the immediate defense of the State of Missouri, but to co-operate with the troops in the service of the United States in military operations within the State or necessary to its defense, and when officers of the State Militia act with officers in the service of the United States of the same grade, the officers of the United States service shall command the combined force; the State Militia to be armed, equipped, clothed, subsisted, transported, and paid by the United States during such time as they shall be actually engaged as an embodied military force in service in accordance with Regulations of the United States Army or general orders as issued from time to time.

"In order that the Treasury of the United States may not be burdened with the pay of unnecessary officers, the Governor proposes that, although the State law requires him to appoint upon the general staff an adjutant-general, a commissary-general, an inspector-general, a quarter-master-general, a paymaster-general, and a surgeon-general, each with the rank of colonel of cavalry, yet he proposes that the Government of the United States pay only the adjutant-general, the quarter-master general, and inspector-general, their services being necessary in the relations which would exist between the State Militia and the United States. The Governor further proposes that, while he is allowed by the State law to appoint aides-de-camp to the Governor at his discretion, with the rank of colonel, three only shall be reported to the United States for payment. He also proposes that the State Militia shall be commanded by a single major-general and by such number of brigadier-generals as shall allow one for a brigade of not less than four regiments, and that no greater number of staff officers shall be appointed for regimental, brigade, and division duties than is provided for in the act of Congress of the 22d July, 1861, and that whatever be the rank of such officers as fixed by the law of the State the compensation that they shall receive from the United States shall only be that which belongs to the rank given by said act of Congress to officers in the United States service performing the same duties.

"The field officers of a regiment in the State militia are 1 colonel, 1 lieutenant-colonel, and 1 major, and the company officers are a captain, a first lieutenant, and a second lieutenant.

"The Governor proposes that, as the money to be disbursed is the money of the United States, such staff officers in the service of the United States as may be necessary to act as disbursing officers for the State Militia shall be assigned by the War Department for that duty; or, if such cannot be spared from their present duty, he will appoint such persons disbursing officers for the State Militia as the President of the United States may designate. Such regulations as may be required, in the judgment of the President, to insure regularity of returns and to protect the United States from any fraudulent practices, shall be observed and obeyed by all in office in the State Militia.

"The above propositions are accepted on the part of the United States, and the Secretary of War is directed to make the necessary orders upon the Ordnance, Quartermaster, Commissary, Pay, and Medical Departments to carry this agreement into effect. He will cause the necessary staff officers in the United States service to be detailed for duty in connection with the Missouri State Militia, and will order them to make the necessary provision in their respective offices for fulfilling this agreement. All requisitions upon the different officers of the United States under this agreement to be made in substance in the same mode for the Missouri State Militia as similar requisitions are made for troops in the service of the United States, and the Secretary of War will cause any additional regulations that may be necessary to insure regularity and economy in carrying this agreement into effect to be adopted and communicated to the Governor of Missouri for the government of the Missouri State Militia." *(Ibid.,* pp. 454-56).

To Simon Cameron[1]

November 7, 1861

Secretary of War, please see Dr. Boyd Pendleton of Va. and, if you can, let him be examined at once to be a Brigade Surgeon. I very much wish to appoint him at once.   A. LINCOLN

Nov. 7, 1861.

[1] Tracy, p. 196. Dr. E. Boyd Pendleton was appointed April 4, 1862, and resigned June 10, 1862.

To William H. Seward[1]

[November 7, 1861]

All right   A.L.

[1] AES, owned by Hamilton Hutton, Wilmington, Delaware. Lincoln's endorsement is written on a note from Seward, November 7, 1861, proposing ". . . to present . . . tomorrow, two Foreign Ministers—one at half past 2 o'clock, the other at 3. . . ." See Lincoln's reply to the minister from Sweden, November 8, *infra.*

To Simon Cameron[1]

November 8, 1861

Respectfully submitted to the War Department, with the request that it be remembered as a recommendation from Gov. Morton.

A. LINCOLN.

[1] American Art Association Anderson Galleries Catalog 4255, April 30, 1936, No. 265. According to the catalog description, Lincoln's endorsement is written on a letter from Oliver P. Morton recommending appointment of George B. Ripley as paymaster. There is no record of the appointment. See further, Lincoln to Stanton, August 9, 1862, *infra.*

Reply to Edward Count Piper[1]

November 8, 1861.

SIR: I receive with great pleasure a Minister from Sweden. That pleasure was enhanced by the information which preceded your arrival here, that his Majesty, your sovereign, had selected you to fill the mission upon the grounds of your derivation from an ancestral stock, identified with the most glorious era in your country's noble history, and your own eminent social and political standing in Sweden.

This country, Sir, maintains, and means to maintain, the rights of human nature and the capacity of man for self-government. The history of Sweden proves that this is the faith of the people of Sweden, as we know that it is the faith and practice of their respected Sovereign. Rest assured, therefore, that we shall be found always just and fraternal in our transactions with your Government, and that nothing will be omitted on my part to make your residence in this capital agreeable to yourself and satisfactory to your Government.

[1] New York *Tribune*, November 9, 1861. Edward Count Piper, minister resident from Sweden and Norway, was certainly one of the two foreign ministers for whom Seward made appointments (see Lincoln to Seward, November 7, *supra*). No report has been found of the second minister's presentation.

To James W. Ripley[1]

Gen: Ripley   Executive Mansion
Sir   Nov. 8. 1861.

Please see Gov. Wood and Mr. Woodruff, bearers of this, and make the arrangements for arms which they desire if you possibly can. Do not turn them away lightly; but either provide for their getting the arms, or write me a clear reason why you can not. Yours truly   A. LINCOLN

[1] ALS, DLC-Cameron Papers. Ex-Governor John Wood of Illinois, was quartermaster general of the state. Woodruff was probably his fellow townsman Mayor Isaac O. Woodruff of Quincy. Since there is no reply from General Ripley in the Lincoln Papers, it may be assumed the arms were provided.

Memorandum:
Appointment of Richard C. Vaughan[1]

The head of any Department, or Bureau, will oblige me, by obliging Attorney General Bates in the matter mentioned within. Nov. 9, 1861.   A. LINCOLN.

[1] Thomas F. Madigan Catalog, First Issue, 1937, No. 158. According to the catalog description, Lincoln's endorsement is written on a letter from Edward Bates recommending an appointment for Colonel Vaughan. Richard C. Vaughan of Lexington, Missouri, was Bates' friend, but seems to have received no federal appointment; his son John M. Vaughan, however, was appointed by Bates himself to a clerkship in the attorney general's office.

To José Joaquin Perez[1]

November 9, 1861

Abraham Lincoln,
President of the United States of America,

To His Excellency Jose Joaquin Perez,
President of the Republic of Chile.

Great and Good Friend: I have received the autograph letter of your Excellency dated the 24th. September last apprizing me of your elevation to the Supreme Magistracy of the Republic by the vote of the Chilean nation, and assuring me of your Excellency's best disposition to increase and strengthen the friendly and fraternal relations so happily subsisting between our respective countries.

I offer my sincere congratulations to your Excellency upon the event which you have communicated to me, and I am happy to believe that the sentiments which inspire your Excellency and which the Government and people of the United States cordially reciprocate cannot fail to be productive of the largest benefits to your own Nation, while they will promote the best understanding and harmony with others.

Accept my best wishes for your Excellency's personal happiness, with the assurances of my profound interest in the welfare and prosperity of the Chilean Nation.

May God have your Excellency always in His safe and holy keeping.

Written at the City of Washington the ninth day of November, in the year of our Lord one thousand eight hundred and sixty-one. Your Good Friend, ABRAHAM LINCOLN.

By the President:

WILLIAM H. SEWARD, Secretary of State.

[1] Copy, DNA FS RG 59, Communications to Foreign Sovereigns and States, III, 134-35; copy, DLC-Thomas H. Nelson Papers.

To Simon Cameron[1]

[c. November 10, 1861]

Mr. Bingham has not been much obliged by appointments; so that I think the first PayMaster hereafter appointed in Ohio should be his man, named within. A. LINCOLN

[1] AES, DLC-Cameron Papers. Lincoln's endorsement is written on the envelope of a letter from Representative John A. Bingham of Ohio, November 10, 1861, recommending Alexander J. McDonall of Steubenville for a paymastership. No record has been found of McDonall's appointment.

To George B. McClellan[1]

November 10, 1861

Gen: McClellan, please see Hon: Mr. Washburne, M.C. who has been on an investigating committee at St. Louis, for sixteen days recently, & can really give more accurate & fuller information on material matters there, than any one I have seen.

Nov. 10. 1861.   A. LINCOLN

[1] ALS, RPB. Representatives Elihu B. Washburne, William S. Holman, Henry L. Dawes, and William G. Steele of a House committee appointed July 8, 1861, to investigate government contracts, met in St. Louis, October 15-29, and at Cairo, Illinois, October 31. Washburne's report of December 17, 1861, is printed in Thirty-seventh Congress, Second Session, *House Reports*, No. 2.

To John A. McClernand[1]

Brigadier General McClernand   Washington. Nov. 10. 1861

My Dear Sir   This is not an official but a social letter. You have had a battle, and without being able to judge as to the precise measure of its value, I think it is safe to say that you, and all with you have done honor to yourselves and the flag and service to the country. Most gratefully do I thank you and them. In my present position, I must care for the whole nation; but I hope it will be no injustice to any other state, for me to indulge a little home pride, that Illinois does not disappoint us.

I have just closed a long interview with Mr. Washburne in which he has detailed the many difficulties you, and those with you labor under. Be assured, we do not forget or neglect you. Much, very much, goes undone: but it is because we have not the power to do it faster than we do. Some of your forces are without arms, but the same is true here, and at every other place where we have considerable bodies of troops. The plain matter-of-fact is, our good people have rushed to the rescue of the Government, faster than the government can find arms to put into their hands.

It would be agreeable to each division of the army to know its own precise destination: but the Government cannot immediately, nor inflexibly at any time, determine as to all; nor if determined, can it tell its *friends* without at the same time telling its *enemies*.

We know you do all as wisely and well as you can; and you will not be deceived if you conclude the same is true of us. Please give my respects and thanks to all   Yours very truly

A LINCOLN.

[1] Copy, DLC-RTL. The copy is in John Hay's handwriting and the envelope containing it bears Lincoln's endorsement, "Copy of letter to Gen. McClernand."

Under the command of General Ulysses S. Grant, General McClernand fought at Belmont, Missouri, on November 7, 1861. His command included the Twenty-seventh, Thirtieth, and Thirty-first Illinois Regiments, with additional units of cavalry and artillery.

To Simon Cameron[1]

Sec. of War, please see Mrs. Major Oakes.   A. LINCOLN
Nov. 11. 1861.

[1] ALS, DLC-Cameron Papers. Major James Oakes of the Fifth Cavalry was promoted to lieutenant colonel, November 12, 1861.

To John A. Dahlgren[1]

Capt. Dahlgren, please see the bearer, and learn if you have any thing for him to do   He is well vouched as an honest, & business man.   A. LINCOLN
Nov. 11. 1861

[1] ALS-P, ISLA. Written on a small card, Lincoln's note gives no indication of the bearer's name, the verso being inscribed by Lincoln merely "Navy-Yard."

Appointment of Delano T. Smith[1]

Washington   November 12th. 1861
Delano T. Smith, is hereby appointed to discharge the duties of Third Auditor of the Treasury, during the absence of Robert J. Atkinson.   ABRAHAM LINCOLN

[1] DS, owned by Melville A. Tinkham, Milwaukee, Wisconsin. Smith was chief clerk in the office of the Third Auditor.

To Joseph Holt[1]

Hon. Joseph Holt   Washington, D.C.
My dear Sir: Nov. 12. 1861

Yours of the 2nd., written at Louisville, never reached me till yesterday, and Gen McClellan had already so nearly completed his plans for the Departments of the West, and of the Cumberland, that I could scarcely ask him to re-arrange them. Halleck goes to St. Louis, and Buell goes to Louisville.[2] Sherman's wishes are being consulted, & I hope & believe he will be placed not unsatisfactorily to himself.[3]

You are not mistaken in supposing I am gratified extremely by the excellent conduct of *your* general at Camp Wildcat.

[21]

You have with you my good friend Judge David Davis; and allow [me] to assure you, you were never associated with a better man. Please present him my respects. Yours very truly

A. LINCOLN

[1] ALS, owned by Joseph Holt Rose, Pasadena, California. Joseph Holt, David Davis, and Hugh Campbell of St. Louis, were appointed commissioners to examine unsettled claims against the military Department of the West at St. Louis. Holt wrote to Lincoln from Louisville on his way to St. Louis, November 2, commending General William T. Sherman, recommending that he be placed in command of "one of the columns into Tennessee," suggesting General Henry W. Halleck for command of the Department of the Cumberland, and reporting that the "bearing of Genl. [Albin] Schoepf . . . excited great enthusiasm" at the battle at Camp Wildcat, Rockcastle Hills, Kentucky.

[2] Henry W. Halleck was placed in command of the Department of the Missouri, Don C. Buell in command of the Department of the Ohio with headquarters at Louisville, and David Hunter in command of the Department of Kansas, November 9, 1861 (OR, I, IV, 349).

[3] William T. Sherman was transferred to the Department of the Missouri under Halleck.

Appointment of George Harrington[1]

November 13, 1861

George Harrington, is hereby appointed to discharge the duty of Secretary of the Treasury, during the absence of Salmon P. Chase, from Washington.   ABRAHAM LINCOLN

Washington, November 13, 1861.

[1] Benjamin J. Selkirk & Sons Catalog, November 15, 1939, No. 119.

To Simon Cameron[1]

Hon. Sec. of War.   Executive Mansion
My dear Sir   Nov. 13. 1861.

Please have the Adjutant General ascertain whether 2nd. Lieut. of Co. D. 2nd. Infantry—Alexander E. Drake, is not entitled to promotion. His wife thinks he is. Please have this looked into.
Yours truly   A. LINCOLN

[1] ALS, NNP. Alexander E. Drake's promotion to first lieutenant (as of May 14) and to captain (as of October 9) were announced in AGO General Orders No. 106, December 5, 1861.

To Simon Cameron[1]

Hon. Sec. of War.   Executive Mansion
My dear Sir: Nov. 13. 1861

This will be presented by Hon. Charles S. Todd, of Ky, a gentleman of high standing, as you will remember, and distantly re-

lated to Mrs. L. He was once "Chargé de affaires" at Bogota, and once Minister to Russia. He will present strong recommendations from Kentuckians; and I hope you will, if possible, find some employment for him, in which he can help in our present troubles.
Yours truly   A. LINCOLN

[1] ALS, DLC-Cameron Papers. Although Charles S. Todd was also strongly recommended by John J. Crittenden in a letter of November 6, 1861 (DLC-RTL), there is no record of his appointment.

To Gideon Welles[1]

Sec. of Navy, please see Mr. Redfield   A. LINCOLN
Nov. 13, 1861

[1] ALS, owned by Cornelia H. Hill, Washington, D.C. According to the owner of this autograph note, Alexander H. Redfield of Detroit, Michigan, wished an appointment in the Marine Corps for his son, but failed to obtain it.

To Simon Cameron[1]

War Department, please preserve this dispatch, and answer it.
Nov. 14. 1861.   A. LINCOLN

[1] AES, DLC-RTL. Lincoln's endorsement is written on the back of a telegram received from William A. Barstow, Janesville, Wisconsin, November 13, 1861, asking why his authority to raise a cavalry regiment had been revoked. Cameron's reply, November 16, copied below Lincoln's endorsement, was that authority had been revoked "by request of Investigating Committee after their session in St. Louis." Colonel Barstow's Third Wisconsin Cavalry was finally mustered into service January 31, 1862.

To Simon Cameron[1]

November 14, 1861
I have no recollection of authorizing Gen. Anderson to appoint commissaries—think I did not—yet I should strongly incline to ratify acts of Gen. Anderson, when I shall *know* them to be his
Nov. 14, 1861   A. LINCOLN

[1] AES, IHi. Lincoln's endorsement is written on the back of a letter from Marshall H. Bright, captain and commissary of subsistence of Volunteers, Louisville, Kentucky, November 2, 1861, stating that although appointed by General Robert Anderson, he could not draw pay because his appointment was regarded as unauthorized. Lincoln's nomination of Bright for the appointment (as of October 25, 1861) was made under date of December 31, 1861, and confirmed by the Senate, March 26, 1862.

Reply to Delegation of Baltimore Citizens[1]

November 15, 1861

GENTLEMEN: I thank you for the address you have presented to me in behalf of the people of Baltimore. I have deplored the calamities which the sympathies of some misguided citizens of Maryland had brought down upon that patriotic and heretofore flourishing State. The prosperity of Baltimore up to the 19th of April last, was one of the wonders produced by the American Union. He who strangles himself, for whatever motive, is not more unreasonable than were those citizens of Baltimore who, in a single night, destroyed the Baltimore and Ohio Railroad, the Northern Pennsylvania Railroad, and the railroad from Baltimore to Philadelphia. From the day when that mad transaction occurred, the Government of the United States has been diligently engaged in endeavoring to restore those great avenues to their former usefulness, and, at the same time, to save Baltimore and Maryland from the danger of complete ruin through an unnecessary and unnatural rebellion.

I congratulate you upon the declaration which the people of Baltimore and Maryland have made in the recent election, of their recent approbation of the Federal Government, and of their enduring loyalty to the Union. I regard the results of these elections as auspicious of returning loyalty throughout all the insurrectionary States.

Your wishes for a fair participation by the mechanics and laboring men of Baltimore in the benefits of supplying the Government with materials and provisions are reasonable and just. They have deserved that participation. Loyalty has involved them in some danger, and has demanded of them some sacrifices. Their wishes, as you have communicated them, shall be referred to the proper Departments, and I am sure that every member of the Administration will cheerfully lend his aid to carry them out so far as it can be done consistently with the prudence and economy which ought always to regulate the public service.

[1] New York *Tribune*, November 16, 1861. A delegation of prominent citizens of Baltimore presented an address lamenting the suspension of trade and manufacture and the resulting unemployment and suffering which "has brought famine to their doors, and aroused the most gloomy forebodings of the approaching Winter; but amid all their sufferings the patriotism of the industrial classes has been proof against the insidious arguments of those who sought to involve them in hostility to the Government. . . ."

To Simon Cameron[1]

Sec. of War, please see Mr. Darling, who was a Presidential elector last year in New-York. A. LINCOLN

Nov. 16. 1861

[1]ALS, DLC-Cameron Papers. The purpose of William A. Darling's call may have been the same as on his previous visit. See Lincoln to Cameron, August 16, *supra*.

To Simon Cameron[1]

November 16, 1861

The appointment of Mr. W. W. Leland, is desired by the Irish Brigade, including much of the elements of the late 69th. & of Col. Mulligan's regiment. If it is possible to oblige them in this, let it be done. A. LINCOLN

Nov. 16. 1861.

[1] AES, owned by Charles W. Olsen, Chicago, Illinois. Lincoln's endorsement is written on a letter from Governor Edwin D. Morgan, November 13, 1861, recommending appointment of William W. Leland of New York City as brigade commissary designated by Thomas F. Meagher acting brigadier general of the Irish Brigade. Leland was appointed with rank of captain from November 16, 1861.

To Lorenzo Thomas[1]

Adjutant General Executive Mansion,
Sir: Nov. 16, 1861

Lieut. John Watt who, I believe, has been detailed to do service about the White-House, is not needed for that purpose, and you assign him to his proper place in Regiment. Yours truly

A. LINCOLN.

[1] Hertz, II, 846. John Watt, public gardener at the White House under Buchanan, had been appointed first lieutenant, September 9, 1861, but the appointment was revoked February 3, 1862, following charges of disloyalty and an adverse report by the Potter investigating committee. Lincoln's request to Thomas may or may not have been the result of Representative John F. Potter's letter of September 12, forwarding to the president the testimony against Watt. In any event, Watt re-enlisted as a private in the Thirteenth New York Artillery, August 12, 1863, and gained promotion from the ranks to second lieutenant, May 20, 1865, and first lieutenant, January 17, 1866.

To George Bancroft[1]

Executive Mansion, Washington, Nov 18, 1861.

My dear Sir: I esteem it a high honor to have received a note from Mr. Bancroft, inclosing the report of proceedings of a New

York meeting, taking measures for the relief of Union people of North Carolina. I thank you, and all others participating, for this benevolent and patriotic movement.

The main thought in the closing paragraph of your letter is one which does not escape my attention, and with which I must deal in all due caution, and with the best judgment I can bring to it. Your obt. Servt.   [A. LINCOLN.]

Hon. Geo. Bancroft.

¹ Copy, DLC-RTL. The copy is in Nicolay's handwriting without signature. George Bancroft, historian and former minister to Great Britain (1846-1849), wrote Lincoln on November 15, 1861, enclosing a clipping from the New York *Times*, November 8, which gave an account of the meeting at Cooper Institute for the relief of loyal citizens of Hatteras, North Carolina, represented by Reverend T. W. Conway and Reverend Marble N. Taylor (see Lincoln to Cameron, October 25, *supra*). The closing paragraph of Bancroft's letter is as follows: "Your administration has fallen upon times, which will be remembered as long as human events find a record. I sincerely wish to you the glory of perfect success. Civil war is the instrument of Divine Providence to root out social slavery; posterity will not be satisfied with the result, unless the consequences of the war shall effect an increase of free states. This is the universal expectation and hope of men of all parties." (DLC-RTL).

To Edward Everett¹

Hon. Edward Everett   Washington,
My dear Sir: Nov. 18. 1861

Your kind note of the 15th. inclosing a copy of a letter to yourself from Mr. Donnell, is received, and I am greatly obliged for both. There was a gentleman of that name in congress from North-Carolina, when I was a member (from Dec./47 to March/49) but I think this is not the same. His letter, however, is an interesting one, and on a very interesting subject.

The items of news coming in last week were all satisfactory, except the very last—the capture of one of our foraging parties across the river from here, on Saturday, consisting of about 50 men. The success at Port-Royal was both splendid and important. The military men are taking what they consider all necessary steps to hold the places taken. And then the capture of Mason & Slidell! Your Obt. Servt.   A. LINCOLN.

¹ ALS, MHi. Everett's letter of November 15, 1861, with enclosure, is not in the Lincoln Papers, but a copy preserved in the Everett letterbook (MHi) explains that Everett enclosed a communication from ". . . a gentleman living in New York. . . . He is a brother of Judge Donnell of New Bern, formerly I believe Chief Justice, certainly one of the Superior judges of North Carolina, a gentleman of wealth and influence. . . ." Richard S. Donnell of New Bern, North Carolina, was a Whig member of congress 1847-1849, but in the absence of the letter which Everett forwarded, accurate identification of Everett's correspondent has not been possible.

To William H. Seward[1]

If the Sec. of State can and will find a consulate for Rev. Mr. Carothers, I have no objection & shall even be pleased.

Nov. 18. 1861   A. LINCOLN

[1] AES, DNA FS RG 59, Appointments, Box 248. Lincoln's endorsement is written on the back of a letter from Reverend John C. Smith, pastor of the Fourth Presbyterian Church of Washington, November 15, 1861, asking a consulship for Reverend Andrew G. Carothers, who had been removed as consul at Turks Islands (Bahamas) ". . . in the hurry and pressure of public business . . . and *not because* of any objections to him, politically, or *officially*. . . ." (*Ibid.*). For Carothers' appointment, see Lincoln to Seward, December 19, *infra*.

To Hiram Walbridge[1]

Washington,
Gen. H. Walbridge, New-York City.   Nov. 18, 1861.

Dear Sir: Your note reminding me of the fact that, as early as April last, you pointed out to me on the map Port Royal and Beaufort as advantageous places to make lodgments on the Southern coast, is received. I am free to confess you were the first who called my attention to that particular locality. I also remember that you insisted we should call six hundred thousand men into the field, a considerable length of time before I had brought my own mind up to anything near so large a scale. Yours truly,

A. LINCOLN.

[1] New York *Tribune*, November 22, 1861. Walbridge's letter is not in the Lincoln Papers.

To George B. McClellan[1]

November 21, 1861.

If General McClellan and General Halleck deem it necessary to declare and maintain martial law at Saint Louis the same is hereby authorized.   A. LINCOLN.

[1] OR, II, I, 230. Lincoln's qualified authorization was endorsed on a telegram from Halleck to McClellan, St. Louis, November 20, 1861, reading as follows: "No written authority is found here to declare and enforce martial law in this department. Please send me such written authority and telegraph me that it has been sent by mail." Lorenzo Thomas to Halleck, November 25, communicated McClellan's request for more information before issuing the authority, and on November 30 Halleck replied, citing the insurrection in Northern Missouri: ". . . I cannot arrest such men and seize their papers without exercising martial law for there is no civil law or civil authority to reach them . . . . if the President is not willing to intrust me with it he should relieve me from the command. . . ." (*Ibid.*, 232). See Lincoln to Halleck, December 2, *infra*.

To Caleb B. Smith[1]

Hon. Sec. of Interior   Executive Mansion
My dear Sir   Nov. 21, 1861

Can you, by any possibility, find some place for Judge Taft? I shall be greatly obliged if you can & will. Yours truly

A. LINCOLN

[1] ALS, MH. Judge Taft was probably Horatio N. Taft who retained his position as chief examiner in the Patent Office although appointed by President Buchanan. Taft's children, Halsey and Horatio, Jr., were playmates of Willie and Tad Lincoln. See Lincoln's memorandum, July 4, *supra*.

To Simon Cameron[1]

Sec. of War, please see Admiral Zerman.

Nov. 23. 1861   A. LINCOLN

[1] ALS, DLC-Cameron Papers. Juan Napoleon Zerman took part in the French revolution of July, 1830, was banished from France as a Republican in 1848, and migrated to the United States. Having commanded the Turkish Black Sea Fleet (1842-1847), he found employment as admiral in the Mexican Navy (1854-1859), and upon the outbreak of the Civil War sought a commission in the Union Army. Lincoln nominated him March 15, 1862, on Cameron's recommendation, for appointment as brigadier general in the Volunteer service. The Senate confirmed the appointment on May 5, recalled the confirmation the next day, and tabled the nomination on June 12, 1862. A letter from Zerman to Lincoln dated August 14, 1862 (DLC-RTL) blamed the recall of his appointment on intrigues of foreign politicians.

To Simon Cameron[1]

November 25, 1861

I take the occasion of Gen. Cooper's letter within, to call attention again to Mr. Jones application to enter the Army. I really feel some interest for him.   A. LINCOLN

Nov. 25. 1861.

[1] AES, DLC-Cameron Papers. Lincoln's endorsement is written on a letter from General James Cooper, November 21, 1861, recommending Alfred H. Jones for appointment as an officer of cavalry. There is no record of the appointment.

To Thomas A. Scott[1]

November 25, 1861

I know I have expected General Keim, upon certain conditions, to be appointed a Brigadier General but I do not remember particulars. If his case is now presented mature, according to the understanding, let him be appointed.

1 *The Collector*, May, 1941, No. 1392. According to the catalog description, Lincoln's endorsement is written on a letter from William H. Keim, November 21, 1861, referring to organization of four unattached companies over and above previous requisitions for troops from Pennsylvania. Governor Curtin had suggested that Keim write the president asking a commission to command this brigade. Keim was appointed December 20, 1861.

Drafts of a Bill for
Compensated Emancipation in Delaware[1]

[November 26? 1861]

[No. 1]

Be it enacted by the State of Delaware, that on condition the United States of America will, at the present session of Congress, engage by law to pay, and thereafter faithfully pay to the said State of Delaware, in the six per cent bonds of said United States, the sum of seven hundred and nineteen thousand and two hundred dollars, in five equal annual instalments, there shall be neither slavery nor involuntary servitude, at any time after the first day of January in the year of our Lord one thousand, eight hundred and sixtyseven, within the said State of Delaware, except in the punishment of crime, whereof the party shall have been duly convicted: *Provided*, that said State shall, in good faith prevent, so far as possible, the carrying of any person out of said State, into involuntary servitude, beyond the limits of said State, at any time after the passage of this act; and shall also provide for one fifth of the adult slavery becoming free at the middle of the year one thousand eight hundred an[d] sixtytwo; one fourth of the remainder of said adults, at the middle of the year one thousand eight hundred and sixtythree; one third of the remainder of said adults, at the middle of the year one thousand eight hundred and sixtyfour; one half the remainder of said adults at the middle of the year one thousand eight hundred and sixtyfive; and the entire remainder of adults, together with all minors, at the beginning of the year one thousand eight hundred and sixtyseven, as hereinbefore indicated. And *provided* also that said State may make provision of apprenticeship, not to extend beyond the age of twenty-one years for males, nor eighteen for females, for all minors whose mothers were not free, at the respective births of such minors.

[No. 2]

Be it enacted by the State of Delaware that on condition the United States of America will, at the present session of Congress, engage by law to pay, and thereafter faithfully pay to the said

State of Delaware, in the six per cent bonds of said United States, the sum of seven hundred and nineteen thousand, and two hundred dollars, in thirty one[2] equal annual instalments, there shall be neither slavery nor involuntary servitude, at any time after the first day of January in the year of our Lord one thousand eight hundred and ninety three,[3] within the said State of Delaware, except in the punishment of crime, whereof the party shall have been duly convicted; nor, except in the punishment of crime as aforesaid, shall any person who shall be born after the passage of this act, nor any person above the age of thirty five years, be held in slavery, or to involuntary servitude, within said State of Delaware, at any time after the passage of this act.

And be it further enacted that said State shall, in good faith prevent, so far as possible, the carrying of any person out of said state, into involuntary servitude, beyond the limits of said State, at any time after the passage of this act.

And be it further enacted that said State may make provision of apprenticeship, not to extend beyond the age of twentyone years for males, nor eighteen for females, for all minors whose mothers were not free at the respective births of such minors.

On reflection, I like No. 2 the better. By it the Nation would pay the State $23,200 per annum for thirtyone years— and

All born after the passage of the act would be born free— and

All slaves above the age of 35 years would become free on the passage of the act— and

All others would become free on arriving at the age of 35 years, until January 1893— when

All remaining of all ages would become free, subject to apprenticeship for minors born of slave mothers, up to the respective ages of 21 and 18.

If the State would desire to have the money sooner, let the bill be altered only in fixing the time of final emancipation earlier, and making the annual instalments correspondingly fewer in number, by which they would also be correspondingly larger in amount. For instance, strike out "1893," and insert "1872"; and strike out "thirtyone" annual instalments, and insert "ten" annual instalments. The instalments would then be $71,920 instead of $23,200 as now. In all other particulars let the bill stand precisely as it is.

1 AD, CSmH. The date of the four sheets of manuscript comprising the two drafts and Lincoln's comments is that assigned by Nicolay and Hay. Representative George P. Fisher of Delaware undertook to promote the bill among the Union men of his state. Lincoln's drafts were rewritten and printed for

circulation among members of the Delaware legislature, but the bill was never introduced.   2 "Ten" has been written with pencil above "thirty one."
3 "Seventytwo" has been written with pencil above "ninety three."

To George B. McClellan[1]

The within is the copy of a letter from Mr. Guthrie, which perhaps it is well for Gen. McClellan to see.   A. LINCOLN
Nov. 26. 1861

1 AES, DLC-RTL. Lincoln's endorsement is written on a copy of a letter from James Guthrie to Joshua F. Speed, November 22, 1861, endorsed by Speed November 26, giving information on construction and gauge of the Nashville Railroad and on Middle Tennessee. Guthrie's letter expressed fear that ". . . the directing spirits at Washington still think of an invasion of East Tennessee . . . and are disposed to allow [Leonidas] Polk Johnson [Albert S. Johnston] & [Simon] Buckner to . . . threaten the whole Ohio border for the next six months. . . . The Federal armies must advance and advance within a month. . . ." (DLC-RTL). Although Lincoln's endorsement is one day earlier than that to McClellan on another of Guthrie's letters to Speed bearing the same date, November 22, it is obvious that the matter covered in Guthrie's letter bearing Lincoln's endorsement of the 27th was written prior to this one. See Lincoln to McClellan, November 27, *infra*.

To George B. McClellan[1]

November 27, 1861

If Gen. McClellan thinks it proper to make Buell a Major General, enabling Sherman to return to Kentucky, it would rather please me. As Buell, by the letter shown me to-day, agrees with Mr. Guthrie about half a dozen more Brig. Genls. being needed in Ky, that, also might be attended to at the same time.
Nov. 27. 1861.   A. LINCOLN

1 AES, DLC-RTL. Lincoln's endorsement is written on the back of a copy of a letter from James Guthrie to Joshua F. Speed, November 22, 1861, expressing the wish of himself and many Union men that William T. Sherman should remain in Kentucky to lead troops in the field, and stating that "We want more Brigadier generals of the best military schools." Although dated on the same day as Guthrie's letter to Speed which Lincoln endorsed to Mc-Clellan on November 26 (*supra*), Guthrie's letter carrying Lincoln's endorsement of November 27 seems obviously of prior composition. Speed carried both letters to Washington for Lincoln's consideration.

To George B. McClellan[1]

Gen. McClellan, if you think the erection of a foot-bridge over the Potomac, is expedient, please see the bearer.   A. LINCOLN
Nov. 27, 1861

1 ALS, NSk. Written on a small card, Lincoln's communication gives no hint as to the bearer.

[31]

Memorandum:
Advice to Mrs. Stephen A. Douglas[1]

Executive Mansion, Nov. 27– 1861

Yesterday Mrs. Douglas called, saying she is guardian of the minor children of her late husband; that she is being urged, against her inclination, to send them South, on the plea of avoiding the confiscation of their property there, and asking my counsel in the case.

I expect the United States will overcome the attempt to confiscate property, because of loyalty to the government; but if not, I still do not expect the property of absent minor children will be confiscated. I therefore think Mrs. Douglas may safely act her pleasure in the premises.

But it is especially dangerous for my name to be connected with the matter; for nothing would more certainly excite the secessionists to do the worst they can against the children.

[1] AD, DLC-RTL. Douglas' children by his first wife (Martha Denny Martin Douglas) were Robert M. Douglas, born January 28, 1849, and Stephen A. Douglas, Jr., born November 3, 1850.

Order for Day of Thanksgiving[1]

Executive Mansion. Washington, 27th. November, 1861.

The Municipal authorities of Washington and Georgetown in this District, have appointed tomorrow, the 28th. instant, as a day of thanksgiving, the several Departments will on that occasion be closed, in order that the officers of the government may partake in the ceremonies. ABRAHAM LINCOLN.

[1] Copy, DNA FI RG 56, General Records, Treasury Department, Series AB, 1861, II, 7; copy, DNA WR RG 107, Secretary of War, Letters Received, P 536.

To William H. Seward[1]

Respectfully submitted to the Secretary of State, with the accompanying recommendation of Senator McDougal.

Nov. 27. 1861.   A. LINCOLN

[1] AES, DNA FS RG 59, Appointments, Box 356. Lincoln's endorsement is written on a letter from John P. O'Sullivan, Union Place Hotel, New York City, November 25, 1861, to Senator James A. McDougall, asking a recommendation for the consulship at Calcutta, India. There is no record of his appointment.

To Salmon P. Chase[1]

Hon. Sec. of Treasury   Executive Mansion
My dear Sir: Nov. 29. 1861
You remember kindly asking me, some time ago whether I really desired you to find a place for William Johnson, a colored boy who came from Illinois with me. If you can find him the place shall really be obliged. Yours truly   A. LINCOLN

[1] ALS, DNA WR RG 56, Treasury Department, Personnel Records. William H. Johnson was given a place as laborer in the Treasury Department at $600 per year. See also Lincoln to whom it may concern, March 7, *supra*.

To Simon Cameron[1]

Respectfully submitted to the Sec. of War, remarking that it be very agreeable to me for Mr. Fillmore to be obliged.
Nov. 30, 1861   A. LINCOLN.

[1] Argosy Book Shop Catalog, April, 1942. According to the catalog description, Lincoln's endorsement is written on a letter from ex-President Millard Fillmore, November 16, 1861, to his nephew George M. Fillmore, advising him how to proceed about getting an appointment as a lieutenant. Corporal Fillmore of the Second Minnesota Infantry was appointed second lieutenant of the Third Artillery, Regular Army, as of November 30, 1861.

Memorandum:
Appointment of Isaac E. Pearson[1]

[December, 1861]
Isaac E. Pearson, of Westminster Md. for West-Point. Will be 18, August 25, 1862.

[1] AE, DNA WR RG 94, U.S. Military Academy, 1861, No. 661, Box 79. Lincoln's endorsement is written on an envelope containing recommendations of Isaac E. Pearson for West Point. There is no record of Pearson's appointment.

To Gideon Welles[1]

[c. December, 1861?]
Sec. of Navy please send me the contract (if there is one) with the man who is *pretending* to build the Engine in the Pensacola.
                               A. LINCOLN.

[1] Stan. V. Henkels Catalog 1342, January 4, 1924, No. 48k. The date assigned by the editors is conjectured from an item in the New York *Tribune*, December 23, 1861, reading in part as follows: "The steam sloop Pensacola made her first trial trip yesterday. . . . Her machinery worked well, much

better than was anticipated. Mr. Sickles, who built the engine a year ago in the Washington Navy-Yard, but was so long in getting it into working order that the Department lost patience and confined him on board, is still shut up and will remain there until the vessel gets to sea."

Memorandum to George B. McClellan on Potomac Campaign[1]

[c. December 1, 1861]

If it were determined to make a forward movement of the Army of the Potomac, without awaiting further increase of numbers, or better drill & discipline, how *long* would it require to actually get in motion?[2]

After leaving all that would be necessary, how many troops could join the movement from South-West of the river?[3]

How many from North-East of it?[4]

Suppose, then, that of those South-West of the river 50,000[5] move forward and menace the enemy at Centerville.

The remainder of the moveable force on that side move rapidly to the crossing of the Ocoquan by the road from Alexandria towards Richmond; there to be joined by the whole moveable force from North-East of the river, having landed from the Potomac just below the mouth of the Ocoquan, moved by land up the South side of that stream to the crossing point named; then the whole move together, by the road thence to Brentsville, and beyond, to the railroad just South of it's crossing of Broad Run, a strong detachment of cavalry having gone rapidly ahead to destroy the railroad bridges South and North of the point.

If the crossing of the Ocoquan by those from above be resisted, those landing from the Potomac below to take the resisting force of the enemy in rear; or, if the landing from the Potomac be resisted, those c[r]ossing the Ocoquan from above to take that resisting force in rear. Both points will probably not be successfully resisted at the same time.

The force in front of Centreville, if pressed too hardly, should fight back slowly into the intrenchments behind them.

Armed vessels and transportation should remain at the Potomac landing to cover a possible retreat.

[1] AD, DLC-RTL. See also the related memorandum enclosed with Lincoln to McClellan, February 3, 1862, *infra*. The document bears an endorsement written by John Hay and Lincoln which reads (with Lincoln's additions given in italics): "Memoranda of the President on Campaign of Potomac—*without date, but about Dec. 1, 1861* and letter of Genl. McClellan—*date Dec. 10, 1861*." McClellan's letter is as follows:

"I inclose the paper you left with me—filled as requested. In arriving at the numbers given I have left the minimum number in garrison & observation.

"Information received recently leads me to believe that the enemy could meet us in front with equal forces nearly—& I have now my mind actively turned towards another plan of campaign that I do not think at all anticipated by the enemy nor by many of our own people."

2 Following this question is McClellan's answer in pencil: "If bridge trains ready—By Dec. 15.—probably 25th."

3 McClellan has written in pencil, "71,000."

4 McClellan has written in pencil, "33,000."

5 In the blank left by Lincoln is written in pencil "50,000." Presumably this figure was not supplied by McClellan.

To Henry W. Halleck[1]

To Major General, Henry W. Halleck,   December 2, 1861

Commanding in the Department of Missouri.

General: As an insurrection exists in the United States and is in arms in the State of Missouri, you are hereby authorized and empowered to suspend the Writ of Habeas Corpus within the limits of the military division under your command and to exercise martial law as you find it necessary in your discretion to secure the public safety and the authority of the United States.

In witness whereof, I have hereunto set my hand and caused the seal of the United States to be affixed at Washington, this second day of December, A D 1861.   ABRAHAM LINCOLN

By the President:

WILLIAM H. SEWARD   Secretary of State.

1 DS, DLC. See Lincoln to George B. McClellan, November 21, *supra.*

Annual Message to Congress[1]

December 3, 1861

Fellow Citizens of the Senate and House of Representatives:

In the midst of unprecedented political troubles, we have cause of great gratitude to God for unusual good health, and most abundant harvests.

You will not be surprised to learn that, in the peculiar exigencies of the times, our intercourse with foreign nations has been attended with profound solicitude, chiefly turning upon our own domestic affairs.

1 DS, DNA RG 233, Thirty-seventh Congress, Second Session, Original Annual Message of the President—Interior. Pages 14-20 and 27 of the manuscript are missing. For these passages our text follows the printing in *Senate Executive Document No. 1.* The manuscript was copied by several different amanuenses. Only the date line and the signature are in Lincoln's handwriting. No trace of Lincoln's original manuscript has been found.

A disloyal portion of the American people have, during the whole year, been engaged in an attempt to divide and destroy the Union. A nation which endures factious domestic division, is exposed to disrespect abroad; and one party, if not both, is sure, sooner or later, to invoke foreign intervention.

Nations, thus tempted to interfere, are not always able to resist the counsels of seeming expediency, and ungenerous ambition, although measures adopted under such influences seldom fail to be unfortunate and injurious to those adopting them.

The disloyal citizens of the United States who have offered the ruin of our country, in return for the aid and comfort which they have invoked abroad, have received less patronage and encouragement than they probably expected. If it were just to suppose, as the insurgents have seemed to assume, that foreign nations, in this case, discarding all moral, social, and treaty obligations, would act solely, and selfishly, for the most speedy restoration of commerce, including, especially, the acquisition of cotton, those nations appear, as yet, not to have seen their way to their object more directly, or clearly, through the destruction, than through the preservation, of the Union. If we could dare to believe that foreign nations are actuated by no higher principle than this, I am quite sure a sound argument could be made to show them that they can reach their aim more readily, and easily, by aiding to crush this rebellion, than by giving encouragement to it.

The principal lever relied on by the insurgents for exciting foreign nations to hostility against us, as already intimated, is the embarrassment of commerce. Those nations, however, not improbably, saw from the first, that it was the Union which made as well our foreign, as our domestic, commerce. They can scarcely have failed to perceive that the effort for disunion produces the existing difficulty; and that one strong nation promises more durable peace, and a more extensive, valuable and reliable commerce, than can the same nation broken into hostile fragments.

It is not my purpose to review our discussions with foreign states, because whatever might be their wishes, or dispositions, the integrity of our country, and the stability of our government, mainly depend, not upon them, but on the loyalty, virtue, patriotism, and intelligence of the American people. The correspondence itself, with the usual reservations, is herewith submitted.[2]

I venture to hope it will appear that we have practiced prudence, and liberality towards foreign powers, averting causes of irrita-

[2] See Thirty-seventh Congress, Second Session, *Senate Executive Document No. 1*, I, 21-441.

tion; and, with firmness, maintaining our own rights and honor.

Since, however, it is apparent that here, as in every other state, foreign dangers necessarily attend domestic difficulties, I recommend that adequate and ample measures be adopted for maintaining the public defences on every side. While, under this general recommendation, provision for defending our sea-coast line readily occurs to the mind, I also, in the same connexion, ask the attention of Congress to our great lakes and rivers. It is believed that some fortifications and depots of arms and munitions, with harbor and navigation improvements, all at well selected points upon these, would be of great importance to the national defence and preservation. I ask attention to the views of the Secretary of War, expressed in his report,[3] upon the same general subject.

I deem it of importance that the loyal regions of East Tennessee and western North Carolina should be connected with Kentucky, and other faithful parts of the Union, by railroad. I therefore recommend, as a military measure, that Congress provide for the construction of such road, as speedily as possible. Kentucky, no doubt, will co-operate, and, through her legislature, make the most judicious selection of a line. The northern terminus must connect with some existing railroad; and whether the route shall be from Lexington, or Nicholasville, to the Cumberland Gap; or from Lebanon to the Tennessee line, in the direction of Knoxville; or on some still different line, can easily be determined. Kentucky and the general government co-operating, the work can be completed in a very short time; and when done, it will be not only of vast present usefulness, but also a valuable permanent improvement, worth its cost in all the future.

Some treaties, designed chiefly for the interests of commerce, and having no grave political importance, have been negotiated, and will be submitted to the Senate for their consideration.

Although we have failed to induce some of the commercial powers to adopt a desirable melioration of the rigor of maritime war, we have removed all obstructions from the way of this humane reform, except such as are merely of temporary and accidental occurrence.

[3] *Ibid.*, II, 8: "It is of great importance that immediate attention should be given to the condition of our Fortifications upon the seaboard and the Lakes, and upon our exposed frontiers. They should at once be placed in perfect condition for successful defence. Aggressions are seldom made upon a nation ever ready to defend its honor and to repel insults; and we should show to the world, that while engaged in quelling disturbances at home we are able to protect ourselves against attacks from abroad. . . ."

I invite your attention to the correspondence between her Britannic Majesty's minister accredited to this government, and the Secretary of State, relative to the detention of the British ship Perthshire in June last, by the United States steamer Massachusetts, for a supposed breach of the blockade.[4] As this detention was occasioned by an obvious misapprehension of the facts, and as justice requires that we should commit no belligerent act not founded in strict right, as sanctioned by public law, I recommend that an appropriation be made to satisfy the reasonable demand of the owners of the vessel for her detention.

I repeat the recommendation of my predecessor, in his annual message to Congress in December last, in regard to the disposition of the surplus which will probably remain after satisfying the claims of American citizens against China, pursuant to the awards of the commissioners under the act of the 3rd of March, 1859.[5] If, however, it should not be deemed advisable to carry that recommendation into effect, I would suggest that authority be given for investing the principal, over the proceeds of the surplus referred to, in good securities, with a view to the satisfaction of such other just claims of our citizens against China as are not unlikely to arise hereafter in the course of our extensive trade with that Empire.

By the act of the 5th of August last, Congress authorized the President to instruct the commanders of suitable vessels to defend themselves against, and to capture pirates. This authority has been exercised in a single instance only.[6] For the more effectual protection of our extensive and valuable commerce, in the eastern seas especially, it seems to me that it would also be advisable to authorize the commanders of sailing vessels to re-capture any prizes which pirates might make of United States vessels and their cargoes, and the consular courts, now established by law in eastern countries, to adjudicate the cases, in the event that this should not be objected to by the local authorities.

4 *Ibid.*, I, 177-81. The *Perthshire* left Mobile with a cargo of cotton within the time granted by Proclamations of Blockade (q.v. April 19 and 27, *supra*). On June 9, she was seized and boarded by the U.S.S. *Massachusetts* off Pensacola, but was released on June 12, 1861.

5 Under the convention with China of November 8, 1858, settlement of claims of U.S. citizens was to come from one-fifth of the receipts for tonnage and export and import duties levied on American vessels at Canton, Shanghai, and Foochow. Buchanan's Annual Message of December 4, 1860, suggested that the surplus of more than $200,000, remaining after the awards and belonging in equity to China, should be appropriated to "some benevolent object in which the Chinese may be specially interested."

6 See Authorization for the *Pembroke*, October 28, *supra*.

If any good reason exists why we should persevere longer in withholding our recognition of the independence and sovereignty of Hayti and Liberia, I am unable to discern it. Unwilling, however, to inaugurate a novel policy in regard to them without the approbation of Congress, I submit for your consideration the expediency of an appropriation for maintaining a chargé d'affaires near each of those new states. It is [sic] does not admit of doubt that important commercial advantages might be secured by favorable commercial treaties with them.[7]

The operations of the treasury during the period which has elapsed since your adjournment have been conducted with signal success. The patriotism of the people has placed at the disposal of the government the large means demanded by the public exigencies. Much of the national loan has been taken by citizens of the industrial classes, whose confidence in their country's faith, and zeal for their country's deliverance from present peril, have induced them to contribute to the support of the government the whole of their limited acquisitions. This fact imposes peculiar obligations to economy in disbursement and energy in action.

The revenue from all sources, including loans, for the financial year ending on the 30th June, 1861, was eighty six million, eight hundred and thirty five thousand, nine hundred dollars, and twenty seven cents, ($86,835,900.27,) and the expenditures for the same period, including payments on account of the public debt, were eighty four million, five hundred and seventy eight thousand, eight hundred and thirty four dollars and forty seven cents, ($84,578,834.47;) leaving a balance in the treasury, on the 1st July, of two million, two hundred and fifty seven thousand, sixty five dollars and eighty cents, ($2,257,065.80.) For the first quarter of the financial year, ending on the 30th September, 1861, the receipts from all sources, including the balance of first of July, were[8] $102,532,509.27, and the expenses $98,239,733.09; leaving a balance on the 1st of October, 1861, of $4,292,776.18.

Estimates for the remaining three quarters of the year, and for the financial year 1863, together with his views of ways and means for meeting the demands contemplated by them, will be submitted to Congress by the Secretary of the Treasury. It is gratifying to know that the expenditures made necessary by the rebellion are not beyond the resources of the loyal people, and to believe that

[7] Senator Charles Sumner of the committee on Foreign Affairs on February 4, 1862, reported a bill, authorizing appointment of diplomatic representatives to Haiti and Liberia, which was approved and signed by Lincoln on June 5.
[8] From this point to footnote 12 the text is taken from *Senate Executive Document No. 1.*

the same patriotism which has thus far sustained the government will continue to sustain it till Peace and Union shall again bless the land.

I respectfully refer to the report of the Secretary of War for information respecting the numerical strength of the army, and for recommendations having in view an increase of its efficiency and the well being of the various branches of the service intrusted to his care.[9] It is gratifying to know that the patriotism of the people has proved equal to the occasion, and that the number of troops tendered greatly exceeds the force which Congress authorized me to call into the field.

I refer with pleasure to those portions of his report which make allusion to the creditable degree of discipline already attained by our troops, and to the excellent sanitary condition of the entire army.

The recommendation of the Secretary for an organization of the militia upon a uniform basis, is a subject of vital importance to the future safety of the country, and is commended to the serious attention of Congress.

The large addition to the regular army, in connexion with the defection that has so considerably diminished the number of its officers, gives peculiar importance to his recommendation for increasing the corps of cadets to the greatest capacity of the Military Academy.

By mere omission, I presume, Congress has failed to provide chaplains for hospitals occupied by volunteers. This subject was brought to my notice, and I was induced to draw up the form of a letter, one copy of which, properly addressed, has been delivered to each of the persons, and at the dates respectively named and stated, in a schedule, containing also the form of the letter, marked A, and herewith transmitted.[10]

These gentlemen, I understand, entered upon the duties designated, at the times respectively stated in the schedule, and have labored faithfully therein ever since. I therefore recommend that they be compensated at the same rate as chaplains in the army. I further suggest that general provision be made for chaplains to serve at hospitals, as well as with regiments.

The report of the Secretary of the Navy[11] presents in detail the operations of that branch of the service, the activity and energy which have characterized its administration, and the results of measures to increase its efficiency and power. Such have been the

---

[9] *See Senate Executive Document No. 1*, II, 3-4, 15-56.   [10] *Vide infra.*
[11] See *Senate Executive Document No. 1*, III.

additions, by construction and purchase, that it may almost be said a navy has been created and brought into service since our difficulties commenced.

Besides blockading our extensive coast, squadrons larger than ever before assembled under our flag have been put afloat and performed deeds which have increased our naval renown.

I would invite special attention to the recommendation of the Secretary for a more perfect organization of the navy by introducing additional grades in the service.

The present organization is defective and unsatisfactory, and the suggestions submitted by the department will, it is believed, if adopted, obviate the difficulties alluded to, promote harmony, and increase the efficiency of the navy.

There are three vacancies on the bench of the Supreme Court—two by the decease of Justices Daniel and McLean, and one by the resignation of Justice Campbell. I have so far forborne making nominations to fill these vacancies for reasons which I will now state. Two of the outgoing judges resided within the States now overrun by revolt; so that if successors were appointed in the same localities, they could not now serve upon their circuits; and many of the most competent men there, probably would not take the personal hazard of accepting to serve, even here, upon the supreme bench. I have been unwilling to throw all the appointments northward, thus disabling myself from doing justice to the south on the return of peace; although I may remark that to transfer to the north one which has heretofore been in the south, would not, with reference to territory and population, be unjust.

During the long and brilliant judicial career of Judge McLean his circuit grew into an empire—altogether too large for any one judge to give the courts therein more than a nominal attendance—rising in population from one million four hundred and seventy-thousand and eighteen, in 1830, to six million one hundred and fifty-one thousand four hundred and five, in 1860.

Besides this, the country generally has outgrown our present judicial system. If uniformity was[12] at all intended, the system requires that all the States shall be accommodated with circuit courts, attended by supreme judges, while, in fact, Wisconsin, Minnesota, Iowa, Kansas, Florida, Texas, California, and Oregon, have never had any such courts. Nor can this well be remedied without a change of the system; because the adding of judges to the Supreme Court, enough for the accommodation of all parts of the country, with circuit courts, would create a court altogether too numerous

12 At this point the manuscript resumes.

for a judicial body of any sort. And the evil, if it be one, will increase as new States come into the Union. Circuit courts are useful, or they are not useful. If useful, no State should be denied them; if not useful, no State should have them. Let them be provided for all, or abolished as to all.

Three modifications occur to me, either of which, I think, would be an improvement upon our present system. Let the Supreme Court be of convenient number in every event. Then, first, let the whole country be divided into circuits of convenient size, the supreme judges to serve in a number of them corresponding to their own number, and independent circuit judges be provided for all the rest. Or, secondly, let the supreme judges be relieved from circuit duties, and circuit judges provided for all the circuits. Or, thirdly, dispense with circuit courts altogether, leaving the judicial functions wholly to the district courts and an independent Supreme Court.[13]

I respectfully recommend to the consideration of Congress the present condition of the statute laws, with the hope that Congress will be able to find an easy remedy for many of the inconveniences and evils which constantly embarrass those engaged in the practical administration of them. Since the organization of the government, Congress has enacted some five thousand acts and joint resolutions, which fill more than six thousand closely printed pages, and are scattered through many volumes. Many of these acts have been drawn in haste and without sufficient caution, so that their provisions are often obscure in themselves, or in conflict with each other, or at least so doubtful as to render it very difficult for even the best informed persons to ascertain precisely what the statute law really is.

It seems to me very important that the statute laws should be made as plain and intelligible as possible, and be reduced to as small a compass as may consist with the fullness and precision of the will of the legislature and the perspicuity of its language. This, well done, would, I think, greatly facilitate the labors of those whose duty it is to assist in the administration of the laws, and would be a lasting benefit to the people, by placing before them, in a more accessible and intelligible form, the laws which so deeply concern their interests and their duties.

[13] An act approved July 15, 1862, created nine circuits including all the states except California and Oregon and repealed all acts giving District Courts the power of circuit courts. Further changes were brought about by the act approved March 3, 1863, which fixed the number of justices of the Supreme Court at nine plus the chief justice, and created the Tenth Circuit consisting of California and Oregon.

I am informed by some whose opinions I respect, that all the acts of Congress now in force, and of a permanent and general nature, might be revised and re-written, so as to be embraced in one volume (or at most, two volumes) of ordinary and convenient size. And I respectfully recommend to Congress to consider of the subject, and, if my suggestion be approved, to devise such plan as to their wisdom shall seem most proper for the attainment of the end proposed.[14]

One of the unavoidable consequences of the present insurrection is the entire suppression, in many places, of all the ordinary means of administering civil justice by the officers and in the forms of existing law. This is the case, in whole or in part, in all the insurgent States; and as our armies advance upon and take possession of parts of those States, the practical evil becomes more apparent. There are no courts nor officers to whom the citizens of other States may apply for the enforcement of their lawful claims against citizens of the insurgent States; and there is a vast amount of debt constituting such claims. Some have estimated it as high as two hundred million dollars, due, in large part, from insurgents, in open rebellion, to loyal citizens who are, even now, making great sacrifices in the discharge of their patriotic duty to support the government.

Under these circumstances, I have been urgently solicited to establish, by military power, courts to administer summary justice in such cases. I have thus far declined to do it, not because I had any doubt that the end proposed—the collection of the debts—was just and right in itself, but because I have been unwilling to go beyond the pressure of necessity in the unusual exercise of power. But the powers of Congress I suppose are equal to the anomalous occasion, and therefore I refer the whole matter to Congress, with the hope that a plan may be devised for the administration of justice in all such parts of the insurgent States and Territories as may be under the control of this government, whether by a voluntary return to allegiance and order or by the power of our arms. This, however, not to be a permanent institution, but a temporary sub-

14 Senator Charles Sumner introduced a resolution on December 12, asking that the Committee on the Judiciary consider establishing by law a commission to revise, correct, arrange, and simplify the public statutes, and on January 28, 1862, introduced a bill (S. 174) to effect the object. The bill was sent to the Committee on the Judiciary whence it was reported on May 31 by Senator Lyman Trumbull without amendment for consideration by the Committee of the Whole. Further consideration was postponed "until 1st Monday in December next," and the bill was not revived. Not until June 27, 1866, was a law approved giving the president authority to appoint three commissioners to accomplish the revision.

stitute, and to cease as soon as the ordinary courts can be re-established in peace.

It is important that some more convenient means should be provided, if possible, for the adjustment of claims against the government, especially in view of their increased number by reason of the war. It is as much the duty of government to render prompt justice against itself, in favor of citizens, as it is to administer the same, between private individuals. The investigation and adjudication of claims, in their nature belong to the judicial[15] department; besides it is apparent that the attention of Congress, will be more than usually engaged, for some time to come, with great national questions. It was intended, by the organization of the court of claims, mainly to remove this branch of business from the halls of Congress; but while the court has proved to be an effective, and valuable means of investigation, it in great degree fails to effect the object of its creation, for want of power to make its judgments final.

Fully aware of the delicacy, not to say the danger, of the subject, I commend to your careful consideration whether this power of making judgments final, may not properly be given to the court, reserving the right of appeal on questions of law to the Supreme Court, with such other provisions as experience may have shown to be necessary.[16]

I ask attention to the report of the Postmaster General, the following being a summary statement of the condition of the department:

The[17] revenue from all sources during the fiscal year ending June 30. 1861, including the annual permanent appropriation of seven hundred thousand dollars ($700,000) for the transportation of "free mail matter," was nine million, forty nine thousand, two hundred and nin[e]ty six dollars and forty cents ($9,049,296.40) being about two per cent. less than the revenue for 1860.

The expenditures were thirteen million, six hundred and six thousand, seven hundred and fifty nine dollars and eleven cents. ($13,606,759.11) showing a decrease of more than eight per cent. as compared with those of the previous year, and leaving an excess of expenditure over the revenue for the last fiscal year of four million, five hundred and fifty seven thousand, four hun-

---

15 Page twenty-seven of the manuscript is missing at this point. The text here follows *Senate Executive Document No. 1.*

16 A bill introduced on January 9, 1862, by Senator Daniel Clark to amend the Act of February 24, 1855, in accord with Lincoln's suggestion, was not finally approved and signed by the president until March 3, 1863.

17 The manuscript resumes with this paragraph.

dred and sixty two dollars and seventy one cents ($4,557,462.71.)

The gross revenue for the year ending June 30, 1863, is estimated at an increase of four per cent. on that of 1861, making eight million, six hundred and eighty three thousand dollars ($8,683,000) to which should be added the earnings of the department in carrying free matter, viz: seven hundred thousand dollars ($700,000.) making nine million, three hundred and eighty three thousand dollars, ($9,383,000.)

The total expenditures for 1863 are estimated at $12,528,000, leaving an estimated deficiency of $3,145,000, to be supplied from the treasury, in addition to the permanent appropriation.

The present insurrection shows, I think, that the extension of this District across the Potomac river, at the time of establishing the capital here, was eminently wise, and consequently that the relinquishment of that portion of it which lies within the State of Virginia was unwise and dangerous. I submit for your consideration the expediency of regaining that part of the District, and the restoration of the original boundaries thereof, through negotiations with the State of Virginia.[18]

The report of the Secretary of the Interior,[19] with the accompanying documents, exhibits the condition of the several branches of the public business pertaining to that department. The depressing influences of the insurrection have been especially felt in the operations of the Patent and General Land Offices. The cash receipts from the sales of public lands during the past year have exceeded the expenses of our land system only about $200,000. The sales have been entirely suspended in the southern States, while the interruptions to the business of the country, and the diversion of large numbers of men from labor to military service, have obstructed settlements in the new States and Territories of the northwest.

The receipts of the Patent Office have declined in nine months about $100,000, rendering a large reduction of the force employed necessary to make it self sustaining.

The demands upon the Pension Office will be largely increased by the insurrection. Numerous applications for pensions, based upon the casualties of the existing war, have already been made. There is reason to believe that many who are now upon the pension rolls and in receipt of the bounty of the government, are in the ranks of the insurgent army, or giving them aid and comfort. The

[18] The regaining of that portion of the District of Columbia retroceded to Virginia by act of Congress, July 9, 1846, was the subject of a bill introduced in the House by Representative Charles H. Upton of Virginia, December 4, 1861, but nothing came of it. [19] See *Senate Executive Document No. 1*, I.

Secretary of the Interior has directed a suspension of the payment of the pensions of such persons upon proof of their disloyalty. I recommend that Congress authorize that officer to cause the names of such persons to be stricken from the pension rolls.

The relations of the government with the Indian tribes have been greatly disturbed by the insurrection, especially in the southern superintendency and in that of New Mexico. The Indian country south of Kansas is in the possession of insurgents from Texas and Arkansas. The agents of the United States appointed since the 4th. of March for this superintendency have been unable to reach their posts, while the most of those who were in office before that time have espoused the insurrectionary cause, and assume to exercise the powers of agents by virtue of commissions from the insurrectionists. It has been stated in the public press that a portion of those Indians have been organized as a military force, and are attached to the army of the insurgents. Although the government has no official information upon this subject, letters have been written to the Commissioner of Indian Affairs by several prominent chiefs, giving assurance of their loyalty to the United States, and expressing a wish for the presence of federal troops to protect them. It is believed that upon the repossession of the country by the federal forces the Indians will readily cease all hostile demonstrations, and resume their former relations to the government.

Agriculture, confessedly the largest interest of the nation, has, not a department, nor a bureau, but a clerkship only, assigned to it in the government. While it is fortunate that this great interest is so independent in its nature as to not have demanded and extorted more from the government, I respectfully ask Congress to consider whether something more cannot be given voluntarily with general advantage.[20]

Annual reports exhibiting the condition of our agriculture, commerce, and manufactures would present a fund of information of great practical value to the country. While I make no suggestion as to details, I venture the opinion that an agricultural and statistical bureau might profitably be organized.

The execution of the laws for the suppression of the African slave trade, has been confided to the Department of the Interior. It is a subject of gratulation that the efforts which have been made for the suppression of this inhuman traffic, have been recently attended with unusual success. Five vessels being fitted out for the

[20] The bill establishing the Department of Agriculture was approved and signed by Lincoln on May 15, 1862.

slave trade have been seized and condemned.[21] Two mates of vessels engaged in the trade, and one person in equipping a vessel as a slaver, have been convicted and subjected to the penalty of fine and imprisonment, and one captain, taken with a cargo of Africans on board his vessel, has been convicted of the highest grade of offence under our laws, the punishment of which is death.[22]

The Territories of Colorado, Dakotah and Nevada, created by the last Congress, have been organized, and civil administration has been inaugurated therein under auspices especially gratifying, when it is considered that the leaven of treason was found existing in some of these new countries when the federal officers arrived there.

The abundant natural resources of these Territories, with the security and protection afforded by organized government, will doubtless invite to them a large immigration when peace shall restore the business of the country to its accustomed channels. I submit the resolutions of the legislature of Colorado, which evidence the patriotic spirit of the people of the Territory. So far the authority of the United States has been upheld in all the Territories, as it is hoped it will be in the future. I commend their interests and defence to the enlightened and generous care of Congress.

I recommend to the favorable consideration of Congress the interests of the District of Columbia. The insurrection has been the cause of much suffering and sacrifice to its inhabitants, and as they have no representative in Congress, that body should not overlook their just claims upon the government.

At your late session a joint resolution was adopted authorizing the President to take measures for facilitating a proper representation of the industrial interests of the United States at the exhibition of the industry of all nations to be holden at London in the year 1862. I regret to say I have been unable to give personal attention to this subject,—a subject at once so interesting in itself, and so extensively and intimately connected with the material prosperity of the world. Through the Secretaries of State and of the Interior a plan, or system, has been devised, and partly matured, and which will be laid before you.[23]

[21] The vessels and dates of seizure are listed as follows: *Nightingale,* June 20, 1861; *Augusta,* June 19, 1861; *Falmouth,* August 2, 1861; *Triton,* July 12, 1861; *Augusta,* November 11, 1861. The *Augusta* had been released and reseized (*Senate Executive Document No. 53,* May 29, 1862).

[22] Captain Nathaniel Gordon of the *Erie,* convicted November 30, 1861, and hanged February 21, 1862. See Stay of Execution, February 4, 1862, *infra.*

[23] See Lincoln's Message of December 20, *infra.*

Under and by virtue of the act of Congress entitled "An act to confiscate property used for insurrectionary purposes," approved August, 6, 1861, the legal claims of certain persons to the labor and service of certain other persons have become forfeited; and numbers of the latter, thus liberated, are already dependent on the United States, and must be provided for in some way. Besides this, it is not impossible that some of the States will pass similar enactments for their own benefit respectively, and by operation of which persons of the same class will be thrown upon them for disposal. In such case I recommend that Congress provide for accepting such persons from such States, according to some mode of valuation, in lieu, *pro tanto*, of direct taxes, or upon some other plan to be agreed on with such States respectively; that such persons, on such acceptance by the general government, be at once deemed free; and that, in any event, steps be taken for colonizing both classes, (or the one first mentioned, if the other shall not be brought into existence,) at some place, or places, in a climate congenial to them. It might be well to consider, too,—whether the free colored people already in the United States could not, so far as individuals may desire, be included in such colonization.[24]

To carry out the plan of colonization may involve the acquiring of territory, and also the appropriation of money beyond that to be expended in the territorial acquisition. Having practiced the acquisition of territory for nearly sixty years, the question of constitutional power to do so is no longer an open one with us. The power was questioned at first by Mr. Jefferson, who, however, in the purchase of Louisiana, yielded his scruples on the plea of great expediency. If it be said that the only legitimate object of acquiring territory is to furnish homes for white men, this measure effects that object; for the emigration of colored men leaves additional room for white men remaining or coming here. Mr. Jefferson, however, placed the importance of procuring Louisiana more on political and commercial grounds than on providing room for population.

On this whole proposition,—including the appropriation of money with the acquisition of territory, does not the expediency amount to absolute necessity—that, without which the government itself cannot be perpetuated? The war continues. In considering the policy to be adopted for suppressing the insurrection, I have been

24 Lincoln probably had the Chiriqui project in mind (see Lincoln to Caleb B. Smith, October 23 and 24, *supra*). Smith's "Report on the Transportation, Settlement, and Colonization of Persons of the African Race," May 9, 1862, may be found in Thirty-ninth Congress, First Session, *Senate Executive Document No. 55.*

anxious and careful that the inevitable conflict for this purpose shall not degenerate into a violent and remorseless revolutionary struggle. I have, therefore, in every case, thought it proper to keep the integrity of the Union prominent as the primary object of the contest on our part, leaving all questions which are not of vital military importance to the more deliberate action of the legislature.

In the exercise of my best discretion I have adhered to the blockade of the ports held by the insurgents, instead of putting in force, by proclamation, the law of Congress enacted at the late session, for closing those ports.[25]

So, also, obeying the dictates of prudence, as well as the obligations of law, instead of transcending, I have adhered to the act of Congress to confiscate property used for insurrectionary purposes. If a new law upon the same subject shall be proposed, its propriety will be duly considered.

The Union must be preserved, and hence, all indispensable means must be employed. We should not be in haste to determine that radical and extreme measures, which may reach the loyal as well as the disloyal, are indispensable.

The inaugural address at the beginning of the Administration, and the message to Congress at the late special session, were both mainly devoted to the domestic controversy out of which the insurrection and consequent war have sprung. Nothing now occurs to add or subtract, to or from, the principles or general purposes stated and expressed in those documents.

The last ray of hope for preserving the Union peaceably, expired at the assault upon Fort Sumter; and a general review of what has occurred since may not be unprofitable. What was painfully uncertain then, is much better defined and more distinct now; and the progress of events is plainly in the right direction. The insurgents confidently claimed a strong support from north of Mason and Dixon's line; and the friends of the Union were not free from apprehension on the point. This, however, was soon settled definitely and on the right side. South of the line, noble little Delaware led off right from the first. Maryland was made to *seem* against the Union. Our soldiers were assaulted, bridges were burned, and railroads torn up, within her limits; and we were many days, at one time, without the ability to bring a single regiment over her soil to the capital. Now, her bridges and railroads

[25] The Act of July 13, 1861, had provided that if the duties could not be collected in any district the president was empowered to close such ports and give notice by proclamation.

are repaired and open to the government; she already gives seven regiments to the cause of the Union and none to the enemy; and her people, at a regular election, have sustained the Union, by a larger majority, and a larger aggregate vote than they ever before gave to any candidate, or any question. Kentucky, too, for some time in doubt, is now decidedly, and, I think, unchangeably, ranged on the side of the Union. Missouri is comparatively quiet; and I believe cannot again be overrun by the insurrectionists. These three States of Maryland, Kentucky, and Missouri, neither of which would promise a single soldier at first, have now an aggregate of not less than forty thousand in the field, for the Union; while, of their citizens, certainly not more than a third of that number, and they of doubtful whereabouts, and doubtful existence, are in arms against it. After a somewhat bloody struggle of months, winter closes on the Union people of western Virginia, leaving them masters of their own country.

An insurgent force of about fifteen hundred, for months dominating the narrow peninsular region, constituting the counties of Accomac and Northampton, and known as eastern shore of Virginia, together with some contiguous parts of Maryland, have laid down their arms; and the people there have renewed their allegiance to, and accepted the protection of, the old flag. This leaves no armed insurrectionist north of the Potomac, or east of the Chesapeake.

Also we have obtained a footing at each of the isolated points, on the southern coast, of Hatteras, Port Royal, Tybee Island, near Savannah, and Ship Island; and we likewise have some general accounts of popular movements, in behalf of the Union, in North Carolina and Tennessee.

These things demonstrate that the cause of the Union is advancing steadily and certainly southward.

Since your last adjournment, Lieutenant General Scott has retired from the head of the army. During his long life, the nation has not been unmindful of his merit; yet, on calling to mind how faithfully, ably and brilliantly he has served the country, from a time far back in our history, when few of the now living had been born, and thenceforward continually, I cannot but think we are still his debtors. I submit, therefore, for your consideration, what further mark of recognition is due to him, and to ourselves, as a grateful people.

With the retirement of General Scott came the executive duty of appointing, in his stead, a general-in-chief of the army. It is a fortunate circumstance that neither in council nor country was there, so far as I know, any difference of opinion as to the proper person to be selected. The retiring chief repeatedly expressed his judgment in favor of General McClellan for the position; and in this the nation seemed to give a unanimous concurrence. The designation of General McClellan is therefore in considerable degree, the selection of the Country as well as of the Executive; and hence there is better reason to hope there will be given him, the confidence, and cordial support thus, by fair implication, promised, and without which, he cannot, with so full efficiency, serve the country.

It has been said that one bad general is better than two good ones; and the saying is true, if taken to mean no more than that an army is better directed by a single mind, though inferior, than by two superior ones, at variance, and cross-purposes with each other.

And the same is true, in all joint operations wherein those engaged, *can* have none but a common end in view, and *can* differ only as to the choice of means. In a storm at sea, no one on board *can* wish the ship to sink; and yet, not unfrequently, all go down together, because too many will direct, and no single mind can be allowed to control.

It continues to develop that the insurrection is largely, if not exclusively, a war upon the first principle of popular government —the rights of the people. Conclusive evidence of this is found in the most grave and maturely considered public documents, as well as in the general tone of the insurgents. In those documents we find the abridgement of the existing right of suffrage and the denial to the people of all right to participate in the selection of public officers, except the legislative boldly advocated, with labored arguments to prove that large control of the people in government, is the source of all political evil. Monarchy itself is sometimes hinted at as a possible refuge from the power of the people.

In my present position, I could scarcely be justified were I to omit raising a warning voice against this approach of returning despotism.

It is not needed, nor fitting here, that a general argument should be made in favor of popular institutions; but there is one point, with its connexions, not so hackneyed as most others, to which I ask a brief attention. It is the effort to place *capital* on an equal footing with, if not above *labor*, in the structure of government. It is assumed that labor is available only in connexion with capital; that nobody labors unless somebody else, owning capital, somehow by the use of it, induces him to labor. This assumed, it is next considered whether it is best that capital shall *hire* laborers, and thus induce them to work by their own consent, or *buy* them, and drive them to it without their consent. Having proceeded so far, it is naturally concluded that all laborers are either *hired* laborers, or what we call slaves. And further it is assumed that whoever is once a hired laborer, is fixed in that condition for life.

Now, there is no such relation between capital and labor as assumed; nor is there any such thing as a free man being fixed for life in the condition of a hired laborer. Both these assumptions are false, and all inferences from them are groundless.

Labor is prior to, and independent of, capital. Capital is only the fruit of labor, and could never have existed if labor had not first existed. Labor is the superior of capital, and deserves much the higher consideration. Capital has its rights, which are as worthy of protection as any other rights. Nor is it denied that there is, and probably always will be, a relation between labor and capital, producing mutual benefits. The error is in assuming that the whole labor of community exists within that relation. A few men own capital, and that few avoid labor themselves, and, with their capital, hire or buy another few to labor for them. A large majority belong to neither class—neither work for others, nor have others working for them. In most of the southern States, a majority of the whole people of all colors are neither slaves nor masters; while in the northern a large majority are neither hirers nor hired. Men with their families—wives, sons, and daughters—work for themselves, on their farms, in their houses, and in their shops, taking the whole product to themselves, and asking no favors of capital on the one hand, nor of hired laborers or slaves on the other. It is not forgotten that a considerable number of persons mingle their own labor with capital—that is, they labor with their own hands, and also buy or hire others to labor for them; but this is only a mixed, and not a distinct class. No principle stated is disturbed by the existence of this mixed class.

Again: as has already been said, there is not, of necessity, any such thing as the free hired laborer being fixed to that condition for life. Many independent men everywhere in these States, a few years back in their lives, were hired laborers. The prudent, penniless beginner in the world, labors for wages awhile, saves a surplus with which to buy tools or land for himself; then labors on his own account another while, and at length hires another new beginner to help him. This is the just, and generous, and prosperous system, which opens the way to all—gives hope to all, and consequent energy, and progress, and improvement of condition to all. No men living are more worthy to be trusted than those who toil up from poverty—none less inclined to take, or touch, aught which they have not honestly earned. Let them beware of surrendering a political power which they already possess, and which, if surrendered, will surely be used to close the door of advancement against such as they, and to fix new disabilities and burdens upon them, till all of liberty shall be lost.

From the first taking of our national census to the last are seventy years; and we find our population at the end of the period eight times as great as it was at the beginning. The increase of those other things which men deem desirable has been even greater. We thus have at one view, what the popular principle applied to government, through the machinery of the States and the Union, has produced in a given time; and also what, if firmly maintained, it promises for the future. There are already among us those, who, if the Union be preserved, will live to see it contain two hundred and fifty millions. The struggle of today, is not altogether for today—it is for a vast future also. With a reliance on Providence, all the more firm and earnest, let us proceed in the great task which events have devolved upon us.

December 3, 1861   ABRAHAM LINCOLN

Form Letter to Chaplains[1]

December 3, 1861

Schedule A.

Executive Mansion,

Washington, D.C.,   1861

Rev.—— ——.

Sir: Having been solicited by Christian ministers, and other pious people, to appoint suitable persons to act as chaplains at the hospitals for our sick and wounded soldiers, and feeling the intrinsic propriety of having such persons to so act, and yet believing there is no law conferring the power upon me to appoint them, I think fit to say that if you will voluntarily enter upon and perform the appropriate duties of such position, I will recommend that Congress make compensation therefor at the same rate as chaplains in the army are compensated.

The following are the names and dates, respectively, of the persons and times to whom and when such letters were delivered:

Rev. G. G. Goss . . . . September 25, 1861.

Rev. John G. Butler . . . . . . September 25, 1861.

Rev. Henry Hopkins . . . . . . September 25, 1861.
Rev. F. M. Magrath . . . . October 30, 1861.
Rev. F. E. Boyle . . . . October 30, 1861.
Rev. John C. Smith . . . . . . November 7, 1861.
Rev. Wm. Y. Brown . . . . . . November 7, 1861.

¹ Thirty-seventh Congress, Second Session, *Senate Executive Document No. 1,*
p. 20. This form letter is printed as "Schedule A." immediately following the
Annual Message. See also Lincoln to Magrath, October 30, 1861, *supra.*

Endorsement on Bill
Rendered by Daniel B. Pond[1]

I advise that the above account be paid.   A. LINCOLN
Dec. 3. 1861

¹ Copy, DLC-RTL. Lincoln's endorsement is on a copy of the following bill,
certified by Lincoln's secretary William O. Stoddard:

	Washington, Nov. 29th 1861	
The United States Government		Dr.
	To Daniel B. Pond	
To	Twenty Ellsworth Guns	
	Carriages and appointments	
	at $350.–	$7000.00
"	Four thousand rounds of am-	
	munition at 40 c	1600.00
"	Transportation from Worcester	
	to New York	78.87
"	Transhipment	13.00
"	Transportation from New	
"	York to Washington	120.00
		————
		$8811.87

To George B. McClellan[1]

December 3, 1861
Please read and consider this letter.   A.L.

¹ OR, I, VII, 469, 470. There are two identical endorsements of this date on
two letters from Samuel P. Carter to Horace Maynard, November 21, and 25,
1861. Carter, as acting brigadier general of the East Tennessee Brigade at
Camp Calvert near London, Kentucky, requested Representative Maynard of
East Tennessee to get action in moving troops (his brigade in particular) to
the defense of East Tennessee and Kentucky. McClellan forwarded the letters
to General Buell, December 3, 1861, ordering him to "send . . . with the least
possible delay, troops enough to protect these men. . . . You may fully rely
on my full support in . . . the liberation of Eastern Tennessee. . . ." (*Ibid.,*
p. 468.)

[54]

To Simon Cameron[1]

This letter is worth preserving; and, being addressed to the Secretary of War, I return it to him.   A. LINCOLN
Dec. 4. 1861.

[1] AES, DLC-Cameron Papers. Lincoln's endorsement is written on a letter from Leonard Haskins, Starksboro, Vermont, November 4, 1861, stating that he had followed Cameron's suggestion by naming his triplet infant sons for Abraham Lincoln, Gideon Welles, and Simon Cameron. The verso of the letter contains also Cameron's endorsement of November 13.

To Simon Cameron[1]

Hon. Sec. of War   Executive Mansion
My dear Sir   Dec. 4. 1861
    Mr. Senator Rice says he would be personally obliged by the appointment of Joel D. Cruttenden, of Minn. as a Q.M. or Com. and I would be glad to oblige Senator Rice. If this can not be done at once, lay it by for one of the first that can. Yours truly
                                A. LINCOLN

[1] ALS, DLC-Cameron Papers. Joel D. Cruttenden was appointed captain and quartermaster of Volunteers, February 19, 1862.

To the House of Representatives[1]

To the House of Representatives: December 4, 1861
    I transmit, herewith, a report from the Secretary of State, in reply to the Resolution of the House of Representatives of the 13th. July, last, in relation to the correspondence between this Government and foreign nations respecting the rights of blockade, privateering and the recognition of the so called Confederate States.
    Washington, 4 December 1861.   ABRAHAM LINCOLN

[1] DS, DNA RG 233, Thirty-seventh Congress, Second Session, Original Executive Document No. 2. Seward's communication merely reported that the correspondence called for by the House Resolution of July 13, 1861, had been submitted with the president's Annual Message of December 3.

To the House of Representatives[1]

To the House of Representatives: December 4, 1861
    I transmit, herewith, a report from the Secretary of State, in reply to the Resolution of the House of Representatives of the 31st. July, last, upon the subject of increasing and extending trade and commerce of the United States with Foreign Countries.
    Washington, December 4, 1861.   ABRAHAM LINCOLN

[1] DS, DNA RG 233, Thirty-seventh Congress, Second Session, Original Executive Document No. 3. In reply to the House Resolution of July 31, 1861, requesting what "legislation is necessary for the increase and extension of the trade and commerce of the United States with foreign countries," Seward reported that "The Secretary of State . . . is not aware that any legislation of the character suggested could now be wisely adopted, beyond such as has been already recommended in the President's annual message. . . ."

To George B. McClellan[1]

December 4, 1861

I am somewhat anxious that Gen. *Van Antwerp* shall be appointed to go into Gen. Halleck's staff, unless Gen. McClellan knows some objection, or difficulty. Will he please attend to it?

Dec. 4, 1861.   A. LINCOLN

[1] AES, IHi. Lincoln's endorsement is written on a letter from Senator James Harlan and other members of the Iowa delegation, November 20, 1861, recommending appointment of Verplanck Van Antwerp of Burlington, Iowa, to General Halleck's staff. Van Antwerp was appointed major and aide-de-camp, January 29, 1862. His appointment as general was probably in the state militia.

Memorandum:
Appointment of Henry D. Wallen[1]

[December 4, 1861?]

Henry D. Wallen, now a Major in the regular Army, is pressed by his friends to be an Inspector General, or Brigadier General.

[1] AD, IHi. The date on the memorandum is not in Lincoln's hand. Lieutenant Henry D. Wallen of the Fourth Infantry had been stationed on the West Coast and on detached service in Panama with 30,000 stand of arms for the Eastern armies. Promoted to major November 25, 1861, he was assigned to the Seventh Infantry and served 1862-1864 in New Mexico. See also Lincoln to Stanton, January 18, 1862, *infra.*

To William H. Seward[1]

December 4, 1861

As this appointment of a consul is desired by Mr. Hickman, who is much of a man, and does not trouble us much, I wish it to be made if it is within reasonable possibility.   A. LINCOLN

Dec. 4, 1861.

[1] AES, DNA FS RG 59, Appointments, Box 281. Lincoln's endorsement is written on a letter from John Hickman of West Chester, Pennsylvania, to Seward, November 19, 1861, recommending Daniel Evans, formerly of Pennsylvania but at the time a resident of Illinois, for a consulship. Evans is listed in the *U.S. Official Register,* 1863, as consul at Bilbao, Spain.

To Mrs. Susannah Weathers[1]

Executive Mansion,
My dear Madam   Washington, Dec. 4, 1861.
I take great pleasure in acknowledging the receipt of your letter
of Nov. 26; and in thanking you for the present by which it was
accompanied. A pair of socks so fine, and soft, and warm, could
hardly have been manufactured in any other way than the old
Kentucky fashion. Your letter informs me that your maiden name
was Crume, and that you were raised in Washington county, Kentucky, by which I infer that an uncle of mine by marriage was a
relative of yours. Nearly, or quite sixty years ago, Ralph Crume
married Mary Lincoln, a sister of my father, in Washington
county, Kentucky.[2]
Accept my thanks, and believe me   Very truly   Your friend
Mrs. Susannah Weathers   A. Lincoln.
Rossville, Clinton Co, Ind.

[1] ALS, ORB.
[2] Mary Lincoln, born in 1775, was a year older than her brother Thomas Lincoln.

To Edward Bates[1]

December 5, 1861
The writer of this intimates that he has appealed to me before. I
have no recollection of it. Has the Attorney General a transcript of
record or other papers concerning it?
The gentleman who brings me the letter says it is a "Slave-
trade" conviction, of a minor grade.   A. Lincoln
Dec. 5. 1861.

[1] AES, DNA RG 204, U.S. Pardon Attorney, Case A 358. Lincoln's endorsement is written on a letter from Thomas Morgan, "Newbury Port Gaol," Massachusetts, December 1, 1861, requesting a pardon. There is no prior letter from
Thomas Morgan in the Lincoln Papers, and no reference to further executive
action.

To Simon Cameron[1]

December 5, 1861
Respectfully submitted to the Secretary of War with the sugges-
tion that the claims already adjusted by the commission at St.
Louis, might, and I think ought to, be paid at once.
Dec. 5. 1861.   A. Lincoln

1 AES, DLC-RTL. Lincoln's endorsement is written on a petition dated November 27, 1861, from banks and savings institutions in St. Louis, Missouri, requesting prompt settlement of claims already adjusted by the commission appointed by the president. See Lincoln to Joseph Holt, November 12, *supra*. The claims grew out of seizure of funds by military commanders in the Department of the West.

To the Senate[1]

To the Senate of the United States   December 5, 1861

I transmit to the Senate, for its consideration with a view to ratification, a treaty between the United States of America and His Majesty the King of Hanover, concerning the abolition of the Stade or Brunshausen Dues, signed at Berlin on the 6th November, 1861.   ABRAHAM LINCOLN

Washington, December 5th, 1861.

1 DNA RG 46, Senate 37B B8. The treaty was ratified by the Senate, February 3, 1862.

To Joseph G. Totten[1]

December 5, 1861

This young man, George H. Palmer, fought with Col. Mulligan at Lexington, & is now recommended by him & others for a Cadetship. He will be twenty one April 16, 1862. Is he too old to be admitted, as matters now stand? Will Gen. Totten please answer?

Dec. 5. 1861.   A. LINCOLN

1 AES, DNA WR RG 77, Office of the Chief of Engineers, Letters Received, P 1054. Lincoln's endorsement is on an envelope addressed by Lincoln to "Gen. Totten," containing recommendations of George H. Palmer for a West Point cadetship. See Lincoln's memorandum *infra*.

Memorandum:
Appointment of George H. Palmer[1]

[December 5, 1861]

But this young man is not 21, till April 16, 1862. Is there no vacancy to which he could be appointed before that time?   A.L.

1 AES, DLC-RTL. Lincoln's endorsement is written on Joseph G. Totten's reply to Lincoln's note *supra*, that "the *Law* is explicitly against the appointment of Mr. Geo. H. Palmer to the military academy," because candidates must not be "under the age of fourteen, nor above the age of twenty one years." George H. Palmer had served as bugler with Colonel James A. Mulligan's First Illinois Cavalry, April 24 to October 9, 1861, and was commissioned first lieutenant in the Eighty-third Illinois Infantry, August 21, 1862. On March 10, 1896, he was awarded the Medal of Honor for most distinguished gallantry at the battle of Lexington, Missouri, September 18-20, 1861.

To Gideon Welles[1]

This day, Dec. 5, 1861, Mrs. Nininger, sister of Gov. Ramsey, calls, with her son, Alexander R. Nininger, 17 2nd. Augt. last, asking to have him placed at the Naval School. Will the Sec. of Navy please preserve this, and give it favorable consideration at the proper time? A. LINCOLN

[1] ADS, PHi. The request of Mrs. John Nininger, sister of Governor Alexander Ramsey of Minnesota, was apparently not fulfilled. There is no record of Alexander R. Nininger's appointment.

To Gideon Welles[1]

Will the Secretary of the Navy please examine this, and inform me what, according to the rules of the Department I should do.
Dec. 5. 1861 A. LINCOLN

[1] AES, DLC-RTL. Lincoln's endorsement is written on a letter from William Chandler, November 30, 1861, protesting his dismissal as commander in the U.S. Navy, October 17, 1861. Welles replied December 16, listing Chandler's several previous trials by court-martial (in 1834-1835, and 1849) and concluding, "I cannot . . . recommend his restoration." (DLC-RTL).

To Simon Cameron[1]

Sec. of War, please see the bearer, who is Marshal of the S. District of Illinois. A. LINCOLN
Dec. 6. 1861

[1] ALS, RPB. David L. Phillips, marshal of Southern Illinois, was in Washington seeking authority to arrest secessionists (New York *Tribune*, December 3, 1861).

To George B. McClellan[1]

Gen. McClellan, please see Col. Hawkins, who comes from Gen. Wool. A. LINCOLN
Dec. 6. 1861.

[1] ALS, RPAB. Colonel Rush C. Hawkins of the Ninth New York Infantry was sent to Fortress Monroe on charges of insubordination about October 15, but was returned to command of his regiment on December 22.

To George B. McClellan[1]

December 6, 1861

Gen. McClellan, please see Senator Johnson & friends. I think you might show him Gen. Buell's letter. You will judge—I think, if it

prove true that Brownlow has had a success, we must push a column to join him. A. LINCOLN

Dec. 6. 1861

¹ ALS-P, ISLA. Andrew Johnson and friends probably wished to discuss action to relieve Union forces under "Parson" William G. Brownlow which were reported to have fought "a great battle" at Morristown in East Tennessee on December 1 (New York *Tribune*, December 6, 1861). Brownlow was arrested by Confederates, December 6, on charges of state-wide burning of railroad bridges.

To George B. McClellan¹

Majr. Genl. McClellan: Executive Mansion. Dec. 6. 1861

My dear Sir: Capt. Francis G. Young, of the California regiment (Col. Baker's) is in some difficulty—I do not precisely understand what. I believe you know I was unfavorably impressed towards him because of apparently contradictory accounts he gave me of some matters at the battle of Ball's Bluff. At length he has brought me the paper which accompanies this, showing, I think, that he is entitled to respectful consideration. As you see, it is signed by several senators and representatives, as well as other well known and respectable gentlemen. I attach considerable consequence to the name of Lt. Col. Shaler, late Major Shaler of the New-York 7th.² These things and his late connection with Col. Baker, induce me to ask you if, consistently with the public service, the *past* whatever it is, can not be waived, and he be placed in service, and given another chance? Yours truly   A. LINCOLN.

¹ ALS copy, DLC-RTL. Captain Francis G. Young of the Seventy-first Pennsylvania (Colonel Edward D. Baker's "California Regiment") wrote Lincoln on December 7 that he could not deliver the letter which Lincoln had given him to General McClellan because ". . . you have misunderstood my case & . . . unintentionally done me injustice . . . . I did not then know that you thought me untruthful. . . . If you could know . . . all the facts of the Battle of Balls Bluff you would have no trouble in recalling all my statements to you. . . . I wish to remain in the service to the end of the war. . . ." (*Ibid.*). Young was found guilty by court-martial of leaving camp without permission and dismissed from service on McClellan's order, January 2, 1862. See further Lincoln to Holt, April 11, 1864, *infra.*

² "7th" has been written with pencil in the blank space which Lincoln left. Lieutenant Colonel Shaler was Major Alexander Shaler of the Seventh New York, who became lieutenant colonel of the Sixty-fifth New York, dating from June 11, 1861.

To Joseph G. Totten¹

Gen. Totten, please see Mr. Prentice, and, if you conveniently can, fix up the business he wishes. A. LINCOLN

Dec. 7, 1861.

[1] ALS, Speed Art Museum, Louisville, Kentucky. George D. Prentice, editor of the Louisville *Journal*, had written Lincoln from Washington on November 16, 1861, asking financial aid for the *Journal* and government contracts for himself (DLC-RTL). His next letter in the Lincoln Papers, dated December 19 from Louisville, indicated that he had in the interim remained in Washington on business.

To Simon Cameron[1]

December 9, 1861

The writers of these two letters are democrats earnestly and efficiently supporting the War; and I would be pleased for them to be obliged in the matter mentioned so soon as it can consistently be done.   A. LINCOLN

Dec. 9. 1861.

[1] AES, DLC-Cameron Papers. Lincoln's endorsement is written on a letter from Isaac B. Curran, Springfield, Illinois, November 2, 1861, enclosing another letter from former Governor John Moore, both introducing and recommending Samuel C. Gibson, attorney and real estate agent at Springfield, to Senator Orville H. Browning. Browning forwarded the letters to Lincoln with his own letter recommending Gibson for appointment as assistant quartermaster and making other recommendations. There is no record of Gibson's appointment.

To the House of Representatives[1]

To the House of Representatives: December 9, 1861

I transmit herewith a report from the Secretary of State in reply to the resolution of the House of the 4th. instant, relative to the intervention of certain European Powers in the affairs of Mexico.

Washington, December 9, 1861.   ABRAHAM LINCOLN

[1] DS, DNA RG 233, Thirty-seventh Congress, Second Session, Original Executive Document No. 4. Seward's report deemed it ". . . inexpedient, at this juncture, to make public the papers referred to." The resolution called for copies of communications from the governments of England, Spain, and France, in regard to armed intervention in Mexico.

To George B. McClellan[1]

December 9, 1861

Is it true that Schofield is, or is to be ordered East?

My expectation & wish was for him to remain in Mo.

Please answer.   A. LINCOLN

Dec. 9. 1861.

[1] AES, DLC-RTL. Lincoln's endorsement is written on the back of a copy of a telegram from Governor Hamilton R. Gamble, December 7, 1861, to Edward Bates: "Halleck tells me Schoefield is to be ordered East, he is now in actual

command of the Missouri State Militia . . . taking him away will postpone organization indefinitely." McClellan's endorsement follows Lincoln's: "This is the first I have heard of it. There has not been any intention of ordering him away from Missouri." Brigadier General John M. Schofield remained in Missouri.

To William H. Seward[1]

Respectfully submitted to the State Department, with reference to Consular application of Prof. J. H. McChesney   A. LINCOLN
Dec. 9. 1861.

[1] AES, DNA FS RG 59, Appointments, Box 335. Lincoln's endorsement is on a letter from Orville H. Browning, December 4, 1861, forwarding letters recommending several appointments, among them that of Samuel C. Gibson (q.v. supra), and "our mutual friend Prof: J. H. McChesney" for a consulship. Joseph H. McChesney who had been assistant state geologist of Illinois, was appointed consul to New Castle, England. Browning's letter contains also marginal endorsements "Left with Adjt. Genl." and "Sent to War Department" which indicate Lincoln's disposal of the other enclosures.

To William H. Seward[1]

Hon: Sec. of State   Executive Mansion
My dear Sir: Dec. 9. 1861
    Hon: Mr. Blair of Pennsylvania had reason to expect a Consular appointment for one of his friends, and has been disappointed. Please see him, & show him what remains, & if there is anything he will accept for his friend, let him have it. Yours truly

A. LINCOLN

[1] ALS, NAuE. See Lincoln's memorandum concerning the appointment of Thomas P. Campbell, March 27, 1861, supra.

Draft of a Dispatch
in Reply to Lord John Russell
Concerning the Trent Affair[1]

[December 10?] 1861
    The despatch of Her Majesty's Secretary for Foreign Affairs, dated the 30th. of November 1861, and, of which your Lordship kindly furnished me a copy, has been carefully considered by the President; and he directs me to say that if there existed no fact, or facts pe[r]tinent to the case, beyond those stated in said despatch, the reparation sought by Great Brittain from the United States, would be justly due, and should be promptly made. The

President is unwilling to believe that Her Majesty's Government will press for a categorical answer upon what appears to him to be only a partial record, in the making up of which, he has been allowed no part. He is reluctant to volunteer his view of the case, with no assurance that Her Majesty's Government will consent to hear him; yet this much he directs me to say, that this government has intended no affront to the British flag, or to the British nation; nor has it intended to force into discussion, an embarrassing question, all which is evident by the fact, hereby asserted, that the act complained of was done by the officer, without orders from, or expectation of, the government. But being done, it was no longer left to us to consider whether we might not, to avoid a controversy, waive an unimportant, though a strict right; because we too, as well as Great Brittain, have a people justly jealous of their rights, and in whose presence our government could undo the act complained of, only upon a fair showing that it was wrong, or, at least, very questionable. The United States government and people, are still willing to make reparation upon such showing.

Accordingly I am instructed by the President to inquire whether Her Majesty's government will hear the United States upon the matter in question. The President desires, among other things, to bring into view, and have considered, the existing rebellion in the United States—the position Great Brittain has assumed, including Her Majesty's proclamation, in relation thereto—the relation the persons, whose seizure is the subject of complaint, bore to the United States, and the object of their voyage at the time they were seized—the knowledge which the master of the *Trent* had of their relation to the United States, and of the object of their voyage, at the time he received them on board for the voyage—the place of the seizure—and the precedents, and respective positions assumed, in analagous cases, between Great Brittain and the United States.

Upon a Submission, containing the foregoing facts, with those set forth in the before mentioned despatch to your Lordship, together with all other facts which either party may deem material, I am instructed to say the government of the United States will, if agreed to by Her Majesty's government, go to such friendly arbitration as is usual among nations, and will abide the award.

Or, in the alternative, Her Majesty's government may, upon the same record, determine whether any, and if any, what reparation is due from the United States; *provided,* no such reparation shall be different in character from, nor transcend, that proposed by your Lordship, as instructed in and by the despatch aforesaid; and, *provided further,* that the determination thus made shall be the law for all future analagous cases, between Great Brittain and the United States.

1 ADf, DLC-RTL. The date is that assigned by Nicolay and Hay. Lincoln's reply to Lord John Russell's dispatch of November 30, 1861, was never sent. On November 8, 1861, the warship *San Jacinto* commanded by Captain Charles Wilkes had stopped the British ship *Trent* and forcibly removed Confederate emissaries James M. Mason (accredited to Britain) and John Slidell (accredited to France) and their secretaries James E. McFarland and George Eustis, Jr. Detailed studies of the *Trent* affair may be found in J. G. Randall's *Lincoln the President* (II, 37 ff.) and other sources. An autograph memorandum which accompanies the draft of Lincoln's despatch reads as follows: "'Orozembo'/ 1807– 6. Ch. Rob. 430/ Atalanta/ Carolina 1808."

To Simon Cameron[1]

Hon. Sec. of War.   Executive Mansion
My dear Sir.   Dec. 12. 1861

I do not remember what letters, or notes of mine may be on file, in regard to applications for Pay-Masters in the Regular Army; but I wish the son of the Pay-Master General—Charles T. Larned —to have the first vacancy, which he can have consistently with my former letters, and notes. Yours truly   A. LINCOLN

1 ALS, DLC-Cameron Papers. Charles T. Larned, son of Paymaster General Benjamin F. Larned, had been appointed additional paymaster of Volunteers as of June 1, 1861, and was nominated for the Regular Army on December 17, and confirmed February 3, 1862, to rank as major from August 30, 1861.

To Simon Cameron[1]

Sec. of War please preserve this, until the question shall be acted on.   A. LINCOLN
Dec. 12. 1861.

1 AES, RPB. Lincoln's endorsement is written on a letter signed by Representative John W. Crisfield of Baltimore and others, recommending Colonel Robert C. Buchanan for appointment as inspector general. See also Lincoln to Cameron, November 2, *supra*. Buchanan did not receive the appointment.

To Simon Cameron[1]

Hon. Sec. of War.   Executive Mansion   Dec. 12, 1861

Gov. Morton tells me that Bishop Ames, of high standing in the Methodist church, wishes his son—Edwin R. Ames—appointed a Lieutenant in the regular Army. Let this be done if possible. Yours truly   A. LINCOLN
P.S. If done, notify Gov. Morton.   A L.

1 ALS, DLC-Cameron Papers. Bishop Edward R. Ames' son Edwin R. Ames was appointed a second lieutenant and assigned to the Seventh Infantry, March 6, 1862.

To Simon Cameron[1]

If Dr. Boyd Pendleton, has passed an examination, to be a Brigade Surgeon, I would like to appoint him at once.　　　　A. LINCOLN
Dec. 12. 1861.

[1] ALS-P, ISLA. On the back of the small card bearing Lincoln's note is a reply in an unidentified handwriting as follows: "Two days since it was decided that the number of Brig. Surgs. shd. be carried up to 125, as a max. limit—& that number was completed by nomination." Concerning Dr. E. Boyd Pendleton, see Lincoln to Cameron, November 7, *supra*; see also Lincoln to Stanton, February 5, 1862, *infra*.

To Simon Cameron[1]

December 12, 1861

Senators have told me this young man was not confirmed last session simply because nobody seemed to know him. I would like to re-nominate him if it will not derange things.
Dec. 12, 1861　　　　　　　　　　A. LINCOLN

[1] William D. Morley, Inc., Catalog, October 13, 1944, No. 274. According to the catalog description Lincoln's endorsement is written on a letter from Richard T. Gill, a resident of Atlanta, Illinois, whose nephew John W. Hamilton had been appointed a first lieutenant in the Regular Army but had been rejected by the Senate on August 5, 1861. There is no record of Hamilton's reappointment to the Regular Army, but he served from June 20 to September 26, 1862, as first lieutenant in the Sixty-eighth Illinois Infantry, a three-months regiment.

To Samuel R. Curtis[1]

Private

Brig. Genl. S. R. Curtis.　　　　　　Washington, D.C.
My dear Sir.　　　　　　　　　　Dec. 12. 1861
I snatch a moment to both thank you, and apologise to you. In all sincerity I thank you for the complete and entirely satisfactory manner in which you executed the trusts I confided to you by letter.

You, and others, particularly, and the public service generally, were wronged, and injured by the publication of Gen. Thomas' report, on his return from the West. I have no apology only to say it never would have been done, if I had had the least suspicion it was to be done. Being done, I thought the maxim "least said, soonest mended" applied to the case. Yours very truly　　A. LINCOLN

[1] ALS, IHi. Publication by the newspapers of Lorenzo Thomas' report to Cameron, October 21, 1861, on conditions in Missouri which led to the removal of Frémont, prompted Curtis to write Lincoln on November 16, "I regret the publicity of General Thomas' report of conversations drawn out of me by your con-

fidential assurance. . . . But I do not murmur at my fate . . . and I trust that in alienating the friends of General Fremont I have not lost the respect of those who best know all the circumstances." (DLC-RTL).

To William M. Dunn[1]

December 12, 1861

I, as President, am not entitled by law, to appoint to the Naval school, either at large or otherwise. Mr Dunn will see that I have kindly indorsed Mr. Hayden's letter; so that it may be sent to the Secretary of the Navy.   A. LINCOLN

Dec. 12. 1861.

[1] AES, NN. Lincoln's endorsement is written on a letter from Representative William M. Dunn, December 12, 1861, enclosing a letter, presumably from "Mr. Hayden," which has not been located.

Memorandum: Appointment of August Willich and George W. Hazzard[1]

December 12, 1861

To-day—Dec. 12. 1861. Gov. Morton calls, and asks, Col. Willech and Capt. Hazzard, whom I know, for Brig. Genls. He says Col. Willech resides in New-York, but is in command of an Indiana regiment, having heretofore served as a Colonel in Prussia.

[1] AD, IHi. Colonel August Willich of the Thirty-second Indiana Infantry was appointed brigadier general of Volunteers, July 17, 1862. Colonel George W. Hazzard of the Thirty-seventh Indiana Infantry died August 14, 1862, of wounds received at White Oak Swamp, Virginia, June 30, 1862.

To William H. Seward[1]

Will the Sec. of State please look at this & mention in Cabinet to-morrow?   A. LINCOLN

Dec. 12. 1861.

[1] AES, DNA FS RG 59, Miscellaneous Letters. Lincoln's endorsement is written on the back of a copy, forwarded by the clerk of the House of Representatives, of Clement L. Vallandigham's resolution of December 9, asking for copies of "all proclamations, or orders, issued and published in the press, or otherwise made public, by himself, or any Head of Department, or any Military or Naval officer of the United States, since the Fourth of March last, relating to the pending contest. . . ." Seward's report of December 14 deeming it not expedient to comply with the request, and an unsigned letter of transmittal of the same date, are both in the Lincoln Papers. From this evidence and the lack of reference to any reply in the *House Journal* or *Congressional Globe*, it seems probable that Lincoln simply withheld the matter to avoid controversy.

To George H. Stuart[1]

Rev. George H. Stuart   Executive Mansion, Washington,
Chairman of Christian Commission   Dec. 12, 1861.
My dear Sir: Your letter of the 11th. Inst. and accompanying plan, both of which are returned as a convenient mode of connecting this with them, have just been received. Your christian and benevolent undertaking for the benefit of the soldiers, is too obviously proper, and praise-worthy, to admit any difference of opinion. I sincerely hope your plan may be as successful in execution, as it is just and generous in conception. Your Obt. Servt.

     A. LINCOLN.

[1] ALS, DLC-Stuart Papers. Stuart's letter of December 11, 1861, submitted for Lincoln's approval a plan for religious work among the armed forces adopted by a committee appointed at the convention of the Young Men's Christian Association and denominated a "Christian Commission . . . to promote the spiritual and temporal welfare of the soldiers . . . the sailors and marines . . ." See Lemuel Moss, *Annals of the United States Christian Commission* (1868), pp. 108-109. Lincoln erred in supposing Stuart to be a cleric.

To Simon Cameron[1]

Sec. of War, please give Mr. Anderson, of Ky. an interview. He is amply recommended.   A. LINCOLN
Dec. 13. 1861.

[1] ALS, DLC-Cameron Papers. George W. Anderson of Louisville, Kentucky, wrote at Washington, D.C., December 23, 1861, in behalf of his neighbor William E. Culver, who had been dismissed as paymaster and wished to be restored to office (DLC-RTL). This may be the same Anderson on the same mission.

To Simon Cameron[1]

Hon. Sec. of War.   Executive Mansion
My dear Sir: Dec. 13. 1861
At the request of Senator Callamer [*sic*], Gov. Fairbanks & other gentlemen of Vermont, I wish, as a special case, to appoint Dr. Edward E. Phelps, a Brigade Surgeon, to serve with the Vermont Brigade, now commanded by Gen. Brooks.[2] Please take steps to have this done at once. Yours truly   A. LINCOLN

[1] ALS-P, ISLA. On the bottom of the letter Cameron has endorsed, "This case is peculiar—and in consideration that no officer of the grade has been selected from the state of Vermont, Dr Phelps will be appointed after examination and approval by the medical board." The appointment was made February 4, 1862.
[2] William T. H. Brooks, appointed brigadier general of Volunteers, September 28, 1861.

Memorandum: Appointment of George May[1]

December 13, 1861

I knew George May, when a boy, and young man, then a little inclined to dissipation. If free from that now, he has intellect enough for almost any place. I suppose the within names ought to be a sufficient voucher, as to that.   A. LINCOLN

Dec. 13, 1861.

[1] Copy, ISLA. Lincoln's endorsement is written on a recommendation signed by Joseph F. Wilson, James Harlan, and James W. Grimes in favor of George May of Plattsmouth, Nebraska Territory, for a judgeship in Utah. There is no record of May's appointment. May had moved from Sangamon County, Illinois, in the eighteen-forties.

Note on Photographs
of Members of Lincoln's Cabinet[1]

These likenesses, so far as I know the originals, are very good.

Dec. 13. 1861.   A. LINCOLN.

[1] Facsimile, Hertz, II, 612. The photographs are reproduced in the source, as mounted with Lincoln's card beneath.

To Caleb B. Smith[1]

Hon. Sec. of Interior   Executive Mansion   Dec. 13. 1861.

My dear Sir: George S. Pomeroy of Illinois, tells me he was a clerk in the Census Bureau, & has been removed. Will you please ascertain, & tell me the circumstances. Yours truly   A. LINCOLN

[1] ALS, CSmH. Smith replied on the same day that "The facts in his case are these. Mr. O E Dake of Ill. was appointed Clk in the Census in April last. Some time this fall Dake being unwell requested me to allow him to go to Ill. to spend some months and to appoint a substitute . . . . he sent Mr Pomeroy . . . . he . . . was not fit to be left on the files. . . ." (DLC-RTL).

To Whom It May Concern[1]

Whom it may concern   Washington, D.C. Dec. 13. 1861

It having been represented to me that Jno.[2] Pope, a citizen of the United States, engaged in the present rebellion against the government thereof, is desirous of returning to his proper allegiance, this may be his full pardon for all political offences committed by him against said government, prior to the first day of January one thousand, eight hundred and sixty two, provided he shall, on or before said day, leave the ranks of said rebellion, and

[68]

not thereafter do, aid, or encourage anything against the said government of the United States.   ABRAHAM LINCOLN
President of the United States of America.

1 ADS, owned by Mrs. R. F. Mattingly, Louisville, Kentucky. As of December 5, 1861, Major John Pope was chief quartermaster under General William J. Hardee of the Confederate Army at Bowling Green, Kentucky (OR, I, VII, 737). The circumstances under which Lincoln issued this document are obscure. There seems to be no record of Pope's capture or parole. According to information furnished by the present owner of the document, Pope was born (1830) John Pope Cocke, the grandson of John Pope (1770-1845), U.S. senator and representative from Kentucky and governor of Arkansas Territory, but changed his name to John Pope in compliance with stipulations in his grandfather's will.

2 Lincoln left a blank for the first name which is filled in by another hand.

To Arnold Fischel[1]

Rev. Dr. A. Fischel   Executive Mansion, December 14, 1861.

My dear Sir: I find that there are several particulars in which the present law in regard to Chaplains is supposed to be deficient, all of which I now design presenting to the appropriate Committee of Congress. I shall try to have a new law broad enough to cover what is desired by you in behalf of the Israelites. Yours truly,

A. LINCOLN.

1 Isaac Markens, *Abraham Lincoln and the Jews* (1909), p. 9. Dr. Fischel wished to be appointed chaplain of a New York regiment composed largely of Jews, but was informed by Secretary Cameron that the law provided only for ordained ministers of Christian denominations. On March 12, 1862, the law was amended to authorize employment of Jewish chaplains.

To John F. Lee[1]

Assuming the within statement to be true, will the Judge Advocate please say what are Gen. Benham's rights in the case?

Dec. 14. 1861.   A. LINCOLN

1 AES, DLC-RTL. Lincoln's endorsement is written on a letter from Assistant Adjutant General Alfred B. Ely, counsel for Brigadier General Henry W. Benham, December 13, 1861, setting forth that some twenty days had elapsed since Benham's arrest, November 24, on orders of General William S. Rosecrans, and that since no charges had been preferred, law required General Benham's release. Judge Advocate General Lee replied, December 19, in an endorsement immediately following Lincoln's, that there was just cause for delaying the trial, but recommending Benham's release and return to duty. Below Lee's endorsement, General McClellan wrote "Since the charges preferred . . . involve the question of his fitness to command troops in presence of the enemy I beg to reserve my opinion in the matter until I see the specifications. The charges are so serious that Genl Benham should cause an investigation." Rosecrans to Lorenzo Thomas, November 29, 1861, reported as follows: "On the 26th [*sic*] instant I found it necessary to arrest Brig. Gen. H. W. Benham for unofficer-like neglect of duty.

He applied for a leave of absence on a medical certificate, with permission to visit a city, and has gone to New York. . . ." (OR, I, V, 669). The arrest had been ordered because Benham failed to cut off the retreat of General John B. Floyd in West Virginia. The case dragged out (see New York *Herald*, March 22, 1862), but Benham was finally ordered to report for duty on March 17 and was later assigned to Major General David Hunter's command at Port Royal, South Carolina. See also Lincoln to McClellan, January 22, 1862, *infra*.

To John F. Lee[1]

Judge Advocate: Dec 14, 1861

Please see Mr. Schell and Mr Johnson on business of which I spoke this morning. ABRAHAM LINCOLN.

[1] Tracy, p. 199. Probably Augustus Schell of New York, a Democrat active in seeking release of political prisoners, was one of Lincoln's callers, but "Mr Johnson" cannot be positively identified.

To the Senate[1]

Executive Mansion, Washington,

To the Senate of the United States: December 14, 1861.

In compliance with the resolution of your honorable body, "that the President be requested to furnish to the Senate copies of the charges, testimony and finding of the recent court of inquiry, in the case of Colonel Dixon S. Miles, of the United States army," I have the honor to transmit herewith the copies desired, which have been procured from the War Department.

ABRAHAM LINCOLN.

[1] Thirty-seventh Congress, Second Session, *Senate Executive Document No. 7*. The resolution referred to was submitted by Senator James W. Grimes on December 4, 1861. Colonel Dixon S. Miles of the Second Infantry was accused of drunkenness on the evening of July 21, 1861, at Bull Run, by General Israel B. Richardson. The court of inquiry found Richardson justified in calling Miles drunk, but gave the opinion that insufficient evidence existed for a court-martial. Both officers died of wounds received in September, 1862.

To Gideon Welles[1]

December 14, 1861

If it is legally possible, and can be done with safety to the service, I would be glad for Commander Overton Carr, to be put on shore duty. A. LINCOLN

Dec. 14. 1861.

[1] ALS, The Rosenbach Company, Philadelphia and New York. Commander Carr had been put on the retired list, December 3, 1861. There is no further record of his service.

Memorandum: Appointment of
Harrison G. Fitzhugh or Captain Johnson[1]

[c. December 15, 1861?]

Has it ever occurred to Mr. Fitzhugh, or Captain Johnson, that in addition to the difficulty of appointing one of them coming from Illinois, possibly Mrs. Lincoln (with whom the Commissioner of Public Buildings has much to do) objects?

[1] Copy, DLC-Nicolay Papers. The original manuscript has not been located. The copy in Nicolay's handwriting, labeled by him as of an autograph manuscript, is without date. The supplied date is inferred from the fact that the post of commissioner of public buildings was a matter of considerable controversy from July, 1861, when the Senate held up Lincoln's appointment of William S. Wood, until January 27, 1862, when the appointment of Benjamin B. French was confirmed. Since Lincoln did not nominate French until December 15, 1861, it would seem that the question of the appointment was open until then. Letters from Shelby M. Cullom, December 16, and Edward L. Baker, December 23, 1861, press the claim of Harrison G. Fitzhugh of Springfield, Illinois (DLC-RTL), but "Captain Johnson" has not been identified.

To Simon Cameron[1]

Hon. Sec. of War.   Executive Mansion.
My dear Sir: Dec. 16. 1861

I wish Hon: James H. Lane to be appointed a Brigadier General of Volunteers, to report to Gen: Hunter, and to be so assigned to duty as not to be under, over, or in immediate contact with Gen. Denver. Yours truly   A. LINCOLN

[1] ALS, IHi. Lane's appointment as brigadier from December 18, 1861, was cancelled March 21, 1862. His letter to Lincoln October 9, 1861, narrating his difficulties in enlisting the Kansas Brigade due to what he termed a conspiracy between Governor Charles Robinson and the commandant at Fort Leavenworth, concluded with the statement that if he could not have command of the new Department of Kansas and the Indian Territory he would be compelled to "quit the field." For Lane's continuing difficulties, see Lincoln to Stanton, January 31, 1862, *infra*.

To Simon Cameron[1]

This appointment I suppose can be made with propriety.
Dec. 16. 1861.   A. LINCOLN

[1] AES-P, ISLA. Lincoln's endorsement is written on a letter from Joshua F. Speed and Robert Mallory, December 14, 1861, requesting appointment of William P. Graves as a first or second lieutenant on the staff of Brigadier General William Nelson. In Speed's letter Lincoln also inserted a phrase as follows: "in order to be appointed aid-de camp." Graves was appointed second lieutenant March 24, 1862. See Lincoln to Stanton, March 13, 1862, *infra*.

Draft of Letter to the Senate
Prepared for Ward H. Lamon[1]

To the Senate of the United States   [December 16, 1861]

In obedience to the resolution of your Honorable body, a copy of which accompanies this, I have the honor to state that since I have held the office of Marshal of the District of Columbia, three persons claimed to be slaves, have been admitted into the jail of said District on the requests, respectively, of the persons claiming to be their owners; that this has been acquiesced in by me, upon an old and uniform custom here, based as I supposed upon some valid law, but of which supposed law I have made no investigation.

[1] AD, CSmH. Lamon wrote the letter (dated December 16, 1861), following Lincoln's draft, but added two polite closing sentences (DNA RG 46, Senate Communications on District of Columbia, Thirty-seventh Congress, Second Session). The Senate resolution of December 9 had directed Marshal Lamon "to inform the Senate by what authority he receives slaves into the jail of the District at the request of their masters and holds them in confinement until discharged by their masters." Bills introduced in the Senate to appoint a warden of the District jail (February 12, 1862) and to abolish the office of marshal and create the office of sheriff (May 8, 1862) were obviously aimed at Lamon. The first of these contained an amendment (February 14) as follows: "That whenever the marshal or other officer . . . shall commit any person to said jail, he shall leave with said warden a certified copy of the precept by which said person was committed; and no person shall be committed . . . unless by virtue of some process or order from some magistrate. . . ." (*Senate Journal*, p. 210). Both bills failed to become law.

To George B. McClellan[1]

If Gen. McClellan thinks it proper, let the appointment be made as requested by Gen. Halleck.   A. LINCOLN

Dec. 16. 1861.

[1] AES, owned by Carl E. Dorr, Fayetteville, New York. Lincoln's endorsement is written on a telegram from General Henry W. Halleck to George B. McClellan, requesting appointment of Lieutenant Colonel William S. Ketchum as brigadier general. McClellan endorsed "I respectfully recommend Col Ketchum as a Brig Genl." Ketchum was appointed February 3, 1862.

To the Senate[1]

To the Senate of the United States: December 16, 1861

I submit to the Senate for consideration with a view to ratification, the amendments introduced by the Constituent National Assembly of Bolivia, in its decree of ratification, into the Treaty of Peace, Friendship, Commerce and Navigation concluded with that Republic on the 13th. May, 1858; an official translation of which decree accompanies this message with the original Treaty.

As the time within which the exchange of ratifications should be effected is limited, I recommend, in view of the delay which must necessarily occur, and of the difficulty of reaching the Seat of Government of that Republic, that the time within which such exchange shall take place be extended in the following terms— "within such period as may be mutually convenient to both Governments." ABRAHAM LINCOLN.

Washington, 16 December, 1861.

[1] DS, DNA RG 46, Senate 37B B1. The treaty was ratified February 3, 1862.

To William H. Seward[1]

If any charges should come against Col. Russell let us give him a hearing before acting. A. LINCOLN

Dec. 16. 1861.

[1] AES, DNA FS RG 59, Appointments, Box 375. Lincoln's endorsement is written on a letter from Elisha Whittlesey, first comptroller of the Treasury, December 16, 1861, enclosing a letter from his friend William H. Russell, consul at Trinidad de Cuba, to Lincoln December 7, in which Russell recounts circumstances under which he had been obliged to remove a consular agent at Cienfuegos by the name of "Cross" and of that gentleman's threats "to array me before your Excellency."

To William H. Seward[1]

Sec. of State, please see Lieut. Webb, of the British Army.

Dec. 16. 1861. A. LINCOLN

[1] ALS, owned by Dale Carnegie, Forest Hills, New York. Lieutenant Webb has not been identified.

To the Senate[1]

To the Senate of the United States: December 17, 1861

I transmit to the Senate for its advice, a copy of a draft for a Convention with the Republic of Mexico, proposed to the Government of that Republic by Mr. Corwin, the Minister of the United

[73]

States accredited to that Government, together with the correspondence relating to it.

As the subject is of momentous interest to the two Governments at this juncture, the early consideration of it by the Senate is very desirable.

Washington, 17th December, 1861   ABRAHAM LINCOLN

1 DS, DNA RG 46, Senate 37B B11. See Lincoln's further message to the Senate, January 24, 1862, *infra.*

To the Senate and House of Representatives[1]

December 17, 1861

To the Senate and House of Representatives:

I transmit to the Senate and House of Representatives copies of the correspondence between the Secretary of State, Secretary of War, and the Governor of the State of Maine, on the subject of the fortification of the seacoast and Lakes.   ABRAHAM LINCOLN

Washington, December 17, 1861.

1 DS, DNA RG 46, Senate 37A F2; DS, DNA RG 233, Thirty-seventh Congress, Second Session, Original Executive Document No. 14. The correspondence transmitted is printed in *H.R. Executive Document No. 14,* and includes Israel Washburn Jr. to Seward, October 23, 1861, endorsed by Lincoln to Cameron, November 4, 1861, *supra.*

To Alexander II[1]

December 18, 1861

Abraham Lincoln
President of the United States of America,

To His Majesty Alexander II
Emperor and Autocrat of all the Russias,
    &c.,   &c.,   &c.

Great and Good Friend: I have received the letter which Your Imperial Majesty addressed to me on the 21st. of October last, informing me that Her Imperial Highness the Grand Duchess Olga Teodorowra, Spouse of Your Majesty's well beloved brother, His Imperial Highness the Grand Duke Michel Nicolaewitsch was happily delivered of a son on the 4th. of that month who has received the name of Michel.

I pray Your Majesty to accept my cordial congratulations upon this event, and to be assured that I take a lively interest in all that concerns the happiness and prosperity of Your Imperial House:

And so I recommend Your Imperial Majesty and Your Royal Family to the protection of the Almighty. Your Good Friend.

Washington, 18th. Decr. 1861   ABRAHAM LINCOLN

By the President

WILLIAM H. SEWARD   Secretary of State

[1] Copy, DNA FS RG 59, Communications to Foreign Sovereigns and States, III, 136-37.

Appointment of George Harrington[1]

Washington, December 18th. 1861

George Harrington, is hereby appointed to discharge the duties of Secretary of the Treasury, during the absence of Salmon P. Chase, from Washington.   ABRAHAM LINCOLN

[1] DS, OClWHi.

To Montgomery C. Meigs[1]

Will the Quarter-Master-General please see this worthy man, who wishes to work?   A. LINCOLN.

Dec. 19, 1861

[1] Anderson Galleries Catalog 1583, May 9, 1921, No. 449. According to the catalog description Lincoln's note is written on a piece of envelope. There is no identification of the bearer.

Memorandum:
Appointment of Richard C. Churchill[1]

I do not know a case more strongly presented than this.

Dec. 19. 1861.   A. LINCOLN

[1] AES, DNA WR RG 94, U.S. Military Academy, 1861, No. 199, Box 77. Lincoln's endorsement is written on a letter from Colonel Ebenezer S. Sibley, December 14, 1861, asking appointment of his stepson, son of Captain William H. Churchill who had died during the Mexican War. Richard C. Churchill entered West Point July 1, 1862.

To James W. Ripley[1]

Let the fifty guns be ordered on the terms above recommended by Genl. McClellan & not otherwise.   A LINCOLN

Dec. 19. 1861.

[1] AES copy, DLC-RTL. Lincoln copied McClellan's recommendation and his own endorsement for preservation in his file. The original, sent to General Ripley, has not been located. McClellan's undated recommendation as copied by Lincoln

is as follows: "I would recommend that fifty of the 'Coffee Mill' guns be furnished at 20% advance on cost price, which cost may be ascertained by competent ordnance officers. I think $1200, entirely too high. Geo. B. McClellan Maj. Genl. Commg." Although this early machine gun was successfully tested and certified by Colonel Charles P. Kingsbury of the Ordnance Department (November 30, 1861, *ibid.*), the guns ordered were never used.

To William H. Seward[1]

This is forwarded merely to back a nomination already made, as I understand   A. LINCOLN
    Dec. 19, 1861.

[1] AES, DNA FS RG 59, Appointments, Box 248. Lincoln's endorsement is written on a petition of New York City merchants and underwriters, December 7, 1861, asking appointment of Reverend Andrew G. Carothers as consul to Martinique. See also Lincoln to Seward, November 18, *supra.* Carother's appointment was confirmed by the Senate December 20, 1861.

To William H. Seward[1]

If the consulate at Cape Town is open, I perceive no objection to the appointment within recommended.   A. LINCOLN
    Dec. 19. 1861.

[1] AES, DNA FS RG 59, Appointments, Box 256. Lincoln's endorsement is written on a petition signed by members of congress from Pennsylvania, recommending H. Crawford Coates of Philadelphia, a merchant residing at Cape Town, Africa, for the consulship at that place. There is no record of the appointment.

To Simon Cameron[1]

Hon. Sec. of War   Executive Mansion
My dear Sir: Dec. 20. 1861.
    Let Thomas Francis Meagher, be appointed a Brigadier General of volunteers   Yours truly   A. LINCOLN.

[1] ALS, IHi. On the bottom of the letter is Cameron's approval dated December 20. The appointment was made February 3, 1862.

To George B. McClellan[1]

    December 20, 1861
Senator Sherman spoke to me verbally about the within matter, upon which I desired him to put it in writing. Can there be any-

thing for the two officers to do in *Oregon* equal in importance to them remaining with the volunteer regiments, under the peculiar circumstances?

I hope Gen. McClellan will say not.   A. LINCOLN

Dec. 20, 1861.

[1] AES, IHI. Lincoln's endorsement appears on a letter of Lorenzo Thomas to John Sherman, December 14, 1861: "In reply to your letter of 5th inst. addressed to Major General McClellan, I am directed to say that the services of Captains [James W.] Forsyth and [Charles G.] Harker are required with their regiment now in Oregon, and that permission cannot be granted them to command the regiments of Ohio Volunteers as requested by you."

Captain Charles G. Harker, appointed colonel of the Sixty-fifth Ohio Volunteers as of November 11, 1861, and brigadier general as of September 20, 1863, was killed at the battle of Kenesaw Mountain, June 27, 1864. Captain James W. Forsyth remained in temporary command of the Sixty-fourth Ohio Volunteers until February, 1862, when he became acting inspector general to the provost marshal of the Army of the Potomac. He served in this capacity until May, 1863, when he became acting assistant adjutant general of the Regular Brigade of Infantry in the Tennessee campaign. He was appointed major and assistant adjutant general of Volunteers as of April 7, 1864, and brigadier general of Volunteers as of May 19, 1865.

To the Senate and House of Representatives[1]

December 20, 1861

To the Senate and House of Representatives:

I transmit to Congress a letter from the Secretary of the Executive Committee of the Commission appointed to represent the interests of those American citizens who may desire to become exhibitors at the Industrial Exhibition to be held in London in 1862, and a Memorial of that Commission, with a report of the Executive Committee thereof, and copies of circulars announcing the decisions of Her Majesty's Commissioners in London, giving directions to be observed in regard to articles intended for exhibition, and also of circular forms of application, demands for space, approvals, &c., according to the rules prescribed by the British Commissioners.

As these papers fully set forth the requirements necessary to enable those citizens of the United States who may wish to become exhibitors to avail themselves of the privileges of the Exhibition, I commend them to your early consideration, especially in view of the near approach of the time when the Exhibition will begin.

Washington, 20th. Decr., 1861.   ABRAHAM LINCOLN

[1] DS, DNA RG 46, Senate 37A F2; DS, DNA RG 233, Thirty-seventh Congress, Second Session, Original Executive Document No. 15. The enclosures are printed in *H.R. Executive Document 15.*

To John F. Lee[1]

Judge Advocate   Executive Mansion
My dear Sir: Dec. 21. 1861
A lady is here saying she is the wife of Capt. or Lieut. Robert
Hunter, lately cashiered from the regular Army by a court martial.
If you have a transcript of the record, I will thank you to send it
to me, to be returned in due time. Yours truly   A. LINCOLN

[1] ALS, DNA WR RG 153, Judge Advocate General, Letters Received, No. 102.
First Lieutenant Robert F. Hunter was cashiered for drunkenness on duty, November 19, 1861. There is no record of his return to service.

To Caleb B. Smith[1]

Sec. of Interior, send me a nomination of Mr. Calvin H. Hale, as
within recommended.   A. LINCOLN
Dec. 21. 1861

[1] AES, DNA NR RG 48, Appointments, Indian Agencies, Box 1274. Lincoln's
endorsement is written on a letter from William H. Wallace, December 20, 1861,
recommending Calvin H. Hale for superintendent of Indian affairs in Washington
Territory. Hale is listed by the *U.S. Official Register* in the office named as of September 30, 1863.

To Simon Cameron[1]

Hon. Sec. of War   Executive Mansion
My dear Sir: Dec. 23. 1861
Let Napoleon T. J. Dana of Minnesota be appointed a Brigadier
General of volunteers. Yours truly   A. LINCOLN

If Gen. McClellan perceives no objection to the above, will he
please approve it, & forward, the paper to the War Department?
A.L.

[1] ALS, owned by Edward C. Stone, Boston, Massachusetts. On the bottom of
the letter McClellan endorsed: "I cordially recommend the promotion of Col.
Dana." Colonel Napoleon Jackson Tecumseh Dana of the First Minnesota Infantry was appointed brigadier February 3, 1862.

To Simon Cameron[1]

Hon. Sec. of War   Executive Mansion
My dear Sir.   Dec. 23. 1861
By the 1st. of June next, I wish to appoint Jesse W. Fell, of Illinois, as Paymaster in the Army, & I wish this placed on file to be
a remembrance on the subject. Yours truly   A. LINCOLN

[1] ALS, IHi. Lincoln's old friend Jesse W. Fell was appointed major and paymaster June 30, 1862, after Lincoln had reminded Edwin M. Stanton of his wish on March 29, 1862, *infra*.

To the House of Representatives[1]

December 23, 1861

To the House of Representatives: In compliance with the resolution of the House of Representatives of the 13th July last, requesting information respecting the Asiatic coolie trade, I transmit a report from the Secretary of State, with the documents which accompanied it.   ABRAHAM LINCOLN.

Washington, December 23, 1861.

[1] Thirty-seventh Congress, Second Session, *H.R. Executive Document No. 16.* The documents transmitted are printed with Lincoln's letter and are chiefly letters dealing with the attempt of Chinese coolies to seize the American merchant vessels *Staghound* and *Leonidas.*

To Simon Cameron[1]

I have before said, and now repeat, I would like Dr. Breckenridges son to be appointed as soon as he consistently can.

Dec. 24. 1861.   A. LINCOLN

[1] AES, RPB. Lincoln's endorsement is written on a letter from Robert J. Breckinridge, Danville, Kentucky, to Representative Henry Grider, December 13, 1861, asking a commission for his son Joseph C. Breckinridge, serving as aide-de-camp without rank or pay under General George H. Thomas. Joseph C. Breckinridge was appointed first lieutenant dating from August 30, 1861.

To Simon Cameron[1]

December 25, 1861

Within is the list of persons whom Gen. T. F. Meagher wishes appointed to his staff. He is very anxious, & I promised him to urge compliance so far as consistent with the service. Please have Adjt. Genl. look to it.   A. LINCOLN

Dec. 25. 1861

[1] AES, owned by Arnold Goldsborough, Wilmington, Delaware. Meagher recommended Sergeant Joseph McCoy of the Fifth Cavalry for his assistant adjutant general and Dr. Francis Reynolds as his brigade surgeon. McCoy had saved Meagher's life at Bull Run, and Dr. Reynolds, "Fellow of the Royal College of Surgeons, Dublin . . . Brigade and Division Surgeon all through the Crimean War," was acting as "Surgeon of the 4th. Regt. of the Irish Brigade."

To Simon Cameron[1]

December 27, 1861

This inchoate Brigade, was set on foot by particular friends of mine some time ago. I expect they will have to be completed by consolidation. I wish the very best done for them that can be consistently with the public service   A. LINCOLN

Dec. 27. 1861

[1] AES, IHi. Lincoln's endorsement is written on a letter from Major Augustus H. Chapman, Charleston, Illinois, December 17, 1861, asking certain appointments to be made in the "Kentucky Brigade." Chapman was a major in the Fifty-fourth Illinois regiment of that brigade.

Endorsement[1]

The writer of this is a most worthy young man, with an excellent education & good business qualifications. I personally know him.

Dec. 27. 1861.   A. LINCOLN

[1] AES, DLC-RTL. Lincoln's endorsement is written on what appears to be a blank covering page which has become detached from a letter and hence is without reference.

Memorandum:
Henry W. Halleck and James H. Lane[1]

December 27, 1861.

An excellent letter; though I am sorry General Halleck is so unfavorably impressed with General Lane.   A.L.

[1] OR, I, VIII, 450. Lincoln's note is an endorsement on a letter from Henry W. Halleck to George B. McClellan, December 19, 1861, reporting on the military situation in Missouri. Halleck wrote, "The conduct of the forces under Lane . . . has done more for the enemy than could have been accomplished by 20,000 of his own army. I receive almost daily complaints of outrages committed by these men in the name of the United States. . . . It is rumored that Lane has been made a brigadier-general. I cannot conceive of a more injudicious appointment. . . ."

To Simon Cameron[1]

Please see Gov. Crittenden, & appoint Dr. Bradford, a Surgeon for Gen. Nelson's Brigade, if it is legally possible.   A. LINCOLN

Dec. 28. 1861

[1] ALS, DLC-Cameron Papers. John J. Crittenden's request was granted by appointment of Joshua T. Bradford as major and surgeon of Volunteers, April 4, 1862.

To Henry Liebman[1]

Executive Mansion, Washington, D.C.

Henry Liebman   Dec. 28, 1861.

My dear Sir: Your private letter in regard to Mr. Burtwell is received.

I have no power to remove a Lieut-Colonel appointed by the Governor of New York. The appeal must be made, if at all, to the Governor. Yours, etc.,   A. LINCOLN

[1] Tracy, pp. 199-200. The letter from Henry Liebman is not in the Lincoln Papers, and no Lieutenant Colonel Burtwell has been identified. Henry Liebman of New York City was appointed first lieutenant and quartermaster in the Seventy-first New York Infantry, September 6, 1862, but that he was the same as Lincoln's correspondent is uncertain.

Memorandum:
Appointment of George R. Edwards[1]

I do not know the position into which I could put Mr. Edwards.
Dec. 28. 1861.   A.L.

[1] AES, DLC-RTL. Lincoln's endorsement is written on a letter from George R. Edwards, Washington, D.C., December 27, 1861, enclosing recommendations from "the most prominent men in the state of Illinois." According to the recommendations, Edwards had published a Republican paper at Shawneetown, Illinois, in 1860, had lost his right arm and was needy.

To William H. Seward[1]

Might we not let Gov. Moorehead loose?   A. LINCOLN
Dec. 28, 1861

[1] ALS, ORB. Lincoln's note is written on a small card. Former Governor Morehead was released on January 6, 1862. See Lincoln to Seward, October 4, 1861, *supra.*

To Joseph G. Totten[1]

Do we have need of the property this good old patriot so kindly offers us?   A. LINCOLN
Dec. 28. 1861

[1] AES, DLC-RTL. Lincoln's endorsement is written on a letter from Representative James K. Moorhead, December 28, 1861, enclosing a letter from Philip Winebiddle offering land at Erie or Pittsburgh, Pennsylvania, as an armory site. Totten's reply of December 30, pointed out that "Until Pittsburg or Erie shall have been selected . . . it would seem to be inappropriate . . . to receive the property. . . ." (*Ibid.*).

To Edward Bates[1]

What thinks the Attorney-General about the proposed court in
Arkansas?   A. LINCOLN
Dec. 30. 1861.

[1] AES, DLC-RTL. Lincoln's endorsement is written on a letter from John S.
Phelps, Rolla, Missouri, December 19, 1861, recommending abolition of the two
U.S. District Courts in Arkansas and the establishment of one only, in Northern
Arkansas. Bates' reply, also written on the letter, deemed any action at the time
premature: "*We* have not yet a spot of ground in Arkansas, on which *one* court
can sit. . . . When we get a foothold in Arkansas . . . it will be proper to ap-
point officers, and then, I would be glad to see Congress abolish the *two* District
Courts, & establish *one*. . . ."

Note[1]

Not having the Act of Congress before me, I know not whether
I am to do anything with the paper, other than to read & return.
Dec. 30, 1861   A. LINCOLN

[1] American Art Association Anderson Galleries Catalog 4079, January 17-18,
1934, No. 535. According to the catalog description the note is on a small card,
but there is no indication as to what it concerns.

To Andrew Porter[1]

December 30, 1861
. . . please my intimate personal friend, Geo. C. Beilor.

[1] *The Collector*, April, 1950, p. 86. According to the catalog description Lincoln's note is "addressed to the Provost Marshal." The text given is incomplete
and probably inaccurate as to the name "Beilor." George C. Bestor, mayor of
Peoria, Illinois, in 1853 and state senator in 1858, was probably the person to
whom Lincoln gave the card. Colonel Andrew Porter was provost marshal of
Washington and the Army of the Potomac, October, 1861 to June, 1862. Concerning Bestor, see Lincoln to Meigs, March 15, 1862, *infra*.

To the Senate and House of Representatives[1]

December 30, 1861
To the Senate and House of Representatives:
I transmit to Congress a correspondence which has taken place
between the Secretary of State and authorities of Great Britain
and France, on the subject of the recent removal of certain citizens
of the United States from the British mail-steamer Trent, by order
of Captain Wilkes, in command of the United States war-steamer
San Jacinto.   ABRAHAM LINCOLN.
Washington, December 30, 1861.

[82]

1 Thirty-seventh Congress, Second Session, *Senate Executive Document No. 8.*
The correspondence transmitted is printed with the letter of transmittal.

To William H. Seward[1]

[December 30, 1861?]

What thinks the Sec. of State, of the within?   A. LINCOLN

1 AES, DLC-RTL. Lincoln's endorsement is written on a letter from Charles H. Middleton, Washington, D.C., December 30, 1861, suggesting an intricate scheme to offset the British demand for surrender of Mason and Slidell by arresting a former fugitive slave, residing in Washington but a citizen of Canada, in order to surrender him immediately upon demand by the British government and thus embarrass Britain in her support of the Confederacy. The former slave, not named, is described as "near purely a white man." Seward's reply endorsed below Lincoln's query is as follows: "The Secretary of State thinks that the scheme proposed would be injudicious."

To Simon Cameron[1]

December 31, 1861

These very ample recommendations are respectfully submitted to the War Department, being quite willing the appointment shall be made if it consistently can.   A. LINCOLN

Dec. 31. 1861.

1 AES, RPB. Lincoln's endorsement is written on a letter from the Maine delegation in congress, December 23, 1861, recommending George W. Wood, formerly of Winthrop, Maine, for appointment to a lieutenancy in the First Infantry Regiment. No appointment for George W. Wood is listed prior to February 23, 1866, when he became second lieutenant in the Eighteenth Infantry.

To Agénor-Etienne Gasparin[1]

Executive Mansion,

My Dear Sir   Washington, December 31, 1861.

It gives me great pleasure to acknowledge the receipt of your favour of the 2nd of December. Although the matter to which it related was decided before your letter was received, I am none the less grateful at your manifestation of kindly interest. Allow me to assure you, Sir, that our people are not unmindful of your cordial sympathy and eloquent championship. I have the honor to be Your Obedient Servant   ABRAHAM LINCOLN

1 Copy (?), DLC-Nicolay Papers. In John Hay's handwriting, this document may be either a copy or a draft composed by Hay. Whether Lincoln ever signed or sent such a letter is uncertain. Count Gasparin's letter from Geneva, December 2, 1861, commented on the *Trent* affair, that although the right of search was beyond question, the arrest of Mason and Slidell on a British ship influenced the opinion of Europe as well as England against the United States.

To Henry W. Halleck and Don C. Buell[1]

General Halleck   Washington, D.C.,
St. Louis, Mo.:   December 31, 1861.

General McClellan is sick. Are General Buell and yourself in concert? When he moves on Bowling Green, what hinders it being re-enforced from Columbus? A simultaneous movement by you on Columbus might prevent it.   A. LINCOLN.

(Similar despatch to Buell same date.)

[1] OR, I, VII, 524. Halleck replied January 1, 1862, "I have never received a word from General Buell. I am not ready to co-operate with him. Hope to do so in few weeks. . . . Too much haste will ruin everything." (*Ibid.*, p. 526). Buell replied on the same date, "There is no arrangement between General Halleck and myself. I have been informed by General McClellan that he would make suitable disposition for concerted action. . . ." (*Ibid.*). See Lincoln to Halleck and Buell, January 1, 1862.

To David Hunter[1]

Executive Mansion, Washington,
Major General Hunter.   Dec. 31, 1861.

Dear Sir: Yours of the 23rd. is received; and I am constrained to say it is difficult to answer so ugly a letter in good temper. I am, as you intimate, losing much of the great confidence I placed in you, not from any act or omission of yours touching the public service, up to the time you were sent to Leavenworth, but from the flood of grumbling despatches and letters I have seen from you since. I knew you were being ordered to Leavenworth at the time it was done; and I aver that with as tender a regard for your honor and your sensibilities as I had for my own, it never occurred to me that you were being "humiliated, insulted and disgraced"; nor have I, up to this day, heard an intimation that you have been wronged, coming from any one but yourself. No one has blamed you for the retrograde movement from Springfield, nor for the information you gave Gen. Cameron; and this you could readily understand, if it were not for your unwarranted assumption that the ordering you to Leavenworth must necessarily have been done as a *punishment* for some *fault*. I thought then, and think yet, the position assigned to you is as respo[n]sible, and as honorable, as that assigned to Buell. I know that Gen. McClellan expected more important results from it. My impression is that at the time you were assigned to the new Western Department, it had not been determined to re-place Gen. Sherman in Kentucky; but of this I am not certain, because the idea that a command in Kentucky was very desireable, and one in the farther West, very

[84]

undesireable, had never occurred to me. You constantly speak of
being placed in command of only 3000. Now tell me, is not this
mere impatience? Have you not known all the while that you are
to command four or five times that many?

I have been, and am sincerely your friend; and if, as such, I dare
to make a suggestion, I would say you are adopting the best possible way to ruin yourself. "Act well your part, there all the honor
lies." He who does *something* at the head of one Regiment, will
eclipse him who does *nothing* at the head of a hundred. Your friend
as ever, A. LINCOLN

1 ALS, CSmH. Major General Hunter's endorsement on the envelope containing Lincoln's letter is as follows: "The President in reply to my 'ugly letter.'—
This letter was kept on his table for more than a month, and then sent by a private conveyance, with directions to hand it to me only when I was in a good
humor!!!!.—" Hunter's letter of December 23, 1861, is in part as follows: "I am
very deeply mortified, humiliated, insulted and disgraced. . . . I am sent here
[Fort Leavenworth] into banishment, with not three thousand effective men
under my command, while one of the Brigadiers, General Buell, is in command of
near one hundred thousand men in Kentucky. The only sin I have committed is
my carrying out your views in relation to the retrograde movement from Springfield. . . . So it appears that I have been deprived of a command, suitable to my
rank, for presuming to answer . . . official questions put to me by the Secretary
of War . . . for in no other way was I connected with the Fremont
troubles. . . ." (DLC-RTL).

To William H. Seward[1]

Sec. of State, please see, Mr. Gerard. A. LINCOLN
Dec. 31. 1861

1 ALS, IHi. George Gerard of Pennsylvania was nominated consul to Brunswick, but on February 20, 1862, Lincoln withdrew the previous nomination and
nominated him for the consulate at St. Helena, which appointment the Senate
confirmed on March 19, 1862.

To Joseph G. Totten[1]

Will Gen Totten, please see Mr Hitchcock A. LINCOLN
Dec. 31, 1861.

1 Stan. V. Henkels Catalog 1372, March 19, 1925, No. 87. The bearer of Lincoln's note has not been identified.

To George D. Ramsay[1]

[1862?]

Col. Ramsey [*sic*], please see Mr. Hegon [Hecon?],[2] and show
him one of the little breech-loading cannons I got of Hon. Eli
Thayer.[3] A LINCOLN

1 ALS, CSmH-Eldridge Collection. 2 Unidentified.
3 See Lincoln's memorandum about guns, September 24, 1861, *supra*.

Memorandum Concerning Sylvester R. Knight[1]

[c. January, 1862?]

The President sympathizes deeply with Mrs. Knight & her husband, and the many others in like condition—but he is sure she does not appreciate the difficulty of what she asks.

[1] AD, DLC-RTL. This item is misdated [Feb. ? 1863] in the Lincoln Papers. Although the memorandum is written on a separate sheet of paper, an endorsement written below it in an unidentified handwriting describes the memorandum as an endorsement "upon the letter of a lady who wished her husband released from jail at Richmond where he is held a prisoner of war. Lt. S R Knight 1st R.I. Regt." Mrs. Knight's letter has not been located. Lieutenant Sylvester R. Knight, captured at Bull Run, was exchanged on January 13, 1862, and mustered out of service on January 20, 1862.

To Don C. Buell[1]

Washington City,

Brigadier-General Buell, Louisville:　　　　January 1, 1862.

General McClellan should not yet be disturbed with business. I think you better get in concert with General Halleck at once. I write you to-night. I also telegraph and write Halleck.

A. LINCOLN.

[1] OR, I, VII, 526. See also the telegram and letter to Halleck of this date, *infra.* The letter which Lincoln promised to write Buell has not been located, but Buell acknowledged its receipt on January 6. Upon receipt of Lincoln's telegram, Buell telegraphed Halleck. Halleck replied on January 2, "All my available troops are in the field except those at Cairo and Paducah, which are barely sufficient to threaten Columbus, &c. A few weeks hence I hope to be able to render you very material assistance. . . ." (*Ibid.,* p. 527).

Draft of a Proclamation to People of Maryland[1]

[c. January 1, 1862?]

In view of the recent declaration of the people of Maryland of their adhesion to the Union so distinctly made in their recent election,[2] the President directs that all the political prisoners who having heretofore been arrested in that State are now detained in military custody by the President's authority be released from their imprisonment on the following conditions, namely: That if they were holding any civil or military offices when arrested the terms of which have not expired they shall not resume or reclaim such offices; and secondly, all persons availing themselves of this proclamation shall engage by oath or parole of honor to maintain the Union and the Constitution of the United States, and in no way to aid or abet by arms, counsel, conversation or information of any kind the existing insurrection against the Government of the United States.

To guard against misapprehension it is proper to state that this proclamation does not apply to prisoners of war.

[1] OR, II, I, 617. According to the source, this undated draft marked "File: January 1, 1862," was "found among the files of the State Department." The original has not been located by the editors. No such proclamation was issued by President Lincoln, but see Lincoln's endorsement of January 30, *infra*.

[2] The Maryland election was held on November 6, 1861.

To Henry W. Halleck[1]

Majr. Genl. Halleck   Washington, D.C.
St. Louis, Mo.   Jany. 1. 1861 [1862]

Gen. McClellan should not yet be disturbed with business. I think Gen. Buell and yourself should be in communication and concert at once. I write you to-night, and also Telegraph and write him.   A. LINCOLN.

[1] ALS, NHi. Lincoln misdates this communication sent by telegraph to both Halleck and General Don C. Buell. See also Lincoln to Halleck, December 31, 1861, *supra*.

To Henry W. Halleck[1]

Executive Mansion, Washington, January 1, 1862.

My dear General Halleck: General McClellan is not dangerously ill, as I hope, but would better not to be disturbed with business. I am very anxious that, in case of General Buell's moving toward Nashville, the enemy shall not be greatly re-enforced, and I think there is danger he will be from Columbus. It seems to me that a real or feigned attack upon Columbus from up-river at the same time would either prevent this or compensate for it by throwing Columbus into our hands. I wrote General Buell a letter similar to this, meaning that he and you shall communicate and act in concert, unless it be your judgment and his that there is no necessity for it. You and he will understand much better than I how to do it. Please do not lose time in this matter. Yours, very truly,   A. LINCOLN.

[1] OR, I, VII, 926. Halleck replied on January 6, ". . . I immediately communicated with Genl Buel and have since sent him all the information I could obtain of the enemy's movements about Columbus and Camp Beauregard. No considerable force has been sent from those places to Bowling Green. They have about 22,000 men at Columbus. . . . I have at Cairo, Fort Holt & Paducah only about 15,000. . . . I cannot . . . withdraw any from Missouri. . . ." (DLC-RTL).

To George B. McClellan[1]

My dear General   Executive Mansion   Jany. 1. 1862

I hear that the doings of an Investigating Committee, give you some uneasiness. You may be entirely relieved on this point. The gentlemen of the Committee were with me an hour and a half last night; and I found them in a perfectly good mood.

As their investigation brings them acquainted with facts, they are rapidly coming to think of the whole case as all sensible men would. Yours as ever   A. LINCOLN

Gen. McClellan.

[1] ALS-F, ISLA. The Joint Committee on the Conduct of the War was composed of Senators Benjamin F. Wade, Zachariah Chandler, and Andrew Johnson, and Representatives Daniel W. Gooch, John Covode, George W. Julian, and Moses F. Odell. According to the Journal of the committee, all members met with the president on December 31 except Covode and Julian (*Report*, Part I, p. 72).

To Salmon P. Chase[1]

January 2, 1862

I have just been with General McClellan; and he is very much better.   A. LINCOLN.

[1] NH, VII, 71. Warden's *Chase* (p. 395) gives this brief communication without the word "very."

To the Senate and House of Representatives[1]

January 2, 1862

To the Senate and House of Representatives:

I transmit to Congress a copy of a letter to the Secretary of State, from James R. Partridge, Secretary to the Executive Committee to the Industrial Exhibition to be held in London in the course of the present year, and a copy of the correspondence to which it refers, relative to a vessel for the purpose of taking such articles as persons in this country may wish to exhibit on that occasion. As it appears that no naval vessel can be spared for the purpose, I recommend that authority be given to charter a suitable merchant vessel, in order that facilities similar to those afforded by the Government for the exhibition of 1851, may also be extended to those citizens of the United States who may desire to contribute to the exhibition of this year.   ABRAHAM LINCOLN

Washington, 2d. Jany. 1862.

[1] DNA RG 46, Senate 37A F2; DS, DNA RG 233, House Original Executive Document No. 25. A joint resolution of July 27, 1861, had approved participation in the exhibition and authorized $2,000 for expenses.

Appointment[1]

Let the appointment within requested be made, unless some valid reason to the contrary is known at the Department.

Jan. 3. 1862.   A. LINCOLN

1 AES, IHi. Lincoln's endorsement has been clipped from the letter on which it was written and is without further reference.

Appointment of Thomas Feran[1]

Washington   January 3rd. 1862

Thomas Feran, is hereby appointed to discharge the duties of Commissioner of Customs, during the absence of N. Sargent, from Washington.   ABRAHAM LINCOLN

1 DS, CSmH. Feran was chief clerk in the commissioner's office.

To Simon Cameron[1]

My views are that the appointment should be made, or a Quarter-Master—already appointed, be assigned to Gen. Mitchell

Jan. 3. 1862.   A. LINCOLN

1 AES, owned by Stephen M. Adams, Danville, Illinois. Lincoln's endorsement is written on a letter from Brigadier General Ormsby M. Mitchel at Camp Jefferson, Bacon Creek, Kentucky, December 25, 1861, requesting that Joseph J. Slocum be appointed brigade quartermaster and assigned to Mitchel's brigade. Montgomery C. Meigs endorsed on January 16 that no brigade quartermaster was "at present assignable." Slocum was appointed commissary with rank of captain on January 15 and confirmed by the Senate on February 19, 1862, but his assignment to Mitchel's command has not been verified.

To the Senate[1]

To the Senate   Washington, D. C.
of the United States: January 3. 1862.

I transmit to the Senate, for its constitutional action thereon, a treaty, concluded on the 15th. November 1861, between Wm. W. Ross, Agent, on the part of the United States and the Chiefs and head men of the tribe of Pottowatomie Indians, with accompanying communications from the Secretary of the Interior and Commissioner of Indian Affairs the latter of which proposes certain modifications of said treaty, which are also referred for the consideration of the Senate.   ABRAHAM LINCOLN

1 DNA RG 46, Senate 37B C3. The treaty was ratified with amendments on April 15, 1862.

[89]

To Don C. Buell[1]

Brig. Gen. Buell   Washington, D.C.
Louisville, Ky.   Jan. 4. 1862
Have arms gone forward for East-Tennessee? Please tell me the
progress and condition of the movement, in that direction. Answer.

A. LINCOLN

[1] ALS, DLC-Cameron Papers. Buell answered Lincoln's telegram on January
5: "Arms can only go forward for East Tennessee under the protection of an
army. My organization of the troops has had in view two columns with reference
to that movement. . . . But it was necessary also to have regard to contingencies
which . . . might require a modification. . . . I will confess . . . I have been
bound to it more by . . . sympathy for the people of Eastern Tennessee, and
the anxiety with which yourself and the General in Chief have desired it, than
by my opinion of its wisdom. . . ." (DLC-RTL). Buell also expressed the view
that an attack upon Nashville, Tennessee, would be preferable to the movement
into East Tennessee. See Lincoln to Buell, January 6, *infra.*

To George B. McClellan[1]

Majr. Gen. McClellan   Executive Mansion
My dear Sir   Jan 4. 1862.
I have been informed that you wish Francis E. Patterson, of
Penn. to be appointed a Brigadier General; and if this is so, so
write at the bottom of this, & it shall be done at once. Yours truly

A. LINCOLN

[1] ALS, owned by Emanuel A. Gardiner, New York City. McClellan endorsed
the letter as follows: "I recommended Col Patterson some time since, & would be
glad to have him appointed." Lincoln endorsed on the back of the letter: "Let
the appointment be made according to the within. A. Lincoln/Jan. 6. 1862."
Francis E. Patterson, son of Major General Robert Patterson, was appointed
brigadier general of Volunteers, April 11, 1862.

To Montgomery C. Meigs[1]

January 4, 1862
I am willing to oblige him [Gen. Cooper], only that I have an
impression that you have some objections. If you have not, so
write below this, and say he may be appointed.

[1] William D. Morley, Inc., Catalog, September 26, 1945, No. 178. According
to the catalog description, this is a partial text of an autograph letter signed, on
which Meigs wrote his approval. General James Cooper wrote Lincoln January
6 as follows: "The answer of Gen. Meigs to the note which your Excellency had
the kindness to address to him on the subject of the appointment of A. A. Mc-
Gaffey, as assistant Qr. Master of my Brigade was a refusal to lend his approval
to the appointment . . . on the belief that McGaffey is a gambler. . . ." (DLC-

RTL). This letter would seem to refer to the same matter, but does not agree with the catalog description of Meigs' endorsement. There is no record of McGaffey's appointment.

To Don C. Buell[1]

Executive Mansion,

Brig. Gen. Buell   Washington, January 6th, 1862.

My dear Sir Your despatch of yesterday has been received, and it disappoints and distresses me. I have shown it to Gen. McClellan, who says he will write you to-day. I am not competent to criticise your views; and therefore what I offer is merely in justification of myself. Of the two, I would rather have a point on the Railroad south of Cumberland Gap, than Nashville, first, because it cuts a great artery of the enemies' communication, which Nashville does not, and secondly because it is in the midst of loyal people, who would rally around it, while Nashville is not. Again, I cannot see why the movement on East Tennessee would not be a diversion in your favor, rather than a disadvantage, assuming that a movement towards Nashville is the main object.

But my distress is that our friends in East Tennessee are being hanged and driven to despair, and even now I fear, are thinking of taking rebel arms for the sake of personal protection. In this we lose the most valuable stake we have in the South. My despatch, to which yours is an answer, was sent with the knowledge of Senator Johnson and Representative Maynard of East Tennessee, and they will be upon me to know the answer, which I cannot safely show them. They would despair—possibly resign to go and save their families somehow, or die with them.

I do not intend this to be an order in any sense, but merely, as intimated before, to show you the grounds of my anxiety. Yours very Truly   A. LINCOLN

1 LS, ORB; ADfS, DLC-RTL. See Lincoln to Buell, January 4, *supra*. McClellan wrote Buell, January 6, "My own general plans . . . make the speedy occupation of East Tennessee . . . of absolute necessity. . . . Interesting as Nashville may be to the Louisville interests, it strikes me that its possession is of very secondary importance. . . ." (OR, I, VII, 531).

To Don C. Buell[1]

Brigr. General Buell   Washington, D.C.

Louisville, Ky.   Jan. 7. 1862

Please name as early a day as you safely can, on, or before which you can be ready to move Southward in concert with Gen.

Halleck. Delay is ruining us; and it is indispensable for me to have something definite. I send a like despatch to Halleck.

A. LINCOLN.

¹ ALS, DLC-RTL. See also Lincoln to Halleck, *infra.* There is no reply from Buell in the Lincoln Papers or in the *Official Records,* but see Lincoln to McClellan, January 9, *infra.* Anson Stager, manager of the Telegraph Department wrote Lincoln on January 8, ". . . I made special inquiry as to the cause of the delay of Telegraphic despatches to and from Louisville. The manager at Louisville states that Gen'l Buell was absent from the city and beyond the reach of the Telegraph. . . . An order has been issued to give precedence to all your telegrams and also to acknowledge by telegraph that they have reached their destination. Your telegram of yesterday reached Louisville at 3 P.M." (DLC-RTL).

To Henry W. Halleck¹

Major General Halleck.   Washington, D.C.
St. Louis, Mo.   Jan. 7. 1862.

Please name as early a day as you safely can, on, or before which, you can be ready to move Southward in concert with Gen. Buell. Delay is ruining us; and it is indispensable for me to have something definite. I send a like despatch to Buell.

A. LINCOLN.

¹ ALS, IHi. Halleck replied on January 8, "I have asked Gen Buel to designate a day for a demonstration to assist him. It is all I can do till I get arms. I have no arms. I have sent two unarmed Regiments to assist in the feint. . . ." (DLC-RTL).

To Francis T. King and Others¹

                                    Executive Mansion,
Gentlemen: Washington, January 7, 1862.

It gives me great pleasure to acknowledge the receipt through you of the Memorial of the English Friends, in relation to the matter in question between the Government of Great Britain and that of the United States of America. Although I trust that any fears entertained of serious derangement of our amicable relations have been without foundation. I cannot but gratefully appreciate your prompt and generous suggestions in the interests of peace and humanity.

I have the honor to be   With great respect   Your Obt Servt

A LINCOLN

¹ LS, Friends Library, Friends House, London, England. The three-page printed "Memorial of the English Friends," December 9, 1861, bears Lincoln's endorsement "Francis T. King, Baltimore," but the covering letter from King and his associates is no longer in the Lincoln Papers.

To Hiram Barney[1]

January 8, 1862

While I know nothing of Mr. Meade, the writer of this is an old friend of mine, once residing in Illinois, though now in New-York. I can do no other than to refer the case to the Collector.

Jan. 8. 1862. A. LINCOLN

[1] AES-P, ISLA. Lincoln's endorsement is written on a letter from George T. M. Davis, January 3, 1862, asking that Abraham B. Meade, who had been removed as appraiser's clerk in the New York Custom House after twenty-eight years' service "without any apparent cause than that his place was wanted for another," be restored to his position. Barney replied on January 16, 1862, "I referred the letter of Geo. T. M. Davis respecting the removal of Mr. Meade . . . to Judge [John T.] Hogeboom. . . . I have no power over the action of the appraisers . . . however . . . Mr. Meade . . . could not be retained with benefit . . . and ought not . . . except on the ground of having long held the place & worn himself out in the service." (DLC-RTL). Meade is listed in the *U.S. Official Register* as appraiser's clerk in the New York Customs House in 1861, but not in 1863.

To Simon Cameron[1]

January 8, 1862

It seems by the accompanying papers that a Brig. Genl. for Cavalry service, is needed; and also in conjunction with the within, that Maj. Davidson is a suitable man. Let him be appointed.

Jan. 8. 1862. A. LINCOLN

[1] AES, IHi. Lincoln's endorsement is written on a letter from Major John W. Davidson of the Second Cavalry to General McClellan, January 6, 1862, asking recommendation for appointment as brigadier general of cavalry. McClellan's undated note, "Most certainly I say *Yes* from the bottom of my heart," is with the letter, and Cameron's endorsement, "Let this be done," is below Lincoln's. Davidson was appointed brigadier general of Volunteers, February 3, 1862.

To Seth Williams[1]

Gen. Seth Williams   Executive Mansion
My dear Sir   Jan. 8. 1862

Major Thomas Duncan, now on duty on the border of Mexico, is an Illinoisian, and I had some acquaintance with him when he was young. His wife, whose father resides in this city, is now here, and tells me you know her husband. She is very anxious, as in duty bound, for him to be promoted, but especially for him to be assigned to duty here. Please write me what you know of him as an officer; and, if you can, tell me whether he can be brought here. Yours truly A. LINCOLN

[1] ALS, RPAB. Adjutant General Seth Williams of the Army of the Potomac apparently turned Lincoln's letter over to the Adjutant General's Office. Lorenzo

Thomas answered on February 13, 1862, that "Major Duncan cannot now be withdrawn from New Mexico without serious prejudice to the public interests. . . . With reference to the promotion of Major Duncan . . . there is no vacancy. . . ." (DLC-RTL). Duncan was a former resident of McLean County, Illinois. The *Official Records* do not indicate his transfer from New Mexico until April 25, 1863, when he was appointed assistant provost marshal for Iowa (III, III, 169).

To Simon Cameron[1]

January 9, 1862

This man William Martin, it seems has been imprisoned on some charge of suspicion of kidnapping and as Senator Pomeroy and Hon. Green Adams ask his release, let him be released.

[1] Copy, DNA WR RG 107, Secretary of War, Letters Received, P 35, Irregular Book 5. The copy is in the register of letters received, but Lincoln's original manuscript is missing from the file. Green Adams of Kentucky was auditor of the Treasury for the Post Office Department. William Martin has not been identified.

To George B. McClellan[1]

Majr. Genl. McClellan.   Executive Mansion

My dear Sir: Jan. 9. 1862

I think you better go before the Congressional Committee the earliest moment your health will permit—to-day, if possible. Yours as ever   A. LINCOLN

[1] ALS, owned by Louis Bamberger, Newark, New Jersey. McClellan wrote Lincoln on January 15, "I am so much better this morning that I am going before the Joint Committee. If I escape alive I will report when I get through." (DLC-RTL). McClellan's anticipation that the committee would give him a rough time was fully borne out. General belief that McClellan's prolonged illness was a subterfuge and that the inaction of his army was inexcusable, combined to make the committee somewhat less than sympathetic, in spite of Lincoln's assurance to the contrary (see Lincoln to McClellan, January 1, *supra*).

To George B. McClellan[1]

January 9, 1862

I send the within copy of dispatch from Gen. Buell, with the remark that neither he nor Halleck meets my request to name the DAY when they can be ready to move.

[1] American Art Association Anderson Galleries Catalog, January 14-15, 1936, No. 352. According to the catalog description Lincoln's endorsement is written on the back of a telegram from General Don C. Buell which reads as follows: ". . . undoubtedly there ought to be more and better artillery and better cavalry, but I shall work with what I have, and as soon as possible. Concert of action by which the enemy may be prevented from concentrating his whole force from Columbus to Bowling Green . . . would have the same and better effect than more troops . . ." See Lincoln to Buell, January 7, *supra*, and to Cameron, January 10, *infra*.

To William Vandever[1]

January 9, 1862

It would afford me great pleasure to oblige Mr. Vandever in the within matter, if I knew it would not be disagreeable to the other Iowa members. Will he please procure their names with his own & send them to me?   A. LINCOLN

Jan. 9. 1862.

[1] AES, DLC-RTL. Lincoln's endorsement is written on a letter from Representative William Vandever, January 4, 1862, recommending Henry O'Conner of Muscatine and William B. Fairfield of Charles City, Iowa, for appointment as commissioners to adjust allotment of Iowa soldiers. Vandever's undated reply, below Lincoln's endorsement, regrets that he cannot get concurrent recommendations from the other Iowa members of congress and asks that if other recommendations are made, his own be given "such weight as you think them justly entitled to."

To Simon Cameron[1]

January 10, 1862

The within is a copy of a letter just received from General Halleck. It is exceedingly discouraging. As everywhere else, nothing can be done.   A. LINCOLN.

January 10, 1862.

[1] OR, I, VII, 533. Lincoln's endorsement is on a copy of Halleck's letter to Lincoln, January 6, 1862, the original of which is in the Lincoln Papers. Explaining in great detail the status of affairs in Missouri which made it impossible for him to send a force against Columbus, Kentucky, Halleck added his opinion of the proposed movement of Buell's force: "To operate on *exterior* lines against an enemy occupying a central position, will fail, as it always has failed, in ninety-nine cases out of a hundred. It is condemned by every military authority I have ever read."

To the Senate and House of Representatives[1]

January 10, 1862

To the Senate and House of Representatives:

I transmit to Congress a translation of an instruction to the minister of his Majesty the Emperor of Austria accredited to this government, and a copy of a note to that minister from the Secretary of State, relative to the questions involved in the taking from the British steamer Trent of certain citizens of the United States, by order of Captain Wilkes, of the United States navy. This correspondence may be considered as a sequel to that previously communicated to Congress relating to the same subject.[2]

Washington, January 10, 1862.   ABRAHAM LINCOLN.

¹ Thirty-seventh Congress, Second Session, *Senate Executive Document No. 14.* The Austrian message of December 18, 1861, expressed that nation's concurrence with England's demands. Seward's reply of January 9, 1862, forwarded a copy of the correspondence between the U.S. and Great Britain and France and gave assurance that "the United States are not only incapable . . . of seeking to disturb the peace of the world, but are deliberately just and friendly in their intercourse with all foreign nations. . . ." (*Ibid.*).

² See Lincoln's communication of December 30, 1861, *supra.*

To John A. Andrew¹

Governor John A. Andrew,   Washington, D.C.,
Boston: January 11, 1862.

I will be greatly obliged if you will arrange somehow with General Butler to officer his two un-officered regiments.

A. LINCOLN.

¹ OR, III, I, 862. Governor Andrew replied on January 11 that ". . . if the Federal Government wishes me to organize those men into companies and regiments, and to appoint and commission officers . . . I will . . . undertake it. . . . But I must frankly say that there are names . . . whom to commission would offend both my sense of honor and of duty. . . ." (DLC-RTL).

To Simon Cameron¹

Hon. Simon Cameron,   Executive Mansion,
Secretary of War,   Washington, January 11, 1862.

My dear Sir   As you have, more than once, expressed a desire for a change of position, I can now gratify you, consistently with my view of the public interest. I therefore propose nominating you to the Senate, next monday, as minister to Russia. Very sincerely   Your friend   A. LINCOLN.

¹ ALS, DLC-Cameron Papers; ALS copy, DLC-RTL. This was Lincoln's "official" letter. See the private letter *infra.* Upon Cameron's resignation Lincoln appointed Edwin M. Stanton to succeed him on January 13, and on January 17 Cameron received his appointment as minister to Russia.

To Simon Cameron¹

     Private   Executive Mansion,
Dear Sir   Washington, Jan. 11, 1862.

Though I have said nothing hitherto in response to your wish, expressed long since, to resign your seat in the cabinet, I have not been unmindful of it. I have been only unwilling to consent to a change at a time, and under circumstances which might give occasion to misconstruction, and unable, till now to see how such misconstruction could be avoided.

But the desire of Mr. Clay to return home and to offer his services to his country in the field enables me now to gratify your wish, and at the same time evince my personal regard for you, and my confidence in your ability, patriotism, and fidelity to public trust.

I therefore tender to your acceptance, if you still desire to resign your present position, the post of Minister to Russia. Should you accept it, you will bear with you the assurance[2] of my undiminished confidence, of my affectionate esteem, and of my sure expectation that, near the great sovreign whose personal and hereditary friendship for the United States, so much endears him to Americans, you will be able to render services to your country, not less important than those you could render at home. Very sincerly Your friend   A. LINCOLN

[1] ALS, DLC-Cameron Papers. Cameron's letter of the same date accepting Lincoln's offer reads in part as follows:

"I have devoted myself, without intermission, to my official duties; I have given to them all my energies; I have done my best. It was impossible, in the direction of operations so extensive, but that some mistakes happen, and some complications and complaints arise. In view of these recollections, I thank you from a full heart, for the expression of your 'confidence in my ability, patriotism, and fidelity to public trust.' Thus my own conscientious sense of doing my duty by the Executive and by my Country, is approved by the acknowledged head of the Government himself.

"When I became a member of your administration, I avowed my purpose to retire from the Cabinet, as soon as my duty to my country would allow me to do so. In your letter of this day's date, so illustrative of your just and upright character, you revive the fact that I sometime ago, expressed the same purpose to you, and in reminding me of this you proffer for my acceptance one of the highest diplomatic positions in your gift, as an additional mark of your confidence and esteem.

"In retiring from the War Department, I feel that the mighty Army of the United States, is ready to do battle for the Constitution—that it is marshalled by gallant and experienced leaders—that it is fired with the greatest enthusiasm for the good cause; and also, that my successor, in this department, is my personal friend, who unites to wonderful intellect and vigor, the grand essential of being in earnest in the present struggle, and of being resolved upon a speedy and overwhelming triumph of our arms. I therefore gratefully accept the new distinction you have conferred upon me, and as soon as important and long neglected private business has been arranged, I will enter upon the important duties of the mission to which you have called me." (DLC-RTL).

[2] Lincoln deleted "evidence" and inserted "assurance."

To William H. Seward[1]

January 11, 1862

As appears within, I am requested to indorse the accompanying Commission. As the Sec. of State has given some attention to this subject, and I have not, I think fit to ask him, "Is this proper?" and "What is the form of doing it?"   A. LINCOLN

Jan. 11. 1862.

1 AES, DNA FS RG 59, Miscellaneous Letters. Lincoln's endorsement is written on a letter from W. B. Hubbard, president of the U.S. Agricultural Society, to whom it may concern, January 9, 1862, appointing John H. Klippart, vice-president of the society, a commissioner delegated to represent the society at the London Exhibition. No reply from Seward has been located.

To Don C. Buell[1]

C O P Y — one also sent to Gen. Halleck.

Brig. Genl. Buell.   Executive Mansion,
My dear Sir: Washington, Jan. 13, 1862.

Your despatch of yesterday is received, in which you say "I have received your letter and Gen. McClellan's; and will, at once devote all my efforts to your views, and his." In the midst of my many cares, I have not seen, or asked to see, Gen. McClellan's letter to you. For my own views, I have not offered, and do not now offer them as orders; and while I am glad to have them respectfully considered, I would blame you to follow them contrary to your own clear judgment—unless I should put them in the form of orders. As to Gen. McClellan's views, you understand your duty in regard to them better than I do. With this preliminary, I state my general idea of this war to be that we have the *greater* numbers, and the enemy has the *greater* facility of concentrating forces upon points of collision; that we must fail, unless we can find some way of making *our* advantage an over-match for *his;* and that this can only be done by menacing him with superior forces at *different* points, at the *same* time; so that we can safely attack, one, or both, if he makes no change; and if he *weakens* one to *strengthen* the other, forbear to attack the strengthened one, but seize, and hold the weakened one, gaining so much. To illustrate, suppose last summer, when Winchester ran away to re-inforce Mannassas, we had forborne to attack Mannassas, but had seized and held Winchester. I mention this to illustrate, and not to criticise. I did not lose confidence in McDowell, and I think less harshly of Patterson than some others seem to. In application of the general rule I am suggesting, every particular case will have its modifying circumstances, among which the most constantly present, and most difficult to meet, will be the want of perfect knowledge of the enemies' movements. This had it's part in the Bull-Run case; but worse, in that case, was the expiration of the terms of the three months men. Applying the principle to your case, my idea is that Halleck shall menace Columbus, and "down river" generally; while you menace Bowling-Green, and East Tennessee. If the enemy shall concentrate at Bowling-Green, do not retire from his front; yet do not fight him there, either, but seize Columbus and East Tennessee, one or both, left exposed by the concentration at Bowling Green. It is matter of no small anxiety to me and one which I am sure you will not over-look, that the East Tennessee line, is so long, and over so bad a road. Yours very truly

A. LINCOLN.

[1] ALS copy, DLC-Stanton Papers. The original copy sent to Halleck has not been located, but see Lincoln's endorsement *infra*.

To Henry W. Halleck[1]

Having to-day written Gen. Buell a letter, it occurs to me to send Gen. Halleck a copy of it.   A. LINCOLN
Jan 13, 1862.

[1] Copy, DLC-RTL. The copy of this endorsement is on a copy of Lincoln's letter to Buell, *supra*, endorsed. "(Official Copy) H.Q.A. May 4, 64 D.C. WAGER A.A.G." Why Lincoln requested a copy in 1864 is not clear. The official copy is in an envelope addressed "To the President" from "H. W. Halleck" and endorsed by Lincoln "Copy of letter to Buell & Halleck, Jan. 13. 1862."

To Thomas A. Scott[1]

Col Thomas A. Scott.   Executive Mansion,
Assistant Secretary of War: Washington, January 14, 1862
My dear Sir, Understanding that it is the wish of several military gentlemen to witness a formal test of Mr. Knorr's[?] invention, and further understanding that it will not incur either expense or inconvenience to the War Department, I would recommend that such a test be made.   A. LINCOLN

[1] LS, ORB. Written by John Hay and signed by Lincoln, the penmanship of this letter is not clear as to the name of the inventor. The reading "Knorr's" is the editors' effort to decipher the name, but no reference to such a man has been found. It seems possible that the name may have been intended as "Ferriss," with reference to a cannon of wrought iron known as the "Ferriss Gun," upon which O. O. Macomber reported to Lincoln on January 28, 1862 (DLC-RTL). No reply from Scott has been found.

To Henry W. Halleck[1]

      Washington, D.C.,
Major-General Halleck: January 15, 1862.
My dear Sir: This will introduce Gov. G. Koerner, of Illinois, who is my personal friend, and who calls on you at my particular

request. Please open the sealed letter he will hand you before he leaves you and confer with him as to its contents. Yours, very truly, A. LINCOLN.

[Inclosure.]

Executive Mansion,
Major-General Halleck: Washington, January 15, 1862.

My dear Sir: The Germans are true and patriotic, and so far as they have got cross in Missouri it is upon mistake and misunderstanding. Without a knowledge of its contents Governor Koerner, of Illinois, will hand you this letter. He is an educated and talented German gentleman, as true a man as lives. With his assistance you can set everything right with the Germans. I write this without his knowledge, asking him at the same time, by letter, to deliver it. My clear judgment is that, with reference to the German element in your command, you should have Governor Koerner with you; and if agreeable to you and him, I will make him a brigadier-general, so that he can afford to so give his time. He does not wish to command in the field, though he has more military knowledge than many who do. If he goes into the place he will simply be an efficient, zealous, and unselfish assistant to you. I say all this upon intimate personal acquaintance with Governor Koerner. Yours, very truly, A. LINCOLN.

[1] OR, I, VIII, 826. On January 21, Halleck replied to this and the enclosed letter that he had "nominated Gov. K. some time ago . . . as aide de camp with the rank of Col. the highest authorized . . . as a staff officer. Should your Excellency see fit to make him a Brig. Gen., I will use my best endeavors to give him such employment as may best suit him.

"The difficulty with the Germans results from . . . 1st the want of pay, the Pay Dept. here being out of funds . . . 2d They are continually tampered with by designing politicians. . . . A part of the scheme is the story about the ill-treatment of Genl Sigel. . . .

"All these difficulties are being satisfactorily arranged. A firm and decided course will end them forever . . . . if the Govt does not interfere, I can reduce these disaffected elements to order & discipline." (DLC-RTL). Instead of appointing Koerner a brigadier, Lincoln nominated him minister to Spain, June 6, 1862.

To Gustave P. Koerner[1]

Washington, D.C.
My dear Gov. Koerner Jan. 15, 1862

Herewith is an open letter of introduction of yourself to Gen. Halleck, and also, a sealed one. Please deliver them both to him, in person, as soon as you conveniently can. The sealed letter contains matter I wish him to confer with you about, relative to the germans in his command. Yours as ever A. LINCOLN

1 ALS, MoSHi. Koerner replied on January 26 with an account of his conference with Halleck, and expressed his opinion that if Halleck had had "an extensive knowledge of what . . . happened . . . before he took command . . . if he had known the temper of the Germans just at this time smarting under some real and partly imaginary wrongs . . . if he had known the great admiration in which Sigel is held . . . [he] would never have made the unfortunate move in supplying his place . . . by Gen. Curtis . . . . the appointment of Genl. Sigel as Major General would give general and unbounded satisfaction, even if he should be appointed on the Potomac. . . ." (DLC-RTL). Franz Sigel was nominated major general March 3, and confirmed by the Senate, March 21, 1862.

To Gideon Welles[1]

Executive Mansion,
My Dear Sir   Washington, January 15, 1862.
Please inform me, if in your opinion, a delay of action in the case of B. F. Gallagher,[2] Paymaster, for one month, will endanger the ultimate collection of the government funds for which he is accountable. If not I would like to grant such delay. Yours truly

The Secretary of the Navy   A. LINCOLN

1 LS, owned by W. Easton Louttit, Jr., Providence, Rhode Island. Welles' letter of January 9, 1862, submitted the case of Paymaster Benjamin F. Gallaher, who had failed to render his accounts within the time prescribed by law and therefore was subject to dismissal. No reply from Welles to Lincoln's question has been found, but Gallaher was not dismissed until August 22, 1862.

2 Secretary John Hay misspelled Gallaher's name.

To Edwin M. Stanton[1]

If a clerkship can be given Mr Goodwin I shall be very glad   I am very earnest about this.   A. LINCOLN
Jany. 16th 1862

1 Copy, DNA WR RG 107, Secretary of War, Personnel Appointments, Box 34. Concerning Richard D. Goodwin's earlier efforts to get a commission, see Lincoln to Cameron, June 25, and to Goodwin, July 8, 1861, supra. There is no record of Goodwin's appointment to a clerkship.

To the Senate[1]

To the Senate   Washington, D.C.
of the United States.   January 17 1862
I transmit herewith, for the consideration of the Senate, a petition of certain members of the Pottowatomie tribe of Indians, complaining of the treaty made by W. W. Ross,[2] on the 15th November last, with that tribe; which treaty was laid before the Senate for

its constitutional action, in my communication to that body dated the 6th instant.

A letter of the 16th instant from the Secretary of the Interior, enclosing a report of the Commissioner of Indian Affairs dated the 15th. inst. in relation to the subject, is also, herewith, transmitted.

ABRAHAM LINCOLN

1 DS, DNA RG 46, Senate 37B C3. The treaty with the Pottawatomie Indians was considerably amended and ratified by the Senate on April 15, 1862.
2 William W. Ross, agent for the Pottawatomies.

To the Senate and House of Representatives[1]

January 17, 1862

To the Senate and House of Representatives:

I transmit to Congress a translation of an instruction to the minister of his Majesty the King of Prussia accredited to this government, and a copy of a note to that minister from the Secretary of State, relating to the capture and detention of certain citizens of the United States, passengers on board the British steamer Trent, by order of Captain Wilkes, of the United States navy.

Washington, January 17, 1862.   ABRAHAM LINCOLN.

1 Thirty-seventh Congress, Second Session, *Senate Executive Document No. 18.* The Prussian message of December 25, 1861, expressed Prussia's support of Great Britain, and Seward's reply, enclosing copies of the correspondence between Great Britain and the United States, was much the same as that sent to Austria. See Lincoln to the Senate and House of Representatives, January 10, *supra.*

To William H. Seward[1]

Deal with a man in Illinois, as you would if he were in any other state.   A.L.

Jan. 17. 1862

1 AES, NBLiHi. Lincoln's endorsement is written below the following undated note from Seward: "Will Mr. Mastern[?] please consult with the President on the within subject. W.H.S." The papers referred to have not been located, and the name "Mastern" is the editors' effort to decipher Seward's scrawl.

To Edwin M. Stanton[1]

Hon. Sec. of War   Executive Mansion
My dear Sir   Jan. 17. 1862.

    If you can do anything for Col. Wampole, I shall be glad. Yours truly   A. LINCOLN

¹ ALS, DNA FS RG 59, Appointments, Box 398. Concerning Elias Wampole's appointment, see Lincoln to Cameron, October 28, 1861, *supra*, and to Seward, January 30, 1862, *infra*.

To John F. Lee¹

Will the Judge Advocate please tell me whether anything, & what I ought to do in this case.   A. LINCOLN

Jan. 18. 1862.

¹ AES, DNA WR RG 153, Judge Advocate General, Letters Received, No. 112. Lincoln's endorsement is written on a copy of a letter from Captain Morgan H. Chrysler of the Thirtieth New York Volunteers to John H. Corey, January 6, 1862, setting forth the extenuating circumstances in the arrest of Captain Miles T. Bliven, who had left his post upon hearing of the illness and death of his child but had believed that a furlough was to be granted. Judge Advocate Lee replied to Lincoln's request on January 22, that in addition to having absented himself without leave Bliven had proved "not a good officer." (DLC-RTL). Bliven was not reinstated, but was later appointed first lieutenant and adjutant of the Thirtieth New York, September 26, 1862, from which post he resigned January 17, 1863. He enrolled as a private in the Second New York Veteran Cavalry, August 8, 1863, and was commissioned first Lieutenant October 24, 1863.

To Edwin M. Stanton¹

Executive Mansion   Jan. 18. 1862

To-day Gov. Crittenden, Senators Hale, Lane of Ia, and Nesmith,² call and beg that Major Wallen may not be sent to New-Mexico for duty, but that he may be retained in service on this side.

I sincerely desire this to be done, if it can be without too much derangement of the public service. Yours truly   A. LINCOLN

¹ ALS, IHi. See also Lincoln's memorandum December 4, 1861, *supra*. On February 3, Adjutant General Lorenzo Thomas endorsed Lincoln's letter with a full report on why Major Henry D. Wallen should report for duty with his troops in New Mexico.

² Senators Henry S. Lane of Indiana and James W. Nesmith of Oregon.

To Joseph G. Totten¹

January 18, 1862

I wish it to [be] definitely settled, that the appointment within requested is to be made, as one of the ten at large for this year; and I will thank Gen. Totten to remind me of it at the proper time.

Jan. 18. 1862.   A. LINCOLN

1 AES, DNA WR RG 94, U.S. Military Academy, Box 80, No. 908. Lincoln's endorsement is written on a note signed by John P. Hale, Henry Wilson, and Lot M. Morrill, January 16, 1862, requesting appointment of Henry D. Wallen, Jr., to West Point. Wallen entered West Point July 1, 1862.

Appointment of Charles E. Mix[1]

Executive Mansion
Washington January 20/1862

I hereby appoint Charles E. Mix, Chief Clerk of the Office of Indian Affairs, to be acting Commissioner of Indian Affairs, during the absence of Commissioner Dole from the Seat of Government. ABRAHAM LINCOLN.

1 DS, CSmH.

To Montgomery C. Meigs[1]

Respectfully submitted to Q. M. General.   A. LINCOLN
Jan. 21. 1862.

P.S. I feel some more than ordinary interest in this case.
Jan. 21. 1862.   A. L.

1 AES, IHi. Lincoln's endorsements are written on a letter from George Robertson, January 7, 1862, recommending John L. Elbert of Lexington, Kentucky, for some appointment. The letter bears concurring endorsements by John J. Crittenden, Leslie Cowles, and Garrett Davis. Elbert wrote on February 27 that he had failed to see Meigs but had seen Secretary Stanton, who "said he would let me hear from him." (DLC-RTL). There is no record of Elbert's appointment.

To Luiz I[1]

January 22, 1862

Abraham Lincoln,
President of the United States of America.

To His Majesty Dom Luiz I,
King of Portugal,
&c., &c., &c.

Great and Good Friend: I have received the letter which Your Majesty was pleased to address to me on the 22nd. of November, last, communicating intelligence of the demise of Your Majesty's honored brothers, His late Majesty Dom Pedro V and His Highness the Most Serene Infante Dom Fernando, and of your accession to the throne of Portugal. Assuring you of my deep sympathy at the death of your august brother, who was the constant friend

of the United States and also at the melancholy loss of your beloved brother, His Highness Dom Fernando, I beg leave to offer
to Your Majesty my sincere and hearty congratulations upon your
accession to the throne of your ancestors, with my best wishes that
your reign may be happy and glorious to yourself and prosperous
to your realm. Permit me also to assure Your Majesty of my constant and earnest desire to maintain the amity and good correspondence which have always subsisted and still prevail between
the two nations, and that nothing shall be omitted on my part to
cultivate and promote the friendly sentiments always entertained
and cherished by this Government in its relations with His late
Majesty. And so I recommend Your Majesty to the protection of
the Almighty. Your Good Friend, ABRAHAM LINCOLN.
Washington, January 22, 1862.
By the President:
WILLIAM H. SEWARD, Secretary of State.

[1] Copy, DNA FS RG 59, Communications to Foreign Sovereigns and States,
III, 183.

To Luiz I[1]

January 22, 1862

Abraham Lincoln,
President of the United States of America.

To His Majesty Dom Luiz I,
King of Portugal,
&c., &c., &c.

Great and Good Friend: I have received the letter which Your
Majesty was pleased to address to me on the 22nd. of November,
last, announcing the marriage of Her Highness the Most Serene
Princess Doña Antonia, Your Majesty's beloved sister, with His
Highness the Prince Leopold, son of His Royal Highness the
Prince of Hohenzollern Sigmaringen.

I participate in the satisfaction afforded by this happy event
and pray Your Majesty to accept my sincere congratulations upon
the occasion,

May God have Your Majesty always in His safe and holy keep-
ing! Your Good Friend, ABRAHAM LINCOLN.
Washington, January 22, 1862.
By the President.
WILLIAM H. SEWARD, Secretary of State.

[1] Copy, DNA FS RG 59, Communications to Foreign Sovereigns and States,
III, 184.

To George B. McClellan[1]

Majr. Genl. McClellan   Executive Mansion
My dear Sir   Jan. 22. 1862

Gen. Benham appeals to me to be either assigned, to duty, or given an immediate hearing upon the charges against him. I think this is but reasonable. What say you? Yours truly

A. Lincoln

[1] ALS, DLC-RTL. McClellan replied on the bottom of Lincoln's letter, "Genl Benham is well aware that his case is under consideration by the Secty of War & myself . . . I would suggest that Genl B be advised to exercise patience." On February 11 Benham wrote Lincoln, "The 'patience' that Gen. McClellan wrote you I 'must have' I have had, not only for these three weeks, but for the *nearly three months*, that this persecution has existed. . . ." (*Ibid.*) See also Lincoln to John F. Lee, December 14, 1861, *supra.*

Memorandum[1]

I wish to remember this young man for 1863, & to appoint him, unless there shall be over-bearing reasons to the contrary

Jan. 22, 1862.   A. Lincoln

[1] AES, DLC-RTL. Lincoln's endorsement is written on the envelope of a letter from Secretary Seward, January 21, 1862, introducing "Mrs Schermerhorn and her son whom she wishes to put into the Academy at West Point." Mrs. Schermerhorn's son, F. Augustus Schermerhorn, was not appointed to West Point. See Lincoln's memorandum of April 1, 1864, *infra.*

Note to Admit German Committee[1]

Let the German committee from N.Y send in this card
Jan. 22. 1862.   A. Lincoln

[1] ADS, DLC-Nicolay Papers. Friedrich Kapp, Weil Von Gernsbach, and Andreas Willmann were named as a committee to call on Lincoln in protest against the supposed bad treatment of General Franz Sigel (New York *Times*, January 17, 1862). Lincoln was reported to have told the committee that Sigel would be made "a General of Division. Also that Col. Koerner of Iowa [*sic*] will be made a Brigadier General." (New York *Tribune*, January 23, 1862).

To the Senate[1]

To the Senate   Washington, D.C.
of the United States.   January [22], 1862.

I transmit, herewith, for the constitutional action of the Senate, articles of agreement and convention concluded at Niobrarah,

Nebraska territory, on the 14th day of November 1860, between J. Shaw Gregory, Agent on the part of the United States, and the Chiefs, and head men, of the Poncas tribe of Indians, being supplementary to the treaty with said tribe, made on the 12th day of March 1858.

I also transmit a letter dated the 4th instant, from the Secretary of the Interior enclosing a copy of a report of the commissioner of Indian Affairs, of the 20th September 1861, in relation to the subject.   ABRAHAM LINCOLN

[1] DS, DNA RG 46, Senate 37B C4. The supplementary agreement and convention to the treaty with the Poncas was referred to the committee on Indian Affairs and ordered to be printed on January 22, but was not ratified until March 2, 1867.

To William H. Seward[1]

I wish first to see Senators Pomeroy & Sumner, who recommended Holmes. If they do not object we will appoint Arney at once.

Jan. 22. 1862.   A. LINCOLN

[1] AES, NAuE. Lincoln's endorsement appears on a letter from Seward, January 22, 1862:
"The Secretary of New Mexico ought to be removed.
"You have thought of Judge Arny for the place. Shall I nominate him at once?"
William F. M. Arny of Kansas, formerly of Illinois, had been confirmed by the Senate on July 16, 1861, as agent for the Indians in the Territory of New Mexico. Not until January 7, 1863, was Arny nominated to replace James H. Holmes as secretary. His appointment was confirmed on February 18, 1863.

To Edwin M. Stanton[1]

Executive Mansion,
Secretary of War.   Washington, Jan. 22, 1862.
My dear Sir: Richard M. Corwine was appointed Judge Advocate by Gen. Frémont on the 20th of July last, and served as such till the 18th of November last. He never had a Commission, but his services were as valuable, and his conduct as meritorious, as if his appointment had been entirely regular. His is but one of a class of cases, which class has been under consideration at the War Department, but what has been done with it I do not know. The meritorious ones ought to have Commissions, *nunc pro tunc*, as an honorable recognition of them, and should also be paid.

I hope this may be done, including Major Corwine in the arrangement. Yours truly,   A. LINCOLN.

¹ Tracy, p. 200. Richard M. Corwine was appointed major and additional aide-de-camp March 31, 1862.

To Edwin M. Stanton[1]

(COPY).

Hon Sec of War   Executive Mansion
My Dear Sir   January 22. 1862
On reflection I think it will not do as a rule for the Adjutant General to attend me wherever I go; not that I have any objection to his presence, but that it would be an uncompensating incumbrance both to him and me. When it shall occur to me to go anywhere, I wish to be free to go at once, and not to have to notify the Adjutant General, and wait till he can get ready. It is better too, for the public service, that he shall give his time to the business of his office, and not to personal attendance on me. While I thank you for the kindness of the suggestion, my view of the matter is as I have stated. Yours truly   A. LINCOLN

¹ Copy, DLC-RTL. The copy is in John Hay's handwriting, but is marked "Copy" by Lincoln. There is no communication from Stanton in regard to this letter in the Lincoln Papers.

To Andrew H. Foote[1]

[January 23, 1862]
The President wishes the rafts with their 13 inch mortars and all appointments to be ready for use at the earliest possible moment. What can we do here to advance this? What is lacking? What is being done, so far as you know? Telegraph us every day, showing the progress, or lack of progress in this matter.

¹ AD-P, ISLA. The following endorsement was written by Henry A. Wise of the Navy Bureau of Ordnance on the bottom of Lincoln's message: "Telegraphic dispatch written by President Lincoln for Flag Officer Foote and sent by H. A. Wise U.S.N. 23 Jan 1862 3.15 P.M." Wise enclosed the autograph message with a letter of the same date as follows: "My dear Foote, I am just from the President, who is stirring up the army ordnance with a sharp stick about mortars. He said to me, 'Now I am going to devote a part of every day to these mortars and I wont leave off until it fairly rains Bombs.' I send you his autograph which may interest you." (ALS-P, *ibid.*). Foote replied by telegraph on January 24, "Telegraph of 23d. received last evening. I have sent an officer to Pittsburgh, to ascertain the condition of the mortars and mortar beds, and to hurry their completion. My last dispatch, from Pittsburgh, states that but one is ready. . . ." (DLC-RTL). Foote was preparing the iron-plated gunboats built by James B. Eads for support of Brigadier General Ulysses S. Grant's movement up the Tennessee River. The movement began on February 6. See Lincoln to Stanton, January 24, *infra*, for further developments.

To Heads of Departments and Bureaus[1]

January 23, 1862

This man wants to *work*—so uncommon a want that I think it ought to be gratified. I shall be obliged by any Head of of [*sic*] a Bureau, or Department who can and will find work for him.

Jan. 23. 1862.   A. LINCOLN

[1] ALS, CSmH. The bearer has not been identified.

To the Senate[1]

To the Senate: January 24, 1862

I lay before the Senate a despatch which has just been received from Mr. Corwin, our Minister in Mexico.

It communicates important information concerning the war which is waged against Mexico by the combined powers of Spain, France, and Great Britain.

Mr. Corwin asks instructions by which to regulate his proceedings so as to save our national interests in the case of an adjustment of the difficulties between the belligerents.

I have heretofore submitted[2] to the Senate a request for its advice upon the question pending by treaty for making a loan to Mexico, which Mr. Corwin thinks will, in any case be expedient. It seems to me to be my duty now to solicit an early action of the Senate upon the subject, to the end that I may cause such instructions to be given to Mr. Corwin as will enable him to act in the manner which, while it will most carefully guard the interests of our country, will at the same time be most beneficial to Mexico.

Washington, 24 January 1862.   ABRAHAM LINCOLN

[1] DNA RG 46, Senate 37B B12. Lincoln's message was referred to the Committee on Foreign Relations, whence Senator Sumner reported at length on February 19. On February 25 the Senate adopted a resolution "That in reply to the two several messages of the President with regard to a treaty with Mexico, the Senate express the opinion that it is not advisable to negotiate a treaty that will require the United States to assume any portion of the principal or interest of the debt of Mexico, or that will require the concurrence of European powers." (*Executive Journal*, p. 134. For Sumner's report see pp. 121-26).

[2] *Vide supra*, December 17, 1861.

To the Senate and House of Representatives[1]

January 24, 1862

To the Senate and House of Representatives.

I submit to Congress the accompanying copy of a correspondence between the Secretary of State, the Spanish Minister and the Secretary of the Navy, concerning the case of the barque "Providencia," —a Spanish vessel seized, on her voyage from Havana to New York, by a Steamer of the United States' blockading squadron, & subsequently released. I recommend the appropriation of the amount of the award of the referee.   ABRAHAM LINCOLN

Washington, January 24th, 1862.

1 DS, DNA RG 233, Thirty-seventh Congress, Second Session, Original Executive Document No. 38. The correspondence submitted is printed in *House of Representatives Executive Document No. 38*. Moses Taylor, referee, awarded damages of $2,501.91 plus $290 to master and crew as an act of courtesy. The total amount was appropriated by an act approved May 12, 1862.

To Edwin M. Stanton[1]

[January 24, 1862]

The Secretary of War has my authority to exercise his discretion in the matter within mentioned.   A. LINCOLN.

1 NH, VII, 88-89. Lincoln's endorsement is on a letter from Stanton, January 24, 1862, reading as follows: "In my opinion the success of military operations and the safety of the country require some changes to be made in the Bureau of Ordnance, and perhaps some others, in order to secure more vigor and activity; and I desire to have your sanction for making them."

To Edwin M. Stanton[1]

Executive Mansion, January 24, 1862.

My dear Sir: On reflection, I think you better make a peremptory order on the ordnance officer at Pittsburg to ship the ten mortars and two beds to Cairo instantly, and all others as fast as finished, till ordered to stop, reporting each shipment to the department here. Yours truly,   A. LINCOLN.

1 NH, VII, 89. See Lincoln to Foote, January 23, *supra*. Colonel John Symington, Allegheny Arsenal, telegraphed Lincoln on January 24: "There is some misapprehension or misrepresentation with regard to the thirteen inch mortar beds . . . . twelve beds have been made & forwarded to Hilton Head S.C. under hurried orders from the War Dept two more are now finished & two others will be completed tomorrow in all sixteen. The next order for beds was a telegram from the War Dept dated the 22nd inst directing thirty eight beds to be sent to Cairo Ill. This order is being pushed forward with all the force that can be applied." (DLC-RTL).

Memorandum:
Appointment of Harvey C. Johns[1]

January 25, 1862

I personally know Dr. Johns, to be a most worthy gentleman; and far more than an ordinarily capable and energetic business man. I shall be very glad to appoint him as soon as it can consistently be done.   A. LINCOLN

Jan. 25. 1862.

1 ADS, IHi. Lincoln's memorandum, perhaps an endorsement, has been clipped from an attendant document. Dr. Harvey C. Johns of Decatur, Illinois, was probably the person concerned.

To Edwin M. Stanton[1]

As Gov. Curtin is so anxious to have Col. D. B. Birney appointed a Brigadier General of Volunteers, let it be done.

Jan. 25, 1862.   A. LINCOLN

1 AES, owned by Emanuel A. Gardiner, New York City. Lincoln's endorsement is written on the back of a letter from Governor Andrew G. Curtin to Simon Cameron, January 16, 1862, recommending Colonel David B. Birney of the Twenty-seventh Pennsylvania Volunteers for appointment as brigadier general. Cameron endorsed his concurrence on January 20. Birney was nominated by Stanton January 29 and confirmed by the Senate February 3, 1862.

To Edwin M. Stanton[1]

Executive Mansion

Hon. Sec. of War: Jan. 25. 1862.

Let Henry M. Judah of the Regular Army, be appointed a Brigadier General of Volunteers. Yours truly   A. LINCOLN

1 ALS, NHi. Colonel Henry M. Judah was appointed brigadier general of Volunteers March 21, 1862.

President's General War Order No. 1[1]

Executive Mansion,

President's general }   Washington, January 27, 1862.
War Order No. 1 }

Ordered that the 22nd. day of February 1862, be the day for a general movement of the Land and Naval forces of the United States against the insurgent forces.

That especially—

The Army at & about, Fortress Monroe.

The Army of the Potomac.

The Army of Western Virginia

The Army near Munfordsville [sic], Ky.

The Army and Flotilla at Cairo.

And a Naval force in the Gulf of Mexico, be ready for a movement on that day.

That all other forces, both Land and Naval, with their respective

commanders, obey existing orders, for the time, and be ready to
obey additional orders when duly given.

That the Heads of Departments, and especially the Secretaries
of War and of the Navy, with all their subordinates; and the General-in-Chief, with all other commanders and subordinates, of
Land and Naval forces, will severally be held to their strict and
full responsibilities, for the prompt execution of this order.

ABRAHAM LINCOLN

Draft[2] of Order sent to Army & Navy Departments respectively
this day.   A. LINCOLN
Jan. 27. 1862.

The[3] Secretary of War will enter this Order in his Department,
and execute it to the best of his ability.   A. LINCOLN
Jan. 27, 1862.

[1] ADfS, DLC-RTL; DS, DLC-Stanton Papers.
[2] This endorsement appears on the back of the second page of the draft in the
Lincoln Papers.
[3] This endorsement appears on the manuscript in the Stanton Papers.

To Henry A. Wise[1]

If Flag-officer Foote, can find a suitable Boat which he can purchase
at a fair price, let him purchase it at once.   A. LINCOLN
Jan. 27. 1862.

[1] AES, IHi. Lincoln's endorsement appears on a letter from Lieutenant Henry
A. Wise, Navy Department, January 27, 1862: "You directed me last evening,
to call your attention today, to the requisition of Flag Officer [Andrew H.]
Foote for the purchase or charter of a Steamer for the Mortar Flotilla, as referred to in his telegram of yesterday. . . ." An endorsement following Lincoln's reads: "In accordance with above Telegraphed Com Foote Jany 27th/62."

To John P. Hale[1]

January 28, 1862

Capt. Dahlgren gave his views in this letter, at my request. I have
so much confidence in him in Naval matters that I inclose it to you
as Chairman of the Naval Committee.   A. LINCOLN
Jan. 28. 1862.

[1] AES-P, ISLA. Lincoln's endorsement is written on an undated memorandum
from Captain John A. Dahlgren reading as follows:
"The present organisation of the Navy Bureau of Ordnance is not suited to
present necessities.
"The practice & custom of the office make it purely administrative, whereas
the Head of this Department should himself participate in the various operations
and be present personally as far as circumstances permit.

"He should have a proper Assistant to take charge of the office affairs and sustain the communication with the Navy Department

"There should also be a corps of Inspectors to supervise the practical details at the Foundries and Navy Yards.

"The Secretary of the Navy in his Report upon the Meeting of Congress on the 4 July last struck out the general features of the new arrangement & recommended it to you

"The Chairman of Naval Affairs in the Senate embodied the same in a Bill which he presented to the Senate during this session—it was referred to the Naval Committee, and there remains, and may be forgotten until some exigency again brings it under consideration.

"I would urge its immediate adoption. . . ."

The bill introduced on January 24 to reorganize the Navy Department and create the Bureau of Ordnance was approved on July 5, 1862.

To the Senate[1]

To the Senate of the United States: January 28, 1862

I submit to the Senate for it's consideration, with a view to ratification, a Treaty of Extradition concluded by Mr. Corwin with the Mexican Government on the 11th. December, last.

I also submit a Postal Convention concluded by that gentleman, at the same time, and a copy of his despatch of the 24th. of the same month, explanatory of the provisions of both these instruments, and the reasons for the non-ratification by Mexico of the Postal Convention concluded in this city on the 31st. July last, and approved by the Senate on the 6th. August.

A copy of a letter from the Postmaster General to the Secretary of State in relation to Mr. Corwin's Postal Convention, is, also, herewith communicated. The advice of the Senate as to the expediency of accepting that Convention as a substitute for the one of the 31st. July, last, is requested.   ABRAHAM LINCOLN

Washington 28 January 1862.

1 DS, DNA RG 46, Senate 37B B13. The convention was ratified without amendment on February 10; the treaty was reported with amendments on February 19 and after further amendment on April 8 was ratified on April 9, 1862. The delay in ratification of the treaty made necessary an extension of the time limit for exchange of ratifications. See Lincoln to the Senate, April 15, *infra*.

Endorsement: Letter of James Speed[1]

The letter I mentioned to you some time ago. Please read & return to me.   A. LINCOLN

Jan. 29, 1862.

1 AES, DLC-RTL. Lincoln's endorsement is written on the back of a lengthy letter from James Speed, December 22, 1861, reporting on affairs in Kentucky, with particular reference to the obstructionist activities of Governor Beriah Magoffin and the general loyalty of the legislature and citizens of the state. There is no hint as to whom Lincoln forwarded the letter.

To Edwin M. Stanton[1]

Hon. Sec. of War   Executive Mansion
My dear Sir   Jan. 29. 1862
    Let Samuel D. Sturgis, of the Regular Army, be appointed a
Brigadier General of Volunteers; and, if possible let the appointment take date of August 10th. 1861, corresponding with the
battle of Springfield, or Wilson's creek, in which he done a con-
spicuous & honorable part. Yours truly   A. LINCOLN

[1] ALS, owned by Harry G. Golden, Richmond, Indiana. Major Samuel D.
Sturgis was nominated to the Senate on January 29 and confirmed on March 5,
1862, his rank of brigadier general dating from August 10, 1861.

Endorsement[1]

[c. January 30, 1862]
    Suggestions of members of Cabinet, made on request, upon
proclamation of Jan. 30, 1862.
Cabinet

[1] AE, DLC-RTL. Lincoln's endorsement is written on an envelope from the
Department of State. The contents have not been found. No proclamation of
January 30, 1862, was issued. That the draft of the Proclamation to People of
Maryland (*supra*, January 1) may have been intended for issuance on January
30 seems probable, but the editors have not been able to ascertain why it was
withheld.

To William H. Seward[1]

If the within statement be correct, let Mr. Wampole be Consul at
Amoor [Amur] River.   A. LINCOLN
Jan. 30, 1862.

[1] AES, DNA FS RG 59, Appointments, Box 398. Lincoln's endorsement is
written on a letter from Cameron, January 30, 1862, stating that Seward had
agreed to appoint Elias Wampole consul to "Amoor River, Rus[s]ia . . . . if the
President would indicate the same. . . ." See also Lincoln to Stanton, January
17, *supra*.

To John Z. Goodrich[1]

January 31, 1862
The bearer of this, Mr. Jesse R. Clark, is an old friend of mine, for
some years residing in Illinois, now residing at Lawrence, Mass.
and well spoken, of, as you see, by his neighbors there. If the

Collector at Boston could find some employment for him I should be much obliged   A. LINCOLN

Jan. 31. 1862

¹ AES-P, ISLA. Lincoln's endorsement has been removed from the recommendations of Clark which originally accompanied it. John Z. Goodrich, the collector at Boston, appointed Clark night inspector in the customhouse (*U.S. Official Register*, 1863).

President's Special War Order No. 1 [1]

Executive Mansion

Presidents special ⎰   Washington January 31, 1862
War Order, No. 1. ⎱

Ordered that all the disposable force of the Army of the Potomac, after providing safely for the defense of Washington, be formed into an expedition, for the immediate object of siezing and occupying a point upon the Rail Road South Westward of what is known of Manassas Junction, all details to be in the discretion of the general-in-chief, and the expedition to move before, or on, the 22nd. day of February next.   ABRAHAM LINCOLN

¹ Copy, DNA WR RG 94, Adjutant General, Letters Received, P 1295.

To the Senate and House of Representatives[1]

January 31, 1862

To the Senate and House of Representatives:

As a sequel to the correspondence on the subject, previously communicated, I transmit to Congress extracts from a despatch of the 20th. ultimo, from Mr. Adams, United States Minister at London, to the Secretary of State, and a copy of an instruction from Earl Russell to Lord Lyons, of the 10th. instant, relative to the removal of certain citizens of the United States from the British mail steamer Trent, by order of the Commander of the United States war steamer San Jacinto.   ABRAHAM LINCOLN

Washington, 31st. Jany. 1862.

¹ DS, DNA RG 46, Senate 37A F2. The enclosures are printed in *House of Representatives Executive Document No. 46.*

To Edwin M. Stanton[1]

Executive Mansion,

Hon. Sec. of War   Washington, January 31, 1862.

My dear Sir: It is my wish that the expedition commonly called the "Lane Expedition" shall be as much as has been promised at

the Adjutant General's Office, under the supervision of Gen. Mc-
Clellan, *and not any more.* I have not intended, and do not now
intend that it shall be *a great exhausting affair;* but a snug, sober
column of 10,000 or 15,000. Gen. Lane has been told by me many
times that he is under the command of Gen. Hunter, and assented
to it as often as told. It was the distinct agreement between him
& me when I appointed him, that he was to be under Hunter.
Yours truly   A. LINCOLN

[1] ALS, owned by Richard Helms, Chevy Chase, Maryland. General James H.
Lane's earlier difficulties (see Lincoln to Cameron, December 16, 1861, *supra*)
were rapidly compounding. On January 24, 1862, Lorenzo Thomas wrote General David Hunter that "Brig. Gen. J. H. Lane . . . has urged upon the President and Secretary of War an expedition to be conducted by him from Fort
Leavenworth against the region west of Missouri and Kansas [Arkansas]. The
outlines of his plan were stated by him to be in accordance with your own
views. . . . The General-in-Chief . . . desires it to be understood that a command independent of you is not given to General Lane, but he is to operate . . .
under your supervision and control, and if you deem proper you may yourself
command the expedition. . . ." (OR, I, VIII, 525). On January 27 Hunter
issued *General Orders No. 11,* "In the expedition . . . called in the newspapers
General Lane's expedition, it is the intention of the major-general commanding
the department to command in person. . . ." (*Ibid.,* 529-30). Lane thereupon
wrote Representative John Covode to "See the President, Secretary of War, and
General McClellan, and answer what I shall do. . . ." (*Ibid.*). Hunter telegraphed Lincoln for a copy of Lincoln's communication which Lane claimed to
have left in Washington with his baggage (Hunter to Lincoln, January 27, 1862,
DLC-RTL). For further developments see Lincoln to Hunter and Lane, February 10, *infra.*

To John F. Lee[1]

Would it be proper for me to order a Court Martial, as within requested.   A. LINCOLN
Feb. 1. 1862.

[1] AES, DLC-RTL. Lincoln's endorsement is written on a letter from Jackson
Grimshaw, January 31, 1862, asking the president to order a court of inquiry
into the official conduct of Captain Reuben B. Hatch, quartermaster at Cairo,
Illinois. Lee's reply, written below Lincoln's endorsement, recommended that
Lincoln not interpose, since ". . . Genl. Grant has authority to appoint a court.
He can do so more conveniently than higher authority, because on the spot. . . ."
Lee forwarded to Lincoln a communication from Montgomery C. Meigs, February 3, 1862, which explained that Hatch's trial on a charge of fraud and speculation had been delayed by Grant because "there are other matters alleged which
he [Grant] thinks should be investigated. . . . He thinks . . . great frauds will
be developed . . . I fear that such a court would be long employed and that the
services of the officers upon it could be ill spared. . . ." Hatch was released from
arrest in April, and the War Claim Commission, investigating Hatch's claims in
July, allowed them, "the investigation not having established anything of fraud
or corruption in them." (Washington *Evening Star,* August 6, 1862).

To Edwin M. Stanton[1]

February 1, 1862

I wish an order, such as indicated within, to be made, so that justice, and honorable recognition, be extended to those who served on Gen. Sigel's staff.   A. LINCOLN

Feb. 1. 1862.

[1] AES, IHi. Lincoln's endorsement is written on a letter from Francis P. Blair, Jr., January 29, 1862, reminding Lincoln of his promise to issue an order for the payment of General Franz Sigel's staff. Below Lincoln's endorsement Stanton directed the adjutant general to make the payments.

To Queen Victoria[1]

February 1, 1862

Abraham Lincoln,
President of the United States of America.

To Her Majesty Victoria,
        Queen of the United Kingdom
                of Great Britain and Ireland,
                        &c., &c., &c., Sendeth Greeting!

Great and Good Friend: By a letter from your son, His Royal Highness, the Prince of Wales, which has just been received, I am informed of the overwhelming affliction which has fallen upon Your Majesty, by the untimely death of His Royal Highness the late Prince Consort, Prince Albert, of Saxe Coburg.

The offer of condolence in such cases is a customary ceremony, which has its good uses, though it is conventional, and may sometimes be even insincere. But I would fain have Your Majesty apprehend, on this occasion, that real sympathy can exist, as real truthfulness can be practised, in the intercourse of Nations. The People of the United States are kindred of the People of Great Britain. With all our distinct national interests, objects, and aspirations, we are conscious that our moral strength is largely derived from that relationship, and we think we do not deceive ourselves when we suppose that, by constantly cherishing cordial friendship and sympathy with the other branches of the family to which we belong, we impart to them not less strength than we derive from the same connection. Accidents, however, incidental to all States, and passions, common to all nations, often tend to disturb the harmony so necessary and so proper between the two countries, and to convert them into enemies. It was reserved for Your Majesty in sending your son, the Heir Apparent of the British Throne, on a visit among us, to inaugurate a policy destined

[117]

to counteract these injurious tendencies, as it has been Your Majesty's manifest endeavor, through a reign already of considerable length and of distinguished success, to cultivate the friendship on our part so earnestly desired. It is for this reason that you are honored on this side of the Atlantic as a friend of the American People. The late Prince Consort was with sufficient evidence regarded as your counsellor in the same friendly relation. The American People, therefore, deplore his death and sympathize in Your Majesty's irreparable bereavement with an unaffected sorrow. This condolence may not be altogether ineffectual, since we are sure it emanates from only virtuous motives and natural affection. I do not dwell upon it, however, because I know that the Divine hand that has wounded, is the only one that can heal: And so, commending Your Majesty and the Prince Royal, the Heir Apparent, and all your afflicted family to the tender mercies of God, I remain   Your Good Friend,   ABRAHAM LINCOLN.

Washington, 1st. Feby., 1862.
By the President:
WILLIAM H. SEWARD, Secretary of State.

1 Copy, Public Record Office, London; Copy, DNA FS RG 59, Communications to Foreign Sovereigns and States, III, 137-39. The death of Prince Albert occurred on December 14, 1861.

To William H. Herndon[1]

                                        Executive Mansion,
Dear William: Washington, Feb. 3. 1862.
    Yours of January 30th. is just received. Do just as you say about the money matters. As you well know, I have not time to write a letter of respectable length.
    God bless you, says   Your friend   A. LINCOLN

1 ALS, PHi. Herndon's letter is not in the Lincoln Papers, and no further reference to its contents has been found.

To George B. McClellan[1]

                                        Executive Mansion,
Major General McClellan   Washington, Feb. 3, 1862.
    My dear Sir: You and I have distinct, and different plans for a movement of the Army of the Potomac—yours to be down the Chesapeake, up the Rappahannock to Urbana, and across land to the terminus of the Railroad on the York River—, mine to move directly to a point on the Railroad South West of Manassas.

If you will give me satisfactory answers to the following questions, I shall gladly yield my plan to yours.

1st. Does not your plan involve a greatly larger expenditure of *time*, and *money* than mine?

2nd. Wherein is a victory *more certain* by your plan than mine?

3rd. Wherein is a victory *more valuable* by your plan than mine?

4th. In fact, would it not be *less* valuable, in this, that it would break no great line of the enemie's communications, while mine would?

5th. In case of disaster, would not a safe retreat be more difficult by your plan than by mine? Yours truly   A. LINCOLN

[*Memorandum accompanying Letter of President to General McClellan, dated February 3, 1862*][2]

1. Suppose the enemy should attack us in force *before* we reach the Ocoquan, what? In view of the possibility of this, might it not be safest to have our entire force to move together from above the Ocoquan.

2. Suppose the enemy, in force, shall dispute the crossing of the Ocoquan, what? In view of this, might it not be safest for us to cross the Ocoquan at Colchester rather than at the village of Ocoquan? This would cost the enemy two miles more of travel to meet us, but would, on the contrary, leave us two miles further from our ultimate destination.

3. Suppose we reach Maple valley without an attack, will we not be attacked there, in force, by the enemy marching by the several roads from Manassas? and if so, what?

[1] ALS and AD (enclosure?), DLC-Stanton Papers. The supposition that the memorandum was enclosed with this letter is based upon the fact that the memorandum is so described in the *Official Records*. The undated memorandum is not, however, with the letter in the Stanton Papers, and the particular references in it to crossing the Occoquan suggest that it may have antedated the letter, as a memo of questions which Lincoln intended to put to McClellan verbally during a conference later than the memorandum of c. December 1, 1861 (*supra*), but prior to the issuing of his Special War Order of January 31, 1862 (*supra*). The memorandum may have been jotted down as early as January 13, on which day Lincoln held a council of war with McClellan and several other generals, as well as cabinet members, but could scarcely have been written on February 3, since by that date Lincoln was already aware that McClellan would not favor his plan.

Upon receipt of Lincoln's Special War Order, McClellan wrote Stanton a twenty-two page letter under the same date, January 31. Although there is no mistaking the date as McClellan wrote it on the letter, the containing envelope is endorsed by Lincoln "From Gen. McClellan Jan. 30. 1862." Lincoln's endorsement is certainly dated one day too soon, unless both the Special Order and McClellan's letter were prepared in advance of the dates which they bear. Beyond reasonable doubt, however, the date under which McClellan incorporated his letter in his official "report of the operations of Army of the Potomac while under my charge," is wrong. McClellan's report, dated at New York, August 4, 1863, prints the letter with numerous details at variance with the original letter in the Lincoln Papers, and in dating his letter February 3, instead of January 31, McClellan either deliberately falsified the record in an effort to support his own case or inadvertently committed an error which had the same effect.

McClellan's report (OR, I, V, 41 ff.) stated that, after receiving Lincoln's Special Order, "I asked his excellency whether this order was to be regarded as final, or whether I could be permitted to submit in writing my objections to his plan and my reasons for preferring my own. Permission was accorded, and I therefore prepared the letter to the Secretary of War which is given below [under date of February 3 in McClellan's report, but dated January 31 in the original in the Lincoln Papers].

"Before this had been submitted to the President he addressed me the following note: [Lincoln's letter of February 3, but without the enclosure, is here given by McClellan.]

"These questions were substantially answered by the following letter of the same date to the Secretary of War:"

Immediately following, under date of February 3, is the letter of January 31, altered somewhat in minor details in the early paragraphs and marked by the significant omission of important passages toward the end. The letter is too long for reproduction here in its entirety, but because the original contains important passages not in the *Official Records*, and because of the strange circumstances surrounding the question of date, the heart of McClellan's statement is reproduced below. Portions in italic type are the passages which McClellan omitted in his official report:

"Two bases of operations seem to present themselves for the advance of the Army of the Potomac.—

I. That of Washington—its present position—involving a direct attack upon the enemy's entrenched positions at Centreville, Manassas etc, or else a movement to turn one or both flanks of those positions, or a combination of the two plans.

"The relative force of the two armies will not justify an attack on both flanks.

"An attack on his left flank alone involves a long line of wagon communication & cannot prevent him from collecting for the decisive battle all the detachments now on his extreme right & left.

"Should we attack his right by the line of the Occoquan & a crossing of the Potomac below the Occoquan & near his batteries, we could perhaps prevent the junction of the enemy's extreme right with his centre (we *might* destroy the former), we would remove the obstructions to the navigation of the Potomac, reduce the length of wagon transportation by establishing new depots at the nearest points of the Potomac, & strike more directly his main railway communication.

"The fords of the Occoquan below the mouth of Bull Run are watched by the rebels, batteries are said to be placed on the heights in rear (concealed by the woods), & the arrangement of his troops is such that he can oppose some considerable resistance to a passage of the stream. Information has just been received to the effect that the enemy are entrenching a line of heights extending from the vicinity of Sangster's (Union Mills?) towards Evansport. Early in Jany. Sprigg's ford was occupied by Genl Rhodes with 3600 men & 8 guns; there are strong reasons for believing that Davis' Ford is occupied.

"These circumstances indicate, or prove, that the enemy anticipate the movement in question & are prepared to resist it. Assuming for the present that this operation is determined upon, it may be well to examine briefly its probable progress.

"In the present state of affairs our columns (for the movement of so large a force must be made in several columns, at least 5 or 6) can reach the Accotinck without danger; during the march thence to the Occoquan our right flank becomes exposed to an attack from Fairfax Station, Sangster's & Union Mills;— this danger must be met by occupying in some force either the two first named places, or, better, the point of junction of the roads leading thence to the village of Occoquan—this occupation must be continued so long as we continue to draw supplies by the roads from this city, or until a battle is won.

"The crossing of the Occoquan should be made at all the fords from Wolf's Run to the mouth, the points of crossing not being necessarily confined to the fords themselves. Should the enemy occupy this line in force we must, with what assistance the flotilla can afford, endeavor to force the passage near the mouth, thus forcing the enemy to abandon the whole line or be taken in flank himself.

"Having gained the line of the Occoquan, it would be necessary to throw a column by the shortest route to Dumfries, partly to force the enemy to abandon his batteries on the Potomac, partly to cover our left flank against an attack from the direction of Acquia, & lastly to establish our communication with the river by the best roads, & thus give us new depots.

"The enemy would by this time have occupied the line of the Occoquan above Bulls Run, holding Brentsville in force & perhaps extending his lines somewhat farther to the S.W.

"Our next step would be to prevent the enemy from crossing the Occoquan between Bull Run & Broad Run, to fall upon our right flank while moving on Brentsville; this might be effected by occupying Bacon [?] Church & the cross roads near the mouth of Bull Run, or still more effectually by moving to the fords themselves & preventing him from debouching on our side. These operations would probably be resisted, & would require some time to effect them. As nearly at the same time as possible we should gain the fords necessary to our purposes above Broad Run.

"Having secured our right flank it would become necessary to carry Brentsville at any cost, for we could not leave it between our right flank & main body. The final movement on the Railroad must be determined by circumstances existing at the time.

"This brief sketch brings out in bold relief the great advantage possessed by the enemy in the strong central position he occupies, with roads diverging in every direction, & a strong line of defence enabling him to remain on the defensive with a small force on one flank, while he concentrates everything on the other for a decisive action.

"Should we place a portion of our force in front of Centreville while the rest crosses the Occoquan we commit the error of dividing our Army by a very difficult obstacle & by a distance too great to enable the two portions to support each other, should either be attacked by the masses of the enemy while the other is held in check.

"I should perhaps have dwelled more decidedly on the fact that the force left near Sangster's must be allowed to remain somewhere on that side of the Occoquan, until the decisive battle is over, to cover our retreat in the event of disaster, unless it should be decided to select & entrench a new base somewhere near Dumfries—a proceeding involving much time.

"After the passage of the Occoquan by the main army, this covering force could be drawn in to a more central & less exposed position, say Brimstone Hill or nearer the Occoquan. In this latitude the weather will for a considerable period be very uncertain, & a movement commenced in force on roads in tolerably firm condition will be liable, almost certain, to be much delayed by rains & snow. It will therefore be next to impossible to surprise the enemy, or take him at a disadvantage by rapid manoeuvres;—our slow progress will enable him to divine our purposes & take his measures accordingly. The probability is, from the best information we possess, that he has improved the roads leading to his lines of defense, while we must work as we advance.

"Bearing in mind what has been said, & the present unprecedented, & impassable condition of the roads, it will be evident that no precise period can be fixed upon for the movement on this line, nor can its duration be closely calculated; it seems certain that many weeks *may* elapse before it is possible to commence the march.

"Assuming the success of this operation & the defeat of the enemy as certain, the question at once arises as to the importance of the results gained.

"I think these results would be confined to the possession of the field of battle, the evacuation of the line of the upper Potomac by the enemy, & the moral effect of the victory—important results it is true, but not decisive of the war, nor securing the destruction of the enemy's main army; for he could fall back upon other positions, & fight us again & again, should the condition of his troops permit.

"If he is in no condition to fight us again out of range of the entrenchments at Richmond we would find it a very difficult & tedious matter to follow him up there—for he would destroy the railroad bridges & otherwise impede our progress through a region where the roads are as bad as they well can be; & we would probably find ourselves forced at last to change the entire theatre of war, or to seek a shorter land route to Richmond with a smaller available force & at an expenditure of much more time than were we to adopt the short line at once.

"We would also have forced the enemy to concentrate his forces & perfect his defensive measures at the very points where it is desirable to strike him where least prepared.

"II. The second base of operations available for the Army of the Potomac is that of the lower Chesapeake Bay, which affords the shortest possible land routes to Richmond, & strikes directly at the heart of the enemy's power in the East.

"The roads in that region are passable at all seasons of the year.

"The country now alluded to is much more favorable for offensive operations than that in front of Washington (which is *very* unfavorable)—much more level —more cleared land—the woods less dense—soil more sandy—the spring some two or three weeks earlier.

"A movement in force on that line obliges the enemy to abandon his entrenched position at Manassas, in order to hasten to cover Richmond & Norfolk.

"He *must* do this, for should he permit us to occupy Richmond his destruction can be averted only by entirely defeating us in a battle in which he must be the assailant.

"This movement if successful gives us the capital, the communications, the supplies of the rebels; Norfolk would fall; all the waters of the Chesapeake would be ours; all Virginia would be in our power; & the enemy forced to abandon Tennessee & North Carolina

"The alternatives presented to the enemy would be to beat us in a position selected by ourselves; disperse; or pass beneath the Caudine Forks. [McClellan referred to a well-known episode in military history when the Samnites hemmed in the Romans at the "Caudine Forks" in southern Italy, in 321 B.C.] Should we be beaten in a battle, we have a perfectly secure retreat down the Peninsula upon Fort Monroe, with our flanks perfectly secured by the fleet. During the whole movement our left flank is covered by the water, our right is secure for the reason that the enemy is too distant to reach us in time—he can only oppose us in front; we bring our fleet into full play.

"After a successful battle our position would be—Burnside forming our left, Norfolk held securely, our centre connecting Burnside with Buell, both by Raleigh & Lynchburg, Buell in Eastern Tennessee & Northern Alabama, Halleck at Nashville & Memphis. The next movement would be to connect with Sherman on the left, by reducing Wilmington & Charleston; to advance our centre into South Carolina & Georgia; to push Buell either towards Montgomery, or to unite with the main army in Georgia; to throw Halleck southward to meet the Naval Expedition from New Orleans.

"We should then be in a condition to reduce at our leisure all the southern sea-ports; to occupy all the avenues of communication; to use the great outlet of the Mississip[p]i; to reestablish our Govt & arms in Arkansas, Louisiana & Texas; to force the slaves to labor for our subsistence instead of that of the rebels;—to bid defiance to all foreign interference. Such is the object I have ever had in view: this is the general plan which I have hoped to accomplish. For many long months I have labored to prepare the Army of the Potomac to play its part in the programme; from the day when I was placed in command of all our armies, I have exerted myself to place all the other armies in such a condition that they too could perform their allotted duties. Should it be determined to operate from the lower Chesapeake, the point of landing which promises the most brilliant results is Urbana on the lower Rappahanock. This point is easily reached by vessels of heavy draught, it is neither occupied nor observed by the enemy; it is but one long march from West Point, the Key of that region, & thence but two marches to Richmond.

"A rapid movement from Urbana would probably cut off Magruder in the *Peninsula*, & enable us to occupy Richmond before it could be strongly rein-forced. Should we fail in that we could, with the cooperation of the Navy, cross the James & throw ourselves in rear of Richmond, thus forcing the enemy to come out & attack us—for his position would be untenable, with us on the south-ern bank of the river.

"Should circumstances render it not advisable to land at Urbana we can use Mob Jack Bay,—or—the worst coming to the worst—we can take Fort Monroe as a base, & operate with complete security, altho' with less celerity & brilliancy of results, up the Peninsula. To reach whatever point may be selected as the base, a large amount of cheap water transportation must be collected—consisting mainly of canal boats, barges, wood boats, schooners etc towed by small steamers —all of a very different character from those required for all previous expedi-tions. This can certainly be accomplished within 30 days from the time the order is given.

"I propose, as the best possible plan that can, in my judgment, be adopted, to select Urbana as the landing place of the first detachments. To transport by water four (4) Divisions of Infantry, with their batteries, the Regular Infty, a few wag-ons, one bridge train & a few squadrons of cavalry—making the vicinity of Hooker's position the place of embarkation for as many as possible. To move the Regular Cavalry, & Reserve Artillery, the remaining bridge trains, & wagons to a point somewhere near Cape Lookout, then ferry them over the river by means of North River ferry boats, march them over to the Rappahannock (covering the movement by an Infantry force placed near Heathsville), cross the Rappahan-nock in a similar way. The expense & difficulty of the movement will thus be much diminished (a saving of transportation of about 10,000 horses!), & the result none the less certain.

"The concentration of the cavalry etc in the lower counties of Maryland can be effected without exciting suspicion, & the movement made without delay from that cause. This movement, if adopted, will not at all expose the city of Wash-ington to danger. The total force to be thrown upon the new line would be (ac-cording to circumstances) from 110,000 to 140,000. I hope to use the latter number, by bringing fresh troops into Washington, & still leaving it quite safe.

"I fully realize that, in all projects offered, time is probably the most valuable consideration—it is my decided opinion that in that point of view the 2nd plan should be adopted. It is possible, nay highly probable, that the weather & state of the roads may be such as to delay the direct movement from Washington, with its unsatisfactory results & great risks, far beyond the time required to complete the second plan.

"IN THE FIRST CASE, we can fix no definite time for an advance—the roads have gone from bad to worse—nothing like their present condition has ever been known here before—they are impassable at present, *we are entirely at the mercy of the weather. In the second plan, we can calculate almost to a day, & with but little regard to the season.*

"If at the expense of 30 days delay we can gain a decisive victory which will probably end the war, it is far cheaper than to gain a battle tomorrow that produces no final results, & may require years of warfare & expenditure to follow up.

"Such, I think, is precisely the difference between the two plans discussed in this long letter. A battle gained at Manassas will result merely in the possession of the field of combat—at best we can follow it up but slowly, unless we do what I now propose, viz:—change the line of operations.

"On the Mannassas line the rebels can, if well enough disciplined (& we have every reason to suppose that to be the case) dispute our advance, over bad roads, from position to position.

"When we have gained the battle, if we do gain it, the question will at once arise— 'What are we to do next?'—

"It is by no means certain that we can beat them at Manassas.

"On the other line I regard success as certain by all the chances of war.

"We demoralize the enemy, by forcing him to abandon his prepared position for one which we have chosen, in which all is in our favor, & where success must produce immense results. My judgement as a General is clearly in favor of this project.

"Nothing is CERTAIN in war—but all the chances are in favor of this movement.

"So much am I in favor of the southern line of operations, that I would prefer the move from Fort Monroe as a base, as a certain, tho' less brilliant movement than that from Urbana, to an attack upon Manassas.

"I know that his Excellency the President, you & I all agree in our wishes— & that our desire is to bring this war to as prompt a close as the means in our possession will permit. I believe that the mass of the people have entire confidence in us—I am sure of it—let us then look only to the great result to be accomplished, & disregard everything else.

"In conclusion I would respectfully, but firmly, advise that I may be authorized to undertake at once the movement by Urbana

"I believe that it can be carried into execution so nearly simultaneously with the final advance of Buell & Halleck that the columns will support each other

"I will stake my life, my reputation on the result—more than that, I will stake upon it the success of our cause.

"I hope but little from the attack on Manassas;—my judgment is against it. Foreign complications may entirely change the state of affairs, & render very different plans necessary. In that event I will be ready to submit them." (DLC-RTL).

McClellan's report (*loc. cit.*, p. 45) continued as follows:

"This letter must have produced some effect upon the mind of the President, since the execution of his order was not required, although it was not revoked as formally as it had been issued. . . ."

As a possible solution to the apparent contradictions in dates, it may be concluded that McClellan composed his letter of January 31 following a prior conference with Lincoln at which the two plans were discussed, that Stanton failed to forward McClellan's letter to the president until after Lincoln had written McClellan on February 3, and that McClellan changed the date of his letter from January 31 to February 3 when he drew up his report in 1863, in order to avoid the apparent contradiction in dates. If this conclusion is correct, the error of one day appearing in Lincoln's endorsement on the envelope containing McClellan's letter becomes more understandable, in that Lincoln probably so endorsed it upon receiving it from Stanton sometime after February 3. In this event McClellan never did specifically reply to Lincoln's questions of February 3, but on January 31 had anticipated them in some degree and in part answered them before Lincoln put them in writing. In conclusion it may be noted that the questions posed in Lincoln's undated memorandum, which the *Official Records* describe as an enclosure with Lincoln's letter, are more adequately disposed of by McClellan than are the questions posed by Lincoln in the letter itself. This fact tends to confirm the supposition that the memorandum was written prior to both Lincoln's letter of February 3 and McClellan's letter of January 31.

² The bracketed title is not on the autograph document but is given to the memorandum as printed in the *Official Records* (I, V, 713). It is worth noting also that McClellan's report does not include this memorandum along with the letter of February 3, the two items being related by means of a footnote.

To Charles Rehm¹

Executive Mansion,
My Dear Sir   Washington, February 3, 1862.

It gives me great pleasure to acknowledge the receipt of your favour of the 29th January, accompanying copies of your "National Union March."

Permit me to thank you cordially for the honor done me, and the kind feeling evinced by you.

I am very truly   Your Obt Servt   A. LINCOLN
   Chas Rehm Esq
   Govrs. Id. N.Y.

¹ LS-P, ISLA. Charles Rehm's "National Union March" was published in 1862. His letter of January 29 has not been located.

To the King of Siam¹

February 3, 1862
Abraham Lincoln,
President of the United States of America.

To His Majesty Somdetch Phra Paramendr Maha Mongut,
King of Siam,
&c.,   &c.

Great and Good Friend: I have received Your Majesty's two letters of the date of February 14th., 1861.

I have also received in good condition the royal gifts which accompanied those letters,—namely, a sword of costly materials and exquisite workmanship; a photographic likeness of Your Majesty and of Your Majesty's beloved daughter; and also two elephants' tusks of length and magnitude such as indicate that they could have belonged only to an animal which was a native of Siam.

Your Majesty's letters show an understanding that our laws forbid the President from receiving these rich presents as personal treasures. They are therefore accepted in accordance with Your Majesty's desire as tokens of your good will and friendship for the American People. Congress being now in session at this capital, I have had great pleasure in making known to them this manifestation of Your Majesty's munificence and kind consideration.

Under their directions the gifts will be placed among the archives of the Government, where they will remain perpetually as tokens of mutual esteem and pacific dispositions more honorable to both nations than any trophies of conquest could be.

I appreciate most highly Your Majesty's tender of good offices in forwarding to this Government a stock from which a supply of elephants might be raised on our own soil. This Government would not hesitate to avail itself of so generous an offer if the object were one which could be made practically useful in the present condition of the United States.

Our political jurisdiction, however, does not reach a latitude so low as to favor the multiplication of the elephant, and steam on land, as well as on water, has been our best and most efficient agent of transportation in internal commerce.

I shall have occasion at no distant day to transmit to Your Majesty some token of indication of the high sense which this Government entertains of Your Majesty's friendship.

Meantime, wishing for Your Majesty a long and happy life, and for the generous and emulous People of Siam the highest possible prosperity, I commend both to the blessing of Almighty God. Your Good Friend,   ABRAHAM LINCOLN.

Washington, February 3, 1862.
By the President:
    WILLIAM H. SEWARD, Secretary of State.

[1] Copy, DNA FS RG 59, Communications with Foreign Sovereigns and States, III, 184-86. See Lincoln's message to congress, February 26, *infra*.

To Edwin M. Stanton[1]

Gov. Morton calls to-day, and asks to withdraw his recommendation of Col. Hazzard for a Brigadier General.   AL.
Feb. 3. 1862

[1] ALS, IHi. Colonel George W. Hazzard of the Thirty-seventh Indiana Infantry resigned from the Volunteer Service on March 5, 1862, and returned to the Regular Army in which he held rank as captain. According to an item in the New York *Tribune*, February 19, 1862, his furlough from the Regular Army was terminated at the request of the Indiana delegation in congress because of "great tyranny to his troops." He died August 14, 1862, of wounds received at White Oak Swamp, Virginia, June 30.

To Lazarus W. Powell[1]

Executive Mansion

Hon. L. M. Powell   Feb. 4, 1862

My dear Sir: I herewith return the letters and printed paper submitted by you in behalf of Mr. Samuel B. Churchill. While I would be glad to oblige you, I can not now interfere with the case. Yours truly   A. LINCOLN

[1] ALS, CSmH. Senator Powell of Kentucky wrote on January 29, 1862, requesting the president to "look into" the case of Samuel B. Churchill of St. Louis, arrested October 19, 1861, for aiding and abetting the enemy and "who had been assessed by military authorities at St. Louis, for the purpose of providing certain persons said to have been driven from their homes." (DLC-RTL).

To the Senate[1]

To the Senate of the United States: February 4, 1862

The Third Section of the "Act further to promote the efficiency of the Navy," approved 21 December 1861, provides:

"That the President of the United States, by and with the advice and consent of the Senate, shall have the authority to detail from the retired list of the Navy for the command of Squadrons and single ships such officers as he may believe that the good of the service requires to be thus placed in command; and such officers may, if upon the recommendation of the President of the United States they shall receive a vote of thanks of Congress for their services and gallantry in action against an enemy, be restored to the active list and not otherwise."

In conformity with this law Captain Samuel F. DuPont, of the Navy, was nominated to the Senate for continuance as the Flag Officer in command of the Squadron which recently rendered such important service to the Union in the expedition to the Coast of South Carolina.

Believing that no occasion could arise which would more fully correspond with the intention of the law, or be more pregnant with happy influence as an example, I cordially recommend that Captain Samuel F. DuPont receive a vote of thanks of Congress for his services and gallantry, displayed in the capture of Forts Walker and Beauregard, commanding the entrance of Port Royal Harbor, on the 7 November 1861.   ABRAHAM LINCOLN

Washington City

4 February 1862.

[1] DS, DNA RG 46, Senate 37A F2. On February 7, Senator John P. Hale of the Committee on Naval Affairs introduced a joint resolution tendering thanks

to Captain Samuel F. Du Pont. The resolution passed both houses and was approved by the president on February 22. Du Pont's appointment as flag officer of the North Atlantic Blockading Squadron was approved by the Senate March 6.

Stay of Execution for Nathaniel Gordon[1]

February 4, 1862

Abraham Lincoln,
President of the United States of America,

To all to whom these Presents shall come Greeting:

Whereas, it appears that at a Term of the Circuit Court of the United States of America for the Southern District of New York held in the month of November A.D. 1861, Nathaniel Gordon was indicted and convicted for being engaged in the Slave Trade, and was by the said Court sentenced to be put to death by hanging by the neck, on Friday the 7th. day of February, A.D. 1862;

And whereas, a large number of respectable citizens have earnestly besought me to commute the said sentence of the said Nathaniel Gordon to a term of imprisonment for life, which application I have felt it to be my duty to refuse;

And whereas, it has seemed to me probable that the unsuccessful application made for the commutation of his sentence may have prevented the said Nathaniel Gordon from making the necessary preparation for the awful change which awaits him:

Now, therefore, be it known, that I, Abraham Lincoln, President of the United States of America, have granted and do hereby grant unto him, the said Nathaniel Gordon, a respite of the above recited sentence, until Friday the twenty-first day of February, A.D. 1862, between the hours of twelve o'clock at noon and three o'clock in the afternoon of the said day, when the said sentence shall be executed.

In granting this respite, it becomes my painful duty to admonish the prisoner that, relinquishing all expectation of pardon by Human Authority, he refer himself alone to the mercy of the common God and Father of all men.

In testimony whereof, I have hereunto signed my name and caused the Seal of the United States to be affixed.

Done at the City of Washington, this Fourth day of
[L.S.]   February A.D. 1862, and of the Independence of the
United States the Eighty-sixth.

By the President: ABRAHAM LINCOLN.
WILLIAM H. SEWARD Secretary of State.

[1] DS, ORB. Attorney General Bates replied on February 4, 1862, to a note, presumably not extant, from Lincoln on the same date requesting an opinion as

to whether the executive could lawfully grant to a convict a "respite of his sentence, without relieving him altogether of the death penalty." Bates gave his opinion that "I have no doubt that you can. . . . A reprieve does not annul the sentence. . . . It only prolongs the time." (DLC-RTL). Although many previous seizures of slave ships had been made, Captain Nathaniel Gordon of Maine was the only slave-trader ever convicted and hanged in accordance with federal law. So numerous were the failures of juries to convict, that many believed Gordon entitled to executive clemency as a victim of unprecedented juridical rigor. The language of Lincoln's reprieve leaves no doubt of his concurrence in the justice of the sentence, but indicates his awareness that public sympathy had encouraged Gordon to believe a pardon would be granted.

To Edwin M. Stanton[1]

February 5, 1862

It has been my wish for some time that Dr. E. Boyd Pendleton of Va. be appointed a Surgeon of Volunteers. I still wish it to be done, if it can be done consistently.   A. LINCOLN.

Feb. 5, 1862.

[1] Stan. V. Henkels Catalog 1442, April 10, 1930, No. 82. According to the catalog description Lincoln's endorsement is written on the back of a letter from Surgeon General Clement A. Finley, February 5, recommending Pendleton's appointment. Lincoln had recommended Dr. Pendleton to Secretary Cameron on November 7, 1861 (*supra*), but the appointment was not made until April 4, 1862.

To Gideon Welles[1]

Hon. Sec. of Navy   Executive Mansion,
My dear Sir.   Washington, Feb. 5, 1862.

Hon. Mr. Veree, of Penn. makes such representation, as to the Naval Agent, at Philadelphia, and a sort of *factotum* of his,— one Derringer—as makes me think your Department better look to it. Yours truly   A. LINCOLN

[1] ALS-P, ISLA. There is no reply from Welles in the Lincoln Papers. James S. Chambers was naval agent at Philadelphia, but we have been unable to identify "one Derringer" about whom Representative John P. Verree registered his complaint.

To Edward Bates[1]

Hon. Attorney General   Executive Mansion,
My dear Sir   Washington, Feb. 6, 1862

As you see, Gen. McClellan, approves the finding of the Court-Martial in the case of which the accompanying is a Copy of the Record. Please give me your opinion. Yours truly   A. LINCOLN

[1] ALS, MHi. There is no reply from Bates in the Lincoln Papers, and the case cannot be identified.

To the Senate[1]

To the Senate of the United States: February 7, 1862

In answer to the resolution of the Senate of the 5th instant, requesting a communication of any recent correspondence relating to the presentation of American citizens to the court of France, I transmit a copy of a despatch of the 14th ultimo, from the United States minister at Paris, to the Secretary of State, and of an instruction of Mr. Seward to Mr. Dayton, of the 3d instant.

Washington, February 7, 1862. ABRAHAM LINCOLN.

1 Thirty-seventh Congress, Second Session, *Senate Executive Document No. 19.* William L. Dayton's letter of January 14, 1862, recounted the refusal of the French Court to admit Americans for presentation on the night of the court ball unless "the social quality" of each person was specified. This Dayton refused to do, on the ground that "The French minister at Washington presents . . . to his excellency [the president] any or as many of his countrymen as he may choose . . . without question to their quality, social position, or profession." Seward's reply of February 3 advised Dayton, "Let the Emperor and Empress receive whom they will . . . and let all others, as well as those who are admitted, turn their attention to . . . how they can serve their country abroad; and if they find no better way to do it than by making their attendance in the saloons of the Tuileries, let them return home. . . ." (*Ibid.*).

To George B. McClellan[1]

Major Genl. McClellan Executive Mansion,
My dear Sir— Washington, Feb, 8, 1862

Have you any farther news from the West?

Have you heard from the Canal-boats?

Have you determined, as yet, upon the contemplated movement we last talked of? Yours truly A. LINCOLN

1 ALS, IHi. McClellan replied on the same day "Saturday Evng," "I had a long conversation with Genl Hooker about the roads etc in the region we were speaking of, & would beg until Monday morning to give a final opinion. I have not yet heard from the canal boats above. The experiment of arranging the two will be completed on Monday, when I can make the necessary calculations with exactness. I have nothing new from Halleck or Buell tonight. . . ." (DLC-RTL). Lincoln's plan to use canal boats coupled together to form a bridge across the Potomac at Liverpool Point (near Harpers Ferry) proved impossible when the boats proved to be too wide by some four or six inches to permit their passage through the lift lock (OR, I, V, 49).

To Edwin M. Stanton[1]

Hon. Sec. of War Executive Mansion
My dear Sir Feb. 8, 1862

If there be a vacant majority in the Regular Army, not already promised, nor to which any officer is entitled by regular promo-

[130]

tion, let it be given to Thomas E. Noell, of Missouri, now a Major in the State service. Yours truly   A. LINCOLN

P.S. Or a Captaincy either   A.L.

[1] Copy, ISLA. Thomas E. Noell was nominated captain in the Nineteenth Infantry in a list sent to the Senate under date of February 10, 1862. His appointment was confirmed by the Senate on March 6.

To David Hunter and James H. Lane[1]

Gen. Hunter   Executive Mansion,
Leavenworth, Kansas.   Washington, Feb. 10, 1862.

My wish has been,—and is, to avail the government of the services of both Gen. Hunter and Gen. Lane; &, so far as possible, to personally oblige both. Gen. Hunter is the senior officer, and must command when they serve together; though, in so far as he can, consistently with the public service, and his own honor, oblige Gen. Lane, he will also oblige me. If they can not come to an amicable understanding, Gen. Lane must report to Gen. Hunter for duty, according to the rules, or decline the service.

A. LINCOLN

[1] ALS (copy?), DLC-RTL. Although the autograph letter in the Lincoln Papers is addressed only to Hunter, the *Official Records* (I, VIII, 551) has this letter addressed to both generals. General Hunter wrote Stanton on February 1, 1862, that Lane had not accepted the appointment as brigadier general and that "on his arrival . . . he stated . . . that he was 'my visitor as a Senator of the United States and a member of the Senate Military Committee' . . . . I find myself compelled . . . to request that some definite character shall be given to Senator Lane. . . . I am satisfied that Senator Lane feels aggrieved and disappointed . . . at the position to which his acceptance of his commission would assign him." (DLC-RTL). Hunter also wrote Lincoln on February 4, asking that Lane be "called upon either to accept his position as Brigadier General and report for duty, or have his appointment to that position withdrawn, or be transferred to some other Department. . . ." (*Ibid.*). See also Lincoln to Stanton, January 31, *supra*.

To the Senate and House of Representatives[1]

February 12, 1862

To the Senate and House of Representatives.

I transmit to Congress a copy of a special Treaty between the United States and His Majesty the King of Hanover for the abolition of the Stade Dues, which was signed at Berlin on the 6th of November last. In this Treaty, already approved by the Senate and ratified on the part of the United States, it is stipulated that the sums specified in Articles III and IV to be paid to the Hanoverian Government, shall be paid at Berlin on the day of the exchange of the ratifications. I therefore recommend that seasonable provision be made to enable the Executive to carry this stipulation into effect. ABRAHAM LINCOLN.

Washington, 12th February, 1862.

1 DS, DNA RG 46, Senate 37A F2; DS, DNA RG 233, House Original Executive Document No. 52. An act approved March 13, 1862, appropriated funds to fulfill the treaty, which provided for a lump payment to Hanover in consideration of the abolition of the "Stade dues"—tolls levied on vessels ascending the Elbe and passing the mouth of the Schwinge River.

To George B. McClellan[1]

February 14, 1862

Gen. McClellan, please see the bearer, who, with his Regiment, was forced back from the Burnside Expedition, because of their vessel drawing too much water. They are now at Anapolis, and wish to follow up the Expedition. Can they be provided to do so? Or, what disposition can be made of them? A. LINCOLN

Feb. 14, 1862

1 ALS, CSmH. General Ambrose E. Burnside's expedition to Hatteras Inlet, North Carolina, sailed January 11, 1862. Colonel Lionel J. D'Epineuil's Fifty-third New York Zouaves assigned to the expedition arrived at Fort Monroe aboard the *John Trucks* the day after Burnside sailed, but followed immediately. Upon arriving at Hatteras, the *John Trucks* was found to draw too much water to pass over the bar and was sent back (OR, I, IX, 361-62). D'Epineuil's request could not be fulfilled because the capture of Roanoke Island by Burnside had already been effected February 7-10, and D'Epineuil's regiment was mustered out March 21, 1862, at Washington, D.C.

To Salmon P. Chase[1]

February 15, 1862

I shall be obliged if the Sec. of the Treasury will in his discretion give Mr. Pierce such instructions in regard to Port Royal contrabands as may seem judicious. A. LINCOLN

Feb. 15, 1862

1 Copy, DLC-RTL. The copy is attested by John G. Nicolay. Edward L. Pierce had been appointed by the secretary of the Treasury as "special Government agent, with duties relating both to negroes and cotton" (New York *Tribune*, February 14, 1862).

To Isabel II[1]

February 15, 1862

Abraham Lincoln,
President of the United States of America.

To Her Majesty Doña Isabel II,
   By the Grace of God and the Constitution
   of the Spanish Monarchy, Queen of Spain,
         &c.,   &c.

Great and Good Friend: I have received the letter which Your Majesty was pleased to address to me on the 28th. of October, last, announcing that Her Royal Highness the Infanta Doña Maria Christina, spouse of His Royal Highness the Infante Don Sebastian Gabriel, had on the 20th. of the preceding August safely given birth to a Prince upon whom at the baptismal font had been bestowed the names of Francisco Maria Isabel Gabriel Pedro.

I participate in the satisfaction which this happy event has afforded to Your Majesty's Royal Family, and offer my sincere congratulations upon the occasion.

May God have Your Majesty always in His safe and holy keeping! Your Good Friend,   ABRAHAM LINCOLN.
Washington, February 15, 1862.
By the President:
   WILLIAM H. SEWARD, Secretary of State.

[1] Copy, DNA FS RG 59, Communications to Foreign Sovereigns and States, III, 186-87.

To Isabel II[1]

February 15, 1862

Abraham Lincoln,
President of the United States of America.

To Her Majesty Doña Isabel II,
   By the Grace of God and the Constitution
   of the Spanish Monarchy, Queen of Spain,
         &c.,   &c.

Great and Good Friend: I have received the letter which Your Majesty was pleased to address to me on the 30th. of October, last, conveying the melancholy tidings of the decease of Her Royal Highness the Infanta Doña Maria de la Concepcion Your Majesty's beloved daughter.

[133]

I participate in the grief occasioned by this sad event, and offer to Your Majesty my sincere condolence.

May God have Your Majesty always in His safe and holy keeping! Your Good Friend, ABRAHAM LINCOLN.

Washington, February 15, 1862.

1 Copy, DNA FS RG 59, Communications to Foreign Sovereigns and States, III, 187.

To the Senate and House of Representatives[1]

February 15, 1862

To the Senate and House of Representatives of the United States:—

The Third Section of the "Act further to promote the efficiency of the Navy," approved 21st. December 1861, provides,

"That the President of the United States, by and with the advice and consent of the Senate, shall have the authority to detail from the retired list of the Navy for the command of Squadrons and single ships such officers as he may believe that the good of the service requires to be thus placed in command; and such officers may, if upon the recommendation of the President of the United States, they shall receive a vote of thanks of Congress for their services and gallantry in action against an enemy, be restored to the active list and not otherwise."

In conformity with this law Captain Louis M. Goldsborough, of the Navy, was nominated to the Senate for continuance as the Flag Officer in command of the North Atlantic Blockading Squadron, which recently rendered such important service to the Union in the expedition to the Coast of North Carolina.

Believing that no occasion could arise which would more fully correspond with the intention of the law or be more pregnant with happy influence as an example, I cordially recommend that Captain Louis M. Goldsborough, receive a vote of thanks of Congress for his services and gallantry displayed in the combined attack of the Forces commanded by him and Brigadier General Burnside in the capture of Roanoke Island and the destruction of Rebel Gun Boats, on the 7th., 8th. and 10th. February 1862.

Washington City, ABRAHAM LINCOLN

15 February 1862.

1 DS, DNA RG 233, Original Executive Document No. 66. A joint resolution giving thanks to Louis M. Goldsborough was approved July 11, 1862; his appointment as flag officer was confirmed by the Senate on March 6.

To Henry W. Halleck[1]

Major General Halleck   Executive Mansion,
St. Louis, Mo.   Washington, Feb. 16, 1862

You have Fort Donelson safe, unless Grant shall be overwhelmed from outside, to prevent which latter will, I think, require all the vigilance, energy, and skill of yourself & Buell, acting in full co-operation. Columbus will not get at Grant, but the the [*sic*] force from Bowling-Green will. They hold the Railroad from Bowling-Green to within a few miles of Donelson, with the Bridge at Clarksburg [Clarksville] undisturbed. It is unsafe to rely that they will not dare to expose Nashville to Buell. A small part of their force can retire slowly towards Nashville, breaking up the Railroad as they go, and keep Buell out of that city twenty days. Mean time Nashville will be abundantly defended by forces from all South & perhaps from here at Manassas. Could not a cavalry force from Gen. Thomas on the upper Cumberland, dash across, almost unresisted, and cut the Railroad at or near Knoxville, Tenn.? In the midst of a bombardment at Donnelson, why could not a Gun-boat run up and destroy the Bridge at Clarksburg [Clarksville]? Our success or failure at Donnelson is vastly important; and I beg you to put your soul in the effort. I send a copy to Buell.

                                        A. LINCOLN

[1] ADfS, DLC-RTL. Fort Donelson surrendered unconditionally to General Grant on the morning of February 16. Halleck telegraphed McClellan on the same day "Every thing looks well. Grant says we can keep them in till mortar boats arrive Com Foote will immediately return from Cairo with two more gun boats. Troops are moving very rapidly to Fort Donelson." (DLC-RTL). Clarksville, Tennessee, was occupied by naval forces under Captain Andrew H. Foote on February 19.

To Edwin M. Stanton[1]

                                        Executive Mansion,
Hon. Sec. of War: Washington, Feb. 17, 1862

Some time ago I directed Henry M. Judah, of the regular Army, to be appointed a Brig. Genl. of volunteers. I understand my note on the subject, is lost or mislaid; and I now renew the direction. Yours truly   A. LINCOLN

[1] ALS, owned by Max Thorek, Chicago, Illinois. See Lincoln to Stanton, January 25, *supra*.

To William A. Newell[1]

Hon. W. A. Newell,   Executive Mansion,
My dear Sir: Feb. 18, 1862.

Your note on the other half of this sheet is exactly true so far as is within my power to know. Your advocacy of Col. Hatfield for a Brigadier-General has been earnest, without reservation, oft repeated, and persistent, so that I can and do know it was not in your power to do more for Col. Hatfield with me than you have done.

You never urged Col. Allen, except with the express reservation that his appointment should in no wise interfere with Col. Hatfield. Yours truly,   A. LINCOLN

[1] Angle, p. 289. On February 18, 1862, Governor Newell of New Jersey wrote Lincoln that "Col. Hatfield is impressed with the belief that I have not faithfully urged his appointment to a Brigadiership with your Excellency chiefly on account of the few words I said to you in relation to Col. Allen. . . . I beg you to write on this note that I have acted in good faith with him, and urged his success to the best of my ability." (*Ibid.*). The officers referred to were probably Colonel James T. Hatfield of the Sixth New Jersey Volunteers who resigned April 27, 1862, and Colonel Joseph W. Allen of the Ninth New Jersey Volunteers, who was drowned at Hatteras Inlet on January 15, 1862, on Burnside's expedition.

Proclamation for Celebration of Washington's Birthday[1]

February 19, 1862

By the President of the United States.
A Proclamation.

It is recommended to the People of the United States that they assemble in their customary places of meeting for public solemnities on the twenty-second day of February instant, and celebrate the anniversary of the birth of the Father of His Country by causing to be read to them his immortal Farewell address.

[L.S.]   Given under my hand and the seal of the United States at Washington, the nineteenth day of February, in the year of our Lord one thousand eight hundred and sixty-two, and of the Independence of the United States of America the eighty-sixth.

By the President: ABRAHAM LINCOLN
WILLIAM H. SEWARD, Secretary of State.

[1] DS, DNA FS RG 11, Proclamations. On February 17, 1862, Representative Edward Haight of New York wrote Lincoln to suggest that the "Commander in

Chief order that the Farewell Address of Washington be read on his next birthday, at the head of Armies & Navies—and that the Loyal people of the *United States* in all their states, cities & hamlets—their churches, houses & hearts be requested to devote that day to Exaltation for victory and gratitude to the Almighy protector of the Republic." (DLC-RTL).

To the Senate and House of Representatives[1]

February 25, 1862

To the Senate and House of Representatives:

I transmit to Congress a copy of an instruction from Prince Gortchacow to Mr. de Stoeckl, the minister of his Imperial Majesty the Emperor of Russia, accredited to this government, and of a note of the Secretary of State to the latter, relative to the adjustment of the question between the United States and Great Britain, growing out of the removal of certain of our citizens from the British mail steamer Trent, by order of the commander of the United States war steamer San Jacinto.

Washington, February 25, 1862.   ABRAHAM LINCOLN.

[1] Thirty-seventh Congress, Second Session, *Senate Executive Document No. 22.* The enclosed communication from Russia, January 9, 1862, expressed "the highest satisfaction that his Imperial Majesty has found his foresight confirmed by the determination which the federal government has . . . taken." Seward's reply of February 18, observed that "The relations of mutual confidence and friendship between a republican power in the west and a great and enterprising and beneficent monarchy in the east will afford new and important guarantees of peace, order, and freedom to the nations. . . ."

To the Senate and House of Representatives[1]

February 26, 1862

To the Senate and House of Representatives:

In transmitting to Congress the accompanying copy of two letters, bearing date the 14th of February, 1861, from his Majesty the Major King of Siam to the President of the United States, and of the President's answer thereto, I submit for their consideration the question as to the proper place of deposit of the gifts received with the royal letters referred to.   ABRAHAM LINCOLN.

Washington, February 26, 1862.

[1] Thirty-seventh Congress, Second Session, *Senate Executive Document No. 23.* See Lincoln's letter to the King of Siam, February 3, *supra.* A joint resolution approved March 15 provided that the letter from His Majesty the Major King of Siam and the accompanying gifts (a sword and scabbard, a photograph of the king, and a pair of elephant tusks) "be deposited in the collection of curiosities at the Department of the Interior."

To Edwin M. Stanton[1]

I should be much gratified for the appointment within requested to be made—if not possible immediately, at least before long.
Feb. 26. 1862. A. LINCOLN

[1] AES, DNA WR RG 107, Secretary of War, Personnel Appointments, Box 13. Lincoln's endorsement is written on a letter from Nathan M. Knapp, Winchester, Illinois, January 24, 1862, requesting appointment of Edward Baker Jerome, nephew of the late Colonel Edward D. Baker, as second lieutenant in the Regular Army. Stanton's nomination of Jerome on March 7 was confirmed by the Senate March 24, 1862.

To the Senate[1]

To the Senate of the United States: February 27, 1862

Lieutenant-General Scott has advised me that, while he would cheerfully accept a commission as additional minister to Mexico, with a view to promote the interests of the United States and of peace, yet his infirmities are such that he could not be able to reach the capital of that country by any existing mode of travel, and he therefore deems it his duty to decline the important mission I had proposed for him. For this reason I withdraw the nomination in this respect heretofore submitted to the Senate. It is hardly necessary to add that the nomination was made without any knowledge of it on his part. ABRAHAM LINCOLN.

Washington, February 27, 1862.

[1] Senate Executive Journal, XII, 136. On February 22, 1862, Lincoln had nominated General Winfield Scott to be additional envoy extraordinary and minister plenipotentiary to Mexico.

To Edwin M. Stanton[1]

Let Elliott Beardsley be appointed as within recommended.
Feb. 27, 1862 A. LINCOLN.

[1] Stan. V. Henkels Catalog 1373, May 19, 1925, No. 144. The catalog entry does not describe the letter on which Lincoln's endorsement is written, but the register of letters received by the Secretary of War lists this missing item (DNA WR RG 107, P 112, Irregular Book 5). No further record or identification of Beardsley has been found.

To Edwin M. Stanton[1]

February 27, 1862

This, as is seen, is a most meritorious case; and I shall really be obliged, if the Secretary of War can and will find a situation—a clerkship, perhaps—for the "little sergeant." A. LINCOLN
Feb. 27, 1862.

[1] AES, CSmH. Lincoln's endorsement has been clipped from a letter or petition in favor of the "little sergeant," who remains unidentified.

Order Relating to Commercial Intercourse[1]

By the President of the United States   February 28, 1862

Considering that the existing circumstances of the country allow a partial restoration of Commercial intercourse between the inhabitants of those parts of the United States heretofore declared to be in insurrection, and the citizens of the loyal States of the Union; and exercising the authority and discretion confided to me by the Act of Congress, approved July 13th., 1861, entitled "An Act further to provide for the collection of duties on imports, and for other purposes;" I hereby license and permit such commercial intercourse in all cases within the Rules and Regulations which have been, or may be, prescribed by the Secretary of the Treasury for the conducting and carrying on of the same, on the inland waters and ways of the United States   ABRAHAM LINCOLN

Washington Feb. 28th. 1862.

[1] DS, DNA FI RG 56, General Records, Treasury Department, Series AB, 1862, Letters from Executive Officers, I, 2.

Memorandum:
Appointment of Samuel E. Gross[1]

[March ?] 1862

West-Point

Samuel E. Gross.—Mt. Carroll—Ills. Says he enlisted in vols.—is 19 in Nov. Is very anxious. Came all the way here by himself.

[1] AE, DNA WR RG 94, U.S. Military Academy, 1862, No. 110, Box 80. Samuel E. Gross served from August 5 to August 16, 1861 in the Forty-first Illinois Infantry. There is no record of his appointment to West Point.

To Park Benjamin[1]

My Dear Sir   Executive Mansion   March 1. 1862

I have the honor to acknowledge the receipt of your kind favour of the 24 February; and I beg that you will accept the assurance of my sincere gratitude for your expression of friendly sympathy.

Yours very truly   A. LINCOLN

Park Benjamin Esq

[1] LS, owned by Henry R. Benjamin, New York City. Except for the signature the letter is in John Hay's handwriting. The letter from Benjamin is not in the Lincoln Papers.

To Edwin M. Stanton[1]

Hon. Sec. of War   Executive Mansion,
My dear Sir   Washington, March 1. 1862.
Dr. Isaac I. Hayes, of Dr. Kane's Arctic expedition, and more recently of an Arctic expedition headed by himself, is an applicant for Brigade Surgeon; and I would like for him to be appointed at once, if consistent with the rules. Yours truly   A. LINCOLN

[1] ALS, DNA WR RG 107, Secretary of War, Personnel Appointments, Box 12. Dr. Isaac I. Hayes sailed in 1853 as surgeon on the second expedition of Elisha K. Kane to the Arctic. From June 9, 1860, to October, 1861, he was on an Arctic expedition of his own. Appointed surgeon of Volunteers April 4, 1862, he served until July 3, 1865.

To the House of Representatives[1]

March 3, 1862

To the House of Representatives of the United States
I transmit herewith a communication of the Secretary of War, enclosing a report of the Adjutant General in answer to a Resolution of the House of Representatives of the 22d. of January 1862.

Washington   }   [ABRAHAM LINCOLN]
March 3. 1862 }

[1] DS, DNA RG 233, House of Representatives Original Executive Document No. 65. Lincoln's signature has been clipped from the document. The resolution introduced on January 22 by Francis P. Blair, Jr., requested the president "to inform the House whether the act of Congress, requiring that the officers of the regular army appointed in the new regiments should be assigned to duty in the field . . . has been complied with; and whether any officers of the regular army . . . have been employed in recruiting service. . . ." The adjutant general's report of February 11 listed eighteen officers employed in recruiting.

To the Senate[1]

To the Senate of the United States: March 3, 1862
I transmit to the Senate a translation of a note addressed to the Secretary of State, on the 1st. instant, by General P. A. Herran,[2] Envoy Extraordinary and Minister Plenipotentiary of the Granadian Confederation, with a translation of the communication accompanying that note from the Special Commissioner of that Republic, together with a copy of a letter from the Special Commissioner of the United States of the 26th. ultimo, under the Convention of 10 September, 1857, setting forth the impracticability of disposing of the cases submitted to the Joint Commission now in session under the Convention within the period described therein.

I recommend therefore, that the Senate consent to the extension of time for   days from and after the expiration of the time limited by the Convention.   ABRAHAM LINCOLN

Washington 3 March, 1862.

[1] DS, DNA RG 46, Senate 37B B5. On March 5, Senator Sumner's resolution was unanimously adopted extending "the time fixed for the termination of the labors of the joint commission . . . for the additional period of six months: *Provided,* That the Government of the Granadian Confederation shall duly assent . . . and that meanwhile it shall not be discharged from liability for claims before the commission . . ." (*Executive Journal,* XII, 151).

[2] Pedro A. Herran, Colombian general and statesman, president of New Granada 1841-1845.

To the Senate and House of Representatives[1]

March 3, 1862

To the Senate and House of Representatives:

I transmit to Congress a copy of a despatch to the Secretary of State from the minister resident of the United States at Lisbon, concerning recent measures which have been adopted by the government of Portugal intended to encourage the growth and to enlarge the area of the culture of cotton in its African possessions.

Washington, March 3, 1862.   ABRAHAM LINCOLN.

[1] Thirty-seventh Congress, Second Session, *Senate Executive Document No. 29.* The dispatch from James E. Harvey, minister to Portugal, January 28, 1862, gave an account of the Portuguese government's plans for increasing cotton culture in Mozambique and Angola, and enclosed translations of two royal decrees offering concessions and subsidies which applied to foreigners as well as to subjects of Portugal.

To the Senate and House of Representatives[1]

March 3, 1862

To the Senate and House of Representatives:

I transmit to Congress a translation of an instruction to the minister of his Majesty the King of Italy accredited to this government, and a copy of a note to that minister from the Secretary of State, relating to the settlement of the question arising out of the capture and detention of certain citizens of the United States, passengers on board the British steamer Trent, by order of Captain Wilkes, of the United States navy.   ABRAHAM LINCOLN.

Washington, March 3, 1862.

[1] Thirty-seventh Congress, Second Session, *Senate Executive Document No. 30.* The communication from the Italian government, January 21, 1862, expressed satisfaction with "the happy solution of a question which . . . put in doubt the peace of the world."

To Edwin M. Stanton[1]

Hon. Sec. of War   Executive Mansion,
My dear Sir: Washington, March 3. 1862.
   Let Irvin McDowell, Ambrose E. Burnside, Don Carlos Buell,
John Pope, Samuel R. Curtis, Franz Sigel, John A. McClernand,
Charles F. Smith, and Lewis Wallace, be appointed Major generals
of volunteers.
   Also, let John Cook, Richard J. Oglesby, William H. L. Wal-
lace[,] John McArthur, Jacob G. Lauman and John A. Logan, (all
of whom fought at Fort Donnelson, with commissions of Colonels,
but all except the last, commanded brigades) be appointed Briga-
dier generals of volunteers.
   Also, let Hiram G. Berry, of Maine, Hon. Orris S. Ferry, of
Connecticut, and Hon. James Craig, of Missouri, be appointed
Brigadier generals of volunteers.
   Please send me the formal nominations at once. Yours truly
                                                   A. LINCOLN

   [1] ALS, IHi. All the promotions were made as listed. General Charles F. Smith
died on April 25 shortly after his promotion was confirmed. Those not previously
identified: Colonel John McArthur of the Twelfth Illinois, Colonel Jacob G.
Lauman of the Seventh Iowa, Colonel Hiram G. Berry of the Fourth Maine,
Colonel Orris S. Ferry of the Fifth Connecticut, and ex-congressman James Craig
of Missouri, who had been a captain of Militia in the Mexican War.

To Green Adams[1]

Hon. Green Adams   Executive Mansion,
My dear Sir   Washington, March 4, 1862.
   Please send me the list of names desired to be commissioned, by
the enclosed letters. Of course, what office each is to have, must
be indicated. Yours truly   A. LINCOLN
   [1] ALS, owned by John S. Adams, Sr., Wayne, Pennsylvania. There is no reply
from Green Adams in the Lincoln Papers, but a letter from Thomas E. Bramlette,
Louisville, Kentucky, March 21, 1862, which Adams forwarded to Lincoln, indicated Bramlette's willingness "to take any position" and named General James
M. Shackelford as willing to raise troops. Colonel W. T. Scott of Lexington was
also recommended for provost marshal "for this district." (DLC-RTL). On February 21, 1863, Lincoln nominated Bramlette district attorney for Kentucky, and
on January 2, 1863, nominated Shackelford for brigadier general of Volunteers.
Bramlette's appointment was confirmed February 27, and Shackelford's on March
11, 1863. Presumably these were among the appointments to which Lincoln
refers.

Reply to Federico Barreda[1]

                                          March 4, 1862
   The United States have no enmities, animosities, or rivalries,
and no interests which conflict with the welfare, safety and rights

[142]

or interests of any other nation. Their own prosperity, happiness and aggrandizement are sought most safely and advantageously through the preservation, not only of peace on their own part, but peace among all other nations. But while the United States are thus a friend to all other nations, they do not seek to conceal the fact that they cherish especial sentiments of friendship for, and sympathies with, those who, like themselves, have founded their institutions on the principle of the equal rights of men; and such nations, being more prominently neighbors of the United States, the latter are co-operating with them in establishing civilization and culture on the American continent. Such being the general principles which govern the United States in their foreign relations, you may be assured, sir, that in all things this government will deal justly, frankly, and, if it be possible, even liberally, with Peru, whose liberal sentiments towards us you have so kindly expressed.

[1] New York *Herald*, March 5, 1862. Federico Barreda presented his credentials as minister from Peru.

To Edwin M. Stanton[1]

Hon. Sec. of War   Executive Mansion,
My dear Sir   Washington, March 4. 1862.
  Send me at once a nomination of Daniel Tyler of Connecticut as a Brigadier General of Volunteers. Let it date as of yesterday, so as to be part of the lot then sent to the Senate. Yours truly
                          A. LINCOLN

[1] ALS-P, ISLA. Stanton's nomination of Daniel Tyler was dated March 4 rather than March 3 as Lincoln suggested. (*Executive Journal*, XII, 147.)

To Whom It May Concern[1]

                          Executive Mansion,
Whom it may concern   Washington, March 4. 1862
  Edward Burke, the bearer of this, was at service in this Mansion for several months now last past; and during all the time he appeared to me to be a competent, faithful, and very genteel man. I take no charge of the servants about the house; but I do not understand that Burke leaves because of any fault or misconduct.
                          A. LINCOLN

[1] ALS, The Rosenbach Company, Philadelphia and New York. The following endorsement is written on the bottom of the letter: "If Mr Newton can do any thing for Edward Burke, the bearer of this, I will be obliged to him I think him worthy O H BROWNING." No further record of Burke's employment has been found until January and February, 1865, when he received $100 for services

as doorkeeper at the White House. Later references to "Edward McManus" seem to indicate the same person who was known both as "Burke" and "McManus." Presumably Browning's endorsement, added later, was to Isaac Newton, whom Lincoln nominated commissioner of Agriculture on May 16, 1862.

To the Senate[1]

To the Senate of the United States: March 5, 1862

I submit to the Senate for its consideration a copy of a message addressed to that body by my immediate predecessor, on the 12th February, 1861, relating to the award made by the joint commission under the convention between the United States and Paraguay of the 4th February, 1859, together with the original "journal of the proceedings" of the commission, and a printed copy of the "statements and arguments —— and for the Republic," and request the advice of the Senate as to the final acquiescence in, or rejection of, the award of the commissioner, by the Government of the United States. As the "journal" is an original document, pertaining to the archives of the Department of State, it is proper, when the Senate shall have arrived at a conclusion on the subject, that the volume be returned to the custody of the Secretary of State.   ABRAHAM LINCOLN.

Washington, 5 March, 1862.

[1] *Executive Journal*, XII, 152-53. The message from President Buchanan, of which Lincoln enclosed a copy, may be found in the *Executive Journal*, XI, 268. See also Lincoln to the Senate, March 14, *infra*.

To William H. Seward[1]

Hon. Sec. of State   Executive Mansion
My dear Sir   March 5, 1862

Please summon the Cabinet to meet me here at 7 o'clock this evening. Yours truly   A. LINCOLN

[1] ALS, owned by Perc S. Brown, Newark, New Jersey. Although the diaries of Gideon Welles and Edward Bates have nothing on this meeting, Lincoln probably presented for discussion his message recommending compensated emancipation, which he sent to congress March 6 (*infra*).

Message to Congress[1]

March 6, 1862

Fellow-citizens of the Senate, and House of Representatives,

I recommend the adoption of a Joint Resolution by your honorable bodies which shall be substantially as follows:

"Resolved that the United States ought to co-operate with any state which may adopt gradual abolishment of slavery, giving to such state pecuniary aid, to be used by such state in it's discretion, to compensate for the inconveniences[2] public and private, produced by such change of system"

If the proposition contained in the resolution does not meet the approval of Congress and the country, there is the end; but if it does command such approval, I deem it of importance that the states and people immediately interested, should be at once distinctly notified of the fact, so that they may begin to consider whether to accept or reject it. The federal government would find it's highest interest in such a measure, as one of the most efficient means of self-preservation.[3] The leaders of the existing insurrection entertain the hope that this government will ultimately be forced to acknowledge the independence of some part of the disaffected region, and that all the slave states North of such part will then say "the Union, for which we have struggled, being already gone, we now choose to go with the Southern section." To deprive them of this hope, substantially ends the rebellion; and the initiation of emancipation completely deprives them of it, as to all the states initiating it. The point is not that *all* the states tolerating slavery would very soon, if at all, initiate emancipation; but that, while the offer is equally made to all, the more Northern shall, by such initiation, make it certain[4] to the more Southern, that in no event, will the former ever join the latter, in their proposed confederacy. I say "initiation" because, in my judgment, gradual, and not sudden emancipation, is better for all. In the mere financial, or pecuniary view, any member of Congress,[5] with the census-tables and Treasury-reports before him, can readily see for himself how very soon the current expenditures of this war would purchase, at fair valuation, all the slaves in any named State. Such a proposition, on the part of the general government, sets up no claim of a right, by federal authority, to interfere with slavery within state limits, referring, as it does, the absolute[6] control of the subject, in each case, to the state and it's people, immediately interested. It is proposed as a matter of perfectly free choice with them.[7]

In the annual message last December, I thought' fit to say "The Union must be preserved; and hence all indispensable means must be employed." I said this, not hastily, but deliberately. War has been made, and continues to be, an indispensable means to this end. A practical re-acknowledgement of the national authority would render the war unnecessary, and it would at once cease. If, however, resistance continues, the war must also continue; and it is impossible to foresee all the incidents, which may attend[8] and all the ruin which may follow[9] it. Such as may seem indispensable, or may obviously promise great efficiency towards ending the struggle, must and will come.

The proposition now made, though an offer only, I hope it may be esteemed no offence to ask whether the pecuniary consideration tendered would not be of more value to the States and private persons concerned,[10] than are the institution, and property in it, in the present aspect of affairs.[11]

While it is true that the adoption of the proposed resolution would be merely initiatory, and not within itself a practical measure, it is recommended in the hope that it would soon lead to important practical results. In full view of my great responsibility to my God, and to my[12] country, I earnestly[13] beg the attention of Congress and the people to the subject.   ABRAHAM LINCOLN

March 6. 1862.

[1] ADf, DLC-RTL; DS, DNA RG 46, Senate 37A F2; DS, RG 233, House of Representatives Original Executive Document No. 69. A joint resolution of April 10 declared that "the United States ought to co-operate with any State which may adopt gradual abolishment of slavery giving to such State pecuniary aid, to be used by such State in its discretion to compensate for the inconveniences, public and private, produced by such change of system." A further resolution of April 14 ordered the printing of ten thousand copies of the message and resolutions. Emendations not in Lincoln's handwriting appear in the draft and were probably made at the cabinet meeting on March 5. Those which Lincoln adopted are indicated in succeeding footnotes, as also are Lincoln's significant deletions.

[2] "Inconveniences" substituted for "evils."

[3] "Self-preservation" substituted for "preserving it's own existence."

[4] "Make it certain to" substituted for "convince."

[5] "Any member of Congress" substituted for "any honorable member."

[6] "The absolute" substituted for "entire."

[7] The following sentence appears at this point in the autograph draft, but is bracketed for deletion: "Should the people of the insurgent districts now reject the councils of treason, revive loyal state governments, and again send Senators and Representatives to Congress, they would, at once find themselves at peace, with no institution changed, and with their just influence in the councils of the nation, fully re-established."   [8] "Which may attend" inserted.

[9] "Follow" substituted for "attend."

[10] "Persons concerned" substituted for "owners."

[11] The following sentence is deleted at this point: "I believe it would assist us much in returning to peace, and to all our rights under the Constitution, and the laws."   [12] "Afflicted" deleted at this point.

[13] Substitution of "respectfully" for "earnestly" not adopted.

To Edward Bates[1]

Respectfully submitted to the Attorney General with the request of as early an examination as possible.   A. LINCOLN

March 7. 1862.

[1] AES, owned by C. Norton Owen, Glencoe, Illinois. Lincoln's endorsement is written on an undated letter signed "Miss Gould," pleading for a pardon for her unnamed fiancé. Since the letter has been removed from associated papers in the National Archives, no identification is available.

To the Senate[1]

To the Senate   Washington, D. C.
of the United States.   March 7 1862.

I transmit, herewith, for the constitutional action of the Senate, thereon, a Treaty concluded at Paola, Kansas, on the 18th day of August 1860, between Seth Clover, Commissioner, on the part of the United States, and the delegates of the united tribes of Kaskia and Peoria Piankeshaw and Wea Indians.

I also transmit a communication, of the Secretary of the Interior, of the 6th instant, and accompanying papers from the Acting Commissioner of Indian Affairs in relation to the subject.

ABRAHAM LINCOLN

[1] DS, DNA RG 46, Senate 37B C5. The treaty was amended and ratified by the Senate, February 12, 1863.

To William H. Seward[1]

Executive Mansion,
Hon. Sec. of State   Washington, March 7, 1862.

My dear Sir: Mr. James F. B. Marshall, of Mass. is now with me on the question of the Honolulu Commissioner. It pains me some that this tilt for the place of Col. Baker's friend grows so fierce, now the Col. is no longer alive to defend him. I presume, however, we shall have no rest from it. Mr. Marshall appears to be a very intelligent gentleman, and well acquainted with the affairs of the Sandwich Islands. The California delegation also expect the place for some one of their citizens. In self-defence I am disposed to say "Make a selection and send it to me." Yours truly

A. LINCOLN.

[1] ALS, NAuE. Lapsley (VI, 264) misdates this letter March 7, 1863. Seward had requested in a note on March 5, 1862, that Lincoln "see Mr Marshall, at some time, a little at leisure" on the subject of the Hawaiian Islands. James F. B. Marshall of Boston had resided in Hawaii since 1838 and had established a business there. Presumably he represented strong opposition to Thomas J. Dryer, whom Lincoln had appointed commissioner on March 20, 1861, for Dryer was recalled and James McBride of Oregon was appointed to replace him on January 26, 1863. See also Lincoln to Seward, March 15, *infra*.

To Edwin M. Stanton[1]

Respectfully submitted to the War Department with the remark that I think the appointment would be a good one.

March 7. 1862.   A. LINCOLN

[1] AES, IHi. Lincoln's endorsement is written on a letter from Governor Richard Yates and others, February 18, 1862, recommending the promotion of Captain William W. Leland, commissary of subsistence on General U. S. Grant's staff, to rank of major. Numerous later endorsements and accompanying letters from Grant and Halleck dated July 25 and August 9, 1862, are concerned with Leland's having been mustered out of service on suspicion of later misconduct, and Halleck's letter, approved by Stanton, recommended that he not be reappointed.

To Edwin M. Stanton[1]

Let the Commission be vacated according to Senator Harlan's request.   A. LINCOLN

March 7. 1862.

[1] AES, IHi. Lincoln's "endorsement appears on an undated letter from Senator James Harlan: "Learning from the accompanying letter of Governor Jayne of Dekotah [February 21, 1862], and other reliable sources that the United States has commissioned one William T Lyman as Major of Dekotah volunteers, and placed him in command of Fort Randall garrisoned chiefly by Iowa volunteers, in violation of their rights and wishes, I respectfully request that said commission may be abrogated."

The following endorsement appears below Lincoln's: "(Revoked March 7, 62.)."

To Gideon Welles[1]

The Sec. of the Navy.   March 7, 1862
          Will oblige me by appointing
Hanscum, Naval constructor at Boston if no valid objection is known one of the commissioners to examine River Boats.

March 7th 1862—   A. LINCOLN

[1] LS, owned by Emanuel A. Gardiner, New York City. Lincoln inserted the phrase "if no valid objection is known." William L. Hanscom is listed as a naval constructor at the Boston Navy Yard.

To James Cooper and Others[1]

                                                            March 8, 1862
These two young men, Richard Middleton and Thomas F. Goodwin seem to have a very meritorious case; and I respectfully com-

mend them to Gen. Cooper, and to others to whom this may be presented.   A. LINCOLN
March 8, 1862.

Mr. Middleton states, he has heretofore been employed for several years on the Capitol. I shall be pleased if he can be again employed upon it.

[1] AES, RPB. Lincoln's endorsement has been clipped from the attendant papers, but is accompanied by an additional endorsement as follows: "Richard Middleton for Superintendent Marble Work/ By Rev: Jno. C. Smith/ Favorably endorsed by the President." No further record of this matter has been found. Richard Middleton of Elmira, New York, was appointed captain in the Fiftieth New York Volunteer Engineers, February 19, 1864. Sergeant Major Thomas F. Goodwin of the Eleventh New York Infantry was wounded at Bull Run and discharged for disability on December 27, 1861; on March 1, 1862 he was appointed first lieutenant of Company I of the same regiment.

Memorandum:
Appointment of William H. Upham[1]

[c. March 8, 1862]

Senator Doolittle wishes William H. Upham, appointed a cadet. He will be 20 next May, was wounded at Bull Run, the ball entering less than an inch from the left collar-bone & jugular, and coming out at his back the two scars being five inches apart.

[1] AD, DLC-RTL. This memorandum is incorrectly dated [Feb. ? 1863] in the Lincoln Papers. See Lincoln's letter to Totten, *infra*. Private William H. Upham, Company F, Second Wisconsin Infantry served from April 23, 1861, to May 5, 1862. Entering West Point July 1, 1862, he graduated June 18, 1866.

President's General War Order No. 2[1]

President's General ⎱   Executive Mansion
War-Order, No. 2 ⎰   Washington, March 8, 1862

Ordered

1st. That the Major General commanding the Army of the Potomac proceed forthwith to organize that part of said Army destined to enter upon active operations (including the reserve, but excluding the troops to be left in the fortifications about Washington) into four Army corps to be commanded according to seniority of rank as follows:

1st. Corps, to consist of four Divisions & to be commanded by Major General McDowell.

2nd. Corps, to consist of three Divisions, & to be commanded by Brigadier General E. V. Sumner.

3rd. Corps, to consist of three Divisions & to be commanded
by Brigadier General Heintzelman

4th. Corps, to consist of three Divisions, & to be commanded
by Brigadier General E. D. Keyes.

2. That the Divisions now commanded by the officers above
assigned to the command of corps, shall be embraced in, and form
parts of their respective corps.

3 The forces left for the defence of Washington will be placed
in command of Brigadier General James Wadsworth, who shall
also be Military Governor of the District of Columbia.

4. That this order be executed with such promptness and despatch as not to delay the commencement of the operations already
directed to be undertaken by the Army of the Potomac.

5. A fifth Army Corps, to be commanded by Major General
Banks will be formed from his own, and Gen. Shields, late Gen.
Lander's Division. ABRAHAM LINCOLN.

[1] ADS, DLC-Stanton Papers. All but the heading "Executive Mansion/ Washington, March 8, 1862" is in Lincoln's handwriting. Upon receiving this order,
McClellan replied to Stanton, March 9, 1862, "In the arrangements for the advance of to-morrow it is impossible to carry into effect the arrangements for the
formation of army corps. I am obliged to take groups as I find them and to move
them by divisions. I respectfully ask a suspension of the order directing it till the
present movement be over." (OR, I, V, 739).
To this Stanton replied on the same day, "I think it is the duty of every officer
to obey the President's orders, nor can I see any reason why you should not obey
them in present instance. I must therefore decline to suspend them." (*Ibid.*).
At 1 A.M. on March 10, McClellan replied, "You have entirely misunderstood
me, and the idea I intended to convey was simply that I could not, under the
pressure of the new aspect of affairs, immediately carry out the President's orders
as to the formation of army corps. . . . I regard it as a military necessity that
the divisions should move to the front at once, without waiting for the formation
of army corps. . . . If the leave to suspend the order be granted, there will be
no unreasonable delay in the formation of army corps. I await your reply. . . ."
(*Ibid.*, p. 740).
Stanton replied immediately, ". . . if you think the terms of the order as it
stands would . . . retard or . . . restrain movements that circumstances require to be made before the army corps are formed, I will assume the responsibility of suspending the order for that purpose. . . ." (*Ibid.*, p. 741).
McClellan replied at 2:50 A.M., "Your reply received. The troops are in motion.
I thank you for your dispatch. It relieves me much, and you will be convinced
that I have not asked too much of you." (*Ibid.*).
The corps assignments were issued in McClellan's *General Orders No. 151,*
March 13, 1862. McClellan's General Report, August 4, 1863, made the following comment on *Lincoln's General War Order No. 2:* ". . . I had always been in
favor of the principle of . . . army corps, but preferred deferring its practical
execution until some little experience in . . . battle should show what general
officers were most competent. . . . These views had frequently been expressed by
me to the President and . . . Cabinet. It was therefore with as much regret as
surprise that I learned the existence of this order. . . ." (*Ibid.*, p. 50).

President's General War Order No. 3[1]

President's General War ⎱   Executive Mansion
Order No. 3   ⎰   Washington, March 8, 1862.

Ordered, that no change of the base of operations of the Army of the Potomac shall be made without leaving in, and about Washington, such a force as, in the opinion of the General-in-chief, and the commanders of all the Army corps, shall leave said City entirely secure.

That not more than two Army corps, (about fifty thousand troops) of said Army of the Potomac, shall be moved *en route* for a new base of operations until the navigation of the Potomac, from Washington to the Chesapeake bay shall be freed from enemies batteries and other obstructions, or, until the President shall hereafter give express permission.

That any movement, as aforesaid, *en route* for a new base of operations, which may be ordered by the General-in-chief, & which may be intended to move upon the Chesapeake-bay, shall begin to move upon the bay as early as the 18th. day of March Inst.; and the General-in-chief shall be responsible that it so move as early as that day.

Ordered that the Army and Navy co-operate in an immediate effort to capture the enemies batteries upon the Potomac between Washington and the Chesapeake-bay.   ABRAHAM LINCOLN.

[1] ADS, DLC-Stanton Papers. All but "General" and "3" in the "President's General War Order No. 3" is in Lincoln's handwriting. On April 2, Stanton submitted to the adjutant general and to General Ethan A. Hitchcock, who had been made a major general on February 10, with advisory duties in the War Department, the records of McClellan's troop movements and directed that they determine whether the terms of Lincoln's order to keep Washington "entirely secure" had been complied with. They reported on the same day that the order had not been obeyed. (OR, I, XI, III, 57-62.)

To Edwin M. Stanton[1]

March 8, 1862.

The within is from the governor of Illinois. I understand the seven additional batteries now sought are to be six-gun batteries; and the object is to mix them with the fourteen batteries they already have, so as to make each battery consist of four 6-pounders and two 12-pounders. I shall be very glad to have the requisition filled if it can be without detriment to the service.

A. LINCOLN.

[1] Thirty-seventh Congress, Second Session, *Senate Executive Document No. 72,* p. 546. Lincoln's endorsement is on a letter from Governor Richard Yates to Stanton, March 1, 1862, requesting "seven batteries of 12-pounder calibre James

rifled guns . . . complete and ready for field service, together with . . . ammunition. . . ." Following Lincoln's endorsement Stanton wrote, "The within application has been considered by the War Department, and cannot be complied with at present without detriment to the service."

To Joseph G. Totten[1]

Executive Mansion
Dear Sir: Washington March 8, 1862.
I hereby appoint the following persons Cadets to the Military Academy at West Point for the year 1862:

At Large.

Edward W. Baker	Barry	Ill.
Albert S. Bayless	Flemingsburg	Ky.
William H. Upham		Wis.
Frederick A. Mahan		N. Y.
Henry Davis Wallen, Jr.		Ga.
Arthur Tracy Lee		Mass.
Edward Everett Sharp	Danville	Mo.
Erasmus D. Gaines	Freeport	Ill.
Francis Jones		Pa.
Charles Woodson Bates		Mo.

For the District of Columbia:
Richard Cuyler Churchill D.C.
Yours truly ABRAHAM LINCOLN
Gen. J. G. Totten
Chief Engineer Bureau.

[1] LS, DNA WR RG 77, Office of the Chief of Engineers, Letters Received, P 1091. Lincoln's letter was accompanied by one from Nicolay of the same date, instructing General Totten to "send the appointments of Baker and Gaines to me; that of Bayless to Senator Wright of Indiana; that of Upham to Senator Doolittle; that of Sharp to Hon. J. S. Rollins, M. C.; and that of Bates to the Attorney General." Of the several appointees the following are not of record as entering West Point: Edward W. Baker, Edward Everett Sharp, Erasmus D. Gaines, and Francis Jones. Charles Woodson Bates, the son of Attorney General Bates, entered but failed his examinations in 1866 (see Bates' *Diary*, January 23, 1866). A list of these appointees, in Lincoln's handwriting, is preserved in the Lincoln Papers, but supplied with an incorrect date "[1861]" (DLC-RTL, 13649).

To Henry J. Raymond[1]

COPY.
Private
Executive Mansion,
Hon. Henry J. Raymond: Washington, March 9, 1862.
My dear Sir: I am grateful to the New-York Journals, and not less so to the Times than to others, for their kind notices of the

late special Message to Congress. Your paper, however, intimates that the proposition, though well-intentioned, must fail on the score of expense. I do hope you will reconsider this. Have you noticed the facts that less than one half-day's cost of this war would pay for all the slaves in Delaware, at four hundred dollars per head?—that eighty-seven days cost of this war would pay for all in Delaware, Maryland, District of Columbia, Kentucky, and Missouri at the same price? Were those states to take the step, do you doubt that it would shorten the war more than eighty seven days, and thus be an actual saving of expense. Please look at these things, and consider whether there should not be another article in the Times? Yours very truly,   A. LINCOLN

¹ ADfS, DLC-RTL; LS, owned by Jacob J. Podell, New York City. With the autograph draft of this letter in the Lincoln Papers are extracts from the New York *Times, Tribune, Evening Bulletin, Herald, World,* and *Evening Post* of March 7—all supporting the message recommending compensated emancipation. Upon receiving Lincoln's letter, Raymond replied, March 15, "You will have seen long before this reaches you . . . that the Times has published several articles in support of your special message. As soon as I saw the one to which you allude, I telegraphed to the office to sustain the message *without qualifications or cavil,* and I believe the paper has done so since. . . . I regard the message as a master-piece of practical wisdom and sound policy. . . ." (DLC-RTL).

To Don C. Buell¹

Washington, March 10, 1862.

General D. C. Buell: The evidence is very strong that the enemy in front of us here is breaking up and moving off. General McClellan is after him. Some part of the force may be destined to meet you. Look out and be prepared. I telegraphed Halleck, asking him to assist you, if needed.   A. LINCOLN.

¹ OR, I, X, II, 612. There is no reply from Buell in the *Official Records* or in the Lincoln Papers.

To Salmon P. Chase¹

Executive Mansion   Washington D.C.
Hon. Sec. of Treasury.   March 10, 1862.
My dear Sir. Thomas H. Campbell bearer of this, has several times been our auditor of State; and I personally know him to be an honest man, of thorough business capacity. He is here now to do something in adjusting the accounts of the State and U.S. growing out of the war. He is thoroughly disinterested, not even receiving

pay for what he does. No man can be more safely trusted. I beg you to afford him all proper facilities, with perfect assurance that no confidence reposed in him will be abused. Yours truly

A. LINCOLN.

[1] Copy, IHi-Nicolay and Hay Papers. Thomas H. Campbell, auditor of public accounts for the State of Illinois, 1846-1857, was assisting State Treasurer William Butler in adjusting accounts.

Check to "Tad" Lincoln[1]

No. 79   Washington, D.C. March 10, 1862
                         RIGGS & Co.
Pay to "Tad" (when he is well enough to present) or bearer
Five —————————————————————— Dollars
$5/oo   A. LINCOLN

[1] ADS, owned by William H. Townsend, Lexington, Kentucky. Early in February, Thomas ("Tad") Lincoln and his brother William Wallace ("Willie") had contracted a fever. On February 20, Willie died, and "Tad" remained in a serious condition for many days. Lincoln's check is a memento of "Tad's" gradual recuperation.

To Gideon Welles[1]

Hon. Sec. of Navy   Executive Mansion
My dear Sir   March 10, 1862
    I have just seen Lieut. Worden, who says the "Monitor" could be boarded and captured very easily—first, after boarding, by wedging the turret, so that it would not turn, and then by pouring water in her & drowning her machinery. He is decidedly of opinion she should not go sky-larking up to Norfolk. Yours truly

A. LINCOLN

[1] ALS, U. S. Naval Academy Museum, Annapolis, Maryland. Following Lincoln's direction, Welles on the same day telegraphed Captain Gustavus V. Fox at Fort Monroe, "It is directed by the President that the Monitor be not too much exposed, and that in no event shall any attempt be made to proceed with her unattended to Norfolk. If vessels can be procured and loaded with stone and sunk in the channel it is important that it should be done. The San Jacinto and Dacotah have sailed from Boston for Hampton Roads and the Sabine in tow of Baltic and a tug from New York. Gun Boats will be ordered forthwith   Should it not be well to detain the Minnesota until other vessels arrive." (Copy, DLC-RTL). Fox communicated his reply to Montgomery Blair, March 11, ". . . tell the President that the Monitor shall take no risk excepting with the Merrimac." (Ibid.). On March 8, the Merrimac had sunk the Cumberland and Congress in Hampton Roads.

President's War Order No. 3[1]

President's War⎱   Executive Mansion
Order, No. 3 ⎰   Washington, March 11, 1862.

Major General McClellan having personally taken the field at the head of the Army of the Potomac, until otherwise ordered, he is relieved from the command of the other Military departments, he retaining command of the Department of the Potomac.

Ordered further that the two departments now under the respective commands of Generals Halleck, and Hunter together with so much of that under General Buell as lies West of a North and South line indefinitely drawn through Knoxville, Tennessee, be consolidated, and designated the Department of the Mississippi; and that, until otherwise ordered, Major General Halleck have command of said department.

Ordered also, that the country West of the Department of the Potomac, and East of the Department of the Mississippi be a Military department to be called the Mountain Department; and that the same be commanded by Major General Fremont.

That all the commanders of departments, after the receipt of this order by them respectively, report severally and directly to the Secretary of War, and that prompt, full, and frequent reports will be expected of all and each of them. ABRAHAM LINCOLN

[1] ADS, IHi. A preliminary draft of this order prepared by Stanton is as follows:

"In view of active operations by the Army of the Potomac which will demand the presence & supervision of its Commanding General in the field and that he should be relieved from all other duties is ordered by the President

"1st. That Major General George B McClellan be and he is hereby relieved from & after this date from duty as General Commanding and directed to devote his attention exclusively to the operations of the Army of the Potomac

"2. The Adjutant General is directed to give immediate notice of this order to all Generals commanding Armies expeditions or Departments and instruct them from and after the receipt of this order to make their reports to & receive their instruction from the President through the War Department." (DLC-Stanton Papers).

The issuing of War Order No. 3 was also recommended by Bates in the cabinet meeting of March 11 (see *Diary of Edward Bates*, p. 239). On March 12 McClellan sent a letter by Governor Dennison of Ohio which he marked "Unofficial," reading in part as follows:

"I have just seen Gov. Dennison who has detailed to me the conversations he held with you yesterday and today.

"I beg to say . . . that I cordially endorse all that he said to you in my behalf, and . . . I thank you . . . for the official confidence & kind personal feelings you entertain for me. I believe I said to you some weeks since . . . that no feeling of self interest or ambition should ever prevent me from devoting myself to your service. I am glad to have the opportunity to prove it, & you will find that under present circumstances I shall work just as cheerfully as ever before & that no consideration of self will in any manner interfere with the discharge of my public duties. . . ." (DLC-RTL).

To Edwin M. Stanton[1]

There are potent reasons why this young man should be made a Lieut. if it can be done consistently with the public service

March 11, 1862. A. LINCOLN

1 AES, RPB. Lincoln's endorsement is written on a letter from Senator Garrett Davis recommending Joseph C. Breckinridge for a lieutenancy. He was appointed second lieutenant in the Second Artillery, April 14, 1862.

To Gideon Welles[1]

Hon. Sec. of Navy Executive Mansion
My dear Sir March 11. 1862
Comodore Foote's telegram of the 10th. has just been sent me. Please have the requisition made in it, filled as soon as possible.

Yours truly A. LINCOLN

1 ALS, OCHP. Foote's telegram of March 10 was transmitted to Lincoln by Henry A. Wise of the Navy Department on March 11, with the comment that "the requests contained therein have been complied with." Foote requested "9 extra chains for gun boats of 1¼ ins, sent immediately. . . . 4 Dahlgren rifled guns of 8000 pounds weight, fitted complete with carriages and all. They are for the 'Eastport' Prize Gunboat; with 300 shells for each of the Rifled guns. . . ." (DLC-RTL). In an earlier telegram to Wise, March 1, Foote called attention to the fact that he had received no reply to his request to have "the Rebel Gun boat 'Eastport,' lately captured in the Tennessee River, fitted up as a Gun boat." (*Ibid.*).

To John A. Dahlgren[1]

Capt. Dahlgren, please see the bearer. A. LINCOLN
March 12, 1862.

1 ALS, CCamStJ. The bearer has not been positively identified, but a letter from Senator Preston King, March 12, introduced "Mr. Pascal Plant of this city. . . . Mr. Plant has an invention which he supposes can with security . . . be navigated and can destroy any vessel whether iron clad or not. . . ." (DLC-RTL).

To the Senate[1]

To the Senate of the United States: March 12, 1862

In compliance with the resolution of the Senate of the 11th instant, requesting a "copy of any correspondence on the records or files of the Department of State in regard to railway systems in Europe," I transmit a report from the Secretary of State, and the papers by which it was accompanied. ABRAHAM LINCOLN.

Washington, March 12, 1862.

[156]

¹ Thirty-seventh Congress, Second Session, *Senate Executive Document No.* 32. Seward's report enclosed an analysis of French railroads made by N. M. Beckwith and referred to previously published documents on the subject.

To Hiram Barney[1]

March 13, 1862

I do not remember Curtis H. Hall, the writer of the within; but Daniel E. Ruckel, mentioned, was a dear friend of mine; and any favor done a member of his family would be appreciated by me. March 13, 1862. A. LINCOLN

¹ AES, RPB. Lincoln's endorsement is written on a letter from Curtis H. Hall, Hackensack, New Jersey, March 10, 1862, asking for a recommendation to a place in the New York Customs House. Hall's wife was the daughter of the late Daniel E. Ruckel of Springfield, Illinois. There is no record of Hall's appointment.

To Henry A. Brown[1]

Executive Mansion,

My Dear Sir Washington, March 13, 1862.

I have the pleasure to acknowledge the receipt of three engravings of General McClellan, two of which I have sent as you requested. Please accept my thanks for the present. The Engraving is very beautifully executed, and the likeness is perfect. I have the honor to be Your Obt Servt A. LINCOLN

H. A. Brown Esq

35 Winter St

¹ LS, owned by Mrs. Harris P. Mosher, Marblehead, Massachusetts. The letter, excepting signature, is in John Hay's handwriting. Henry A. Brown was representative in Boston of London Printing and Publishing Company, Ltd.

To George B. McClellan[1]

War Department, March 13, 1862.

The President having considered the plan of operations agreed upon by yourself and the commanders of army corps, makes no objection to the same, but gives the following directions as to its execution:

1st. Leave such force at Manassas Junction as shall make it entirely certain that the enemy shall not repossess himself of that position and line of communication.

2d. Leave Washington secure.

3d. Move the remainder of the force down the Potomac, choosing a new base at Fortress Monroe, or anywhere between here and there; or, at all events, move such remainder of the army at once in pursuit of the enemy by some route.　EDWIN M. STANTON,

Seven o'clock, forty minutes.　Secretary of War.

Major General George B. McClellan.

[1] Thirty-seventh Congress, Third Session, *Senate Reports*, No. 108, Part I, p. 313. This item is misdated "1863" in Hertz (II, 917-18). The evidence is that Lincoln composed the body of this communication, but the original is missing (DNA WR RG 94, Adjutant General, Letters Received, P 1254).

To William H. Seward[1]

If the Consulate named within stands as is assumed, I shall be glad for Dr. Bettelheim to have it.　A. LINCOLN

March 13, 1862

[1] AES, DNA FS RG 59, Appointments, Box 230. Lincoln's endorsement is written on a letter from V. L. Conrad, Urbana, Ohio, February 18, 1862, to Dr. B. J. Bettleheim, suggesting that since John H. Cowden of Pinegrove, Pennsylvania, has declined appointment as consul to Nagasaki, Japan, Bettleheim may obtain the place and carry on his missionary work. Dr. B. J. Bettleheim of Cayuga, Illinois, had been a missionary in Japan and China prior to 1856. There is no record of his appointment.

Speech to a Massachusetts Delegation[1]

March 13, 1862.

I thank you, Mr. TRAIN, for your kindness in presenting me with this truly elegant and highly creditable specimen of the handiwork of the mechanics of your State of Massachusetts, and I beg of you to express my hearty thanks to the donors. It displays a perfection of workmanship which I really wish I had time to acknowledge in more fitting words, and I might then follow your idea that it is suggestive, for it is evidently expected that a good deal of whipping is to be done. But, as we meet here socially, let us not think only of whipping rebels, or of those who seem to think only of whipping negroes, but of those pleasant days which it is to be hoped are in store for us, when, seated behind a good pair of horses, we can crack our whips and drive through a peaceful, happy and prosperous land. With this idea, gentlemen, I must leave you for my business duties.

[1] New York *Times*, March 22, 1862. Lincoln replied to a short speech by Representative Charles R. Train, who presented "an elegant whip, made by a Massachusetts whip company." Among the delegation was Nathaniel Hawthorne, who had come to Washington to gather impressions for an article to appear in the *Atlantic Monthly* for July, 1862, but being unable to get a personal appointment with the president, thus availed himself of the best opportunity.

To Edwin M. Stanton[1]

March 13, 1862

It is said I some time ago recommended *William P. Graves* of Ky, for a Lieutenancy in the Army, at the particular instance of Hon. Mr. Mallory, and that his name was placed on the list at the War Department, and he notified by Mr. Mallory that he was appointed. It now appears his name was taken off the list. Under these circumstances, I wish him appointed at once if there is any vacancy. A. LINCOLN

March 13. 1862.

[1] AES, RPB. Lincoln's endorsement is written on an envelope franked by Representative Robert Mallory enclosing recommendations for Graves. Graves was appointed second lieutenant in the Second Artillery, March 24, 1862. See also Lincoln to Cameron, December 16, 1861, *supra*.

To Orville H. Browning[1]

Will Mr. Senator Browning please see Mr. Muller, who I believe to be a correct & honest man. Give him a fair show, if possible.

March 14, 1862 A LINCOLN

[1] AES-P, ISLA. Lincoln's endorsement is written on a letter from "Ab. Hall," steamship owner and merchant of Baltimore, to George Harrington, assistant secretary of the Treasury, March 13, 1862, commending James N. Muller's attendance to duty as supervising inspector of steamboats at Baltimore, and asking that he be retained in office. See Lincoln to Chase, May 9, 1861, *supra*.

To George B. McClellan[1]

Washington City, D.C.

Major Genl. McClellan March 14, 1862.

As Gen Richardson takes Gen. Sumner's old Division, can he have an exchange of Brigades so as to take his old Brigade with him?

EDWIN M STANTON
Sec of War

[1] AL, RPB. The telegram is in Lincoln's handwriting, in pencil except for "Richardson" which he had omitted and later wrote in with ink, but is signed by Stanton. It was written in reply to McClellan's telegram to Stanton of March 14, 11:30 A.M., "Have placed Gen'l [Israel B.] Richardson in command of Gen'l [Edwin V.] Sumners Division instead [of?] Genl Kearney who prefers remaining with his old brigade Please inform the President." (DLC-RTL). At 3:45 P.M. McClellan again telegraphed "I would advise that no change be made now in the organization of Divisions. It would be very pernicious at such a moment as this. . . . The third word omitted in your despatch & I do not know whether you mean Kearney or Richardson, but it makes no difference, as my opinion is based on general principles. I am hard at work." (*Ibid.*).

To James A. McDougall[1]

Hon. James A. McDougal   Executive Mansion
U.S. Senate   Washington, March 14, 1862

My dear Sir: As to the expensiveness of the plan of gradual emancipation with compensation, proposed in the late Message, please allow me one or two brief suggestions.

Less than one half-day's cost of this war would pay for all the slaves in Delaware at four hundred dollars per head:

Thus, all the slaves in Delaware,

by the Census of 1860, are...............	1798
	400

Cost of the slaves, ...	$ 719,200.
One day's cost of the war.....................	"2,000,000.

Again, less than eighty seven days cost of this war would, at the same price, pay for all in Delaware, Maryland, District of Columbia, Kentucky, and Missouri.

Thus, slaves in Delaware	1798
" " Maryland	87,188
" " Dis. of Col.	3,181
" " Kentucky	225,490
" " Missouri	114,965
	432,622
	400

Cost of the slaves...........................	$173,048,800
Eightyseven days' cost of the war.............................	"174,000,000.

Do you doubt that taking the initiatory steps on the part of those states and this District, would shorten the war more than eighty-seven days, and thus be an actual saving of expense?

A word as to the *time* and *manner* of incurring the expence. Suppose, for instance, a State devises and adopts a system by which the institution absolutely ceases therein by a named day—say January 1st. 1882. Then, let the sum to be paid to such state by the United States, be ascertained by taking from the Census of 1860, the number of slaves within the state, and multiplying that number by four hundred—the United States to pay such sum to the state in twenty equal annual instalments, in six per cent. bonds of the United States.

The sum thus given, as to *time* and *manner*, I think would not be half as onerous, as would be an equal sum, raised *now*, for the indefinite prossecution of the war; but of this you can judge as well as I.

I inclose a Census-table for your convenience. Yours very truly

A. LINCOLN

[1] ALS, owned by Mrs. Ben Sperry, Bushnell, Illinois; LS copy, DLC-RTL. On March 14, Joseph C. G. Kennedy, superintendent of census, supplied Lincoln with census tables upon which Lincoln based this letter (*ibid.*). Senator McDougall continued, however, to oppose compensated emancipation and on March 26 delivered in the Senate a speech which questioned the constitutionality of using federal money for such purposes.

To John G. Nicolay[1]

Memorandum.   Executive Mansion   March 14. 1862

To-day I nominated the ten cadets at large and one for the District of Columbia—for this year.

I have concluded that the next three I nominate shall be as follows—

One for Gov. Seward.

One for Mr. Sec. Welles

One for H. T. Duncan of Kentucky, his candidate's name being "Thomas Collins, Timberlake"

I wish Mr. Nicolay to keep this, and call my attention to it whenever I have an appointment to make.   A. LINCOLN

[1] ADS, DLC-RTL. Henry Timberlake Duncan was a lawyer of Paris, Kentucky. No record of the appointment of either Thomas Collins or Thomas Collins Timberlake has been found.

To the Senate[1]

To the Senate of the United States: March 14, 1862

With reference to my recent Message on the subject of claims of citizens of the United States on the Government of Paraguay, I transmit a copy of three Memorials of the Claimants, and of their closing argument in the case, together with extracts from a despatch from Mr. Bowlin,[2] the late Commissioner of the United States to that country. These extracts show that President Lopez[3] offered and expected to pay a large sum of money as a compromise of the claims.   ABRAHAM LINCOLN

Washington 14th. March 1862.

[1] DS, DNA RG 46, Senate 37B B16. See Lincoln's messages to the Senate, March 5, *supra*, and June 4, *infra*.   [2] James B. Bowlin.

[3] Carlos Antonio Lopez, president and dictator of Paraguay 1840-1862.

To the Senate and House of Representatives[1]

March [14], 1862

To the Senate and House of Representatives.

I submit to Congress the accompanying copy of a correspondence between the Secretary of State, the Danish Chargé d'Affaires and the Secretary of the Navy, concerning the case of the barque "Jorgen Lorentzen," a Danish vessel seized, on her voyage from Rio Janeiro to Havana, by the United States ship "Morning Light," and subsequently released. I recommend the appropriation of the amount of the award of the referees.   ABRAHAM LINCOLN

Washington, March [14], 1862.

[1] DS, DNA RG 46, Senate 37A F2; DS, DNA RG 233, House of Representatives Original Executive Document No. 78. The enclosed correspondence concerned the seizure on December 26, 1861, of the *Jorgen Lorentzen* in the Gulf of Mexico. Lieutenant Henry T. Moore, commanding the *Morning Light*, believed the Danish ship was trying to run the blockade into New Orleans. Moses Taylor, U.S. referee, and Horace Dollner, Danish consul at New York, awarded damages of $1,850, an appropriation for which amount was approved April 25.

To Montgomery C. Meigs[1]

Gen. Meigs   Executive Mansion   March 15. 1862

My dear Sir   The bearer of this—George C. Bestor—is my friend. Please look at his model of Boat, before letting boat-contracts. Yours truly   A. LINCOLN

[1] ALS, IHi. Concerning George C. Bestor, see Lincoln to Andrew Porter, December 30, 1861, *supra*. No further reference to his boat has been found.

To William H. Seward[1]

Hon. Sec. of State.   Executive Mansion. March 15. 1862.

My dear Sir, I am very glad of your note saying "recent despatches from him" (Dryer at Honolulu,) "are able, judicious, and loyal" and that if I agree we will leave him there. I am glad to agree so long as the public interest does not seem to require his removal. Yours truly—   A. LINCOLN.

[1] Copy, DLC-RTL. This item is misdated "1863" in Lapsley (VI, 267). Seward's undated note to which Lincoln is replying is also supplied with an incorrect date "March, 1865," in the Lincoln Papers. See Lincoln to Seward, March 7, *supra*, and memorandum, January 9, 1863, *infra*.

[162]

To Edwin M. Stanton[1]

Executive Mansion Washington,

Hon. Sec. of War—   March 15, 1862.

My dear Sir It is represented to me that Messrs. Hedden & Hoey had a contract with the government, closed on the 26th. of October last, to deliver *fifty* thousand arms by the 15th. of the then next January—that within the time they delivered *twenty-eight* thousand which were accepted and paid for—that, *not on time,* but ten days *after* time, they were ready, and offered to deliver the remaining twenty two thousand, which were refused *simply* on the question of time.

If this statement be true, and these men acted in good faith, I think they should not be ruined by the transaction, but that the guns should be accepted & paid for. Of course I understand the principle of strict law, would not oblige the govt. to take them, even if it were an individual. Yours truly   A. LINCOLN

[1] ADfS, DLC-RTL. Josiah Hedden and John Hoey were contractors in New York City. See Lincoln's letter to Stanton, March 19, *infra.*

To Edwin M. Stanton[1]

This comes from Wilmington, Delaware; and is respectfully submitted to the Secretary of War.   A. LINCOLN

March. 15. 1862.

[1] AES, DLC-RTL. Lincoln's endorsement is written on a telegram from Arthur H. Grimshaw, postmaster at Wilmington, Delaware, March 15, 5:20 P.M: "Col [James] Wallace of Maryland regiment is here to disarm a disloyal company headed by T F Bayard. . . . The arms were procured to use against the United States   Shall Bayard be released & over ride The U S on a pretense of state authority"   General John A. Dix advised Brigadier General Henry H. Lockwood on the same date, that on instructions from Stanton, Wallace was to release Bayard on parole (OR, II, II, 268-69).

To Edward Bates[1]

March 18, 1862

Senator Nesmith concurring with the writer of the within, as he tells me [he] does, the Attorney General will please send me a nomination for William H. Bennett, as Marshal of Oregon

March. 18. 1862.   A. LINCOLN

[1] AES, DNA RG 60, Papers of Attorney General, Appointments, Box 819. Lincoln's endorsement is written on a letter from Lincoln's old friend Simeon Francis, Portland, Oregon, January 17, 1862, to Senator James W. Nesmith, recommending William H. Bennett, "of Washington County, late Sheriff of that County." Bennett's appointment was confirmed by the Senate on April 10, 1862.

To Edwin M. Stanton[1]

March 18, 1862

Let the removal & appointment within requested by Senators
Pomeroy & Lane be made, unless there be some reason to the contrary unknown to me.   A. LINCOLN

March 18. 1862.

[1] AES, DLC-RTL. Lincoln's endorsement is written on a letter from Mark
W. Delahay, March 14, 1862, signed also by Senators Samuel C. Pomeroy and
James H. Lane, recommending "Michael J. Gulish [Greelish?] Esq as a valuable Irish Republican . . . to the Position of Forage Master at Fort Leavenworth in Place of George McGlouflin the Present incumbent for whose removal
we respectfully now ask." The letter also is endorsed in John Hay's handwriting "Referred back from the Secretary of War." No further reference to this
removal and appointment has been found.

To Edwin M. Stanton[1]

United States Military Telegraph,
Head Quarters Army of the Potomac,
Washington, D.C., March 18, 1862.

In going to Fortress-Monroe, Gen. McClellan gets into Gen. Wool's
Department. He must not be interfered with by Gen. Wool. Yet I
do not wish Gen. Wool's feelings hurt, and I am ready to make him
a Major Genl. if it will do any good.

[1] AD, DLC-Ethan A. Hitchcock Papers. The presence of this document,
which is probably a memorandum even though written on a telegraph blank,
in General Ethan A. Hitchcock's papers may be accounted for by reason of the
fact that on April 2 Stanton submitted to Adjutant General Thomas and
General Hitchcock the papers concerned with McClellan's operations in order
that an examination and report might be made on the question of whether
McClellan had followed Lincoln's orders, particularly with reference to the defenses of Washington (OR, I, XI, III, 57). On March 18, McClellan wrote
Stanton, "In order to carry out the object of this army it has now become
necessary that its commander should have the entire control of affairs around
Fort Monroe. I would . . . suggest that the . . . method . . . would be to
merge the Dept of Virginia into that of the Potomac. . . . I . . . request . . .
the present Comdr of the Dept Virginia be assigned to some other command. . . ." (DLC-RTL). This suggestion was not followed, but on March 26
McClellan was given command over Fort Monroe and all Wool's forces, Wool
agreeing to co-operate to the full. On April 3, however, when it became apparent that McClellan was unable to command all that he was taking over, and
perhaps because of growing uneasiness on the part of both Lincoln and Stanton
at McClellan's overweening dispatches, Wool was ordered to "continue in command of Fort Monroe and the troops heretofore assigned to the Department of
Virginia, and General McClellan will command the troops constituting the
Army of the Potomac." (OR, I, XI, III, 65). Wool was promoted to major general for gallant conduct in taking the city of Norfolk on May 10, rather than
for the reason indicated in Lincoln's memorandum to Stanton on March 18.

To Edwin M. Stanton[1]

Executive Mansion, Washington, March 19, 1862.

My Dear Sir: Messrs. Hedden & Hoey having had a contract with the United States government, closed on the 26th day of November last, to deliver fifty thousand arms to the government by the 15th day of January then next, upon specified terms and conditions, and having actually delivered above twenty-eight thousand within the time, which were accepted and paid for, and having been ready and offered to deliver the remainder, not within, but about ten days after, the contract time, which were refused solely on the question of time, and they having acted in good faith, and the arms being still needed by the government, I think fit to order that the question of time be waived by the government, and that the arms be accepted, if again tendered in conformity to the contract in all respects. Yours truly,   A. LINCOLN.

Hon. Secretary of War.

[1] Thirty-seventh Congress, Second Session, *Senate Executive Document No. 72*, p. 57. Upon Stanton's failure to follow Lincoln's instructions of March 15 (*supra*), George Ashmun as a friend of Hedden and Hoey wrote Lincoln on March 19, "Most unaccountably he [Stanton] still hesitates in the matter notwithstanding the plain justice of the case, & your strong letter to him; but says that he shall be glad to be relieved by an order from you for the acceptance of the arms. . . . I . . . am quite sure that unless such an order be given by you inevitable ruin will fall upon the young men in whom I am so much interested." (DLC-RTL).

To Samuel B. Tobey[1]

Executive Mansion,

Dr. Samuel Boyd Tobey: Washington, March 19, 1862.

My dear Sir: A domestic affliction, of which doubtless you are informed, has delayed me so long in making acknowledgment for the very kind and appropriate letter, signed, on behalf, and by direction of a Meeting of the Representatives of the Society of Friends for New-England, held at Providence, Rhode Island the 8th. of second month 1862, by Samuel Boyce, clerk, and presented to me by yourself and associates.

Engaged, as I am, in a great war, I fear it will be difficult for the world to understand how fully I appreciate the principles of peace, inculcated in this letter, and everywhere, by the Society of Friends. Grateful to the good people you represent for their prayers in behalf of our common country, I look forward hopefully to an early end of war, and return of peace. Your obliged friend

A. LINCOLN

[1] AD*f*S, DLC-RTL. William Sprague wrote Lincoln on February 8, 1862, introducing "the bearer Dr Samuel Boyd Tobey and his associates. . . . Dr Tobey is the foremost member of the Society of Friends in New England. . . ." (*Ibid.*). With this letter in the Lincoln Papers is an autograph copy of an address to the president from the meeting of the representatives of the Society of Friends at Providence, Rhode Island, February 5, 1862, expressing loyalty and thanks to the president for his administration, particularly in the settlement of the *Trent* affair. Lincoln confused the date of Sprague's letter with that of the address.

To Francis H. Peirpoint[1]

Hon. F. H. Peirpoint   Executive Mansion,
My dear Sir: Washington, March 20, 1862.
    Yours of the 14th. received. Make haste slowly. Things are improving by time. Draw up your proclamation carefully, and, if you please, let me see it before issuing. Yours very truly

A. LINCOLN

[1] ALS, WvU. On March 14, 1862, Governor Peirpoint wrote that "Owing to the favorable advance of the Federal troops into Virginia, and, I think, the certainty of the rebellion being shortly put down in the State, I deem it important that I should issue a circular letter to the people . . . calling upon them to co-operate with me in restoring the government of the State in accordance with the Ordinance of the convention . . . at Wheeling on the 11th of June 1861. . . ." (DLC-RTL).

To the Senate and House of Representatives[1]

March 20, 1862

To the Senate and House of Representatives:
    The third Section of the "Act further to promote the efficiency of the Navy," approved 21 December 1861, provides,
    "That the President of the United States, by and with the advice and consent of the Senate, shall have the authority to detail from the Retired List of the Navy for the command of Squadrons and single ships such Officers as he may believe that the good of the service requires to be thus placed in command; and such Officers may, if upon the recommendation of the President of the United States they shall receive a vote of thanks of Congress for their services and gallantry in action against an enemy, be restored to the Active List and not otherwise."
    In conformity with this law Captain Samuel F. DuPont, of the Navy, was nominated to the Senate for continuance as the Flag Officer in command of the Squadron which recently rendered such important service to the Union in the Expedition to the coasts of South Carolina, Georgia and Florida.
    Believing that no occasion could arise which would more fully

correspond with the intention of the law or be more pregnant with happy influence as an example, I cordially recommend that Captain Samuel F. DuPont receive a vote of thanks of Congress for his services and gallantry, displayed in the capture, since the 21st. December 1861, of various points on the coasts of Georgia and Florida, particularly Brunswick, Cumberland Island and Sound, Amelia Island, the towns of St. Mary's, St. Mary's [sic] St. Augustine and Jacksonville, and Fernandina.

Washington City,   ABRAHAM LINCOLN
20 March 1862.

[1] DS, DNA RG 233, House of Representatives Original Executive Document No. 82. See Lincoln's similar communication of February 4, *supra*. Since only one vote of thanks was necessary to return Du Pont to the active list and since Du Pont's appointment as flag officer had received Senate approval on March 6, there was no necessity for a further resolution. A joint resolution passed the House on July 2, however, and was read the first and second time in the Senate before being stopped.

To William H. Seward[1]

Secretary of State: March 20, 1862.
Please read this and speak with me about [it] at our next interview.   A. LINCOLN.

[1] OR, II, II, 981. The brackets are in the source. Lincoln's endorsement is written on a letter from L. D. Stickney of Florida, March 19, 1862, asking that James McKay, a wealthy and loyal cattle-raiser of Tampa Bay who was in Washington on parole after having been in Fort Lafayette on charges of blockade running, be permitted to return to Florida. McKay returned to his state, and wrote to Lorenzo Thomas from Key West on April 2, 1862 (*ibid.*).

To Edwin M. Stanton[1]

Hon. Sec. of War   Executive Mansion   March 20. 1862.
My dear Sir: Let George W. B. Tompkins, of New-York, be appointed a Brigadier General of volunteers. Yours truly
A. LINCOLN

[1] ALS, IHi. Stanton replied on March 28, enclosing papers in relation to the promotion of Colonel George W. B. Tompkins of the Eighty-second New York Infantry. Under date of March 17, George T. Brown, sergeant-at-arms to the Committee on the Conduct of the War, reported that Colonel Tompkins had been useful in testifying when Brown was gathering evidence against General Charles P. Stone, and that Tompkins should be protected against reprisals from Stone (DLC-RTL). A letter from General McClellan to Stanton dated March 24 in relation to Brown's report, stated that Stone's charges against Tompkins were misbehavior before the enemy at Bull Run and a set of charges involving a false muster, and that since the papers were with General Nathaniel P. Banks and Stone no longer in command, Tompkins need fear no injustice (*ibid.*). Tompkins was not made a brigadier and left the service May 26, 1862.

[167]

To Henry W. Halleck[1]

Major General Halleck,   Washington,
St. Louis, Mo.   March 21. 1862.

Please suspend the order sending Gen. Denver to Kansas until you hear from the Secretary of War, or myself.

                                       A. Lincoln

[1] ALS (copy?), DLC-RTL. *General Orders No. 7*, Headquarters Department of the Mississippi, March 19, 1862, assigned Brigadier General James W. Denver to command the District of Kansas. *General Orders No. 77*, April 6, 1862, assigned Brigadier General Samuel D. Sturgis to Kansas, and Halleck instructed Sturgis on April 6, to send General Denver "to Fort Scott to take . . . command in that vicinity, and particularly to take the general charge of the Indian tribes. . . ." (OR, I, VIII, 668).

To Mrs. Irvin McDowell[1]

My dear Madam   Executive Mansion   March 21. 1862.

Gen. McDowell did me the honor yesterday to enquire when you could see Mrs. L. If you please she will see you to-day at 2.o'clock.
Yours truly   A. Lincoln

[1] ALS, ORB. The inference that this note was addressed to the wife of General Irvin McDowell is drawn from its contents. Mrs. Lincoln was distraught for a considerable period following the death of her son William Wallace Lincoln, and kept in seclusion from all but intimate friends.

To John C. Frémont[1]

Major General Fremont   Executive Mansion
My dear Sir.   Washington, D.C. March 22. 1862.

This will introduce my friend, Col. Thomas W. Sweeney, of Philadelphia, who has already done some service with volunteers, and is a gentleman of great intelligence and good principles. He would be glad to serve on your staff; but I do not know whether that is possible. Yours truly   A. Lincoln

[1] ALS, owned by Roy A. Heymann, Philadelphia, Pennsylvania. There is no record of Colonel Thomas W. Sweeney's service following his resignation from command of the Ninety-ninth Pennsylvania Infantry on January 24, 1862.

To Edwin M. Stanton[1]

                                 March 22, 1862

I personally know Gen. Palmer, and John Condit Smith; and as the former wants the latter for a Quarter-Master, let the appointment be made.   A Lincoln
   March. 22. 1862.

¹ AES, IHi. Lincoln's endorsement appears on a letter from Brigadier General John M. Palmer, Camp near New Madrid, Missouri, March 12, 1862, recommending an appointment as quartermaster with the rank of captain for "Lieutenant John Condit Smith whom you know personally." Smith was nominated assistant quartermaster on March 26 and confirmed by the Senate on April 1, 1862.

To Horace Greeley¹

Private

Hon. Horace Greeley— Executive Mansion,
My dear Sir: Washington, March 24, 1862.

Your very kind letter of the 16th. to Mr. Colfax, has been shown me by him. I am grateful for the generous sentiments and purposes expressed towards the administration. Of course I am anxious to see the policy proposed in the late special message, go forward; but you have advocated it from the first, so that I need to say little to you on the subject. If I were to suggest anything it would be that as the North are already for the measure, we should urge it *persuasively,* and not *menacingly,* upon the South. I am a little uneasy about the abolishment of slavery in this District, not but I would be glad to see it abolished, but as to the time and manner of doing it. If some one or more of the border-states would move fast, I should greatly prefer it; but if this can not be in a reasonable time, I would like the bill to have the three main features—gradual—compensation—and vote of the people—I do not talk to members of congress on the subject, except when they ask me. I am not prepared to make any suggestion about confiscation. I may drop you a line hereafter. Yours truly A. LINCOLN

¹ ALS, NNP. Greeley's letter to Colfax has not been located, but his reply to Lincoln, presumably incorrectly dated by Greeley "Mar. 24," and certainly incorrectly cataloged in the Lincoln Papers as "Nov. 24, 1862," reads as follows:
"I thank you for your kind letter of yesterday.
"I am sure you will find great patience in the country as well as in Congress with regard to all action respecting slavery if it can only be felt that *things are going ahead.* The stagnation of the grand Army has given life to all manner of projects which would be quiet if the War had been going vigorously on. If you think it best that the bill for Emancipation in the district shall embody a clause of submission to the people of the district, it can easily be so amended. I will advocate it in the Tribune if you desire it. If such vote be deemed requisite, I hope it may be taken on the 4th of July next.
"I hear with regret that there is danger of difference between the Secretary of War and Gen. Fremont. I pray you to see that this be obviated. I do not know that F. is a great general; but I *do* know that our loyal people, with scarcely an exception, are anxious that he should be permitted to *show* what he is. Now if he is left without a decent force—Army *corps*—or not allowed to select his own staff, it will be generally thought that he has been crippled, and the government will be blamed for whatever ill [?] fortune [?] may befall. Pray look to this." (DLC-RTL).

To Edwin M. Stanton[1]

Hon. Sec. of War.   Executive Mansion
My dear Sir   March 24, 1862
Let Ward B. Burnett be appointed a Brigadier General of vol-
unteers. Yours truly   A. LINCOLN

[1] ALS, owned by Charles W. Olsen, Chicago, Illinois. Ward B. Burnett of
New York was nominated a brigadier general on the General Staff, March 25,
but his appointment was tabled by the Senate on July 16.

To Edward Bates[1]

Respectfully submitted to the Attorney General with a strong inclination on my part to grant the pardon requested
March 25. 1862.   A. LINCOLN

[1] AES, DNA RG 204, U.S. Pardon Attorney, A 334. Lincoln's endorsement is
written on an envelope containing letters from John J. Crittenden and others
asking a pardon for Tunstall G. Carter of Kentucky, convicted of stealing
stamped envelopes and sentenced to twenty years' imprisonment. There is no
further record of Lincoln's action.

To John F. Lee[1]

I wish to grant the suspension within requested. Will the Judge
Advocate please carry it into effect.   A. LINCOLN
March 25. 1862.

[1] AES, DNA WR RG 153, Judge Advocate General, Letters Received, No.
136. Lincoln's endorsement is written on the back of a telegram from Governor Beriah Magoffin to John J. Crittenden, March 24, 1862, asking a suspension of the sentence of his brother Ebenezer Magoffin, until "I can get it fairly
before them [Lincoln and Stanton]. I think I can prove . . . he is innocent."
On February 20, 1862, a military commission had sentenced Ebenezer Magoffin to death on a charge of violation of parole, after finding him not guilty on
a charge of murder. Lincoln ordered the sentence suspended, and in April
Lee recommended dismissal of the sentence and release on parole. The prisoner
subsequently escaped at Alton, Illinois, on July 24, 1862 (OR, II, I, 283-374
and II, IV, 487-89). See also Lincoln to Henry W. Halleck, April 9, infra.

To John F. Lee[1]

                                                    March 25, 1862
I wish to grant a pardon in this case, and will be obliged to the
Judge Advocate of the Army, if he will inform me as to the *way*
in which it is to be done.   A. LINCOLN
March 25. 1862

[1] AES, DNA WR RG 153, Judge Advocate General, Letters Received, No.
137. Lincoln's endorsement is written on a petition signed by officers of the
Twenty-third Pennsylvania Volunteers for pardon of Private John James of

Company D, sentenced to three years imprisonment and dishonorable discharge. The petition sets forth that James was but eighteen and in ill health. James received a discharge by order of the president.

To Edwin M. Stanton[1]

The Vice President leaves this with me; & I hope he can be obliged.
March 25. 1862.   A. LINCOLN

[1] AES, DNA WR RG 107, Secretary of War, Personnel Appointments, Box 12. Lincoln's endorsement is written on a memorandum reading "Augustus C. Hamlin Brigade Surgeon," above which Lincoln had written, "Left by the Vice-President." A nephew of the vice-president, Dr. Augustus C. Hamlin was appointed brigade surgeon of Volunteers, April 4, 1862.

To Edwin M. Stanton[1]

Hon. Sec. of War.   Executive Mansion   March 25. 1862
    Sir   Send me a nomination of Amiel W. Whipple, as a Brigadier General of volunteers.   A. LINCOLN

[1] ALS, owned by Charles W. Olsen, Chicago, Illinois. Major Amiel W. Whipple of the Corps of Topographical Engineers was appointed brigadier general April 14, 1862.

To the Senate and House of Representatives[1]

March 26, 1862

To the Senate and House of Representatives:

I transmit a copy of a communication of the 21st of December last, addressed to the Secretary of State by the governor of the Territory of Nevada, and commend to the particular attention of Congress those parts of it which show that further legislation is desirable for the public welfare in that quarter.

Washington, March 26, 1862.   ABRAHAM LINCOLN

[1] Thirty-seventh Congress, Second Session, *Senate Executive Document No. 36*. Governor James W. Nye's communication of December 21, 1861, requested a private secretary and an increase in salaries of federal officials in the territory to meet the high cost of living. No action was taken in either the Senate or the House.

To Edwin M. Stanton[1]

Sec. of War please see the bearer Rev. Mr. Jerome.
March 26. 1862.   A. LINCOLN

[1] ALS-P, ISLA. Reverend John A. Jerome was appointed hospital chaplain of Volunteers, June 20, 1862, but whether he was the bearer of Lincoln's note is not known.

To Edwin M. Stanton[1]

March 26, 1862

I understand a requisition has been made by Governor Yates, according to the memorandum at the bottom of this contract, and that the requisition is refused. Will the Secretary of War please tell me why is this?   A. LINCOLN.

March 26, 1862.

[1] Thirty-seventh Congress, Second Session, *Senate Executive Document No. 72.* Lincoln's endorsement is on a letter from Brigadier General James W. Ripley·to George H. Penfield, dated in error October 11, 1862, but obviously written in 1861, as follows: "By direction of the Secretary of War, I offer you an order for fourteen field batteries. . . . It is understood that an additional quantity of ammunition for the batteries will be supplied hereafter, on requisitions from the Governor of Illinois, when wanted." Stanton's reply follows Lincoln's endorsement:

"The Secretary of War has the honor to report that the above-mentioned requisition is not complied with—

"1st. Because, if necessary for the army, the commanding general . . . is the proper person to make the requisition, in the regular manner, through the Ordnance department.

"2d. It involves large expenditures of public money, when the treasury is in straitened circumstances, which can only be justified through requisitions in the proper official channels." (*Ibid.*, pp. 545-46).

To George D. Ramsay[1]

Col. Ramsay, please find work for the bearer if possible. He will tell you what he can do.   A. LINCOLN

March 27, 1862.

[1] ALS, RPB. The bearer is unidentified.

To Edwin M. Stanton[1]

Sec. of War, please send me a nomination of William B. Lebo as a commissary of subsistence.   A. LINCOLN

March. 27. 1862.

[1] AES, owned by C. L. Mulfinger, Los Angeles, California. Lincoln's endorsement is written on the back of a letter from Senator Henry Wilson, March 27, 1862, suggesting that Lincoln renominate William B. Lebo of Pennsylvania, who "was rejected, not on charges but at the suggestion of a gentleman of Pa." On the bottom of the letter is a concurring note signed by David Wilmot. Lebo's appointment was confirmed by the Senate on April 14, 1862.

To Edwin M. Stanton[1]

March 27, 1862

I wish Major James B. M. Potter, to be appointed a Paymaster in the Regular Army so soon as it can be done without interference

with any former recommendation of mine. Please look on the other side of this scrap.   A. LINCOLN
March 27, 1862.

[1] AES, RPB. Lincoln's endorsement is written on the other side of the same scrap of paper which bears his note to Cameron of June 11, 1861, *supra*. Potter's appointment as major and paymaster in the Regular Army was made July 15, 1864.

To Henry B. Whipple[1]

Executive Mansion, Washington,
Right Reverend Sir   March 27, 1862.
I have the honor to acknowledge the receipt of your esteemed favour of the 6th of March and to state in reply that I have commended the matter of which it treats to the special attention of the Secretary of the Interior.

I have &c &c   Your Obt Servt   A. LINCOLN
H.B. WHIPPLE
Bishop of Minnesota

[1] LS, MnHi. Bishop Whipple's letter of March 6 was concerned with "the sad condition of the Indians of this State, who are my heathen wards. . . . I ask only justice for a wronged and neglected race. . . . The United States has virtually left the Indian without protection. . . . The first thing needed is *honesty*. . . . The second . . . is to frame instructions so that the Indian shall be the ward of the Government. . . ." (Henry B. Whipple, *Lights and Shadows of a Long Episcopate*, pp. 510-14).

To George B. McClellan[1]

Gen. McClellan, please see the bearer, Hon. J. S. Greene, of Mo. He will tell his own story. Oblige him, if you consistently can.
March. 28. 1862   A. LINCOLN

[1] ALS, owned by R. E. Burdick, New York City. James S. Green was U.S. representative from Missouri (1847-1851) and senator (1857-1861). No further reference to his business with General McClellan has been found.

To William H. Seward[1]

March 28, 1862
I believe Dr. Evans has already been appointed Governor of Colorado. If not, let it be done at once, while, at all events, the within is a good voucher to place on file.   A. LINCOLN
March. 28. 1862.

[1] AES, DNA FS RG 59, Appointments, Box 282. Lincoln's endorsement is written on the back of a letter signed by Senator Lyman Trumbull and others, February 19, 1862, recommending John Evans of Evanston, Illinois, for gover-

nor of Colorado. Lincoln had already removed William Gilpin and had nominated John Evans to replace him, March 18, 1862. On March 10, Francis P. Blair, Jr. had written Lincoln concerning the necessity for removing Gilpin, "I feel myself constrained to say that from conversations with Governor Gilpin himself & his own statements to me of his actions there, I am decidedly of opinion that he should be removed & some man of plain common sense put in his place." (DLC-RTL).

To Joseph Smith, John Lenthall, Edward Hartt and Benjamin F. Isherwood[1]

Washington March 28. 1862

To Com. Smith, Constructor Lenthall, Constructor Hart and Engineer in Chief Isherwood

Commissioners to examine Plans and award contracts for building Western Gun-Boats.

Gentlemen   Capt. Joseph Brown is well known to me, as one of the most successful Boat Builders on the Western Waters having built some of the finest, as well as the fastest Boats on the Mississippi River, & he is also a man of great energy.

The commission will do me a personal favor, as well as the country at large by giving the plans presented by him, that attention, which I have no doubt thier merits entitle them to.

ABRAHAM LINCOLN

[1] LS, RPB. Joseph Brown was a builder of steamboats at Cincinnati, Ohio, who subsequently built the *Chillicothe* and *Indianola* for the government.

To Edwin M. Stanton[1]

Hon. Sec. of War.   Executive Mansion   March 28. 1862.

Sir   Let Col. Charles Devens, of Massachusetts be appointed a Brigadier General of Volunteers. Yours truly   A. LINCOLN

[1] ALS-P, ISLA. Devens' appointment was confirmed by the Senate on April 15, 1862.

Pass for James F. Harney[1]

Let Mr. J. F. Harney, bearer of this, proceed to Gen. Wool, at Fortress Monroe.   A. LINCOLN

March 29. 1862.

[1] AES, Lane Collection, Crawfordsville, Indiana. Lincoln's endorsement is written on the back of a letter from Henry S. Lane and James A. Wright, March 28, 1862: "Genl John E Wool   Dear Sir the bearer of this letter Col. [James F.] Harney is an excellent Gentleman true & loyal citizen   he visits Fortress Monroe in order if possible to forward a letter to a Miss Harris at Bedford Virginia   we commend him to your favorable consideration. . . ."

According to a note which accompanies this document, Mary Harris was a kinswoman of Nathan Harris of Indiana, killed in battle. She undertook to escort his body back to Indiana, but being unable to pass through the lines, appealed to James F. Harney for assistance.

To Edwin M. Stanton[1]

Hon. Sec. of War   Executive Mansion   March 29. 1862
Sir: I really wish Jesse W. Fell, of Illinois, to be appointed a Paymaster in the Regular Army, at farthest, as early as the 1st. of July 1862. I wish nothing to interfere with this; and I have so written as much as two months ago, I think. Yours truly

A. LINCOLN

[1] ALS, IHi. On December 23, 1861, Lincoln had written Cameron about Fell's appointment. The appointment was made on June 30, 1862.

To Edward L. Baker[1]

E. L. Baker, Esq   Executive Mansion,
My dear Sir: Washington. March 31. 1862.
Your note to Mr. Edwards, together with that from the War Department to yourself, has been handed to me by your brother John.[2] For me to appoint "Joe"[3] to the Army, and then let him resign his present position is what is objectionable, because it is a substantial transfer. The objection is the setting of examples by which every body in all arms of the service, are set to studying whether they can not squirm round into a position more satisfactory to themselves. A rule, to cut off this, is a necessity. Yours truly

A. LINCOLN

[1] ALS, owned by Philip R. Baker, Pasadena, California. The correspondence mentioned by Lincoln has not been found. "Mr. Edwards" may have been Ninian W. Edwards, Baker's father-in-law.

[2] First Lieutenant John P. Baker of the First Cavalry, who was promoted to captain July 17 and appointed aide-de-camp to Major General William B. Franklin on August 20, 1862.

[3] Probably Joseph F. Baker whom Lincoln had just nominated as a second lieutenant in the Marine Corps on March 19.

To George B. McClellan[1]

Private

Major General McClellan   Executive Mansion,
My dear Sir   Washington, March 31, 1862.
This morning I felt constrained to order Blenker's Division to Fremont; and I write this to assure you that I did so with great pain, understanding that you would wish it otherwise. If you

could know the full pressure of the case, I am confident you would justify it—even beyond a mere acknowledgment that the Commander-in-chief, may order what he pleases. Yours very truly

A. LINCOLN

1 ALS, DLC-McClellan Papers. This letter is misdated March 21, 1862, in Nicolay and Hay (VII, 138). *McClellan's Own Story* (p. 165) states that "the President . . . informed me that the pressure was only a political one to swell Frémont's command" in the Mountain Department in Western Virginia. No more specific details are available, although General Louis Blenker was under considerable political fire at the time in connection with charges of his having illegally assessed the officers and men of his division with "a monthly tax of $500." (New York *Tribune,* March 21, 22, 1862).

To the Senate[1]

To the Senate of the United States: March 31, 1862

I transmit to the Senate, for its consideration with a view to ratification, a treaty of commerce and navigation between the United States and the Ottoman Empire, signed at Constantinople on the 25th. of last month. Extracts from a despatch of the same date upon the subject of the treaty, from Mr. Morris, the United States Minister at Constantinople, to the Secretary of State, are also herewith communicated.

It will be noticed that the exchange of ratifications is to take place within three months from the date of the instrument. This renders it desirable that the Senate should decide in regard to it as soon as this may be convenient; for, if that decision should be favorable, the ratification of this Government must reach Constantinople prior to the expiration of the three months adverted to.

Washington, 31st. March, 1862.   ABRAHAM LINCOLN

1 DS, DNA RG 46, Senate 37B B15. The treaty was ratified on April 9, 1862.

To Edwin M. Stanton[1]

The Secretary of War please discharge this gentleman's son, on such terms (parol, or oath of allegiance) as he (the Sec.) sees fit March 31. 1862.   A. LINCOLN

1 AES, Herbert Wells Fay Collection. Lincoln's endorsement has been removed from the attendant papers and the case cannot be identified.

To Joseph G. Totten[1]

Will Gen. Totten please look over this, and the accompanying drawings, & give me his opinion of them.   A. LINCOLN
April 1. 1862.

1 AES, DNA WR RG 77, Office of Chief of Engineers, P 1099. Lincoln's endorsement is written on a letter from B. Severson, March 31, 1862, criticizing the army engineers for faulty calculation on the construction of the Capitol and adding that "I am quite confident that I could make important improvements in military and naval matters. That I could sink the Merrimac in ten minuites, The Monitor in fifteen minuites, and that I could have reduced the rebel works on Island Number 10 in half the time our forces have already spent. . . ." General Totten replied on April 12, "I have examined the papers of Mr. Severson . . . his claims are so superlative, and . . . so unsupported, that, I can only avow myself unable to credit them." (DLC-RTL).

To Michael Crock[1]

My dear Sir   Executive Mansion   April 2. 1862
     Allow me to thank you in behalf of my little son for your present of White Rabbits. He is very much pleased with them. Yours truly   ABRAHAM LINCOLN
Michael Crock Esq
860 N Fourth St. Philada.

1 LS, ORB. This letter is in John Hay's handwriting except for Lincoln's signature. There is no letter from Michael Crock in the Lincoln Papers, and he has not been further identified.

To Edwin M. Stanton[1]

April 2, 1862
I would suggest that Hon. Stephen T. Logan of Springfield, Illinois, and Col. James Mitchell . . . be appointed as commissioners to examine into claims, etc. at Cairo . . . I would also suggest that John R. Shepley, Esq. of St. Louis be selected as attorney to the said commission.

1 Parke-Bernet Catalog 662, April 16-17, 1945, No. 237. According to the catalog description this is a partial text of an autograph letter signed. The register of letters received by the secretary of War (DNA WR RG 107, P 39) lists this missing letter of April 2. Logan, Mitchell, and Shepley were appointed. On August 1, 1862, the commission closed its hearings at Cairo, having allowed claims in the amount of $451,105.81, among them the claims of Quartermaster Reuben B. Hatch (see Lincoln to John F. Lee, February 1, 1862).

To Henry W. Halleck[1]

Majr. Genl. Halleck   Executive Mansion,
St. Louis, Mo.   Washington, April 3. 1862.
     Col. James A. Barret, with a Cavalry Regiment now at St. Louis, wishes to be ordered to New-Mexico. Let him go, if, in your discretion, you think it not inconsistent with the public interest.
                                      A. LINCOLN

¹ ALS, DLC-RTL; copy, RPB. The copy in John Hay's handwriting was originally in the files of the War Department telegraph office and bears the operator's endorsement "11 54 a m to Philada." Colonel James A. Barret of the Tenth Illinois Cavalry at Benton Barracks near St. Louis telegraphed Lincoln on April 3, "My regiment wishes to be assigned to New Mexico   A word from you to Gen Halleck will suffice." (DLC-RTL).

To Henry W. Halleck¹

Maj Gen Halleck   Washington
Saint Louis   Mo.   April 3. 1862
    Your despatch in regard to Col. Barret's regiment is received. Use your own judgement in the matter.   A LINCOLN.

¹ Copy, RPB. The copy of this telegram is in John Hay's handwriting. General Halleck had replied to Lincoln's preceding telegram (*supra*) that "Col Barretts regt is here under orders to join Gen Curtis in Arkansas   To make the change will require two 2 weeks & will cost . . . about thirty three thousand . . . dollars. I do not feel authorized to make this exchange unless ordered to do so." (DLC-RTL).

To Montgomery C. Meigs¹

April 3, 1862

I do not personally know Capt. Eddy, so as to be able to ask a personal favor for him: yet I protest now, as heretofore, that my asking to have him relieved from duty . . . shall, to no extent, be set down to his disadvantage. I neither *know,* nor have allowed myself to *believe* anything against him. And I shall be glad for you to so place him *that he may not be able to think that he has suffered any by my action.*

¹ Nodle Book Nook Catalog (1940), No. 17. According to the catalog description this letter was written at the request of George Ashmun. This incomplete text is all that is available. Captain Asher R. Eddy of Rhode Island served as quartermaster for Illinois and Wisconsin, at Springfield, from September 27, 1861, to January 25, 1862. On February 27, 1862, Jesse K. Dubois telegraphed Lincoln, "In defiance of your authority Quartermaster Eddy is still here and is making mischief   I urge that he & all his Assistants be immediately sent away." (DLC-RTL).

To William H. Seward¹

Respectfully submitted to the Secretary of State, Mr. Bennett, the Delegate, presents this & is for the appointment.
April 3. 1862.   A. LINCOLN

¹ AES, DNA FS RG 59, Appointments, Box 263. Lincoln's endorsement is written on an envelope containing a series of recommendations of George

E. Crater. Hiram P. Bennet, delegate to congress from Colorado Territory, apparently favored Crater for appointment as secretary of state for Colorado in place of Lewis L. Weld, resigned, but see Lincoln to Seward, April 7, *infra*.

To Edwin M. Stanton[1]

Executive Mansion, April 3. 1862

The Secretary of War will order that one, or the other of the corps, of Gen. McDowell and Gen. Sumner, remain in front of Washington until further orders from the Department,—to operate at, or in the direction of Ma[na]ssas junction, or otherwise as occasion may require; that the other corps, not so ordered to remain, go forward to Gen. McClellan as speedily as possible; that Gen. McClellan commence his forward movement from his new base at once; and that such incidental modifications as the foregoing may render proper, be also made.   ABRAHAM LINCOLN

[1] ADS, DLC-Stanton Papers. On April 2, 1862, Brigadier General James S. Wadsworth reported to Stanton a total of 19,022 troops present for the defense of Washington and stated that "looking at the numerical strength and character of the force under my command, it is in my judgment entirely inadequate to and unfit for the important duty to which it is assigned." (OR, I, XI, III, 60-61). On the same day, Stanton requested Adjutant General Lorenzo Thomas and Major General Ethan A. Hitchcock "to report to me whether the President's order and instructions have been complied with in respect to . . . the defense of Washington. . . ." (*Ibid.*, p. 57). Thomas and Hitchcock replied also on the same day, that the president's order "has not been fully complied with." (*Ibid.*, p. 62).

To Edwin M. Stanton[1]

Respectfully submitted to the Secretary of War, with the request that the appointment be made so soon as it consistently can.

April 3. 1862.   A. LINCOLN

[1] AES, DNA WR RG 107, Secretary of War, Personnel Appointments, Box 14. Lincoln's endorsement is written on a letter from William A. Newell, April 2, 1862, asking appointment of Nehemiah Merritt of New Brunswick, New Jersey, as a lieutenant in the Regular Army. Nehemiah Merritt was appointed captain and additional aide-de-camp to General Frémont, May 13, 1862.

To Edwin M. Stanton[1]

If the whole, or any part of the within request of Gen. Cook can consistently be complied with, let it be done.   A. LINCOLN

April 3. 1862.

[1] AES, IHi. Lincoln's endorsement is written on a letter of Brigadier General John Cook, Springfield, Illinois, March 26, 1862, to Senator Lyman Trumbull, requesting his assistance in obtaining appointments "to my staff, viz. Dr.

R. L. Metcalfe, Surgeon 7th Inf'y. Ills. vols. to be Brigade Surgeon and Lieut Benjamin F. Smith, same Regt. to be Capt and Asst Adjt Genl." Benjamin F. Smith was nominated to Cook's staff on April 9 and confirmed by the Senate on April 21. Dr. Richard L. Metcalf remained surgeon of the Seventh Illinois until he resigned on September 15, 1863.

To Henry W. Halleck[1]

Major Gen. Halleck   Executive Mansion,
St. Louis, Mo.   Washington, April 4, 1862.

I am sorry to learn that, after all, Gen. Denver has gone to Kansas. Can not Gen. Davies go there. There is a hard pressure on me in this matter.   A. LINCOLN

[1] ALS, DLC-RTL; copy, RPB. The copy in John Hay's handwriting was originally in the files of the War Department telegraph office. Brigadier General Thomas A. Davies had been assigned to the Department of the Mississippi on March 25, and Brigadier General James W. Denver on orders from Halleck had assumed command at Fort Leavenworth on April 2. Major General Ethan A. Hitchcock had written Halleck on March 22, that Secretary Stanton "conversationally told me that Jim Lane had been to him to-day with an order from the President for you not to put Denver in command in Kansas, but that Davies . . . was to be assigned to that command. He told me that his answer to Lane was a positive refusal to attend to any such order. . . ." (OR, I, VIII, 832-33). There is no reply from Halleck in the Lincoln Papers, but on April 7, he reported to Stanton that Denver had been assigned to the Indian Territory (*ibid.*, p. 672).

To Montgomery C. Meigs[1]

April 4, 1862

Q. M. General, please let the bearer, Geo. C. Bestor, withdraw the papers of Lt. Ferguson.

[1] Parke-Bernet Catalog 304, October 22-24, 1941, No. 697a. "Lt. Ferguson" has not been identified.

To Edwin M. Stanton[1]

If Mr. Clemens can be sent to Gen. McClernand, on the terms indicated, let it be done.   A. LINCOLN

Appril 4, 1862

[1] AES, RPB. Lincoln's endorsement is written on a letter from Sherrard Clemens, former member of Congress (1852-1853, 1857-1861), Wheeling, Virginia, March 26, 1862, to Stanton requesting that he "be allowed to act, (*at my own expense*) as a volunteer aid, to Genl. McClernand, with whom I served in Congress, or as aid to some other General, who will have command at New Orleans. . . ." On April 9, Lorenzo Thomas endorsed that "Mr. Clemens could not, without military rank, act in the capacity of Aide. . . ." No action was taken by Stanton, and Clemens later served in the Confederate Army.

To Edwin M. Stanton[1]

April 4, 1862

The within I know to be a genuine letter of the late Col. Baker. The young man has *not* been appointed; but he must be as soon as he consistently can   A. LINCOLN

April 4. 1862.

[1] AES, IHi. Lincoln's endorsement appears on a letter of Edward D. Baker to Lieutenant George Williams of Oregon, July 11, 1861:

"The Secretary of War has just promised me to appoint you a Second Lieutenant in the Regular Army.

"I hope to send you your commission in a few days. Go to work and study tactics."

George Williams was nominated a second lieutenant in the Fourth U.S. Infantry on April 5 and was confirmed by the Senate on April 14, 1862.

To the House of Representatives[1]

To the House of Representatives: April 5, 1862

In compliance with the resolution of the House of Representatives of yesterday, requesting any information which may have been received at the Department of State showing the system of revenue and finance now existing in any foreign country, I transmit a copy of a recent despatch from Mr. Pike, the United States Minister at the Hague. This is understood to be the only information on the subject of the resolution, recently received, which has not been made public.   [ABRAHAM LINCOLN][2]

Washington, 5th. April, 1862.

[1] DS, DNA RG 233, Original Executive Document No. 99. The resolution requesting "any information which may have been received at the Department of State showing the system of revenue and finance in any foreign countries" is in the *House Journal* under date of April 3 rather than April 4, as Lincoln designates it. On April 9, Lincoln's communication and the copy of James S. Pike's letter of March 12, 1862, summarizing the methods of taxation in the Netherlands, were referred to the Committee on Ways and Means and ordered to be printed.   [2] Signature has been clipped.

To George B. McClellan[1]

United States Military Telegraph.

Received Apl 6th. 1862.

To Maj. Gen McClellan   From Washington Apl 6th.

If you wish anything from Mr Short[2] in the way of fire shells or the like telegraph to the Department or to me designating what it is   A LINCOLN

1 Copy, DLC-McClellan Papers. The received copy of Lincoln's telegram in the McClellan Papers has no endorsement and there is no reply in the Lincoln Papers. See further, Lincoln's memorandum of March 23, 1863.
2 Levi Short, a chemist and inventor of Buffalo, New York.

To George B. McClellan[1]

Majr. Genl. McClellan   Washington,
Fortress Monroe—   April 6. 1862. [8 P.M.]

Yours of 11. A.M. to-day received. Sec. of War informs me that the forwarding of transportation, amunition, & Woodburys, brigade, under your orders, is not, and will not be interfered with. You now have over one hundred thousand troops, with you independent of Gen. Wool's command. I think you better break the enemies' line from York-town to Warwick River, at once. They will probably use *time*, as advantageously as you can   A. LINCOLN

1 ALS, RPB. McClellan's telegram of 11 A.M. complained that "The order forming new Departments, if rapidly enforced, deprives me of the power of ordering up wagons & troops absolutely necessary. . . . I respectfully request I may not be placed in this position, but that my orders for wagon trains ammunition, and other material that I have prepared and necessarily left behind, as well as [Daniel P.] Woodbury's brigade, may at once be complied with. . . ." (DLC-RTL). In an earlier dispatch from near Yorktown, 7:30 P.M., April 5, received by Lincoln the morning of the 6th, McClellan reported that the enemy were "in large force" and "being reinforced daily," and that "Under these circumstances I beg that you will reconsider the order detaching the first corps from my command. . . . I am now of the opinion that I shall have to fight all of the available force of the Rebels, not far from here. Do not force me to do so with diminished numbers. . . ." (*Ibid.*). In reply to Lincoln's telegram, McClellan telegraphed on April 7, "I have the honor to state that my entire force for duty, only amounts to about eighty five thousand. . . . Genl Wools command . . . has been taken out of my control. . . . The only use that can be made of his command, is to protect my communication in rear. . . ." (*Ibid.*).

To William H. Seward[1]

Let Samuel H. Elbert, of Nebraska be appointed Secretary of Colorado, in place of ——— Weld, resigned   A. LINCOLN
April 7, 1862.

1 AES, DNA FS RG 59, Appointment Papers, Resignations. Lincoln's endorsement is written on a letter of resignation from Lewis L. Weld, secretary of State for Colorado, April 7, 1862. Samuel H. Elbert's appointment was confirmed by the Senate on April 14, 1862.

To Edwin M. Stanton[1]

April 7, 1862

Hon. John A. Gurley says there is a necessity of this appointment, owing to the condition of things at Cincinnati; and that the Sec. of

War is willing to make it, if I consent. If so, I consent. One appointee[2] at Cincinnati, resigns I understand.   A. LINCOLN

April. 7. 1862.

[1] AES, DNA WR RG 107, Secretary of War, Personnel Appointments, Box 13. Lincoln's endorsement is written on a letter of recommendation signed by Governor William Dennison and others for the appointment of Colonel A. E. Jones "late Aid-de-Camp to Governor Dennison" as a brigadier general of Volunteers to be assigned to command of Camp Dennison at Cincinnati. The letter also bears John A. Gurley's concurring endorsement. For further developments, see Lincoln to Stanton, April 29, *infra*.
[2] General Melancthon S. Wade.

To Edwin M. Stanton[1]

Discharge this boy   A. LINCOLN

April 7, 1862

[1] AES, owned by J. L. Balderson, Beverly Hills, California. Lincoln's endorsement is scrawled on a letter from William H. Purnell, postmaster at Baltimore, April 6, 1862, introducing a Mrs. Dalrymple who sought the discharge of her younger brother, Charles T. M. Duvall, a private in Company E of the Purnell Legion of Maryland Infantry, because she was a widow dependent on him for her support. Stanton's endorsement, above Lincoln's, is as follows: "This case has been presented to the Secretary of War who regrets that official duty compels him to deny the application." A clerk's notation on the back of the letter reads "Dis. ordered April 7/62."

To Edwin M. Stanton[1]

April 7 [8?], 1862

Respectfully submitted to the War Department. I personally know Mr. Manly to be a good man. The within are excellent, and ample recommendations. His application has been before the Department half a year, and he should be appointed a Quarter-Master, so soon as it can consistently be done.   A. LINCOLN

April 7 [8?], 1862.

[1] AES, IHi. The date appears to be a "7" written over an "8," but may be the reverse. The endorsement is written on an envelope containing recommendations of Uri Manly of Marshall, Illinois, for appointment as assistant quartermaster. See further, Lincoln to Stanton, December 23, *infra*.

To Henry W. Halleck[1]

Major General Halleck   Executive Mansion
Saint Louis Mo: Washington, April 9, 1862.

If the rigor of the confinement of Magoffin at Alton, is endangering his life, or materially impairing his health, I wish it mitigated so far as it can be, consistently with his safe detention.

                   A. LINCOLN.

[183]

¹ Copy, RPB. The copy in John Hay's handwriting, originally in the files of the War Department telegraph office, carries Hay's endorsement "Please send above, by order of President." See Lincoln to John F. Lee, March 25, *supra*.

To George B. McClellan¹

Major General McClellan.   Washington,
My dear Sir.   April 9. 1862

Your despatches complaining that you are not properly sustained, while they do not offend me, do pain me very much.

Blencker's Division was withdrawn from you before you left here; and you knew the pressure under which I did it, and, as I thought, acquiesced in it—certainly not without reluctance.

After you left, I ascertained that less than twenty thousand unorganized men, without a single field battery, were all you designed to be left for the defence of Washington, and Manassas Junction; and part of this even, was to go to Gen. Hooker's old position. Gen. Banks' corps, once designed for Manassas Junction, was diverted, and tied up on the line of Winchester and Strausburg, and could not leave it without again exposing the upper Potomac, and the Baltimore and Ohio Railroad. This presented, (or would present, when McDowell and Sumner should be gone) a great temptation to the enemy to turn back from the Rappahanock, and sack Washington. My explicit order that Washington should, by the judgment of *all* the commanders of Army corps, be left entirely secure, had been neglected. It was precisely this that drove me to detain McDowell.

I do not forget that I was satisfied with your arrangement to leave Banks at Mannassas Junction; but when that arrangement was broken up, and *nothing* was substituted for it, of course I was not satisfied. I was constrained to substitute something for it myself. And now allow me to ask "Do you really think I should permit the line from Richmond, *via* Mannassas Junction, to this city to be entirely open, except what resistance could be presented by less than twenty thousand unorganized troops?" This is a question which the country will not allow me to evade.

There is a curious mystery about the *number* of the troops now with you. When I telegraphed you on the 6th. saying you had over a hundred thousand with you, I had just obtained from the Secretary of War, a statement, taken as he said, from your own returns, making 108,000 then with you, and *en route* to you. You now say you will have but 85,000, when all *en route* to you shall have reached you. How can the discrepancy of 23,000 be accounted for?

As to Gen. Wool's command, I understand it is doing for you

precisely what a like number of your own would have to do, if that command was away.

I suppose the whole force which has gone forward for you, is with you by this time; and if so, I think it is the precise time for you to strike a blow. By delay the enemy will relatively gain upon you—that is, he will gain faster, by *fortifications* and *re-inforcements*, than you can by re-inforcements alone.

And, once more let me tell you, it is indispensable to *you* that you strike a blow. *I* am powerless to help this. You will do me the justice to remember I always insisted, that going down the Bay in search of a field, instead of fighting at or near Mannassas, was only shifting, and not surmounting, a difficulty—that we would find the same enemy, and the same, or equal, intrenchments, at either place. The country will not fail to note—is now noting— that the present hesitation to move upon an intrenched enemy, is but the story of Manassas repeated.

I beg to assure you that I have never written you, or spoken to you, in greater kindness of feeling than now, nor with a fuller purpose to sustain you, so far as in my most anxious judgment, I consistently can. *But you must act.* Yours very truly

A. LINCOLN

1 ALS, DLC. See Lincoln to McClellan, April 6, *supra*, for excerpts from McClellan's dispatches.

Memorandum[1]

What possible injury can this lad work upon the cause of this great Union? I say let him go. A. LINCOLN.

April 10, 1862.

1 Leslie J. Perry, "Appeals to Lincoln's Clemency," *The Century Magazine*, LI (December, 1895), 255. Perry describes Lincoln's endorsement merely as being "on a large bundle of papers covering but a single case, and that unimportant."

Proclamation of Thanksgiving for Victories[1]

April 10, 1862

By the President of the United States of America.

A Proclamation.

It has pleased Almighty God to vouchsafe signal victories to the land and naval forces engaged in suppressing an internal rebellion, and at the same time to avert from our country the dangers of foreign intervention and invasion.

It is therefore recommended to the People of the United States that, at their next weekly assemblages in their accustomed places of public worship which shall occur after notice of this proclamation shall have been received, they especially acknowledge and render thanks to our Heavenly Father for these inestimable blessings; that they then and there implore spiritual consolations in behalf of all who have been brought into affliction by the casualties and calamities of sedition and civil war, and that they reverently invoke the Divine Guidance for our national counsels, to the end that they may speedily result in the restoration of peace, harmony, and unity throughout our borders, and hasten the establishment of fraternal relations among all the countries of the earth.

In witness whereof, I have hereunto set my hand and caused the seal of the United States to be affixed.

[L.S.]   Done at the City of Washington, this tenth day of April, in the year of our Lord one thousand eight hundred and sixty-two, and of the Independence of the United States the eighty-sixth.

By the President: ABRAHAM LINCOLN
WILLIAM H. SEWARD, Secretary of State.

[1] DS, DNA FS RG 11, Proclamations.

To the Senate[1]

To the Senate of the United States: April 10, 1862

I transmit to the Senate, for its consideration, with a view to ratification, a treaty between the United States and Her Britannic Majesty, for the suppression of the slave trade. A copy of the correspondence between the Secretary of State and Lord Lyons, on the subject of the treaty, is also herewith transmitted.

Washington, 10th. April, 1862.   ABRAHAM LINCOLN

[1] DS, DNA RG 46, Senate 37B B7. This letter, accompanied by the correspondence between Seward and Lord Lyons, was printed as *Senate Executive Document No. 57*. The treaty was unanimously ratified by the Senate on April 24, 1862.

To Richard Yates and William Butler[1]

Hon. R. Yates, & Wm. Butler   Washington,
Springfield, Ills.   April 10. 1862

I fully appreciate Gen. Pope's splendid achievements with their invaluable results; but you must know that Major Generalships in the Regular Army, are not as plenty as blackberries.

A. LINCOLN

[1] ALS, DLC-RTL. Governor Yates and State Treasurer William Butler telegraphed on April 9, 1862, "We appeal to you to transfer Maj Genl John Pope to the regular army with his present rank as a token of gratitude to Illinois. Give one of her sons a position in the U.S. army who has so gloriously achieved the just reward we ask for him." (DLC-RTL). On April 7-8 Pope's command, together with six ironclads and ten mortar boats under command of Andrew H. Foote, had captured Island No. 10 in the Mississippi below Cairo, Illinois.

Memorandum:
Appointment of John C. Robinson[1]

[c. April 11, 1862]

To-day Mr. Duell, of New-York, personally asks to have Col. John C. Robinson, appointed a Brig. Genl. Resides in N.Y. & is W.P. Says Maryland men are for him. Hon. Mr. Calvert personally calls and endorses.

[1] AD, IHi. Although undated, this memorandum must have been written about April 11, on which day Colonel John C. Robinson of the First Michigan Volunteers was nominated brigadier. His nomination was confirmed by the Senate on April 28. Although Lincoln specifies that Robinson "is W.P.," Robinson did not graduate at West Point, but was a cadet from 1835 to 1838. Robert H. Duell was a congressman from New York.

To Edwin M. Stanton[1]

April 11, 1862

Col. Harvey Brown wishes his brevet of date, Nov. 22nd 1861, be conferred to take date as of the 16th of April 1861—the day on which he relieved Fort Pickens. If this be at all admissable, let it be done.

[1] Parke-Bernet Catalog 841, February 25, 1947, No. 165. According to the catalog description, this communication is an autograph letter signed. No record has been found of the requested modification in the date of Brown's brevet as brigadier general.

To William H. Seward[1]

These are excellent, and ample recommendations; and I hope something worthy of the applicant may be found for him ere long.

April 12, 1862.   A. LINCOLN

[1] AES, DNA FS RG 59, Appointments, Box 291. Lincoln's endorsement is written on an envelope containing a letter from Edward D. Gazzam, April 10, 1862, enclosing recommendations for an appointment to foreign service. Gazzam was a Republican of Pittsburgh, Pennsylvania. No record of his appointment has been found.

To William H. Seward[1]

Sec. of State, please see the bearer, Miss Alice Lightner.
April 12, 1862.   A. LINCOLN

[1] Ben Bloomfield List DI 2 (1949), No. 98. According to the catalog description Lincoln's note is written on a small card and accompanied by a note from Seward to Stanton, "The President refers Miss Lightner to me, but you have absorbed my functions. I refer her to you with commendations." Miss Lightner's business with Seward and Stanton probably had to do with a state prisoner, and a likely possibility is that the person was A. S. Lightner of Alexander County, Illinois, who had been arrested and released on oath June 23, 1861 (OR, II, II, 35).

To Whom It May Concern[1]

Executive Mansion,
Whom it may concern.   Washington, April 12, 1862
Mr. Charles C. Lathrop, bearer of this, is vouched to me as a worthy and loyal gentleman; He wishes to serve as a volunteer aid to some of our generals, and I am quite willing for him to do so, with any one of them who may see fit to avail himself of his services.   A. LINCOLN

[1] ALS, RPB. There is no record of Lathrop's military service. He was from New Jersey and later was a member of the legislature of that state.

To the House of Representatives[1]

To the House of Representatives: April 14, 1862
In compliance with the resolution of the House of Representatives of the 3d ultimo, requesting information in regard to the present condition of Mexico, I transmit a report from the Secretary of State and the documents by which it was accompanied.
Washington, April 14, 1862.   ABRAHAM LINCOLN.

[1] Thirty-seventh Congress, Second Session, House of Representatives Executive Document No. 100. Seward's report transmitted by Lincoln is printed in the source, pp. 5-434.

Memorandum Concerning Stephen Baker[1]

[April 15—May 3, 1862?]
Hon. Mr. Baker, writer of the within, says he has had no appointment, little or large, from his District, except the local ones, and he particularly wishes these. I desire that he may be obliged.
Yours truly,   A. LINCOLN

[1] Tracy, p. 205. This item is placed by Tracy between April 15 and May 3, 1862. The original has not been located, and no further references have been found to appointments desired by Representative Stephen Baker of Poughkeepsie, New York.

To James W. Ripley[1]

April 15, 1862

What reason is there that the appraisement made by Major Hagner, and adopted & acted upon by Capt. Crispin, should not stand, so far as it went   A. LINCOLN

April 15, 1862.

[1] AES, RPB. Lincoln's endorsement is written on a letter from Captain Silas Crispin, ordnance officer at New York, to Messrs. S. Dingee & Co., April 1, 1862, "In accordance with instructions received from Ordnance Department this day I have to offer you a voucher for that portion of last inspected lot of your arms. . . . As regards the balance of the lot I conceive it to be clearly my duty . . . to assess their value before issuing voucher, and as you have expressed yourself unwilling to submit to any other basis of settlement than that heretofore offered you by Maj [Peter V.] Hagner I have referred the matter to Washington for decision." For further developments, see Lincoln to Ripley, April 23, *infra*.

To the Senate[1]

To the Senate   Washington, D.C.
of the United States.   April 15. 1862.

I transmit herewith, for the consideration and such constitutional action as the Senate may deem proper to take, a treaty negotiated on the 6th March 1861, between late Agent Vanderslice,[2] on the part of the U.S. and certain delegates of the Sac and Fox, of the Missouri, and the Iowa tribes, of Indians; also certain petitions of said tribes praying that the treaty may be ratified with an amendment as set forth in said petitions.

A letter of the Secretary of the Interior, with a report of the Comr. of Indian Affairs and letter of the present agent of the Indians accompany the treaty and petitions.

ABRAHAM LINCOLN.

[1] DS, DNA RG 46, Senate 37B C6. On February 3, 1863, the treaty was reported with amendments and unanimously ratified as amended.
[2] Daniel Vanderslice of Kentucky.

To the Senate[1]

To the Senate of the United States: April 15, 1862

In consequence of the delay attending the approval by the Senate of the Extradition Treaty with Mexico, signed on the 11th. December last, it is impossible to effect the exchange of ratifications of that, and the Postal Convention of the same date, within the period assigned by those instruments.

I recommend therefore the passage of a Resolution, at the earliest practicable moment, extending the time specified in the 8th. Article of the Extradition Treaty, and in the 12th. Article of the Postal Convention for the exchange of ratifications, for sixty days from and after the 11th. June, next, the date of the expiration of the period named for that purpose in both instruments.

Washington, 15 April 1862.   ABRAHAM LINCOLN

1 DS, DNA RG 46, Senate 37B B13. See Lincoln's earlier communications concerning the treaty and the convention with Mexico, December 17, 1861, and January 28, 1862, *supra*. The Senate had amended the treaty before ratifying it, and additional time was required to obtain Mexico's ratification. On April 15 the Senate adopted a resolution extending the time for ratification.

To the Senate[1]

To the Senate of the United States: April 15, 1862

On the 26th. June 1860, the Senate approved of the Treaty of Friendship and Commerce between the United States and Nicaragua signed on the 16th. March, 1859, with certain amendments.

On the next day, namely, 27th. June, 1860, the Senate adopted a resolution extending the period for the exchange of the ratifications of the Treaty, for six months from that day, that is, until the 27th. December, 1860.

Altho' the amendments of the Senate were immediately transmitted to our Minister in Nicaragua for submission to the Government of that Republic, he failed, notwithstanding earnest efforts, to induce that government to call an extra session of Congress, to take into consideration the amendments of the Senate of the United States, within the supplementary time named in the Resolution of 27th. June, 1860, for the exchange of ratifications.

It was not until the 25th. March, 1861—nearly three months after the expiration of the six months extended by the Senate Resolution, that the Congress of Nicaragua acted favorably upon the amendments of the Senate of the United States.

A translation of the decree of the Nicaraguan Government approving the Treaty as amended, with an additional amendment is herewith enclosed.

It will be perceived that while the ratification of Nicaragua recites literally the *second* amendment of the Senate, and accepts it with an additional clause, it does not, in explicit terms, accept the *first* amendment of the Senate, striking out the last clause of the 16th. Article.

[190]

That amendment is of so much importance, that the adoption or rejection of it by the Government of Nicaragua should not be left to construction or inference.

The final amendment of that government properly extended the time of exchanging ratifications for an additional twelve months. That time has expired. For obvious reasons connected with our internal affairs, the subject has not sooner been submitted to the Senate, but the Treaty is now laid before that Body, with this brief historical sketch and the decree of the Nicaraguan Government, for such further advice as may be deemed necessary and proper in regard to the acceptance or rejection of the amendments of Nicaragua. ABRAHAM LINCOLN

Washington, 15th. April 1862.

[1] DS, DNA RG 46, Senate 37B B14. On May 7, 1862, Senator Sumner reported a resolution consenting to the adoption and ratification of the amendment proposed by Nicaragua and extending the time for ratification. The resolution was unanimously agreed to on May 9.

To Edwin M. Stanton[1]

April 15, 1862

I do not sign the within, because I do not know but there is good reason, known to the Secretary of War, why the course indicated should not be taken. But if no such reason is known, I think that course should be adopted; and therefore I respectfully submit the subject to the Secretary of War. A. LINCOLN

April 15, 1862.

[1] AES, IHi. Lincoln's endorsement is written on a memorandum from Montgomery C. Meigs, April 15, 1862, recommending that the War Department "take immediately all necessary measures to have all boats, scows, and other property used in repairing and navigating the [Chesapeake and Ohio] Canal restored to their rightful owners. If boats have been used for the uses of the Army or Navy and cannot be restored, they are forthwith to be paid for, so that trade on the Canal may be revived." Meigs' endorsement dated April 18 is as follows: "Secy directs that all but about 36—including those sent down the river . . . be released." *General Orders No. 44*, April 21, 1862, made the restoration.

To Edwin M. Stanton[1]

April 15, 1862

Respectfully submitted to the Secretary of War, with the remark that Mr. Blair says the writer's word is good to the utmost hair's-breadth for what he says. A. LINCOLN

April 15, 1862.

[1] AES, RPB. Lincoln's endorsement is written on a letter from Major Robert Allen, quartermaster at St. Louis, to Montgomery Blair, April 4, 1862, requesting aid in getting an appointment as brigadier general. "The rank to which I attached no value a little while ago has become desirable by the change in the geography of the Department since it takes in Col. [Thomas] Swords who ranks me and I become subordinate to him." Allen's appointment as brigadier general of Volunteers was confirmed by the Senate on June 11, 1862.

Message to Congress[1]

April 16, 1862

Fellow citizens of the Senate, and House of Representatives.

The Act entitled "An Act for the release of certain persons held to service, or labor in the District of Columbia" has this day been approved, and signed.

I have never doubted the constitutional authority of congress to abolish slavery in this District; and I have ever desired to see the national capital freed from the institution in some satisfactory way. Hence there has never been, in my mind, any question upon the subject, except the one of expediency, arising in view of all the circumstances. If there be matters within and about this act, which might have taken a course or shape, more satisfactory to my jud[g]ment, I do not attempt to specify them. I am gratified that the two principles of compensation, and colonization, are both recognized, and practically applied in the act.

In the matter of compensation, it is provided that claims may be presented within ninety days from the passage of the act "but not thereafter"; and there is no saving for minors, femes-covert, insane, or absent persons. I presume this is an omission by mere over-sight, and I recommend that it be supplied by an amendatory or supplemental act.   ABRAHAM LINCOLN

April 16. 1862.

[1] ADS, ORB. Lincoln's suggestion concerning supplemental legislation was carried out by Senate Bill 351, approved July 12, 1862.

To James W. Ripley[1]

I shall be very much obliged, if Mr. Ellsworth can be assigned to duty where the work will be lighter.   A. LINCOLN

April 16. 1862.

[1] AES, owned by C. Norton Owen, Glencoe, Illinois. Lincoln's endorsement is written on a letter from First Lieutenant Thomas G. Baylor at Fort Monroe Arsenal to General Ripley, April 15, 1862, asking that Ephraim D. Ellsworth, assigned to the Arsenal as military storekeeper, be relieved because of health. The father of Elmer E. Ellsworth remained in government employment until he was retired on a pension.

To Edwin M. Stanton[1]

Sec. of War, please oblige Gen. Fremont, as within, if consistent with the public service. A. LINCOLN

April 17. 1862.

[1] AES, owned by Dale Carnegie, New York City. Lincoln's endorsement is written on a letter from Major General John C. Frémont to Senator Samuel C. Pomeroy, April 14, 1862, asking his influence to have D. Henry Burtnete appointed to Frémont's staff. Burtnete, who had been dismissed as lieutenant colonel of the Second New York Artillery on December 9, 1861, was appointed major and assistant aide-de-camp on Frémont's staff, June 10, 1862, but was dismissed again on November 25, 1862, for absence without leave, breach of arrest, and conduct unbecoming an officer.

To John Eastham[1]

Executive Mansion,
My Dear Sir Washington, April 18., 1862.

I have the honor to acknowledge the receipt from you of a very fine copy of your Photograph of the "Treaty of Commerce."

Be good enough, my dear Sir, to accept the assurance of my grateful appreciation of your kindness, and believe me Very Sincerely Yours ABRAHAM LINCOLN

To Mr John Eastham
22 St. Ann's Square
Manchester

[1] LS, ICHi. There is no letter from John Eastham in the Lincoln Papers, and he has not been further identified.

To the Senate and House of Representatives[1]

April 18, 1862

To the Senate and House of Representatives:

I transmit to Congress a copy of a correspondence between the Secretary of State and Benjamin E. [H.] Brewster, of Philadelphia, relative to the arrest, in that city, of Simon Cameron, late Secretary of War, at the suit of Pierce Butler, for trespass, *vi et armis,* assault and battery, and false imprisonment.

Washington, April 18, 1862. ABRAHAM LINCOLN.

[1] Thirty-seventh Congress, Second Session, *Senate Executive Document No. 43.* The correspondence between Cameron's attorney, Benjamin H. Brewster, and Secretary Seward, April 16 and 18, 1862, was referred to the Committee on the Judiciary in each house. Pierce Butler of Philadelphia, a South Carolinian by birth and a secession sympathizer who was accused of accepting a Confederate commission, was arrested August 15, 1861, on Secretary Cameron's order, and imprisoned at Fort Lafayette from August 20 to September 24, 1861, when he was released on pledge that he would do no act hostile to the U.S. and would not visit South Carolina without a passport from the Department of

State. Butler brought suit against Cameron as a "result of consultation among the Breckinridge leaders, who intend to divide and conquer your administration, and thus bring themselves into power. The Governor of Penna. has directed his law adviser to examine our constitution and laws, with the determination to avert the proceedings, if he can do so—but I apprehend Congress only can apply the proper remedy. . . ." (Cameron to Lincoln, April 17, 1862, DLC-RTL). The case was dropped before coming to trial.

To Edwin M. Stanton[1]

Executive Mansion   April 18 [?] 1862

It is impossible for me to devote sufficient time to the consideration of this case to determine as to its merits. I can only refer the case of Mr. Meyer to the attention of the Secretary of War.

A. LINCOLN

[1] ES, ORB. The endorsement in John Hay's hand but signed by Lincoln, is written on a letter from Henry F. Meyer to Lincoln, April 8, 1862. The date is indistinct but appears to be April 18. The petition and documents attached show that the case had already gone to Stanton, and that no action had been taken. Meyer, an architect and civil engineer, was a member of the Engineer Corps of the Fifth New York Militia, who at the end of a three months' enlistment in the spring of 1861, had been briefly employed by the Coastal Survey and had then returned to New York City to organize as captain a company in a new regiment. Being attacked and seriously wounded one night by unidentified assailants in Central Park, Meyer was confined to a hospital for a long time. Upon his release, he found himself mustered out of service. His petition was for back pay and expenses for recruiting his company.

To Edward Bates[1]

April 19, 1862

Will the Attorney General please examine this case and give me his opinion whether the accounting officers should pay this claim, the Resolution of Congress to the contrary notwithstanding.

April 19. 1862.   A. LINCOLN.

[1] AES, DNA GE RG 60, Papers of Attorney General, Segregated Lincoln Material. Lincoln's endorsement is written on an unsigned memorandum to the Attorney General, April 18, 1862, asking a decision in regard to an act of congress for the relief of the widow and other heirs of George Fisher of Florida. Bates' opinion has not been located. A joint resolution approved on March 2, 1861, had repealed earlier legislation of June 1, 1860, and June 3, 1858, regarding claims for destruction of property by U.S. troops in suppressing Indian hostilities in 1813.

Memorandum[1]

April 19, 1862

I scarcely think the son can be made a Brigadier General, under the circumstances but I should be glad for the father to be breveted

a Brigadier General, if it can be done consistently with the Army
rules. A. LINCOLN
April 19. 1862.

[1] ADS, owned by C. M. Rogers, Chicago, Illinois. Lincoln's memorandum
has been removed from attendant papers, and the identity of the persons concerned has not been established.

To Edward Bates[1]

If the Attorney General thinks proper, I have no objection to the
leave of absence being given as asked. A. LINCOLN
April 21. 1862.

[1] AES, DNA GE RG 60, Papers of Attorney General, Segregated Lincoln
Material. Lincoln's endorsement is written on a letter from Senators James
A. McDougall and Milton S. Latham asking a leave of absence for Mathew
H. McAllister, judge of the U.S. Circuit Court at San Francisco. Attorney
General Bates granted the leave for a period of six months. See Lincoln's
communication to the House of Representatives June 12, *infra*, for further
developments.

To George B. McClellan[1]

Major Gen. McClellan Washington City, D.C.
Near York-Town. April 21, 1862

Your despatch of the 19th. was received that day. Fredericksburg is evacuated and the bridges destroyed by the enemy—and a
small part of McDowell's command occupies this side of the Rappahannock opposite the town. He purposes moving his whole force
to that point. A. LINCOLN

[1] ALS, RPB. McClellan's dispatch of April 18, 11:30 P.M., but with date
line Washington, D.C., April 19, 9 A.M., reads in part as follows: "Confidential—
If compatible with your impressions as to the security of the Capital and not
interfering with operations of which I am ignorant I would be glad to have
[George A.] McCall's Division so as to be enabled to make a strong attack
upon West Point. . . . After all that I have heard of things which have occurred since I left Washington and before I would prefer that Genl McDowell
should not again be assigned to duty with me." (DLC-RTL).

To James G. Berret[1]

Executive Mansion,
Hon. James G. Berret. Washington, April 22. 1862.

My dear Sir: With some reluctance and in accordance with the
request made in your letter of the 17th, I have withdrawn the
nomination of yourself to the Senate to be one of the commissioners under the act of congress abolishing slavery in the District of

Columbia. In so far as your letter assumes that the tendering you the office without your solicitation or knowledge, attests my confidence in your loyalty to the United States, now and heretofore, you are entirely right. So far, however, as it assumes that, in my judgment, your imprisonment mentioned, was wholly undeserved, an explanatory word from me is due. I think you made a mistake which justified men having less evidence to the contrary than I had, to suspect your loyalty, and to act accordingly. The arrest, though made by my general authority, was in fact made without my knowledge at the time; but being done, the question of undoing it was a little different from that of the original making; and required a little time to solve it satisfactorily.

[1] ADf, DLC-RTL. Lincoln's draft was probably never completed, nor the letter sent. Berret's letter of April 17 is not in the Lincoln Papers. Mayor Berret had been arrested in August, 1861, and confined at Fort Lafayette until September 14, when he was released on oath and upon condition that he resign from office (OR, II, II, 598-99).

To John A. Dahlgren[1]

Capt. Dahlgren, please see Mr. Hitchcock, & appoint a time to meet him & me here   A. LINCOLN
April 22, 1862

[1] ALS, American Swedish Historical Museum, Philadelphia. "Mr. Hitchcock" may have been Ethan A. Hitchcock.

To Edwin M. Stanton[1]

April 22, 1862.

I personally know Julius White, and that he is worthy. Having successfully commanded a Brigade at Pea Ridge, I think he should be made a Brigadier General.   A. LINCOLN
April 22. 1862.

[1] AES, IHi. Lincoln's endorsement appears on a letter from Representative Isaac N. Arnold, April 22, 1862, requesting appointment of Colonel Julius White, Thirty-seventh Illinois Volunteers, as a brigadier general. White was nominated brigadier general of Volunteers on April 22 and was confirmed by the Senate on June 9, 1862.

To James W. Ripley[1]

Executive Mansion, Washington, April 23, 1862.

It is said that in the case of the contract of S. Dingee & Co. in relation to arms a dispute has arisen as to the proper construction of a clause in an order signed by me, which clause is in these words: "and that all not conforming thereto" (the contract) "be appraised by the ordnance officer at New York, and received at such price as he may determine."

This order was prepared with reference to *a definite number* of arms expected to be delivered within a *definite time*, and not in reference to an *indefinite* number to be delivered in an *indefinite time*. I certainly did not expect that under the clause in question a lot of guns would be appraised at one price at one time, and another lot of precisely the same quality appraised at different prices at another time. I expected that when under the clause the price of a particular quality of gun was fixed it would stand throughout the transaction, neither going down or up. I still think this is the just construction.   A. LINCOLN.

[1] Thirty-seventh Congress, Second Session, *Senate Executive Document No. 72*, p. 116. Solomon Dingee and Company of New York had a contract to deliver 53,500 Austrian-made Enfield rifles at $19 each. On January 10, 1862, Cameron wrote Ripley that "After a careful examination . . . it has been determined that you shall receive the guns offered in accordance with terms of contract. . . . The guns that may not conform to terms . . . you will purchase at their value, of which such ordnance officer as you may designate shall be the judge. . . ." (*Ibid.*, p. 106). Major Peter V. Hagner, ordnance officer at New York, had set valuations on certain arms offered but not conforming to terms of contract. Captain Silas Crispin (see Lincoln to Ripley, April 15, *supra*), who replaced Hagner, refused to allow the valuations placed on the arms, interpreting Cameron's letter of January 10 to mean that the ordnance officer in charge should evaluate in accordance with the market value at the time of offering. The case was finally settled by Dingee's offer, accepted by Stanton, June 25, 1862, to substitute English Enfield rifles at $19 in sufficient numbers to complete the contract within ninety days.

To Montgomery Blair[1]

Hon. Post-Master-General   Executive Mansion,
My dear Sir   Washington, April 24, 1862

The member of Congress from the District including Tiffin O calls on me about the Post-Master at that place. I believe I turned over a despatch to you from some persons there, asking a suspension, so as for them to be heard, or something of the sort. If nothing, or nothing amounting to anything, has been done, I think the suspension might now be suspended, and the commission go forward. Yours truly   A. LINCOLN

[1] ALS, IaHA. Warren P. Noble, Democrat of Tiffin, Ohio, was the representative, and William Gallup was the postmaster as listed in the *U.S. Official Register*, 1863.

To David P. Holloway[1]

I join in asking an early examination.   A. LINCOLN
April 24, 1862.

[1] AES, DNA IR RG 241, Patent No. 35,311. Lincoln's endorsement is written on a note from Senator Benjamin F. Wade requesting Commissioner of Patents David P. Holloway to give an early examination to an application for a patent filed on April 23 by William F. Goodwin of Powhatan, Ohio. Goodwin's patent, described as an "Improvement in Breech-loading Ordnance," was issued on May 8, 1862.

Reply to Lorenzo Montufar[1]

April 24, 1862

Mr. MONTUFAR: At any time the arrival of a Minister from San Salvador would be an interesting event. It is peculiarly so now. Republicanism is demonstrating its adaptation to the highest interests of society—the preservation of the State itself against the violence of faction. Elsewhere on the American continent it is struggling against the inroads of anarchy, which invites foreign intervention.

Let the American States, therefore, draw closer together and animate and reassure each other, and thus prove to the world that, although we have inherited some of the errors of ancient systems, we are nevertheless capable of completing and establishing the new one which we have now chosen. On the result largely depends the progress, civilization, and happiness of mankind.

[1] New York *Tribune*, April 26, 1862. Upon presenting his credentials to the president, Don Lorenzo Montufar, minister from San Salvador, made an appropriate speech to which Lincoln replied.

To the Senate[1]

Executive Mansion, Washington, April 24th. 1862.

To the Senate of the United States:—In obedience to your resolution of the 17th. inst. I herewith communicate the testimony and judgment of the recent Naval Court of Inquiry in the case of Lieutenant Charles E. Fleming of the United States Navy. Also the testimony and finding of the Naval Retiring Board in the case of said Lieutenant Fleming.

I have the honor to state that the judgment and finding aforesaid have not been approved by me.   ABRAHAM LINCOLN

[1] DS, DNA RG 46, Senate 37A F2. The resolution introduced by Senator Grimes on April 17 not only requested the testimony and finding of the court, but also whether the judgment had been approved by the president. Dismissed

from the Navy in 1857 for drunkenness and disobedience to orders, Fleming was reappointed lieutenant in 1859. A court of inquiry again found him guilty of intemperance and incompetence. He was, however, promoted to lieutenant commander on July 16, 1862. Secretary Welles recorded in his *Diary* on August 10 (I, 77) that the promotion was "most objectionable."

To Luiz I[1]

April 25, 1862

Abraham Lincoln,
President of the United States of America.

To His Majesty Dom Luiz I,
    King of Portugal,
        &c., &c., &c.

Great and Good Friend: I have received the letter which Your Majesty was pleased to address to me on the 7th. of January, last, conveying the melancholy tidings of the decease of His Royal Highness the Most Serene Infante Dom Joao [*sic*], Your Majesty's beloved brother.

I participate in the grief occasioned by this sad event and offer to Your Majesty and to your royal household my sincere condolence.

May God have Your Majesty always in His safe and holy keeping! Your Good Friend,   ABRAHAM LINCOLN.

Washington, April 25, 1862.
By the President:
    WILLIAM H. SEWARD, Secretary of State.

[1] Copy, DNA FS RG 59, Communications to Foreign Sovereigns and States, III, 189.

To the House of Representatives[1]

To, The House of Representatives,   April 26, 1862

In compliance with the Resolution of the House of Representatives of the 24th. of February last, requesting information in regard to insurgent privateers, in foreign ports, I transmit a Report from the Secretary of State and the documents by which it was accompanied.   [ABRAHAM LINCOLN.]

[Washington, April 26, 1862.]

[1] DS, DNA RG 233, Original Executive Document No. 104. The signature and date have been clipped from the document, but are restored from the printing in *House of Representatives Executive Document No. 104*. Seward's report of April 26, 1862, transmitted by Lincoln, may also be found in the printed document pp. 5-211.

To Edwin M. Stanton[1]

Sec. of War please make an order carefully in accordance with the within.   A. LINCOLN

April 26. 1862.

[1] AES, NHi. Lincoln's endorsement is written on a letter from Milton S. Latham, April 26, 1862, requesting that authority be given "to Brigham Young in Salt Lake City to raise, arm & equip one hundred men for ninety days service to be used in protecting the property of the Telegraph & overland mail companies" against hostile Indians until "our own troops can reach the point where they are so much needed." Adjutant General Lorenzo Thomas issued the authorization to Brigham Young on April 28, 1862 (OR, III, II, 27).

To Andrew Johnson[1]

Gov. Andrew Johnson   Washington City, D.C.
Nashville, Tenn.   April 27. 1862.

Your despatch of yesterday just received—as also, in due course, was your former one. The former one, was sent to Gen. Halleck, and we have his answer, by which I have no doubt he, Gen. Halleck, is in communication with you before this. Gen. Halleck understands better than we can here, and he must be allowed to control in that quarter. If you are not in communication with Halleck, telegraph him at once, fully, and frankly.

A. LINCOLN

[1] ALS, RPB. This telegram is misdated April 27, 1861, in Hertz (II, 830). On April 24 Governor Johnson had telegraphed Horace Maynard that an order transferring the Third Minnesota Regiment from Nashville was "subtantially surrendering the country to the rebels." Stanton communicated the telegram to Halleck on April 25, and Halleck replied from Pittsburg Landing on April 26, "Troops cannot be detached from here on the eve of a great battle. . . . We cannot hunt up disloyalists at present. We are now at the enemy's throat, and cannot release our great grasp to pare his toe-nails." On April 26, Johnson telegraphed Lincoln that the Sixty-ninth Ohio, ordered to Nashville, had upon arrival been ordered to another point. "I hope you will send an order at once . . . that the regiment remain at this place. . . . (OR, I, X, II, 126, 128-29).

To Lulu Waldron[1]

Executive Mansion, Washington, April 27, 1862.

My Dear Young Friend   Allow me to express to you my very sincere thanks for your kindness in sending me those elegant studs of Pipestone. Very truly   Your friend   A. LINCOLN

[1] LS, owned by Mrs. Max Robertson, Rapid City, South Dakota. Lulu Waldron, the daughter of Judge George P. Waldron of Yankton, Dakota Territory, sent Lincoln some shirt studs which she had carved from pipestone.

To Henry W. Bellows[1]

Dr. Bellows, of Sanitary Commission, please see Mr. Nellis, the bearer.   A. LINCOLN
April 28, 1862

[1] Stan. V. Henkels Catalog 1384, December 18, 1925, No. 297. According to the catalog description, Lincoln's note is on a card. "Mr. Nellis" has not been identified. The Reverend Henry W. Bellows, D.D., of New York, was president of the U.S. Sanitary Commission.

To Hannibal Hamlin[1]

War Department
Washington City, D.C. April 28th. 1862
Sir; In answer to the Resolution of the Senate in relation to General Charles Stone, I respectfully state that he was arrested and imprisoned under my authority and with my sanction, upon evidence which, whether he be guilty or innocent, required in my judgment such proceedings to be had against him for the safety and welfare of the Country. He has not been tried because in the state of Military operations at the time of his arrest, and ever since, the Officers to constitute a Court, and for Witnesses, could not be withdrawn from duty, without serious injury to the service. He will be tried without any unnecessary delay, the Charges and Specifications will be furnished him in due season, and every facility for his defence will be afforded by the War Department.
Respectfully Yours,   ABRAHAM LINCOLN
Hon. Hannibal Hamlin.
President of the Senate.

[1] LS, DLC-RTL. On April 30, 1862, Senator Henry Wilson of the committee on military affairs wrote Lincoln, "I notice that your note is dated at the War Department and I would suggest that it might cause some comment when printed. Would it not be better to change it." (DLC-RTL). Recopying and revising the letter somewhat, Lincoln sent it again addressed to the Senate on May 1, *infra.*

To Edwin M. Stanton[1]

Respectfully submitted to the Sec. of War, requesting a fair hearing for the applicant.   A. LINCOLN
April. 28. 1862.

[1] AES, owned by Dale Carnegie, New York City. Lincoln's endorsement has been removed from attendant papers in the War Records, but immediately following Lincoln's endorsement is a concurring endorsement by Isaac N. Arnold which provides a clue. The Register of letters received by the Secretary

of War (DNA WR RG 107 P 61) lists a letter of this date, "Endorsed and submitted for Col. William S. Johnston, Jr. Endorsed by I. N. Arnold, introducing and recommending Lt. William Goldie who comes to settle account of Mechic. Fusilliers." William Goldie served as first lieutenant and quartermaster of the Fifty-sixth Illinois Infantry, October 1, 1861—February 1, 1862. The "Mechanic Fusilliers" formed a portion of this regiment. Goldie was nominated captain and quartermaster of Volunteers, May 2, 1862, and confirmed by the Senate on June 30.

To George B. McClellan[1]

Major General McClellan.   Executive Mansion,
Near York-Town, Va.   Washington, April 29, 1862.

Would it derange, or embarrass your operations, if I were to appoint Capt. Charles Griffin, a Brigadier General of volunteers? Please answer.   A. LINCOLN

(Send in Cypher)

[1] ALS-P, ISLA; LS, RPB. McClellan replied on April 30, 9 P.M., "It will not at all embarrass or interfere with my arrangements if you appoint Capt Chas Griffin. . . . All goes well." (DLC-RTL). Captain Charles Griffin of the Fifth Artillery was nominated brigadier general of Volunteers on May 1 and confirmed by the Senate on June 9, 1862.

To Edwin M. Stanton[1]

I think as much as two weeks ago, I directed the appointment of Col. Jones, named within. Let it be done.   A. LINCOLN
April 29. 1862.

[1] AES, owned by C. L. Mulfinger, Los Angeles, California. Lincoln's endorsement is written on a letter from John A. Gurley addressed to "Mr. Hay, Private Secretary of the President," April 28, 1862, calling attention to the fact that the recommendation for appointment of Colonel A. E. Jones (see Lincoln to Stanton, April 7, supra) had been misplaced, and requesting that the appointment be made as soon as possible. Colonel A. E. Jones was nominated brigadier general of Volunteers on April 29, but failed to get confirmation by the Senate when his nomination was tabled on July 16, 1862.

To Edward Bates[1]

May 1, 1862
If Mr.   Anconia, Rep. of the Reading District & Mr. Stevens, Rep. of Lancaster District,[2] will investigate this case and say in writing, they wish the young man pardoned, I will do it.
May 1. 1862.   A. LINCOLN

[1] AES, DNA RG 204, U.S. Pardon Attorney, A 413. Lincoln's endorsement is written on a letter from Representative James H. Campbell of Pottsville, Pennsylvania, April 29, 1862, asking a pardon for Emanuel Riffert (Rifford,

[202]

Rifferd) convicted in the District of Columbia on charges of larceny. See Lincoln to Bates May 13, *infra*.
2 Sydenham E. Ancona and Thaddeus Stevens were the representatives.

To John A. Dahlgren[1]

Thomas Fitzgerald, the bearer, wants to work. I shall be obliged if Capt. Dahlgren can find employment for him.

May. 1, 1862.   A. LINCOLN

[1] ALS-P, ISLA. There is no reply in the Lincoln Papers, and Thomas Fitzgerald has not been identified.

To Henry W. Halleck[1]

War Department, May 1, 1862.

Major-General Halleck, Pittsburg Landing, Tenn:

I am pressed by the Missouri members of Congress to give General Schofield independent command in Missouri. They insist that for want of this their local troubles gradually grow worse. I have forborne, so far, for fear of interfering with and embarrassing your operations. Please answer, telling me whether anything, and what, I can do for them without injuriously interfering with you.

A. LINCOLN.

[1] OR, I, XIII, 368. Halleck replied by telegraph from Pittsburg, Tennessee, May 2, that Brigadier General John M. Schofield "has entire command of the Missouri Militia in United States service and the Volunteers in two thirds of the State He has been informed that his District will comprise the entire state as soon as Genl Curtis comes south. This is more than his rank entitles him to If he is intriguing for more he is not honest I would rather resign than to have him given an independent command in my Department. I have yielded much to the importunities of his friends but they ask still more." (DLC-RTL).

To George B. McClellan[1]

(CYPHER)

Major Gen. McClellan   Executive Mansion,
Near York-Town, Va.   Washington, May 1, 1862.

Your call for Parrott guns from Washington alarms me—chiefly because it argues indefinite procrastination. Is anything to be done?   A. LINCOLN

[1] ALS, DLC-RTL; copy, RPB. The copy of this message is in John Hay's handwriting, and was originally in the files of the telegraph office of the War Department. McClellan's dispatch to Stanton of 11 P.M., April 28, announced that he would "soon be ready to open. Would be glad to have the 30-pounder Parrotts in the works around Washington at once." (OR, I, XI, III, 126). His

reply to Lincoln of 9:30 P.M., May 2, explained, "I asked for the Parrott guns from Washington for the reason that some expected had been two weeks nearly on the way and could not be heard from They arrived last night My arrangements had been made for them and I thought time might be saved by getting others from Washington My object was to hasten not procrastinate. All is being done that human labor can accomplish" (DLC-RTL).

To the Senate[1]

Executive Mansion, Washington,
To the Senate of the United States: May 1– 1862
   In answer to the Resolution of the Senate in relation to Brigadier General Stone, I have the honor to state that he was arrested, and imprisoned under my general authority, and upon evidence which, whether he be guilty or innocent, required, as appears to me, such proceedings to be had against him for the public safety. I deem it incompatable with the public interest, as also perhaps, unjust to General Stone, to make a more particular statement of the evidence.
   He has not been tried because in the state of military operations, at the time of his arrest and since, the officers to constitute a court-martial, and for witnesses, could not be withdrawn from duty without serious injury to the service. He will be allowed a trial without any unnecessary delay; the charges and specifications will be furnished him in due season; and every facility for his defence will be afforded him by the War Department.

   [1] ADf, DLC-RTL. This message is a revision of Lincoln's letter to Hamlin, April 28, *supra*, in answer to a resolution passed by the Senate on April 22. It was read in the Senate on May 2, and ordered to lie on the table and be printed. General Charles P. Stone was not released from arrest until August 16, 1862, and did not return to duty until May, 1863.

To the Senate[1]

To the Senate of the United States: May 1, 1862
   In accordance with the suggestion of the Secretary of the Treasury contained in the accompanying letter, I have the honor to transmit the enclosed petition and report thereon of the Third Auditor for the consideration of Congress.
   Executive Mansion,   ABRAHAM LINCOLN.
   Washington, May 1, 1862.

   [1] Thirty-seventh Congress, Second Session, *Senate Executive Document No. 46*. The petition, dated November 1, 1861, from Oregon and Washington Territory, complained that the Third Auditor was wrong in reducing an award

to citizens for goods advanced to the U.S. during the Indian uprising in 1855-1856, and also complained that no bonds had yet been received to take care of the award as specified in an act of congress approved March 2, 1861. Third Auditor Robert J. Atkinson's report called attention to the fact that congress had accepted the reduced award and passed the act of March 2 based on it, and that $941,219.38 had been paid of the total $2,800,000 awarded.

To Edward Bates[1]

May 3, 1862

This petition for pardon is presented by Senator Chandler, and earnestly urged by him.

May 3. 1862. A.L.

The Attorney General will please make out a pardon in this case.

May 16, 1862. A. LINCOLN

[1] AES, DNA RG 204, U.S. Pardon Attorney, A 380. Lincoln's endorsements are written on an envelope containing the petition presented by Senator Zachariah Chandler for pardon of James Ranking of Washington, D.C., sentenced in June, 1861, to three years on charges of robbery.

Memorandum:
Appointment of George W. Garrett[1]

Executive Mansion, Washington, May 3, 1862.

To-day Mr. Senator Wright introduces a Committee of Citizens of this District consisting of William Dixon, William Wise, Henry Lee, Reuben Bacon, Henry D. Gannell [Grinnell?], W. J. Murta[u]gh, James H. Lusby who asks the appointment of George W. Garrett as Warden of Penitentiary. A. LINCOLN.

[1] Tracy, p. 206. Senator Joseph A. Wright of Rockville, Indiana, was appointed to fill the vacancy in the Senate caused by expulsion of Senator Jesse D. Bright and served from February 24, 1862 to January 14, 1863. No further record concerning the appointment of George W. Garrett has been found.

To Edwin M. Stanton[1]

Executive Mansion,

Hon. Sec. of War. Washington, May. 3. 1862.

Let Stephen G. Burbridge, of Kentucky, be appointed a Brigadier General of volunteers. Yours truly A. LINCOLN

[1] ALS, owned by C. Norton Owen, Glencoe, Illinois. Colonel Stephen G. Burbridge of the Twenty-sixth Kentucky Infantry was appointed brigadier general of Volunteers June 9, 1862.

[205]

To Edwin M. Stanton[1]

May 5, 1862

On enquiry into this case I think it due to Lt. Colonel G. Montagu Hicks that he be appointed an Aide de Camp of General Wool with the rank of Colonel as upon his recommendation and assigned to General McDowell. Let it be done.

May 5th. 1862.   A. LINCOLN.

[1] Copy, DLC-RTL. The copy is contained in a letter from George Montagu Hicks, Metropolitan Hotel, Washington, D.C., May 22, 1862, complaining that "This order the Secretary of War refuses to carry out, thus not only placing me in the position of inability to act on the instructions of the Commander in Chief, but also leaving the inference that the highest power in this country is not vested in its President." For Lincoln's comment see the memorandum of May 22, *infra*. No record of Hicks' military service or further identification has been found.

To Edwin M. Stanton[1]

I think it would be proper to appoint Eugene Sullivan a Lieutenant in the regular Army, if there be any vacancy not committed to any other.   A. LINCOLN

May 5. 1862.

[1] AES, IHi. Lincoln's endorsement appears on a letter from Captain Charles H. Tompkins, Fifth U.S. Cavalry, May 5, 1862, recommending Private Eugene Sullivan of Company B for a commission. Stanton endorsed: "Referred to the Adjutant General."

To Edwin M. Stanton[1]

May 5, 1862

Sec. of War please give fair and respectful consideration to the within recommendations of Miss Dix.

[1] Parke-Bernet Catalog 760, April 9, 1946, No. 60. The Register of letters received by the secretary of War (DNA WR RG 107 P 60) lists this missing endorsement and indicates that the persons recommended by Dorothea L. Dix, superintendent of women nurses in army hospitals, were Dr. John M. Cuyler and Dr. Joseph R. Smith. On June 11, Cuyler was promoted to medical inspector with rank of lieutenant colonel and Smith to surgeon with rank of major. Miss Dix also gave praise to Surgeon Meredith Clymer for his management of a hospital in Philadelphia.

To Edwin M. Stanton[1]

May 6, 1862

The enclosed recommendation from the Govr. of Pennsylvania is respectfully referred to the consideration of the Secretary of War.   A. LINCOLN

May 6. 1862

[1] ES, RPB. The endorsement was written by John Hay and signed by Lincoln on a letter from Governor Andrew G. Curtin, May 5, 1862, recommending a promotion for Colonel George H. Crosman, quartermaster at Philadelphia and Schuylkill Arsenal. George H. Crosman was brevetted brigadier general October 1, 1862, for meritorious and faithful services in charge of depot of clothing and equipment at Philadelphia.

To Louis M. Goldsborough[1]

Head-quarters, Department of Va.
Flag officer Goldsborough   Fort Monroe, Va. May 7, 1862.

Sir   Major General McClellan telegraphs that he has ascertained by a reconnaisance that the battery at Jamestown at Jamestown [sic] has been abandoned, and he again requests that gunboats may be sent up the James River.

If you have tolerable confidence that you can successfully contend with the Merrimac without the help of the Galena and two accompanying gunboats send the Galenana [sic] and two gunboats up the James River at once. Please report your action on her to me at once. I shall be found either at Gen Wools Head Quarters or on board the Miami   Your Obedient Servt.   A. LINCOLN.

[1] Copy, DLC-Stanton Papers. The copy is in Stanton's handwriting. McClellan's message to Stanton, Williamsburg, May 7, 1862, requested the "Galena and other gunboats to move up James River." The message also replied to a request for a meeting, "I dare not leave my command in the present state of affairs, so that it is really impossible for me to go to the rear to meet the President and yourself." (OR, I, XI, III, 146). Flag Officer Goldsborough's reply to Lincoln's message has not been located, but Stanton's dispatch to McClellan, May 7, midnight, promised, "An expedition under command of Captain Rodgers will . . . be sent up the James River to-night, consisting of the Galena and two gunboats. . . . Is there anything else you want?" (Ibid., p. 147).

To Edwin M. Stanton[1]

[May 7, 1862]
Let this appointment be made if there be any vacancancy [sic] not already committed to any other.   A. LINCOLN

[1] AES, owned by Charles W. Olsen, Chicago, Illinois. Lincoln's endorsement is written on a letter signed by Senator Zachariah Chandler and several members of Congress, May 7, 1862, recommending appointment of Simeon J. Davenport as second lieutenant of cavalry. There is no record of his appointment.

To George B. McClellan[1]

Major General McClellan   Head-quarters, Department of Va.
Williamsburg: Fort Monroe, Va. May 9. 1862.

The President is unwilling to have the Army corps organization broken up; but also unwilling that the commanding General shall be trammelled, and embarrassed, in actual skirmishing collision with the enemy, and on the eve of an expected great battle; you therefore may temporarily suspend that organization, in the Army now under your immediate command, and adopt any you see fit until further orders. He also writes you privately.

¹ ADf, DLC-Stanton Papers. The draft is entirely in Lincoln's handwriting, but the telegram was sent over Stanton's signature.

To George B. McClellan¹

Major General McClellan.   Fort Monroe, Va.
My dear Sir: May 9, 1862.

I have just assisted the Secretary of War in framing the part of a despatch to you, relating to Army Corps, which despatch of course will have reached you long before this will. I wish to say a few words to you privately on this subject. I ordered the Army Corps organization not only on the unanimous opinion of the twelve Generals whom you had selected and assigned as Generals of Division, but also on the unanimous opinion of every *military man* I could get an opinion from, and every modern military book, yourself only excepted. Of course, I did not, on my own judgment, pretend to understand the subject. I now think it indispensable for you to know how your struggle against it is received in quarters which we cannot entirely disregard. It is looked upon as merely an effort to pamper one or two pets, and to persecute and degrade their supposed rivals. I have had no word from Sumner, Heintzelman, or Keyes.² The commanders of these Corps are of course the three highest officers with you, but I am constantly told that you have no consultation or communication with them; that you consult and communicate with nobody but General Fitz John Porter, and perhaps General Franklin.³ I do not say these complaints are true or just; but at all events it is proper you should know of their existence. Do the Commanders of Corps disobey your orders in any thing?

When you relieved General Hamilton⁴ of his command the other day, you thereby lost the confidence of at least one of your best friends in the Senate. And here let me say, not as applicable to you personally, that Senators and Representatives speak of me in their places as they please, without question; and that officers of the army must cease addressing insulting letters to them for taking no greater liberty with them.

But, to return, are you strong enough—are you strong enough, even with my help—to set your foot upon the necks of Sumner,

Heintzelman, and Keyes all at once? This is a practical and very serious question for you.

The success of your army and the cause of the country are the same; and of course I only desire the good of the cause. Yours truly   A. LINCOLN.

¹ Copy, DLC-RTL; copy, DLC-Stanton Papers. The copy in the Stanton Papers is in Stanton's handwriting. McClellan's dispatch to Stanton, received May 9, 12:19 A.M., reads in part as follows: "I respectfully ask permission to reorganize the army corps. I am not willing to be held responsible for the present arrangement, experience having proved it to be very bad, and it having very nearly resulted in a most disastrous defeat. I wish either to return to the organization by division or else be authorized to relieve incompetent commanders of army corps. Had I been one-half hour later on the field on the 5th we would have been routed. . . . Notwithstanding my positive orders I was informed of nothing that had occurred. . . . At least a thousand lives were really sacrificed by the organization into corps.

"I have too much regard for the lives of my comrades and too deep an interest in the success of our cause to hesitate for a moment. I learn that you are equally in earnest, and I therefore again request full and complete authority to relieve from duty with this army commanders of corps or divisions who prove themselves incompetent." (OR, I, XI, III, 153-54). No reply from McClellan has been located. The Army Corps organization was retained, but on May 18 *General Orders No. 125* established the Fifth and Sixth Provisional Corps under Generals Fitz-John Porter and William B. Franklin.

² Brigadier General Edwin V. Sumner commanded the Second Corps, Brigadier General Samuel P. Heintzelman the Third Corps, and Brigadier General Erasmus D. Keyes the Fourth Corps.

³ Brigadier General Fitz-John Porter was a division commander in Heintzelman's Third Corps and Brigadier General William B. Franklin a division commander in Major General Irvin McDowell's First Corps.

⁴ On April 30 Brigadier General Charles S. Hamilton was replaced as commander of the Third Division of the Third Corps by Brigadier General Philip Kearny.

To Louis M. Goldsborough¹

Flag officer Goldsborough   Fort Monroe Va   May 10 1862

My dear Sir   I send you this copy of your report of yesterday for the purpose of saying to you in writing that you are quite right in supposing the movement made by you and therein reported was made in accordance with my wishes verbally expressed to you in advance. I avail myself of the occasion to thank you for your courtesy and all your conduct so far as known to me during my brief visit here   Yours very truly   A LINCOLN

¹ Copy, DLC-Stanton Papers. The copy is in Stanton's handwriting, written on the back of Goldsborough's report of May 9, which summarized the action of the *Monitor* and other vessels in shelling the batteries on Sewell's Point, and calling attention to the fact that "the Merrimac did not engage the Monitor, nor did she place herself where she could have been assailed by our ram vessels. . . ." Lincoln witnessed the action from Fort Wool (OR, I, XI, III, 153-56).

To Henry W. Halleck[1]

Major Gen. Halleck   Fort. Monroe, Va.
Pittsburg Landing, Tenn.   May. 11. 1862

Norfolk in our possession, Merrimac blown up, & Monitor & other boats going up James River to Richmond. Be very sure[2] to sustain no reverse in your Department.   A. LINCOLN

[1] ALS, NHi. This communication was sent by telegraph. The *Merrimac* was blown up by the Confederates on the morning of May 11 and the order sending the *Monitor* and two other boats up the James River was given the same afternoon (OR, I, XI, III, 163-64).
[2] "Sure" deleted and "careful" written in by Stanton.

Proclamation Raising the Blockade of Certain Ports[1]

May 12, 1862

By the President of the United States of America.

A Proclamation.

Whereas, by my Proclamation of the nineteenth of April, one thousand eight hundred and sixty-one, it was declared that the ports of certain States, including those of Beaufort in the State of North Carolina, Port Royal in the State of South Carolina, and New Orleans in the State of Louisiana, were, for reasons therein set forth, intended to be placed under blockade; and whereas, the said ports of Beaufort, Port Royal, and New Orleans, have since been blockaded; but as the blockade of the same ports may now be safely relaxed with advantage to the interests of commerce:

Now, therefore, be it known, that I, Abraham Lincoln, President of the United States, pursuant to the authority in me vested by the fifth section of the Act of Congress, approved on the 13th. of July, last, entitled "An Act further to provide for the Collec‑ tion of Duties on Imports, and for other Purposes,"—do hereby declare that the blockade of the said ports of Beaufort, Port Royal, and New Orleans, shall so far cease and determine from and after the first day of June, next, that commercial intercourse with those ports, except as to persons, things, and information, contraband of war, may, from that time, be carried on, subject to the laws of the United States and to the limitations and in pursuance of the regulations which are prescribed by the Secretary of the Treasury in his order of this date, which is appended to this proclamation.

In witness whereof, I have hereunto set my hand and caused the seal of the United States to be affixed.

[210]

Done at the City of Washington this twelfth day of
May, in the year of our Lord one thousand eight hundred
[L.S.]   and sixty two, and of the Independence of the United
States the eighty sixth.   ABRAHAM LINCOLN
By the President:
WILLIAM H. SEWARD   Secretary of State.

1 DS, DNA FS RG 11, Proclamations. A list of regulations relating to trade
with the ports opened by Lincoln's proclamation, dated May 12 and signed
by Salmon P. Chase, accompanied the proclamation.

To Lorenzo Thomas[1]

For special reasons, let George F. Gardiner, now a Major of Volunteers, be appointed a Second Lieutenant in the Regular Army.
May 12, 1862.   A. LINCOLN

1 AES, IHi. Lincoln's endorsement appears on a letter from Lorenzo Thomas,
March 28, 1862:
"The letters of application in the case of Major Geo. F. Gardiner, 7th Conn.
Vols., recommending him for an appointment as Captain in the regular army,
have been received and submitted to the Secretary of War, and I am instructed
by him to say that there is now no vacancy of that grade in the Army. There
are a few vacancies, however, of the grade of 2nd Lieutenant, and if Major
Gardiner is not yet too old he could be appointed to one of these.
"He will please forward a statement of his age, should he desire the appointment. . . ."
Nominated second lieutenant in the First U.S. Artillery, Gardiner failed to
be confirmed by the Senate, but was promoted to lieutenant colonel of the
Seventh Connecticut Volunteers on June 20, 1862.

To Edward Bates[1]

Attorney-General, please make out a pardon in this case.
May 13, 1862.   A. LINCOLN

1 AES, DNA RG 204, U.S. Pardon Attorney, A 413. Lincoln's endorsement
is written on the copy of the record of "United States vs Emanuel Rifferd"
(Rifford, Riffert). See Lincoln to Bates, May 1, supra.

To Charles L. Flint[1]

Executive Mansion, Washington, May 13, 1862.
My dear Sir   Allow me to thank you very cordially for the copy
of your work on "Insects Injurious to Vegetation" which you have
had the kindness to send me, and believe me Yours very sincerely
Charles L. Flint Esq   A. LINCOLN

[211]

¹ LS, RPB. This letter, in John Hay's handwriting but signed by Lincoln, is incorrectly dated May 18, 1862, in the *Complete Works* (NH, VII, 170). Charles L. Flint was secretary of the Massachusetts State Board of Agriculture and became an authority on agricultural subjects, later serving as president of Massachusetts Agricultural College.

To Abraham Hart[1]

Executive Mansion, Washington, May 13, 1862.

My dear Sir Permit me to acknowledge the receipt of your communication of April 23d containing a copy of a Prayer recently delivered at your Synagogue, and to thank you heartily for your expressions of kindness and confidence. I have the honor to be Your Obt. Servt   A. LINCOLN

A Hart Esq
Prest. Congn. Hope of Israel
Phila.

¹ LS, PPDrop. The letter is in John Hay's handwriting but signed by Lincoln. Abraham Hart, a publisher at Philadelphia and president of the congregation Hope of Israel, wrote Lincoln on April 23 enclosing a copy of the address and prayer delivered by the Reverend Sabato Morais in "accordance with your Proclamation. . . ." (DLC-RTL).

Response to Evangelical Lutherans[1]

May 13, 1862

GENTLEMEN: I welcome here the representatives of the Evangelical Lutherans of the United States. I accept with gratitude their assurances of the sympathy and support of that enlightened, influential, and loyal class of my fellow-citizens in an important crisis which involves, in my judgment, not only the civil and religious liberties of our own dear land, but in a large degree the civil and religious liberties of mankind in many countries and through many ages. You well know, gentlemen, and the world knows, how reluctantly I accepted this issue of battle forced upon me, on my advent to this place, by the internal enemies of our country. You all know, the world knows the forces and the resources the public agents have brought into employment to sustain a Government against which there has been brought not one complaint of real injury committed against society, at home or abroad. You all may recollect that in taking up the sword thus forced into our hands this Government appealed to the prayers of the pious and the good, and declared that it placed its whole dependence upon the favor of God. I now humbly and reverently, in your presence, reiterate the acknowledgment of that dependence, not doubting that, if it shall please the Divine Being who determines the destinies of nations that this shall remain a united people, they will, humbly seeking the Divine guidance, make their prolonged national existence a source of new benefits to themselves and their successors, and to all classes and conditions of mankind.

1 Washington *National Intelligencer*, May 14, 1862. This speech is misdated May 6 in the *Complete Works* (NH, VII, 153) and misdated August, 1864, by Hertz (II, 940). A committee of the General Synod of the Evangelical Lutheran Church called to present resolutions adopted by the Synod concerning the suppression of the rebellion and maintenance of the Constitution and Union. Lincoln received them at 11 A.M. and responded to speeches by the Reverend Professor L. Sternberg of Hartwick Seminary and the Reverend Dr. H. N. Pohlman of Albany, New York, who headed the committee.

Speech to the Twelfth Indiana Regiment[1]

May 13, 1862

Soldiers of the Twelfth Indiana Regiment!

It has not been customary heretofore, nor will it be hereafter, for me to say something to every regiment passing in review. It occurs too frequently for me to have speeches ready on all occasions. As you have paid such a mark of respect to the Chief Magistrate, it appears proper that I should say a word or two in reply.

Your Colonel[2] has thought fit, on his own account and in your name, to say that you are satisfied with the manner in which I have performed my part in the difficulties which have surrounded the nation. For your kind expressions I am extremely grateful, but, on the other hand, I assure you that the nation is more indebted to you, and such as you, than to me. It is upon the brave hearts and strong arms of the people of the country that our reliance has been placed in support of free government and free institutions.

For the part that you and the brave army of which you are a part have, under Providence, performed in this great struggle, I tender more thanks—greatest thanks that can be possibly due— and especially to this regiment, which has been the subject of good report. The thanks of the nation will follow you, and may God's blessing rest upon you now and forever. I hope that upon your return to your homes you will find your friends and loved ones well and happy. I bid you farewell.

1 New York *Evening Post*, May 15, 1862. The Twelfth Indiana was a regiment enlisted for one year whose term had expired and who were in Washington waiting to be mustered out on May 19.
2 Colonel William H. Link, who died of wounds on September 20, 1862.

To the Senate and House of Representatives[1]

May 14, 1862

To the Senate and House of Representatives:

The third section of the "Act further to provide the efficiency of the navy," approved 21st December, 1861, provides: "That the President of the United States, by and with the advice and consent of the Senate, shall have the authority to detail from the retired list of the navy for the command of squadrons and single ships such officers as he may believe that the good of the service requires to be thus placed in command; and such officers may, if upon the recommendation of the President of the United States they shall receive a vote of thanks of Congress for their services and gallantry in action against an enemy, be restored to the active list and not otherwise."

In conformity with this law, Captain David G. Farragut was nominated to the Senate for continuance as the flag-officer in command of the squadron which recently rendered such important service to the Union, by his successful operations on the lower Mississippi and capture of New Orleans.

Believing that no occasion could arise which would more fully correspond with the intention of the law, or be more pregnant with happy influence as an example, I cordially recommend that Captain D. G. Farragut receive a vote of thanks of Congress for his services and gallantry displayed in the capture, since the 21st December, 1861, of Forts Jackson and St. Philip, city of New Orleans, and the destruction of various rebel gunboats, rams, &c.

Washington, D.C., May 14, 1862.   ABRAHAM LINCOLN.

[1] Thirty-seventh Congress, Second Session, *Senate Executive Document No. 48.* A resolution of thanks to Flag Officer David G. Farragut was approved July 11, 1862. Farragut's appointment as flag officer had been confirmed by the Senate on March 19.

To the Senate and House of Representatives[1]

May 14, 1862

To the Senate and House of Representatives:

I submit, herewith, a list of naval officers who commanded vessels engaged in the recent brilliant operations of the squadron commanded by Flag-Officer Farragut, which led to the capture of Forts Jackson and St. Philip, city of New Orleans, and the destruction of rebel gunboats, rams, &c., in April, 1862. For their services and gallantry on those occasions I cordially recommend that they should, by name, receive a vote of thanks of Congress.

[214]

LIST.

Captain Theodorus Bailey.
Captain Henry W. Morris.
Captain Thomas T. Craven.

Commander Henry H. Bell.   Commander John DeCamp.
Commander Samuel Phillips Lee.   Commander James Alden.
Commander Samuel Swartwout.   Commander David D. Porter.
Commander Melancton Smith.   Commander Richard Wainwright.
Commander Charles Stewart Boggs. Commander William B. Renshaw.

Lieutenant Commanding Abram D. Harrell.
Lieutenant Commanding Edward Donaldson.
Lieutenant Commanding George H. Preble.
Lieutenant Commanding Edward T. Nichols.
Lieutenant Commanding Jonathan M. Wainwright.
Lieutenant Commanding John Guest.
Lieutenant Commanding Charles H. B. Caldwell.
Lieutenant Commanding Napoleon B. Harrison.
Lieutenant Commanding Albert N. Smith.
Lieutenant Commanding Pierce Crosby.
Lieutenant Commanding George M. Ransom.
Lieutenant Commanding Watson Smith.
Lieutenant Commanding John H. Russell.
Lieutenant Commanding Walter W. Queen.
Lieutenant Commanding K. Randolph Breese.
Acting Lieutenant Commanding Selim E. Woodworth.
Acting Lieutenant Commanding Charles H. Baldwin.

Washington, D.C., May 14, 1862.   ABRAHAM LINCOLN.

[1] Thirty-seventh Congress, Second Session, *Senate Executive Document No. 49.* The resolution approved July 11, 1862, expressed thanks to Flag Officer Farragut and to "the officers and men under his command. . . ."

To I. A. Gere, A. A. Reese, and George D. Chenoweth[1]

[May 15?] 1862

Rev. I. A. Gere, A. A. Reese, D.D., G. D. Chenoweth:—

Gentlemen:—Allow me to tender to you, and through you to the East Baltimore Conference of the Methodist Episcopal Church, my grateful thanks for the preamble and resolutions of that body, copies of which you did me the honor to present yesterday. These kind words of approval, coming from so numerous a body of intelligent Christian people, and so free from all suspicion of sinister motives, are indeed encouraging to me. By the help of an all-wise Providence, I shall endeavor to do my duty; and I shall expect

[215]

the continuance of your prayers for a right solution of our national difficulties, and the restoration of our country to peace and prosperity. Your obliged and humble servant, A. LINCOLN.

¹ Edward McPherson, *A Political History of the United States During the Great Rebellion.* . . . (second edition, 1865), p. 496. As printed in the source this letter is without date but given under the title "Reply to Resolutions of the East Baltimore Methodist Conference of 1862." The date [May 15?] assigned in the *Complete Works* (NH, VII, 163) has been retained for lack of better information.

To George B. McClellan¹

Major General McClellan   Washington City, D.C.
Cumberland, Va.   May 15 1862

Your long despatch of yesterday is just received. I will answer more fully soon. Will say now that all your despatches to the Secretary of War have been promptly shown to me. Have done, and shall do, all I could and can to sustain you—hoped that the opening of James River, and putting Wool and Burnside in communication, with an open road to Richmond, or to you, had effected something in that direction. I am still unwilling to take all our force off the direct line between Richmond and here.

A. LINCOLN

¹ ALS, RPB. McClellan's dispatch of May 14 complained that although he had "more than once Telegraphed to the Secretary of War stating that in my opinion the enemy were concentrating all their available force to fight this army. . . . I have received no reply whatever. . . ." Continuing, McClellan reported that he could not bring into battle more than 80,000 men against "a much larger force, perhaps double my number," and asked to be reinforced "without delay by all the disposable troops of the Government. . . . Any commander of the reinforcements . . . will be acceptable to me whatever expressions I may have heretofore addressed to you on that subject. . . ." (DLC-RTL).

To Edwin M. Stanton¹

If another Brigade Quarter-Master is needed let Mr. Bowen be appointed.   A. LINCOLN
May. 15. 1862.

¹ AES, RPB. Lincoln's endorsement is written on a letter from New York State Senator Lysander Farrar, April 17, 1862, recommending John J. Bowen of Rochester, New York, for appointment "to such an office, civil or military, as will enable him to do the most efficient service. . . ." Concurring endorsements were written by U.S. Representative Alfred Ely, Governor Edwin D. Morgan, and others. Bowen's appointment as assistant quartermaster of Volunteers was confirmed by the Senate on June 30, 1862.

To Edwin M. Stanton[1]

Hon. Sec. of War   Executive Mansion
My dear Sir   May 15, 1862.
Capt. Symmes Gardner, was nominated to the Senate as Assistant Quarter-Master, and rejected. My impression is that I directed his renomination, on information from Senators, that the rejection probably resulted from mistake. If there be such direction of mine on file, please send me the re-nomination at once. Yours truly

                                     A. LINCOLN

If Gen. Meigs will say in writing that this re-nomination may properly be made, I will do it.   A. LINCOLN
Dec. 11. 1862

If there is a vacancy of Asst. Q. M. not already promised—let Capt. Gardner have it. Dec. 15. 1862   A. LINCOLN

[1] ALS-P, ISLA. Adjutant General Lorenzo Thomas endorsed this letter on the same day, "This officer is a 1st Lieut 18 Infantry. He was nominated as Assistant Quartermaster with the rank of Captain to fill an original Vacancy. He was rejected by the Senate, and the vacancy filled by another officer. There is now no vacancy in the Quartermasters Department, to which he could be re-nominated." Gardner had been rejected by the Senate on February 3, 1862. Lincoln's later endorsements of December 11 and 15, 1862, brought no results, but Gardner was promoted to captain June 30, 1863.

To Edwin M. Stanton[1]

I really wish the appointment within recommended, to be made.
May 15. 1862.   A. LINCOLN

[1] AES, RPB. Lincoln's endorsement is written on a letter signed by members of the Missouri delegation in congress, May 15, 1862, recommending appointment of John E. Phelps as a lieutenant of cavalry or artillery in the Regular Army. Phelps was appointed second lieutenant in the Third Cavalry June 11, 1862.

To Henry Wilson[1]

Hon. Henry Wilson   Executive Mansion
My dear Sir: May 15, 1862.
I would gladly say a word for the two establishments at Philadelphia, one called the "Union Volunteer Refreshment Saloon" and the other the "Cooper Shop" if I could do so with propriety and good taste. But I know nothing of the facts myself, and could only say hypothetically, that if they have dealt so generously with

our volunteers, as I have frequently heard, and believe, they are indeed worthy of all praise. Yours very truly   A. LINCOLN.

[1] ALS, RPB. The Union Volunteer Refreshment Saloon was organized formally on May 27, 1861, with a committee headed by Arad Barrows, and operated until December 1, 1865, distributing food, coffee, etc., and operating a hospital, to take care of troops in transit through Philadelphia. Cooper Shop served in a similar manner from May 26, 1861. Both operated on funds raised by public subscription and spent respectively about $100,000 and $70,000 (Frank H. Taylor, *Philadelphia in the Civil War 1861-1865*, pp. 207-12).

To Valentine B. Horton[1]

Hon. V. B. Horton,   Executive Mansion,
M.C. from Ohio,   Washington, May 16, 1862.

My dear Sir: Herewith is a copy of your letter with a copy of my Endorsement upon it.

You perceive I did exactly what you requested. Neither more nor less. Yours truly,   A. LINCOLN.

I authorize the Secretary of War to appoint Capt. R. F. Hunter, as I am within requested to do by Hon. V. B. Horton.

[1] Tracy, pp. 206-207. First Lieutenant Robert F. Hunter was cashiered for drunkenness on duty, November 19, 1861. There is no record of his reappointment.

To Irvin McDowell[1]

Major-General McDowell: Washington, May 16, 1862.

What is the strength of your force now actually with you?
                                           A. LINCOLN.

[1] OR, I, XII, III, 195. On the same day General McDowell telegraphed that he had "Thirty thousand one hundred and twelve officers and men for duty. At Belle Plain and Aquia Creek as guards, and unloading stores, repairing railroad and wharf &c, one thousand three hundred and sixty one, officers and men." (DLC-RTL).

To the Senate[1]

To the Senate   Executive Office
of the United States—   May [16] 1862

I transmit herewith for the constitutional action of the Senate, a treaty negotiated on the 13th. of March 1862, between H. W. Farnsworth, a Commissioner on the part of the United States, and the authorized representatives of the Kansas tribe of Indians.

[218]

A communication from the Secretary of the Interior, together with a letter of the Commissioner of Indian affairs suggesting certain amendments to the treaty, and enclosing papers relating thereto, are also transmitted. ABRAHAM LINCOLN

[1] DS, DNA RG 46, Senate 37B C7. The day of month has been supplied on the basis of the date the message appears in the *Executive Journal*. The treaty was finally ratified with amendments on February 6, 1863.

To Salmon P. Chase[1]

[May 17, 1862]

No commanding general shall do such a thing, upon *my* responsibility, without consulting me. A. LINCOLN.

[1] Robert B. Warden, *An Account of the Private Life and Public Services of Salmon Portland Chase* (1874), p. 434. This note was in reply to a letter from Chase, May 16, 1862, "Obliged to go to Philadelphia this afternoon I cannot confer with you as I wish in relation to the Military order of Maj. Gen. Hunter. . . . it seems to me of the highest importance . . . that this order be not revoked." (DLC-RTL). See Lincoln's proclamation of May 19, *infra*, revoking Hunter's order.

To Irvin McDowell[1]

[May 17, 1862]

You will retain the separate command of the forces taken with you; but while co-operating with Gen. McClellan you will obey, his orders, except that you are to Judge, and are not to allow your force to be disposed otherwise than so as to give the greatest protection to this capital which may be possible from that distance.

[1] AD, IHi. At the top of the page preceding Lincoln's instructions, Montgomery C. Meigs wrote: "Prepared in addition to the instructions to Gen McDowell of 17. May '62." On the bottom and verso Meigs continued:
"17 May 62
"The President having shown this to me I suggested that it is dangerous to direct a subordinate not to obey the orders of his superior in any case & that to give instructions to Gen McClellan to this same end & furnish Gen McDowell with a copy thereof would effect the object desired by the President. He desired me to say that the sketch of instructions to Gen McClellan herewith he thought made this addition unnecessary. Respy. MCM
"To the Secretary of War"
The order prepared by Meigs "on consultation of the President, Generals Totten, Meigs and Ripley, and Colonel [Joseph P.?] Taylor" and issued to McDowell on May 17 by Secretary Stanton is as follows:
"General: Upon being joined by General Shields' division, you will move upon Richmond by the general route of the Richmond and Fredericksburg Railroad, cooperating with the forces under General McClellan now threatening Richmond from the line of the Pamunkey and York Rivers.

[219]

"While seeking to establish as soon as possible a communication between your left wing and the right wing of General McClellan, you will hold yourself always in such position as to cover the capital of the nation against a sudden dash of any large body of the rebel forces.

"General McClellan will be furnished with a copy of these instructions, and will be directed to hold himself in readiness to establish communication with your left wing and to prevent the main body of the enemy's army from leaving Richmond and throwing itself upon your column before a junction of the two armies is effected.

"A copy of his instructions in regard to the employment of your force is annexed." (OR, I, XI, I, 28).

The order which Stanton issued to McClellan, as indicated by Meigs' note accompanying Lincoln's autograph addition to the instructions to McDowell, was prepared at the same consultation, but may have been issued a day later. In the *Official Records* it is dated as follows:

"Washington, May 18 [17]—2 P.M.

"General: Your dispatch to the President asking re-enforcements has been received and carefully considered.

"The President is not willing to uncover the capital entirely, and it is believed that even if this were prudent, it would require more time to effect a junction between your army and that of the Rappahannock by the way of the Potomac and York rivers than by a land march. In order, therefore, to increase the strength of the attack upon Richmond at the earliest moment General McDowell has been ordered to march upon that city by the shortest route. He is ordered—keeping himself always in position to save the capital from all possible attack—so to operate as to put his left wing in communication with your right wing, and you are instructed to co-operate, so as to establish this communication as soon as possible, by extending your right wing to the north of Richmond. It is believed that this communication can be safely established either north or south of the Pamunkey River. In any event you will be able to prevent the main body of the enemy's forces from leaving Richmond and falling in overwhelming force upon General McDowell. He will move with between 35,000 and 40,000 men.

"A copy of the instructions to General McDowell are with this. The specific task assigned to his command has been to provide against any danger to the capital of the nation.

"At your earnest call for re-enforcements he is sent forward to co-operate in the reduction of Richmond, but charged, in attempting this, not to uncover the city of Washington; and you will give no order, either before or after your junction, which can put him out of position to cover this city. You and he will communicate with each other by telegraph or otherwise as frequently as may be necessary for efficient co-operation. When General McDowell is in position on your right his supplies must be drawn from West Point, and you will instruct your staff officers to be prepared to supply him by that route.

"The President desires that General McDowell retain the command of the Department of the Rappahannock and of the forces with which he moves forward." (*Ibid.*, p. 27).

To Mary Motley[1]

Executive Mansion,

Miss Mary Motley—   Washington, May 17, 1862.

A friend of yours (a young gentleman of course) tells me you do me the honor of requesting my autograph. I could scarcely refuse any young lady—certainly not the daughter of your distinguished father. Yours truly   A. LINCOLN

[1] ALS, The Rosenbach Company, Philadelphia and New York. Mary Motley was the daughter of the historian John Lothrop Motley, nominated minister to Austria on December 23, 1861, and confirmed by the Senate on January 22, 1862.

To Edwin M. Stanton[1]

May 17, 1862

Let Frederick Salomon, of Wisconsin, be appointed a Brigadier General of volunteers.

[1] American Art Association Anderson Galleries Catalog 3913, May 6, 1931, No. 49. Colonel Frederick Salomon of the Ninth Wisconsin Infantry was appointed brigadier general of Volunteers July 16, 1862.

Appointment of George Harrington[1]

Washington, May 19th. 1862.

George Harrington, is hereby appointed to discharge the duties of Secretary of the Treasury, during the absence of Salmon P. Chase, from Washington.   ABRAHAM LINCOLN

[1] DS, OClWHi.

To John A. Dix[1]

This is a copy of a letter said to be written by a reliable man now a prisoner in Richmond.   A. LINCOLN

May 19, 1862.

[1] AES, owned by Joseph L. Eisendrath, Jr., Highland Park, Illinois. Lincoln's endorsement is written on a copy of a letter from an unnamed Maryland man in prison at Richmond, May 11, 1862, setting forth information of a Confederate plot engineered by Maryland secessionists who are returning from Richmond to their homes but organized in a secret society with "5000 rifles concealed" in Baltimore in "one house alone" and "vast sums of money" raised for the purpose of insurrection and an attack on Washington. General Dix acknowledged receipt of the document on May 21, commenting, "It has some truth, and a good deal of error. . . . there are not in any one . . . place in Baltimore or Maryland '5000 rifles' secreted—nor do I think there are 500. . . . I do not believe in any concerted scheme here to rise up against the government . . ." (DLC-RTL). On May 23, Dix wrote that he had caused the arrest of "Mr. Emack" of Baltimore who was named in the Richmond letter, and that "Nothing treasonable was found. . . ." (Ibid.).

Proclamation Revoking General Hunter's Order of Military Emancipation of May 9, 1862[1]

May 19, 1862

By the President of The United States of America.

A Proclamation.

Whereas there appears in the public prints, what purports to be a proclamation, of Major General Hunter, in the words and figures following, towit:[2]

> *Headquarters Department of the South,* }
> Hilton Head, S.C., May 9, 1862.

General Orders No. 11.—The three States of Georgia, Florida and South Carolina, comprising the military department of the south, having deliberately declared themselves no longer under the protection of the United States of America, and having taken up arms against the said United States, it becomes a military necessity to declare them under martial law. This was accordingly done on the 25th day of April, 1862. Slavery and martial law in a free country are altogether incompatible; the persons in these three States—Georgia, Florida and South Carolina—heretofore held as slaves, are therefore declared forever free.　　　　　　　　　　　　　　DAVID HUNTER,
(Official)　　　　　　　　　　Major General Commanding.
ED. W. SMITH, Acting Assistant Adjutant General.

And whereas the same is producing some excitement, and misunderstanding: therefore

I, Abraham Lincoln, president of the United States, proclaim and declare, that the government of the United States, had no knowledge, information, or belief, of an intention on the part of General Hunter to issue such a proclamation; nor has it yet, any authentic information that the document is genuine. And further, that neither General Hunter, nor any other commander, or person, has been[3] authorized by the Government of the United States, to make proclamations declaring the slaves of any State free; and that the supposed proclamation, now in question, whether genuine or false, is altogether void, so far as respects such declaration.

I further make known that whether it be competent for me, as Commander-in-Chief of the Army and Navy, to declare the Slaves of any state or states, free, and whether at any time, in any case, it shall have become a necessity indispensable to the maintainance of the government, to exercise such supposed power, are questions which, under my responsibility, I reserve to myself, and which I can not feel justified in leaving to the decision of[4] commanders in the field. These are totally different questions from those of police regulations in armies and camps.

On the sixth day of March last, by a special message, I recommended to Congress the adoption of a joint resolution to be substantially as follows:[5]

Resolved, That the United States ought to co-operate with any State which may adopt a gradual abolishment of slavery, giving to such State pecuniary aid, to be used by such State in its discretion to compensate for the inconveniences, public and private, produced by such change of system.

The resolution, in the language above quoted, was adopted by large majorities in both branches of Congress, and now stands an authentic, definite, and solemn proposal of the nation to the States and people most immediately interested in the subject matter. To the people of those states I now earnestly appeal. I do not argue. I beseech you to make the arguments for yourselves. You[6] can not if you would, be blind to the signs of the times. I beg of you a calm and enlarged consideration of them, ranging, if it may be, far above personal and partizan politics. This proposal makes common cause for a common object, casting no reproaches upon any. It acts[7] not the pharisee. The change it contemplates would come gently as the dews of heaven, not rending or wrecking anything. Will you not embrace it? So much good has not been done, by one effort, in all past time, as, in the providence of God, it is now your high previlege to do. May the vast future not have to lament that you have neglected it.[8]

In witness whereof, I have hereunto set my hand, and caused the seal of the United States to be affixed.

[L.S.] Done at the City of Washington this nineteenth day of May, in the year of our Lord one thousand eight hundred and sixty-two, and of the Independence of the United States the eighty-sixth. ABRAHAM LINCOLN.

By the President:

WILLIAM H. SEWARD, Secretary of State.

[1] ADfS, DLC-RTL; DS, DNA FS RG 11, Proclamations.
[2] The draft in the Lincoln Papers has General Orders No. 11 clipped from a newspaper and pasted on the center of the page at this point.
[3] Lincoln deleted "expressly, or implicitly" at this point in the draft.
[4] Lincoln inserted the remainder of this paragraph in place of the following phraseology deleted in the draft, "will permit to be decided for me by neither any, nor all of my military subordinates."
[5] The following resolution in the draft is a newspaper clipping pasted in the center of the page.
[6] Lincoln inserted this sentence and the next in place of the following phraseology deleted in the draft, "The strong tendency to a total disruption of

MAY 19, 1862

society in the South, is apparent. *You* can stay [it?] without your [act?], possibly *I* can not. You can stay it without harming a hair of white or black."

7 "Plays" deleted and "acts" inserted by Lincoln in the draft.

8 Lincoln signs and dates the draft at this point, but both date and signature have been deleted and the remainder of the document added in the handwriting of a clerk. Lincoln's signature appears, of course, on the official copy in the Archives.

Reply to Maryland Slaveholders[1]

May 19, 1862

The President, in reply, assured them he had entire confidence in Gen. Wadsworth's ability and intention to do right, but would take their representations into consideration, and see that no injustice was done.

[1] New York *Tribune*, May 20, 1862. Lincoln replied to a committee representing "about one hundred slaveholders from Prince George's County, Maryland," who "complained concerning the non-enforcement of the Fugitive Slave law in the District, and of the hindrances alleged to have been thrown in their way by Gen. Wadsworth, who, it seems, does not show much alacrity in aiding its execution, refusing wholly except when the claimants prove themselves loyal citizens, and on that point taking the evidence of the slaves." (*Ibid.*).

To Edwin M. Stanton[1]

If there be a vacancy such as mentioned within, and it be not in the regular Army, let it be filled as herein requested.   A. LINCOLN

May 19. 1862.

[1] AES, IHi. Lincoln's endorsement appears on a letter from Representatives Luther Hanchett and Timothy O. Howe and Senator James R. Doolittle, May 1, 1862, reminding Lincoln of his promise to appoint Moses S. Gibson of Hudson, Wisconsin, a paymaster. Gibson was nominated paymaster on May 24 and was confirmed by the Senate on June 30, 1862.

To George B. McClellan[1]

United States Military Telegraph,
Washington 20   Head-Quarters, Department Potomac
Maj Gen McClellan   May 20th 1862.

Telegraph being open tell us the situation & suggest if you can anything about batteries at Fort Darling   A LINCOLN

[1] Copy, DLC-McClellan Papers. The copy is the one received at McClellan's headquarters. For McClellan's reply see note, Lincoln to McClellan, May 21, *infra*.

To Edwin M. Stanton[1]

Hon. Sec. of War　　　　　Executive Mansion　May 20, 1862
　Hon. Mr. Wadsworth of Ky. wishes five hundred arms for reasons which he will explain to you. Unless you know some strong objection, please let him have them. Yours truly,

A. LINCOLN

[1] Copy, ISLA. The Register of letters received by the Office of Chief of Ordnance (DNA WR RG 156, WF 1046 Z) lists this missing item as referred to General James W. Ripley. Representative William H. Wadsworth served as aide to Brigadier General William Nelson.

To Lady Villiers[1]

Executive Mansion, Washington, May 20, 1862.
　Mr. Lyon has informed me that Lady Villiers has expressed a wish for my autograph. I beg that her Ladyship will accept the assurance of my sincere gratification at this oppertunity of subscribing myself　Very truly, Her Ladyship's obedient servant,

A. LINCOLN.

[1] ALS, RPB. Lady Villiers (Sarah Sophia Fane, 1785-1867), the widow of George C. Villiers (1773-1859), Fifth Earl of Jersey and Eighth Viscount Grandison, was a collector of autographs. Her request was undoubtedly presented by Lord Lyons the British minister to the United States.

To James G. Bennett[1]

Private

James G. Bennett, Esq　　　　　　Executive Mansion
Dear Sir:　　　　　　　　　　　　May 21, 1862.
　Thanking you again for the able support given by you, through the Herald, to what I think the true cause of the country, and also for your kind expressions towards me personally, I wish to correct an erroneous impression of yours in regard to the Secretary of War. He mixes no politics whatever with his duties; knew nothing of Gen. Hunter's proclamation; and he and I alone got up the counter-proclamation. I wish this to go no further than to you, while I do wish to assure you it is true. Yours truly

A. LINCOLN

[1] ALS-P, ISLA. In a highly uninformed editorial entitled "President Lincoln and His Happy Cabinet," the New York *Herald* of May 18, 1862, speculated on the possibility that divisions in the cabinet over Hunter's proclamation might necessitate some changes in its personnel. Seward and Chase were dismissed as

possibilities because they "have given up the nigger business," Welles also, because he wanted only to be allowed "to doze in peace," but Stanton seemed a likely prospect: "Who, then, remains? Only Secretary Stanton, to whom both Seward and Chase have thrown their dirty linen—the newspapers and the niggers—and who has since been kept at the wash-tub, splashing and scolding in a style more ridiculous than imposing. We do not think Stanton will go. Much as he may admire Hunter's proclamation, he will not risk his office by opposing the President's wishes. . . ." Bennett replied to Lincoln's letter on June 6, 1862, that he had availed himself "at the earliest moment of the hints you gave me relative to the Secretary of war a gentleman and a patriot of whom I have a high opinion. . . . In order to . . . aid and assist you . . . I have a great mind to pay you a short visit. . . ." (DLC-RTL).

To George B. McClellan[1]

Washington City, D C   May 21, 1862

Major General McClellan: Your long despatch of yesterday just received. You will have just such control of Gen. McDowell and his force as you therein indicate. McDowell can reach you by land sooner than he could get aboard of boats if the boats were ready at Frederick'sburg,—unless his march shall be resisted, in which case, the force resisting him, will certainly not be confronting you at Richmond. By land he can reach you in five days after starting, whereas by water he would not reach you in two weeks, judging by past experience. Franklin's single Division did not reach you in ten days after I ordered it.   A. LINCOLN

[1] ALS-P, ISLA. There has been some confusion about the date of this telegram. Nicolay and Hay printed it under date of May 22 (VII, 174-75). The received copy in the McClellan papers is dated May 24. Lincoln's autograph is clearly May 21, and the received copy of McClellan's "long despatch of yesterday" in the Lincoln Papers supports the correctness of Lincoln's date by being dated May 21, 1862, received 5 A.M. McClellan's ten-page telegram reads in part as follows: "Your despatch of yesterday respecting our situation & the batteries at Fort Darling was recd while I was absent with the advance where I have also been all this day. I have communicated . . . with Goldsborough . . . The vessels can do nothing without cooperation on land which I will not be in position to afford for several days. Circumstances must determine the propriety of a land attack. . . . roads incredibly bad. . . . Keyes corps is on the new Kent road. . . . He[i]ntzelman is on the same road. . . . Sumner is on the road connecting right with left. Stoneman with advanced guard is within one mile of New Bridge. Franklin . . . two miles this side of Stonemans. Porters division . . . is within supporting distance. . . . The enemy are in force on every road leading to Richmond . . . . their numbers . . . greatly exceeding our own. . . . I shall advance steadily & carefully to attack. . . . I regret the state of things as to Genl McDowells command. . . . I would still most respectfully suggest the policy of our concentrating here by movements of water. . . . I regret also the configuration of the department of the Rappahannock it includes a portion even of the city of Richmond. I think that my own department should embrace the entire field of active military operations designed for the capture . . . of that city. Again I agree with your Excellency that one bad Genl is better than two good ones. I am not sure that I fully

comprehend your orders of the 17th inst addressed to myself & Genl Mc-
Dowell. If a junction is effected before we occupy Richmond it must necessarily
be east of the RR to Fredericksburg & within my department. . . . my superior rank & the . . . sixty second (62d) article of war will place his command under my orders unless it is otherwise specially directed by your
Excellency & I consider that he will be under my command except that I am
not to detach any portion of his forces or give any orders which can put him
out of position to cover Washington. . . . I believe that there is a great struggle before this army but I am neither dismayed nor discouraged. . . . I trust
that the result may either obtain for me the permanent confidence of my government or that it may close my career."

To George B. McClellan[1]

Major Genl. McClellan   Washington City, D.C. May 21, 1862.

I have just been waited on by a large Committee who present
a petition signed by twenty-three Senators and eightyfour Representatives, asking me to restore Gen. Hamilton to his Division. I
wish to do this, and yet I do not wish to be understood as rebuking
you. Please answer at once.   A. LINCOLN.

Send in Cypher.

[1] ALS, RPB. McClellan's reply, "Cool [Cold] Harbor May 22d. 12.30 Pm.,"
protested that "The discipline of the army will not permit the restoration of
General Hamilton to his Division. . . . Genl Hamilton is not fit to command
a Division. . . . The cause of his removal . . . was ample to justify me in the
course pursued. You cannot do anything better calculated to injure my army
and diminish the probabilities of success . . . than to restore Gen Hamilton. . . ." (DLC-RTL). McClellan's reply and the petition of May 15 are
filed together with Lincoln's endorsement "Petition to have Gen. Hamilton
restored to his command, and protest of Gen. McClellan against it. A.L."
Brigadier General Charles S. Hamilton, replaced by Brigadier General Philip
Kearny as commander of the Third Division of the Third Corps on April 30,
was "sent forward to join Banks and report to him for orders. . . . If he remains at Harper's Ferry and can render any service I desire him to do so, but
not to supersede you [Brigadier General Rufus Saxton] in command." (Stanton to Saxton, May 25, 1862, OR, I, XII, I, 630).

To the Senate[1]

To the Senate: May 21, 1862

In answer to the resolution of the Senate of the 14th instant,
requesting information in regard to arrests in the State of Kentucky, I transmit a report from the Secretary of War, to whom the
resolution was referred.   ABRAHAM LINCOLN.

Washington, May 21, 1862.

[1] Thirty-seventh Congress, Second Session, *Senate Executive Document No.
51.* Stanton's accompanying report deemed it incompatible with public interest
to furnish the requested information.

To James F. Simmons[1]

Hon. Senator Simmons   Executive Mansion   May 21, 1862.

My dear Sir: This distressed girl says she belongs to your state; that she was here with her father and brother, in our Army, till they went with it to the peninsula; that her brother[2] has been killed there and her father made prisoner—and that she is here, wanting employment to support herself. If you can be satisfied that her story is correct, please see if you can not get Mr. Sec. Chase or friend Newton to find her a place. Yours truly

A. LINCOLN.

[1] Copy, DLC-Nicolay Papers. The copy carries a notation "Copy from Sam R. Simmons Jr." The girl has not been identified.

[2] "Brother" has been inserted in the copy. This may indicate an omission in the original manuscript.

To Charles Sumner[1]

May 21, 1862

I know nothing of this case—know not where Mr. Alden is—whether any proceedings are on foot against him. I should not knowingly let him be punished, if shown he has the infirmity stated in the affidavit; though the infirmity may be sufficient reason for dismissing him from the service.   A. LINCOLN

May 21, 1862.

[1] AES, owned by G. Lynn Sumner, New York City. Lincoln's endorsement is written on a letter from Samuel Breck, Bridgewater, Massachusetts, May 17, 1862, to Sumner, "We have an unpleasant report that George C Alden of Company K. Capt Reed 7th Massts Reg. a native and resident of this town is on trial, under arrest or sentence for being found sleeping on his post whilst on guard. . . . He has for many years . . . been subject to a lethargy occasion-[al]ly so that he would fall asleep even when persons were in conversation with him. . . . The accompanying certificate . . . of one of the Physicians who have practiced in the family . . . will give you the necessary assurance. . . ." Alden remained in service and was mustered out June 27, 1864.

To William A. Hammond[1]

Washington, May 22, 1862.

I am personally acquainted with Dr. Stone, the writer of the within paper, and believe him to be a skilful physician, altogether capable of forming a correct opinion on the subject he within has spoken upon. I think it probable the disinfectant would be valuable in our hospitals and camps; and, with the consent of the Surgeon General, I should be glad for Dr. Kidwell to be allowed to introduce it.   A. LINCOLN.

[1] Hertz, II, 868. Dr. Robert K. Stone was the family physician of the Lincolns in Washington. On April 18, 1862, William A. Hammond had been nominated surgeon general with rank of brigadier general and was confirmed by the Senate on April 25. Dr. Kidwell has not been identified, and the specific nature of Dr. Stone's recommendation has not been discovered.

To the House of Representatives[1]

To the House of Representatives.   May 22, 1862
In compliance with the Resolution of the House of Representatives of the 20th. instant requesting information in regard to the indemnity obtained by the Consul General of the United States at Alexandria, Egypt, for the maltreatment of Faris-el-Hakim, an agent in the employ of the American Missionaries in that country, I transmit a Report from the Secretary of State and the documents by which it was accompanied.   ABRAHAM LINCOLN
Washington, 22nd. May, 1862.

[1] DS, DNA RG 233, Original Executive Document No. 117. Concerning the episode referred to, see Lincoln to Pacha Mohammed Said, October 11, 1861, *supra*.

Memorandum:
Appointment of George Montagu Hicks[1]

May 22, 1862
This note, as Col. Hicks did verbally yesterday, attempts to excite me against the Secretary of War, and therein is offensive to me. My "order" as he is pleased to call it, is plainly no order at all.
May 22, 1862.   A. LINCOLN

[1] AES, DLC-RTL. See Lincoln to Stanton May 5, *supra*.

To Edwin M. Stanton[1]

Hon. Sec. of War   Executive Mansion
My dear Sir   May 22. 1862.
The bearer of this, Dr. Tarrant A. Perkins, was appointed a Brigadier Surgeon by me, and was serving in Western Virginia, when wishing to be transferred West, under bad advice, he resigned, expecting to get a new appointment, and thus to effect his object. Of course this simply got him out of the service. He is, however, my personal friend, for whom, and whose family I have great kindness of feeling. I shall be personally obliged, if it can

[229]

be arranged to re-appoint him, and order him to report for duty anywhere in Gen. Halleck's Department. Yours truly

A. LINCOLN

1 ALS, owned by A. H. Greenly, Hoboken, New Jersey. Dr. Tarrant A. Perkins of Chicago, Illinois, had been appointed September 4, 1861, and resigned March 24, 1862. There is no record of his reappointment.

To the House of Representatives[1]

To the House of Representatives: May 23, 1862
I transmit a Report from the Secretary of State in answer to the Resolution of the House of Representatives of the 22d instant, calling for further correspondence relative to Mexican Affairs.

Washington, 23d May 1862. ABRAHAM LINCOLN

1 DS, DNA RG 233, Original Executive Document No. 120. The resolution of May 22, 1862, called for copies of such correspondence as had been received since Lincoln's message of April 14, *supra*. Seward's report deemed it not expedient to furnish the correspondence "at the present time."

To John C. Frémont[1]

War Department
Major General Fremont Washington City, D.C.
Franklin. May 24th. 1862

You are authorized to purchase the four hundred horses or take them wherever and however you can get them.

The exposed condition of General Banks makes his immediate relief a point of paramount importance. You are therefore directed by the President to move against Jackson at Harrisonberg and operate against the enemy in such way as to relieve Banks. This movement must be made immediately. You will acknowledge the receipt of this order and specify the hour it is received by you.

A. LINCOLN

1 Copy, DNA WR RG 92 Quartermaster General, P 26. Frémont's telegram to Stanton, received at 2:30 P.M., May 24, 1862, reads in part as follows: "General Banks informs me this morning of an attack by enemy. This is probably by [Thomas J. "Stonewall"] Jackson. . . . [Richard S.] Ewell's force with him. General Banks says he should be re-enforced immediately. My own movements are being directed to the object proposed in plan approved, and in connection to the speediest possible support of General [J.D.] Cox. . . . Under the circumstances my force cannot be divided, and if I abandon this line and move eastward to the support of General Banks this whole country to the Ohio would be thrown open, and General [J.D.] Cox also immediately exposed to disaster. . . . May I ask if you will support him? . . . Needing much the use of my cavalry. I telegraph to General Meigs asking that he authorize the . . . purchase immediately, wherever they can be had, 400 horses. Will you approve the requisition?" (OR, I, XII, I, 642-43).

To John C. Frémont[1]

Major Genl. Fremont
Franklin, Va.

Washington City, D.C.
May 24, 7¼ P.M. 1862

Many thanks for the promptness with which you have answered that you will execute the order. Much—perhaps all—depends upon the celerity with which you can execute it. Put the utmost speed into it. Do not lose a minute. A. LINCOLN

[1] ALS, RPB. Frémont replied to Lincoln's telegram sent at 4 P.M., as follows: "Your telegram received at five (5) oclock this afternoon will move as ordered & operate against the Enemy in such way to afford prompt relief to genl Banks." (DLC-RTL).

To Henry W. Halleck[1]

Major Genl. Halleck
Near Corinth, Tenn. [Mississippi]

Washington City, D.C.
May 24, 7½ P.M. 1862

Several despatches from Assistant Secretary Scott, and one from Gov. Morton, asking re-inforcements for you have been received. I beg you to be assured we do the best we can. I mean to cast no blame when I tell you each of our commanders along our line from Richmond to Corinth supposes himself to be confronted by numbers superior to his own. Under this pressure we thinned the line on the upper Potomac until yesterday it was broken, at heavy loss to us, and Gen. Banks put in great peril, out of which he is not yet extricated, and may be actually captured. We need men to repair this breach, and have them not at hand.

My dear general, I feel justified to rely very much on you. I believe you and the brave officers and men with you, can and will get the victory at Corinth. A. LINCOLN

[1] ALS, RPB. Oliver P. Morton telegraphed from "Camp near Corinth," May 23, 9 A.M., "General Hallecks army has been greatly reduced by sickness The enemy are in great force at Corinth and have recently received reinforcements They evidently intend to make a desperate struggle at that point and from all I can learn their leaders have utmost confidence in the result They are constantly at work upon their entrenchments which are becoming of a formidable character It is fearful to contemplate the consequences of a defeat at Corinth In the opinion of many officers our forces are at present outnumbered I would most earnestly ask that if it be possible ten more [sic] be at once detached from Points and sent here and also that no time be lost doing this if it can be." (DLC-RTL).

To George B. McClellan[1]

Washington City, D.C.
May 24. 1862

Major General McClellan

I left Gen. McDowell's camp at dark last evening. Shields'[2] command is there but is so worn that he can not move before

[231]

Monday morning the (26th.) twenty sixth. We have so thinned our line to get troops for other places that it was broken yesterday at Front-Royal with a probable loss to us of a Regiment infantry, two companies of cavalry, putting Banks in some peril. The enemies forces under Gen. Anderson[3] now opposing Gen. Mc-Dowell's advance have, as their line of supply and retreat, the Road to Richmond. If in conjunction with McDowell's movement against Anderson you could send a force from your right to cut off the enemies supplies from Richmond, preserve the Rail Road bridges across the two forks of the Pamunkey and intercept the enemies retreat you will prevent the army now opposed to you from receiving an accession of numbers of nearly fifteen thousand men—and if you succeed in saving the bridges you will [se]cure a line of Rail Road for supplies in addition to the one you now have. Can you not do this almost as well as not, while you are building the Chicahomany bridges? McDowell and Shields both say they can, and positively will, move monday morning. I wish you to move cautiously and safely. You will have command of Gen. McDowell after he joins you, precisely as you indicate in your long despatch to me of the twentyfirst.   A. LINCOLN

1 ALS, RPB. No reply to this telegram has been located in the Lincoln Papers.
2 Brigadier General James Shields.   3 Brigadier General Joseph R. Anderson.

To George B. McClellan[1]

Washington City, D.C.
Major Gen. McClellan   May 24. 4. P.M. 1862
In consequence of Gen. Banks' critical position I have been compelled to suspend Gen. McDowell's movement to join you. The enemy are making a desperate push upon Harper's Ferry, and we are trying to throw Fremont's force & part of McDowell's in their rear.   A. LINCOLN

1 ALS, RPB. McClellan replied the same day, "Telegram of 4 p.m. received. I will make my calculations accordingly." (OR, I, XI, III, 190).

To Irvin McDowell[1]

Major Gen McDowell   Washington City, D.C.
Fredericksburg   24 May 1862 [5 P.M.]
Gen Fremont has been ordered by Telegraph to move from Franklin on Harrisonburg to relieve Gen Banks and capture or destroy Jackson & Ewell's force.
You are instructed laying aside for the present the movement

on Richmond to put twenty thousand men (20000) in motion at once for the Shenandoah moving on the line or in advance of the line of the Manassas Gap R Road. Your object will be to capture the forces of Jackson & Ewell, either in cooperation with Gen Fremont or in case want of supplies or of transportation interferes with his movement, it is believed that the force with which you move will be sufficient to accomplish the object alone.

The information thus far received here makes it probable that if the enemy operates actively against Gen Banks you will not be able to count upon much assistance from him but may even have to release him.

Reports received this moment are that Banks is fighting with Ewell (8) Eight miles from Winchester.

ABRAHAM LINCOLN

[1] LS, RPB. At 11:12 A.M., Stanton telegraphed McDowell, "In view of the operations of the enemy on the line of General Banks the President thinks the whole force you designed to move from Fredericksburg should not be taken away, and he therefore directs that one brigade in addition to what you designed to leave at Fredericksburg should be left there; this brigade to be the least effective of your command." (OR, I, XII, III, 219). McDowell replied: "Your order to leave an additional brigade at Fredericksburg has been received. Shields' ammunition has been landed and will be up this afternoon or evening. The enemy, attracted by the movement of our troops yesterday, drew in his right to the railroad. . . ." (Ibid.). In reply to Lincoln's telegram of 5 P.M. McDowell telegraphed Stanton, "The President's order has been received and is in process of execution. This is a crushing blow to us." (Ibid., p. 220).

To Irvin McDowell[1]

Washington City, D.C.   May 24 1862 [8 P.M.]

Major General McDowell   I am highly gratified by your alacrity in obeying my order. The change was as painful to me as it can possibly be to you or to any one. Every thing now dependes upon the celerity and vigor of your movement.

A. LINCOLN

[1] LS, RPB. McDowell's reply, received at 9:30 P.M., reads in part as follows: "I obeyed your orders immediately . . . perhaps as a subordinate there I ought to stop; but. . . . I beg to say that co-operation between General Fremont and myself to cut Jackson and Ewell there is not to be counted upon, even if it is not a practical impossibility. Next, that I am entirely beyond helping distance of General Banks; no celerity or vigor will avail so far as he is concerned. . . . It will take a week or ten days for the force to get to the valley by the route which will give it food and forage, and by that time the enemy will have retired. I shall gain nothing for you there, and shall lose much for you here. . . . I have ordered General Shields to commence the movement by to-morrow morning. A second division will follow in the afternoon. Did I understand you aright, that you wished that I personally should accompany this expedition? I hope to see Governor Chase to-night and express myself more fully to him." (OR, I, XII, III, 220-21).

To Dixon S. Miles[1]

Col. Miles,   Washington, D.C.,
Harper's Ferry, Va   May 24, 1862. [1.30 P.M.]
Could you not send scouts from Winchester, who would tell whether enemy are North of Banks, moving on Winchester? What is the latest you have?   A. LINCOLN

[1] ALS, RPB. Colonel Miles, commanding the Railroad Brigade, replied at 2 P.M., "Early this morning directed Colonel [George L.] Beal, Tenth Maine, to withdraw First Maryland Cavalry from the road to Romney and place them on the Middletown turnpike. The telegraph has been working to-day to Winchester. For the last two hours, for some reason, it has ceased to do so." (OR, I, XII, III, 225).

To Rufus Saxton[1]

Gen. Saxton: Washington City, D.C. May 24, 1862 1. P.M.
Geary[2] reports Jackson with twenty thousand, moving from Ashby's Gap, by the Little River Turnpike through Aldie toward's Centerville. This he says is reliable. He is also informed of large forces South of him. We know a force of some fifteen thousand broke up Saturday-night, from in front of Fredericks'burg, & went we know not where. Please inform us, if possible, what has become of the force which pursued Banks yesterday. Also, any other information you have.   A. LINCOLN

[1] ALS, RPB. No reply to this telegram has been located.
[2] Brigadier General John W. Geary.

To the Senate[1]

May 24, 1862
To the Senate of the United States: I transmit a report from the Secretary of State in answer to the resolution of the Senate of the 22d instant, calling for further correspondence relative to Mexican affairs.   ABRAHAM LINCOLN.
Washington, May 24, 1862.

[1] *Journal of the Senate*, p. 530. See Lincoln's message to the House, May 23, *supra.* Seward's report was the same transmitted therewith.

To Salmon P. Chase[1]

Secretary Chase   Washington City, D.C.
Fredericksburg, Va.   May 25. 1862
It now appears that Banks got safely in to Winchester last night, and is, this morning, retreating on Harper's Ferry. This justifies

the inference that he is pressed by numbers superior to his own. I think it not improbable that Ewell Jackson and Johnson, are pouring through the gap they made day-before yesterday at Front-Royal, making a dash Northward. It will be a very valuable, and very honorable service for Gen. McDowell to cut them off. I hope he will put all possible energy and speed into the effort.

A. LINCOLN

[1] ALS, RPB. General Banks telegraphed Lincoln May 24, 8 P.M., that he had occupied Winchester (OR, I, XII, I, 527). Chase's reply to Lincoln from Falmouth, Virginia, received at 11:20 A.M., May 25, reads in part as follows: ". . . General McDowell appreciates, as you do, the importance of the service he is called on to perform. All possible exertion is being made. . . . Having done all I can here, I shall come immediately to Washington with General Shields. . . ." (OR, I, XII, III, 230).

To John W. Geary[1]

War Department, May 25, 1862—1.45 P.M.

General Geary, White Plains: Please give us your best present impression as to the number of the enemy's forces north of Strasburg and Front Royal. Are the forces still moving north through the Gap at Front Royal and between you and there?

A. LINCOLN.

[1] OR, I, XII, III, 240. Brigadier General Geary replied the same day that ". . . The enemy are passing up from Front Royal, Between the Blue [Ridge] Mountains and the river, to Ashby's Gap . . . . contrabands . . . say their force intends crossing by Snickersville to Leesburg, there to seize the fortifications and maintain a position. . . . My information shows the enemy to be in full possession of the country between Front Royal and Ashby's Gap between the mountains and the river . . . . the number thus travelling cannot be short of 7,000 or 8,000. . . . supported by large forces at Front Royal. . . . The forces moving between me and the mountains are not in heavy bodies. . . . Forces have crossed at Manassas Gap and are now in front of me. Contrabands have told me that they have heard letters read . . . stating that 10,000 cavalry are about passing through this valley from the direction of Warrenton." (Ibid., p. 241).

To George B. McClellan[1]

United States Military Telegraph
War Department, Washington, D.C.

To/   May 25, 1862.

General McClellan: The enemy is moving North in sufficient force to drive Banks before him in precisely what force we can not tell. He is also threatening Leesburgh and Geary on the Manassas Gap Rail Road from both north and south in precisely what force we can not tell. I think the movement is a general and concerted one, such as could not be if he was acting upon the purpose of a very desperate defence of Richmond. I think the time is near when you must either attack Richmond or give up the job and come to the defence of Washington. Let me hear from you instantly.

A. LINCOLN.

¹ Copies, DLC-McClellan Papers and Stanton Papers; copy, DNA WR RG 94, Adjutant General, Letters Received, P 1353. McClellan's reply of 5 P.M., received at 7 P.M. reads as follows: "Telegram received. Independently of it the time is very near when I shall attack Richmond. The object of Enemys movements is probably to prevent reinforcements being sent to me. All the information obtained from balloon, deserters, prisoners and contrabands agrees in the statement that the mass of rebel troops are still in immediate vicinity of Richmond, ready to defend it. I have no knowledge of Genl Bank's position and force, nor what there is at Manassas, therefore cannot form a definite opinion as to force against him. I have two Corps across the Chickahominy, within six miles of Richmond. The others on this side at other crossings within same distance, and ready to cross when Bridges completed." (DLC-RTL).

To George B. McClellan¹

(Send in Cypher). War Department Washington City, D.C.
Major Gen. McClellan   May 25. 1862 8½ P.M.

Your despatch received. Banks was at Strausburg with about six-thousand men, Shields having been taken from him to swell a column for McDowell to aid you at Richmond, and the rest of his force scattered at various places. On the 23rd. a rebel force of seven to ten thousand fell upon one regiment and two companies guarding the bridge at Front-Royal, destroying it entirely, crossed the Shenandoah, and on the 24th. (yesterday) pushed to get North of Banks on the Road to Winchester. Banks ran a race with them, beating them into Winchester yesterday evening. This morning a battle ensued between the two forces in which Banks was beaten back into full retreat towards Martinsburg, and probably is broken up into a total route. Geary, on the Manassas Gap R.R. just now reports that Jackson is now near Front-Royal with ten thousand following up & supporting as I understand, the force now pursuing Banks. Also that another force of ten thousand is near Orleans following on in the same direction. Stripped bare, as we are here, it will be all we can do to prevent them crossing the Potomac at Harper's Ferry, or above. We have about twenty thousand of McDowell's force moving back to the vicinity of Front Royal; and Gen. Fremont, who was at Franklin, is moving to Harrisonburg, both these movements intended to get in the enemies rear. One more of McDowells Brigades is ordered through here to Harper's Ferry. The rest of his force remains, for the present, at Fredericksburg. We are sending such regiments and dribs from here and Baltimore, as we can spare, to Harper's Ferry, supplying their places, in some sort, by calling in Militia from the adjacent States. We also have eighteen cannon on the road to Harper's Ferry of which arm, there is not a single one yet at that point. This is now our situation. If McDowell's force was now beyond our reach, we should be utterly helpless. Apprehension of something like this, and no unwillingness to sustain you, has always been my reason for withholding McDowells force from you. Please understand this, and do the best you can with the force you have.

A LINCOLN

[1] ADfS, DLC-RTL. Lincoln endorsed on the back of the document "Draft of Tel. Despatch to Gen. McClellan, May 25, 1862." General Banks had telegraphed from Martinsburg at 2:40 P.M.: "The rebels attacked us this morning at daybreak in great force. Their number was estimated at 15000. consisting of Ewells & Jackson's divisions the fire of pickets began with light, was followed by the artillery until the lines were fully under fire on both sides. The left wing stood firmly, holding its ground well & right did the same for a time when two regiments broke the lines under the fire of the enemy. The right wing fell back & was ordered to withdraw & the troops pressed through the town in considerable confusion. They were quickly reformed on the other side, & continued their march in good order to Martinsburg where they arrived at 2.40 P.M. a distance of twenty-two miles. Our trains are in advance & will cross the river in safety. Our entire force engaged was less than 4000 consisting of [George H.] Gordon's & [Dudley] Donnelly's brigades, with two reg'ts of cavalry under Gen. [John P.] Hatch. & two batteries artillery. Our loss is considerable as was that of the enemy, but cannot now be stated. We were reinforced by 10th Maine which did good service, & a regt. of cavalry" (DLC-RTL).

To Rufus Saxton[1]

War Department, May 25, 1862—4.15 P.M.

General Saxton, Harper's Ferry: If Banks reaches Martinsburg, is he any the better for it? Will not the enemy cut him off from thence to Harper's Ferry? Have you sent anything to meet him and assist him at Martinsburg? This is an inquiry, not an order.

A. LINCOLN.

[1] OR, I, XII, I, 628. A telegram from Saxton at Harper's Ferry, received at 2:25 P.M., described Banks as "hotly pressed and in full retreat toward Martinsburg. There is a panic. . . ." (Ibid.). Saxton's reply to Lincoln's questions received at 6 P.M., was as follows: "General Banks cannot reach Harper's Ferry from Martinsburg. He had two lines of retreat—one to Harper's Ferry, one to Martinsburg. He took the latter. . . . It is 19 miles from Winchester to Martinsburg, and 23 miles from here to Martinsburg, and 11 or 12 from Williamsport. His only chance is to go there. We could do nothing to assist him, as we could not ascertain line of retreat until it was too late. The whole force here does not amount to over 2,500 men, and 1,000 of these did not get ready to march before 12 o'clock to-day. I am looking anxiously for artillery." (Ibid., p. 629).

To Rufus Saxton[1]

Gen. Saxton   Washington City, D.C.
Harper's Ferry   May 25, 1862. 6.50 P.M.

One good six-gun battery, complete in it's men and appointments, is now on it's way to you from Baltimore. Eleven other guns of different sorts are on their way to you from here. Hope they will all reach you before morning.

As you have but twentyfive hundred men at Harper's Ferry, where are the rest which were in that vicinity, and which we have sent forward? Have any of them be[en] cut off?

                                          A. LINCOLN

[1] ALS, RPB. Saxton's reply was received at 10:10 P.M., as follows: "All the troops which were in this vicinity . . . are here. None of the troops which have arrived since I came here have been cut off. . . . the First Regiment District Volunteers . . . . arrived at Winchester just as . . . Banks commenced retreating. Three companies only got out of the cars. The train returned with the regiment, with the above-mentioned line of retreat, until it was too late. . . ." (OR, I, XII, I, 630).

To Rufus Saxton[1]

Gen. Saxton   Washington City, D.C.
Harper's Ferry   May 25, 1862. 10½ P.M.

I fear you have mistaken me. I did not mean to question the correctness of your conduct. On the contrary I approve what you have done. As the 2500, reported by you seemed small to me, I feared, some had got to Banks and been cut off with him. Please tell me the exact number you now have in hand.

                                          A LINCOLN

[1] ALS, RPB. Saxton replied May 26, "I have had as careful an estimate made of the force here as is possible at present. It amounts to 6,700 men. Many more are on the way. A portion of the artillery has arrived, including one light battery. . . ." (OR, I, XII, I, 632).

To Edward Bates[1]

                                 May 26, 1862

Will the Attorney General please give his opinion whether this claim of William H. DeGroot, should be paid, the resolution of Congress to the contrary notwithstanding.   A. LINCOLN
May 26, 1862.

[1] ALS, ORB. An endorsement in another hand reads as follows: "6 June 1862/Opinions Sent." The opinions are not in the Lincoln Papers. A joint resolution approved June 15, 1860, called for settlement by the secretary of War of damages, losses, and liabilities incurred by William H. DeGroot in connection

with the building of the Washington Aqueduct. A joint resolution approved February 21, 1861, repealed the resolution of June 15, 1860. A resolution reported in the House on July 9, 1861, requiring adjustment of DeGroot's claim, failed of passage.

To Andrew G. Curtin[1]

His Excellency A. G. Curtin   Executive Mansion
Gov. of Penn.   May 26. 1862

The bearer of this, Edward D. Baker, is the son of my very dear friend Col. Baker, who fell at Ball's Bluff. He thinks you might be induced to make him a field officer in a Pennsylvania Regiment. Disclaiming all wish to interfere in a matter so purely belonging to you and your State, I still say I would be much pleased, if he could be obliged. Yours truly   A. LINCOLN

[1] ALS, CSmH. Governor Curtin replied May 28, 1862, "Your letter by Lieutenant Baker was handed me yesterday. I have every desire to give the young gentleman a place in one of our Pennsylvania regiments not only from my respect to the memory of his father but my disposition to oblige you personally.

"I make all appointments . . . from the men in service and wherever possible in the order of seniority. To make an exception to my order the application must come from the regiment and I have advised Lieut. Baker to a course in reference to places now, or soon to be vacant in the California regiment under which I have reason to hope he will soon receive a commission." (DLC-RTL). Second Lieutenant Edward D. Baker, Jr., of the Fourth Cavalry in the Regular Army was promoted to first lieutenant on July 17, 1862, but did not receive an appointment from Curtin.

To George B. McClellan[1]

United States Military Telegraph,
Head-Quarters, Department Potomac
Maj Gen McClellan—   Washington May 26th 1862. 12 40 AM

We have Genl Banks official report. He has saved his army & baggage & has made a safe retreat to the river & is probably safe at Williamsport. He reports the attacking force at fifteen thousand (15000).   ABRAHAM LINCOLN

[1] Copy, DLC-McClellan Papers. No "official report" from Banks has been located. The probability is that Lincoln referred to Banks' message of May 25, 2:40 P.M. (see note, Lincoln to McClellan, May 25, 8½ P.M., *supra*).

To George B. McClellan[1]

Washington City, D.C.
Major Genl. McClellan.   May 26, 1862 10¼ P.M.

Can you not cut the Acquia Creek Railroad also? What impression have you, as to intrenchments—works—for you to contend

with in front of Richmond? Can you get near enough to throw shells into the city? A. LINCOLN

(Send in cypher).

¹ ALS, RPB. The received copy of McClellan's reply is dated May 26, 1862, 2 P.M. The discrepancy of its having been received before Lincoln's telegram was sent may represent an error of the telegraph office. The telegram reads as follows: "Have cut the Virginia Central Rail Road in three places between Hanover C.H. and the Chickahominy. Will try to cut the other. I do not think Richmond entrenchments formidable, but am not certain. Hope very soon to be within shelling distance. Have Rail road in operation from White House to Chickahominy. Hope to have Chickahominy bridge repaired tonight. Nothing of interest today." (DLC-RTL).

To Irvin McDowell¹

Major Genl. McDowell   Washington City, D.C.
Falmouth, Va.   May 26, 1862 1. P.M.

Despatchs from Geary, just received, have been sent you.² Should not the remainder of your force except sufficient to hold the point at Frederick'sburg, move this way—to Manassas junction, or to Alexandria? As commander of this Department should you not be here? I ask these questions. A. LINCOLN

¹ ALS, RPB. General Geary telegraphed Stanton from White Plains at 12:10 P.M. that Stonewall Jackson was advancing with a large force through Middleburg, and again from Broad Run at 12:30 which confirmed the information. McDowell replied that he thought the available forces sufficient and added, "I have not thought my presence needed elsewhere as much as here, but since there is a sufficient doubt to cause you to ask the question I will immediately leave here to go to Washington and will arrive early to-morrow morning, but will not move my headquarters till I have seen you. . . ." (OR, I, XII, III, 243).

² This sentence was revised by Stanton from Lincoln's, "I send you a despatch from Geary, just received."

To the Senate and House of Representatives¹

May 26, 1862

To the Senate and House of Representatives:

The insurrection which is yet existing in the United States, and aims at the overthrow of the federal Constitution and the Union,

¹ Thirty-seventh Congress, Second Session, Senate Executive Document No. 50. Cameron wrote Lincoln from St. Petersburg, June 26, 1862, "I must begin this my first letter from Russia, by thanking you for your Message to Congress, in relation to the N. York agencies. It was a good act, bravely done. Right, in itself, as it was, very many men, in your situation, would have permitted an innocent man to suffer rather than incur responsibility. I am glad to see that the leading papers of Europe speak of it, in high terms, as an act of 'nobleness'. . . ." (DLC-RTL).

was clandestinely prepared during the winter of 1860 and 1861, and assumed an open organization in the form of a treasonable provisional government at Montgomery, in Alabama, on the 18th day of February, 1861. On the 12th day of April, 1861, the insurgents committed the flagrant act of civil war by the bombardment and capture of Fort Sumter, which cut off the hope of immediate conciliation. Immediately afterwards all the roads and avenues to this city were obstructed, and the capital was put into the condition of a siege. The mails in every direction were stopped, and the lines of telegraph cut off by the insurgents, and military and naval forces, which had been called out by the government for the defence of Washington, were prevented from reaching the city by organized and combined treasonable resistance in the State of Maryland. There was no adequate and effective organization for the public defence. Congress had indefinitely adjourned. There was no time to convene them. It became necessary for me to choose whether, using only the existing means, agencies, and processes which Congress had provided, I should let the government fall at once into ruin, or whether, availing myself of the broader powers conferred by the Constitution in cases of insurrection, I would make an effort to save it with all its blessings for the present age and for posterity.

I thereupon summoned my constitutional advisers, the heads of all the departments, to meet on Sunday, the 20th [21st] day of April, 1861, at the office of the Navy Department, and then and there, with their unanimous concurrence, I directed that an armed revenue cutter should proceed to sea, to afford protection to the commercial marine, and especially the California treasure ships then on their way to this coast. I also directed the commandant of the navy yard at Boston to purchase or charter, and arm as quickly as possible, five steamships, for purposes of public defence. I directed the commandant of the navy yard at Philadelphia to purchase, or charter and arm, an equal number for the same purpose. I directed the commandant at New York to purchase, or charter and arm, an equal number. I directed Commander Gillis[2] to purchase, or charter and arm, and put to sea two other vessels. Similar directions were given to Commodore DuPont,[3] with a view to the opening of passages by water to and from the capital. I directed the several officers to take the advice and obtain the aid and efficient services in the matter of his excellency Edwin D. Morgan, the governor of New York, or, in his absence, George D. Morgan, William M. Evarts, R. M. Blatchford, and Moses H. Grinnell, who

[2] John P. Gillis.   [3] Samuel F. Du Pont.

were, by my directions, especially empowered by the Secretary of the Navy to act for his department in that crisis, in matters pertaining to the forwarding of troops and supplies for the public defence.

On the same occasion I directed that Governor Morgan and Alexander Cummings, of the city of New York, should be authorized by the Secretary of War, Simon Cameron, to make all necessary arrangements for the transportation of troops and munitions of war, in aid and assistance of the officers of the army of the United States, until communication by mails and telegraph should be completely re-established between the cities of Washington and New York. No security was required to be given by them, and either of them was authorized to act in case of inability to consult with the other.

On the same occasion I authorized and directed the Secretary of the Treasury to advance, without requiring security, two millions of dollars of public money to John A. Dix, George Opdyke, and Richard M. Blatchford, of New York, to be used by them in meeting such requisitions as should be directly consequent upon the military and naval measures necessary for the defence and support of the government, requiring them only to act without compensation, and to report their transactions when duly called upon.

The several departments of the government at that time contained so large a number of disloyal persons that it would have been impossible to provide safely, through official agents only, for the performance of the duties thus confided to citizens favorably known for their ability, loyalty, and patriotism.

The several orders issued upon these occurrences were transmitted by private messengers, who pursued a circuitous way to the seaboard cities, inland, across the States of Pennsylvania and Ohio and the northern lakes. I believe that by these and other similar measures taken in that crisis, some of which were without any authority of law, the government was saved from overthrow. I am not aware that a dollar of the public funds thus confided without authority of law to unofficial persons was either lost or wasted, although apprehensions of such misdirection occurred to me as objections to those extraordinary proceedings, and were necessarily overruled.

I recall these transactions now because my attention has been directed to a resolution which was passed by the House of Representatives on the 30th day of last month, which is in these words:

"*Resolved*, That Simon Cameron, late Secretary of War, by investing Alexander Cummings with the control of large sums of the public money, and authority to purchase military supplies without restriction, without requiring from him any guarantee for the faithful performance of his duties, when the services of competent public officers were available, and by involving the government in a vast number of contracts with persons not legitimately engaged in the business pertaining to the subject-matter of such contracts, especially in the purchase of arms for future delivery, has adopted a policy highly injurious to the public service, and deserves the censure of the House."

Congress will see that I should be wanting equally in candor and in justice if I should leave the censure expressed in this resolution to rest exclusively or chiefly upon Mr. Cameron. The same sentiment is unanimously entertained by the heads of departments, who participated in the proceedings which the House of Representatives has censured. It is due to Mr. Cameron to say that, although he fully approved the proceedings, they were not moved nor suggested by himself, and that not only the President but all the other heads of departments were at least equally responsible with him for whatever error, wrong, or fault was committed in the premises.   ABRAHAM LINCOLN.

Washington, May 26, 1862.

To John C. Frémont[1]

Major General Fremont.   Washington City, D.C.
Moorefield   May 27 1862. [9.58 P.M.]

I see you are at Moorefield. You were expressly ordered to march to Harrisonburg   What does this mean?

A. LINCOLN

[1] LS, RPB. This telegram is in Stanton's handwriting signed by Lincoln. Frémont replied May 28, 6 A.M., "My troops were not in condition to execute your order—otherwise than has been done. They have marched day & night to do it. The men had had so little to eat that many were weak for want of food & so reported by the Chief Surgeon   Having for main object as stated in your telegram, the relief of Genl Banks the line of march followed was a necessity. In executing any order rec'd I take it for granted that I am to exercise discretion concerning it's literal execution according to circumstances if I am to understand that literal obedience to orders is required please say so. I have no desire to exercise any power which you do not think belongs of necessity to my position in the field." (DLC-RTL). On Lincoln's direction Stanton telegraphed Frémont three separate times on May 28 to "move against the enemy." An undated message from Frémont to Stanton in reply to one of these telegrams reads as follows: "Your telegram conveying information from General Hamilton was received at seven this evening. The President's order will be obeyed accordingly." (DLC-RTL).

To George B. McClellan[1]

Major Gen. McClellan   Washington, May 28. 1862.

What of F. J. Porter's expedition? Please answer.

A LINCOLN

(Send in Cypher)

[1] ALS, RPB. Apparently this message was not received at McClellan's head-quarters until after McClellan had telegraphed a report of General Fitz-John Porter's action of the previous day. McClellan's report dated May 28, 2 P.M., is as follows: "Porter's action of yesterday was truly a glorious victory. Too much credit cannot be given to his magnificent division and its accomplished leader. The route of rebels was complete—not a defeat, but a complete rout. Prisoners are constantly coming in; two companies have this moment arrived, with excellent arms.

"There is no doubt that the enemy are concentrating everything on Richmond. I will do my best to cut off Jackson, but am doubtful whether I can.

"It is the policy and duty of the Government to send me by water all the well-drilled troops available. I am confident that Washington is in no danger. Engines and cars in large numbers have been sent up to bring down Jackson's command. I may not be able to cut them off, but will try. We have cut all but the Fredericksburg and Richmond Railroad. The real issue is in the battle about to be fought in front of Richmond. All our available troops should be collected here—not raw regiments, but the well-drilled troops. It cannot be ignored that a desperate battle is before us. If any regiments of good troops remain unemployed it will be an irreparable fault committed." (OR, I, XI, I, 35).

Randolph B. Marcy replied to Lincoln's prior query at 11 P.M., as follows: "Your despatch to Gen McClellan this moment received and despatched by special messenger to him. In his absence directing operations in front I have the honor to state . . . that the troops under Gen F J Porter marched more than twenty (20) miles yesterday through rain and mud fought six hours and were at the close of the action encumbered with some six hundred (600) killed and wounded including those of the enemy to be buried & cared for with five or six hundred prisoners to be guarded which prevented Genl Porter from pressing forward last night to cut the Fredericksburg and Richmond Rail Road   This will be done tomorrow   The prisoners that were taken yesterday and are here now say that they were ordered to reinforce Jackson via Hanover Junction and were ordered back to Richmond   It is therefore presumed that this is the same force referred to by Genl King" (DLC-RTL).

To George B. McClellan[1]

Washington City, D.C.

Maj. Gen. McClellan   May 28, 1862. 8.40 P.M.

I am very glad of Gen. F. J. Porter's victory. Still, if it was a total rout of the enemy, I am puzzled to know why the Richmond and Fredericksburg Railroad was not seized. Again, as you say you have *all* the Railroads but the Richmond and Fredericksburg, I am puzzled to see how, lacking that, you can have any, except the scrap from Richmond to West-Point. The scrap of the Virginia

Central from Richmond to Hanover Junction, without more, is simply nothing.

That the whole force of the enemy is concentrating in Richmond, I think can not be certainly known to you or me. Saxton, at Harper's Ferry, informs us that a large force (supposed to be Jackson's and Ewells) forced his advance from Charlestown today. Gen. King telegraphs us from Frederick'sburg that contrabands give certain information that fifteen thousand left Hanover Junction monday morning to re-inforce Jackson. I am painfully impressed with the importance of the struggle before you; and I shall aid you all I can consistently with my view of due regard to all points.[2]   A. LINCOLN

[1] ALS, RPB. McClellan's reaction to this message is indicated by his reply to Stanton on May 30, "From the tone of your dispatches and the President's I do not think that you at all appreciate the value and magnitude of Porter's victory. It has entirely relieved my right flank . . . routed and demoralized a considerable portion of the rebel forces; taken over 750 prisoners; killed and wounded large numbers. . . . It was one of the handsomest things in the war. . . . I regard the burning of South Anna bridges as the least important result of Porter's movement. . . ." (I, XI, I, 37).

[2] Lincoln deleted an additional clause: "and last I must be the Judge as to the *duty*, of the government in this respect."

To Irvin McDowell[1]

Gen. McDowell   Washington City, D.C.
Manassas Junction   May 28, 1862. 1 P.M

Gen. McClellan, at half past six P.M. yesterday telegraphed that Fitz John Porter's Division had fought and driven thirteen thousand of the enemy, under Gen. Branch[2] from Hanover Court-House, and was driving them from a stand they had made on the Rail-Road, at the time the messenger left. Two hours later he telegraphed that Stoneman had captured an Engine and six cars on the Virginia Central which he at once sent to communicate with F. J. Porter. Nothing further from McClellan.

If Porter effects a lodgement on both R.R. near Hanover C.H. consider whether your force in front of Fredericksburg should not push through and join him.   A. LINCOLN

[1] ALS, RPB. McDowell's reply, received at 5:45 P.M., reads as follows: "I beg leave to report, in reply to your telegram of this morning directing me to consider whether my force in front of Fredericksburg should not push through and join the army under General McClellan, that I do not think, in the present state of affairs, it would be well to attempt to push through a part of that force, or to leave Fredericksburg otherwise than strongly held which could not be done as the troops are now posted. I trust in a few days to be able to effect the object you have in view, and which no one desires more than I do." (OR, I, XII, III, 267-68).   [2] Lawrence O. Branch.

To Irvin McDowell[1]

Major-General McDowell: Washington, May 28, 1862.

Following received from Brigadier-General Hamilton:
Harper's Ferry, May 28, 1862.

Hon. E. M. Stanton, Secretary of War:

There is very little doubt that Jackson's force is between Winchester and Charlestown. His troops were too much fatigued to pursue Banks. A large body of rebel cavalry is near Charlestown now. Jackson and Ewell were near Bunker Hill yesterday at noon. Of this there is no doubt. A. LINCOLN.

[1] OR, I, XII, III, 269. McDowell's reply, received at 7:20 P.M., reads as follows: "In reply to your last telegram acquainting me with the position of Jackson and Ewell I beg leave to report that I am pushing Generals Shields and [Edward O.C.] Ord upon Front Royal with all expedition possible. As soon as the railroads can be unloaded I will use them to get the troops forward, so that nothing shall be left undone to catch them. To guard against all chances please have the water transportation retained at Aquia Creek sufficient to bring up a division, with its artillery, from below if it should be needed. I will have one held ready to move up at short notice." (Ibid.).

To Irvin McDowell[1]

Gen. McDowell Washington,
Mannassas Junction May 28. 1862. 4. P.M.

You say Gen. Geary's scouts report that they find no enemy this side of the Blue Ridge. Neither do I. Have *they* been *to* the Blue Ridge looking for them? A. LINCOLN

[1] ALS, RPB. McDowell had telegraphed Stanton, "General Geary reports this a.m. that his scouts find nothing of the enemy this side of the Blue Ridge. Nothing else of importance." (OR, I, XII, III, 267).

To Irvin McDowell[1]

Gen. McDowell Washington City, D.C.
Mannassas Junction May 28, 1862—5.40. P.M.

I think the evidence now preponderates that Ewell and Jackson are still about Winchester. Assuming this, it is, for you a question of legs. Put in all the speed you can. I have told Fremont as much, and directed him to drive at them as fast as possible. By the way, I suppose you know, Fremont has got up to Moorefield, instead of going to Harrisonburg. A. LINCOLN

[1] ALS, RPB. McDowell's reply, received at 11:18 P.M., reads as follows: "I beg to assure you that I am doing everything which legs and steam are capable of to hurry forward matters in this quarter. I shall be deficient in wagons when I get out of the way of the railroad for transporting supplies, but shall push on nevertheless." (OR, I, XII, III, 270).

[246]

Recommendation for Ward H. Lamon[1]

May 28, 1862

The bearer of this, W. H. Lamon, is Marshal of D.C,—my particular friend, born & raised at Bunker-Hill, an excellent horseman, and, I think, will be most valuable for scouting purposes.
May 28, 1862.   A. LINCOLN

[1] ADS, CSmH. No reference has been found as to the use Lamon made of this recommendation or pass.

To Nathaniel P. Banks[1]

Maj. Gen. Banks   Washington City, D.C.
Williamsport, Md.   May 29, 1862. 12. M.

Gen. McDowell's advance should & probably will be at or near Front Royal at 12. M to-morrow. Gen. Fremont will be at or near Strasburg as soon. Please watch the enemy closely, and follow & harrass and detain him, if he attempts to retire. I mean this for Gen. Saxton's force as well as that immediately with you.
A. LINCOLN

[1] ALS, RPB. Banks replied upon receipt of Lincoln's message at 3:30 P.M., "My command is much disabled, but we will do what we can to carry out your views." (OR, I, XII, I, 533).

To John C. Frémont[1]

Maj. Gen. Fremont   Washington City, D.C.
Moorefield, Va.   May 29, 1862. 12.M.

Gen. McDowell's advance, if not checked by the enemy, should, and probably will, be at Front-Royal by 12 (noon) to-morrow. His force, when up, will be about twenty thousand. Please have your force at Strasburg, or (if the route you are moving on does not lead to that point) as near Strasburg as the enemy may be, by the same time. Your despatch No. 30, received, and satisfactory.
A. LINCOLN

[1] ALS, RPB. At 11 P.M. on May 28, Stanton telegraphed Lincoln's direction that Frémont should halt at Moorefield and await orders unless the enemy should be in the general direction of Romney, in which case Frémont should move upon him. Frémont telegraphed to Stanton the following day that Lincoln's order, "will be obeyed as promptly as possible, and I am now engaged in drawing forward my force. My reconnoitering parties out last night 22 miles, to Wardensville, report Jackson's force 4 miles below Winchester; rear guard at Strasburg; headquarters, Winchester. Reconnaissance returned to Romney at 11 last night from 15 miles out. Report Jackson, [Edward] Johnson, and Ewell at Chester, and rebel cavalry sent from Winchester toward Harper's Ferry and Martinsburg." (OR, I, XII, I, 647).

[247]

To George B. McClellan[1]

(Cypher)

Washington City, D.C.

Major General McClellan: May 29, 1862. 10½ A.M.

I think we shall be able, within three days, to tell you certainly, whether any considerable force of the enemy, Jackson, or any one else is moving onto Harper's Ferry, or vicinity. Take this expected developement into your calculations.   A. LINCOLN—

[1] ALS, RPB.

To Irvin McDowell[1]

Maj. Gen. McDowell   Washington City, D.C.

Manassas Junction   May 29 1862.   12.M.

Gen. Fremont's force should, and probably will, be at or near Strasburg by twelve (noon) to-morrow. Try to have your force, or the advance of it, at Front-Royal, as soon.   A. LINCOLN.

[1] ALS, RPB. McDowell's telegram to Stanton, received at 5:45 P.M., reads in part as follows: ". . . Shields reported an accident on the railroad at Thoroughfare Gap which he feared could not be repaired under twenty-four hours. . . . I sent him the President's telegram and he reports he will make such arrangements that will enable him to be in Front Royal before 12 o'clock m. to-morrow, with his other two brigades within 4 miles of the town by the same hour. Since then the locomotive and force sent from here have repaired the break in the road. . . ." (OR, I, XII, III, 277).

To Randolph B. Marcy[1]

Gen. R. B. Marcy   Washington,

McClellan's Head Quarters   May 29, 1862. 10. A.M.

Yours just received. I think it can-not be certainly known whether the force which fought Gen. Porter is the same which recently confronted McDowell. Another item of evidence bearing on it is that Gen. Branch commanded against Porter, while it was Gen. Anderson who was in front of McDowell. He and McDowell were in correspondence about prisoners.   A. LINCOLN

[1] ALS, RPB. Marcy replied, "In answer to your dispatch of this morning I have the honor to state that several rebel officers, taken prisoners on the 27th, say they confidently expected to have been re-enforced on that day by Anderson's command. General Porter reports that South Anna railroad bridge was fired this morning, and a large amount of Confederate property destroyed at Ashland. General Porter's command is now on its march back to this place, having executed his instructions." (OR, I, XI, III, 199).

To Randolph B. Marcy[1]

Gen. R. B. Marcy   Washington City, D.C.
McClellans Head Quarters   May 29, 1862. 1.20 P.M.

Your despatch, as to South Anna, and Ashland being seized by our forces this morning, is received. Understanding these points to be on the Richmond and Fredericksburg Railroad, I heartily congratulate the country, and thank Gen. McClellan and his army for their seizure.   A. LINCOLN

[1] ALS, RPB.

To Edwin M. Stanton[1]

May 29, 1862

This boy is said to be only nineteen years of age, and so diseased as to be unfit for Military duty. As nearly the entire Congressional delegations from Ky. & Va. ask his release, the Secretary of War will please bail him to the bearer, who is his brother-in-law.

May 29, 1862.   A. LINCOLN.

[1] Thomas F. Madigan, *A Catalogue of Lincolniana* (1929), No. 34. According to the catalog description, this is an autograph document signed. The Register of letters received by the secretary of War on this date lists a missing item of this description concerning the release of James Lindsay of Virginia (DNA WR RG 107, P 63).

To an Unidentified Person[1]

Please see Mr. Smith the bearer, a moment.   A. L.

May 29, 1862

[1] Parke-Bernet Catalog 841, February 25, 1947, No. 166.

To Nathaniel P. Banks[1]

Majr. Gen. Banks   Washington City, D.C.
Williamsport, Md.   May 30, 1862 10¼ A.M.

If the enemy, in force, is in or about Martinsburg, Charlestown, and Winchester, or any or all of them, he may come in collision with Fremont; in which case I am anxious that your force, with you, and at Harper's Ferry, should so operate as to assist Fremont, if possible. The same, if the enemy should engage McDowell. This was the meaning of my despatch yesterday.   A. LINCOLN

[1] ALS, RPB. Banks' reply, received at 4:45 P.M., reads as follows: "Your communication received. Have sent part of our force to Antietam Ford, near Shepherdstown. Will do all we can to harass the enemy's rear. No indication of enemy this side of Martinsburg, and we believe no considerable force there." (OR, I, XII, I, 535).

To John C. Frémont[1]

Maj. Gen. Fremont   Washington City, D.C.
Moorefield, Va.   May 30. 1862 11½ A.M.

Yours of this morning from Moorefield, just received. There can not be more than twenty, probably not more than fifteen thousand of the enemy, at or about Winchester. Where *is* your force? It ought this minute to be near Strasburg. Answer at once.

                                      A. LINCOLN

[1] ALS, RPB. Frémont's telegram received at 11:30 A.M. reads as follows: "Scouts and men from Winchester represent Jackson's force variously at 30,000 to 60,000. With him Generals Ewell and [James] Longstreet." (OR, I, XII, I, 648).

To John C. Frémont[1]

Major Gen. Fremont   Washington City, D.C.
Moorefield, Va.   May 30, 1862   2½ P.M.

Yours saying you will reach Strasburg, or vicinity, at five PM, saturday, has been received and sent to Gen. McDowell, & he directed to act in view of it. You must be up to time you promise if possible. Corinth was evacuated last night and is occupied by our troops to-day—the enemy gone South to Okalona [*sic*] on the Railroad to Mobile.   A. LINCOLN

[1] ALS, RPB. Frémont's despatch of May 29, reads in part as follows: "My command is not yet in marching order. It has been necessary to halt to-day to bring up parts of regiments and to receive stragglers, hundreds of whom from Blenker's division strewed the roads. You can conceive the condition of the command from the fact that the medical director this morning protested against its farther advance without allowing one day's rest. . . . I could not venture to proceed with it in disorder, and cannot with safety undertake to be at the point you mention earlier than by 5 o'clock on Saturday afternoon. At that hour I will be at or near it, according to position of the enemy. . . . Will be on the road early to-morrow . . . and couriers will be provided to bring on your answer, which please send to-night, and let me know if General McDowell's force can be so controlled as to make this combination." (OR, I, XII, I, 647). Lincoln made a copy of this reply (DLC-RTL) and forwarded the original to the telegraph office with his message to McDowell sent at 2:30 P.M., *infra*.

To John C. Frémont[1]

Maj. Gen. Fremont   Washington City, D.C.
Moorefield[2]   May 30. 1862 9 ½ P.M

I send you a despatch just received from Gen. Saxton at Harper's Ferry.

                  (Here insert it at length)

[250]

It seems the game is before you. Have sent a copy to Gen. Mc-Dowell.   A. LINCOLN

[1] ALS, RPB. The telegram from General Saxton which was inserted in this message and also in the message to McDowell dispatched at 9:30 P.M. (*infra*), reads as follows:

"The rebels are in line of battle in front of our lines. They have nine pieces of artillery in position and cavalry. I shelled the woods in which they were, and they in return threw a large number of shells into the lines and tents from which I moved last night to take up a stronger position. I expect a great deal from the battery on the mountain, having here 9-inch Dahlgren's bearing directly on the enemy's approaches. The enemy appeared this morning, and then retired with the intention of driving us out. I shall act on the defensive, as my position is a strong one. In a skirmish which took place this afternoon I lost 1 horse; the enemy lost 2 men killed and some wounded." (OR, I, XII, I, 648-49). Frémont replied to Lincoln's telegram, "Your telegram of thirty first [thirtieth] received. Main column at this place[2] Roads heavy and weather terrible Heavy storm of rain most of yesterday and all last night Our cavalry and scouts have covered the roads ten to fifteen miles ahead The enemy's cavalry and ours now in sight of each other on the Strasburg road. Engagement expected today The army is pushing forward and I intend to carry out operations proposed" (DLC-RTL).   [2] "Moorefield" inserted, not in Lincoln's handwriting.

To Irvin McDowell[1]

Maj. Gen. McDowell.   Washington City, D.C.
Manassas Junction.   May 30. 1862. 10. A.M.

I somewhat apprehend that Fremont's force, in it's present condition, may not be quite strong enough in case it comes in collision with the enemy. For this additional reason, I wish you to push forward your column as rapidly as possible. Tell me what number your force reaching Front Royal will amount to.

A. LINCOLN

[1] ALS, RPB. McDowell's reply received at 12:30 P.M. reads in part as follows: "I am pushing forward every thing to the utmost as I telegraphed the Secy of War last night. Major General Shields did not think he could make Front Royal before tonight. I sent him your telegraph and asked what could be done by extraordinary exertions, towards accomplishing your wishes that the advance of my force should be at Front Royal by twelve oclock noon today I informed him of the position of affairs and how necessary it was to forward He fully appreciated the course and said he would . . . be at Front Royal by noon and two other Brigades within five miles of Front Royal by the same time. It will require driving to accomplish this and the day is hot. I am urging Genl Ord forward with all the physical power of the Rail Road & of the moral power of a strong representation of the urgency of the cause. he may be beyond Rectorstown tonight. Genl Shields has ten thousand nine hundred . . . men & Genl Ord nine thousand about 20000 between them Bayards cavalry brigade will amount to about two thousand 2000 Gearys will amount to about fifteen hundred (1500) All this will give me about twenty one thousand 21000 men for offensive purposes—the others being required to guard Bridges and Rail road in the rear. . . . May I ask the force which . . . Fremont will have with him at Strasburg. . . . Will Blenker form part. . . . " (DLC-RTL).

[251]

To Irvin McDowell[1]

Major Gen. McDowell   Washington City, D.C.
Rectortown   May 30, 1862. 12.40. [P.M.]

Your despatch of to-day received, and is satisfactory. Fremont has nominally twenty-two thousand, really about seventeen thousand. Blencker's Division is part of it. I have a despatch from Fremont this morning, not telling me where he is, but he says "Scouts and men from Winchester represent Jacksons force variously at thirty to sixty thousand. With him Gen. Ewell and Longstreet." The high figures erroneous of course. Do you not know where Longstreet is?

Corinth is evacuated and occupied by us.[2]   A. LINCOLN.

[1] ALS, RPB. Lincoln's address "Manassas Junction" was deleted and "Rectortown" substituted in the telegraph office.
[2] This sentence has been added in an unidentified handwriting.

To Irvin McDowell[1]

                        Washington City, D.C.
Major Gen. McDowell   May 30. 1862. 2½ P.M.

Herewith I send a telegram just received from Gen. Fremont. The despatch is dated of last night, and the point he says he will be at, five o'clock Saturday afternoon, is "Strasburg, or as near it, as it may be to the enemy at that time." I direct Fremont to come to time as fixed by himself, and you will act your discretion, taking this information into your calculation.   A. LINCOLN

[1] ALS, RPB. McDowell's telegram to Meigs, May 30, acknowledged receipt of "the President's telegram, sending me a copy of a dispatch from General Fremont." (OR, I, XII, III, 292). The dispatch from Frémont is given in the note to Lincoln's telegram to Frémont of 2:30 P.M., *supra*.

To Irvin McDowell[1]

Maj. Gen. McDowell   Washington City. D.C.
Rectortown, Va   May 30. 1862. 9½ P.M.

I send you a despatch just received from Gen. Saxton at Harper's Ferry—

         (Here insert it at length)

It seems the game is before you. Have sent a copy to Gen. Fremont   A. LINCOLN

[1] ALS, RPB. For the text of Saxton's dispatch see note to Lincoln's telegram to Frémont 9 ½ P.M., *supra*.

[252]

To the Senate[1]

To the Senate of the United States.   May 30, 1862

I transmit to the Senate, for its consideration with a view to ratification, a Treaty of Amity, Commerce, Consular privileges and Extradition between the United States and the Republic of Salvador, signed in this City on the 29th. instant. It is believed that, though this instrument contains no stipulation which may not be found in some subsisting Treaty between the United States and Foreign Powers, it will prove to be mutually advantageous. Several of the Republics of this hemisphere, among which is Salvador, are alarmed at a supposed sentiment tending to reactionary movements against Republican institutions on this continent. It seems therefore to be proper that we should show to any of them who may apply for that purpose, that, compatibly with our cardinal policy and with an enlightened view of our own interests, we are willing to encourage them by strengthening our ties of good will and good neighborhood with them.   ABRAHAM LINCOLN

Washington, 30 May 1862.

[1] DS, DNA RG 46, Senate 37B B19. The treaty was amended and unanimously ratified by the Senate on June 23, 1862.

To Edwin M. Stanton[1]

Let the appointment be made as within requested by Senator Henderson.   A. LINCOLN

May 30. 1862.

[1] AES, IHi. Lincoln's endorsement appears on a letter from Senator John B. Henderson, May 29, 1862, recommending William K. Kennedy of Louisiana, Missouri, for appointment as assistant quartermaster with rank of captain. Kennedy was nominated on June 4 and was confirmed by the Senate on June 11, 1862.

To Elihu B. Washburne[1]

May 30, 1862

The President directs Mr. Washburne to say to his German friends in N.Y. that Col. Willich has already been appointed a brigadier General   A. LINCOLN

Executive Mansion,
May 30, 1862.

[1] DS-P, ISLA. Colonel August Willich of the Thirty-second Indiana Volunteers was nominated brigadier general on May 17 and confirmed by the Senate on July 17, 1862.

To George A. McCall[1]

Washington, May 31, 1862—3.35.
Brigadier-General McCall, Commanding, Fredericksburg:
Are you about to withdraw from Fredericksburg; and, if so,
why, and by whose orders?   A. LINCOLN.

[1] OR, I, XII, III, 305. McCall replied as follows: "Despatch received   I am
not about to withdraw from Fredericksburg but I have received the following
orders from Genl McDowell
" 'Draw in your force moving them on the left bank of the River — holding
yourself on the defensive   Keeping Fredericksburg   Guard the bridges to
Aquia Creek by completing the Block Houses near them'
"I have in obedience to these orders withdrawn all my forces except a sufficient
guard for the city police and the out pickets from the right bank of the River
and have made such disposition of my command as seems to me best calculated
to resist an attack from any quarter   I have no idea of withdrawing from
this position without orders   I have scouts out in the direction of Spotsylvania
Court House and the forks of the Rappahannock and will report the result of
their observations on their return" (DLC-RTL). To this Stanton replied that
"The President directs me to say to you that there can be nothing to justify a
panic at Fredericksburg. He expects you to maintain your position there as becomes a soldier and a general." (OR, I, XII, III, 306).

To George B. McClellan[1]

Washington City, D.C.
Major Gen. McClellan   May 31, 1862. 10.20 P.M.
   A circle whose circumference shall pass through Harper's Ferry,
Front-Royal, and Strasburg, and whose center shall be a little
North East of Winchester, almost certainly has within it this
morning, the forces of Jackson, Ewell, and Edward Johnson. Quite
certainly they were within it two days ago. Some part of these
forces attacked Harper's Ferry at dark last evening, and are still
in sight this morning. Shields—with McDowell's advance, re-took
Front Royal at 11 A.M. yesterday, with a dozen of our own prisoners taken there a week ago, one hundred and fifty of the enemy,
two locomotives and eleven cars, some other property and stores,
and saved the bridge. Fremont, from the direction of Moorefield,
promises to be at or near Strasburg at 5. P.M. to-day. Banks, at
Williamsport, with his old force, and his new force at Harpers
Ferry, is directed to co-operate. Shields, at Front-Royal, reports a
rumor of still an additional force of the enemy, supposed to be Anderson's, having entered the valley of Virginia. This last may or
may not be true. Corinth is certainly in the hands of Gen. Halleck.   A. LINCOLN

[1] ALS, RPB.

[254]

To George B. McClellan[1]

Washington City, D.C.

Major Gen. McClellan   June 1. 1862. 9½ [A.M.]

You are probably engaged with the enemy. I suppose he made the attack. Stand well on your guard—hold all your ground, or yield any only, inch by inch and in good order. This morning we merge Gen. Wool's department into yours, giving you command of the whole, and sending Gen. Dix to Fortress-Monroe, and Gen. Wool to Fort-McHenry. We also send Gen. Sigel to report to you for duty.   A. LINCOLN

[1] ALS, RPB. The Battle of Fair Oaks was fought May 31-June 1.

To George B. McClellan[1]

Washington City, D.C.

Major Gen. McClellan.   June 1, 1862. 1.15. P.M.

You are already notified that Gen. Sigel is to report to you for duty. I suggest—(do not order) that he have command of such of the forces about Fort-Monroe, Norfolk, Newports-News, &c. as you may see fit to put into active service, or such other command as may be suitable to his rank.   A. LINCOLN

[1] ALS, RPB.

To George B. McClellan[1]

Washington City, D.C.

Major Gen. McClellan.   June 1, 1862. 5. P.M.

Thanks for what you *could,* and *did* say, in your despatch of noon to-day to the Sec. of War. If the enemy shall not have renewed the attack this afternoon, I think the hardest of your work is done.

Shields' advance came in collision with part of the enemy yesterday evening six miles from Front-Royal in a direction between Winchester & Strausburg, driving them back, capturing a few prisoners and one rifled cannon. Firing in that direction to-day, heard both from Harper's Ferry and Front Royal, indicate a probability that Fremont has met the enemy.

We have concluded to send Gen. Sigel to Harper's Ferry, so that what I telegraphed you about him this morning, is revoked.[2] Dix goes to Fort-Monroe to-night.   A. LINCOLN

[255]

1 ALS, RPB. McClellan reported to Stanton at 12 o'clock, June 1, "We have had a desperate battle, in which the corps of Sumner, Heintzelman, and Keyes have been engaged against greatly superior numbers. Yesterday, at 1, the enemy . . . attacked our troops on the right bank. . . . [Silas] Casey's division . . . gave way unaccountably. . . . Heintzelman and Kearny . . . checked the enemy . . . [John] Sedgwick's and [Israel B.] Richardson's divisions . . . drove back the enemy at the point of the bayonet. . . .

"This morning the enemy attempted to renew the conflict, but was everywhere repulsed. . . . Our loss is heavy, but that of the enemy must be enormous. . . ." (OR, I, XI, I, 749).

2 Stanton telegraphed Banks that Sigel had been assigned to command "troops at Harper's Ferry, numbering about 10,000, and directed to report to you. . . . the President desires you to assume actively the offensive against the retreating enemy without the loss of an hour. . . ." (OR, I, XII, I, 538).

To Edward Bates[1]

Hon. Attorney General   Executive Mansion,
My dear Sir   Washington, June 2, 1862.

Judge Pettis having resigned, as appears by his letter herewith inclosed please send me a nomination for Allen A. Bradford as his successor. Yours truly   A. LINCOLN

1 ALS, DNA GE RG 60, Papers of Attorney General, Segregated Lincoln Material. Allen A. Bradford of Colorado Territory, nominated associate justice for that territory replacing S. Newton Pettis, was confirmed by the Senate on June 6, 1862.

To Salmon P. Chase[1]

Hon. Sec. of Treasury   Executive Mansion
My dear Sir.   Washington June 2. 1862

Please send a nomination for George W. Lane of Indiana as Superintendent of the Mint at Denver, Colorado Territory. Yours truly   A. LINCOLN.

1 Copy, IHi-Nicolay and Hay Papers. Chase replied the same day, "I have just received your note in relation to the appointment of Superintendent of the Mint at Denver . . . together with the letter addressed to you by Messrs. Lane and Wright, of Indiana, and General J.H. Lane of Kansas urging the appointment of a brother of General Lane residing in Indiana. . . . All these gentlemen, I think — the two last named certainly — have called on me separately in reference to this appointment; and I have explained to each the grounds on which I felt obliged to decline recommending the nomination. . . . The right of making the appointment is unquestionably yours; but I am confident you will not direct it to be made without at least considering what I have to say in regard to it." (DLC-RTL). After some delay Lincoln appointed George W. Lane during the recess of the Senate and sent in his nomination on January 5, 1863. The appointment was confirmed on January 16, 1863.

To Montgomery C. Meigs[1]

Executive Mansion,
Dear Sir   Washington, June 2, 1862.
This will introduce to you Judge Nathaniel Niles of Belleville,
Illinois, a personal friend of mine, and one of our most estimable
citizens. Yours Truly   A. LINCOLN
Gen. M. C. Meigs
     Quarter Master General.

[1] LS, IHi. Judge Nathaniel Niles organized the One Hundred Thirtieth
Illinois Volunteers and served as colonel from its muster on October 25, 1862,
until he resigned on May 6, 1864.

Memorandum[1]

[c. June 2, 1862]
Profoundly laid by.

[1] AE, DLC-RTL. Lincoln's endorsement is written on an envelope containing
a report from Seward, June 2, 1862, concerning a message from the governor of
Washington Territory asking interference in the plan of France to seize Acapulco
and Western Mexico.

To James W. Ripley[1]

Will Gen. Ripley please consider whether this Musket-shell, would
be a valuable missile in battle?   A. LINCOLN
June 2. 1862.

[1] ALS, RPB. This note is misdated June 2, 1861, in Tracy, p. 186.

To Edwin M. Stanton[1]

Will the Secretary of War please have this claim investigated, and
if found just and lawful have it paid.   A. LINCOLN
June. 2. 1862.

[1] AES, owned by L. E. Dicke, Evanston, Illinois. Lincoln's endorsement is
written on a letter from Gustavus A. Seidel of New York, presenting a claim for
expenses in recruiting a regiment (Lincoln Guards) in July, 1861, the order
for recruiting having been revoked on August 10 before the regiment was full.
No further record of the case has been found.

To George B. McClellan[1]

Washington City, D.C.
Majr. Gen. McClellan   June 3 1862
With these continuous rains, I am very anxious about the Chickahominy so close in your rear, and crossing your line of communication. Please look well to it.   A. LINCOLN

[257]

1 ALS, RPB. McClellan telegraphed at 8:30 P.M., "Your despatch of Five PM just received. As the Chickahominy has been almost the only obstacle in my way for several days your Excellency may rest assured that it has not been overlooked Every effort has been made and will continue to be to perfect the communication across it Nothing of importance except that it is again raining." (DLC-RTL).

To Irvin McDowell[1]

Majr. Genl. McDowell Washington City, D.C.
Front-Royal, Va June 3, 1862 6.15 P.M.

Anxious to know whether Shields can head or flank Jackson. Please tell about where Shields and Jackson respectively are, at the time this reaches you. A. LINCOLN

1 ALS, RPB. McDowell telegraphed June 4, 12:10 A.M., that he could only infer the position of "Stonewall" Jackson's army, "as I have nothing on that point from either Genl Fremont or Genl Shields Since Fremont has been in Woodstock Jackson has had time to be south of Mt Jackson with macadamized turnpike. Shields is at Luray—his advance at the Shenandoah on the road to New Market with an indifferent road which the constant rains are making bad and with the Shenandoah impassable and rising." (DLC-RTL).

To Edward Bates[1]

June 4, 1862

Let a pardon be issued in this case agreeably to the recommendation of the Secretary of War. A. LINCOLN

1 ES, DNA RG 204, U.S. Pardon Attorney, A 412. The endorsement is signed but not written by Lincoln, on a recommendation for remission of punishment of Private Thomas F. Kelley (Kelly) of the Fortieth New York Volunteers, found guilty of insubordination and sentenced to hard labor and dishonorable discharge.

To Edward Bates[1]

June 4, 1862

I said yesterday if the Kentucky delegation or a majority of them, would ask in writing, for the pardon of Franks, I would grant it. Having so asked, then the Attorney General will please make out the pardon.

Also exercise his discretion as to directing *"Nolle prossequis"*
June 4. 1862. A. LINCOLN

1 AES, DNA RG 204, U.S. Pardon Attorney, A 417. Lincoln's endorsement is written on a petition signed by the Kentucky delegation and Joshua F. Speed asking pardon for Herman Franks of New Orleans, and *nolle prosequi* for his sureties, Emanuel and Simon Bamberger of Louisville. Franks had been indicted for treason on November 4, 1861, but was unable to appear and his bond became forfeited. No further reference has been located.

To Henry W. Halleck[1]

Majr. Gen. Halleck.   Washington, D.C.,
Hallecks Head Quarters   Corinth—   June 4, 1862.
Your despatch of to-day to Sec. of War received. Thanks for
the good news it brings. Have you anything from Memphis or
other parts of the Mississippi river? Please answer.

A. LINCOLN.

[1] ALS, RPB. "Hallecks Head Quarters   Corinth" is not in Lincoln's handwriting. Halleck had telegraphed Stanton on June 4 that General John Pope
was thirty miles south of Corinth and "already reports 10,000 prisoners and deserters . . . and 15,000 stand of arms captured." (OR, I, X, I, 669). Pope later
denied ever having made such a report (OR, I, X, II, 635), but Halleck maintained that he had telegraphed "the exact language of General Pope. If it was
erroneous, the responsibility is his, not mine." (OR, I, X, I, 671). On June 5
Halleck telegraphed that "A dispatch from Grand Junction says it was reported
there that Memphis was evacuated on Saturday   I have nothing to confirm
the report & can hear nothing of the flotilla in the Mississippi River." (DLC-
RTL).

To William A. Hammond[1]

Surgeon-General please see Mrs. Bradley, whom I do not know,
& redress her grievance, if she have any real one.
June. 4. 1862.   A. LINCOLN

[1] AES, owned by Alfred M. Hellman, New York City. Lincoln's endorsement
is written on a letter from S.H. Swetland to Major General Wool, May 28, 1862,
asking that "Mrs. Bradley" be assigned to some new field of labor, "Mrs. Dix
having rendered her former field obnoxious—one not controlled by her is desired. Any aid you may give will I think benefit the soldiery. . . ." The letter
also bears a recommendation of Mrs. Bradley, May 30, 1862, signed by Lieutenant Colonel William D. Whipple, chief of staff at Fort Monroe. Miss, not
Mrs., Amy M. Bradley of Maine served during May, 1862, in the Hospital
Transport Service at Fort Monroe. No further record of her differences with
Miss Dorothea Dix has been found.

To the House of Representatives[1]

Washington City, D.C.
To the House of Representatives: June 4th, 1862
I transmit herewith a Report of the Secretary of War, in answer
to the Resolution of the House of Representatives of the 2d. of
June, in relation to the authority and action of the Honorable Ed-
ward Stanly, Military Governor of North Carolina.

ABRAHAM LINCOLN.

[1] DS, DNA RG 233, Original Executive Document No. 123. The resolution of
June 2 requested information concerning Edward Stanly, former Whig congressman from North Carolina (1837-1843, 1849-1853), appointed military governor

of North Carolina May 26, 1862, who was purported to have prevented the education of negro children in the state. Stanton reported that Stanly had not been instructed by the government to prevent the education of children, white or black, and that the War Department had no official information that he had, but that Stanly had been requested to give a report on the subject which would be communicated to the House. See further, Lincoln to Stanly, September 29, *infra*.

To Andrew Johnson[1]

Hon. Andrew Johnson
Nashville, Tenn.

Washington, D.C.,
June 4, 1862.

Do you really *wish* to have control of the question of releasing rebel prisoners so far as they may be Tennesseeans? If you do, please tell us so distinctly. Your answer not to be made public.

A. LINCOLN

[1] ALS, RPB. This telegram is misdated May 4, 1862, in Hertz (II, 929). Johnson replied on June 5, "I have to state that I do believe we can prescribe such terms of release & so dispose of the question as to exert a powerful influence throughout the State in our favor. . . . I do desire the disposition of . . . releasing the Tennessee prisoners. . . ." (DLC-RTL). In a second telegram of the same date Johnson explained that he proposed to exchange the secession prisoners for East Tennesseans held by the Confederacy in Mobile. Stanton telegraphed Johnson on June 7, that the president ". . . holds the question as to the time when executive clemency shall be exercised under consideration. It has always been the design of the Government to leave the exercise of that clemency to your judgment and discretion whenever the period arrives that it can properly be exercised." (OR, II, III, 659). See further, Lincoln's telegram to Johnson on June 9, *infra*.

To the Senate[1]

To, the Senate of the United States. June 4, 1862

In compliance with the resolution of the Senate of the 29th. ultimo, adopted in Executive Session, requesting information in regard to the claims of Citizens of the United States on Paraguay, and the correspondence relating thereto, I transmit a report from the Secretary of State and the documents by which it was accompanied. ABRAHAM LINCOLN

Washington, June, 4th. 1862.

[1] DS, DNA RG 46, Senate 37B B16. The correspondence transmitted was referred to the committee on foreign relations and ordered to be printed.

To Henry W. Halleck[1]

Washington City, D.C.

Major Gen. Halleck June 5, 1862 9½ PM

I have received the following despatch from Gen. McClellan, which I transmit for your consideration. A. LINCOLN

[260]

[1] ALS, RPB. McClellan's telegram of 4 P.M., June 5, reads as follows: "May I again invite your Excellency's attention to the great importance of occupying Chatanooga and Dalton, by our Western forces. The evacuation of Corinth would appear to render this very easy. The importance of this move in force cannot be exaggerated." (DLC-RTL). See Lincoln to McClellan, June 7, *infra*.

To Edwin M. Stanton[1]

PRIVATE   War Department
Hon. Sec. of War.   Washington City, D.C.
My dear Sir   June 5. 1862

Herewith I return you the papers in relation to the proposed re-appointment of William Kellogg, Jr. to a Cadetship. Upon Gen. Totten's statement of the case I think it is natural that he should feel as he expresses himself. And yet the case comes upon me in the very strongest way to be painful to me. Hon. William Kellogg, the father, is not only a member of Congress from my state, but he is my personal friend of more than twenty years' standing, and of whom I had many personal kindnesses. This matter touches him very deeply—the feelings of a father for a child—as he thinks, all the future of his child. I can not be the instrument to crush his heart. According to strict rule he has the right to make the re-nomination. Let the appointment be made. It needs not to become a precedent. Hereafter let no resignation be accepted under demerit amounting to cause for dismissal, unless upon express stipulation in writing that the cadet resigning shall not be re-nominated. In this I mean no censure upon Gen. Totten; and although I have marked this note *"private"* I am quite willing for him to see it. Yours truly   A. LINCOLN.

[1] ALS, NHi. William Kellogg, Jr., was re-appointed but never graduated.

To Edwin M. Stanton[1]

June 5, 1862

As Brigadier General McKean, now resigning, was appointed at the request of the Iowa Senators, I think it not unreasonable that his vacancy should be filled as within requested.

June 5. 1862.   A. LINCOLN

[1] AES, DNA WR RG 107, Secretary of War, Personnel Appointments, Box 16. Lincoln's endorsement is written on a letter from James W. Grimes and James Harlan recommending appointment of Colonel Nicholas Pretzel [Perczel ?] of the Tenth Iowa Infantry as a brigadier general in the place of Thomas J. McKean, who was supposedly resigning. McKean did not resign, however, and Pretzel was not appointed.

To Edwin M. Stanton[1]

June 5, 1862

If the War Department or Major Gen. Halleck can assign Col. Woodruff to the command of a Brigade, without injustice to any other, I shall be gratified.　　　　　　　　　　A. LINCOLN
June 5. 1862.

Let Col. Woodruff be appointed a Brig. Genl. of vols.
June 9. 1862.　　　　　　　　　　　　　　　A LINCOLN

[1] AES, IHi. Lincoln's endorsements are written on a letter from John B. Temple, president of the Military Board, Frankfort, Kentucky, May 28, 1862, asking appointment of William E. Woodruff, formerly colonel of the Second Kentucky, as a brigadier general. While he was held a prisoner by the Confederates, Colonel Woodruff's place had been filled by another man. Although Woodruff was nominated on June 10, there is no record of his confirmation by the Senate.

To Caleb B. Smith[1]

Sec. of Interior please send me a nomination according to the within.　　　　　　　　　　　　　A. LINCOLN
June 6. 1862.

[1] AES, DNA NR RG 48, Applications, General Land Office, California, Box 1276. Lincoln's endorsement is written on a letter from the California delegation in congress, June 4, 1862, recommending appointment of Alvan Flanders as register of the Land Office at Humboldt, California. Flanders' appointment was confirmed by the Senate on June 18, 1862.

To Edwin M. Stanton[1]

Hon. Sec. of War　　　　　　　　　Executive Mansion,
My dear Sir　　　　　　　　Washington, June 6. 1862.

I need not tell you how much I would like to oblige Capt. Dahlgren. I now learn, not from him, that he would be gratified for his son Ulric Dahlgren, to be appointed a lieutenant in the Army. Please find a place for him. Yours truly　　　　　A. LINCOLN

[1] ALS, NHi. Ulric Dahlgren was appointed captain of Volunteers and additional aide-de-camp on the staff of General Frémont, as of May 29, 1862.

To Edwin M. Stanton[1]

June 6, 1862

I am quite willing, and even should be pleased, for Capt. Edwards to be transferred as he desires, if it can be done consistently with the public interest.　　　　　　　　　　A. LINCOLN
June 6. 1862

[1] AES, NHi. Lincoln's endorsement is written on a letter from A. Edwards, assistant quartermaster on General Wadsworth's staff, June 6, 1862, asking to be assigned to duty upon the staff of the military governor of either South Carolina or Georgia, where he had "extensive acquaintance."

To Edwin M. Stanton[1]

Let the appointment be made, as within requested.
June 6. 1862. A. LINCOLN

[1] AES, IHi. Lincoln's endorsement appears on a letter from Senator Ira Harris, June 3, 1862, asking an endorsement ordering appointment of John H. Nichols, Jr., as a second lieutenant in the army. Nichols was nominated second lieutenant in the First U.S. Cavalry on June 6, and was confirmed by the Senate on July 14, 1862.

To George B. McClellan[1]

Washington, D.C.,
Majr. Gen. McClellan June 7th 1862.
Your despatch about Chattanooga and Dalton was duly received and sent to Gen. Halleck. I have just received the following answer from him. We have Fort-Pillow, Randolph, and Memphis.

A LINCOLN

[1] ALS, RPB. "June 7th" is not in Lincoln's handwriting. See Lincoln to Halleck, June 5, *supra*. Halleck's telegram of June 7 reported, "Preparations for Chattanooga made five days ago & troops moved in that direction." (DLC-RTL).

Recommendation for Edward Burke[1]

June 7, 1862
The bearer of this, Edward Burke [Benke?], has been here at the White-House, several months, during my residence here, and has appeared to me to be a quiet, orderly, and faithful man.
June 7, 1862 A. LINCOLN

[1] ADS, ORB. The name may be "Burke" or "Benke." No record of an "Edward Benke" has been found, but see Lincoln to whom it may concern, March 4, *supra*, for Edward Burke.

To John A. Dahlgren[1]

Capt. Dahlgren, will be interested to accompany the bearer of this to see a new patern of gun. A. LINCOLN
June 8. (1862)

[1] ALS, RPB. The year date in parentheses is not in Lincoln's handwriting.

To Henry W. Halleck[1]

Majr. Gen. Halleck.   Washington, D.C.,
Corinth, Miss.   June 8, 1862.

We are changing one of the departmental lines so as to give you all of Kentucky and Tennessee. In your movement upon Chattanooga &c I think it probable that you include some combination of the force near Cumberland Gap under Gen. Morgan. Do you?

       A. LINCOLN

[1] ALS, RPB. AGO *General Orders No. 62*, June 8, 1862, extended the Department of the Mississippi to include the whole of Tennessee and Kentucky. No reply from Halleck to Lincoln's question has been located, but Brigadier General George W. Morgan was at Bowman, Tennessee, on June 13 (OR, I, XVI, II, 21).

To Nathaniel P. Banks[1]

Major Gen. Banks   Washington City, D.C.
Winchester   June 9. 1862

We are arranging a general plan for the valley of the Shenandoah; and, in accordance with this, you will move your main force to the Shenandoah at or opposite Front-Royal as soon as possible.

       A. LINCOLN

[1] ALS, RPB. "Winchester" is not in Lincoln's handwriting. Banks replied at 10:50 P.M., "Your orders shall be faithfully executed. . . ." (DLC-RTL).

To John C. Frémont[1]

       Washington City, D.C.
Maj. Gen. Fremont   June 9. 1862

Halt at Harrisonburg, pursuing Jackson no farther; get your force well in hand, and stand on the defensive, guarding against a movement of the enemy either back towards Strasburg, or towards Franklin, and await further orders which will soon be sent you.

       A. LINCOLN

[1] ALS, RPB. Frémont's telegram of June 7, to Stanton, received at 9 A.M., June 9, reported arrival of his army at Harrisonburg "at 2 o'clock yesterday afternoon, driving out the enemy's rear guard. . . . The condition of the force is extremely bad, for want of supplies. . . ." (OR, I, XII, I, 652).

To Andrew Johnson[1]

Hon. Andrew Johnson   Washington, D.C.,
Nashville, Tenn.   June 9 1862.

Your despatch about seizing seventy rebels to exchange for a like number of Union men, was duly received. I certainly do not disapprove the proposition.   A. LINCOLN

1 ALS, RPB. The copy of this telegram in the Johnson Papers (DLC) is incorrectly dated May 9. Johnson's second telegram of June 5 in reply to Lincoln's telegram of June 4 (*supra*) proposed to arrest "seventy 70 vile secessionists in this vicinity & offer them in exchange" for "seventy east Tennesseeans now lying in prison at Mobile . . . . & if they refuse to exchange I will at once send them South at their own expense . . . with the . . . understanding that if they . . . come again within said lines . . . they shall be treated as spies and with death. . . . It is no punishment now to send secessionist north   In most instances they would rather go to the Infernal regions than to be sent South. . . ." (DLC-RTL).

To Edward Bates[1]

June 10, 1862

Unless the Attorney-General knows some reason to the contrary, he will please send me a nomination for A. Cameron Hunt, of Colorado Territory, to be Marshal of that District, in place of Copeland Townsend, removed.   A. LINCOLN

June. 10. 1862.

1 AES, THaroL. Lincoln's endorsement is written on a letter from Elihu B. Washburne, June 2, 1862, recommending A. Cameron Hunt, formerly mayor of Freeport, Illinois, for Marshal of Colorado Territory. Hunt's appointment was confirmed by the Senate on June 18.

To the Senate and House of Representatives[1]

June 10, 1862

To the Senate and House of Representatives:

I transmit to Congress a copy of a treaty for the suppression of the African slave trade, between the United States and her Britannic Majesty, signed in this city on the 7th of April last, and the ratifications of which were exchanged at London on the 20th ultimo.

A copy of the correspondence which preceded the conclusion of the instrument, between the Secretary of State and Lord Lyons, her Britannic Majesty's envoy extraordinary and minister plenipotentiary, is also herewith transmitted.

It is desirable that such legislation as may be necessary to carry the treaty into effect should be enacted as soon as may comport with the convenience of Congress.   ABRAHAM LINCOLN.

Washington, June 10, 1862.

1 Thirty-seventh Congress, Second Session, *Senate Executive Document No. 57*. In response to Lincoln's suggestion, congress passed the act approved July 11, providing for the appointment of one judge and one arbitrator to reside at New York, one each at Sierra Leone, and one each at the Cape of Good Hope, to carry into effect the terms of the treaty.

To Edward Bates[1]

The Attorney-General will please make out a pardon, according to the within petition of the Judges who tried the case, and others.

June. 11. 1862.   A. LINCOLN

1 AES, DNA RG 204, U.S. Pardon Attorney, A 419. Lincoln's endorsement is written on a petition for pardon of Josephus M. Clark, May 28, 1862, signed by Judge Samuel H. Treat and others. Although a minor and afflicted with "an affection of the head," Clark had been sentenced to ten years for opening letters.

To Edward Bates[1]

June 11, 1862

Our little disinterested woman of last year, is again upon me for the pardon of Isaac Lambert. I propose to the Attorney General, that the pardon be granted.   A. LINCOLN

June 11, 1862.

1 AES, DNA RG 204, U.S. Pardon Attorney, A 354. See also Lincoln to Bates, October 15, 1861, supra. Lincoln's endorsement is written on a recommendation for pardon of Isaac Lambert, February 27, 1862, signed by George W. Garrett and Henry M. Hurdle, two of the jurors who had convicted him on charges of larceny at the December, 1857, term of the Criminal Court of the District of Columbia. "Our little disinterested woman" was Mrs. Ellen V. McLane, who had written Bates on October 19, 1861, on Lambert's behalf (DLC-RTL). Lambert was pardoned June 19, 1862.

To Edward Bates[1]

I incline to grant a pardon in this case; and if the Attorney-General does not dissent, he will please have the pardon made out

June 11. 1862.   A. LINCOLN

1 AES, DNA RG 204, U.S. Pardon Attorney, A 367. Lincoln's endorsement is written on a petition signed by members of the Indiana delegation in congress, recommending the pardon of George W. Sullivan sentenced by the Criminal Court of the District of Columbia to five years on conviction of larceny.

To Edwin M. Stanton[1]

June 11, 1862

Mrs. Harwood is very anxious for her brother, William Luce, to be appointed a Lieutenant of Engineers; and, as the within testimonials seem to be ample, I shall be glad for her to be obliged, if there is a vacancy to which he can be appointed.

June. 11. 1862.   A. LINCOLN

1 AES, owned by Wilson F. Harwood, Washington, D.C. Mrs. Harwood was the wife of Captain Andrew A. Harwood, chief of the Navy Bureau of Ordnance and Hydrography. No record of William Luce's appointment has been found.

To Edwin M. Stanton[1]

June 11, 1862.

The President respectfully refers the inclosed to the Secretary of War, with the expression of his confidence in the energy and faithfulness of General White.

[1] OR, III, II, 71. Lincoln's endorsement is on a letter of Colonel Julius White of the Thirty-seventh Illinois Volunteers, Cassville, Missouri, May 25, 1862, endorsed by Governor Richard Yates to the president, June 6. White suggested that a regiment be recruited from the northwestern counties of Arkansas.

To Edward Bates[1]

[June 12, 1862]

Will the Attorney General please furnish me the information sought by the within resolution so far as the means for so doing may be in his Department?   A. Lincoln

[1] AES, DNA GE RG 60, Papers of Attorney General, Segregated Lincoln Material. Lincoln's endorsement, undated, is written on a copy of a House resolution of June 9, reading as follows: "On motion of Mr Low   Resolved. That the President be requested to furnish this House with any information he may have concerning the interruption of business in the Circuit Court of the United States for the State of California; whether or not the Judge of said Court has left the State of California, and if he has left, for what reason and for what length of time and by what authority of law he has absented himself from his official duties." An endorsement by Nicolay dated June 13, states that "the President this day sent to the House of Representatives, the letter of the Hon. Attorney General, and accompanying papers." Lincoln's message to the House (*infra*), however, bears the date of June 12.

To John C. Frémont[1]

Washington City, D.C.

Maj. Gen. Fremont.   June 12. 1862

Accounts which we do not credit, represent that Jackson is largely reinforced, and is turning upon you. Stand well on your guard, get your forces well in hand, and keep us well and frequently advised; and if you find yourself really pressed by a superior force of the enemy, fall back cautiously towards, or to, Winchester, according to circumstances; and we will in, due time, have Gen. Banks in position to sustain you. Do not fall back of Harrisonburg, unless upon tolerably clear necessity. We understand Jackson is on the other side of the Shenandoah from you, and hence can not, in any event, press you into any necessity of a precipitate withdrawal.   A. Lincoln.

[267]

P.S. Yours, preferring Mount Jackson, to Harrisonburg is just received. On this point, use your discretion, remembering that our object is to give such protection as you can to Western Virginia. Many thanks to yourself, officers, and men, for the gallant battle of last sunday. A. L.

¹ ALS, RPB. Frémont had telegraphed from Harrisonburg, Virginia, June 11, "Will you allow me to halt at Mount Jackson instead of Harrisonburg, which is not a line of defense, and exposes me to be cut off. . . . My troops are very much distressed for want of supplies. . . ." (OR, I, XII, I, 656). Generals Mc-Dowell and Sigel reported to Stanton June 12, that "Jackson has been re-enforced to the number of 30,000 or 35,000 men." (OR, I, XII, III, 372). Stanton telegraphed Sigel on June 12 that "It cannot be possible that Jackson has any such re-enforcement as 30,000 or 35,000. . . . The President directs that your forces and Banks' shall not fall back from Front Royal and their present positions until further developments." (Ibid., p. 378).

To the House of Representatives¹

Executive Mansion, Washington, June 12, 1862.

The Honorable House of Representatives—

In obedience to the resolution of your honorable body, of the 9th. Inst. requesting certain information in regard [to] the Circuit Court of the United States for the State of California, and the judge of said Court, I have the honor to transmit a letter of the Attorney General, with copies of two other letters, and of an indorsement of my own upon one of them, all which, taken together, contain all the information within my power to give upon the subject. ABRAHAM LINCOLN

¹ ADS, MB; DS, DNA RG 233, Original Executive Document No. 129. See Lincoln's endorsement to Bates, supra. Bates forwarded to Lincoln a copy of the letter from Senators McDougall and Latham endorsed by Lincoln on April 21 (supra) and a copy of Bates' letter to McAllister, April 21, granting leave of absence. Bates admitted in his covering letter in regard to the question of authority that ". . . I am not, at this moment, prepared to answer it. . . . Ever since your accession to the presidency, such letters of license have been granted without any minute scrutiny of the law . . . under the belief that you were but following numerous precedents. . . ." (Ibid.).

To Benjamin F. Larned¹

Pay-Master-General   Executive Mansion,
My dear Sir: Washington, June 12. 1862.

The bearer of this, a french lady, so far as I can understand her, had a son in our volunteer Army, who was made a prisoner at Bull-Run, and has since died, at Mobile. He was only seventeen years of age; and she wishes, if possible, to draw what is due him, or some part of it. You will know, while I do not, whether this is possible. She is in great distress; and I shall be glad if you will kindly hear her, & do for her the best you can. Yours truly

A. LINCOLN

[1] ALS, IHi. Paymaster General Larned became inactive because of illness in July, 1862, and died the following September. No reply to this letter has been found.

To John C. Frémont[1]

Washington City, D.C.

Major Gen. Fremont   June 13 1862

We can not afford to keep your force, and Banks', and McDowell's, engaged in keeping Jackson South of Strasburg and Front-Royal. You fought Jackson alone, and worsted him. He can have no substantial reinforcement, so long as a battle is pending at Richmond. Surely you and Banks in supporting distance are capable of keeping him from returning to Winchester. But if Sigel be sent forward to you, and McDowell (as he must) be put to other work, Jackson will break through at Front Royal again. He is already on the right side of the Shenandoah to do it, and on the wrong side of it to attack you. The orders already sent you and Banks place you and him in the proper positions for the work assigned you. Jackson can not move his whole force on either of you, before the other can learn of it, and go to his assistance. He can not divide his force, sending part against each of you because he will be too weak for either. Please do as I directed in the order of the 8th. and my despatch of yesterday, the 12th. and neither you nor Banks will be overwhelmed by Jackson. By proper scouts-look-outs, and beacons of smokes by day, and fires by night, you can always have timely notice of the enemies approach. I know not as to you, but by some, this has been too much neglected.

A. LINCOLN

[1] ALS, RPB. Frémont telegraphed from Mount Jackson on June 12, as follows: "Upon intelligence of Genl Shields defeat and withdrawal towards Richmond I retired upon this place which is a defensible and good position   The Regiments composing my command have been rendered very weak by illness casualties and deaths   I request that orders be given to recruit them to full strength immediately   Their condition necessitates that they have some days rest and good and sufficient food   The demand made upon them in the pursuit of Jackson has exhausted them for the present and they should be supported by fresh troops   At any hour they may be attacked by the Enemy now reported strong [sic] reinforced and I ask that Genl Sigel be telegraphed to report to me with his force without delay   I respectfully suggest to the President that it may prove disastrous to separate the small corps now operating in this region—consolidated they could act offensively and efficiently against the enemy   I also suggest that Gen Shields may be attacked on his march Eastward unless supported   My strength should be sufficient to enable me to occupy the Monteray

passes & aid Gen [J. D.] Cox and Col [George] Crook against whom I think the Enemy is likely to concentrate a superior force   I have asked for Sigel—if possible Banks also should come   A disaster now would have consequences difficult to remedy." (DLC-RTL).

To the Senate and House of Representatives[1]

Executive Mansion   Washington June 13, 1862.
Fellow-citizens of the Senate and House of Representatives:
I herewith transmit a Memorial addressed, and presented to me, in behalf of the State of New York, in favor of enlarging the locks of the Erie and Oswego canals. While I have not given, nor have leisure to give the subject a careful examination, its great importance is obvious and unquestionable. The large amount of valuable statistical information which is collated and presented in the memorial, will greatly facilitate the mature consideration of the subject, which I respectfully ask for it at your hands.

ABRAHAM LINCOLN

[1] DS, DNA RG 46, Senate 37A F2; DS, DNA RG 233, Original Executive Document No. 128; ADfS, IHi. The autograph draft is dated June 12, but the date of the official signed documents in the Senate and House files is followed. The printed Memorial of the New York General Assembly which Lincoln transmitted may be found in *House of Representatives Executive Document No. 128*. Neither Senate nor House took further action.

To Edward Bates[1]

June 14, 1862
If the Attorney General is of opinion that the President has the legal power to remit the fine in this case, let it be considered as done, and let any necessary paper for that object be prepared.

June. 14. 1862.   A. LINCOLN

[1] AES, DNA RG 204, U.S. Pardon Attorney, A 421. Lincoln's endorsement is written on the petition of Hermann Kirchner, restaurateur of Washington, D.C., June 5, 1862, for remission of a fine of twenty dollars imposed on charges of selling spirituous liquor to a soldier. Kirchner avowed that he had sent brandy to a wounded soldier in a neighboring house, but had never dispensed liquor to soldiers in his restaurant. Further endorsements indicate Bates' remission of the fine.

To John C. Frémont[1]

War Department,
Washington City, D.C.,
Major-General Frémont: June 15, 1862.
My Dear Sir: Your letter of the 12th, by Colonel Zagonyi, is just received. In answer to the principal part of it I repeat the

substance of an order of the 8th and one or two telegraphic despatches sent you since.

We have no indefinite power of sending re-enforcements; so that we are compelled rather to consider the proper disposal of the forces we have than of those we could wish to have. We may be able to send you some dribs by degrees, but I do not believe we can do more. As you alone beat Jackson last Sunday I argue that you are stronger than he is to-day, unless he has been re-enforced; and that he cannot have been materially re-enforced, because such re-enforcement could only have come from Richmond, and he is much more likely to go to Richmond than Richmond is to come to him. Neither is very likely. I think Jackson's game—his assigned work—now is to magnify the accounts of his numbers and reports of his movements, and thus by constant alarms keep three or four times as many of our troops away from Richmond as his own force amounts to. Thus he helps his friends at Richmond three or four times as much as if he were there. Our game is not to allow this. Accordingly, by the order of the 8th, I directed you to halt at Harrisonburg, rest your force, and get it well in hand, the objects being to guard against Jackson's returning by the same route to the Upper Potomac, over which you have just driven him out, and at the same time give some protection against a raid into West Virginia. Already I have given you discretion to occupy Mount Jackson instead, if, on full consideration, you think best. I do not believe Jackson will attack you, but certainly he cannot attack you by surprise; and if he comes upon you in superior force you have but to notify us, fall back cautiously, and Banks will join you in due time. But while we know not whether Jackson will move at all, or by what route, we cannot safely put you and Banks both on the Strasburg line, and leave no force on the Front Royal line, the very line upon which he prosecuted his late raid. The true policy is to place one of you on one line and the other on the other, in such positions that you can unite on either once you actually find Jackson moving upon it. And this is precisely what we are doing. This protects that part of our frontier, so to speak, and liberates McDowell to go to the assistance of McClellan. I have arranged this, and am very unwilling to have it deranged. While you have only asked for Sigel I have spoken only of Banks, and this because Sigel's force is now the principal part of Banks's force.

About transferring General Schenck's command, the purchase of supplies, and the promotion and appointment of officers[2] mentioned in your letter, I will consult with the Secretary of War to-morrow. Yours, truly,   A. LINCOLN.

1 OR, I, XII, I, 661. Frémont's letter delivered by his aide-de-camp Colonel Charles Zagonyi, read as follows: "The situation here gives me some anxiety and I wish therefore to trouble you with a few lines. We have been operating against the enemy with a force greatly inferior to his. He has been still farther re-enforced and my men have been exhausted by the demand made upon them. . . . I have asked you by telegraph which I send forward this afternoon to direct General Sigel with his force immediately to report to me here. . . . In the battle at Cross Keys I do not think I had 10,000 men, the enemy according to all acounts . . . not less than 20,000. . . . I ought to have a moveable corps of not less than 30000 men. . . . I should also have the power . . . to order the proper officer to procure immediately and as they are required such supplies as are necessary. . . . I hope that you will find it agreeable to your views to give me what I ask & that you will be good enough to give me a reply as soon as you have considered the subject. . . . I have to ask that you will have the appointment of Col. Anselm Albert as Brig. Genl. confirmed as well as that of Brig Genl. Stahel. . . . I still continue to desire . . . that you will permit me to raise a cavalry regiment to be commanded by Col. Zagonyi whom I send to you with this letter. . . . The Secretary of War informed me that if there should be officers in this command with whom it was not agreeable to me to act they could be transferred. . . . I avail myself of this assurance to ask that Brig. General Schenck be transferred from my Dept. And it is just to him to say that this request is made on personal grounds and without any reference to his qualities as a soldier. . . ." (DLC-RTL).

2 The appointment of Anselm Albert as brigadier general was confirmed by the Senate on July 17; that of Julius H. Stahel had been confirmed on February 16 but for some reason failed to be entered in the Senate *Executive Journal*.

To George B. McClellan[1]

War Department
Washington City, D.C.

Major General McClellan   June 15, 1862

My dear Sir: The night between your two late battles of Saturday and Sunday, I went earnestly to work to find a way of putting Gen. Wool's force under your control without wounding any one's feelings.[2] But after all, Gen. Dix was a little hurt at being taken from an independent command and put in a dependent one.[3] I could not help this without giving up the principal object of the move. So soon as you can, (which I do not expect is yet,) I wish you to give me the benefit of your suggestions as to how an independent command can be given him without detriment.

The Secretary of War has turned over to me your despatch about sending McDowell to you by water, instead of by land.[4] I now fear he can not get to you either way in time. Shields' Division has got so terribly out of shape, out at elbows, and out at toes, that it will require a long time to get it in again. I expect to see McDowell within a day or two, when I will again talk with him about the mode of moving.

McCall's Division has nearly or quite reached you by now. This, with what you get from Gen. Wool's old command, and the new regiments sent you, must give you an increase since the late battles of over twenty thousand. Doubtless the battles and other causes have decreased you half as much in the same time; but then the enemy have lost as many in the same way.

I believe I would come and see you, were it not that I fear my presence might divert you and the army from more important matters. Yours truly   A. LINCOLN

¹ ALS copy, DLC-RTL.
² AGO *General Orders No.* 57, June 1, 1862, extended McClellan's Department of Virginia to include Wool's command at Fort Monroe, assigned Wool to command the Middle Department at Baltimore, and Dix to command at Fort Monroe and to report to McClellan for orders.
³ Dix telegraphed Lincoln at 6:45 P.M., June 1, asking that his orders to report to McClellan be modified (DLC-RTL).
⁴ On June 8, McDowell had been directed first to provide for the defense of Washington then to "operate with the residue of your force as speedily as possible in the direction of Richmond, to co-operate with . . . McClellan. . . ." (OR, I, XII, III, 354). On June 13, McClellan telegraphed Stanton to advise McDowell to come by water. (DLC-RTL).

To John C. Frémont¹

"Cypher"

Major General Fremont   Washington City, D.C.
Mount Jackson, Va.   June 16, 1862

Your despatch of yesterday reminding me of a supposed understanding that I would furnish you a corps of thirty five thousand men, and asking of me "the fulfillment of this understanding" is received. I am ready to come to a fair settlement of accounts with you on the fulfillment of understandings.

Early in March last, when I assigned you to the command of the Mountain Department, I did tell you I would give you all the force I could, and that I hoped to make it reach thirty five thousand. You, at the same time told me that, within a reasonable time, you would seize the Railroad at, or East of, Knoxville, Tenn. if you could. There was then in the Department a force supposed to be twentyfive thousand—the exact number as well known to you as to me. After looking about two or three days you called and distinctly told me that if I would add the Blecker [Blenker] Division to the force already in the Department, you would undertake the job. The Blecker [Blenker] division contained ten thousand; and at the expense of great dissatisfaction to Gen. McClellan, I took it from his army, and gave it to you. My promise was litterally fulfilled. I had given you all I could, and I had given you very nearly if not quite thirtyfive thousand.

[273]

Now for yours. On the 23rd. of May, largely over two months afterwards, you were at Franklin Va, not within three hundred miles of Knoxville, nor within eighty miles of any part of the Railroad East of it—and not moving forward, but telegraphing here that you could not move for lack of everything. Now, do not misunderstand me. I do not say you have not done all you could. I presume you met unexpected difficulties; and I beg you to believe that as surely as you have done your best, so have I. I have not the power now to fill up your corps to thirtyfive thousand. I am not demanding of you to do the work of thirtyfive thousand. I am only asking of you to stand cautiously on the defensive, get your force in order, and give such protection as you can to the valley of the Shenandoah, and to Western Virginia. Have you received the orders? and will you act upon them?[2]

A. LINCOLN.

[1] ALS, RPB. Frémont's telegram received at 3 P.M. on June 15, reminded Lincoln that "when assigned to this command I was informed that I should have a corps of thirty five thousand men   I now ask from the President the fulfillment of this understanding. . . ." (DLC-RTL).

[2] Frémont telegraphed in reply the same day that he had received the orders and "as a matter of course I will act upon them as I am now doing." (*Ibid.*). Upon reports arriving at the War Department which indicated that Frémont understood his orders to require him to remain at Mount Jackson regardless of circumstances, Stanton at Lincoln's direction telegraphed Frémont on June 17 that the president "does wish you to hold your position at Mount Jackson if you can safely do so; but if pressed beyond your strength that you will then fall back toward Strasburg for support from General Banks. General Banks is now here, and will see you immediately upon his return to his command." (OR, I, XII, I, 663).

To Carl Schurz[1]

Brigadier General Schurz.   Washington City, D.C.
Mount Jackson, Va.   June 16, 1862 [12:30 P.M.]

Your long letter is received. The information you give is valuable. You say it is fortunate that Fremont did not intercept Jackson—that Jackson had the superior force, and would have overwhelmed him. If this is so, how happened it that Fremont fairly fought and worsted him on the 8th.? Or, is the account that he did fight and worst him, false, and fabricated?

Both Gen. Fremont and you speak of Jackson having beaten Shields. By our accounts, he did not beat Shields. He had no engagement with Shields. He did meet, and drive back with disaster, about two thousand of Shields' advance, till they were met by an additional Brigade of Shields, when Jackson himself turned and retreated. Shields himself, and more than half his force, were not nearer than twenty miles of any of it.[2]   A. LINCOLN

¹ ALS, RPB. Schurz's seven-page letter written from Frémont's headquarters on June 12 reads in part as follows: "When I took leave of you, you authorized me to send you a confidential report about the condition of things in this Department. . . . I have already seen and heard enough to give a reliable opinion. . . . It is a fact . . . that, when you ordered Gen. Fremont to march from Franklin to Harrisonburg, it was absolutely impossible to carry out the order. The army was in a starving condition and literally unable to fight . . . . it is undoubtedly a very fortunate circumstance that Gen. Fremont did not succeed in placing himself across Jacksons line of retreat; for Jacksons force was so much superior (all the Generals . . . put at 25,000 as the very lowest) that he would in all probability have been beaten. . . ." (DLC-RTL).

² Schurz replied to Lincoln's questions in a telegram received at 5:40 P.M. on June 16, as follows: "Your Despatch received   About the correctness of Genl Fremonts report there can be no question   When he attacked Jackson at Cross Keyes the cooperation of Genl Shields was expected Jackson being immediately between them when Shields withdrew and Jackson was largely reinforced   The conditions were no longer the same and it was in reference to this new state of things that my letter was written   As to Shields I wrote on the information I had   More by letter" (DLC-RTL). In a four-page letter written on the same day Schurz explained in detail Frémont's strategy and need for withdrawal (DLC-Nicolay Papers).

To the House of Representatives¹

Executive Mansion   Washington City. June 17. 1862
To the Speaker of the House of Representatives.

The Resolution of the House of Representatives of the 9. instant, asking whether any legislation is necessary in order to give effect to the provisions of the Act of April 16, 1862, providing for the re-organization of the Medical Department of the Army, was referred to the Secretary of War, whose report thereon is hereby communicated.   ABRAHAM LINCOLN

¹ DS, DNA RG 233, Original Executive Document No. 134. Stanton reported that no additional legislation was "now needed to give effect to the provisions of that act."

To Edward Bates¹

June 18, 1862

I suppose the question is, "Can the Marshal, accept command of Regt. guarding prisoners without losing the office of Marshal?" What says the Attorney General?   A. LINCOLN
June 18. 1862.

¹ AES, DLC-RTL. Lincoln's endorsement is written on a telegram from Governor Oliver P. Morton, June 17, asking whether Colonel David G. Rose, U.S. marshal for Indiana, could accept command of a regiment guarding prisoners at Camp Morton without vacating his civil appointment. Bates endorsed below Lincoln's query, "There is no incompatibility *in law*. And I know of none *in fact*, in this case." See Lincoln's reply to Morton, *infra*.

To Henry W. Halleck[1]

Major General Halleck—   Washington, D.C.,
Corinth, Miss.   June 18, 1862.

It would be of both interest and value to us here to know how the expedition towards East Tennessee is progressing, if in your judgment you can give us the information with safety.

A. LINCOLN

[1] ALS, RPB. Halleck replied on June 21, "Genl Buell's column is at Tuscumbia As soon [as] the bridge at that place is rebuilt he will move east more rapidly. The enemy has evacuated Cumberland Gap. Must very soon leave all East Tennessee. Our troops have reached Memphis & the Railroad connection will be complete in a few days" (DLC-RTL).

To George B. McClellan[1]

"Cypher"   Washington, D.C.,
Major General McC[lellan]   June 18. 1862.

Yours of to-day making it probable that Jackson has been reinforced by about ten thousand from Richmond, is corroborated by a despatch from Gen. King[2] at Frederick'sburg, saying a Frenchman just arrived from Richmond by way of Gordon'sville, met ten to fifteen thousand passing through the latter place to join Jackson.

If this is true, it is as good as a reinforcement to you of an equal force. I could better dispose of things if I could know about what day you can attack Richmond, and would be glad to be informed, if you think you can inform me with safety.   A. LINCOLN

[1] ALS, RPB. McClellan telegraphed Stanton at 10:30 A.M., June 18, that several deserters had stated that troops including "a considerable portion of Longstreets Division" had left Richmond to reinforce Jackson (DLC-RTL). See further Lincoln to McClellan, June 19, *infra*.
[2] Rufus King.

To Oliver P. Morton[1]

Gov. O. P. Morton   Head Quarters Army of the Potomac,
Indianapolis, Ia.   June 18, 1862.

I suppose it will not vacate the office of Marshal, for the officer to command of a Regiment guarding prisoners at Camp-Morton.

A LINCOLN—

[1] ALS, RPB. See Lincoln to Bates, *supra*.

[276]

To Lorenzo Thomas[1]

Adjutant General.   Executive Mansion,
My dear Sir   Washington, June 18. 1862.
  Please see Gov. Yates and Gov. Wood, and if it be consistent
with regulations, do what they desire about a mustering officer at
Springfield, Illinois. Yours truly   A. LINCOLN

  [1] ALS, IHi. The following endorsement is signed on the bottom of the letter
by Richard Yates, John Wood, and William Kellogg: "We recommend A. J.
Allen." Allen was nominated assistant quartermaster with rank of captain on
June 19 and confirmed by the Senate on June 30, 1862.

To George B. McClellan[1]

                              Washington City, D.C.
Major Genl. McClellan   June 19. 1862
  Yours of last night just received, and for which I thank you. If
large re-inforcements are going from Richmond to Jackson, it
proves one of two things, either that they are very strong at Richmond, or do not mean to defend the place desperately.
  On reflection, I do not see how re-inforcements from Richmond
to Jackson could be in Gordon'sville as reported by the Frenchman. It induces a doubt whether the Frenchman & your deserters
have not all been sent to deceive.   A. LINCOLN

  [1] ALS, RPB. McClellan's reply to Lincoln's telegram of June 18, *supra*, received at 11:30 A.M., June 19, argued that "If ten 10 or fifteen 15 thousand men
have left Richmond to reinforce Jackson it illustrates their strength and confidence. After tomorrow we shall fight the rebel Army as soon as Providence will
permit   We shall await only a favorable condition of the earth and sky and
the completion of some necessary preliminaries" (DLC-RTL).

To the Provost Marshal[1]

                                        June 19, 1862
  Will the Provost Marshal let me know on what charge it is that
Dr. Perkins is arrested?   A. LINCOLN

  [1] Stan. V. Henkels, Jr., Catalog 1492, April 10, 1935, No. 52. According to the
catalog description Lincoln's endorsement is written on the back of a letter from
Isaac N. Arnold. Dr. Tarrant A. Perkins may have been the person arrested, but
no further reference has been found to the case.

To George B. McClellan[1]

                              Washington City, D.C.
Major Gen. McClellan   June 20. 1862
  We have, this morning, sent you a despatch of Gen. Sigel cor-
roborative of the proposition that Jackson is being re-inforced from

Richmond.[2] This may be reality, and yet may only be contrivance for deception; and to determine which, is perplexing. If we knew it were not true, we could send you some more force, but as the case stands, we do not think we safely can. Still we will watch the signs, and do so if possible.

In regard to a contemplated execution of Captains Sprigg and Triplett, the government here has no information whatever, but will inquire and advise you.[3]   A. LINCOLN

[1] ALS, RPB.

[2] Sigel's dispatch to Stanton of 9 P.M., June 19, reported "about 12,000 troops arrived from Richmond, via Lynchburg and Charlottesville." (OR, I, XII, III, 411).

[3] Captain John S. Spriggs and Captain Marshall Triplett of the Virginia Partisan Rangers, guerillas, were being held awaiting trial at Camp Chase, Ohio. General Robert E. Lee notified McClellan June 19 that on information they were to be executed two Union prisoners had been selected for retaliation. Stanton telegraphed McClellan June 20 that Spriggs and Triplett were being treated like other prisoners of war. (OR, II, IV, 43-46).

Remarks to a Delegation of Progressive Friends[1]

June 20, 1862

The President said that, as he had not been furnished with a copy of the memorial in advance, he could not be expected to make any extended remarks. It was a relief to be assured that the deputation were not applicants for office, for his chief trouble was from that class of persons. The next most troublesome subject was Slavery. He agreed with the memorialists, that Slavery was wrong, but in regard to the ways and means of its removal, his views probably differed from theirs. The quotation in the memorial, from his Springfield speech, was incomplete. It should have embraced another sentence, in which he indicated his views as to the effect upon Slavery itself of the resistance to its extension.

The sentiments contained in that passage were deliberately uttered, and he held them now. If a decree of emancipation could abolish Slavery, John Brown would have done the work effectually. Such a decree surely could not be more binding upon the South than the Constitution, and that cannot be enforced in that part of the country now. Would a proclamation of freedom be any more effective?

Mr. Johnson replied as follows:

"True, Mr. President, the Constitution cannot now be enforced at the South, but you do not on that account intermit the effort to enforce it, and the memorialists are solemnly convinced that the abolition of Slavery is indispensable to your success."

[278]

The President further said that he felt the magnitude of the task before him, and hoped to be rightly directed in the very trying circumstances by which he was surrounded.

Wm. Barnard addressed the President in a few words, expressing sympathy for him in all his embarrassments, and an earnest desire that he might, under divine guidance, be led to free the slaves and thus save the nation from destruction. In that case, nations yet unborn would rise up to call him blessed and, better still, he would secure the blessing of God.

The President responded very impressively, saying that he was deeply sensible of his need of Divine assistance. He had sometime thought that perhaps he might be an instrument in God's hands of accomplishing a great work and he certainly was not unwilling to be. Perhaps, however, God's way of accomplishing the end which the memorialists have in view may be different from theirs. It would be his earnest endeavor, with a firm reliance upon the Divine arm, and seeking light from above, to do his duty in the place to which he had been called.

[1] New York *Tribune*, June 21, 1862. Less extended but similar reports appeared in other papers. The delegation called upon the president to present a memorial praying him to decree the emancipation of the slaves, which had been adopted by the annual meeting of the Progressive Friends. Members of the delegation were: Thomas Garrett, Alice Eliza Hambleton, Oliver Johnson, Dinah Mendenhall, William Barnard, and Eliza Agnew.

To George B. McClellan[1]

Washington City, D.C.
Major General McClellan   June 21 1862 [6 P.M.]

Your despatch of yesterday, 2. P.M. was received this morning. If it would not divert too much of your time, and attention from the Army under your immediate command, I would be glad to have your views as to present state of Military affairs throughout the whole country—as you say you would be glad to give them. I would rather it should be by letter, than by Telegraph, because of the better chance of secrecy. As to numbers and position of the troops, not under your command, in Virginia and elsewhere, even if I could do it with accuracy, which I can not, I would rather not transmit either by telegraph or letter, because of the chances of it's reaching the enemy.

I would be very glad to talk with you, but you can not leave your camp, and I can not well leave here.   A. LINCOLN.

[1] ALS, RPB. McClellan's reply to Lincoln's telegram of June 20, *supra*, reported further on the "great . . . difficulties" confronting him and his "inferiority in numbers," and concluded by suggesting that "I would be glad to have

permission to lay before your Excellency by letter or telegram my views as to the present state of Military affairs throughout the whole country. In the mean time I would be pleased to learn the disposition as to numbers and position of the troops not under my command in Virginia and elsewhere" (DLC-RTL). Upon receiving Lincoln's answer, he replied on June 22, "Under the circumstances . . . I perceive that it will be better at least to defer for the present the communication I desired to make." (OR, I, XI, I, 48).

To Edwin M. Stanton[1]

[June 21, 1862]

Tell General McDowell what Banks says. Tell him we incline to have Shields remain a few days at Front Royal, and ask him to state his strongest objections, if he has any.

[1] OR, I, XII, III, 416. The text of this note was incorporated by Stanton in his telegram to Irvin McDowell, June 21, 1862. The original has not been located. Banks had "urgently and repeatedly requested that Shields' should remain a short time at Front Royal." (*Ibid.*). McDowell replied to Stanton's telegram at 2 P.M., "Your telegram requesting that Shields' division should be allowed to remain a few days at Front Royal, is just received. In compliance with the orders given after the President was here (Manassas) the advance of Shields' division reached here last night and has moved to Bristol. The sick, foot weary, and part of the baggage and stores left Front Royal last night; General Shields and the remainder of his division left Front Royal this morning at 5 o'clock.

"My reasons for wishing to get General Shields here were, first, that the movements I am ordered to make depend upon it; second, his position at Front Royal, with nothing in advance of him beyond the support of General Fremont and with a river separating him from General Banks, which General Banks' force seems reluctant to cross, was not such as I wanted him, in the condition he is in, to remain in.

"General Shields' division is, I learn, in a bad state morally and materially. . . .

"I am improving and sitting up, and hope soon to regain my bodily activity." (OR, I, XII, I, 288).

McDowell's horse had fallen on him the afternoon of June 18.

To Nathaniel P. Banks[1]

Major Genl. Banks   Washington City, D.C.
Middletown   June 22 1862

I am very glad you are looking well to the West for a movement of the enemy in that direction. You know my anxiety on that point. All was quiet at Gen. McClellan's Head-Quarters at 2 o'clock to-day.[2]   A. LINCOLN

[1] ALS, RPB. Banks telegraphed Stanton from Middletown, Virginia, 1:45 P.M., ". . . the enemy was in force near Luray. It was fully believed that Jackson was moving toward Manassas Gap Railroad . . . to intercept . . . Shields. Ewell was also said to be at Luray. . . . We are looking well to the west, in which direction the enemy threatens a movement. . . ." (OR, I, XII, III, 423).

2 McClellan telegraphed Stanton at 1:30 P.M., "Some sharp attempts of the enemy last evening and night to drive in Hooker's pickets. They certainly failed and were driven back. . . . Nothing else of interest. . . ." (OR, I, XI, III, 241).

To the Senate[1]

To the Senate of the United States.   June 23, 1862

On the 7th. day of December, 1861, I submitted to the Senate the project of a Treaty between the United States and Mexico, which had been proposed to me by Mr Corwin, our Minister to Mexico, and respectfully requested the advice of the Senate thereupon.

On the 25th. day of February, last, a resolution was adopted by the Senate to the effect, "That it is not advisable to negotiate a Treaty that will require the United States to assume any portion of the principal or interest of the debt of Mexico, or that will require the concurrence of European Powers."

This resolution having been duly communicated to me, notice thereof was immediately given by the Secretary of State to Mr. Corwin, and he was informed that he was to consider his instructions, upon the subject referred to, modified by this resolution, and would gove[r]n his course accordingly. That despatch failed to reach Mr Corwin, by reason of the disturbed condition of Mexico, until a very recent date, Mr Corwin being without instructions or thus practically left without instructions to negotiate further with Mexico.

In view of the very important events occurring there, he has thought that the interests of the United States would be promoted by the conclusion of two treaties which should provide for a loan to that Republic. He has therefore signed such treaties, and they having been duly ratified by the Government of Mexico, he has transmitted them to me for my consideration. The action of the Senate of course is conclusive against an acceptance of the treaties on my part. I have nevertheless thought it just to our excellent Minister in Mexico, and respectful to the Government of that Republic, to lay the treaties before the Senate,—together with the correspondence which has occurred in relation to them. In performing this duty, I have only to add that the importance of the subject thus submitted to the Senate cannot be over estimated, and I shall cheerfully receive and consider with the highest respect any further advice the Senate may think proper to give upon the subject.   ABRAHAM LINCOLN

Washington, June, 23, 1862.

1 DS, DNA RG 46, Senate 37B B11. The message and enclosures were referred to the committee on foreign relations. They were reported without amendment on July 12 and ordered to lie on the table.

To the Senate[1]

To the Senate of the United States: June 23, 1862

The bill which has passed the House of Representatives and the Senate, entitled "An act to repeal that part of an act of Congress which prohibits the circulation of bank notes of a less denomination than five dollars in the District of Columbia,"[2] has received my attentive consideration; and I now return it to the Senate, in which it originated, with the following objections:

1. The bill proposes to repeal the existing legislation, prohibiting the circulation of bank notes of a less denomination than five dollars within the District of Columbia, without permitting the issuing of such bills by banks not now legally authorized to issue them. In my judgment, it will be found impracticable, in the present condition of the currency, to make such a discrimination. The banks have generally suspended specie payments; and a legal sanction given to the circulation of the irredeemable notes of one class of them will almost certainly be so extended, in practical operation, as to include those of all classes, whether authorized or unauthorized. If this view be correct, the currency of the District, should this act become a law, will certainly and greatly deteriorate, to the serious injury of honest trade and honest labor.

2. This bill seems to contemplate no end which cannot be otherwise more certainly and beneficially attained. During the existing war it is peculiarly the duty of the national government to secure to the people a sound circulating medium. This duty has been, under existing circumstances, satisfactorily performed, in part at least, by authorizing the issue of United States notes, receivable for all government dues except customs, and made a legal tender for all debts, public and private, except interest on public debt. The object of the bill submitted to me, namely, that of providing a small note currency during the present suspension, can be fully accomplished by authorizing the issue, as part of any new emission of United States notes made necessary by the circumstances of the country, of notes of a similar character, but of less denomination than five dollars. Such an issue would answer all the beneficial purposes of the bill; would save a considerable amount to the treasury in interest; would greatly facilitate payments, to soldiers and other creditors, of small sums; and would furnish to the people a currency as safe as their own government.[3]

Entertaining these objections to the bill, I feel myself constrained to withhold from it my approval, and return it for the further consideration and action of Congress.

June 23, 1862.   ABRAHAM LINCOLN.

[1] Thirty-seventh Congress, Second Session, *Senate Executive Document No. 65.*

[2] The bill (S.193) passed the Senate on April 4 and the House on June 11, 1862.

[3] An act approved July 11, 1862, authorized an additional issue of United States notes in the amount of $150,000,000 in no-interest notes "of such denominations as he [Secretary of the Treasury] may deem expedient," but that no note for a fractional part of a dollar be issued, nor more than $35,000,000 for denominations less than $5.

To Edwin M. Stanton[1]

June 23, 1862

Gen. Rousseau was our first active practical Military friend in Kentucky, as the within letter shows, & as I knew before. He raised two regiments of Kentuckians over the river in Indiana, before they would allow him to organize them in Kentucky. He fought bravely at Pittsburg Landing. These things entitle him to a fair hearing, which I ask the Secretary of War to give him.

June 23. 1862.   A. LINCOLN

[1] AES, NHi. Lincoln's endorsement is written on a letter from Joshua F. Speed, June 17, 1862, recommending that Rousseau be given a hearing on "the army of the Ohio and the relation of its officers to the Government."

To Edwin M. Stanton[1]

Executive Mansion,
Sir: Washington, June 23, 1862.

We specially request that the nomination of Col. Benjamin S. Roberts, for a Brigadier General of Volunteers, be withdrawn, and that he be nominated as a Brigadier General by brevet, in the regular army, for meritorious service in New Mexico, and distinguished conduct in the battle of Valverde, to date from the 21st of Feb. 1862.   J. COLLAMER   JAS. HARLAN

The President   S. FOOT   O. H. BROWNING
                                       J. T. WATTS

Let it be done.   A. LINCOLN
June 23, 1862.

[1] Copy, ISLA. The body of this letter as well as the endorsement appears in Lincoln's autograph. Benjamin S. Roberts' nomination as brigadier general of Volunteers had been confirmed by the Senate on June 11. No record has been found of his being brevetted a brigadier general in the Regular Army until the Senate confirmed his brevet rank on July 25, 1866, to date from March 13, 1865.

Remarks at Jersey City, New Jersey[1]

June 24, 1862

When birds and animals are looked at through a fog they are seen to disadvantage, and so it might be with you if I were to attempt to tell you why I went to see Gen. SCOTT. I can only say that my visit to West Point did not have the importance which has been attached to it; but it conceived [concerned] matters that you understand quite as well as if I were to tell you all about them. Now, I can only remark that it had nothing whatever to do with making or unmaking any General in the country. [Laughter and applause.] The Secretary of War, you know, holds a pretty tight rein on the Press, so that they shall not tell more than they ought to, and I'm afraid that if I blab too much he might draw a tight rein on me.

[1] New York *Times,* June 26, 1862. On Monday, June 23, Lincoln had left Washington on an unannounced trip to West Point for consultation with General Winfield Scott. Returning late at night, he was met at the Jersey City station by a small crowd who called for a speech. The substance of Lincoln's conference with Scott is indicated in Scott's memorandum in the Lincoln Papers:

"The President having stated to me, orally, the present numbers & positions of our forces in front of the rebel armies, south & South west of the Potomack, has done me honor to ask my views, in writing, as to the further dispositions now to be made, of the former, & particularly of the army under McDowell, towards the suppression of the rebellion.

"Premising that, altho' the statements of the President were quite full & most distinct & lucid—yet from my distance from the scenes of operation, & not having, recently, followed them up, with closeness—many details are still wanted to give professional value to my suggestions—I shall, nevertheless, with great deference, proceed to offer such as most readily occur to me—each of which has been anticipated by the President.

"I consider the numbers & positions of Fremont & Banks, adequate to the protection of Washington against any force the enemy can bring by the way of the Upper Potomack, & the troops, at Manassas junction, with the garrisons of the forts on the Potomack & of Washington, equally adequate to its protection on the South.

"The force at Fredericksburg seems entirely out of position, & it cannot be called up, directly & in time, by McClellan, from the want of rail-road transportation, or an adequate supply train, moved by animals. If, however, there be a sufficient number of vessels, at hand, that force might reach the head of York river, by water, in time to aid in the operations against Richmond, or in the very improbable case of disaster, there, to serve as a valuable reinforcement to McClellan.

"The defeat of the rebels, at Richmond, or their forced retreat, thence, combined with our previous victories, would be a virtual end of the rebellion, & soon restore entire Virginia to the Union.

"The remaining important points to be occupied, by us, are—Mobile, Charleston, Chattanooga. These must soon come into our hands.

"McDowell's force, at Manassas, might be ordered to Richmond, by the Potomack & York rivers, & be replaced, at Manassas, by King's brigade, if there be adequate transports at, or near Alexandria. Most respectfully Submitted

"WINFIELD SCOTT."

To Edward Bates[1]

June 26, 1862

Believing that William Griffin, named within, has been sufficiently punished, he is hereby pardoned of so much of the sentence against him as has not already been executed.   A. LINCOLN

June 26, 1862.

[1] AES, owned by R. E. Burdick, New York City. Lincoln's endorsement is written on the cover of the court-martial record of Private William Griffin of Company K, Fifth New York Volunteers, sentenced by court-martial January 8, 1862, on charges of desertion, to six months' imprisonment wearing ball and chain, and "that he forfeit all pay and allowances now due or which may become due him by reason of his enlistment, except the allowances for clothing and that at the end of said time of six months, one half his head be shaved and that he be dishonorably discharged the service and be drummed out in presence of his regiment."

To John W. Crisfield[1]

Executive Mansion,

Hon. John W. Crisfield.   Washington, June 26. 1862.

My dear Sir: I have been considering the appeal made by yourself, and Senator Pearce in behalf of Judge Carmichael. His charge to the Grand-Jury, was left with me by the Senator, and, on reading it, I must confess I was not very favorably impressed towards the Judge. The object of the charge, I understand, was to procure prossecutions, and punishment of some men for arresting, or doing violence to some secessionists—that is, the Judge was trying to help a little, by giving the protection of law to those who were endevoring to overthrow the Supreme law—trying if he could find a safe place for certain men to stand on the constitution, whilst they should stab it in another place.

But possibly I am mistaken.

The Secretary of War and I have agreed that if the Judge will take the oath of allegiance, usually taken in such cases, he may be discharged. Please ascertain, and inform me whether he will do it. Yours very truly   A. LINCOLN

[1] ADfS, DLC-RTL. The circumstances of the arrest of Judge Richard B. Carmichael, whose release was requested by Representative Crisfield and Senator James A. Pearce of Maryland, are recounted in the report of General John A. Dix to Secretary Stanton, June 25, 1862, which reads in part as follows: "In October [October 3, 1861] last I was authorized by the Secretary of State to arrest Judge R. B. Carmichael of [Talbot County] the Eastern Shore of Maryland, if I should deem it expedient . . . and if necessary in his own Court. In the communication . . . was enclosed a printed memorial . . . to the Legislature of Maryland, signed by him and expressing the most disloyal sentiments. . . . I did not . . . deem it advisable to make the arrest at that time. Soon afterwards a Military arrest was made on the Eastern Shore . . . in a county in Judge Carmichael's

District, by Officer of the Second Regiment of Delaware Volunteers. At the next term of the Court, the Judge charged the Grand jury that it was their duty to present all persons concerned in such arrest. . . . His charges in . . . other Counties as well as this, were of a most disloyal and offensive character. . . . Under the charge referred to the Hon. Henry H. Goldsborough, President of the Senate of Maryland and several officers of the 2nd. Delaware . . . I was informed that bills of indictment had been found against them. The trial of the Hon. Mr. Goldsborough was expected to take place in . . . May last, and four Officers of the Delaware Regiment were summoned as witnesses in his behalf. They came to me and expressed a great unwillingness to obey . . . as they had been presented by the Grand jury . . . and would be arrested if they made their appearance in the county. . . . I dispatched Mr. [Daniel H.] McPhail, Deputy Provost Marshal of the Baltimore Military Police with four police-men to Easton . . . where the Court was in session [May 23-27], to accompany the four officers . . . with instructions to arrest Judge Carmichael, if on consultation with . . . Mr. Goldsborough, it should be thought expedient. . . . It was, on full consideration, deemed expedient that the arrest should be made in Court in order that the proceeding might be the more marked. . . . When Mr. McPhail accompanied by two . . . policemen ascended the bench and respectfully announced to the Judge the order to take him into custody by the authority of the United States, he denied the authority of the Government and made a violent attack on one of the policemen. Mr. McPhail was thus compelled to use force to secure him, and he unluckily received a superficial wound on the head. . . ." (DLC-RTL). Judge Carmichael was released on Stanton's order, December 2, 1862.

To George B. McClellan[1]

Washington, June 26, 1862.

Major-General McClellan: Your three dispatches of yesterday in relation to the affair, ending with the statement that you completely succeeded in making your point, are very gratifying. The later one of 6:15 p.m., suggesting the probability of your being overwhelmed by 200,000, and talking of where the responsibility will belong, pains me very much. I give you all I can, and act on the presumption that you will do the best you can with what you have, while you continue, ungenerously I think, to assume that I could give you more if I would. I have omitted and shall omit no opportunity to send you reenforcements whenever I possibly can.

A. LINCOLN

[1] OR, I, XI, III, 259; copy, DLC-McClellan Papers. In the absence of the original telegram, the received copy in the McClellan Papers establishes satisfactorily that the *Official Records* are in error in printing as a part of this telegram the postscript properly belonging to Lincoln's dispatch to McClellan on June 28, *infra*. McClellan's telegram to Stanton of June 25, 6:15 P.M., reads in part as follows: ". . . I incline to think Jackson will attack my right and rear. The rebel force is stated at 200,000, including Jackson and Beauregard. I shall have to contend against vastly superior odds if these reports be true; but this army will do all in the power of men to hold their position and repulse any attack.

"I regret my great inferiority in numbers, but feel that I am in no way responsible for it, as I have not failed to represent repeatedly the necessity of re-enforcements; that this was the decisive point, and that all the available means of the Government should be concentrated here. I will do all that a general can do with the splendid army I have the honor to command, and if it is destroyed by overwhelming numbers, can at least die with it and share its fate. But if the result of the action, which will probably occur to-morrow, or within a short time, is a disaster, the responsibility cannot be thrown on my shoulders; it must rest where it belongs. . . ." (OR, I, XI, I, 51).

Order Constituting the Army of Virginia[1]

Executive Mansion   Washington, D.C   June 26, 1862

1. . . . . . The forces under Major Generals Fremont, Banks and McDowell, including the troops now under Brigadier General Sturgis at Washington, shall be consolidated and form one army, to be called the Army of Virginia.

2. . . . . The command of the Army of Virginia is specially assigned to Major General John Pope as commanding General. The troops of the Mountain Department, heretofore under command of General Fremont shall constitute the first army corps, under the command of General Fremont; the troops of the Shenandoah Department, now under General Banks, shall constitute the second army corps, and be commanded by him; the troops under the command of General McDowell, except those within the fortifications and city of Washington, shall form the third army corps and be under his command.

3. . . . . The Army of Virginia shall operate in such manner as, while protecting western Virginia and the National Capitol from danger or insult, it shall in the speediest manner attack and overcome the rebel forces under Jackson and Ewell, threaten the enemy in the direction of Charlottesville, and render the most effective aid to relieve General McClellan and capture Richmond.

4. . . . . When the Army of the Potomac and the Army of Virginia shall be in position to communicate and directly cooperate at, or before Richmond, the chief command while so operating together shall be governed as, in like cases, by the rules and Articles of War.   ABRAHAM LINCOLN

[1] DS, DLC-Stanton Papers. This order was sent by telegraph to Banks, Frémont, and McDowell.

To the Senate[1]

To the Senate   Executive Mansion
of the United States.   Washington June 26 1862.

The accompanying treaty made and concluded at the City of Washington, on the 24th day of June, 1862, between the United

States and the United Bands of the Ottawa Indians of Blanchard's Fork, and of Roche de Boeuf, in Kansas, is transmitted for the consideration and constitutional action of the Senate, agreeably to recommendation of the enclosed letter from the Secretary of the Interior of this date. ABRAHAM LINCOLN

[1] DS, DNA RG 46, Senate 37B C8. The treaty was amended and ratified as amended on July 16, 1862.

To Ambrose E. Burnside[1]

Gen Burnside   Washington City, D.C. 28th June 1862.

I think you had better go with any reinforcements you can spare to Gen McClellan   A. LINCOLN

[1] LS, RPB. On June 25 McClellan had ordered Burnside at New Bern, North Carolina, to "advance on Goldsborough [North Carolina] with all your available forces at the earliest practicable moment . . . . destroying all the railroad communications in the direction of Richmond in your power. . . ." (OR, I, XI, III, 252-53). Stanton telegraphed Burnside at 6 P.M. on June 28, "Since the dispatches of the President and myself to you of to-day we have seen a copy of one sent to you by . . . McClellan on the 25th, of which we were not aware. Our directions were not designed to interfere . . . but only to authorize . . . any aid in your power." (*Ibid.*, p. 271).

To Quintin Campbell[1]

Cadet Quintin Campbell   Washington D.C.

My dear Sir   June 28. 1862

Your good mother tells me you are feeling very badly in your new situation. Allow me to assure you it is a perfect certainty that you will, very soon, feel better—quite happy—if you only stick to the resolution you have taken to procure a military education. I am older than you, have felt badly myself, and *know*, what I tell you is true. Adhere to your purpose and you will soon feel as well as you ever did. On the contrary, if you falter, and give up, you will lose the power of keeping any resolution, and will regret it all your life. Take the advice of a friend, who, though he never saw you, deeply sympathizes with you, and stick to your purpose. Sincerely your friend   A. LINCOLN

[1] ALS-F, St. Paul, Minnesota, *Pioneer Press*, February 12, 1909. Quintin Campbell, the son of Mrs. Lincoln's cousin Mrs. Ann Todd Campbell of Boonville, Missouri, had just entered West Point. According to the account published in the *Pioneer Press*, Quintin's mother wrote to Mrs. Lincoln about her son's dissatisfaction, and at his wife's suggestion Lincoln wrote this letter. Quintin graduated at West Point in 1866.

To John A. Dix[1]

Gen. Dix   Washington City, D.C. June 28– 1862
Communication with McClellan by White House is cut-off.
Strain every nerve to open communications with him by James
River, or any way you can. Report to me.   A. LINCOLN

[1] ALS, RPB. McClellan to Stanton, June 28, ". . . Jackson is driving in my
pickets, &c., on the other side of the Chickahominy.
   "It is impossible to tell where re-enforcements ought to go, as I am yet unable
to predict result of approaching battle. . . . It is not probable that I can maintain
telegraphic communications more than an hour or two longer. . . ." (OR, I, XI,
III, 270).
   Dix to McClellan, June 28, ". . . Commodore Goldsborough has been with
me two hours, and no effort will be spared to support you at all points. I will
open a regular communication with you by steam the moment I hear from you.
I have a dispatch from the President expressing an earnest desire that I should
reach you with a message, that I may know your wants. . . ." (*Ibid.*, p. 269).

To Louis M. Goldsborough[1]

Flag Officer Goldsborough: Washington, D.C.
Fort-Monroe   June 28, 1862.
   Enemy has cut McClellan's communications with White-House,
and is driving Stoneman back on that point. Do what you can for
him with Gun-boats at or near that place. McClellan's main force
is between the Chickahominy and the James. Also do what you
can to communicate with him and support him there.

                                        A. LINCOLN

[1] ALS, RPB. Goldsborough replied at 3:30 P.M., "I beg to acknowledge receipt
of your telegram to-day. I knew of General McClellan's position last night, and
sent up orders for gun-boats to go up Chickahominy to protect the general's left
flank and guard vessels with supplies. General Dix and myself will do everything
in our power to communicate with General McClellan and to keep a communication with him open up the James River." (OR, I, XI, III, 270).

To George B. McClellan[1]

                                        Washington City, D.C.
Major Gen. McClellan   June 28– 1862
   Save your Army at all events. Will send re-inforcements as fast
as we can. Of course they can not reach you to-day, to-morrow, or
next day.[2] I have not said you were ungenerous for saying you
needed re-inforcement. I thought you were ungenerous in assuming that I did not send them as fast as I could. I feel any misfortune to you and your Army quite as keenly as you feel it yourself.
If you have had a drawn battle, or a repulse, it is the price we pay

for the enemy not being in Washington. We protected Washington, and the enemy concentrated on you; had we stripped Washington, he would have been upon us before the troops sent could have got to you. Less than a week ago you notified us that reinforcements were leaving Richmond to come in front of us. It is the nature of the case, and neither you or the government that is to blame. Please tell at once the present condition and aspect of things.   A. LINCOLN

P.S. Gen. Pope thinks if you fall back, it would be much better towards York River, than towards the James. As Pope now has charge of the Capital, please confer with him through the telegraph.   A. L.

¹ ALS, IHi. McClellan's dispatch to Stanton, June 28, 12:20 A.M., is as follows: "I now know the full history of the day. On this side of the river (the right bank) we repulsed several strong attacks. On the left bank our men did all that men could do, all that soldiers could accomplish, but they were overwhelmed by vastly superior numbers, even after I brought my last reserves into action. The loss on both sides is terrible. I believe it will prove to be the most desperate battle of the war.

"The sad remnants of my men behave as men. Those battalions who fought most bravely and suffered most are still in the best order. My regulars were superb, and I count upon what are left to turn another battle, in company with their gallant comrades of the volunteers. Had I 20,000 or even 10,000 fresh troops to use to-morrow I could take Richmond, but I have not a man in reserve, and shall be glad to cover my retreat and save the material and *personnel* of the army.

"If we have lost the day we have yet preserved our honor, and no one need blush for the Army of the Potomac. I have lost this battle because my force was too small.

"I again repeat that I am not responsible for this, and I say it with the earnestness of a general who feels in his heart the loss of every brave man who has been needlessly sacrificed to-day. I still hope to retrieve our fortunes, but to do this the Government must view the matter in the same earnest light that I do. You must send me very large re-enforcements, and send them at once. I shall draw back to this side of Chickahominy, and think I can withdraw all our material. Please understand that in this battle we have lost nothing but men, and those the best we have.

"In addition to what I have already said, I only wish to say to the President that I think he is wrong in regarding me as ungenerous when I said that my force was too weak. I merely intimated a truth which to-day has been too plainly proved. If, at this instant, I could dispose of 10,000 fresh men, I could gain a victory to-morrow. I know that a few thousand more men would have changed this battle from a defeat to a victory. As it is, the Government must not and cannot hold me responsible for the result.

"I feel too earnestly to-night. I have seen too many dead and wounded comrades to feel otherwise than that the Government has not sustained this army. If you do not do so now the game is lost.

"If I save this army now, I tell you plainly that I owe no thanks to you or to any other persons in Washington.

"You have done your best to sacrifice this army." (OR, I, XI, I, 61).

McClellan's last two sentences were deleted by Colonel Edward S. Sanford, military supervisor of the telegraph, from the copy delivered to Stanton, and the fact was not known until 1907 when David H. Bates told the story in *Lincoln in the Telegraph Office*. They were included, however, in McClellan's official report as printed in the *Official Records*.

² At Lincoln's direction Stanton telegraphed Halleck on June 28, "immediately to detach 25,000 of your force and forward it by the nearest and quickest route by way of Baltimore and Washington to Richmond. . . . The direction to send these forces immediately is rendered imperative by a serious reverse suffered by General McClellan before Richmond yesterday, the full extent of which is not yet known. . . ." (OR, I, XVI, II, 69).

To Oliver P. Morton¹

Gov. O. P. Morton   Washington, D.C.,
Indianapolis, Ia   June 28. 1862.

Your despatch of to-day is just received. I have no recollection of either John R. Cravens, or Cyrus M. Allen having been named to me for appointment under the tax-law. The latter particularly has been my friend, and I am sorry to learn that he is not yours. No appointment has been, or will be made by me, for the purpose of stabbing you.   A. LINCOLN

¹ ALS, RPB. Governor Morton telegraphed on June 27, "It is reported that Jno R Cravens & Cyrus M Allen are about to receive important appointments under the new tax law. They have become notorious by waging a bitter and unscrupulous opposition to my administration & the appointment of one or both would be mortifying to me & regarded as an endorsement of their course by the people of the state on the part of the administration   There are plenty of good men who have not spent their time in an unscrupulous opposition" (DLC-RTL). John R. Cravens of Indianapolis, Indiana, was appointed additional paymaster of Volunteers on June 30, 1862.

To William H. Seward¹

[c. June 28, 1862?]
None at all   A.L.

¹ AES, OClWHi. Lincoln's endorsement is written on the back of an undated note from Seward: "My dear President: Have you any good or bad news. W. H. S." Although neither note is dated, it seems probable that the exchange took place just before Seward's departure for New York to confer with the Union Defense Committee about raising more troops. McClellan's dispatch of June 28 had not as yet been received.

To William H. Seward¹

Hon. W. H. Seward   Executive Mansion
My dear Sir   June 28. 1862.

My view of the present condition of the War is about as follows:
The evacuation of Corinth, and our delay by the flood in the Chicahominy, has enabled the enemy to concentrate too much

force in Richmond for McClellan to successfully attack. In fact there soon will be no substantial rebel force any where else. But if we send all the force from here to McClellan, the enemy will, before we can know of it, send a force from Richmond and take Washington. Or, if a large part of the Western Army be brought here to McClellan, they will let us have Richmond, and retake Tennessee, Kentucky, Missouri &c. What should be done is to hold what we have in the West, open the Mississippi, and, take Chatanooga & East Tennessee, without more—a reasonable force should, in every event, be kept about Washington for it's protection. Then let the country give us a hundred thousand new troops in the shortest possible time, which added to McClellan, directly or indirectly, will take Richmond, without endangering any other place which we now hold—and will substantially end the war. I expect to maintain this contest until successful, or till I die, or am conquered, or my term expires, or Congress or the country forsakes me; and I would publicly appeal to the country for this new force, were it not that I fear a general panic and stampede would follow—so hard is it to have a thing understood as it really is. I think the new force should be all, or nearly all infantry, principally because such can be raised most cheaply and quickly. Yours very truly   A. LINCOLN

1 ADfS, DLC-RTL. Secretary Seward carried the original letter to New York to show to Union governors in order to get them to issue new calls for troops, but at the New York conference it was decided that a direct official appeal would be preferable, this to be issued in response to a memorial from the governors to the president suggesting the call. See Lincoln's call of June 30 and July 1, *infra*.

To William H. Seward[1]

Hon. W. H. Seward.   Washington City, D.C.
Astor-House—N.Y.   June 29, 1862   6 oclock PM[2]

Not much more than when you left. "Fulton"[3] of Baltimore American, is now with us. He left White House at 11. A.M. yesterday. He conversed fully with a Pay-Master who was with Porter's force during the fight of Friday and fell back to near McClellan's Quarters, just a little sooner that [sic] Porter did, seeing the whole of it; staid on the Richmond side of the Chickahominy over night and left for White House at 5. AM. Saturday. He says Porter retired in perfect order, under protection of guns, arranged for the purpose, under orders, and not from necessity, and, with all other of our forces, except what was left on purpose to go to White House, was safely in position over the Chickahominy before morning; and that there was heavy firing on the Richmond side began at 5 and ceased at 7 AM. Saturday   On the whole, I think we had the better of it up to that point of time. What has happened since we still know not, as we have no communication with Gen. McClellan. A despatch from Col. Ingalls⁴ shows that he thinks McClellan is fighting with the enemy at Richmond to-day, and will be tomorrow. We have no means of knowing upon what Col Ingalls' founds, his opinion. All confirmed about our saving all property. Not a single unwounded straggler came back to the White-House from the field; and the number of wounded reaching there up to 11. A.M. Saturday was not large.

A. LINCOLN

¹ ALS, RPB. Seward telegraphed from New York on June 29, "Have you any later news from McClellan." (DLC-RTL). To Lincoln's reply as given above, Stanton added at the end as follows: "To what the President has above stated I will only add one or two points that may be satisfactory for you to know.

"1st. All the sick and wounded were safely removed from the White House not a man left behind.

"2d A despatch from Burnside shows that he is in condition to afford efficient support and is probably doing so.

"3d The despatch from Col Ingalls impresses me with the conviction that the movement was made by General McClellan to concentrate on Richmond, and was successful to the latest point of which we have any information.

"4th. Mr Fulton says that on Friday night between twelve and one oclock General McClellan telegraphed Commodore Goldsborough that the result of the movement was satisfactory to him.

"5th. From these and the facts stated by the President my inference is, that General McClellan will probably be in Richmond within two days.
"EDWIN M STANTON"

² "6 oclock PM" was added by Stanton.   ³ Charles C. Fulton.

⁴ Rufus Ingalls telegraphed Montgomery C. Meigs from Fort Monroe, 2:45 P.M., June 29, "The White House depot was abandoned by me last night at sunset . . . . moving out from the narrow and tortuous Pamunkey some four hundred vessels laden with supplies, quite all of which I now have with me, *en route* to James River by Fort Monroe, if our arms are successful to-day and to-morrow at Richmond. . . ." (OR, I, XI, III, 273).

Call for Troops¹

New York, June 30, 1862.

To the Governors of the several States: The capture of New Orleans, Norfolk, and Corinth by the national forces has enabled the insurgents to concentrate a large force at and about Richmond, which place we must take with the least possible delay; in fact, there will soon be no formidable insurgent force except at Richmond. With so large an army there, the enemy can threaten us on the Potomac and elsewhere. Until we have re-established the national authority, all these places must be held, and we must keep a respectable force in front of Washington. But this, from the diminished strength of our Army by sickness and casualties, renders an addition to it necessary in order to close the struggle which has been prosecuted for the last three months with energy and success. Rather than hazard the misapprehension of our military condition and of groundless alarm by a call for troops by proclamation, I have deemed it best to address you in this form. To accomplish the object stated we require without delay 150,000 men, including those recently called for by the Secretary of War. Thus re-enforced, our gallant Army will be enabled to realize the hopes and expectations of the Government and the people.

A. LINCOLN.

₁ OR, III, II, 183. This call was drafted by Seward at the New York conference (see Lincoln to Seward, June 28, *supra*) and telegraphed to Lincoln for approval, but was not issued. Governor Morgan and Governor Curtin attended the conference and Seward communicated with the others by telegraph. At 5 P.M. on June 30, Seward telegraphed Lincoln of a new suggestion—a memorial to the president from the governors, asking that a call be made, and a circular from the president in reply, making a call for 150,000 men. Copies of both memorial and circular were telegraphed to Lincoln for approval (*ibid.*, p. 181). Stanton answered at 9 P.M. that the president had "gone to the country very tired. In the morning you shall have his answer." (*Ibid.*, pp. 181-82). On July 1 Stanton telegraphed that Lincoln approved but suggested 200,000 men (*ibid.*, p. 186). Seward replied at 4 P.M., "The Governors respond, and the Union Committee approve. . . . The number of troops to be called is left to the President to fix. . . ." (*Ibid.*, p. 187). Lincoln issued the call on July 1, specifying 300,000 men (*vide infra*).

To John A. Dix[1]

Major Gen. Dix   Washington City, D.C.

Fort-Monroe   June 30, 1862

Is it not probable the enemy have abandoned the line between White House and McClellan's rear? He could have but little object to maintain it; and nothing to subsist upon. Would not Stoneman better move up and see about it. I think a Telegraphic communication can at once be opened to White-House from Williamsburg. The wires must be up still.   A. LINCOLN

₁ ALS, RPB. Dix telegraphed Stanton at 11 A.M., "Will you please say to President Lincoln that the report from Williamsburg is just in. The enemy had not been at White House at 8 o'clock last evening. Our pickets extend to New Kent Court-House, 6 miles this side." (OR, I, XI, III, 278). At 2 P.M. he replied to Lincoln's dispatch, "We have no doubt that McClellan intended to abandon the White House. Our only line of communication with him by telegraph from that point would be along the railroad, which the enemy will hardly give up.

"The communication of . . . Goldsborough, telegraphed to Gideon Welles, will have advised you that the general relies on the James River for all his communications hereafter. The commodore was with me an hour ago. I suggested we should extend our wires from Williamsburg to the mouth of the Chickahominy and there communicate by the James River by steamers or carry them on the left bank of the river to Turkey Island Point. . . . The general has all the materials of the working party with him. . . . We have no material here. I will make a reconnaissance in the vicinity of the White House, to ascertain whether the enemy are there." (*Ibid.*, pp. 278-79).

To Henry W. Halleck[1]

"Cypher"

Major Genl. Halleck   Washington, D.C.

Corinth, Miss.   June 30, 1862.

Would be very glad of twenty five thousand Infantry—no artillery, or cavalry—but please do not send a man if it endangers any place you deem important to hold, or if it forces you to give up, or weaken, or delay the expedition against Chattanooga. To take and hold the Rail-road at, or East of, Cleveland in East Tennessee, I think fully as important as the taking and holding of Richmond.   A. LINCOLN

[1] ALS, RPB. Halleck telegraphed Stanton on June 30, "I think, under the circumstances, the Chattanooga expedition better be abandoned or at least diminished. If not, I doubt our ability to hold West Tennessee after detaching so large a force as that called for. . . ." (OR, I, XI, III, 279). Stanton replied at 3 P.M., "The Chattanooga expedition must not on any account be given up. The President regards that . . . as one of the most important movements of the war. . . . and directs that no force be sent here if you cannot do it without breaking up the operation. . . ." (*Ibid.*, p. 280). Halleck replied to Lincoln (received 9:40 P.M.) that "Your telegram just received saves Western Tennessee; the former order was imperative and I had no alternative but obedience. . . ." (*Ibid.*, p. 285).

To William H. Seward[1]

Hon. W. H. Seward   Washington City, D.C.

New-York—   June 30 1862

We are yet without communication with Gen. McClellan; and this absence of news, is our point of anxiety. Up to the latest point to which we are posted, he effected everything in such exact accordance with his plan contingently announced to us before the battle began, that we feel justified to hope he has not failed since. He had a severe engagement in getting the part of his army on this side of the Chickahominy over to the other side, in which the enemy lost certainly as much as we did. We are not dissatisfied with this, only that the loss of enemies does not compensate for the loss of friends. The enemy did [can?] not come below White-House[,] certainly is not there now, and probably has abandoned the whole line. Dix' pickets are at New-Kent C.H.

A LINCOLN

1 ALS, RPB.

To James S. Wadsworth[1]

I would be glad if Gen. Wadsworth could give this man employment.   A. LINCOLN

June 30. 1862.

1 AES, DLC-RTL. Lincoln's endorsement is written on the back of a letter from William A. Darling, president of the Third Avenue Rail Road Company, New York, June 11, 1862, introducing Charles J. Bertram (Bartram), formerly of the "Highland Guard," who had been wounded at Bull Run and was "disabled from longer service in the Army."

Memorandum: Appointment of A. Keller, Jr.[1]

West-Point—   [c. July? 1862]

Judge Peters says I promised. I dont remember.

1 AE, DNA WR RG 94, U.S. Military Academy, 1862, No. 149, Box 80. Lincoln's endorsement is written on an undated letter on "Executive Mansion" stationery from John H. Peters, reminding the president that "some months —near a year—he said he would appoint a young friend of mine to the West Point School. . . . I would not ask it were not the applicant a young gentleman A. Keller Jr. *a loyal South Carolinian* of more than ordinary mental & moral strength." There is no record of Keller's appointment.

Call for 300,000 Volunteers[1]

Executive Mansion   Washington, July 1, 1862.

To the Governors of Maine, New Hampshire, Vermont, Connecticut, New York, New Jersey, Pennsylvania, Maryland, Virginia, Michigan, Tennessee, Missouri, Indiana, Ohio, Minnesota, Illinois, and Wisconsin, and the President of the Military Board of Kentucky:

Gentlemen: Fully concurring in the wisdom of the views expressed to me in so patriotic a manner by you in the communication of the 28th day of June, I have decided to call into the service an additional force of 300,000 men. I suggest and recommend that the troops should be chiefly of infantry. The quota of your State would be——.[2] I trust that they may be enrolled without delay, so

[296]

as to bring this unnecessary and injurious civil war to a speedy and satisfactory conclusion. An order fixing the quotas of the respective States will be issued by the War Department to-morrow.

ABRAHAM LINCOLN.

[1] OR, III, II, 187-88. See note to Lincoln's Call for Troops, June 30, *supra*. The communication bearing the names of all but three of the Union governors and dated June 28 although prepared by Seward on June 30, was released to the press simultaneously with Lincoln's reply, to appear on July 2. Governors William Sprague of Rhode Island, Samuel J. Kirkwood of Iowa, and John A. Andrew of Massachusetts could not be reached in time for inclusion (Seward to Stanton, July 2, OR, III, II, 198). The text of the governors' communication of June 28 is as follows:

"The undersigned, Governors of States of the Union, impressed with the belief that the citizens of the States which they respectively represent are of one accord in the hearty desire that the recent successes of the Federal arms may be followed up by measures which must insure the speedy restoration of the Union; and believing that in view of the present state of the important military movements now in progress and the reduced condition of our effective forces in the field, resulting from the usual and unavoidable casualties of the service, that the time has arrived for prompt and vigorous measures to be adopted by the people in support of the great interests committed to your charge, we respectfully request, if it meets with your entire approval, that you at once call upon the several States for such number of men as may be required to fill up all military organizations now in the field, and add to the armies heretofore organized such additional number of men as may in your judgment be necessary to garrison and hold all of the numerous cities and military positions that have been captured by our armies, and to speedily crush the rebellion that still exists in several of the Southern States, thus practically restoring to the civilized world our great and good Government. All believe that the decisive moment is near at hand, and to that end the people of the United States are desirous to aid promptly in furnishing all re-enforcements that you may deem needful to sustain our Government." (OR, III, II, 180).

[2] The quotas ranging from twenty-eight regiments (New York) to one regiment (Delaware, Minnesota, and Rhode Island) were sent out by the Adjutant General's Office on July 7 (OR, III, II, 208).

To Benjamin F. Larned[1]

I think Mr. Merwin should be paid, upon the Pay-Master-General being satisfied that he has performed the service as stated.

July 1. 1862.   A. LINCOLN

[1] AES, IHi. Concerning Merwin's appointment see Lincoln to Cameron, July 17, 1861, *supra*. Lincoln's endorsement is written on a letter from James B. Merwin to Owen Lovejoy, June 30, 1862, asking his assistance, "I have been acting as an *ordained* Chaplain since *Sept* 20th. 1861 & I submit herewith a *part* of a great amount of evidence of my labors. I have not been paid a farthing yet. . . . The President appointed me or wrote an order for my appointment *Sept*. 12th. 1861." Larned's endorsement following Lincoln's has been crossed out, but is sufficiently legible to indicate that the Pay Department insisted that either the "President or Secretary of War" should state the date "upon which to base an account."

[297]

To George B. McClellan[1]

Executive Mansion,
Major Genl. McClellan—   Washington, July 1 1862.

It is impossible to re-inforce you for your present emergency. If we had a million of men we could not get them to you in time. We have not the men to send. If you are not strong enough to face the enemy you must find a place of security, and wait, rest, and repair. Maintain your ground if you can; but save the Army at all events, even if you fall back to Fortress-Monroe. We still have strength enough in the country, and will bring it out.

A. LINCOLN

[1] ALS, NN. McClellan telegraphed Stanton at 7 P.M. on June 30, "Another day of desperate fighting. We are hard pressed by superior numbers. . . . You must send me very large reinforcements by way of Fort Monroe and they must come very promptly. . . . My Army has . . . done all that men could do, if none of us escape we shall at least have done honor to the country. I shall do my best to save the Army. . . ." (DLC-RTL).

Proclamation Concerning Taxes In Rebellious States[1]

July 1, 1862

By the President of the United States of America:

A Proclamation.

Whereas, in and by the second section of an Act of Congress passed on the 7th. day of June A.D. 1862, entitled "An Act for the collection of direct taxes in insurrectionary districts within the United States and for other purposes" it is made the duty of the President to declare, on or before the first day of July, then next following, by his proclamation, in what States and parts of States insurrection exists:

Now, therefore, be it known that I, Abraham Lincoln, President of the United States of America, do hereby declare and proclaim that the States of South Carolina, Florida, Georgia, Alabama, Louisiana, Texas, Mississippi, Arkansas, Tennessee, North Carolina; and the State of Virginia, except the following counties:— Hancock, Brooke, Ohio, Marshall, Wetzel, Marion, Monongalia, Preston, Taylor, Pleasants, Tyler, Ritchie, Doddridge, Harrison, Wood, Jackson, Wirt, Roane, Calhoun, Gilmer, Barbour, Tucker, Lewis, Braxton, Upshur, Randolph, Mason, Putnam, Kanawha, Clay, Nicholas, Cabell, Wayne, Boone, Logan, Wyoming, Webster, Fayette and Raleigh, are now in insurrection and rebellion and, by reason thereof, the civil authority of the United States is obstructed so that the provisions of the "Act to provide increased revenue from imports to pay the interest on the public debt, and for other purposes," approved August fifth, eighteen hundred and sixty-one, cannot be peaceably executed, and that the taxes legally chargeable upon Real Estate under the Act last aforesaid, lying within the States and parts of States as aforesaid, together with a penalty of fifty per centum of said taxes shall be a lien upon the Tracts or Lots of the same, severally charged till paid.

In witness whereof, I have hereunto set my hand, and caused the seal of the United States to be affixed.

Done at the City of Washington, this first day of July, [L.S.]   in the year of our Lord one thousand eight hundred and sixty-two, and of the Independence of the United States of America the eighty-sixth.   ABRAHAM LINCOLN

By the President:

F. W. SEWARD, Acting Secretary of State.

[1] DS, DNA FS RG 11, Proclamations; DfS, NAuE.

To the Senate and House of Representatives[1]

July 1, 1862

To the Senate and House of Representatives:—

I most cordially recommend that Captain Andrew H. Foote, of the U.S. Navy, receive a vote of thanks of Congress for his eminent services in organizing the Flotilla on the Western waters, and for his gallantry at Fort Henry, Fort Donelson, Island Number Ten and at various other places, whilst in command of the Naval Forces, embracing a period of nearly Ten months.

Washington, D.C,   ABRAHAM LINCOLN
1 July 1862.

[1] DS, DNA RG 46, Senate 37A F2; DS, DNA RG 233, Original Executive Document No. 141. The resolution (H.R. 102) was approved July 16, 1862.

To Edwin M. Stanton[1]

Executive Mansion, Washington, July 1, 1862.

Dear Sir, Please to make out and send me a nomination of Col. Ralph P. Buckland of Ohio to be Brigadier General of Volunteers. Your obt. Servt.,   ABRAHAM LINCOLN

[1] Thomas F. Madigan, *A Catalogue of Lincolniana* (1929), p. 18. Ralph P. Buckland's appointment as brigadier general was not confirmed by the Senate until March 9, 1863.

To Edwin M. Stanton[1]

July 1, 1862

Sec. of War please oblige Senator Powell, by giving the limits of Cleveland to Charles F. Johnson, on his parole—the Senator pledging me that the parole will not be violated. He is a prisoner now at, or near Sandusky.   A. LINCOLN

July 1, 1862

[1] Parke-Bernet Catalog 905, December 1-2, 1947, No. 277. Charles F. Johnson has not been further identified, but he was presumably from Senator Lazarus W. Powell's state, Kentucky.

To an Unknown Person[1]

July 1, 1862

I suppose this man has been doing something for our sick soldiers, and I think it would be no more than fair that he should have a railroad pass to his home at Albany, N. Y.

July 1, 1862.   A. LINCOLN.

[1] *American Notes and Queries* (Philadelphia), March 5, 1892, Vol. VIII, No. 18, p. 216. The persons are unidentified.

To Edward Bates[1]

Let Calvin [*sic*] Beckwith, named within, be pardoned for so much of his punishment as remains unexecuted   A. LINCOLN

July. 2. 1862.

[1] AES, DNA RG 204, U.S. Pardon Attorney, A 425. Lincoln's endorsement is written on the court-martial record of Private Colvin Beckwith, Company A, Twenty-fifth New York Volunteers, sentenced January 23, 1862, to eighteen months at hard labor on charges of desertion.

To Henry W. Halleck[1]

"Cypher"

Major Gen. Halleck   Washington, D.C.,
Corinth, Miss.   July 2 1862.

Your several despatches of yesterday to Sec. of War, and myself, received. I did say and now repeat, I would be exceedingly glad for some re-inforcements from you, still do not send a man, if, in your judgment, it will endanger any point you deem important to hold, or will force you to give up, or weaken, or delay the Chattanooga expedition.

Please tell me, could you make me a flying visit, for consultation, without endangering the service in your Department?

A. LINCOLN

[1] ALS, RPB. Halleck replied at 6 P.M., "The Enemy attacked us at Booneville yesterday in considerable force. . . . Particulars not yet received—. . . . According to reports . . . [Braxton] Bragg is preparing to attack us. . . . Under these circumstances I do not think I could safely be absent from my Army, although being somewhat broken in health and wearied . . . a trip to Washington would be exceedingly desirable." (DLC-RTL).

To George B. McClellan[1]

Washington, D.C.,

Major Gen. McClellan   July 2 1862.

Your despatch of Tuesday morning induces me to hope your Army is having some rest. In this hope, allow me to reason with you a moment. When you ask for fifty thousand men to be promptly sent you, you surely labor under some gross mistake of fact. Recently you sent papers showing your disposal of forces, made last spring, for the defence of Washington, and advising a return to that plan.[2] I find it included in, and about Washington seventyfive thousand men. Now please be assured, I have not men enough to fill that very plan by fifteen thousand. All of Fremont in the valley, all of Banks, all of McDowell, not with you, and all in Washington, taken together do not exceed, if they reach sixty thousand. With Wool and Dix added to those mentioned, I have not, outside of your Army, seventyfive thousand men East of the mountains. Thus, the idea of sending you fifty thousand, or any other considerable force promptly, is simply absurd. If in your frequent mention of responsibility, you have the impression that I blame you for not doing more than you can, please be relieved of such impression. I only beg that in like manner, you will not ask impossibilities of me. If you think you are not strong enough to take Richmond just now, I do not ask you to try just now. Save the Army, material and personal; and I will strengthen it for the offensive again, as fast as I can. The Governors of eighteen states offer me a new levy of three hundred thousand, which I accept.

A. LINCOLN

[1] ALS, IHi. McClellan telegraphed Lorenzo Thomas at 2:45 A.M., July 1, "Another desperate combat to-day. Our troops repulsed the enemy. . . . I have taken steps to adopt a new line, the left resting on Turkey Island, and thence along a ridge parallel to James River as far as I have the force to hold it. . . . I will probably be obliged to change this line in a few days, when I have rested the men, for one lower down. . . . If it is the intention of the Government to re-enforce me largely it should be done promptly and in mass. I need 50,000 more men, and with them I will retrieve our fortunes. More would be well, but that number sent at once, will . . . enable me to assume the offensive. I cannot too strongly urge the necessity of prompt action in this matter. . . . I must apologize for the probable incoherency of this letter. I am exhausted by want of sleep and constant anxiety. . . ." (OR, I, XI, III, 281).

² On May 26, McClellan had forwarded copies of his instructions to Banks and Wadsworth of March 16 and a copy of his letter to Lorenzo Thomas written on April 1, containing the "plan" which he advised Lincoln to adopt (OR, I, XI, I, 33).

To Edwin D. Morgan[1]

Gov. E. D. Morgan   Washington, D.C.,
Albany, New-York.   July 2 1862.
It was thought safest to mark high enough. It is three hundred thousand.   A. LINCOLN

[1] ALS, RPB. Governor Morgan had telegraphed on July 2, "Is the call for 300,000 or for 200,000 volunteers? It appears in all the New York papers for 300,000." (OR, III, II, 199).

To the Senate[1]

To the Senate of the United States: July 2, 1862

I herewith return to your honorable body, in which it originated, an act entitled "An act to provide for additional medical officers of the Volunteer service," without my approval.

My reason for so doing is that I have approved an act of the same title passed by Congress after the passage of the one first mentioned, for the express purpose of correcting errors in, and superseding the same, as I am informed.

    Executive Mansion   ABRAHAM LINCOLN.
    July 2, 1862.

[1] DS, DNA RG 46, Senate 37A F3. The bill which Lincoln returned (S. 343) had passed the Senate and House on June 11 and 13 respectively. The new bill of the same title (S. 370) passed the Senate on June 25 and was approved by Lincoln on July 2.

To John A. Dix[1]

Major Gen. Dix   Washington City, D.C.
Fort-Monroe—   July 3, 1862
What news, if any, have you from Gen. Burnside?
         A. LINCOLN

[1] ALS, RPB. Dix replied: "I hear nothing whatever from him." (DLC-RTL).

To Andrew Johnson[1]

Hon. Andrew Johnson.   July 3, 1862.

My Dear Sir: You are aware we have called for a big levy of new troops. If we can get a fair share of them in Tennessee I shall value it more highly than a like number most anywhere else, because of the face of the thing, and because they will be at the very place that needs protection. Please do what you can, and do it quickly. Time is everything. A word on another subject. If we could, somehow, get a vote of the people of Tennessee and have it result properly it would be worth more to us than a battle gained. How long before we can get such a vote? Yours truly,

A. LINCOLN.

[1] Hertz, II, 871-72. Governor Johnson replied on July 10, "The number of troops suggested can and will be raised in Tennessee   As to an expression of public opinion as soon as the rebel army can be expelled from East Tennessee there can & will be an expression of public opinion that will surprise you but I am constrained to say one thing as I said to you repeatedly in the fall Genl Buell is not the man to redeem East Tennessee. . . ." (DLC-RTL).

To George B. McClellan[1]

Washington City, D.C.

Major Genl. McClellan   July 3, 1862.

Yours of 5.30. yesterday is just received. I am satisfied that yourself, officers and men have done the best you could. All accounts say better fighting was never done. Ten thousand thanks for it.

On the 28th. we sent Gen. Burnside an order to send all the force he could spare, to you. We then learned that you had requested him to go to Goldsborough, upon which, we said to him our order was intended for your benefit, and we did not wish to be in conflict with your views. We hope you will have help from him soon. Tᴗ day we have ordered Gen. Hunter to send you all he can spare.[2] At last advices Halleck thinks he can not send reinforcements, without endangering all he has gained.[3]

A. LINCOLN

[1] ALS, IHi. McClellan's dispatch of 5:30 P.M., July 2, sent from Berkeley, Harrison's Bar, via Fort Monroe, reads in part as follows: "I have succeeded in getting this army to this place on the banks of the James. . . . I have lost but one gun. . . . An hour and a half ago the rear of the wagon train was within a mile of camp, and only one wagon abandoned. As usual, we had a severe battle yesterday and beat the enemy badly, the men fighting even better than before. We fell back to this position during the night and morning. Officers and men thoroughly worn-out by fighting every day and working every night for a week. They are in good spirits, and after a little rest will fight better than ever. If not attacked during this day I will have the men ready to repulse the enemy to-morrow. . . . Our losses have been very heavy, for we have fought every day since last Tuesday. I have not yielded an inch of ground unnecessarily, but have retired to prevent the superior force of the enemy from cutting me off and to take a different base of operations.

"I thank you for the re-enforcements. Every 1,000 men you send at once will help me much." (OR, I, XI, III, 287-88).

² At Lincoln's direction Stanton ordered Hunter at Hilton Head, South Carolina, to forward "all the infantry force that can be spared. . . . It is believed that you can forward 10,000. . . ." (*Ibid.*, pp. 290-91).

³ Lincoln's final sentence was inserted to replace the following deletion: "I repeat what I have twice before said, 'save the Army, at all events.'"

To Edwin M. Stanton¹

Let Randolph Botts be appointed an Assistant Quarter-Master.
July 3. 1862. A. LINCOLN

¹ AES, owned by H. K. Crofoot, Moravia, New York. Lincoln's endorsement is written below an endorsement by Montgomery C. Meigs, "If Mr Botts is commissioned there will be no difficulty in finding employment for him as asst Quarter-Master where he can be useful to his country." Botts' appointment was confirmed on July 17, 1862.

To Union Governors¹

Gov. E. D. Morgan Washington,
My dear Sir— July 3. 1862. [10:30 A.M.]
I should not want the half of three hundred thousand new troops, if I could have them *now*. If I had fifty thousand additional troops here *now*, I believe I could substantially close the war in two weeks. But *time* is *every-thing;* and if I get fifty thousand new men in a month, I shall have lost twenty thousand old ones during the same month, having gained only thirty thousand, with the difference between old and new troops still against me. The quicker you send, the fewer you will have to send. *Time* is everything. Please act in view of this. The enemy having given up Corinth, it is not wonderful that he is thereby enabled to check us for a time at Richmond. A. LINCOLN.

¹ ALS, RPB. Stanton wrote "Private and *Confidential*" on the top of the manuscript, crossed out "Gov. E.D. Morgan," and inserted "Yours truly" before Lincoln's signature. This letter seems to have been written primarily to Governor Morgan, but was telegraphed to the other governors also, in view of their common problem. Replies from the several governors (OR, III, II, 201-06) indicate difficulties in meeting the call but promise prompt action.

To John A. Dix¹

Major Gen. Dix Washington City, D.C.
Fort-Monroe. July 4, 1862
Send forward the despatch to Col Hawkins, and this also. Our order, and Gen. McClellan's to Gen. Burnside being the same, of course we wish it executed as promptly as possible.
A LINCOLN

[1] ALS, RPB. Dix had forwarded at 3 P.M. on July 3 a dispatch from Colonel Rush C. Hawkins at Roanoke Island, July 2, 6 P.M., in which Hawkins asked further orders for Burnside's command (DLC-RTL). Stanton's reply to Hawkins directed that "General Burnside in person, with all the infantry force he can spare, move by way of Hampton Roads and the James River to General McClellan's headquarters to re-enforce him immediately." (OR, I, XI, III, 290). Dix replied to Lincoln at 8:10 P.M., "Soon after sending you Colonel Hawkins' dispatch I received from General McClellan an order to General Burnside to bring on all the troops he could spare. I sent it off immediately with a letter from myself describing to General Burnside the position of General McClellan's army. The steamer having gone, I cannot send your dispatch to Colonel Hawkins until morning. I will do so then, if you desire it." (*Ibid.*).

To Henry W. Halleck[1]

Major Genl. Halleck   Washington City, D.C.
Corinth– Miss   July 4. 1862.

You do not know how much you would oblige us, if, without abandoning any of your positions, or plans, you could promptly send us even ten thousand infantry. Can you not? Some part of the Corinth Army is certainly fighting McClellan in front of Richmond. Prisoners are in our hands from the late Corinth Army.

A. LINCOLN.

[1] ALS, RPB. Halleck replied on July 5, "For the last week there has been great uneasiness among Union men in Tennessee on account of the secret organizations of insurgents to co-operate in any attack of the enemy on our lines. Every commanding officer from Nashville to Memphis has asked for re-enforcements. . . . I submitted the question of sending troops to Richmond to the principal officers of my command. They are unanimous in opinion that if this army is seriously diminished the Chattanooga expedition must be revoked or the hope of holding Southwest Tennessee abandoned. I must earnestly protest against surrendering what has cost us so much . . . and which in a military point of view is worth more than Richmond. . . ." (OR, I, XVI, II, 95). Lincoln forwarded Halleck's dispatch to McClellan on July 5, *infra*.

To George B. McClellan[1]

            War Department Washington City, D.C.
Major Gen. McClellan: July 4. 1862

I understand your position as stated in your letter, and by Gen. Marcy. To reinforce you so as to enable you to resume the offensive within a month, or even six weeks, is impossible. In addition to that arrived, and now arriving from the Potomac, (about ten thousand, I suppose) and about ten thousand I hope you will have from Burnside very soon, and about five thousand from Hunter a little later, I do not see how I can send you another man within a month. Under these circumstances the defensive, for the present, must be your only care. Save the Army—first, where you are, if you *can;* and secondly, by removal, if you must. You, on the ground, must be the judge as to which you will attempt, and of the means for effecting it. I but give it as opinion, that with the aid of the Gun-Boats, and the re-inforcements mentioned above, you can hold your present position, provided, and so long as, you can keep the James River open below you. If you are not tolerably confident you can keep the James River open, you had better remove as soon as possible. I do not remember that you have expressed any apprehension as to the danger of having your communication cut on the river below you; yet I do not suppose it can have escaped your attention. Yours very truly   A. LINCOLN

P.S. If, at any time, you feel able to take the offensive, you are not restrained from doing so.   A. L.

[1] ADfS, DLC-RTL. McClellan sent his chief of staff Randolph B. Marcy to Washington in order to press his plea for reinforcements. Marcy reported to McClellan on July 4, "I have seen the President and Secretary of War. Ten thousand men from Hunter, 10,000 from Burnside, and 11,000 from here have been ordered to re-enforce you as soon as possible. . . . The President and Secretary speak very kindly of you and find no fault. I will remain here until I hear from you. . . ." (OR, I, XI, III, 294).

Remarks to Delegation of Veterans of 1812[1]

July 4, 1862

MR. PRESIDENT AND GENTLEMEN: I am indeed very grateful for this courtesy which you have thought fit to extend me (for the time being), the head of the Government. I am exceedingly sorry that the continual and intense engrossment of my attention by other matters has not permitted me to devote a moment's thought to the manner in which I should receive you. I have no pretty speech, or any other sort of speech, prepared, with which to entertain you for a single moment. I am indeed surrounded, as is the whole country, by very trying circumstances. I am grateful to you for the approbation which you give me of what I have done, and grateful for the support which the whole country seems to give me. I hope that, although far advanced in life as many of you are, you will, gentlemen, yet live to see better days than those which it is now our misfortune to behold. Thanking you for the support which you in this manner give me, unprepared as I am, I could not with any degree of entertainment detain you longer.

[1] New York *Tribune,* July 7, 1862. These remarks are misdated July 4, 1863, by Hertz (II, 899). Lincoln spoke in reply to a brief speech of introduction made by William W. Seaton, president of the Association of the Surviving Soldiers of the War of 1812.

To George B. McClellan[1]

[July 5, 1862]

United States Military Telegraph.
Received July 6th 1862.
From Washington   9.30 A.M
To Maj. Genl McClellan

I send you the following dispatch received this morning for your
information   A. LINCOLN

[1] Copy, DLC-McClellan Papers. For the text of Halleck's dispatch of July 5,
see note to Lincoln to Halleck, July 4, *supra*.

To George B. McClellan[1]

Washington City, D.C.

Major Genl. McClellan   July 5, 1862.

A thousand thanks for the relief your two despatches of 12 & 1
P.M. yesterday—give me. Be assured the heroism and skill of yourself, officers, and men, are, and forever will be appreciated. If
you can hold your present position, we shall *"hive"* the enemy
yet.   A. LINCOLN

[1] ALS, IHi. McClellan's dispatch of July 4, 12 Noon, reported completion of
his withdrawal to Harrison's Bar, "The spirit of the army is excellent. . . .
Send such reinforcements as you can. I will do what I can. . . . When the circumstances of the case are known it will be acknowledged by all competent
judges that the movement just completed by this army is unparalleled in the
annals of war. . . ." (DLC-RTL). At 1 P.M. he acknowledged receipt of Lincoln's dispatch of July 3, "I will do the best I can with such force as I have
and such aid as you can give me. I think that the Army of Virginia should
keep out cavalry reconnaissances in the direction of Richmond, lest the enemy
should prefer an advance to Washington to attacking this army. I wish to be
advised fully of all matters in front of that army. If the capital be threatened,
I will move this army, at whatever hazard, in such direction as will best divert
the enemy.
"Our whole army is now drawn up for review in its positions, bands playing,
salutes being fired, and all things looking bright." (OR, I, XI, III, 294).

To the Senate[1]

To the Senate   Washington, D. C.
of the United States.   July 5th 1862

I transmit, herewith, for the constitutional action of the Senate,
thereon, a treaty negotiated in this city, on the 3d instant, with
the Sac and Fox Indians of the Mississippi;

Letters from the Secretary of the Interior and Commissioner of
Indian Affairs accompany the treaty.   ABRAHAM LINCOLN

[1] DS, DNA RG 46, Senate 37B C9. The treaty was referred to the committee
on Indian affairs on March 7, 1863.

To Henry W. Halleck[1]

War Department
Major Gen. Halleck   Washington City, D.C.
Corinth, Miss—   July 6th. 1862

My dear Sir: This introduces, Gov. William Sprague, of Rhode-Island. He is now Governor for the third time, and Senator elect of the U.S.

I know the object of his visit to you. He has my cheerful consent to go, but not my direction. He wishes to get you and part of your force, one or both, to come here. You already know I should be exceedingly glad of this if, in your judgment, it could be, without endangering positions and operations in the South-West; and I now repeat what I have more than once said by Telegraph, "Do not come, or send a man, if, in your judgment, it will endanger any point you deem important to hold, or endangers, or delays the Chattanooga expedition.["]

Still, please give my friend, Gov. Sprague, a full and fair hearing. Yours very truly   A. LINCOLN.

[1] ALS, owned by Crown Prince Olaf of Norway. Sprague wrote Lincoln on July 5, "The critical condition of the republic emboldens me. It is in far greater jeopardy than at any previous time. . . . Nothing can save us but the immediate transfer of Halleck and 50 000 men. He will consent to this if he comes with them. . . . This can be done in a week or 10 days with proper energy. I volunteer to go to Halleck [to] explain to him our critical position, or I shall go to the Army of the Potomac and share its fortunes. . . . New recruits are worthless now. . . . Hallecks army will unravel the snarl. . . ." (DLC-RTL). Halleck telegraphed Lincoln on July 10, "Gov Sprague is here. If I were to go to Washington I could advise but one thing—to place all the forces in North Carolina, Virginia, and Washington under one head and hold that head responsible for the result." (*Ibid.*).

To George B. McClellan[1]

United States Military Telegraph,
Head-Quarters, Department Washington
Genl McClellan   July 6th 1862.

I send you the following message received by the secretary of war last evening. Fredericksburg July 5th 62. The Richmond Examiner of yesterday the 4th fourth instant has just been received in Fredericksburg. I am promised the paper Tomorrow morning. A reliable man who had the paper assures me that it censures the confederate Generals severely for failing to capture Genl. McClellan and his army and pronounces McClellans whole movement a masterpiece of strategy. Signed Rufus King Brig Genl.

(Signed)   A. LINCOLN
President U.S.

[1] Copy, DLC-McClellan Papers. The telegram from Rufus King which Lincoln incorporates in this dispatch to McClellan is dated as received at 7:20 P.M. on July 5 (DLC-RTL).

To Hiram P. Bennet[1]

Mr Bennet.   [c. July 7, 1862]

Dear Sir: If I did not endorse upon Judge Pettis' resignation my acceptance of it, it was merely an oversight. I of course intended to do so. Yours very truly

Executive Mansion   A. LINCOLN
July 1862

[1] ES, DNA GE RG 60, Papers of Attorney General, Segregated Lincoln Material. The endorsement is in John Hay's handwriting, signed by Lincoln, and is written on a letter from Hiram P. Bennet, delegate in congress from Colorado Territory, July 7, 1862, calling the president's attention to the fact that his failure to endorse the resignation of Judge S. Newton Pettis "leaves the matter in doubt. . . ." See also Lincoln to Bates, June 2, *supra*.

To John G. Nicolay[1]

Time Received   United States Military Telegraph,
        10 10 Am
                War Department, Washington, D.C. Jul 8th 1862.

J. G. Nicolay Esq   Fort Monroe
Private Secy.   Jul 8th 7 30 Am

Please borrow and send Bob Two hundred and Eighty (280.) Dollars. I forgot to send it before leaving.   A. LINCOLN.

[1] Copy, DLC-Nicolay Papers. On the bottom of the received telegram Nicolay endorsed, "Sent as above requested July 8th 1862. Received payment of the President July 24th 1862."

Memorandum of Interviews Between Lincoln and Officers of the Army of the Potomac[1]

July 8-9, 1862

Gen. McClellan July 8. 1862

What amount of force have you now?

        About 80-000—cant vary much—certainly 75-000.

What is likely to be your condition as to health in this camp?

        Better than in any encampment since landing at Fort Monroe.

[1] AD, DLC-RTL. The interviews took place at Harrison's Landing. Except where noted otherwise, the document is in Lincoln's handwriting.

Where is the enemy now?

>From four to 5. miles from us on all the roads—I think nearly the whole Army. Both Hills—Longstreet, Jackson, Magruder, Huger,

If you desired, could you remove the army safely?

It would be a delicate & very difficult matter.

Cavalry about 5000—

Gen. Sumner—July 9. 1862

What is the whole amount of your corps with you now?

About 16,000

What is the agregate of your killed, wounded, and missing from the attack on the 26th. ult till now?

1175

In your present encampment what is the present and prospective condition as to health?

As good as any part of Eastern Va.

Where, & in what condition do you believe the enemy to now be

I think they have retired from our front, were much damaged, especially in their best troops in the late actions from superiority of our arms

If it were desired to get the Army away, could it be safely effected?

I think we could, but I think we give up the cause if we do it.

Is the Army secure in it's present position?

Perfectly so, in my judgment.

Gen. Heintzelman—July 9, 1862

What is the whole amount of your corps now with you?

15-000 for duty

What is the agregate of your killed, wounded, and missing from the attack on the 26. ult. till now?

Not large. 745.

In your present encampment, what is the present and prospective condition as to health?

Excellent for health & present health improving.

Where, and in what condition do you believe the enemy to now be?

Dont think they are in force in our vicinity.

If it were desired to get the Army away from here could it be safely effected?

Perhaps we could, but think it would be ruinous to the country

Is the Army secure in its present position?[2]
I think it is safe.

Gen. Keyes—July 9. 1862

What is the whole amount of your corps with you now?
About 12-500
What is the agregate of your killed, wounded, and missing, from the attack on the 26th. till now?
Less than 500.
In your present encampment what is the present & prospective condition as to health?
A little improved, but think camp is getting worse
Where, and in what condition, do you believe the enemy to now be?
Think he has withdrawn & think preparing to go to Washington.
If it were desired to get the Army away, could it be safely effected?
I think it could if done quickly.
Is the Army, in its present position, secure?
With help of Gen B. can hold position.

Gen Porter[3]

What is the amount of your corps now with you?
About 23,000
Fully 20-000 fit, for duty.
What is the aggregate of your killed wounded and missing from the attack on the 26th ult. until now?
Over 5000.
In your present encampment, what is the present and prospective condition as to health?
Very good.
Where and in what condition do you believe the enemy now to be?
Believe he is mainly near Richmond. He feels he dare not attack us here.
If it were desired to get the army away from here, could it be safely effected?
Impossible—move the Army & ruin the country.
Is the Army secure in its present position?
Perfectly so. Not only but, we are ready to begin moving forward.

[2] This question is not in Lincoln's handwriting.
[3] The questions to Porter are not in Lincoln's handwriting, but the answers are.

[311]

General Franklin.[4]

What is the whole amount of your corps now with you?
About 15,000.

What is the aggregate of your killed, wounded, and missing, from the attack on the 26th ultimo till now?
Don't think whole will exceed 3,000 men.

In your present encampment what is the present and prospective condition as to health?
Not good.

Where and in what condition do you believe the enemy now to be?
I learn he has withdrawn from our front, and think that is probable.

If it were desired to get the army away from here, could it be safely effected?
I think we could, and think we better—think Rappahannock true line.

Is the army secure in its present position?
Unless we can be closer, it is.

General Sumner[5]	1175
General Heintzelman	745.
General Keyes	500.
Fitz J Porter	5000
Franklin	3000
	10420

[4] The page containing the questions and answers of General Franklin is missing, and is reproduced as printed in the *Complete Works* (VII, 265-66).
[5] The remainder is not in Lincoln's handwriting.

To the Senate[1]

To the Senate of the United States: July 9, 1862

I transmit to the Senate for consideration, with a view to ratification a Postal Convention with Costa Rica concluded at San Jose on the 9th. June, last.   ABRAHAM LINCOLN
Washington, 9th. July 1862.

[1] DS, DNA RG 46, Senate 37B B2. The convention was ratified by the Senate on July 14, 1862.

Order Making Henry W. Halleck General-in-Chief[1]

Executive Mansion, Washington, July 11, 1862.

Ordered that Major General Henry W. Halleck be assigned to command the whole land forces of the United States, as General-in-Chief; and that he repair to this Capital so soon as he can with safety to the positions and operations within the Department now under his special charge. ABRAHAM LINCOLN

¹ ADS, DLC-Stanton Papers. Lincoln's order was published as AGO *General Orders No. 101.* Halleck telegraphed Lincoln at 3 P.M., "Your orders of this are this moment received. Genl Grant next in command is at Memphis   I have telegraphed to him to immediately repair to this place. I will start for Washington the moment I can have a personal interview with Genl. Grant." (DLC-RTL).

To Henry W. Halleck¹

Major Gen. Halleck.   Washington City, D.C.
Corinth   July 11. 1862

Gov. Johnson, at Nashville is in trouble and great anxiety about a raid into Kentucky. The Gov. is a true, and a valuable man—indispensable to us in Tennessee. Will you please get in communication with him, and have a full conference with him, before you leave for here? I have telegraphed him on the subject.

A. LINCOLN

¹ ALS, RPB. No reply from Halleck to Lincoln has been located, but Halleck got in communication with Johnson by July 15. See Lincoln to Halleck July 14, *infra.*

To Andrew Johnson¹

                                                        Washington City, D.C.
Hon. Andrew Johnson.   July 11, 1862.

My dear Sir—Yours of yesterday is received. Do you not, my good friend, perceive that what you ask is simply to put you in command in the West. I do not suppose you desire this. You only wish to control in your own localities; but this, you must know, may derange all other parts. *Can* you, not, and *will* you not, have a full conference with Gen. Halleck? Telegraph him, and meet him at such place as he and you can agree upon. I telegraph him to meet you and confer fully with you.   A. LINCOLN.

¹ ALS, RPB. On the afternoon of July 10, Johnson telegraphed as follows: "Last night I received dispatches from Genl Boyle . . . in Kentucky stating that a raid by a cavalry force of 2000 has been made into Ky & asking me to send one or two Regts to his relief. . . . Capt O D Greene Asst Adjt Genl of Buell's staff who exercises command over the troops here so far as to order them wherever he wishes refuses to take notice . . . & afford the necessary relief for Kentucky & Tennessee. This attack is aimed at the . . . Louisville & Nashville R.R. . . . This Captain Green has not only refused to cooperate

with me but has used his position . . . in locating the troops here directly in opposition to my views. . . . My opinion is that he is at this time in complicity with the traitors here & shall therefor have him arrested & sent beyond the Influence of rebels and traitors if he is not immediately removed. . . . Mr. President since I reached this place there has been a struggle . . . going on between the provost marshalls Brigadier Generals & Staff officers of Genl Buell which has retarded the . . . development of Union sentiment. . . . All I ask is to be sustained by the President & I will sustain the President. . . ." (DLC-RTL).

On the evening of July 10, Johnson sent a second telegram: "Capt Greene. . . . has since my dispatch to you of this afternoon put Lewis D. Campbell, 69th Ohio Vols. & provost marshal under arrest because he obeyed an order I issued to him . . . & has appointed a Provost Marshal in whom I have no confidence. . . . I desire an order from you at once reinstating Col Campbell & a transfer of Capt Greene to some post beyond the limits of this State. . . . The commission I hold as I conceive gives me full & ample power to appoint a Prov. Marshal yet I prefer the order from you. I must have the means to execute my orders or abandon the undertaking. . . ." (DLC-RTL).

On July 12, at Lincoln's direction, Stanton ordered Captain Oliver D. Greene to release Colonel Lewis D. Campbell and to "turn over your command to the officer next in rank, and leave . . . Nashville and report yourself in person to General Buell." (OR, I, XVI, II, 135). Stanton notified Johnson of this order and expressed the president's hope that the action would meet approval, and that Johnson would "use efforts to prevent . . . collision of authority between your subordinates and those of General Buell." (*Ibid.*).

Order Extending the Pacific Railroad[1]

July 11, 1862

Whereas, in the judgment of the President, the public safety does require that the Railroad line, called and known as the South West Branch of the Pacific Railroad in the State of Missouri, be repaired, extended and completed, from Rolla to Lebanon, in the direction to Springfield, in the said State, the same being necessary to the successful and economical conduct of the war, and to the maintenance of the authority of the government, in the South West. Therefore, under and in virtue of the act of Congress entitled "An act to authorise the President of the United States, in certain cases, to take possession of Railroad and Telegraph lines, and for other purposes" Approved January 31, 1862, it is—

Ordered that the portion of the said Railroad line which reaches from Rolla to Lebanon, be repaired, extended and completed, so as to be made available for the military uses of the Government, as speedily as may be. And in as much as, upon the part of the said line from Rolla to the stream called Little Piney, a considerable portion of the necessary work has already been done, by the Railroad Company, and the road, to this extent, may be completed at comparatively small cost, it is ordered that the said line, from

Rolla to and across Little Piney, be first completed, and as soon as possible.

The Secretary is charged with the execution of this order. And, to facilitate the speedy execution of the work, he is directed, at his discretion, to take possession and control of the whole or such part of the said Railroad line, and the whole or each part of the rolling stock, offices, shops, buildings and all their appendages and appertenances, as he may judge necessary or convenient for the early completion of the road, from Rolla to Lebanon.

Done at the City of Washington, July 11th. 1862.

ABRAHAM LINCOLN

[1] DS, RPB. See Lincoln to Curtis, October 12, *infra*. The order was written by Bates. The date had originally been "June 27." The circumstances surrounding Lincoln's communication to Curtis on October 12, however, make it seem improbable that the order was actually issued on July 11, if in fact it was issued at all. See also Lincoln to Samuel T. Glover, January 20, 1863, and to Rosecrans, March 4 and 10, 1864, *infra*.

To the Senate[1]

To the Senate,   Washington, D.C.
of the United States,   July 11th 1862.

I transmit to the Senate, herewith, for its constitutional action, thereon, a treaty negotiated at the Kickapoo Agency, on the 28th of June 1862, between Charles B. Keith, Commissioner on the part of the United States and the Chiefs, Head men and delegates of the Kickapoo, Indians, of Kansas.

A letter of the Commissioner of Indian Affairs, of the 10th. instant, is also transmitted, suggesting amendments to the treaty, for the consideration of the Senate. ABRAHAM LINCOLN

[1] DS, DNA RG 46, Senate 37B C10. The treaty was ratified with amendments on March 13, 1863.

To the Senate and House of Representatives[1]

July 11, 1862

To the Senate and House of Representatives:

I recommend that the thanks of Congress be given to the following Officers of the U.S. Navy:

Captain James L. Lardner, for meritorious conduct at the battle of Port Royal and distinguished services on the coast of the United States against the enemy;

Captain Charles Henry Davis, for distinguished services in conflict with the enemy at Fort Pillow, at Memphis and for successful operations at other points in the waters of the Mississippi River;

Commander John A. Dahlgren, for distinguished service in the line of his profession: improvements in Ordnance and zealous and efficient labors in the Ordnance branch of the service;

Commander Stephen C. Rowan, for distinguished services in the waters of North Carolina, and particularly in the capture of Newbern, being in chief command of the Naval forces;

Commander David D. Porter, for distinguished services in the conception and preparation of the means used for the capture of the Forts below New Orleans, and for highly meritorious conduct in the management of the Mortar Flotilla, during the bombardment of Forts Jackson and St. Philip;

Captain Silas H. Stringham, now on the Retired List, for distinguished services in the capture of Forts Hatteras and Clark.

Washington, D.C.,   ABRAHAM LINCOLN
11 July 1862.

[1] DS, DNA RG 46, Senate 37A F2; DS, DNA RG 233, Original Executive Document No. 147. A resolution of thanks "to James L. Lardner and other officers of the navy" was reported in both House and Senate on July 16. Upon development of objections to the inclusion of James L. Lardner, however, the resolution was held up until January 31, 1863, when Senator Hale reported the resolution with title amended to read "a joint resolution tendering the thanks of Congress to Commodore Charles Henry Davis and other officers. . . ." thus omitting Lardner's name. The resolution was approved as amended on February 7, 1863.

To Caleb B. Smith[1]

Sec. of Interior, send the nomination, as within recommended.

July 11, 1862.   A. LINCOLN

[1] AES, DNA NR RG 48, Applications, General Land Office, Registers and Receivers, Nevada Territory, Box 1285. Lincoln's endorsement is written on a letter from Representative Ambrose W. Clark of New York, July 8, 1862, favorably endorsed by Smith, recommending appointment of Clement T. Rice as register of the Land Office at Carson City. Rice's appointment was confirmed by the Senate on July 17.

To Edwin M. Stanton[1]

Let the within recommendation be carried into effect, if it can be done without inconsistency and collision.   A. LINCOLN
July 11. 1862.

[1] AES, IHi. Lincoln's endorsement appears on a letter from Commissary General of Subsistence, Joseph P. Taylor, July 7, 1862, recommending promotion of Major Amos Beckwith of the Subsistence Department to a colonelcy. Beckwith was nominated colonel on July 17, and was confirmed by the Senate on the same day, his promotion to date from January 1, 1862.

To Edwin M. Stanton[1]

Remembering the rule, I would be pleased if the within could be consistently done.   A. LINCOLN

July 11. 1862.

[1] AES, IHi. Lincoln's endorsement appears on an unsigned order written on Executive Mansion stationery: "Let Lieutenant Edward Wright of the ——— Infantry be made an assistant Quartermaster of the Regular Army, vice Symmes Gardner whose appointment was not confirmed by the Senate." An endorsement by Representative William Kellogg also urged the appointment. Edward Wright was not appointed Quartermaster but was appointed aide-de-camp with rank of major as of November 8, 1862, and was confirmed by the Senate on March 11, 1863.

Appeal to Border State Representatives to Favor Compensated Emancipation[1]

July 12, 1862

Gentlemen. After the adjournment of Congress, now very near, I shall have no opportunity of seeing you for several months. Believing that you of the border-states hold more power for good than any other equal number of members, I feel it a duty which I can not justifiably waive, to make this appeal to you. I intend no reproach or complaint when I assure you that in my opinion, if you all had voted for the resolution in the gradual emancipation message of last March, the war would now be substantially ended. And the plan therein proposed is yet one of the most potent, and swift means of ending it. Let the states which are in rebellion see, definitely and certainly, that, in no event, will the states you represent ever join their proposed Confederacy, and they can not, much longer maintain the contest. But you can not divest them of their hope to ultimately have you with them so long as you show a determination to perpetuate the institution within your own states. Beat them at elections, as you have overwhelmingly done, and, nothing daunted, they still claim you as their own. You and I know what the lever of their power is. Break that lever before their faces, and they can shake you no more forever.

Most of you have treated me with kindness and consideration; and I trust you will not now think I improperly touch what is exclusively your own, when, for the sake of the whole country I ask "Can you, for your states, do better than to take the course I urge? ["] Discarding *punctillio*, and maxims adapted to more manageable times, and looking only to the unprecedentedly stern facts of our case, can you do better in any possible event? You prefer that the constitutional relation of the states to the nation shall be practically restored, without disturbance of the institution; and if this were done, my whole duty, in this respect, under the constitution, and my oath of office, would be performed. But it is not done, and we are trying to accomplish it by war. The incidents of the war can not be avoided. If the war continue long, as it must, if the object be not sooner attained, the institution in your states will be extinguished by mere friction and abrasion—by the mere incidents of the war. It will be gone, and you will have nothing valuable in lieu of it. Much of it's value is gone already. How much better for you, and for your people, to take the step which, at once, shortens the war, and secures substantial compensation for that which is sure to be wholly lost in any other event. How much better to thus save the money which else we sink forever in the war. How much better to do it while we can, lest the war ere long render us pecuniarily unable to do it. How much better for you, as seller, and the nation as buyer, to sell out, and buy out, that without which the war could never have been, than to sink both the thing to be sold, and the price of it, in cutting one another's throats.

I do not speak of emancipation *at once*, but of a *decision* at once to emancipate *gradually*. Room in South America for colonization, can be obtained cheaply, and in abundance; and when numbers shall be large enough to be company and encouragement for one another, the freed people will not be so reluctant to go.

I am pressed with a difficulty not yet mentioned—one which threatens division among those who, united are none too strong. An instance of it is known to you. Gen. Hunter is an honest man. He was, and I hope, still is, my friend. I valued him none the less for his agreeing with me in the general wish that all men everywhere, could be free. He proclaimed all men free within certain states, and I repudiated the proclamation. He expected more good, and less harm from the measure, than I could believe would follow. Yet in repudiating it, I gave dissatisfaction, if not offence, to many whose support the country can not afford to lose. And this is not the end of it. The pressure, in this direction, is still upon me, and is increasing. By conceding what I now ask, you can relieve me, and much more, can relieve the country, in this important point. Upon these considerations I have again begged your attention to the message of March last. Before leaving the Capital, consider and discuss it among yourselves. You are patriots and statesmen; and, as such, I pray you, consider this proposition; and, at the least, commend it to the consideration of your states and people. As you would perpetuate popular government for the best people in the world, I beseech you that you do in no wise omit this. Our common country is in great peril, demanding the loftiest views, and boldest action to bring it speedy relief. Once relieved, it's form of government is saved to the world; it's beloved history, and cherished memories, are vindicated; and it's happy future fully assured, and rendered inconceivably grand. To you, more than to any others, the previlege is given, to assure that happiness, and swell that grandeur, and to link your own names therewith forever.

[1] AD and ADf, DLC-RTL. Lincoln invited the representatives and senators of the Border States to the White House and read his address to them. On July 14, a majority reply argued against compensated emancipation on the ground that the federal government could not stand the expense, that emancipation in any form would further consolidate the spirit of rebellion in the seceded states and fan the spirit of secession among loyal slaveholders in the Border States, and that emancipation in the Border States would not, as the president supposed, lessen the pressure for "unconstitutional" emancipation by proclamation of the remaining three million slaves in the seceded states, which the majority were unwilling to approve. The majority reply was signed by twenty representatives and senators. On July 15, a minority reply in approval of Lincoln's appeal was signed by John W. Noell of Missouri, Samuel L. Casey of Kentucky, George P. Fisher of Delaware, Andrew J. Clements of Tennessee, William G. Brown, Jacob B. Blair, and Waitman T. Willey of West Virginia. Horace Maynard of Tennessee replied individually on July 16, in support of the appeal. The several replies were published in full by the New York *Tribune* (July 19) as well as other papers.

To the House of Representatives[1]

To the House of Representatives: July 12, 1862

I transmit a report of the Secretary of State upon the subject of the resolution of the House of Representatives of the 9th ultimo, requesting information in regard to the relations between the United States and foreign powers.   ABRAHAM LINCOLN.

Washington, July 12, 1862.

[1] Thirty-seventh Congress, Second Session, *House of Representatives Executive Document No. 148*. The House resolution requested that the president submit "whatever information he possesses concerning the relations existing between this country and foreign powers." Seward's report of July 11 informed the president that "considerable progress has been made in preparing an answer to the resolution, but the correspondence . . . is so voluminous, and the indispensable current of business of this department is so pressing in proportion to its force, that it will be impracticable to comply with the resolution at this session. . . ." (*Ibid.*).

To Rufus King[1]

Will Gen. King please see this gentleman, & do the best for him he can?   A. LINCOLN
July 12, 1862.

[1] ALS, IHi. The gentleman has not been identified.

To Edwin M. Stanton[1]

Hon. Sec. of War.   Executive Mansion,
My dear Sir   Washington, July 12, 1862.
    Mr. Senator Hale says you were to appoint Capt. John P. Sherburne, now in Gen. Wadsworth's staff, an Assistant Adjutant General with the rank of Major, if a law should be passed authorizing it. The law is passed; and so let him be appointed. Yours truly
                                                     A. LINCOLN

[1] ALS, NN. Stanton endorsed on the bottom of the letter, "I did promise Mr Hale that Capt Sherburne should have the appointment. I was not aware of any objection by the Adjutant General. I would be glad to have the promise redeemed but yield to whatever the President may think best for the service." John P. Sherburne's appointment as assistant adjutant general with rank of major was confirmed by the Senate on July 17.

To Edwin M. Stanton[1]

Hon. Sec. of War   Executive Mansion,
My dear Sir.   Washington, July 12. 1862.
    Let Thomas L. Crittenden, William Nelson, and Alexander McD. McCook, all now Brigadier generals, be appointed Major Generals of volunteers.   A. LINCOLN

[1] ALS, IHi. All three appointments were confirmed by the Senate on July 17.

To Edwin M. Stanton[1]

Let the appointment, as within requested, for Additional Paymaster, be made.   [A. LINCOLN]
July 12, 1862.

[1] AES, DLC-RTL. Lincoln's signature has been cut off this endorsement written on a letter signed by the Wisconsin delegation in congress, recommending Horace A. Tenney of Madison, Wisconsin, for a paymastership in lieu of the office of collector at Madison for which he had been recommended but which was already filled. Tenney's appointment was confirmed by the Senate on July 14.

To Lorenzo Thomas[1]

Adjt. General Thomas.   Executive Mansion,
My dear Sir—   Washington, July 12, 1862.
   Please see Col. Farnsworth, and restore his man, as he will request, if it can be done consistently with the public service. Yours truly   A. LINCOLN

[1] ALS, owned by Edward C. Stone, Boston, Massachusetts. Whether Colonel Farnsworth was Colonel John F. Farnsworth of the Eighth Illinois Cavalry or Colonel Addison Farnsworth of the Seventy-ninth New York Infantry has not been determined.

To Jeremiah T. Boyle[1]

"Cypher"

Gen. J. T. Boyle.   Washington,
Louisville, Ky   July 13, 1862.
   Your several despatches received. You should call on Gen. Halleck. Telegraph him at once. I have telegraphed him that you are in trouble.   A. LINCOLN

[1] ALS, RPB. From Louisville, Boyle had telegraphed both Halleck and Stanton on July 12 that Confederate General John H. Morgan was reported raiding in the vicinity of Danville, Harrodsburg, and Glasgow, Kentucky, with a cavalry force too large to be driven back with infantry alone. (OR, I, XVI, II, 734).

To Jeremiah T. Boyle[1]

"Cypher"

Gen. J. T. Boyle   Washington, D.C.,
Louisville, Ky.   July 13. 1862.
   We can not venture to order troops from Gen. Buell. We know not what condition he is in. He may be attacked himself. You must call on Gen. Halleck, who commands, and whose business it is to understand and care for the whole field. If you can not telegraph to him, send a messenger to him. A despatch has this moment come from Halleck at Tuscumbia–Alabama.[2]   A. LINCOLN

[1] ALS, RPB. Boyle's dispatches to Stanton on July 13 reported Morgan's force at 2,800 to 3,000, and that requests for reinforcements from Buell remained unanswered. (OR, I, XVI, II, 736-37).
[2] Halleck's dispatches on July 13, so far as they have been located, are dated at Corinth, Mississippi, but General George H. Thomas was operating at Tuscumbia, Alabama.

[321]

To Henry W. Halleck[1]

Major Gen. Halleck.   Washington City, D.C.
Corinth, Miss.   July 13, 1862
They are having a stampede in Kentucky. Please look to it.

                                                    A. LINCOLN

[1] ALS, RPB. On July 14 Halleck ordered Buell to "Do all in your power to put down the Morgain raid even if the Chattanooga expedition should be delayed." (OR, I, XVI, II, 143).

To George B. McClellan[1]

Major General McClellan   Executive Mansion,
My dear Sir—   Washington, July 13 1862.

I am told that over 160-000 men have gone into your Army on the Peninsula. When I was with you the other day we made out 86,500 remaining, leaving 73,500 to be accounted for. I believe 23,500, will cover all the killed, wounded and missing in all your battles and skirmishes, leaving 50-000 who have left otherwise. Not more than 5000 of these have died, leaving 45,000 of your Army still alive, and not with it. I believe half, or two thirds of them are fit for duty to-day. Have you any more perfect knowledge of this than I have? If I am right, and you had these men with you, you could go into Richmond in the next three days. How can they be got to you? and how can they be prevented from getting away in such numbers for the future?   A. LINCOLN

[1] ALS, IHi. McClellan's telegram received at 8 P.M. on July 15, reads in part as follows: ". . . The difference between the effective force of troops and that expressed in returns is considerable in every Army. All commanders find the actual strength less than the strength represented on paper. I have not my own returns for the tri-monthly period since arriving at Fort Monroe at hand at this moment but even on paper I will not . . . be found to have received one hundred and sixty thousand officers and men present although present and absent my returns will be accountable for that number. . . . I find from official reports that I have present for duty—Officers three thousand two hundred fifteen. Enlisted men Eighty Eight thousand four hundred fifty. In all present for duty Eighty Eight thousand six hundred sixty-five. Absent by authority thirty four thousand four hundred seventy two—without authority three thousand seven hundred seventy eight. Present and absent, One hundred forty four thousand four hundred and seven. The number . . . present sick is sixteen thousand six hundred nineteen. . . . Thus the number . . . really absent is thirty eight thousand two hundred fifty. Unquestionably of the number present some one absent, say forty thousand will cover the absentees. I quite agree with you that more than one half these men are probably fit for duty to-day. I have frequently called the attention lately of the War Dept to the evil of absenteeism. . . . It is to be remembered that many of those absent by authority are those who have got off either sick or wounded . . . and

[322]

. . . are still reported absent by authority. If I could receive back the absentees and could get my sick men up I would need but small reinforcements to enable me to take Richmond. . . . I can now control people getting away better for the natural opportunities are better. Leakages by desertion occur in every Army and will occur here of course, but I do not at all . . . anticipate anything like a recurrence of what has taken place." (DLC-RTL).

To Salmon P. Chase[1]

July 14, 1862.

Hon. Secretary of the Treasury: Might not Mr. Bouligny be appointed surveyor of the port of New Orleans? If there be no objections, please send nomination. A. LINCOLN.

[1] NH, VII, 278. There is no reply from Chase in the Lincoln Papers. John E. Bouligny, representative from Louisiana 1859-1861, remained loyal to the Union and retired to private life in Washington. No record of his appointment has been found, but see further, Lincoln's letter to Benjamin F. Butler and others, October 14, *infra*.

To Henry W. Halleck[1]

"Cypher"

Major Gen. Halleck   Washington, D.C.,
Corinth Miss   July 14, 1862.

I am very anxious—almost impatient—to have you here. Having due regard to what you leave behind, when can you reach here? A. LINCOLN

[1] ALS, RPB. "Corinth Miss" is not in Lincoln's handwriting. Halleck replied on July 15, "General Grant has just arrived from Memphis. I am in communication with General Buell and Governor Johnson in Tennessee. Hope to finally arrange disposition of troops and re-enforcements for General Curtis by to-morrow and to leave Thursday morning, the 17th." (OR, I, XVI, II, 150).

To George B. McClellan[1]

War Department,
Washington City, July 14, 1862.

Major-General McClellan: General Burnside's force is at Newport News, ready to move, on short notice, one way or the other, when ordered. A. LINCOLN.

[1] OR, I, XI, III, 320. McClellan telegraphed Lincoln on July 14, 7:30 A.M., "Nothing new of interest. . . . Everything going on very well. I am very anxious to have my old regiments filled up rather than have new ones formed. What of Burnside" (DLC-RTL).

Note Concerning John R. Kenly[1]

If the particular arrangement for exchange which Col. Kenly has made can be effected let it be done.   A LINCOLN

July 14, 1862.

[1] ADS, owned by George T. Kenly, Baltimore, Maryland. Colonel John R. Kenly of the First Maryland Infantry was wounded and captured at Front Royal, Virginia, May 23-24, 1862. The regimental history indicates that prisoners taken at Front Royal were exchanged in November, 1862.

To the Senate and House of Representatives[1]

July 14, 1862

Fellow citizens of the Senate, and House of Representatives

Herewith is the draft of a Bill to compensate any State which may abolish slavery within it's limits, the passage of which, substantially as presented, I respectfully, and earnestly recommend.

July 14. 1862.   ABRAHAM LINCOLN

Be it enacted by the Senate and House of Representatives of the United States of America, in Congress assembled, That whenever the President of the United States shall be satisfied that any State shall have lawfully abolished slavery within and throughout such State, either immediately, or gradually, it shall be the duty of the President, assisted by the Secretary of the Treasury, to prepare and deliver to such State, an amount of six per cent interest bearing bonds, of the United States, equal to the aggregate value, at —— dollars per head, of all the slaves within such State, as reported by the census of the year One thousand, eight hundred and sixty —the whole amount for any one State, to be delivered at once, if the abolishment be immediate, or, in equal annual instalments, if it be gradual—interest to begin running on each bond at the time of it's delivery, and not before.

And be it further enacted, That if any State, having so received any such bonds, shall at any time afterwards, by law, reintroduce, or tolerate slavery within it's limits, contrary to the act of abolishment, upon which such bonds shall have been received, said bonds, so received by said State, shall at once be null and void in whosesoever hands they may be, and such State shall refund to the United States, all interest which may have been paid on such bonds.

[1] ADS, New York Avenue Presbyterian Church, Washington, D.C. On July 16 Representative Albert S. White of Indiana, from the select committee on emancipation to which Lincoln's message and draft were referred, reported a

bill (H.R. 576), granting aid to states adopting a system of emancipation. The bill was read the first and second time, committed to the Committee of the Whole House, and ordered to be printed. Congress adjourned without further action on the bill.

To James W. White, Robert H. McCurdy, and Frederick S. Winston[1]

Messrs. James W. White   Executive Mansion,
Robert H. McCurdy &   Washington,
F. S. Winston—Committee.   July 14. 1862.

Gentlemen: Your letter conveying to me the invitation of several loyal and patriotic bodies in New-York, to attend a mass meeting in that city, on Tuesday the 15th. Inst. is received. While it would be very agreeable to me to thus meet the friends of the country, I am sure I could add nothing to the purpose, or the wisdom with which they will perform their duty; and the near adjournment of Congress makes it indispensable for me to remain here. Thanking you, and those you represent, for the invitation, and the kind terms in which you have communicated it, I remain Your obt. Servt.   A. LINCOLN

[1]ADfS, DLC-RTL. Following White's letter of July 7 (DLC-RTL) extending the invitation, the committee went to Washington to present their request in person. On July 14 White and McCurdy addressed a further letter to Lincoln, reading in part as follows: "Upon leaving for New York we called to pay our respects and to say one word more upon the all engrossing subjects of the hour. . . . You put the question to us then, 'Who should I appoint if I displace McClellan?' We made no definite reply. . . . But we will say now that it appears to us clear that one of the older generals who have been distinguished—Sumner, or Heintzelman, should be appointed. We have heard it intimated that Halleck was to be appointed. Permit us to say that this would be in our judgment a deplorable mistake. . . ." (DLC-RTL).

To Solomon Foot[1]

Hon. Solomon Foot,   Executive Mansion,
President *pro. tem.* of the Senate: Washington, July 15, 1862.

Sir: Please inform the Senate that I shall be obliged if they will postpone the adjournment at least one day beyond the time which I understand to be now fixed for it. Your obt. Servt.

ABRAHAM LINCOLN

[1] LS, DNA RG 46, Senate 37A F2. Foot replied on July 15, "I am advised that it will be exceedingly difficult, if not impossible, to postpone the adjournment, unless some Senator can say *it is necessary*. To this end several Senators desire me to ask that you will state the ground or reason of such necessity. I have the honor to be. . . ." (DLC-RTL).

To Solomon Foot[1]

Hon. S. Foot
Sir

Executive Mansion,
Washington, July 15. 1862.

I am sorry Senators could not so far trust me as to believe I had some real cause for wishing them to remain. I am considering a bill which came to me only late in the day yesterday, and the subject of which has perplexed Congress for more than half a year.[2] I may return it with objections; and if I should, I wish Congress to have the oppertunity of obviating the objections, or of passing it into a law notwithstanding them.

That is all. Your Obt. Servt.   A. LINCOLN

[1] ALS-P, ISLA.
[2] See Lincoln's communication to the Senate and House of Representatives, July 17, *infra*.

To Galusha A. Grow[1]

Executive Mansion, Washington, July 15, 1862.

Sir: Please inform the House of Representatives that I shall be obliged if they will postpone the adjournment at least one day beyond the time which I understand to be now fixed for it. Your obedient servant,   ABRAHAM LINCOLN.

HON. GALUSHA A. GROW,
Speaker of the House of Representatives.

[1] *Congressional Globe*, New Series, No. 211, p. 3364. The resolution adopted on July 14, called for adjournment on July 16 at 12 M. On July 15, the time was extended to July 17 at 12 M.

To Edwin M. Stanton[1]

Hon. Sec. of War
My dear Sir:

Executive Mansion,
Washington, July 15. 1862.

This young man—George K. Pomeroy—is the son of one of the best women I ever knew—a widow who has lost all her other children, and has cheerfully given this one to the war, and devotes herself exclusively to nursing our sick and wounded soldiers. I wish to do something for him, and, even, to strain a point for that object. I wish you would see him, and give him a second Lieutenancy in the regular Army, in the first vacancy not already promised. He has already served nearly a year in the volunteers. This shall be your voucher. Yours truly   A LINCOLN

[1] ALS-F, American Art Association Anderson Galleries Catalog 3873, December 15-16, 1930, No. 277. According to the catalog description the letter is accompanied by an envelope which carried the following endorsement: "Hon. Sec. of War. Please see this young man a moment. A.L." George K. Pomroy was the son of Mrs. Rebecca R. Pomroy, the famous Civil War nurse of Chelsea, Massachusetts, who had nursed "Tad" Lincoln and Mrs. Lincoln in February and March, 1862. He was appointed second lieutenant of the Third Infantry on July 17.

Memorandum: Appointment of John West[1]

[c. July 17, 1862]

John West, to be appointed a Collector—6th. old Dist. 5th. new.

[1] AE, DLC-Nicolay Papers. Lincoln's endorsement is written on the envelope containing a letter from Hannibal Hamlin, July 17, 1862, reminding Lincoln of his promise to appoint John West of Franklin, Maine. The appointment was made after adjournment of congress and confirmed by the Senate on February 3, 1863.

Remarks to Committee
of Reformed Presbyterian Synod[1]

July 17, 1862

Mr. Lincoln then replied. As to the moral character of the institution of Slavery, and as to its political bearing on the institutions of this or any other Nation, he said there was, between him and the committee, no difference of sentiment. He went on to say:

"Had Slavery no existence among us, and were the question asked shall we adopt such an institution? we should agree as to the reply which should be made. If there be any diversity in our views it is not as to whether we should receive Slavery when free from it, but as to how we may best get rid of it already amongst us. Were an individual asked whether he would wish to have a wen on his neck, he could not hesitate as to the reply; but were it asked whether a man who has such a wen should at once be relieved of it by the application of the surgeon's knife, there might be diversity of opinion, perhaps the man might bleed to death, as the result of such an operation.

"Feeling deeply my responsibility to my country and to that God to whom we all owe allegiance, I assure you I will try to do my best, and so may God help me."

[1] Cincinnati Daily Gazette, August 4, 1862. A committee of the Synod of the Reformed Presbyterian Church presented a copy of resolutions on slavery passed by the Synod.

To the Senate and House of Representatives[1]

Fellow-Citizens of the Senate, and House of Representatives,

Considering the bill for "An act to suppress insurrection, to punish treason, and rebellion, to seize and confiscate the property of rebels, and for other purposes" and the Joint Resolution [explanatory of said act,][2] as being substantially one, I have approved and signed both.

Before I was informed of the passage of the Resolution, I had prepared the draft of a Message, stating objections to the bill becoming a law, a copy of which draft is herewith transmitted.

[ABRAHAM LINCOLN.]

[July 17, 1862.]

Fellow citizens of the House of Representatives

I herewith return to your honorable body, in which it originated, the bill for an act entitled "An act to suppress treason and rebellion, to seize and confiscate the property of rebels, and for other purposes" together with my objections to it's becoming a law.

There is much in the bill to which I perceive no objection. It is wholly prospective; and it touches neither person or property, of any loyal citizen; in which particulars, it is just and proper. The first and second sections provide for the conviction and punishment of persons who shall be guilty of treason, and persons who shall "incite, set on foot, assist, or engage in any rebellion, or insurrection, against the authority of the United States, or the laws thereof, or shall give aid or comfort thereto, or shall engage in, or give aid and comfort to any such existing rebellion, or insurrection" By fair construction, persons within these sections are not to be punished without regular trials, in duly constituted courts,

[1] ADf, DLC-RTL; Thirty-seventh Congress, Second Session, *Senate Executive Document No. 70.* A forgery of the first page of this message is in the New York Public Library. The present text follows the autograph draft, which is undated and unsigned. The "Act to suppress insurrection. . . ." presented for Lincoln's approval on July 14, was responsible for Lincoln's request that Congress remain in session an extra day (see Lincoln to Foot and to Grow, July 15, *supra*) in order to receive his message of rejection. On July 15, however, a resolution (H.R. 110) introduced by Representative Horace Maynard correcting portions of the act to which Lincoln most seriously objected, was further amended in the Senate and passed both houses on the same day. Thus Lincoln probably concluded it better to sign the act and the resolution, rather than to reject the act on the other less important objections set forth in his message.

[2] "[Explanatory of said act,]" is in pencil handwriting, not Lincoln's, inserted in the draft in the blank space which Lincoln left for description of the resolution.

under the forms, and all the substantial provisions of law, and of the constitution, applicable to their several cases. To this I perceive no objection; especially as such persons would be within the general pardoning power, and also the special provision for pardon and amnesty, contained in this act. It is also provided, that the slaves of persons convicted under these sections shall be free. I think there is an unfortunate form of expression, rather than a substantial objection, in this. It is startling to say that congress can free a slave within a state; and yet if it were said the ownership of the slave had first been transferred to the nation, and that congress had then liberated, him, the difficulty would at once vanish. And this is the real case. The traitor against the general government forfets his slave, at least as justly as he does any other property; and he forfeits both to the government against which he offends. The government, so far as there can be ownership, thus owns the the [*sic*] forfeited slaves; and the question for Congress, in regard to them is, "Shall they be made free, or be sold to new masters?" I perceive no objection to Congress deciding in advance that they shall be free. To the high honor of Kentucky, as I am informed, she has been the owner of some slaves by *escheat*, and that she sold none, but liberated all. I hope the same is true of some other states. Indeed, I do not believe it would be physically possible, for the General government, to return persons, so circumstanced, to actual slavery. I believe there would be physical resistance to it, which could neither be turned aside by argument, nor driven away by force. In this view I have no objection to this feature of the bill. Another matter involved in these two sections, and running through other parts of the act, will be noticed hereafter.

I perceive no objection to the third and fourth sections.

So far as I wish to notice the fifth, and sixth sections, they may be considered together.[3] That the enforcement of these sections would do no injustice to the persons embraced within them, is clear. That those who make a causeless war should be compelled to pay the cost of it, is too obviously just, to be called in question.

[3] The joint resolution explanatory of the act, which was passed on July 15 while Lincoln was preparing his message of rejection, undertook to remove some of the objections to section 5 to which Lincoln refers. The language of the resolution is as follows: "Resolved. . . . That the provisions of the third clause of the fifth section . . . shall be so construed as not to apply to any act or acts done prior to the passage thereof; nor to include any member of a State legislature, or judge of any State court, who has not in accepting or entering upon his office, taken an oath to support the constitution of the so-called 'Confederate States of America'; nor shall any punishment or proceedings under said act be so construed as to work a forfeiture of the real estate of the offender beyond his natural life."

To give governmental protection to the property of persons who have abandoned it, and gone on a crusade to overthrow that same government, is absurd, if considered in the mere light of justice. The severest justice may not always be the best policy. The principle of seizing, and appropriating the property of the persons embraced within these sections is certainly not very objectionable; but a justly discriminating application of it, would be very difficult, and, to a great extent, impossible. And would it not be wise to place a power of remission somewhere, so that these persons may know they have something to lose by persisting, and something to save by desisting?[4] I am not sure whether such power of remission is or is not within section Thirteen.

Without any special act of congress, I think our military commanders, when, in military phrase, "they are within the enemies country" should in an orderly manner, seize and use whatever of real or personal property may be necessary or convenient for their commands; at the same time, preserving, in some way, the evidence of what they do.

What I have said in regard to slaves, while commenting on the first and second sections, is applicable to the ninth, with the difference, that no provision is made in the whole act for determining whether a particular individual slave does or does not fall within the classes defined in that section. He is to be free upon certain conditions; but whether those conditions do, or do not pertain to him, no mode of ascertaining is provided. This could be easily supplied.

To the tenth section, I make no objection. The oath therein required seems to be proper; and the remainder of the section is substantially identical with an already existing law.

The eleventh section simply assumes to confer discretionary powers upon the executive. Without this law I have no hesitation to go as far in the direction indicated, as I may at any time deem expedient. And I am ready to say now I think it is proper for our military commanders to employ, as laborers, as many persons of African de[s]cent, as can be used to advantage.

The twelfth and thirteenth sections are something better than objectionable; and the fourteenth is entirely proper if all other parts of the act shall stand.

That to which I chiefly object, pervades most parts of the act, but more distinctly appears in the first, second, seventh and eighth

4 At this point Lincoln deleted the following passage in the draft: "When you extinguish hope, you create desperation. Leave to misguided men, some motive for returning to the Union."

sections. It is the sum of those provisions which results in the divesting of title forever. For the causes of treason, and the ingredients of treason, not amounting to the full crime, it declares forfeiture, extending beyond the lives of the guilty parties; whereas the Constitution of the United States declares that "no attainder of treason shall work corruption of blood, or forfeiture, except during the life of the person attainted." True, there is to be no formal attainder in this case; still I think the greater punishment can not be constitutionally inflicted, in a different form, for the same offence. With great respect, I am constrained to say I think this feature of the act is unconstitutional. It would not be difficult to modify it.

I may remark that this provision of the constitution, put in language borrowed from Great Brittain, applies only in this country, as I understand, to real, or landed estate.

Again, this act, by proceedings *in rem* forfeits property, for the ingredients of treason, without a conviction of the supposed criminal, or a personal hearing given him in any proceeding. That we may not touch property lying within our reach, because we can not give personal notice to an owner who is absent endeavoring to destroy the govern[ment,] is certainly not very satisfactory; still the owner may not be thus engaged, and I think a reasonable time should be provided for such parties to appear and have personal hearings. Similar provisions are not uncommon in connection with proceedings *in rem*.

For the reasons stated I return the bill to the House in which it originated.

To the Senate and House of Representatives[1]

July 17, 1862

Fellow citizens of the Senate and House of Representatives:

I have inadvertently omitted so long to inform you that in March last Mr. Cornelius Vanderbilt, of New York, gratuitously presented to the United States the ocean steamer "Vanderbilt," by many esteemed the finest merchant ship in the world. She has ever since been, and still is, doing valuable service to the government. For the patriotic act in making this magnificent and valuable present to the country, I recommend that some suitable acknowledgement be made. ABRAHAM LINCOLN.

July 17, 1862.

[1] Thirty-seventh Congress, Second Session, *Senate Executive Document No. 71.* A joint resolution approved January 28, 1864, offered Vanderbilt the

thanks of congress and directed the president to have a gold medal struck to be presented to him and a copy made for deposit in The Library of Congress. The appropriation bill of February 28, 1865, allowed $3,000 for the medal.

To Salmon P. Chase[1]

Executive Mansion, Washington, July 18, 1862.

My dear Sir: Mr. Senator Doolittle informs me that the Wisconsin delegation have unanimously recommended persons for assessors and collectors throughout their State, and that the paper showing this is filed with you. If so, I am in favor of adopting their "slate" at once, and so disposing of one State. Yours truly,

A. LINCOLN.

[1] NH, VII, 286. No reply from Chase has been located.

Memorandum: Michigan Appointments[1]

[c. July 18, 1862]

Note, Mr. Granger did not sign!

[1] Anderson Auction Company, Catalog 317, June 14, 1904, No. 179. According to the catalog description Lincoln's endorsement is written on a letter dated July 16, 1862, and signed by the "entire" delegation in congress from Michigan. Representative Bradley F. Granger was the lone Democrat in congress from Michigan.

To Edwin M. Stanton[1]

July 18, 1862

I understand the young man mentioned within was forced [to] decline this appointment by reason of some injury or disease about the foot which has now recovered; and that he had the promise of a re-appointment on recovery, from Gen. Cameron. Under these circumstances, I shall be glad if a vacancy of 2nd. Lieutenancy can be found for him, especially as it is said he has been studying and preparing in reliance upon such promise. A. LINCOLN

July 18. 1862.

[1] AES, NHi. Lincoln's endorsement is written on the back of Secretary Cameron's letter to Wharton White of Philadelphia, notifying him of his appointment as first lieutenant in the Sixteenth Infantry, June 14, 1861. There is no record of White's reappointment prior to 1867, when he was appointed second lieutenant in the Twentieth Infantry on March 7.

To Edwin M. Stanton[1]

July 18, 1862

I would desire that in any arrangement for a general exchange of prisoners, (now about being made, as I understand) loyal men now prisoners in our hands should not be indiscriminately, turned back into the power of the enemy; and, if any agent shall be deemed necessary, to make such discrimination and apply it, I doubt not Mr. Rodgers would be a suitable person for such Agency. Will the Secretary of War please consider it?

July 18, 1862 A. LINCOLN

[1] AES, IHi. Lincoln's endorsement is written on an undated petition signed by Representative Andrew J. Clements and other Tennesseans and Kentuckians recommending John B. Rodgers of Tennessee to "visit the places of confinement of Tennessee prisoners, to release all loyal union soldiers, upon such conditions as you shall prescribe." On July 6, Andrew Johnson had telegraphed Lincoln, "I see there is some contest in reference to the appointment of Judge for Tennessee. Rodgers is my personal friend but he will not do for Judge at this time. . . ." (DLC-RTL). No further reference to Rodgers' appointment has been located.

To Edward Bates[1]

Respectfully submitted to the Attorney General for his opinion whether I *can*, and *ought* to remit as requested.

July 19, 1862 A. LINCOLN

[1] AES, DNA RG 204, U.S. Pardon Attorney, A 429. Lincoln's endorsement is written on a letter from Salmon P. Chase to Ephraim Morrison, June 17, 1862, concerning his petition relative to the steamer *Minnesota* owned by Morrison, fined for violation of the Revenue Act of 1852. See further Lincoln's letter to Chase, July 22, *infra*.

To William H. Fry[1]

Executive Mansion,
My Dear Sir Washington, July 19, 1862

A pressure of important business has prevented my earlier acknowledgement of the receipt of your favor of the 9th of this month.

You are in error if you suppose any important portion of my correspondence escapes my notice. Every thing requiring my action or attention is brought to my notice. No letter of yours, which has been received here, has been neglected or left unacknowledged.

Your Obt. Servt. A LINCOLN

W. H. Fry Esq

[1] LS, CtY. The letter is in John Hay's handwriting, signed by Lincoln. Although Fry's letter of July 9 is not in the Lincoln Papers, there is a clipping from the New York *Tribune*, July 8, 1862, containing Fry's communication to Lincoln of July 4, 1862, proposing an "Immediate Increase in Military and Naval Pensions." Fry was music editor of the *Tribune* and a composer and musician of note who dabbled considerably in politics.

[333]

To Edwin M. Stanton[1]

Will the Sec. of War please respond to this? Let Gen. Boyle raise one year's men, unless there be some potent objection.

July 19, 1862.   A. LINCOLN

[1] AES, NHi. Lincoln's endorsement is written on a telegram from Brigadier General Jeremiah T. Boyle, Louisville, 12 o'clock midnight, July 18, asking authority to raise regiments of twelve-months men: "The rebel villains cannot be suppressed by leniency or conciliation. . . . Give me the force and authority & I will rid the State of their presence. . . ." Boyle recruited three regiments of cavalry for one year and two regiments for three years (OR, III, II, 431).

To Edwin M. Stanton[1]

If the service needs another Commissary of Subsistence, let Edwin Henry, named within, be appointed.   A. LINCOLN

July 19, 1862.

[1] AES, IHi. Edwin Henry of New York was appointed captain and commissary of subsistence of Volunteers on November 16, 1863. See Lincoln to Stanton, September 19, infra.

To George B. McClellan[1]

"Cypher"

War Department   Washington City, D.C.

Major Gen. McClellan   July 21 1862

This is Monday. I hope to be able to tell you on Thursday, what is to be done with Burnside.   A. LINCOLN

[1] ALS, owned by Foreman M. Lebold, Chicago, Illinois. McClellan telegraphed on July 20, 1:30 P.M., ". . . If I am to have Burnsides troops I would be glad to avail myself of at least a portion of them to occupy a point on south bank of James River. . . ." (DLC-RTL). Burnside's troops were not to be assigned to McClellan, but to Major General John Pope. Since Burnside ranked Pope, his troops were placed under Major General Jesse L. Reno and assigned to Pope's command on August 1, 1862, with orders to take position near Fredericksburg (OR, I, XII, III, 524).

Order Concerning Subjects of Foreign Powers[1]

July 21, 1862

Representations have been made to the President by the Ministers of various foreign powers in amity with the United States, that subjects of such powers have, during the present insurrection, been obliged or required by military authorities to take an oath of general or qualified allegiance to this Government. It is the duty of all aliens residing in the United States to submit to and obey the laws, and respect the authority of the Government. For any proceeding or conduct inconsistent with this obligation, and subversive of that authority, they may rightfully be subjected to military restraints when this may be necessary. But they cannot be required to take an oath of allegiance to this Government, because it conflicts with the duty they owe to their own sovereigns. All such obligations heretofore taken are, therefore, remitted and annulled. Military Commanders will abstain from imposing similar obligations in future, and will, in lieu thereof, adopt such other restraints of the character indicated as they shall find necessary, convenient, and effectual, for the public safety. It is further directed that whenever any order shall be made affecting the personal liberty of an alien, reports of the same, and of the causes thereof, shall be made to the War Department, for the consideration of the Department of State.

[1] AGO *General Orders No. 82*, July 21, 1862. This order is misdated in Hertz (II, 873-74) as of July 22.

To Edwin M. Stanton[1]

July 21, 1862.

I do not personally know the writer of this; but Senator Harlan thinks the service might be advanced, by sending him into Penn, to assist in raising more forces. Sec. of War, please see Senator Harlan, on the subject.   A. LINCOLN

July 21, 1862.

[1] AES, RPB. Lincoln's endorsement is written on a letter from Colonel Josiah Harlan of the Eleventh Pennsylvania Cavalry to James Harlan, July 21, 1862, stating his wish to recruit a brigade in Pennsylvania and to be appointed brigadier general. Apparently Colonel Harlan was disappointed, for he was mustered out of service by order on August 20, 1862.

To Gideon Welles[1]

Hon. Sec. of Navy   Executive Mansion,
My dear Sir.   Washington, July 21, 1862.

I am induced to think it probable that Mr. William R. Hopkins, lately dismissed from the place of Assistant Professor, in the Naval School, is an entirely loyal man. I shall be glad if you will investigate the case so as to be fully satisfied yourself; and if satisfied that he is loyal, restore him to his place. Yours truly

A. LINCOLN

[1] ALS, IHi. Lieutenant William R. Hopkins was assistant professor of engineering at Annapolis. Welles endorsed on the back of the letter: "Decline to reappoint Mr. H. with regret but he has conducted himself in a manner that precludes [the?] idea of his restoration with his former associates. W"

To Salmon P. Chase[1]

You see by the within what papers the Attorney General wants to enable him to give an opinion in the case.   A. LINCOLN

July 22, 1862.

[1] AES, DNA RG 204, U.S. Pardon Attorney, A 429. Lincoln's endorsement is written on Attorney General Bates' reply of July 21 to Lincoln's communication of July 19, *supra*, concerning the case of Ephraim Morrison. Bates listed the papers sent to him and pointed out that other necessary papers had not been received, "and therefore it is impossible for me to form an opinion whether or not you 'can or ought' to remit the fine or grant a pardon." No further action by Lincoln has been located.

Emancipation Proclamation—First Draft[1]

[July 22, 1862]

In pursuance of the sixth section[2] of the act of congress entitled "An act to suppress insurrection and to punish treason and rebellion, to seize and confiscate property of rebels, and for other purposes" Approved July 17. 1862, and which act, and the Joint Resolution explanatory thereof, are herewith published, I, Abraham Lincoln, President of the United States, do hereby proclaim to, and warn all persons within the contemplation of said sixth section to cease participating in, aiding, countenancing, or abetting the existing rebellion, or any rebellion against the government of the United States, and to return to their proper allegiance to the United States, on pain of the forfeitures and seizures, as within and by said sixth section provided.

And I hereby make known that it is my purpose, upon the next meeting of congress, to again recommend the adoption of a practical measure for tendering pecuniary aid to the free choice or rejection, of any and all States which may then be recognizing and practically sustaining the authority of the United States, and which may then have voluntarily adopted, or thereafter may voluntarily adopt, gradual abolishment of slavery within such State or States—that the object is to practically restore, thenceforward to be maintain[ed], the constitutional relation between the general government, and each, and all the states, wherein that relation is now suspended, or disturbed; and that, for this object, the war, as it has been, will be, prossecuted. And, as a fit and necessary military measure for effecting this object, I, as Commander-in-Chief of the Army and Navy of the United States, do order and declare that on the first day of January in the year of Our Lord one thousand, eight hundred and sixtythree, all persons held as slaves within any state or states, wherein the constitutional authority of the United States shall not then be practically recognized, submitted to, and maintained, shall then, thenceforward, and forever, be free.

> Emancipation Proclamation
> as first sketched and
> shown to the Cabinet in
> July 1862.[3]

[1] ADf, DLC-RTL. The first paragraph of this draft was issued as the proclamation of July 25, *infra*. According to Lincoln's recollection as quoted by Francis B. Carpenter in *Six Months at the White House* (pp. 20-22), Montgomery Blair opposed the proclamation of emancipation on the ground that it would cost the administration the fall election, and Seward approved it but proposed that issuance be postponed until military success gave the administration a more favorable position. Bates' Diary is silent on this discussion, but Nicolay and Hay in *Abraham Lincoln: A History* (VI, 127) record that Bates gave "unreserved concurrence." On the day following the meeting Postmaster General Blair wrote Lincoln a lengthy opinion objecting to the proclamation on political grounds. "There is therefore no public sentiment at the North, even among extreme men which now demands the proposed measure," he wrote. It would "endanger our power in Congress, and put the power in the next House of Representatives in the hands of those opposed to the war, or to our mode of carrying it on," but "if adopted to meet foreign intervention and to make issue between the Governments of Europe and the people there," the measure might be favorably received (D, DLC-Chase Papers). Chase's Diary records the cabinet discussion as follows: "The question of arming slaves was then brought up and I advocated it warmly. The President was unwilling to adopt this measure, but proposed to issue a proclamation, on the basis of the Confiscation Bill, calling upon the States to return to their allegiance . . . adding, on his own part, a declaration of his intention to renew, at the next session of Congress, his recommendation of compensation to States adopting the gradual abolishment of slavery—and proclaiming the emancipation of all slaves within States remaining in insurrection on the first of January, 1863.

"I said that I should give to such a measure my cordial support; but I should prefer that no new expression on the subject of compensation should be made, and I thought that the measure of Emancipation could be much better and more quietly accomplished by allowing Generals to organize and arm the slaves . . . and by directing the Commanders of Departments to proclaim emancipation within their Districts as soon as practicable; but I regarded this as so much better than inaction on the subject, that I should give it my entire support. . . ." (*Diary and Correspondence of Salmon P. Chase*, pp. 48-49).

[2] The sixth section provided that property of persons in States in rebellion, who did not cease to give aid to the rebellion within sixty days after proclamation by the president, would be liable to seizure. At Lincoln's direction Stanton prepared on July 22 the Executive Order authorizing seizure of property "which may be necessary or convenient" and the employment of "so many persons of African descent as can be advantageously used for military or naval purposes." This order was issued by the Adjutant General's Office on August

16, as *General Orders No. 109.* See also Lincoln's memorandum on recruiting Negroes, *infra.*

³ This endorsement was written by Lincoln on the back of the second page of the draft.

Memorandum on Recruiting Negroes[1]

[July 22, 1862?]

To recruiting free negroes, no objection.

To recruiting slaves of disloyal owners, no objection.

To recruiting slaves of loyal owners, *with their consent,* no objection.

To recruiting slaves of loyal owners *without* consent, objection, *unless the necessity is urgent.*

To conducting offensively, while recruiting, and to carrying away slaves not suitable for recruits, objection.

[1] AD, The Rosenbach Company, Philadelphia and New York. This memorandum was probably written during July, 1862, when recruiting of Negroes began under authorization of the Confiscation Act and an act to amend the Force Bill of 1795, both of which were approved by the president on July 17. Negro recruitment was discussed in the cabinet meeting on July 22, when Lincoln submitted the first draft of the Emancipation Proclamation to the cabinet, and this memorandum may well have been written at that time.

To Edwin M. Stanton[1]

Executive Mansion,

Hon. Secretary of War.   Washington, July 22, 1862.

Sir—I think it will be better to do nothing now which can be construed into a demand for troops in addition to the three hundred thousand for which we have recently called. We do not need more, nor, indeed, so many, if we could have the smaller number very soon. It is a very important consideration, too, that one recruit into an old regiment is nearly or quite equal in value to two in a new one. We can scarcely afford to forego any plan within our power, which may facilitate the filling of the old regiments with recruits. If, on consideration, you are of opinion that this object can be advanced, by causing the Militia of the several states to be enrolled, and by drafts therefrom, you are at liberty to take the proper steps, and do so, provided that any number of recruits so obtained from any state within the next three months, shall, if practicable, be an abatement, of the quota of volunteers from such state under the recent call. Yours truly   A. LINCOLN.

[1] ALS, DLC-Stanton Papers. Chase's Diary records that in the cabinet meeting on July 22 Stanton "brought forward a proposition to draft 50,000 men. Mr. Seward proposed . . . 100,000." (*Diary and Correspondence of Salmon P.*

Chase, p. 49). The slowness with which the call for new troops was being met prompted Lincoln to direct Stanton's order of August 4, 1862, calling for a draft of three hundred thousand militia for nine months, which provided that deficiencies in the volunteer quotas under the call of July 1 would be made up by the draft.

To William H. Seward[1]

July 23, 1862

Respectfully submitted to the Secretary of State, with the remark that I have no objection to the appointment of Mr. Brainerd, if the Secretary has none.   A. LINCOLN

July 23. 1862.

[1] AES, DNA FS RG 59, Appointments, Box 238. Lincoln's endorsement is written on a letter from Truman Smith, July 21, 1862, introducing Cephas Brainerd whom he recommended for appointment as arbitrator at New York under the slave trade treaty with Great Britain. Brainerd's appointment was confirmed by the Senate on January 19, 1863.

To Edwin M. Stanton[1]

Hon. Sec. of War   Executive Mansion,
Sir—   Washington, July 23. 1862.

It is a question whether we shall accept the troops under the call of Gov. Curtin for 9 months men & 12 months men. I understand you say it rests with me under the law. Perhaps it does; but I do not wish to decide it without your concurrence. What say you? If we do not take them after what has happened, we shall fail perhaps to get any on other terms from Pennsylvania. Yours truly   A. LINCOLN

[1] ALS, NHi. Stanton's reply has not been located, but sixteen regiments of nine-months men were accepted from Pennsylvania (OR, III, II, 480).

To James Dixon[1]

Executive Mansion,
Hon. Senator Dixon   Washington, July 24, 1862.

My dear Sir   The bearer of this, Mr. Bronson Murray, now resident in the 4th. District of Connecticut, wishes to be Collector for that District. He is my acquaintance and friend, of some years standing, whom I would like to oblige; but I should not like to appoint him against the wish of yourself & other Union friends there.

Please give the case such attention as you reasonably can & write me. Yours truly   A. LINCOLN

[339]

1 ALS (copy?), DLC-RTL. James Dixon was Senator from Connecticut. Bronson Murray had formerly resided at Ottawa, Illinois, and at this time was a resident of Stamford, Connecticut. Senator Dixon's reply to Lincoln's letter has not been located, and there is no record of Murray's appointment.

To William A. Hammond[1]

Surgeon General will send Mr. Merwin wherever he may think the public service may require.   A. LINCOLN
July 24, 1862.

1 ALS, owned by Alfred W. Stern, Chicago, Illinois. Concerning Reverend James B. Merwin, see Lincoln to Cameron, July 17, 1861, and Lincoln to Larned, July 1, 1862, *supra*.

To Edwin M. Stanton[1]

July 24, 1862

I understand it is desired that Joseph M. Bell be appointed a 2nd Lieut. in the Army, in order to his being Assistant Adjutant General on the Staff of Gen. B.S. Roberts. If consistent with the rules, let it be done.   A. LINCOLN.
July 24, 1862.

1 Stan. V. Henkels Catalog 1439, January 31, 1930, No. 71. According to the catalog description, Lincoln's note is written on the back of a letter from John S. Watts, delegate in congress from New Mexico Territory, endorsing appointment of Joseph M. Bell, who had served as second lieutenant in the Second New Mexico Infantry, October 27, 1861 to May 31, 1862. Bell was appointed assistant adjutant general with rank of captain and assigned to the staff of Brigadier General Benjamin S. Roberts, July 24, 1862.

Order for Observance of Death of Martin Van Buren[1]

Washington 25th July. 1862

The President, with deep regret, announces to the people of the United States the decease at Kinderhook, New York, on the 24th instant, of his honored predecessor, Martin Van Buren.

This event will occasion mourning in the nation for the loss of a citizen and a public servant whose memory will be gratefully cherished. Although it has occurred at a time when his country is afflicted with division and civil war, the grief of his patriotic friends will measurably be assuaged by the consciousness that, while suffering with disease and seeing his end approaching, his prayers were for the restoration of the authority of the government of which he had been the head, and for peace and good will among his fellow citizens.

As a mark of respect for his memory, it is ordered that the Executive Mansion and the several Executive Departments, excepting those of War and the Navy, be immediately placed in mourning, and all business be suspended during to morrow.

It is further ordered that the War and Navy Departments cause suitable military and naval honors to be paid on this occasion to the memory of the illustrious dead.   ABRAHAM LINCOLN.

[1] Copy, DNA WR NB RG 45, Naval Records, Executive Letters, No. 110. Lincoln's order was incorporated in AGO *General Orders No. 89*, July 25, 1862.

Proclamation of the Act to Suppress Insurrection[1]

July 25, 1862

By the President of the United States of America,

A proclamation

In pursuance of the sixth section of the act of Congress entitled "An act to suppress insurrection, and to punish treason and rebellion, to seize and confiscate property of rebels, and for other purposes," Approved July 17, 1862; and which act, and the Joint Resolution explanatory, thereof, are herewith published; I, Abraham Lincoln, President of the United States, do hereby proclaim to, and warn all persons within the contemplation of said sixth section to cease participating in, aiding, countenancing, or abetting the existing rebellion, or any rebellion, against the government of the United States, and to return to their proper allegiance to the United States, on pain of the forfeitures and seizures, as within, and by said sixth section provided.

In testimony whereof, I have hereunto set my hand, and caused the seal of the United States to be affixed.

[L.S.]   Done at the City of Washington, this twenty-fifth day of July, in the year of our Lord one thousand eight hundred and sixty-two, and of the Independence of the United States the eighty seventh.

By the President: ABRAHAM LINCOLN.

WILLIAM. H. SEWARD, Secretary of State.

[1] ADf, PP; DS, DNA FS RG 11, Proclamations. The autograph draft in the Free Library of Philadelphia has the first paragraph in Lincoln's handwriting and the remainder in the hand of a clerk. This draft was obtained by James C. Welling, editor of the *National Intelligencer*, for sale at the Great Central

Sanitary Fair in Philadelphia. Welling's letter of transmittal is preserved with the draft. It should be noted that the first paragraph is identical with the first paragraph of the draft presented at the cabinet meeting on July 22, at which meeting Lincoln was dissuaded from issuing the remainder of the proclamation as drafted. Thus it seems probable that Lincoln simply made a copy of the first portion pertaining to the Act to Suppress Insurrection and turned it over to Secretary Seward, whose clerk added the conclusion in customary language. The official signed copy in the National Archives was presumably prepared from this draft.

To Edwin M. Stanton[1]

July 25, 1862

I know there is no vacancy of a pay-mastership in the regular army. If there be now or soon will be for volunteers have Mr. Huey named within because Hon. Mr. Hickman seldom asks for anything and because Mr. Huey is abundantly vouched as a good man.

[1] Copy, ISLA. Lincoln's endorsement is written on the back of a letter from John Hickman recommending appointment of William Huey as paymaster. There is no record of Huey's appointment.

To Lorenzo Thomas[1]

Col. Morrison is above a false pretence, & saying this I leave it to the Adjt. Genl. to say whether he shall have leave of absence.

July 25, 1862.   A. LINCOLN

[1] AES, DLC-Nicolay Papers. Lincoln's endorsement is written on a letter from Governor Richard Yates to John G. Nicolay, July 20, 1862, "Col Wm R. Morrison is now here and is in bad health. He desires to go to Mackinaw. In my opinion it will take a month to recruit his health. Please get him leave of absence immediately or he will be compelled to leave the service. . . ." Nicolay replied to Yates that if Morrison would send the surgeon's certificate required by the War Department, the leave could be granted (*ibid.*). Colonel Morrison of the Forty-ninth Illinois had been severely wounded at Fort Donelson, but recuperated sufficiently to be elected to congress in November, 1862.

To Reverdy Johnson[1]

PRIVATE

Executive Mansion,

Hon Reverdy Johnson   Washington, July 26, 1862.

My Dear Sir. Yours of the 16th. by the hand of Governor Shepley is received. It seems the Union feeling in Louisiana is being crushed out by the course of General Phelps. Please pardon me for believing that is a false pretense. The people of Louisiana— all intelligent people every where—know full well, that I never had a wish to touch the foundations of their society, or any right of theirs. With perfect knowledge of this, they forced a necessity upon me to send armies among them, and it is their own fault, not mine, that they are annoyed by the presence of General Phelps. They also know the remedy—know how to be cured of General Phelps. Remove the necessity of his presence. And might it not be well for them to consider whether they have not already had *time* enough to do this? If they can conceive of anything worse than General Phelps, within my power, would they not better be looking out for it? They very well know the way to avert all this is simply to take their place in the Union upon the old terms. If they will not do this, should they not receive harder blows rather than lighter ones?

You are ready to say I apply to *friends* what is due only to *enemies.* I distrust the *wisdom* if not the *sincerity* of friends, who would hold my hands while my enemies stab me. This appeal of professed friends has paralyzed me more in this struggle than any other one thing. You remember telling me the day after the Baltimore mob in April 1861, that it would crush all Union feeling in Maryland for me to attempt bringing troops over Maryland soil to Washington. I brought the troops notwithstanding, and yet there was Union feeling enough left to elect a Legislature the next autumn which in turn elected a very excellent Union U. S. Senator!

I am a patient man—always willing to forgive on the Christian terms of repentance; and also to give ample *time* for repentance. Still I must save this government if possible. What I *cannot* do, of course I *will* not do; but it may as well be understood, once for all, that I shall not surrender this game leaving any available card unplayed. Yours truly   A LINCOLN

¹ Copy, DLC-RTL. The copy is in John Hay's handwriting. Reverdy Johnson, who had been appointed by the Department of State as a special agent to investigate and report on complaints by foreign consuls against military proceedings in New Orleans under Benjamin F. Butler, wrote that "So far, *for want, mainly,* of adequate military force, little has been done but to obtain the possession of this City, & the Country, immediately surrounding it. . . . Whatever Union feeling (& it is said to have been extensive—) there was . . . has nearly subsided, & principally, from an impression that it is the *purpose* of the Govt. to force the Emancipation of the slaves. This impression grows, in a great measure, from the course of Genl. Phelps. . . . Depend upon it, my Dear Sir, that unless this is at once corrected, this State cannot be, for years, if ever, reinstated in the Union. . . ." (DLC-RTL). Brigadier General John S. Phelps was military governor of Arkansas and Louisiana. In May, Butler placed Colonel George F. Shepley of the Twelfth Maine Volunteers in command at New Orleans, and in June Shepley became military governor of Louisiana.

On September 5, 1862, Reverdy Johnson answered Lincoln's letter, which had been forwarded from New Orleans to Washington, "Your private letter to me of the 26th of July, has been forwarded to me from New Orleans. When, some days since, you read a copy of it to me, in the presence of some Louisiana Gentlemen, I deemed it due to us both, to correct you in a fact that it alleged. It was that I told you 'the day after the Baltimore mob of April '61, that it would crush all union feeling in Maryland, for me to attempt bringing troops over Md. soil to Washington.' You were never more mistaken. I never said so, to you or any one else, nor ever thought so." (DLC-RTL).

To Edwin M. Stanton[1]

Respectfully submitted to the Sec. of War, with the request that he respond, particularly as to Gen. Pope's order.

July 26. 1862.   A. LINCOLN

1 AES, NHi. Lincoln's endorsement is written on a telegram from Andrew Johnson, 12:31 A.M., July 26, 1862, "In the exchange of prisoners reported soon to take place, all Tennessee prisoners who are not willing to take the oath of allegiance . . . should be exchanged first. And if there should be any left I hope they will be at once released upon taking the oath &c, and permitted to return to their homes. . . . I wish the commanding General of this Department would issue an order like that recently issued by Genl Pope, which is universally approved by the Unionists of Tennessee. . . ." Pope's *General Orders No. 11*, July 23, 1862, directed that commanders arrest all disloyal male citizens "within their lines or within their reach in rear of their respective stations. Such as are willing to take the oath of allegiance . . . and will furnish sufficient security for its observance shall be permitted to remain at their homes. . . . Those who refuse shall be conducted south . . . and be notified that if found again anywhere within our lines . . . they will be considered spies. . . ." (OR, II, IV, 271). No reply from Stanton to Lincoln's request has been located.

To Cuthbert Bullitt[1]

PRIVATE

Cuthbert Bullitt Esq   Washington D.C.
New Orleans La.   July 28. 1862

Sir: The copy of a letter addressed to yourself by Mr. Thomas J. Durant, has been shown to me. The writer appears to be an able, a dispassionate, and an entirely sincere man. The first part of the letter is devoted to an effort to show that the Secession Ordinance of Louisiana was adopted against the will of a majority of the people. This is probably true; and in that fact may be found some instruction. Why did they allow the Ordinance to go into effect? Why did they not assert themselves? Why stand passive and allow themselves to be trodden down by a minority? Why did they not hold popular meetings, and have a convention of their own, to express and enforce the true sentiment of the state? If preorganization was against them *then*, why not do this *now*, that the United States Army is present to protect them? The paralysis

—the dead palsy—of the government in this whole struggle is, that this class of men will do nothing for the government, nothing for themselves, except demanding that the government shall not strike its open enemies, lest they be struck by accident!

Mr. Durant complains that in various ways the relation of master and slave is disturbed by the presence of our Army; and he considers it particularly vexatious that this, in part, is done under cover of an act of Congress, while constitutional guaranties are suspended on the plea of military necessity. The truth is, that what is done, and omitted, about slaves, is done and omitted on the same military necessity. It is a military necessity to have men and money; and we can get neither, in sufficient numbers, or amounts, if we keep from, or drive from, our lines, slaves coming to them. Mr. Durant cannot be ignorant of the pressure in this direction; nor of my efforts to hold it within bounds till he, and such as he shall have time to help themselves.

I am not posted to speak understandingly on all the police regulations of which Mr. Durant complains. If experience shows any one of them to be wrong, let them be set right. I think I can perceive, in the freedom of trade, which Mr. Durant urges, that he would relieve both friends and enemies from the pressure of the blockade. By this he would serve the enemy more effectively than the enemy is able to serve himself. I do not say or believe that to serve the enemy is the purpose of Mr. Durant; or that he is conscious of any purpose, other than national and patriotic ones. Still, if there were a class of men who, having no choice of sides in the contest, were anxious only to have quiet and comfort for themselves while it rages, and to fall in with the victorious side at the end of it, without loss to themselves, their advice as to the mode of conducting the contest would be precisely such as his is. He speaks of no duty—apparently thinks of none—resting upon Union men. He even thinks it injurious to the Union cause that they should be restrained in trade and passage without taking sides. They are to·touch neither a sail nor a pump, but to be merely passengers,—dead-heads at that—to be carried snug and dry, throughout the storm, and safely landed right side up. Nay, more; even a mutineer is to go untouched lest these sacred passengers receive an accidental wound.

Of course the rebellion will never be suppressed in Louisiana, if the professed Union men there will neither help to do it, nor permit the government to do it without their help.

Now, I think the true remedy is very different from what is suggested by Mr. Durant. It does not lie in rounding the rough angles of the war, but in removing the necessity for the war. The people of Louisiana who wish protection to person and property, have but to reach forth their hands and take it. Let them, in good faith, reinaugurate the national authority, and set up a State Government conforming thereto under the constitution. They know how to do it, and can have the protection of the Army while doing it. The Army will be withdrawn so soon as such State government can dispense with its presence; and the people of the State can then upon the old Constitutional terms, govern themselves to their own liking. This is very simple and easy.

If they will not do this, if they prefer to hazard all for the sake of destroying the government, it is for them to consider whether it is probable I will surrender the government to save them from losing all. If they decline what I suggest, you scarcely need to ask what I will do. What would you do in my position? Would you drop the war where it is? Or, would you prosecute it in future, with elder-stalk squirts, charged with rose water? Would you deal lighter blows rather than heavier[2] ones? Would you give up the contest, leaving any available means unapplied.

I am in no boastful mood. I shall not do *more* than I can, and I shall do *all* I can to save the government, which is my sworn duty as well as my personal inclination. I shall do nothing in malice. What I deal with is too vast for malicious dealing. Yours truly

A. LINCOLN

[1] LS, DLC-RTL. The original letter, in John Hay's handwriting signed by Lincoln, was returned to John G. Nicolay by General Nathaniel P. Banks, on March 13, 1865, with a request that the president "consent that his letter will be published. Considering the time and circumstances under which it was written, I think it one of the best of his letters. . . ." (*Ibid.*). Also in the Lincoln Papers is a copy of the letter with corrections in Lincoln's handwriting and endorsed on the verso "to be returned." This copy was presumably made for the purpose indicated in Banks' letter of March 13, 1865, but if it was published at that time, the editors have not been able to verify the fact. Cuthbert Bullitt and Thomas J. Durant were loyalists at New Orleans. Bullitt was acting collector of customs in 1863, and U.S. marshal for Louisiana in 1864.

[2] Lincoln deleted "harder" and inserted "heavier."

Appointment of Charles E. Mix[1]

Executive Mansion   Washington July 28th. 1862

I hereby appoint Charles E. Mix, Chief Clerk of the Office of Indian Affairs, to be Acting Commissioner of Indian Affairs, during the absence of Commissioner Dole from the Seat of Government.

ABRAHAM LINCOLN

[1] DS, DNA NR RG 75, Office of Indian Affairs, Letters Received, Miscellaneous, P-520.

To Hamilton R. Gamble[1]

July 28, 1862

You ask four Regiments for Gen. Schofield, and he asks the same of the Sec. of War. Please raise them for me, as I have them not, nor can have, till some governor gives them to me.

[1] Metropolitan Art Association Catalog, January 14, 1914, No. 495. According to the catalog description this communication is an autograph dispatch signed. Governor Gamble telegraphed Attorney General Bates "or, in his absence, President Lincoln," July 27, 1862, "Rebel forces are approaching this State from Arkansas. If they enter far we will have a general rising. General Schofield is urgently in need of four regiments of infantry." (OR, I, XIII, 515). General Schofield's telegram to Stanton was of the same date (*ibid.*, p. 514).

To Edwin M. Stanton[1]

Sec. of War, please put Bob in the way to find where John Reed, of Co. C, 11 Mass. may be found.   A. LINCOLN

July 28. 1862.

[1] ALS, IHi. Lincoln's note is written on a card, the back of which is endorsed by Stanton, "The Adjutant General will please furnish the within information." Robert T. Lincoln's quest for Private John Reed has not been explained. Reed enlisted from Cambridge, Massachusetts, October 16, 1861, and deserted October 28, 1862. His regiment fought on the Peninsula and retired to Harrison's Landing, where it remained until the middle of August.

To Union Governors[1]

Washington, D.C.,
Gov. of "all Loyal States"[2]   July 28, 1862.

It would be of great service here for us to know, as fully as you can tell, what progress is made, and making, in recruiting for old regiments in your State. Also, about what day the first new regiment can move from you—what, the second, what the third, and so on. This information is important to us in making calculations. Please give it as promptly, and accurately as you can.

A. LINCOLN

[1] ALS, RPB. The lengthy replies may be found in the *Official Records*, III, II, 265 ff. In general the reports indicated that new regiments would be ready in August or September and that recruiting for old regiments varied from "slowly" to "satisfactory."
[2] "All Loyal States" not in Lincoln's handwriting.

To Edward Bates[1]

Edward Keinle, named within, is hereby pardoned, for so much of his sentence as remains unexecuted.   A. LINCOLN

July 29, 1862

[347]

[1] AES, DNA RG 204, U.S. Pardon Attorney, A 432. Lincoln's endorsement appears on a letter of Francis P. Blair, Jr., to Montgomery Blair, July 25, 1862, transmitting papers in the case of Sergeant Edward Keinle, Company B, Second U.S. Reserve Corps, Missouri Volunteers, convicted of robbery.

Memorandum:
Appointment of Robert T. Knight[1]

July 29, 1862

To-day, Mrs. Robert T. Knight, calls and asks that her husband be Assessor of this District, in which he resides. She says good papers are on file with Sec. of Treasury. I am to give respectful consideration to the case.   A. LINCOLN

July 29, 1862.

[1] ADS, DLC. Robert T. Knight was not appointed. See Lincoln's endorsement of Mrs. Knight's further request, April 8, 1864, *infra*.

Recommendation of Hawkins Taylor[1]

Washington July 29, 1862

I have some acquaintance with Mr. Taylor and think his appointment would be a good one.   A. LINCOLN

[1] Tracy, p. 209. Tracy describes this note as an endorsement on a letter of Senator James Harlan, recommending appointment of Hawkins Taylor as commissioner to adjust claims for military service.

To Edwin M. Stanton[1]

Hon. Sec. of War.   Executive Mansion,
Sir—   Washington, July 29. 1862.

Gen. John Cook tells me he has never had an Assistant Quarter-Master, and he wants Joseph B. Tully, now First Lieut. in the N.Y. 69th. appointed to that position. Unless there be some insurmountable obstacle, let him be appointed. Yours truly

A. LINCOLN

[1] ALS-P, ISLA. Record of Tully's appointment has not been found. Colonel John Cook of the Seventh Illinois Infantry had been appointed brigadier general of Volunteers March 3, 1862.

To Edwin M. Stanton[1]

If the Secretary of War approves, so do I.   A LINCOLN
July 29 1862

[348]

¹ Copy, DLC-George H. Stuart Papers. Lincoln's endorsement is on a recommendation from Surgeon General William A. Hammond, July 28, 1862, that the Christian Commission be granted transportation for distributing hospital supplies.

To John F. Lee¹

Judge Advocate   Executive Mansion,
Of the Army.   Washington July 30. 1862.

Sir. Please examine once more, the case of Lieutenant Colonel Francis B O'Keefe, and tell me what I, as President, can lawfully do, if anything, to relieve him from the unpleasant attitude he is in. Yours truly   A. LINCOLN

¹ Copy, DNA WR RG 153, Judge Advocate General, Letters Received, No. 196. Lieutenant Colonel Francis B. O'Keefe of the Fifteenth New York Volunteers had been dismissed from the service on September 2, 1861. Lee replied that O'Keefe, who sought a new trial, would "obtain the benefit he seeks . . . if the President will authorize the Assistant Adjutant General to inform the Governor of New York that the President has considered the proceedings of the court martial in Col. O'Keefe's case, and consents that he be re-appointed into the volunteer service." (*Ibid.*). See further, Lincoln to John F. Lee, August 8, *infra*.

To Edwin M. Stanton¹

Hon. Sec. of War   Executive Mansion,
Sir: Washington, July 30, 1862.

These gentlemen desire some order to facilitate recruiting in the City of New-York. I think you may safely give them such as they desire, making it subject to the approval of the Governor of the State. Yours truly   A. LINCOLN

¹ ALS-P, DLC-Stanton Papers. The New York *Tribune* of July 31, 1862, published a dispatch from Washington under date of July 30 which accounts for this letter as follows: "The New-York Committee had a long interview with the President to-day . . . . they urged the issuance of orders from the War Department that should tend to quicker recruiting for the old regiments.

"In the course of conversation . . . the President said that 100,000 men enlisted in the old regiments would be worth more than 300,000 in new organizations, and he sent a note to the War Department requesting the Secretary to issue the orders asked for by the Committee. The President said that arrangements for the creation and continuance of harmonious relations between the recruiting officers of the General Government and the State authorities would be made, and intimated as decidedly his opinion that it would not be necessary to resort to drafting in order to raise the number of men required under the call.

"The Committee, on presenting the President's note to Secretary Stanton, and conferring with him and Gen. Halleck, came to the conclusion that no special action in addition to what had been taken on the part of the State, would be necessary to secure the volunteers required. . . ."

The committee was headed by James W. White.

To Edwin M. Stanton[1]

July 30, 1862

We want the proposed Regiment if we can get it, and, with the concurrence of the Sec. of War, and the Gov. of New-York, and not without, let Capt. Bradley raise the regiment.

July 30. 1862   A. LINCOLN

[1] AES, DLC. Lincoln's endorsement is written on a letter dated July 28, 1862, from Morris Ketchum, New York capitalist who helped organize the Illinois Central Railroad, introducing "Capt. Jas. H. Bradley of 5th N.Y. State Vols. . . . Capt Bradley proposes to raise a regiment. . . ." No record of a regiment by Bradley has been located.

To August Belmont[1]

July 31, 1862.

Dear Sir: You send to Mr. W[eed] an extract from a letter written at New Orleans the 9th instant, which is shown to me. You do not give the writer's name; but plainly he is a man of ability, and probably of some note. He says: "The time has arrived when Mr. Lincoln must take a decisive course. Trying to please everybody, he will satisfy nobody. A vacillating policy in matters of importance is the very worst. Now is the time, if ever, for honest men who love their country to rally to its support. Why will not the North say officially that it wishes for the restoration of the Union as it was?"

And so, it seems, this is the point on which the writer thinks I have no policy. Why will he not read and understand what I have said?

The substance of the very declaration he desires is in the inaugural, in each of the two regular messages to Congress, and in many, if not all, the minor documents issued by the Executive since the inauguration.

Broken eggs cannot be mended; but Louisiana has nothing to do now but to take her place in the Union as it was, barring the already broken eggs. The sooner she does so, the smaller will be the amount of that which will be past mending. This government cannot much longer play a game in which it stakes all, and its enemies stake nothing. Those enemies must understand that they cannot experiment for ten years trying to destroy the government, and if they fail still come back into the Union unhurt. If they expect in any contingency to ever have the Union as it was, I join with the writer in saying, "Now is the time."

How much better it would have been for the writer to have gone at this, under the protection of the army at New Orleans, than to have sat down in a closet writing complaining letters northward! Yours truly,   A. LINCOLN.

[1] NH, VII, 299-300. Belmont, the New York financier, replied on August 10, "I have the honor to acknowledge the receipt of your esteemed favor. Its contents bear the stamp of that statesmanship and patriotism which I know to have guided all your actions. . . . I share entirely your views with regard not only to the duty, but also the policy of the revolted States to return to their allegiance without allowing their unequal struggle . . . to increase in violence. . . . The words *conquest* and *subjugation* have been used to good effect by our opponents. . . . while the rebel leaders can keep up . . . the idea that the North means conquest and subjugation, I fear that there is very little hope for any Union demonstration in the revolted States. . . . My own conviction has always been, that . . . we would have to come to a national convention for the reconstruction of one government over all the States. . . . My impression is, that such a solution would, at the proper time, be acceptable to a majority of the Southern people, and I sent to Mr. Weed the letter which procured me the honor of receiving your note, for the very reason that I saw in it an indication of the writer's desire for a reconstruction of the Union. He is a very wealthy and influential planter . . . ." (August Belmont, *A Few Letters and Speeches of the Late Civil War*, privately printed, New York, 1870, pp. 71-72).

Memorandum:
Appointment of James Farrington[1]

Col. R. W. Thompson, recommends James Farrington of Terre-Haute; for Collector of that District.

July 31. 1862.

[1] AE, DLC-RTL. James Farrington's appointment as assessor of the Seventh District of Indiana was confirmed by the Senate on February 3, 1863.

To Edwin M. Stanton[1]

Let this appointment be made if it consistently can.

July 31. 1862.   A LINCOLN

[1] AES, IHi. Lincoln's endorsement appears on a letter from Governor Richard Yates, July 10, 1862, recommending Lieutenant J. C. Smith, Company C, First Illinois Cavalry, "now being mustered out of service . . . acting Post Quarter Master at Rolla Mo . . . loses this position, and is anxious to continue at such post. . . ." Smith was appointed assistant quartermaster with rank of captain as of November 26, 1862, and was confirmed by the Senate on February 21, 1863.

To Joseph A. Wright[1]

Hon Joseph A. Wright: Executive Mansion,
My dear Sir.   Washington, July 31, 1862.

Our mutual friends, R. W. Thompson, and John P. Usher, assure me that they believe you, more certainly than any other man, can

carry the Terre-Haute District for the Union cause. Please try.
The effort shall not go unappreciated, so far as I am concerned.
Yours truly   A. LINCOLN

¹ ADfS, DLC-RTL; LS, IaHA. No reply from Senator Wright has been located. Democrat Daniel W. Voorhees was reelected to congress from Terre
Haute in 1862.

To Edward Bates¹

James A. Wise is hereby pardoned of all the imprisonment except
as to the first ten days.   A. LINCOLN

Aug. 1. 1862.

¹ AES, DNA RG 204, U.S. Pardon Attorney, A 432. Lincoln's endorsement
is written on a "Short copy of Indictment & sentence of James A. Wise" convicted in the Criminal Court of the District of Columbia, June Term, 1862, of
resisting an officer, fined and sentenced to four months' imprisonment.

To Mary L. Booth¹

                                              Executive Mansion,
Madam   Washington, August 1, 1862.
   Allow me to return my cordial thanks for your kindness in send-
ing me a copy of your translation of the Comte de Gasparin's
"America before Europe." I shall read it with pleasure and with
gratitude. I am very truly   Your Obt. Servt.

   Mary L. Booth   ABRAHAM LINCOLN
     &c.   &c.

¹ LS, NN. The letter is in John Hay's handwriting and signed by Lincoln.
Mary Louise Booth was the author of a *History of the City of New York* (1859),
whose translation of Gasparin's book was published in New York by Scribner
and in London by S. Low and Son. See Lincoln to Gasparin August 4, *infra*.

To Andrew H. Foote¹

Sir.   Executive Mansion   1 August 1862.
   I have the pleasure to transmit, herewith, a certified copy of a
Joint Resolution of Congress, approved July 16th. 1862, tendering
its thanks to you for your eminent services and gallantry at Fort
Henry, Fort Donelson, and Island Number Ten, while in com-
mand of the Naval forces of the United States. I am, respectfully
Your Obdt. Servt.   ABRAHAM LINCOLN

   Rear Admiral Andrew H. Foote,
     U. S. Navy   New Haven, Conn:

¹ DS, MeHi. See Lincoln to the Senate and House of Representatives July 1,
supra.

To Sydney H. Gay[1]

S. H. Gay— of Tribune—   Executive Mansion,
New-York.   Washington, August 1. 1862
   Your letter, and inclosure, received. Please come and see me at once; and, if possible, bring your correspondent with you.

                                                    A. LINCOLN

   [1] ALS, RPB. On July 30, Sydney H. Gay, an editor of the New York *Tribune,* enclosed a letter to the *Tribune* signed *"Enquirer,"* with the comment "I am receiving daily many similar letters . . . . I do not publish them because I know they would exercise a most serious influence upon the public mind." The enclosed letter of July 28, reads in part as follows: "Can you enlighten the people in regard to the real object . . . . of the Administration . . . in relation to the rebellion? The people are uneasy, anxious and suspicious. They begin to fear . . . that we are trifled with, that there is not & never has been any serious determination to put down the rebels. . . . Appearances seem conclusive as to the correctness of this view . . . . the great army of the Potomac, so full of strategy, is hid away under the protection of gun boats & cannot, or dare not or will not move & . . . the President with full power to act . . . hangs back, hesitates, & leaves the country to drift. . . . Does this mean that he does not care what becomes of the country—that he is ready to play conservative to the ruin of the Nation? We fear it. . . . If you know any cause for hope & patience give it to us. Let us once more breathe free." (DLC-RTL). Gay replied to Lincoln's telegram on the same day, that "A death in my family alone prevents my answering to your call instantly. It shall be done as soon as possible." (*Ibid.*). See further Lincoln to Gay, August 9, *infra.*

To Salmon P. Chase[1]

                                                    August 2, 1862
I have but slight personal recollection of Mr. Hall; but the writers of the within letters would not say what they do not know. On their representation, I should be glad if an appointment could be consistently given him.   A. LINCOLN
   Aug. 2. 1862.

   [1] AES, DNA RG 56, Personnel Records. Lincoln's endorsement is written on a letter from Benjamin F. James, U.S. Patent Office, to Isaac Newton, August 2, 1862, recommending Edward H. Hall of Chicago for an appointment. Hall is listed in the *Official Register* (1863) as a clerk in the Internal Revenue Office of the Treasury. In 1857-1858 Hall had been associated with the Waukegan, Illinois, *Gazette.*

To Henry W. Halleck[1]

                                                    August 2, 1862
Gen. Halleck, please see the bearer, Mr. Swett, who will tell you truth only about Wm. W. Orme, whom I also know, to be one of the most active, competent, and best men in the world.

   Aug. 2. 1862.   A. LINCOLN

¹ ALS, owned by Mrs. E. M. Evans, Normal, Illinois. William W. Orme, lawyer and associate of Leonard Swett at Bloomington, Illinois, was colonel of the newly recruited Ninety-fourth Illinois Infantry, mustered in on August 20, 1862.

To Edwin M. Stanton¹

August 2, 1862

If the Secretary of War shall write his name below this, Gen. Dix, commanding at Fort-Monroe, is authorized, in his discretion, to allow Gov. Rencher & family to go to North-Carolina.

Aug. 2. 1862.   A. LINCOLN

¹ ADS, ORB. Below Lincoln's note Stanton endorsed, "I gave Governor Rencher a pass to go to Fortress Monroe that he might get a pass from General Burnside or Governor Stanley [sic] who I supposed to be the best persons to quote in respect to Gov Renchers return to North Carolina The Department has no objection to it being given by Gen Dix if the President thinks proper." Abraham Rencher, governor of New Mexico Territory 1857-1861, was a lawyer of Pittsboro, North Carolina.

To John P. Usher¹

Executive Mansion August 2. 1862

Let the appointment be made as recommended by the Acting Secretary of the Interior.   A. LINCOLN

¹ ES, DNA NR RG 48, Applications, Indian Agencies, New Mexico, Box 1267. Written by John Hay and signed by Lincoln, the endorsement is on a letter from John P. Usher, acting secretary, July 31, 1862, recommending that Levi J. Keithly of New Mexico be appointed "in the place vacated by Judge [William F. M.] Arny." Arny was appointed secretary of New Mexico, and Keithly took his place as agent at the Utah Agency in New Mexico.

To Gideon Welles¹

G. Welles   Executive Mansion
My dear Sir.   Aug. 2, 1862

Allow me to request that you will afford all facilities not inconsistent with public interests to Captain Diller and Dr. Wetherell² for some chemical experiments which they desire to make privately under my direction. Yours truly   A. LINCOLN.

¹ Stan. V. Henkels Catalog 1342, January 4, 1924, No. 25. Lincoln's old friend Isaac R. Diller, a captain in the Illinois Militia and clerk of the Illinois House of Representatives (1851-1854), had obtained a new formula for making gunpowder. For further developments see Lincoln to Holloway August 20 and his endorsement of Diller's papers December 15, infra.
² Dr. Charles M. Wetherell was a chemist in the Bureau of Patents.

To Agénor-Etienne de Gasparin[1]

Executive Mansion   Washington August 4. 1862

Dear Sir: Your very acceptable letter dated Orbe Canton de Vaud, Switzerland 18th of July 1862 is received. The moral effect was the worst of the affair before Richmond; and that has run its course downward; we are now at a stand, and shall soon be rising again, as we hope. I believe it is true that in men and material, the enemy suffered more than we, in that series of conflicts; while it is certain he is less able to bear it.

With us every soldier is a man of character and must be treated with more consideration than is customary in Europe. Hence our great army for slighter causes than could have prevailed there has dwindled rapidly, bringing the necessity for a new call, earlier than was anticipated. We shall easily obtain the new levy, however. Be not alarmed if you shall learn that we shall have resorted to a draft for part of this. It seems strange, even to me, but it is true, that the Government is now pressed to this course by a popular demand. Thousands who wish not to personally enter the service are nevertheless anxious to pay and send substitutes, provided they can have assurance that unwilling persons similarly situated will be compelled to do like wise. Besides this, volunteers mostly choose to enter newly forming regiments, while drafted men can be sent to fill up the old ones, wherein, man for man, they are quite doubly as valuable.

You ask "why is it that the North with her great armies, so often is found, with inferiority of numbers, face to face with the armies of the South?" While I painfully know the fact, a military man, which I am not, would better answer the question. The fact I know, has not been overlooked; and I suppose the cause of its continuance lies mainly in the other facts that the enemy holds the interior, and we the exterior lines; and that we operate where the people convey information to the enemy, while he operates where they convey none to us.

I have received the volume and letter which you did me the honor of addressing to me, and for which please accept my sincere thanks. You are much admired in America for the ability of your writings, and much loved for your generosity to us, and your devotion to liberal principles generally.

You are quite right, as to the importance to us, for its bearing upon Europe, that we should achieve military successes; and the same is true for us at home as well as abroad. Yet it seems unreasonable that a series of successes, extending through half-a-year.

and clearing more than a hundred thousand square miles of country, should help us so little, while a single half-defeat should hurt us so much. But let us be patient.

I am very happy to know that my course has not conflicted with your judgement, of propriety and policy.

I can only say that I have acted upon my best convictions without selfishness or malice, and that by the help of God, I shall continue to do so.

Please be assured of my highest respect and esteem.

¹ Copy, DLC-RTL. The unsigned copy in John Hay's handwriting has "Dear Sir" added in Lincoln's hand. A translation of Count Gasparin's letter of July 18, furnished to Lincoln by Secretary Seward on August 1, reads as follows:

"It is in moments of difficulty that friends should show themselves.

"The check sustained by the federal army before Richmond was certainly a situation of difficulty for the United States. Learn that your friends in Europe do not lose courage, and that they pray for you.

"This, besides, is not a Bull Run. There is nothing in it like defeat. The mischief, please God, will soon be repaired.

"Why is it that the north with her great armies, so often is found, with inferiority in numbers, face to face with the armies of the South? You know that battles are won by the feet! and that the great principle of war is to concentrate forces in place of scattering them. It is necessary that at important points the national troops should always outnumber those of the rebel forces. It seems that the contrary has too often taken place.

"Have you received, recently, the volume and the letter I had the honor to address to you? I have attempted to sustain in Europe a struggle which is not always easy. There, assuredly, the greatest peril of America is to be found; without Europe; without the chances of European intervention, or mediation, the revolt . . . would have been at an end long since.

"That ideas of intervention may be counteracted in our old world, there is need not only of military successes achieved by you, but more than that, a continuation of your wise policy; avoid, I entreat you, the complications you may find in Mexico—avoid also, revolutionary me[a]sures—confiscations—capital punishments—appeals to the negroes—precipitate emancipation.

"You have traced a programme which every upright mind must applaud. Whilst developing it in the spirit of liberty, it tends to the preservation of fundamental principles. On the day when it can be said in Europe that your Government is, either indifferent to abolition, or carried away by the extreme abolitionists, the partizans of intervention, in favor of the South, will succeed in effecting it.

"Pardon me for writing these things to you, my excuse lies in the interest which I take in the cause of which you are the worthy representative.

"Accept Sir the assurance of my devotion and of my respect." (DLC-RTL).

Remarks to Deputation of Western Gentlemen[1]

August 4, 1862

A deputation of Western gentlemen waited upon the President this morning to offer two colored regiments from the State of Indiana. Two members of Congress were of the party. The President received them courteously, but stated to them that he was not prepared to go the length of enlisting negroes as soldiers. He would employ all colored men offered as laborers, but would not promise to make soldiers of them.

The deputation came away satisfied that it is the determination of the Government not to arm negroes unless some new and more pressing emergency arises. The President argued that the nation could not afford to lose Kentucky at this crisis, and gave it as his opinion that to arm the negroes would turn 50,000 bayonets from the loyal Border States against us that were for us.

Upon the policy of using negroes as laborers, the confiscation of Rebel property, and the feeding the National troops upon the granaries of the enemy, the President said there was no division of sentiment. He did not explain, however, why it is that the Army of the Potomac and the Army of Virginia carry out this policy so differently. The President promised that the war should be prosecuted with all the rigor he could command, but he could not promise to arm slaves or to attempt slave insurrections in the Rebel States. The recent enactments of Congress on emancipation and confiscation he expects to carry out.

[1] New York *Tribune*, August 5, 1862. Members of the deputation are not identified.

To Edwin M. Stanton[1]

Hon. Sec. of War   Executive Mansion,
Sir—   Washington, Aug. 4. 1862.

Please see these Texas gentlemen, and talk with them. They think if we could send 2500 or 3000 arms, in a vessel, to the vicinity of the Rio. Grande, that they can find the men there who will re-inaugerate the National Authority on the Rio Grande first, and probably on the Nuesces also. Perhaps Gen. Halleck's opinion should should [*sic*] be asked. Yours truly   A. LINCOLN

[1] ALS, RPB. The Texas gentlemen may have been Edmund J. Davis (judge of the U.S. District Court at Austin, Texas, 1855-1860) and John L. Haynes, whose proposal to rearm unionists in Texas is listed on August 24, 1862, as referred to the War Department (DNA WR RG 107, Register of Letters Received, P 113, Irregular Book 5). Other possibilities are Andrew J. Hamilton and Edward L. Plumb (former minister to Mexico) who in company with Haynes and the "War Committee of the Citizens of New York" headed by John A. Stevens, Jr., pressed a similar proposal on October 9, 1862. (New York *Tribune*, October 8, 1862). The Report of the Stevens' committee, published as a pamphlet sometime later, indicated that Stanton and Lincoln did not find the proposal practicable at the time.

To Lorenzo Thomas[1]

On what ground was Dr. Stipp suspended?   A. LINCOLN
Aug. 4. 1862

[1] AES, RPB. Lincoln's endorsement is written on a letter from Brigade Surgeon George Winfield Stipp, Bloomington, Illinois, July 24, 1862, asking an investigation of his suspension from duty while stationed at Corinth, Mississippi. No reply has been located, but see further Lincoln to the assistant surgeon general, October 6, *infra*.

To Whom It May Concern[1]

Executive Mansion.
Whom it may concern: Aug. 4, 1862
Edward Hall, a Texas gentleman, is a very competent, faithful, and genteel man. Yours truly,   A. LINCOLN.

[1] Dauber & Pine Bookshops Catalog 157, October, 1934, No. 531. Edward Hall has not been further identified, but he was probably one of a group of loyal Texans who were given refuge aboard the U.S.S. *Montgomery* off the mouth of the Rio Grande in June and arrived in Washington in late July or early August. See Lincoln to Stanton, *supra*.

Address to Union Meeting at Washington[1]

August 6, 1862
FELLOW-CITIZENS: I believe there is no precedent for my appearing before you on this occasion, [applause] but it is also true that there is no precedent for your being here yourselves, [applause and laughter;] and I offer, in justification of myself and of you, that, upon examination, I have found nothing in the Constitution against. [Renewed applause.] I, however, have an impression that there are younger gentlemen who will entertain you better, [voices—"No, no; none can do better than yourself. Go on!"] and better address your understanding, than I will or could, and therefore, I propose but to detain you a moment longer. [Cries —"Go on! Tar and feather the rebels!"]

I am very little inclined on any occasion to say anything unless I hope to produce some good by it. [A voice—"You do that; go on."] The only thing I think of just now not likely to be better said by some one else, is *a matter in which we have heard some other persons blamed for what I did myself.* [Voices—"What is it?] There has been a very wide-spread attempt to have a quarrel between

AUGUST 6, 1862

Gen. McClellan and the Secretary of War. *Now, I occupy a position that enables me to observe, at least, these two gentlemen are not nearly so deep in the quarrel as some pretending to be their friends.* [Cries of "Good."] Gen. McClellan's attitude is such that, in the very selfishness of his nature, he cannot but wish to be successful, and I hope he will—and the Secretary of War is in precisely the same situation. If the military commanders in the field cannot be successful, not only the Secretary of War, but myself for the time being the master of them both, cannot be but failures. [Laughter and applause.] I know Gen. McClellan wishes to be successful, and I know he does not wish it any more than the Secretary of War for him, and both of them together no more than I wish it. [Applause and cries of "Good."] Sometimes we have a dispute about how many men Gen. McClellan has had, and those who would disparage him say that he has had a very large number, and those who would disparage the Secretary of War insist that Gen. McClellan has had a very small number. The basis for this is, *there is always a wide difference, and on this occasion, perhaps, a wider one between the grand total on McClellan's rolls and the men actually fit for duty;* and those who would disparage him talk of the grand total on paper, and those who would disparage the Secretary of War talk of those at present fit for duty. Gen. McClellan *has sometimes asked for things that the Secretary of War did not give him.* Gen. McClellan is not to blame for asking what he wanted and needed, and the Secretary of War *is not to blame for not giving when he had none to give.* [Applause, laughter, and cries of "Good, good."] And I say here, as far as I know, *the Secretary of War has withheld no one thing at any time in my power to give him.* [Wild applause, and a voice—"Give him enough now!"] I have no accusation against him. *I believe he is a brave and able man,* [applause,] and I stand here, as justice requires me to do, *to take upon myself what has been charged on the Secretary of War, as withholding from him.*

I have talked longer than I expected to do, [cries of "No, no—go on,"] and now I avail myself of my privilege of saying no more.

1 New York *Times,* August 7, 1862 (brackets in original). The meeting was held in front of the Capitol. Resolutions in support of the Union, regretting "a want of readiness and determination" on the part of "those who direct our military operations," but commending Stanton's order for the draft of 300,000 militia issued on August 4 and calling for "measures . . . which will bear with the most crushing weight upon those in rebellion" were read by Edward Jordan, solicitor of the Treasury, and "unanimously and enthusiastically adopted." Lincoln's speech was preceded by one from Lucius E. Chittenden, register of the Treasury, and followed by one from George S. Boutwell, commissioner of Internal Revenue.

To Edwin M. Stanton[1]

Hon. Sec. of War.   Executive Mansion,
Sir—   Washington, Aug. 6. 1862.
After the late battles before Richmond, we promoted Gen. Israel
B. Richardson to be a Major General. He wishes that Gen. French
may be assigned to his old Division; and that he may be assigned
to a new Division from Michigan, which he thinks he can bring
forward faster than any one else, & which I think is probable. You
and Gen. Halleck must decide these things. Yours &c

A. LINCOLN

[1] ALS, NHi. No reply from Stanton has been found, but Brigadier General
William H. French was not appointed major general until November 29, 1862.

To Salmon P. Chase[1]

Executive Mansion, August 7, 1862.
My dear Sir: I have signed and herewith [return] the papers
sent yesterday for Vermont, New Hampshire, and Michigan, except in the three cases of departure from the congressional recommendations, which, with the brief, I hold to examine a little. Yours
truly,   A. LINCOLN.

[1] NH, VII, 306. Secretary Chase sent papers for appointments in Michigan
on August 5, and for appointments in New Hampshire and Vermont on August 6, recommending L. G. Berry of Adrian, Michigan, for collector in First
District instead of —— Trowbridge; William S. Mills of Lexington, Michigan,
for assessor in Fifth District instead of Luther Stanley of Birmingham; and
Townsend North of Vassar, Michigan, for assessor in Sixth District instead of
—— Bartlett, "who, it seems, is Postmaster." (DLC-RTL). Lincoln followed
Chase's recommendations except in the Fifth District, where Stanley received
the appointment.

To Cary H. Fry[1]

August 7, 1862
I remember nothing of this case; but I desire that it shall be investigated, and that Capt. Bourry, be paid for the services he actually performed, if any. The government can not afford to accept
services, and refuse payment for them.   A. LINCOLN.
Aug. 7. 1862.

[1] AES, NBuHi. Lincoln's endorsement to the acting paymaster general is
written on a copy of a letter from General Louis Blenker, June 25, 1862, recommending that Captain Gotthilf Bourry, "In October last . . . sent to my staff
by order of Major General McClellan," but who had "only received pay as
Aid de Camp since March 20th inst.," be paid for his services. See further, Lincoln to Cary H. Fry, August 20, infra.

To Henry W. Halleck[1]

Executive Mansion
Major Gen. Halleck,   Washington, Aug. 7, 1862.
Please see Gen. Casey. He considers himself aggrieved, and appeals to me for justice. But I do not know what would be justice in the case and have not the time to inquire.   A. LINCOLN
Please hear him.

[1] Tracy, p. 210. Major General Silas Casey's division had made a poor showing on the Peninsula (see note to Lincoln's telegram to McClellan, 5 P.M., June 1, *supra*), and Casey was removed from command. On August 12, he was assigned to receiving and encamping new troops as they arrived in Washington (OR, I, XII, III, 568).

To Amos A. Lawrence[1]

Executive Mansion,
My Dear Sir   Washington, August 7, 1862.
Allow me to thank you sincerely for your kind letter of the 5th of August. Your Obt. Servt.   A. LINCOLN
Hon Amos A. Lawrence
&c   &c

[1] LS, MHi. Amos A. Lawrence, merchant and philanthropist of Boston, Massachusetts, wrote on August 5, 1862, "to assure you that the draft for 300,-000 men is welcomed in this section by *all classes* of citizens." (DLC-RTL).

To Edwin M. Stanton[1]

August 7, 1862
There seems to be a peculiar reason why Mr. Busteed should enter the Military services; & if the Sec. of War concurs, he may be appointed a Brigadier General; and with the concurrence of the Gov. of New-York, may engage in raising troops there.
Aug. 7. 1862.   A. LINCOLN

[1] AES, NN. Lincoln's endorsement is written on the envelope of a letter from William C. Bryant, July 31, 1862, recommending Richard Busteed, a lawyer of New York City. Busteed had served as captain of Battery C, Chicago Light Artillery October 1 - November 7, 1861, and was appointed brigadier general of Volunteers August 7, 1862.

To Salmon P. Chase[1]

Executive Mansion, Washington, August 8, 1862.
Sir: I have signed the paper forming the districts for Rhode Island and Connecticut, and herewith return it. Also two of the

commissions for Connecticut; the others are fiercely contested.
Yours truly,   A. LINCOLN.

1 NH, VII, 306-307. See also Lincoln to Chase, August 14, *infra.*

To John F. Lee[1]

August 8. 1862.

The opinion of the Judge Advocate is approved. I consent that
Colonel O'Keefe be reappointed into the Volunteer service of the
United States if the Governor of New York so inclines.

A. LINCOLN

1 Copy, DNA WR RG 153, Judge Advocate General, Letters Received, No.
196. See Lincoln to Lee, July 30, *supra.* Lee's report of August 4, 1862, pointed
out that Colonel Francis B. O'Keefe "cannot be *restored,* unless his successor
be *removed.*" No record has been found of a reappointment by Governor Morgan.

To John F. Lee[1]

August 8, 1862

Judge Advocate please examine this case.
The evidence appears slight; and the finding, it seems to me, is
equivalent to saying Lieutenant Rowly left "with permission of
the Battallion commander, Captain A. F Bond 2nd U.S. Infantry"
Aug. 8. 1862   A. LINCOLN

1 AES, DLC-RTL. Lincoln's endorsement is written on an official copy of
the court-martial record of Second Lieutenant George A. Rowley of the Second Infantry, sentenced to be cashiered for "misbehavior before the enemy"
during the Battle of Gaines' Mill on June 27, 1862. In reply Lee endorsed at
length on August 9, "The President's suggestion as to the construction to be,
or that *may be* put on the finding, is in accordance with legal logic. . . . But
it is not according to the rule and usage of courts-martial. . . . This would be
bad pleading in a court of common law. It is good in a court martial. . . . The
Presidents authority over the case now, would be to restore or re-appoint . . .
not to vacate the judgment, or annul an executed sentence." See further, Lincoln to McClellan, August 12, *infra.*

To Edwin M. Stanton[1]

Sec. of War, please respond to this.   A. LINCOLN
Aug. 8. 1862.

1 AES, NHi. Lincoln's endorsement is written on a telegram from Andrew
H. Reeder, Easton, Pennsylvania, August 8, 1862, "Our County has raised its
quota of call for Volunteers. Have a surplus on hand and men still coming in.
We want very much to fill our quota of the draft with Volunteers and thus
avoid the draft and furnish better men." Catharinus P. Buckingham replied to
Reeder at 5:30 P.M., that "The General Government apportions the quota of

militia force among the States, but has no regard to counties. . . . It would be right for the State to make a proper allowance to any county that exceeds its proportion, but it must be left to the Executive of the State to make such arrangement." (OR, III, II, 332).

To Queen Victoria[1]

August 8, 1862

Abraham Lincoln,
President of the United States of America,

To Her Majesty Victoria,
    Queen of the United Kingdom
        of Great Britain and Ireland,
            &c.,   &c.,   &c

Sendeth Greeting.

Great and Good Friend: I have received the letter which Your Majesty addressed to me on the fourth day of July last, notifying the pleasing intelligence of the marriage on the first of that month, of Your Majesty's dearly beloved daughter, Her Royal Highness, the Princess Alice Maud Mary with His Grand Ducal Highness, the Prince Frederick William Lewis Charles, eldest son of His Grand Ducal Highness the Prince Charles William Lewis of Hesse, and Nephew of His Royal Highness the Grand Duke of Hesse.

Feeling a lively interest in all that concerns Your Majesty's August Family, I participate in the satisfaction afforded by this happy event and offer to Your Majesty my sincere congratulations upon the occasion, with the assurance that the newly married Prince and Princess have my best wishes for their prosperity and happiness: And so I recommend your Majesty and Your Majesty's Royal Family to the protection of the Almighty.

Written at Washington, the 8th. day of August, in the year of our Lord one thousand eight hundred and sixty-two. Your Good Friend,   ABRAHAM LINCOLN.

    By the President:
    WILLIAM H. SEWARD, Secretary of State.

[1] Copy, DNA FS RG 59, Communications to Foreign Sovereigns and States, III, 143-44.

To John M. Clay[1]

Mr. John M. Clay.   Executive Mansion,
My dear Sir: Washington, August 9, 1862.
    The snuff-box you sent, with the accompanying note, was received yesterday.

Thanks for this *memento* of your great and patriotic father. Thanks also for the assurance that, in these days of dereliction, you remain true to his principles. In the concurrent sentiment of your venerable mother, so long the partner of his bosom and his honors, and lingering now, where he *was*, but for the call to rejoin him where he *is*, I recognize his voice, speaking as it ever spoke, for the Union, the Constitution, and the freedom of mankind. Your Obt. Servt. A. LINCOLN

¹ ALS-F, ISLA; ADfS, DLC-RTL. John M. Clay wrote on August 4, 1862, "I send you through Adams Express a snuff box, not of much intrinsic value, but which belonged to my late father, whose avowed sentiment 'that he owed a higher allegiance to the Constitution and Government of the United States than to the Constitution and Government of any State,' is mine, and whose other noblest sentiment 'that he would rather be right than be President' I hope may ever be yours." (DLC-RTL).

To Sydney H. Gay¹

S. H. Gay, Esq Washington, D.C.,
N.Y. Tribune August 9. 1862.

When will you come? Will your correspondent come with you?

A. LINCOLN

¹ ALS, RPB. See Lincoln to Gay, August 1, *supra.* Gay replied in an undated letter written after August 22, enclosing a letter from his anonymous correspondent dated August 13 declining to come to Washington because "I cannot conceive the object of such a visit. . . . I understand the policy is now finally settled that none but white men are to be allowed to give their lives for the preservation of the country." Gay's letter commented that Lincoln's "letter to Mr. Greeley (August 22, *infra*) has infused new hope among us. . . ." (DLC-RTL).

To Henry W. Halleck¹

August 9, 1862

Respectfully submitted to Major General Halleck.

Aug. 9. 1862. A. LINCOLN

Let John B. S. Todd, be appointed a Brigadier General.

Feb. 6. 1863. A. LINCOLN

¹ AES, IHi. Lincoln's endorsements appear on a letter from John B. S. Todd, August 7, 1862, tendering his military services. His appointment as brigadier general of Volunteers had expired July 17, 1862. On August 11, Halleck endorsed following Lincoln's first endorsement:

"Genl Todd is a well educated and competent officer, thoroughly acquainted with his military duties. He did satisfactory & excellent service while under my command in the west. He was passed over while many inferior officers were confirmed."

On March 9, 1863, the Senate rejected Todd's appointment.

To Edwin M. Stanton[1]

August 9, 1862

If Senator King has investigated, and says William Lilley is "all right" and another assistant Q.M. is needed, let him, Mr. L. be appointed—or—rather, re-instated. A. LINCOLN

Aug. 9, 1862.

[1] ADS, DLC-RTL. William Lilley's appointment as assistant quartermaster with rank of captain, October 16, 1861, was rejected by the Senate on January 15 and revoked on February 3, 1862. No further appointment has been found, but Preston King wrote Lilley on August 20 that "your case is made clear & straight" (DLC-RTL). See also Lincoln's endorsement to Stanton concerning Lilley, March 25, 1863, *infra.*

To Edwin M. Stanton[1]

Hon Sec of War   Executive Mansion
Sir   Washington Aug 9 1862

I have examined and seen tried the "Rafael Repeater" and consider it a decided improvement upon what was called the "Coffee Mill Gun" in these particulars that it dispenses with the great cost and liability to loss of the Steel cartridges and that it is better arranged to prevent the escape of gas. Other advantages are claimed for it upon which I cannot so well speak. While I do not order it into the service I think it well worthy of the attention of the Ordnance Bureau and should be rather pleased if it should be decided to put it into the service Yours Truly A LINCOLN

[1] Copy, NRU-Weed Papers. The copy in the handwriting of James R. Haskell was enclosed by Haskell to Thurlow Weed, October 8, 1862. Haskell was an inventor of New York City who collaborated with the French inventor Rafael in making the Rafael Repeater. The gun was successfully tested on August 7 in presence of Lincoln, John A. Dahlgren and others (New York *Tribune*, August 8, 1862), but was never adopted by the army.

To Edwin M. Stanton[1]

Sec. of War, please respond. I think we better take while we can get. A. LINCOLN

Aug. 9, 1862.

[1] AES, NHi. Lincoln's endorsement is written on a telegram from Ozias M. Hatch and others, Springfield, Illinois, August 8, 1862, "The Governor is absent. An immense number of people are here. Many counties tender a Regiment. Can we say that all will be accepted under call for the War? An immediate answer is very important." On the same day Catharinus P. Buckingham notified Adjutant General Allen C. Fuller at Springfield that "All volunteers for the war will be accepted until August 15. After that all that offer will be accepted for filling up old regiments." (OR, III, II, 324).

To Edwin M. Stanton[1]

If an Additional PayMaster is needed, let Mr. Ripley be appointed.
Aug. 9. 1862   A. LINCOLN

[1] AES, IHi. Lincoln's endorsement appears on a letter from William H. Aspinwall and others, New York, October 30, 1861, recommending George B. Ripley, "a Merchant in this city," for appointment as paymaster. See Lincoln's similar endorsement to Cameron, November 8, 1861, *supra*.

To Edwin M. Stanton[1]

Sec. of War, please respond to this   A. LINCOLN
Aug. 9, 1862.

[1] AES, NHi. Lincoln's endorsement is written on a six-page telegram from Governor John A. Andrew, received at 9 A.M., August 9, concerning enlistments and the draft of militia. No reply from Stanton to Andrew has been found.

To Edward Bates[1]

August 11, 1862

On examination of George Krager's case, I think he was properly convicted; but as he was quite young, was of good character before the offence, and has behaved well in the prison, and has already suffered more than four years, I have concluded to direct his pardon for the remainder of his punishment.   A. LINCOLN
Aug. 11. 1862

[1] AES, DNA RG 204, U.S. Pardon Attorney, A 352. Lincoln's endorsement is written on an envelope from which papers have been removed. No further reference to the case has been found, and George Krager has not been identified.

To Ambrose E. Burnside[1]

Majr. Genl. Burnside   Washington, D.C.,
Falmouth, Va   Aug 11. 1862.
Has King's Division, in part, or in whole, joined Pope yet?
A. LINCOLN.

[1] ALS, RPB. Burnside replied from Falmouth, Virginia, the same day, "General King's advance of two brigades left here day before yesterday, and at 8 o'clock yesterday morning they crossed Ely's Ford. The last of his division left here yesterday morning and probably reached within 15 miles of Culpeper last night." (OR, I, XII, III, 562).

To William H. Seward[1]

August 11, 1862

James A. Briggs. Left with me by Hon. Mr. Ashley, with his commendation of the applicant.

I know James A. Briggs, and believe him to be an excellent man.
Aug. 11. 1862   A. LINCOLN

[1] AES, DNA FS RG 59, Appointments, Box 239. Lincoln's endorsement is written on a letter from James A. Briggs to James M. Ashley, July 9, 1862, "I want the place of 'Arbitrator' in the new court established here [New York] under the recent Slave Trade Treaty." Cephas Brainerd received the appointment. See Lincoln to Seward, July 23, *supra*.

To Edwin M. Stanton[1]

Gov. Morton is one of our best Governors, but I do not think he would be the best Military commander.   A. LINCOLN
Aug. 11. 1862

[1] AES, DNA WR RG 108, HQA, Letters Received, C 210, Box 57. Lincoln's endorsement is written on a telegram from Samuel L. Casey, Indianapolis, Indiana, 9:06 P.M., August 9, recommending that Governor Oliver P. Morton be made military governor of Kentucky in place of General Jeremiah T. Boyle.

To Edwin M. Stanton[1]

Let Dr. Baker's leave of absence be extended to the 20th. of August Inst.   A. LINCOLN
Aug. 11. 1862.

[1] AES, IHi. Lincoln's endorsement appears on a letter from Brigade Surgeon A. C. Baker, Washington, August 11, 1862, asking for an extension of his leave of absence. Lincoln's order was promulgated in AGO *Special Orders No. 190*, August 14, 1862.

To John A. Andrew[1]

Gov. Andrew,   Washington, D.C.,
Boston, Mass.   Aug. 12 1862.

Your despatch saying "I cant get those regts. off because I cant get quick work out of the U.S. disbursing officer & the Paymaster" is received.

Please say to these gentlemen that if they do not work quickly I will make quick work with them. In the name of all that is reasonable, how long does it take to pay a couple of Regts.?

We were never more in need of the arrival of Regts. than now— even to-day.   A. LINCOLN.

[1] ALS, RPB. Governor Andrew's telegram of August 11, 1862, is in the *Official Records* (III, II, 353), but for some reason the copy in the Lincoln Papers has been incorrectly dated May 12, 1861 (DLC-RTL).

To Cassius M. Clay[1]

Executive Mansion,
Hon. Cassius M. Clay. Washington, Aug. 12, 1862.

My dear Sir: I learn that you would not dislike returning to Russia as Minister Plenopotentiary. You were not recalled for any fault of yours, but, as understood, it was done at your own request. Of course there is no personal objection to your re-appointment. Still, Gen. Cameron can not be recalled except by his request. Some conversation passing between him and myself, renders it due that he should not resign without full notice of my intention to re-appoint you. If he resign with such full knowledge, and understanding, I shall be quite willing, and even gratified, to again send you to Russia. Your Obt. Servt. A. LINCOLN.

1 ALS, THaroL; ADfS, DLC-RTL. Clay wrote on August 13, 1862, "I leave for home today, by way of New-York, to visit my family—and await your pleasure—about again entering upon service, as you promise me. If agreeable to you, I will for the present, retain my commission of Majr General, with which you have honored me, till you order me into other service—unless you desire me to resign, which I am ready to do whenever you shall intimate to me your wishes. I have not received your letter as promised me—but I suppose that you have been content to give me your verbal promise, which is sufficient So I have thus written to General Cameron. I trust you will allow him to come home at once on *leave of absence;* and he will resign so you will not lose the public money by such leave.

"Please return my sincere thanks to Mrs. Lincoln for the Photographs of Yourself, and her, with the children. They shall be kept with pride, and handed down to our latest posterity." (DLC-RTL).

To Andrew G. Curtin[1]

Gov. Curtin Washington, D.C.,
Harrisburg, Penn. Aug. 12, 1862.

It is *very* important for some regiments to arrive here at once. What lack you from us? What can we do to expedite matters? Answer. A. LINCOLN

1 ALS, RPB. Governor Curtin replied the same day, "Three regiments will be organized this a.m., and leave as soon as transportation is ready. We have 13,000 men here, and will organize as rapidly as equipments and transportation can be provided. The regiments at Lancaster can go, and expect to hear from Philadelphia that some are ready there." (OR, III, II, 367).

To Cary H. Fry[1]

Pay Master General. Executive Mansion,
Sir— Washington, August 12. 1862

It is happening in many cases that persons do military service for the government without having entered regularly, and gotten upon the pay-rolls. But the service we actually receive we should pay for. Henry D'Ahna claims that he is entitled to something by this rule. I wish his case investigated; and if any thing is due him by such rule, let it be paid, with the distinct understanding that the running of the bill is at an end. Yours &c   A. LINCOLN

¹ ALS, DLM. Cary H. Fry was acting paymaster general July 15-December 10, 1862. Henry C. De Ahna of Missouri was nominated brigadier general of Volunteers on March 11, but rejected by the Senate on April 25, 1862. On May 13, Francis P. Blair, Jr., asked Lincoln to appoint him to McClellan's staff to be detailed to General David Hunter (DLC-RTL). No reply from the paymaster general has been found.

To William Hoffman¹

Wm. Hoffman—   Washington, D.C.
Detroit, Michigan   Aug. 12. 1862
    Have you charge of Confederate prisoners at Detroit? If so, is there a Dr. Joseph J. Williams amongst them?

A. LINCOLN

¹ ALS, RPB. Colonel William Hoffman, commissary general of prisoners at Detroit, telegraphed Captain Henry M. Lazella in command at Camp Chase, August 13, 1862, "At 2 o'clock this afternoon, having received no reply to my telegram of last night to you, I telegraphed Governor [David] Tod to obtain the first name of Doctor Williams, it being a matter which requires immediate attention. As the doctor is reported on parole in Columbus I can't understand where the difficulty is in getting his first name, as he will doubtless give it correctly if he is asked for it. If Governor Tod is unable to give me his name I wish on receipt of this tomorrow you would obtain it from the doctor himself, or in his absence from those who know him, and let me know by telegram. If he is not there say where he has gone to." (OR, II, IV, 385-86). See further Lincoln to Henry M. Lazella, August 14, *infra*.

To George B. McClellan¹

Major General McClellan,   Executive Mansion,
My Dear Sir: Washington, Aug. 12, 1862.
    It seems that several young Lieutenants, of whom Charles L. Noggle and George A. Rowley are two, have been cashiered by Court Martial for misconduct at the battle of June 27th. The records in the cases of the two named are now before me. I suppose that the law and the nature of the service required it, but these cases seem hard. I enclose the copy of an informal letter by the Judge Advocate in regard to them generally. I shall be obliged if you and the Regimental officers can, consistently with your sense of duty to the service, act upon the suggestions of the Judge Advocate's letter. I am very unwilling for these young men to be ruined for so slight causes. Yours Truly,   A LINCOLN

¹ Copies, DLC-RTL. One copy is endorsed by John Hay "A true Copy." The other is endorsed "Respectfully referred to Maj. Genl. F. J. Porter . . . as to the case of Lieut. Rowley. The case of Lieutenant Noggle has been recently passed upon. . . ." Further endorsement by General Porter referred the copy to Brigadier General George Sykes. See Lincoln to Lee, August 8, *supra.* On returning the record of Lieutenant Rowley, Lee wrote John Hay, August 12, 1862, "There are several others like it . . . . all very mortifying. . . . I could not but feel desirous to relieve and serve them if I could see any way. But I did not see it. . . . It is only in sentences of death that the law provides an appeal to the President. . . . I suggest . . . the applicants . . . bring to the President recommendations to his clemency from their military commanders through the general of the army in the field. . . ." (DLC-RTL). The cases of Second Lieutenants Charles L. Noggle and First Lieutenant Frank C. Goodrich of the Second Infantry and Second Lieutenant Thomas S. Wright of the Fourteenth Infantry were similarly treated. Lincoln reappointed Rowley and Noggle on January 31, 1863, and Goodrich on December 23, 1862, but no further record of Wright's service has been found. See further Lincoln's memorandum concerning Rowley, October 11, *infra.*

To Edwin M. Stanton[1]

Sec. of War please respond to this.   A. LINCOLN

Aug. 12. 1862.

¹ AES, NHi. Lincoln's endorsement is written on a telegram from John B. Temple, president of the Military Board at Frankfort, Kentucky, August 12, 1862, protesting "indiscriminate arrests" of "quiet law abiding men holding state rights dogmas" who "are required to take an oath repulsive to them or go to prison." Stanton telegraphed Temple on August 13 that "direction has this day been given to General Boyle to confine arrests to cases where good cause exists." (OR, II, IV, 380-81).

Address on Colonization
to a Deputation of Negroes[1]

August 14, 1862

This afternoon the President of the United States gave audience to a Committee of colored men at the White House. They were in-

¹ New York *Tribune,* August 15, 1862. An act "releasing certain persons held to labor in the District of Columbia" and providing $100,000 for colonization, became law on April 16, 1862, and an act approved on July 16, freed slaves in the hands of the army and granted $500,000 for colonization. Since October, 1861, the Chiriqui Project for colonization had been under cabinet consideration (see Lincoln to Smith October 23 and 24, 1861, *supra*). The appointment of Reverend James Mitchell of Indiana as agent of emigration is not listed in the *Official Register,* but contemporary records indicate that he operated in the Department of Interior as early as May 28, 1862, when he sent Lincoln his long letter on colonization printed by the Government Printing Office. His activity in July and August brought the matter of colonization to a head with the arrangement for an interview between Lincoln and the committee of Negroes headed by Edward M. Thomas on August 14. Thomas was

troduced by the Rev. J. Mitchell, Commissioner of Emigration. E. M. Thomas, the Chairman, remarked that they were there by invitation to hear what the Executive had to say to them. Having all been seated, the President, after a few preliminary observations, informed them that a sum of money had been appropriated by Congress, and placed at his disposition for the purpose of aiding the colonization in some country of the people, or a portion of them, of African descent, thereby making it his duty, as it had for a long time been his inclination, to favor that cause; and why, he asked, should the people of your race be colonized, and where? Why should they leave this country? This is, perhaps, the first question for proper consideration. You and we are different races. We have between us a broader difference than exists between almost any other two races. Whether it is right or wrong I need not discuss, but this physical difference is a great disadvantage to us both, as I think your race suffer very greatly, many of them by living among us, while ours suffer from your presence. In a word we suffer on each side. If this is admitted, it affords a reason at least why we should be separated. You here are freemen I suppose.

A VOICE: Yes, sir.

The President—Perhaps you have long been free, or all your lives. Your race are suffering, in my judgment, the greatest wrong

president of the Anglo-African Institute for the Encouragement of Industry and Art. The committee's reception of Lincoln's views is indicated by a letter from Thomas written on August 16:

"We would respectfully suggest that it is necessary that we should confer with leading colored men in Phila New York and Boston upon the movement of emigration to the point recommended in your address.

"We were entirely hostile to the movement until all the advantages were so ably brought to our view by you and we believe that our friends and colaborers for our race in those cities will when the subject is explained by us to them join heartily in sustaining such a movement. . . ." (DLC-RTL).

Subsequent developments, however, indicated that Negroes in the District of Columbia received the colonization proposal with hostility. A Negro meeting held at Union Bethel Church was reported in the Baltimore Sun on August 23 as protesting against the plan: "Such dissatisfaction had been manifested in regard to the course of the committee who lately waited on the president . . . that they did not attend. It was hinted that they had exceeded their instructions."

Plans were fully matured in August, however, to send Senator Samuel C. Pomeroy with "500 able-bodied negroes as the first colony" to be settled on a site on the Isthmus of Chiriqui to be selected by Pomeroy (New York *Tribune*, September 15, 1862). A letter of authority from Lincoln to Pomeroy was prepared for Lincoln's signature, probably by the State Department, under date of September 10, 1862, but remains unsigned in duplicate copies in the Lincoln Papers. The project was abandoned when first Honduras and later Nicaragua and Costa Rica protested the scheme and hinted that force might be used to prevent the settlement.

inflicted on any people. But even when you cease to be slaves, you are yet far removed from being placed on an equality with the white race. You are cut off from many of the advantages which the other race enjoy. The aspiration of men is to enjoy equality with the best when free, but on this broad continent, not a single man of your race is made the equal of a single man of ours. Go where you are treated the best, and the ban is still upon you.

I do not propose to discuss this, but to present it as a fact with which we have to deal. I cannot alter it if I would. It is a fact, about which we all think and feel alike, I and you. We look to our condition, owing to the existence of the two races on this continent. I need not recount to you the effects upon white men, growing out of the institution of Slavery. I believe in its general evil effects on the white race. See our present condition—the country engaged in war!—our white men cutting one another's throats, none knowing how far it will extend; and then consider what we know to be the truth. But for your race among us there could not be war, although many men engaged on either side do not care for you one way or the other. Nevertheless, I repeat, without the institution of Slavery and the colored race as a basis, the war could not have an existence.

It is better for us both, therefore, to be separated. I know that there are free men among you, who even if they could better their condition are not as much inclined to go out of the country as those, who being slaves could obtain their freedom on this condition. I suppose one of the principal difficulties in the way of colonization is that the free colored man cannot see that his comfort would be advanced by it. You may believe you can live in Washington or elsewhere in the United States the remainder of your life [as easily], perhaps more so than you can in any foreign country, and hence you may come to the conclusion that you have nothing to do with the idea of going to a foreign country. This is (I speak in no unkind sense) an extremely selfish view of the case.

But you ought to do something to help those who are not so fortunate as yourselves. There is an unwillingness on the part of our people, harsh as it may be, for you free colored people to remain with us. Now, if you could give a start to white people, you would open a wide door for many to be made free. If we deal with those who are not free at the beginning, and whose intellects are clouded by Slavery, we have very poor materials to start with. If intelligent colored men, such as are before me, would move in this matter, much might be accomplished. It is exceedingly important that we have men at the beginning capable of thinking as white men, and not those who have been systematically oppressed.

There is much to encourage you. For the sake of your race you should sacrifice something of your present comfort for the purpose of being as grand in that respect as the white people. It is a cheering thought throughout life that something can be done to ameliorate the condition of those who have been subject to the hard usage of the world. It is difficult to make a man miserable while he feels he is worthy of himself, and claims kindred to the great God who made him. In the American Revolutionary war sacrifices were made by men engaged in it; but they were cheered by the future. Gen. Washington himself endured greater physical hardships than if he had remained a British subject. Yet he was a happy man, because he was engaged in benefiting his race—something for the children of his neighbors, having none of his own.

The colony of Liberia has been in existence a long time. In a certain sense it is a success. The old President of Liberia, Roberts, has just been with me—the first time I ever saw him. He says they have within the bounds of that colony between 300,000 and 400,000 people, or more than in some of our old States, such as Rhode Island or Delaware, or in some of our newer States, and less than in some of our larger ones. They are not all American colonists, or their descendants. Something less than 12,000 have been sent thither from this country. Many of the original settlers have died, yet, like people elsewhere, their offspring outnumber those deceased.

The question is if the colored people are persuaded to go anywhere, why not there? One reason for an unwillingness to do so is that some of you would rather remain within reach of the country of your nativity. I do not know how much attachment you may have toward our race. It does not strike me that you have the greatest reason to love them. But still you are attached to them at all events.

The place I am thinking about having for a colony is in Central America. It is nearer to us than Liberia—not much more than one-fourth as far as Liberia, and within seven days' run by steamers. Unlike Liberia it is on a great line of travel—it is a highway. The country is a very excellent one for any people, and with great natural resources and advantages, and especially because of the similarity of climate with your native land—thus being suited to your physical condition.

The particular place I have in view is to be a great highway from the Atlantic or Caribbean Sea to the Pacific Ocean, and this particular place has all the advantages for a colony. On both sides there are harbors among the finest in the world. Again, there is evidence of very rich coal mines. A certain amount of coal is valuable in any country, and there may be more than enough for the wants of the country. Why I attach so much importance to coal is, it will afford an opportunity to the inhabitants for immediate employment till they get ready to settle permanently in their homes.

If you take colonists where there is no good landing, there is a bad show; and so where there is nothing to cultivate, and of which to make a farm. But if something is started so that you can get your daily bread as soon as you reach there, it is a great advantage. Coal land is the best thing I know of with which to commence an enterprise.

To return, you have been talked to upon this subject, and told that a speculation is intended by gentlemen, who have an interest in the country, including the coal mines. We have been mistaken all our lives if we do not know whites as well as blacks look to their self-interest. Unless among those deficient of intellect everybody you trade with makes something. You meet with these things here as elsewhere.

If such persons have what will be an advantage to them, the question is whether it cannot be made of advantage to you. You are intelligent, and know that success does not as much depend on external help as on self-reliance. Much, therefore, depends upon yourselves. As to the coal mines, I think I see the means available for your self-reliance.

I shall, if I get a sufficient number of you engaged, have provisions made that you shall not be wronged. If you will engage in the enterprise I will spend some of the money intrusted to me. I am not sure you will succeed. The Government may lose the money, but we cannot succeed unless we try; but we think, with care, we can succeed.

The political affairs in Central America are not in quite as satisfactory condition as I wish. There are contending factions in that quarter; but it is true all the factions are agreed alike on the subject of colonization, and want it, and are more generous than we are here. To your colored race they have no objection. Besides, I would endeavor to have you made equals, and have the best assurance that you should be the equals of the best.

The practical thing I want to ascertain is whether I can get a number of able-bodied men, with their wives and children, who are willing to go, when I present evidence of encouragement and protection. Could I get a hundred tolerably intelligent men, with their wives and children, to "cut their own fodder," so to speak? Can I have fifty? If I could find twenty-five able-bodied men, with a mixture of women and children, good things in the family relation, I think I could make a successful commencement.

I want you to let me know whether this can be done or not. This is the practical part of my wish to see you. These are subjects of very great importance, worthy of a month's study, [instead] of a speech delivered in an hour. I ask you then to consider seriously not pertaining to yourselves merely, nor for your race, and ours, for the present time, but as one of the things, if successfully managed, for the good of mankind—not confined to the present generation, but as

> "From age to age descends the lay,
> To millions yet to be,
> Till far its echoes roll away,
> Into eternity."

The above is merely given as the substance of the President's remarks.

The Chairman of the delegation briefly replied that "they would hold a consultation and in a short time give an answer." The President said: "Take your full time—no hurry at all."

The delegation then withdrew.

To Salmon P. Chase[1]

Sir: Washington, August, 14, 1862.

I have signed and herewith return the tax commissions for Connecticut, except two, in which I substituted Henry Hammond for Rufus S. Mather [sic], and David F. Hollister for Frederick S. Wildman. Yours truly, A. LINCOLN.

[1] NH, VIII, 9. Concerning the Connecticut appointments Chase wrote on August 7, 1862, "In the Third District, Ezra Dean is recommended by the Governor . . . Henry Hammond by Messrs. Foster and Dixon, and Rufus L. Matherson [sic] by Mr. Burnham, the Representative from the District. . . . After conferring with Secretary Welles and Governor Buckingham, I am satisfied that the Representative . . . should prevail, and . . . advise the appointment of Mr. Matherson [sic].

"In the Fourth District, Frederick S. Wildman is recommended by the Governor . . . for collector; the same gentleman is recommended for Assessor by Senators Dixon and Foster; while David F. Hollister is recommended for Collector. . . . I . . . advise the appointment of . . . Wildman. . . ." (DLC-RTL). On August 11, James Dixon telegraphed, "If Hammond & Hollister are not appointed my humiliation & disgrace will be complete." (Ibid.). See further Lincoln to Dixon, August 15 and 21, infra.

To Salmon P. Chase[1]

Hon. Sec. of Treasury   Executive Mansion,
Sir.   Washington, Aug. 14, 1862.
    I have signed, & herewith return, the Delaware Tax Commissions. Yours truly   A. LINCOLN.

    [1] ALS, owned by L. E. Dicke, Evanston, Illinois. John P. McLear of Wilmington was appointed assessor and Charles H. B. Day of Dover, collector for Delaware.

To Salmon P. Chase[1]

Sir: Executive Mansion, Washington, August 14, 1862.
    I have signed and herewith send the New Jersey tax commissions, so far as laid before me. Yours truly,   A. LINCOLN.

    [1] NH, VIII, 10. Appointments for New Jersey were: First District, Josiah C. Sparks, assessor, William S. Sharp, collector; Second District, George W. Cowperthwait, assessor, Stephen B. Smith, collector; Third District, Robert Rusling, assessor, Elston Marsh, collector; Fourth District, Nathaniel Lane, assessor, Eugene Ayres, collector; Fifth District, George A. Halsey, assessor, Daniel M. Wilson, collector.

To Henry M. Lazella[1]

                                        Washington, D.C., Aug. 14 1862.
Officer in charge of Confederate prisoners at Camp Chase Ohio
    It is believed that a Dr. J. J. Williams is a prisoner in your charge, and if so, tell him his wife is here, and allow him to Telegraph to her.   A. LINCOLN

    [1] ALS, RPB. Captain Lazella replied the same day, "Dr. J. J. Williams is a prisoner at Camp Chase and has been notified of the permission granted him by the President. As the person first inquired for by the commissary-general of prisoners was Joseph J. Williams I have the honor to state that this is Dr. John J. Williams and his wife's maiden name was Virginia Noll." (OR, II, IV, 387). See further Lincoln to Tucker, August 15, *infra*.

To James Dixon[1]

Hon. James Dixon   Executive Mansion,
Hartford, Conn.   Washington, Aug. 15. 1862.
            Come here.   A. LINCOLN

    [1] ALS, RPB. No reply is in the Lincoln Papers. See further Lincoln to Dixon August 21, *infra*. See also Lincoln's letter to Chase concerning the Connecticut appointments, August 14, *supra*.

To Montgomery C. Meigs[1]

Qr Mr Genl: please give the Bearer Mr Foster a pass to New-bern, N.C.   A. LINCOLN

Aug: 15/62

[1] Copy, DNA WR RG 92, Quartermaster General, P 257. The copies (2) preserved in the Quartermaster General's records also give Meigs' order, "All Qr. Mrs. will respect the requests of the President on the card attached." Probably the pass was for Charles H. Foster. See Lincoln to Cameron, August 31, 1861, *supra*.

To Edwin M. Stanton[1]

If another Additional Paymaster is needed, let Gen. Mallett be appointed.   A. LINCOLN

Aug. 15. 1862

[1] AES, RPB. Lincoln's endorsement is written on a letter from Governor William Sprague introducing and recommending Edward J. Mallett of New York. Mallett was not appointed, however, until August 12, 1863.

To Edwin M. Stanton[1]

When an Additional Paymaster is needed let Mr. Newcomer be appointed   A. LINCOLN

Aug. 15, 1862

[1] AES, RPB. Lincoln's endorsement is written on a letter signed by Governor Richard Yates and others, August 6, 1862, recommending Charles Newcomer of Ogle County, Illinois. Newcomer was appointed November 26, 1862.

To Joseph H. Tucker[1]

Executive Mansion, Washington, Aug. 15. 1862.

Officer having prisoners in charge at Camp Douglas, near Chicago, Ills.

Is there a prisoner—Dr. Joseph J. Williams?, and if so, tell him his wife is here, and allow him to Telegraph her.   A. LINCOLN.

[1] ALS, RPB. See Lincoln to Hoffman August 12 and to Lazella August 14, *supra*. Colonel Joseph H. Tucker of the Sixty-ninth Illinois Volunteers was in command at Camp Douglas. Lincoln had probably not yet received the reply from Captain Lazella when he telegraphed Tucker.

To Hiram P. Barney[1]

Hon. Hiram Barney,   Executive Mansion
New-York   Washington, Aug. 16, 1862

Mrs. L. has $1000.00 for the benefit of the hospitals; and she will be obliged, and send the pay, if you will be so good as to select and send her two hundred dollars worth of good lemmons, and one hundred dollars worth of good oranges.   A. LINCOLN

[1] ALS, RPB. No reply has been found.

To George P. Fisher[1]

Hon. Geo. P. Fisher   Executive Mansion
My dear Sir.   Washington, Aug. 16. 1862

I was painfully surprised by your letter, handed me by the P.M.G.; because the Secretary of War, who saw you after I did, had assured me, that you and accompanying friends, were fully satisfied with what he had undertaken to do. Since receiving your letter, I have seen him again, and he again assures me that such was his understanding. I went over your eight points with him to see which he accepted, and which he rejected.

He rejects that about postponing drafting till the 15th. of September.

He accepts that about the 3rd. Delaware Regiment.

He accepts that about Col. Grimshaw's Regiment.

He accepts that about the battery of Artillery, if it be the battery heretofore authorized.

He accepts that about the Battalion of Cavalry.

He accepts that about forces remaining in the State.

He rejects that about drafting being made under the Marshal of the District. He thinks he could not be justified to thus snub the Governor who is apparently doing right, but he will at once check anything which may be apparently wrong.

He accepts that about appointing officers by the War Department—unless some serious, and now unforeseen obstacle shall be presented.

I do hope you will be able to get along upon this. The Secretary feels very sure that Judge Gilpin[2] thinks you can. I mean this as a private letter, but I am quite willing for you to show it to Judge Gilpin.

I do hope you will not indulge a thought which will admit of your saying the administration turns you over to the fury of your enemies.

You certainly know I wish your success as much as you can wish it yourself. Your friend, as ever   A. LINCOLN

[1] ADfS, DLC-RTL. On August 13 the Delaware delegation interviewed Lincoln in regard to drafting in that state. Fisher's letter of August 14 reads as follows:

"You requested our delegation from Delaware, that before leaving this city, they would submit to you in writing the desires of our friends in that state respecting the calls for troops. All of them except myself have left, but before leaving they desired me to express to you our views, which are as follows.

"*1st* That the time for drafting may be extended till the 15th day of September.

"*2d* That the 3d Delaware Regiment (now in the field) which was over and above the quota which we were called upon to furnish, prior to the recent calls may be set down to the credit of the state, as part of the quota required of her under the call for 300,000 additional Volunteers.

"*3d* That Col. [Arthur H.] Grimshaw may have till the 15th day of September to fill up the 4th Delaware Regiment and that it also be credited as above.

"*4th* That the battery of Artillery now just made up by Capt Ben. Nields [Shields?] also be so credited.

"*5th* That the Battallion of Cavalry, for the raising of which an order was yesterday issued to N. B. Knight Esq, when raised may be credited as above if necessary to make up the quota of additional volunteers; or if not so necessary there [then?] that it be set off against an equal number of militia called for under the recent orders.

"*6th* That none of the troops now being organized or hereafter to be raised shall be removed from the State of Delaware until after the election to be held on the 4th day of Novr. next. Let them be placed in a camp of instruction under Genl. Lockwood . . .; or if the new levies shall be removed from the state that they and the three Regts. now in the field may be allowed to return home to vote.

"*7th* That the drafting be made under the Marshall of the district & not by Comrs. &c. appointed by the Governor.

"*8th* That the officers of the Vols. & militia will be appointed by the War Dept. & not by the Governor.

"I deem it my duty to say that. . . . We have but 16,000 voters in the state all told; and of them we have sent already 2,000 men into the field. . . . The present arrangement will diminish our strength from 500 to 1000 votes. Two years ago I had only a *plurality* of 247 votes. . . . You may very readily see how slim will be our chances to carry the election. . . ." (DLC-RTL).

2 Edward W. Gilpin, Chief Justice of Delaware.

To Edwin M. Stanton[1]

If an additional Paymaster is needed, let Mr. Phelps be appointed.

Aug. 16. 1862.   A. LINCOLN

1 AES, RPB. Lincoln's endorsement is written on a petition of July 30, 1862, signed by New York merchants and endorsed by Governor Morgan and Senator Harris, recommending Justus M. Phelps of New York City. Phelps was appointed February 27, 1863.

To Salmon P. Chase[1]

August 18, 1862

Mr. Sec. of the Treasury & Com of Revenue— Please see Mr Talcott—one of the best men there is—and if any difference—one they would like better than they do me.   A. LINCOLN

Aug. 18th 1862

1 Copy, DLC-HW. Lincoln appointed his old friend Wait Talcott collector for the Second District in Illinois. See further Lincoln to Talcott, August 27, *infra*.

To Andrew G. Curtin[1]

August 18, 1862

Under all the circumstances of this case, if the Governor of Pennsylvania shall think fit to appoint Dr. Hays a Surgeon of a Pennsylvania Regiment, he may be mustered into the United States service   A. LINCOLN

Aug. 18. 1862

[1] AES-P, ISLA. Lincoln's endorsement is written on a letter from Governor Andrew G. Curtin, August 16, 1862:

"I respectfully ask of you to revoke 'General Order No. 69 [*sic*]. War Department,' dismissing Surgeon D. S. Hayes of Penna. for neglect of duty.

"Surgeon Hayes has previously enjoyed a good character as an efficient, energetic & kind hearted surgeon. In the late & solitary instance of neglect, exhausted nature & inexperience of military rule, may be pleaded in palliation of his fault.

"He has been deeply mortified—incurred heavy expenses & in common with the service obtained the full benefit of the example intended to be set by his punishment.

"As the Surgeon General of the U. States & that of Pennsylvania agree in asking for his restoration, may not Mr President mercy now temper justice, by your pardoning his fault & restoring him to his command.

"Such a course is earnestly desired by all his Regiment—by his numerous friends & by myself."

AGO *General Orders No. 66*, June 16, 1862, reads: "Surgeon David S. Hays 110th Regiment Pennsylvania Volunteers, having been ordered to conduct to this city a large detachment of sick and wounded men, and having shamefully neglected them after their arrival, the President directs that . . . he be dismissed. . . ."

No record of a further appointment for Hays has been found.

To Cary H. Fry[1]

Executive Mansion   Aug. 18, 1862

If the Paymaster General is satisfied upon examination of this case that Lieut Tosk actually performed the service stated and is kept from his pay by a mere informality which my order will remedy, let him be paid.   A. LINCOLN

[1] ES-P, ISLA. In Hay's handwriting signed by Lincoln, this item seems to be an endorsement, but the editors have not been able to trace the original. Lieutenant Tosk has not been identified.

Invitation to Dinner[1]

Executive Mansion, Washington, August 18, 1862.

I wish the   Secretary of War
                      General Halleck
                      General McCall

Colonel Corcoran
Colonel Wilcox and
Colonel Wood
to dine with me today at half-past six P.M.   A LINCOLN

[1] DS, DLC-Nicolay Papers. The invitation is in John Hay's handwriting signed by Lincoln. The guests of honor were recently exchanged prisoners— Brigadier General George A. McCall, captured in the Seven-Days Battle and exchanged for Confederate General Simon B. Buckner; Brigadier General Michael Corcoran; Colonel Orlando B. Willcox of the First Michigan Volunteers captured at Bull Run; and Colonel Alfred M. Wood of the Eighty-fourth New York Volunteers wounded and captured at Bull Run.

To Seymour B. Moody[1]

S. B. Moody   Executive Mansion,
Springfield   Illinois.   Washington, August 18, 1862.
     Which do you prefer Commissary or Quarter master? If appointed it must be without conditions.   A. LINCOLN

[1] LS, RPB. This telegram is in John Hay's handwriting, signed by Lincoln. On the bottom of the page is Hay's endorsement, "Operator   Please send above for President." Moody replied on the same day, "Would prefer post Commissary if located at Springfield," and on August 22, declined appointment as commissary or quartermaster (DLC-RTL).

To Edwin M. Stanton[1]

August 18, 1862
If another Additional Paymaster is needed let Mr. Wood be appointed. It is thought probable that G. W. Burns, already appointed, may resign, or not qualify, & if so, his place could at once be given Mr. Wood, as they both reside at Quincy, Illinois
     Aug. 18. 1862.   A. LINCOLN

[1] AES, IHi. This endorsement was written on an envelope addressed to Lincoln. George W. Burns was appointed additional paymaster of Volunteers on June 30, 1862, and resigned on March 18, 1864. His law partner John Wood, Jr., was never appointed.

To Anna E. Carroll[1]

Executive Mansion
Dear Miss Carroll   August 19th. 1862
     Like every thing else that comes from you I have read the address to Maryland with a great deal of pleasure and interest.
     It is just what is needed now and you were the one to do it
Yours very truly   A. LINCOLN

1 Copy, DLC-Garfield Papers. The copy in the handwriting of Anna E. Carroll was enclosed in her letter to President James A. Garfield, August 6, 1880, along with a copy of a letter from Attorney General Bates, August 20, 1862: "I have now to thank you for your able and patriotic address of the 5th instant to your State which has equal relevancy to mine and all the border States. I trust and believe its influence will go far to fill the quota now required without resort to a draft on the militia of the several States.

"The President sends you a brief note of thanks."

Lincoln's note was probably an effort to mollify the indignant Miss Carroll, who following an interview with the president had written him on August 14 a very long letter reading in part as follows:

"I am just informed, that at a public dinner . . . in a Washington Hotel, a gentleman . . . stated, that the President had said 'a lady demanded fifty thousand dollars, for writing a document,' &c; meaning myself. . . . I saw . . . that you did not comprehend me . . . at the time of my interview. . . . It is due to myself . . . that I make this statement plain.

"I had a verbal agreement, with Hon Thos. A. Scott . . . to write in defense of the War Policy. . . .

"For the writing and circulating of the copies, accepted, under this agreement, there was no question; as I knew the Government was legally bound, to pay me, its just value.

"But for the circulation of all my documents, that I had written under this agreement, and for what I might write . . . I was advised . . . to bring the matter before you. . . .

"I was also advised . . . that the Government should circulate . . . the 'Reply to Breckinridge' 'The War Powers of the Government.' 'The Relations of the Government to the Revolted Citizens' &c, &c,. . . .

"They all understood, that the amount suggested, was to be used in the circulation of my documents . . . and to write and publish in Europe . . . and they deemed it a very reasonable sum. . . .

"When you said to me, that my proposition, ['] was the most outrageous one, ever made to any government, upon earth,' I remarked, that, the difference between us, was in our views, upon the value of intellectual laber. . . . If the estimate placed upon my writings, be too high, the error is not mine. . . ."

(DLC-RTL). See also Sydney Greenbie and Marjorie Barstow Greenbie, *Anna Ella Carroll and Abraham Lincoln* (1952).

To William A. Hammond[1]

August 19, 1862

Respectfully submitted to the Surgeon General—

Dr. Adolph Mayer [*sic*], says he was a Brigade Surgeon, & resigned because of a hurt, from which he is sufficiently recovered to resume his duties, which he wishes to do. If the Surgeon General has no objection & will point out the way, I will do what is necessary on my part.   A. LINCOLN

Aug. 19. 1862.

1 AES, DLC-RTL. Lincoln's endorsement is written on a letter from Dr. Adolph Majer, late surgeon of the Fourth New York Cavalry, August 18, 1862, asking annulment of his resignation. Majer had resigned on July 22 after suffering injuries in crossing the Rappahannock, but "restored by a three weeks' medical treatment" was ready to re-enter service. Surgeon General Hammond replied to Lincoln on August 19 that as regimental surgeon of the Fourth New

York Cavalry Majer was "not under the immediate assignment of this office" and could be reappointed only by the governor of the state, but that if he wished to make application to the adjutant general he might be appointed anew without reference to his former regiment (*ibid.*). Majer was appointed assistant surgeon on October 4, 1862, and surgeon on February 19, 1863.

Memorandum:
Appointment of William Masten[1]

Executive Mansion, Washington, Aug. 19. 1862.

To-day, Hon. Mr. Steele, of N.Y. comes and expresses great anxiety that William Masten may be appointed Collector in the District including Ulster County. He says Mr. *M.* is a Republican, but one to whom he, Mr. S. is under personal obligations. Mr. S. fully explains about indictments.

[1] AD, DLC-RTL. Representative John B. Steele was a Democrat of Kingston, New York. Senator Ira Harris wrote in support of Masten on August 21, 1862, and added, "He has been indicted. *I know the facts* about it. There is not the *slightest foundation* for the charges made that of *taking illegal fees in office.* . . ." (DLC-RTL). Masten was appointed collector in the Thirteenth District of New York and confirmed by the Senate on February 26, 1863, in spite of memorials of remonstrance from citizens of the district. See Lincoln's letter to Chase and memorandum concerning this appointment, November 8, *infra.*

Memorandum: New York Appointments[1]

[c. August 19, 1862]

Mr. *Halstead* is is [*sic*] Mr. Pomeroy's man.

Mr. *Latham* is Mr. Chamberlin's man. By change of Districts they are thrown together & brought, into collision. Mr. W[eed]. wishes to leave at a ballance with me.

[1] AE, DLC-RTL. Lincoln's endorsement is written on a telegram from congressmen Theodore M. Pomeroy and Jacob P. Chamberlain, Auburn, New York, August 19, to Frederick W. Seward: "We cannot formally changed [*sic*] recommendation   fix as you think best." Lincoln confused the name of John B. Halsted of Castile, New York, appointed collector for the Twenty-ninth District, with that of William A. Halsey of Port Byron, who was Pomeroy's man, and who received the appointment as collector of the Twenty-fourth District.

To William H. Seward[1]

Sec. of State, please see Gov. Koerner, the new Minister to Spain.

Aug. 19. 1862.   A. LINCOLN

[1] ALS, NAuE. Gustave P. Koerner's appointment had been confirmed by the Senate on June 14, 1862.

To Edwin M. Stanton[1]

Sec. of War please confer with Gen. Halleck & respond to them.
Aug. 19. 1862.   A. LINCOLN

[1] AES, NHi. Lincoln's endorsement is written on a telegram from Governor James F. Robinson of Kentucky, August 18, 1862, "Brigade Surgeon Joshua Bradford of Ky is offered the Command of a Regt. of 3 years Infy. His great popularity & worth; his tried courage and his devotion to the Cause impels me to ask in his favor a modification of general orders." Robinson, speaker of the Kentucky House of Representatives, became governor upon the resignation of General Beriah Magoffin on August 16, 1862. No reply by Stanton to this telegram has been found, and there is no record of Joshua T. Bradford's appointment as brigadier general. Bradford had fought a desperate battle with his command of Home Guards against a part of John H. Morgan's cavalry.

To Edwin M. Stanton[1]

Sec. of War, please respond.   A. LINCOLN
Aug. 19, 1862

[1] AES, NHi. Lincoln's endorsement is written on the last page of a telegram containing only the following words "the circumstances? Joseph M. Wightman Mayor." No reply from Stanton has been found, and the remainder of Wightman's telegram is missing, but see Lincoln to Governor John A. Andrew, August 20, *infra*.

To John A. Andrew[1]

Gov. Andrew   Washington, D.C.,
Boston, Mass.   Aug. 20, 1862.

Neither the Secretary of War, nor I, know any thing, except what you tell us, about the "published official document" you mention.   A. LINCOLN

[1] ALS, RPB. This telegram is misdated December 20, 1862 in Lapsley (VI, 222). Governor Andrew telegraphed Lincoln on August 20, "Mayor Wightman, of Boston has this morning in a published official document used these words 'Namely—Every citizen who desires to maintain the honor & reputation of our militia system as established by our fathers must resolve that the quota of Boston shall be filled without resorting to a draft which though sanctioned by an act of Congress is in one of its Elements contrary to the spirit & intent of the Constitution obnoxious to the President of the U.S. & in direct opposition to the constitution & laws of Massachusetts.' It is clear sir that my duty is to yield implicit obedience to the laws of Congress relating to militia organization & to your lawful orders issued thereunder in order to prevent confusion in the public mind—will you please telegraph immediately the authority for the foregoing reference to yourself—also any additional orders or instructions you may think proper." (DLC-RTL).

[384]

To Cary H. Fry[1]

August 20, 1862

I did not ask for information as to whether this man has been *mustered* into service. Have we *accepted* his actual service? If we have, let him be paid for them; unless there is positive law against it.   A. LINCOLN

Aug. 20. 1862.

[1] AES, NBuHi. Upon receipt of Lincoln's communication of August 7, *supra*, Paymaster General Fry forwarded General Blenker's letter to the Adjutant General's Office. Assistant Adjutant General Edward D. Townsend endorsed that Captain de Bourry "never was mustered into service." On August 23 Fry finally endorsed that "Major Rochester will pay this officer from the 16th. Oct. 1861 to the 6th. Feby 1862."

To David P. Holloway[1]

Comr. of Patents   Executive Mansion,
Sir   Washington, Aug. 20, 1862.

My friend, Capt. Diller, bearer of this, wishes the assistance of Dr. Wetherell, Chemist in your Bureau, to make an experiment, in which he Capt. Diller, trusts Dr. Wetherell, the government wishing, as yet, not to be trusted with the secret. Please let Dr. Wetherell give him the assistance. Yours truly   A. LINCOLN

[1] ALS, RPB. See Lincoln to Welles, August 2, *supra*, and endorsement of Diller's papers, December 15, *infra*.

To Ambrose E. Burnside or John G. Parke[1]

To Gen. Burnside   Received Aug. 21st. 1862.
or Gen. Parke: From Washington
What news about arrival of troops?   A. LINCOLN

[1] Copy, DLC-Fitz-John Porter Papers. Major General John G. Parke was Burnside's chief of staff. Burnside replied at 7:55 A.M., "Telegram received. Two brigades of Porter's corps arrived, with [Erastus B.] Tyler's heavy artillery, of over forty pieces. A large number of steamers in sight below Aquia. Will telegraph what troops are on board as soon as I learn. Over 6,000 troops were landed yesterday and I hope double that will be landed to-day. All that I can't land here at once I will send to Alexandria." (OR, I, XII, III, 613).

To James Dixon[1]

PRIVATE   War Department
Hon. James Dixon   Washington City, D.C.
My dear Sir: August 21. 1862

It was with great regret I felt constrained to give the tax appointment, sought for Mr. Hammond, to another. If some arrange-

[385]

ment for his benefit could be made, I should be glad, I hope to find an oppertunity of yet recognizing him. Yours very truly

A. LINCOLN

1 ALS, DNA RG 60, Papers of Attorney General, Appointments. On March 2, 1864, this letter was filed with Henry Hammond's recommendations for U.S. marshal in Connecticut. Apparently Lincoln had promised Dixon in an interview following the telegram of August 15, *supra*, that he would send such a letter to pacify Hammond, for on August 21, Dixon telegraphed, "Very important you send me promised letter immediately   Please reply." (DLC-RTL).

To Mrs. Margaret Preston[1]

Mrs. Margaret Preston   Washington, D.C.,
Lexington, Ky.   Aug. 21. 1862.

Your despatch to Mrs. L. received yesterday. She is not well. Owing to her early and strong friendship for you, I would gladly oblige you, but I can not absolutely do it. If Gen. Boyle and Hon. James Guthrie, one or both, in their discretion, see fit to give you the passes, this is my authority to them for doing so.

A. LINCOLN.

1 ALS, RPB. This telegram is misdated August 21, 1863 in Hertz (II, 907). The telegram to Mrs. Lincoln has not been found. Margaret Wickliffe Preston, daughter of Robert Wickliffe of Lexington, Kentucky, probably wished to go through the Union lines to see her husband, Confederate General William C. Preston.

Recommendation for Mason W. Newell[1]

August 21, 1862

Mr. Mason W. Newell, within recommended for Railroad employment, is personally known to me as a Railroad man. He was engaged in that capacity at Springfield, the place of my residence, for five years, and during that time enjoyed the reputation of a most competent and faithful man. I afterwards saw him at Cincinnati, engaged in the same business. I never heard any thing against him personally or professionally. I shall be very glad if employment can be found for him.   A. LINCOLN

Aug. 21. 1862.

1 ADS-P, ISLA. Newell had been superintendent of the machine shop of the Sangamon and Morgan Railroad and in 1852 was appointed superintendent of the Northern Cross Railroad.

To Edwin M. Stanton[1]

Sec. of War, please respond to this.   A. LINCOLN
Aug. 21, 1862

[386]

1 AES, NHi. Lincoln's endorsement is written on a telegram from Governor James F. Robinson of Kentucky August 20, 1862, asking extension of time to September 20 for recruiting three regiments of infantry in "territory . . . threatened by rebels & occupied by guerrillas so as to retard recruiting" and also that "authorities of the State be permitted to recruit twelve 12. months' men in satisfaction of one half of the Quota of the draft & on first October make draft for remainder." On August 22, Stanton telegraphed Robinson in reply, "Pursuant to the request of the General Assembly of Kentucky, communicated to the President by your telegram of the 20th instant, the time is extended for recruiting the regiments therein mentioned until the period named. The other suggestions contained in your telegram are under consideration, and under the peculiar condition of your State will no doubt be acceded to, as the Government has every disposition to aid you." (OR, III, II, 436).

To Gillet F. Watson[1]

Gillet F. Watson   Executive Mansion,
Williamsburg, Va.   Washington, August 21, 1862.

Your Telegram in regard to the Lunatic Assylum has been received. It is certainly a case of difficulty; but if *you can not* remain, I *can not* conceive *who*, under my authority, can. Remain as long as you safely can, and provide as well as you can for the poor inmates of the Institution.   A. LINCOLN.

1 ALS, RPB. Watson was appointed superintendent of the asylum by Governor Peirpoint after Union forces occupied Williamsburg. He telegraphed Lincoln on August 20 that "Williamsburg is being evacuated by the Union forces. Under these circumstances the safety of my life requires that I shall leave in a very few hours. When I leave all the officers and servants will leave so that the unfortunate inmates will be left locked up without any one to minister unto them. I have made known this condition of things to Genl Dix and Genl McClellan and they have done nothing! I now communicate it to you which is the last effort I can make." (DLC-RTL). McClellan's telegram of the same day explained: "Williamsburg is not evacuated by our forces but will be held . . . for several days. When applied to furnish medical attendance & servants to enable the present employees to run away I took the ground that the superintendent must make these arrangements himself. I recommended that they be required to provide employees who can & will remain. There is time enough to do this."

To Gideon Welles[1]

Sir,   Executive Mansion   August 21st 1862

Under the authority vested in me by the Act approved July 14, 1862. I have "selected the following candidates from the Sons of officers or soldiers who distinguished themselves in the service of the United States" &c. for admission into the Naval Academy as Midshipmen:

1   H. Livingston Mansfield.
2   James McB. Stembel.

3 Wm. H. Emory.
4 R. M. Cutts.
5 Morris A. [Morris R.S.] Mackenzie.
6 George Mansfield Totten, and
7 Henry W. Wessells.

I am, respectfully

Honble Gideon Welles
Secretary of the Navy.

1 D, DLC-RTL. This appears to be a draft or copy of a letter sent. The act referred to had been approved on July 14, 1862. The candidates appointed by this letter graduated at Annapolis with the exception of Mansfield and Stembel, who resigned.

To Horace Greeley[1]

Hon. Horace Greely: Executive Mansion,
Dear Sir   Washington, August 22, 1862.

I have just read yours of the 19th. addressed to myself through the New-York Tribune. If there be in it any statements, or assumptions of fact, which I may know to be erroneous, I do not, now and here, controvert them. If there be in it any inferences which I may believe to be falsely drawn, I do not now and here, argue against them. If there be perceptable in it an impatient and dictatorial tone, I waive it in deference to an old friend, whose heart I have always supposed to be right.

As to the policy I "seem to be pursuing" as you say, I have not meant to leave any one in doubt.

I would save the Union. I would save it the shortest way under the Constitution. The sooner the national authority can be restored; the nearer the Union will be "the Union as it was."[2] If there be those who would not save the Union, unless they could at the same time *save* slavery, I do not agree with them. If there be those who would not save the Union unless they could at the same time *destroy* slavery, I do not agree with them. My paramount object in this struggle *is* to save the Union, and is *not* either to save or to destroy slavery. If I could save the Union without freeing *any* slave I would do it, and if I could save it by freeing *all* the slaves I would do it; and if I could save it by freeing some and leaving others alone I would also do that. What I do about slavery, and the colored race, I do because I believe it helps to save the Union; and what I forbear, I forbear because I do *not* believe it would help to save the Union. I shall do *less* whenever I shall believe what I am doing hurts the cause, and I shall do *more* whenever I shall believe doing more will help the cause. I shall try to correct errors when shown to be errors; and I shall adopt new views so fast as they shall appear to be true views.

I have here stated my purpose according to my view of *official* duty; and I intend no modification of my oft-expressed *personal* wish that all men every where could be free. Yours,

A. LINCOLN

¹ ALS, Wadsworth Atheneum, Hartford, Connecticut. Greeley's communication of August 19, printed in the *Tribune* of August 20, 1862, under the headline "The Prayer of Twenty Millions," expressed disappointment with "the policy you seem to be pursuing with regard to the slaves of Rebels. . . . I. We require of you . . . that you EXECUTE THE LAWS. . . . II. We think you are strangely and disastrously remiss . . . with regard to the emancipating provisions of the new Confiscation Act. . . . III. We think you are unduly influenced by the counsels . . . of certain fossil politicians hailing from the Border Slave States. . . . IV. We think timid counsels in such a crisis calculated to prove perilous. . . . V. We complain that the Union cause has suffered . . . from mistaken deference to Rebel Slavery. . . . VI. We complain that the Confiscation Act which you approved is habitually disregarded by your Generals. . . . VII. Let me call your attention to the recent tragedy in New-Orleans. . . . A considerable body of . . . men, held in Slavery by two Rebel sugar-planters . . . made their way to the great mart of the South-West, which they knew to be in the undisputed possession of the Union forces. . . . They came to us for liberty and protection. . . . They were set upon and maimed, captured and killed, because they sought the benefit of that act of Congress. . . . VIII. On the face of this wide earth, Mr. President, there is not one disinterested, determined, intelligent champion of the Union cause who does not feel that all attempts to put down the Rebellion and at the same time uphold its inciting cause are preposterous and futile. . . . IX. I close as I began with the statement that what an immense majority of the Loyal Millions of your countrymen require of you is a frank, declared, unqualified, ungrudging execution of the laws of the land. . . ."

Greeley printed Lincoln's letter in the *Tribune* on August 25 and followed with a lengthy response, of which the following provides the core: "I never doubted . . . that you desire, before and above all else, to re-establish the now derided authority . . . of the Republic. I intended to raise only this question— *Do you propose to do this by recognizing, obeying, and enforcing the laws, or by ignoring, disregarding, and in effect denying them?*"

2 At this point Lincoln crossed out the following sentence: "Broken eggs can never be mended, and the longer the breaking proceeds the more will be broken."

To Gideon Welles¹

Respectfully submitted to the Navy Department, asking special attention, and as favorable action as may be consistent.

Aug. 22. 1862   A. LINCOLN

¹ AES, NN. Lincoln's endorsement is written on a letter from Rear Admiral Samuel F. Du Pont, Port Royal, South Carolina, August 15, 1862, introducing "my young friend and acting flag Lieutenant Mr [Samuel W.] Preston . . . from Illinois" and recommending him for promotion to "full Lieutenant." Preston was appointed lieutenant dating from August 1, 1862.

To Edward Bates[1]

Let Andrew Jones, named within, be pardoned, as to the remainder [of] the sentence of imprisonment.   A. LINCOLN

Aug. 23. 1862

[1] AES, DNA RG 204, U.S. Pardon Attorney, A 438. Lincoln's endorsement is written on a petition signed by citizens of Washington, D.C., asking pardon of "Andrew Jones, a very respectable and worthy Colored man . . . convicted on the 25th. day of July, 1862 . . . on the charge of assaulting and resisting a Police Officer. . . ." The petition reviews evidence that the police officer attacked Jones and that the arrest was unwarranted.

To Henry W. Halleck[1]

August 23, 1862

Submitted to Gen. Halleck, who probably knows, Capt. Garrard. He is the son of Mrs. Judge McLean, whom I would like to oblige if consistent with law & the public service.   A. LINCOLN

Aug. 23, 1862

[1] AES, IHi. Lincoln's endorsement is written on a letter from Cassius M. Clay, August 19, 1862, recommending that Captain Kenner Garrard, acting colonel in command of cadets at West Point, be appointed brigadier general of Volunteers. Garrard was appointed brigadier general as of July 23, 1863. The widow of Jeptha Garrard became the wife of John McLean.

To Montgomery C. Meigs[1]

August 23, 1862

If a strictly honest man, who has raised and dealt in cattle & horses all his life could be of service in regard to our broken down horses the bearer of this Mr. Cunningham is the very man. Q.M.G. please see him.   A. LINCOLN

Aug 23. 1862.

[1] Copy, DNA WR RG 92, Office of the Quartermaster General, P 291, C 529. "Referred to Col. [Daniel H.] Rucker Chief Quarter Master who has charge of the broken down Horses at this place. M. C. Meigs QM Genl." Cunningham is not identified, but may have been Samuel W. Cunningham of Salem, Illinois, known for his stock breeding.

Memorandum:
Appointment of Gabriel R. Paul[1]

Executive Mansion, Washington. Aug. 23, 1862.

To-day, Mrs. Major Paul, of the Regular Army calls and urges the appointment of her husband as a Brig. Genl. She is a saucy woman and I am afraid she will keep tormenting till I may have to do it.

[1] AD, DLC-RTL. This telegram is misdated "Spring 1861" in Hertz (II, 823). Major Gabriel R. Paul was appointed brigadier general as of September 5, 1862.

To S. Irenaeus Prime[1]

Executive Mansion,
My Dear Sir Washington, Aug 23, 1862.
I have received your letter of the 21st August and the accompanying paper.
Accept my cordial thanks for your good wishes and your courtesy, and believe me, very truly Your Obt. Servt.

A. LINCOLN

[1] LS, owned by W. E. Louttit, Jr., Providence, Rhode Island. This note is in Hay's handwriting, signed by Lincoln. Reverend S. Irenaeus Prime, editor of the New York *Observer* wrote Lincoln on August 21, enclosing a clipping from the *Observer* complimenting the president on his policy.

To William H. Seward[1]

This gentleman, though very plain spoken, in pursuit of an office, is excellently recommended as a worthy gentleman.
Aug. 23. 1862 A. LINCOLN

[1] AES, DNA FS RG 59, Appointments, Box 227. Lincoln's endorsement is written on a letter from Samuel B. Bell of California, August 22, 1862, asking appointment as governor of Nevada Territory, to foreign service, or to a commission in the armed forces. No record of his appointment has been found.

To Edwin M. Stanton[1]

I ask respectful consideration for the within. A. LINCOLN
Aug. 23. 1862.

[1] AES, THaroL. Lincoln's endorsement is written on an envelope franked by Representative James S. Rollins of Missouri, and bearing other endorsements indicating recommendations of Colonel William F. Switzler of Columbia, Missouri, for paymaster. Although there is no record of Switzler's appointment as paymaster he became provost marshal of Missouri in 1863.

To Richard Yates[1]

Hon. R. Yates Washington. D.C.,
Springfield, Ills. Aug. 23 1862. [8 A.M.]
I am pained to hear that you reject the service of an officer we sent to assist in organizing and getting off troops. Pensylvania and

Indiana accepted such officers, kindly; and they now have more than twice as many new troops in the field, as all the other states together. If Illinois had got forward as many troops as Indiana, Cumberland Gap would soon be relieved from it's present peril. Please do not ruin us on *punctilio*.   A. LINCOLN

[1] ALS, RPB. There seems to have been some confusion and conflict in authority between Henry M. Judah and Pitcairn Morrison, as mustering officers at Springfield, which was cleared up by the Adjutant General's Office on the same day (OR, III, II, 435, 441). Yates replied somewhat heatedly to Lincoln's telegram, "I have received your unjust dispatch. I have not rejected the service of any officer. The statement is false. Illinois may be behind in getting her troops into the field because you have sent your paymasters and mustering officers to Pennsylvania and Indiana first, but I assert, sir, that no State has done more in so short a time than Illinois has without aid from your paymasters and mustering officers, and I point with pride to 50,000 men now ready to go into the field, and only delayed, not by me, but for the want of blankets, guns, camp-kettles, &c., which come from your depot. I regard your dispatch as unkind to me and unjust to your State." (OR, III, II, 441). See further Lincoln's telegram to Yates on August 25, *infra*.

To Isabel II[1]

August 25, 1862

Abraham Lincoln,
President of the United States of America.

To Her Majesty Doña Isabel II,
    By the Grace of God and the Constitution
    of the Spanish Monarchy, Queen of Spain,
        &c.,   &c.,   &c.

Great and Good Friend: I have received the letter which Your Majesty was pleased to address to me on the 28th. of May, last, announcing that the Duchess of Montpensier, Your Majesty's beloved sister, had on the 12th. of the same month safely given birth to an Infante, upon whom, in sacred baptism, had been bestowed the names of Felipe Ramon Maria.

I participate in the satisfaction which this happy event has afforded to Your Majesty's Royal Family, and offer my sincere congratulations upon the occasion.

May God have Your Majesty always in His safe and holy keeping! Your Good Friend,   ABRAHAM LINCOLN.

Washington, August 25, 1862.

By the President:
    WILLIAM H. SEWARD, Secretary of State.

[1] Copy, DNA FS RG 59, Communications to Foreign Sovereigns and States, III, 191.

To Isabel II[1]

August 25, 1862

Abraham Lincoln,
President of the United States of America.

To Her Majesty Doña Isabel II,
By the Grace of God and the Constitution
of the Spanish Monarchy Queen of Spain,
&c., &c.

Great and Good Friend: I have received the letter which Your Majesty was pleased to address to me on the 18th. ultimo, announcing the birth of an Infanta upon whom had been bestowed in sacred baptism the names of Maria de la Paz Juana Amalia Adalberta Francisca de Paula Juana Bautista Isabel Francisca de Asis.

I participate in the satisfaction afforded by this happy event, and offer to Your Majesty my sincere congratulations upon the occasion.

May God have Your Majesty always in His safe and holy keeping! Your Good Friend, ABRAHAM LINCOLN.

Washington, August 25, 1862.

By the President:

WILLIAM H. SEWARD, Secretary of State.

[1] Copy, DNA FS RG 59, Communications to Foreign Sovereigns and States, III, 192.

To Richard Yates[1]

Hon. R. Yates, Governor   Executive Mansion,
Springfield, Ills.   Washington, August 25, 1862.

Yours denying that you have rejected the service of an officer sent you by us, is received. Of course I do not question your word; and yet what I said was based upon direct evidence; and I the more readily gave credit to it because I had previously had so much trouble between officers sent to Illinois and the State government there. I certainly can not conceive what it was I said which can be construed as injustice to Illinois. I knew by your despatches that Ills. had raised an unexpectedly large number of troops, and my impatience was that *none* of them could be got forward. I supposed too, and know nothing to the contrary yet, that the government had made the same provision for Illinois as for Pennsylvania and Indiana.   A. LINCOLN

[1] ALS, RPB. See Lincoln to Yates August 23, *supra*, and note. Yates replied on August 27, "I have not had the least difficulty with any of your officers. I have treated them all kindly & attentively." (DLC-RTL).

[393]

To Salmon P. Chase[1]

Executive Mansion   Aug 26. 1862

B. B. French, Esq. Commr. of Public Buildings is hereby authorized to draw on the sum appropriated at the last session of Congress, of $250 for Books for the Executive Mansion, for the sum of ($125 90) one hundred twenty five dollars ninety cents.

To the Secy. of the Treasury.   A. LINCOLN

[1] LS, DNA RG 217, General Accounting Office. This letter and that to Benjamin B. French *infra* are accompanied by invoices from T. J. Crowen of New York and William F. Richstein of Washington, booksellers, for books purchased for the Executive Mansion library. Lincoln paid for part of the books himself and authorized payment out of funds appropriated by congress for the remainder. For a complete analysis see Harry E. Pratt, *Personal Finances of Abraham Lincoln*, pp. 180-81.

To Benjamin B. French[1]

Hon. B. B. French   Washington, Aug. 26. 1862.

Sir   With the sum created by what you draw on the book fund and my private check of $124.25, pay T. J. Crowen of New-York one $175.00, and William F. Richstein, $75.00.   A. LINCOLN

[1] ALS, DNA RG 217, General Accounting Office. See Lincoln to Chase, *supra*.

To Jesse O. Norton[1]

Hon. Jesse O. Norton   Executive Mansion,
Joliet, Ills.   Washington, Aug. 26. 1862.

I can give you Collector, but not Assessor. Which will you have for Collector, Ellsworth, or McIntosh? Answer at once.

A. LINCOLN

[1] ALS, RPB. No reply from Norton has been found. Lewis Ellsworth of Naperville, recommended for collector, was appointed for the Sixth District of Illinois. Alexander McIntosh of Joliet, recommended for assessor, was later to be appointed assistant quartermaster with rank of captain, and was confirmed by the Senate on February 29, 1864.

To Edwin M. Stanton[1]

I would especially like for this appointment to be made if it consistently can be.   A. LINCOLN
Aug. 26. 1862.

[1] AES, IHi. Lincoln's endorsement appears on a letter of Senator Jacob Collamer to William H. Seward, August 21, 1862: "I desire that my son William Collamer . . . receive the appointment of Paymaster . . . of Volunteers.

I presume on your kindness to present this my request to the President. . . ."
William Collamer was appointed additional paymaster as of November 1, 1862,
and was confirmed by the Senate on February 19, 1863.

To Gideon Welles[1]

August 26, 1862

I shall be obliged if the within request can be granted—if not immediately, as soon as possible.   A. LINCOLN.

[1] Anderson Galleries Catalog 2193, November 15, 1927, No. 263. According to
the catalog description Lincoln's endorsement is written on the back of a letter
from Amos Tuck asking appointment for his son, Edward, as assistant paymaster
in the Navy.

To Ambrose E. Burnside[1]

Major Gen. Burnside
Falmouth, Va.   Aug. 27. 4./30 P.M. 1862
Do you hear any thing from Pope?   A. LINCOLN

[1] ALS, RPB. Stonewall Jackson had cut Pope's communications by taking
Manassas on August 26. Burnside replied at 5 P.M., "Nothing from Pope since
his dispatch to Genl Halleck which has just gone through. I sent full dispatches
to Genl Halleck this morning of all that I know." (DLC-RTL). Pope's army
was converging on Jackson at Manassas and Lee was moving around to Jackson's relief.

To Herman Haupt[1]

War Department, August 27, 1862.

Is the railroad bridge over Bull Run destroyed?
Colonel Haupt.   A. LINCOLN.

[1] Thirty-seventh Congress, Third Session, *Senate Reports No. 108*, I, 380.
Haupt's reply was received at 4:20 P.M., "Intelligence recd within 20 minutes
informs me that the enemy are advancing and have crossed Bull Run bridge—
if it is not destroyed it probably will be. The forces sent by us last night held
it until that time." (DLC-RTL).

To Herman Haupt[1]

War Department, August 27, 1862.

What became of our forces which held the bridge till twenty
minutes ago, as you say?   A. LINCOLN.
Colonel Haupt.

[1] Thirty-seventh Congress, Third Session, *Senate Reports No. 108*, I, 380.
Haupt's reply was received at 5 P.M., "Our latest information is 'The Eleventh
Ohio was covering the retreat   had held the Bridge some time and was retreat-
ing' " (DLC-RTL).

To George B. McClellan[1]

Major General McClellan
Alexandria, Va   Aug. 27. 4 P.M. 1862.
What news from the front?   A LINCOLN

[1] ALS, owned by Foreman M. Lebold, Chicago, Illinois. McClellan's telegram notifying Halleck of his arrival in Alexandria was received at 1:20 P.M. (OR, I, XII, III, 689), but no reply to Lincoln's query has been found.

Memorandum:
Appointment of Marshall B. Blake[1]

Executive Mansion, Washington, Aug. 27. 1862.
To-day Hon. F. A. Conkling, asks that Marshall B. Blake be Collector in the 6th. District instead of the 7th. as recommended. The 6.th. is Mr. Conkling's, and Mr. Blake resides in the 6.th & not in the 7th. On something I said to Mr. Conkling, he did not get up recommendations of Mr. B.

Says both are good men. Blake has never had any thing[.] Orton has an office of $1200, in same District. Is for Blake. Says Orton could go to 7th.

[1] AD, DLC-RTL. According to the *U.S. Official Register*, 1863, Marshall B. Blake was appointed collector in the Seventh District of New York and William Orton in the Sixth, Representative Frederick A. Conkling's objection notwithstanding.

Memorandum:
Appointment of John B. Colton[1]

August 27, 1862
To-day, Aug. 27, 1862, Hon: O. Lovejoy, says he would like for John B. Colton, of Galesburg, to be a Paymaster of volunteers, and I should be glad to oblige him when it can consistently be done.
A. LINCOLN

[1] ADS, IHi. Colton was appointed assistant quartermaster on November 26, 1862.

To Alexander Ramsey[1]

Gov. Ramsay   Executive Mansion,
St. Paul   Minnesota.   Washington, Aug. 27, 1862.
Yours received. Attend to the Indians. If the draft can *not* proceed, of course it *will* not proceed. Necessity knows no law. The government can not extend the time.   A. LINCOLN

[1] ALS, RPB. The Sioux were on the warpath and the Cheyennes and Chippewas were in revolt against the government because of frauds practiced by Agent Lucius C. Walker. Governor Ramsey telegraphed at 10 P.M., August 26, "With the concurrence of Commissioner Dole I have telegraphed the Secretary of War for an extension of one month of drafting, &c. The Indian outbreak has come upon us suddenly. Half the population of the State are fugitives. It is absolutely impossible that we should proceed. The Secretary of War denies our request. I appeal to you, and ask for an immediate answer. No one not here can conceive the panic in the State." (OR, I, XIII, 597). John G. Nicolay, whom Lincoln had sent to investigate the Indian troubles in Minnesota in July, joined Senator Morton S. Wilkinson and Commissioner William P. Dole in sending the following telegram from St. Paul on August 27, "We are in the midst of a most terrible and exciting Indian war. Thus far the massacre of innocent white settlers has been fearful. A wild panic prevails in nearly one-half of the State. All are rushing to the frontier to defend settlers." (*Ibid.*, 599).

To Wait Talcott[1]

Hon. Wait Talcott   Executive Mansion
My dear Sir   Washington, Aug. 27, 1862.

I have determined to appoint you Collector. I now have a very special request to make of you, which is that you will make no war upon Mr. Washburne, who is also my friend of longer standing than yourself. I shall even be obliged if you can do something for him if occasion presents. Yours truly   A. LINCOLN

[1] ALS, IaHA. See Lincoln to Chase, August 18, *supra.*

To Ambrose E. Burnside[1]

Major Genl. Burnside
Falmouth, Va   Aug. 28. 2/40 P.M. 1862
     Any news from Gen. Pope?   A. LINCOLN

[1] ALS, RPB. Burnside replied at 3 P.M., "All quiet in our front" and relayed a dispatch sent from the advance telegraph station by Captain James B. McIntyre at 2:30 P.M. as follows: "I heard from Colonel [Thomas C.] Devin at 1.30 P.M. All quiet here. A cavalry force on the Culpeper road, 12 miles from Barnett's Ford; a force of all arms at Stevensburg, 16 miles from the ford. This, he says, is from information gained, but he has seen no enemy, except a small scout on the south side of the river. He reports General Pope, with the main body of his army, at Warrenton Junction. He has sent to Rappahannock Station and will report to me. When the scout returns I will telegraph you. Everything is perfectly quiet in this neighborhood." (OR, I, XII, III, 715).

To Herman Haupt[1]

Col. Haupt.
Alexandria, Va.   Aug. 28. 2/40 P.M. 1862

Yours received. *How* do you learn that the rebel forces at Manassas are large and commanded by several of their best generals?

         A. LINCOLN

[1] ALS, RPB. Haupt had telegraphed at 12:50 P.M., that Colonel Eliakim P. Scammon "is safe & has returned to Alexandria. I went out on Engine to meet him & bring him in. He held Bull Run bridge a long time against a very superior force retired at last in perfect order eluded the efforts of the enemy to surround him & brought off his whole command with but little loss. I have advised Genl McClellan of his presence   he has important information to communicate. The rebels forces at Manassas were large and Several of their best Generals were in command. I have sent out a reconnoitering party of two hundred sharpshooters by Rail with operators and wire to repair telegraph make communication and report observations." (DLC-RTL). Haupt replied to Lincoln's query at 3:15 P.M., "One of Col Scammans surgeons was captured and released   he communicated the information, one of our firemen was captured and escaped, he confirms it & gives important details   Genl McClellan has just seen him also Col Scamman" (*ibid.*).

To Edwin M. Stanton[1]

August 28, 1862

I personally know Thomson R. Webber of Illinois to be an honest and capable man, having for a long time been Clerk of one of the Courts in which I practiced. . . .

[1] American Art Association Anderson Galleries Catalog 3955, March 4, 1932, No. 131. According to the catalog description this incomplete text is from an autograph letter signed, asking the appointment of Webber as a paymaster of Volunteers. Webber served for twenty-five years as clerk of Champaign County Circuit Court. No record of his appointment as paymaster has been found.

To James S. Wadsworth[1]

Gen. Wadsworth, please see the two gentlemen whose names are on the other side. I believe they will not misrepresent

Aug. 28. 1862.   A LINCOLN

[1] ALS, owned by Dale Carnegie, New York City. This note is pasted in an autograph album and the names on the verso are not available.

To Ambrose E. Burnside[1]

Major Genl. Burnside   Washington, D.C.,
Falmouth, Va.   Aug. 29. 2/30 P.M 1862.

Any further news? Does Col. Devin mean that sound of firing was heard in direction of Warrenton, as stated, or in direction of Warrenton Junction?   A. LINCOLN

[1] ALS, RPB. Burnside forwarded to Halleck and McClellan at 1 P.M. a dispatch from Colonel Thomas C. Devin, Barnett's Ford, 10 A.M., with news of "heavy firing this morning, apparently in the direction of Brensville and being at this hour toward Warrenton." (OR, I, XII, III, 732). At 5:15 P.M. he forwarded to Halleck a dispatch from General Porter, Bristol, 6 A.M., which gave more details: "Sigel had severe fight last night; took many prisoners. Banks is

at Warrenton Junction; McDowell near Gainesville; Heintzelman and Reno at Centreville. . . . A large body of enemy reported opposite. . . ." (OR, I, XII, III, 733).

To Herman Haupt[1]

War Department, August 29, 1862.

What news from direction of Manassas? What generally?

Colonel Haupt.   A. LINCOLN

[1] Thirty-seventh Congress, Third Session, *Senate Reports No. 108*, I, 384. Haupt replied, "General Pope was at Centreville this morning at 6 o'clock; seemed to be in good spirits. Hooker driving the enemy before him. McDowell and Sigel cutting off his retreat; army out of forage and subsistence; force of enemy 60,000. This is the substance of information communicated by two ambulance drivers who came from Centreville, and who also gave many particulars confirming previous statements. I have ordered a train of forage and another of subsistence to be got ready to start before daylight, and will notify General Pope to-night by courier, that he can have wagons to receive it at Sangster's Station by daylight to-morrow morning." (*Ibid.*).

To George B. McClellan[1]

War Department,

Major Genl. McClellan   Washington, D.C.,

Alexandria, Va.   Aug. 29. 2/30. 1862.

What news from direction of Mannassas Junction? What generally?   A. LINCOLN

[1] ALS, owned by Foreman M. Lebold, Chicago, Illinois. McClellan replied at 2:45 P.M., "The last news I recd from the direction of Manassas was from stragglers to the effect that the enemy were evacuating Centreville & retirring towards Thorofare Gap this by no means reliable. I am clear that one of two courses should be adopted. First to concentrate all our available forces to open communication with Pope. Second to leave Pope to get out of his scrape & at once use all our means to make the capital perfectly safe. No middle course will now answer. Tell me what you wish me to do & I will do all in my power to accomplish it. I wish to know what my orders & authority are. I ask for nothing but will obey whatever orders you give. I only ask a prompt decision that I may at once give the necessary orders. It will not do to delay longer" (DLC-RTL).

To George B. McClellan[1]

Major Genl. McClellan   Washington, D.C.,

Alexandria, Va   Aug. 29. 1862.

Yours of to-day just received. I think your first alternative, towit, "to concentrate all our available forces to open communication with Pope," is the right one. But I wish not to control. That I now leave to Gen. Halleck, aided by your counsels.   A. LINCOLN

[1] ALS, IHi.

[399]

To Lorenzo Thomas[1]

[c. August 29, 1862]

The Adjutant General will inform the Govr. of Pennsylvania that I will not reject Surgeon Neff from the service, if the Governor chooses to re-appoint him.

[1] E, DLC-RTL. The endorsement is in John Hay's handwriting but with corrections by Lincoln. Hay wrote ". . . I will receive Surgeon Neff again into the service, if the Governor wishes. . . ." The endorsement is written on a letter from Governor Curtin, August 29, 1862, asking restoration to service of Surgeon Henry K. Neff, who had been dismissed. On October 11, Neff was appointed surgeon of the One Hundred Fifty-third Pennsylvania Regiment of nine-months men.

To Nathaniel P. Banks[1]

Major Genl. Banks.

Manassas Junction, Va   August 30. 8/35 PM. 1862
    Please tell me what news.   A LINCOLN

[1] ALS, RPB. Banks replied at 11:45 P.M., "It is represented to me that the engagement yesterday evening was very severe but successful for our arms. Another engagement occurred this afternoon but I have not yet learned the result" (DLC-RTL).

To Henry W. Halleck[1]

August 30, 1862

Gen. Halleck, please see Lieut. Morse who left Centerville at 4.
P.M. yesterday   A. LINCOLN
    Aug 30, 1862

[1] ALS, owned by Richard F. Barker, Dorchester, Massachusetts. First Lieutenant Charles F. Morse of the Thirteenth Massachusetts Infantry carried dispatches from General Banks' headquarters.

To Herman Haupt[1]

Col. Haupt.   Washington, D.C.,
Alexandria, Va.   Aug. 30, 10/20 AM 1862.
            What news?   A. LINCOLN

[1] ALS, RPB. This same telegram appears in Haupt's *Reminiscences* (1901), p. 119, dated "August 30, 1862, 9 A.M." Lincoln may have sent two identical telegrams, since there are three telegrams which may be considered as replies. The first is dated at 11 A.M., "Firing this morning is heard in direction of Centreville. I have sent out four trains. . . . The intelligence last evening was that Hooker and Pope were pushing the enemy toward the gap in the mountains through which they had advanced, and that McDowell and Sigel were heading

them off. This morning the direction of the firing seems to be changing and it is not impossible that the enemy's forces may be changing direction and trying to escape toward Fredericksburg. . . . I await intelligence . . . and will communicate anything of importance that I hear." (OR, I, XII, III, 762). The second is dated as sent at 11:30 A.M., received at 11:35 A.M., "Our opr. has reached Manassas. Hears no firing of importance. I have directed part of the 200 Riflemen to go out as Scouts make observations & report constantly. 2 of [sic] 3 flashes just seen from Manassas in direction of Centreville. Our Expedition this A M appears to have [been] completely successful   We have re-established teleg communication with Manassas & if protected will even have cars running but the Military authorities heretofore have never extended to us the protection that was necessary & we have assumed the responsibility of going ahead without it. Our telegraph operators & Railway Employees are entitled to great credit. They have been advance "pioneers" occupying the posts of danger & the Exploit of penetrating to Fairfax & Bringing off the wounded when they supposed twenty thousand Rebels were in their front & flank was one of the boldest performances I have heard of." (DLC-RTL). The third is dated as received at 11:50 A.M., "One of our men who is just in left Bristoe yesterday noon says our men had nearly finished repairing Kettle-Run Bridge   A large number of cars with four Engines were the other side of Kettle-Run Bridge ready to come over as soon as possible   One of the Engines, the one in advance had 12 cars of ammunition & more behind   After the completion of Kettle Run the Trains can advance to Bristoe   They are probably there now   This intelligence is extremely gratifying   I learn too that Broad Run Bridge has been attempted to be destroyed by cutting off the legs of all the trestles   They could not have done mischief in a way that would render it more easy & Expeditious for us to repair   Very few hours should make Broad Run passable & then Bull Run will remain the only obstacle." (DLC-RTL).

To Herman Haupt[1]

Col. Haupt,
Alexandria, Va   Aug. 30. 1862, 3/50. P.M
    Please send me the latest news.   A. LINCOLN

[1] ALS, RPB. As in the case of the preceding telegram, there may have been two with identical wording sent at different hours. Haupt's *Reminiscences*, p. 119, prints this telegram as sent at 8:50 P.M. Haupt's reply, however, is dated as sent and received at 5 P.M., as follows: "The latest news is that our men are busy building bridges beyond Bull Run. One of my assistants has just returned from Bristoe to Manassas   Reports bridge across Kettle Run finished   A good force at work at Broad Run and another at Bull Run. One train of supplies sent out & unloaded   Another of thirteen cars of bread & meat just starting the track to Bull Run should be clear by this time but I have no advices of the fact. Major [B. F.] Fifield [?] has this moment arrived on return train & gives it as his opinion from the position of affairs when he left that Jackson has by this time surrendered. This is doubtful as we can hear firing" (DLC-RTL).

To Jeremiah T. Boyle[1]

Gen. Boyle   Louisville, Ky   Aug. 31. 1862
    What force, and what the numbers, of it, which Gen. Nelson had in the engagement near Richmond yesterday?   A. LINCOLN

[401]

[1] ALS, RPB. General Horatio G. Wright telegraphed Halleck from his headquarters, Department of the Ohio, at Cincinnati on August 31, "Nelson has been badly beaten, I fear, in an encounter with the enemy near Richmond, Ky.; his force being, as he says, hopelessly broken and scattered. He is in Lexington, Ky., wounded, and I leave for that place in a couple of hours to see what can be done. He gives me no particulars. My orders were to make the Kentucky River the line of defense, and his orders in pursuance seem to have been disregarded. At any rate his force has been routed." (OR, I, XVI, II, 464). To Lincoln's telegram Boyle answered: "I am not accurately informed of the force Gen Nelson had in the Engagement but believe that he had seven or eight thousand men all of them new lev[i]es except eighteenth Ky. His force may have been greater. The Enemys force estimated at fifteen to twenty thousand Morgan has moved from Glasgow in direction of Lebanon. Col Bruce, at Bowling Greene says Buckner, with force of Forest, Stearns & Co is moving from Tomkinsville toward Columbia & Lebanon. We need drilled troops & drilled artillery" (DLC-RTL).

To Herman Haupt[1]

Col. Haupt,   United States Military Telegraph.
Alexandria, Va   Aug. 31. 7/10 A.M. 1862
What news? Do you hear firing this morning?   A. LINCOLN

[1] ALS, owned by Robert Matlock, Owensboro, Kentucky. Haupt replied, "No news received as yet this morning; firing heard distinctly in direction of Bristoe at 6 o'clock" (*Reminiscences*, p. 124). At 10 A.M. Haupt reported, "We escaped any injury to the track or bridges last night. We sent forward trains until 2 am. They all reached their destination which affords I think an ample supply of subsistence & ammunition. We sent 88 cars   The trains were all guarded the tops filled with riflemen & strong guards at all the bridges. We asked Manassas a short time ago if firing was heard   He said no   Fairfax just answered no firing heard. I sent out one of Genl Couches [Darius N. Couch] regiments about 12 last night   The other reported for duty after 2 AM. It was of no use to send it at that hour as no train was ready." (DLC-RTL).

At 10:10 Haupt reported further: "One of our train dispatchers reports from Manassas that he was ordered out of his car at Bristoe this morning by our own troops with the information that they were ordered to destroy the cars & engines & they have been burned. I suppose this was done by command of Genl Banks" (*ibid.*).

The Second Battle of Bull Run was over, and at 8:50 A.M. on September 1 General Pope would advise Halleck that he should order the army to fall back to the entrenchments in front of Washington.

To Salmon P. Chase[1]

[September 1, 1862]
Bring them in a half hour   A.L.

[1] Copy, IHi-Nicolay and Hay Papers. Lincoln's endorsement is written on a note from Chase, September 1, 1862, asking an audience for "Judge Bond, Mr. Goldsborough and two other gentlemen." Judge Hugh L. Bond of Baltimore and Henry H. Goldsborough, president of the Maryland Senate, were probably the men named.

Memorandum
on Criticism of Henry W. Halleck[1]

[c. September 1, 1862]

Gen. Halleck is acting on the proposition that the Army under Pope is not to be sacraficed.

[1] AE, DLC-RTL. Lincoln's endorsement is written on a letter from E. Hinton, Washington, September 1, 1862, reporting a rumor that "Halleck has sent down the whole army to Bull run . . . . it would be none the less a violation of all military principles to risk the battle."

To William H. Seward[1]

If this office has not already been filled, I should be very glad to appoint Mr. Briggs, whom I personally know.   A. LINCOLN

Sept. 1. 1862

[1] AES, DLC-RTL. Lincoln's endorsement is written on a letter from George Opdyke and Hiram Walbridge, August 23, 1862, recommending James A. Briggs for arbitrator under the slave trade treaty with Great Britain. See Lincoln to Seward, August 11, *supra*.

To Edwin M. Stanton[1]

Hon. Sec. of War   Executive Mansion,
Sir.   Washington, Sep. 1. 1862.

I personally know Dr. Levi D Boone, of Chicago, Illinois, who is not in close confinement, but on limits, on parol, under bonds, and oath of allegiance. From my knowledge of him, and the open, and rather marked part he has taken for the war, I think he should be at least, enlarged generally, on the same terms. If the Sec.. of War concurs, let it be done. Yours truly   A. LINCOLN

[1] ALS, IHi. Dr. Boone had been arrested for giving money to a Confederate prisoner E. H. Green at Camp Douglas (OR, II, IV, 339-40). On September 10, Commissary General of Prisoners William Hoffman reported on the case of Dr. Boone that "There seems to be no reason to doubt Doctor Boone's loyalty. . . . I should respectfully suggest that he be released." (*Ibid.*, 503-504).

Meditation on the Divine Will[1]

[September 2, 1862?]

The will of God prevails. In great contests each party claims to act in accordance with the will of God. Both *may* be, and one *must*

be wrong. God can not be *for,* and *against* the same thing at the same time. In the present civil war it is quite possible that God's purpose is something different from the purpose of either party—and yet the human instrumentalities, working just as they do, are of the best adaptation to effect His purpose. I am almost ready to say this is probably true—that God wills this contest, and wills that it shall not end yet. By his mere quiet power, on the minds of the now contestants, He could have either *saved* or *destroyed* the Union without a human contest. Yet the contest began. And having begun He could give the final victory to either side any day. Yet the contest proceeds.

¹ AD-P, ISLA. The bracketed date September [30?], 1862, is given to the meditation by Nicolay and Hay in the *Complete Works* (VIII, 52). According to their account, however, the fragment was written "in September, 1862, while his mind was burdened with the weightiest question of his life. . . . It was not written to be seen of men. . . ." (*Abraham Lincoln: A History,* VI, 341-42). If this comment means anything, September 30 is too late for the meditation. The "weightiest question" must be understood to refer to the issuing of the Preliminary Emancipation Proclamation on September 22, and it is evident that Lincoln's mind was made up on this question some time before the proclamation was actually issued. Quite possibly the meditation was written as early as September 2, at which time, following the Second Battle of Bull Run, Lincoln seems to have plumbed his lowest depths, and was reported by Attorney General Bates to have "seemed wrung by the bitterest anguish—said he felt almost ready to hang himself." (See note to Lincoln's order to Halleck dismissing McClellan, November 5, *infra*). In choosing an approximate date of September 2, rather than September 30, the editors have been prompted by these considerations of milieu.

To Henry W. Halleck¹

Washington, D.C., Sept. 3, 1862.

Ordered that the General-in-chief, Major General Halleck, immediately commence, and proceed with all possible dispatch, to organize an army for active operations, from all the material within, and coming within his control, independent of the forces he may deem necessary for the defense of Washington, when such active army shall take the field.

By order of the President:

EDWIN M. STANTON, Secretary of War.

Indorsement.

Copy delivered to Major General Halleck Sept. 3, 1862 at 10 p.m.

E. D. TOWNSEND Asst. Adjt. Genl

¹ Copy, DLC-RTL. This is a letterpress copy stamped "copied, War Records, 1866," and bearing the following notation: "The original is in President Lincoln's handwriting."

To Henry W. Halleck[1]

Gen. Halleck—please read this, & if he pleases, return it to me.
Sept. 3. 1862.   A. LINCOLN

[1] AES, DLC-RTL. Lincoln's endorsement is written on a letter from General
Erasmus D. Keyes, Yorktown, August 25, 1862, "Having given my opinion in
favor of removing the army from Harrison's Landing when your Excellency
was at that place, and afterwards by letter, I did not learn that my views were
in opposition to those of . . . McClellan and of most . . . the corps commanders until quite recently! . . . . As my corps . . . has been left behind on this
Peninsula, and as two brigades have been detached . . . to Genl. Dix, the main
object of this note is to ask Your Excellency to maintain me in a command
corresponding with my rank. . . ." (DLC-RTL).

To Henry W. Halleck[1]

Gen. Halleck, please see, Gen. Sigel.   A. LINCOLN
Sep. 4. 1862.

[1] ALS, IHi.

To Edwin M. Stanton[1]

September 4, 1862
Capt. Rives, mentioned within by Gen. John A. McClernand, is
the son of John C. Rives, of the Cong. Globe—said to be an excellent
officer, and I should be pleased to give the desired promotion, if
lawful, and consistent with the service.   A. LINCOLN
Sep. 4. 1862.

[1] AES, IHi. Lincoln's endorsement is written on a letter from General John
A. McClernand, Jackson, Tennessee, August 14, 1862, asking promotion of
Captain Wright Rives to colonel in order that he might appoint him "Chief of
my Staff." There is no record of the promotion.

To Edwin M. Stanton[1]

Hon. Sec. of War   Executive Mansion,
Sir—   Washington, Sep. 4. 1862.
There are special reasons, as I suppose, why James Bowen, of
New-York, should be appointed a Brigadier General. Please hear
the particulars from Gov. Seward. Yours truly   A. LINCOLN

[1] ALS copy, DLC-RTL. James Bowen, police commissioner of New York
City who recruited the Metropolitan Brigade with the assistance of the police
department, was appointed brigadier general of Volunteers October 11, 1862.

To James N. Brown[1]

Executive Mansion,
My Dear Sir   Washington, September 5, 1862.
I have the honor to acknowledge the reciept of your favor of the
24th August. I fully appreciate the patriotism and devotion which
dictated the tender of service of the Agricultural Society and have
referred the matter to the consideration of the Secretary of War. I
am very truly   Your Obt. Servt.   A. LINCOLN
    Jas. N. Brown Esq
       &c   &c   &c

[1] LS, owned by Mrs. Mary C. Harmon, Springfield, Illinois. On August 24,
1862, Lincoln's old friend James N. Brown wrote offering the services of the
Illinois State Agricultural Society in organizing one or two brigades of men
over forty-five years of age for special services. On September 5, John Hay
endorsed the letter referring it to the War Department and wrote the letter
of acknowledgment which Lincoln signed.

To Edwin M. Stanton[1]

September 5, 1862
With the concurrence, of the Secretary of War and Gen. Halleck,
I shall be very glad for Gen. Turchin to be given a Brigade, composed as desired, if convenient, and sent where active duty is now
required in Kentucky.   A. LINCOLN
    Sep. 5. 1862.

[1] AES, ORB. Lincoln's endorsement is written on a letter from Governor
Richard Yates, August 29, 1862, in support of an application of the Chicago
Union Defense and War Committee in behalf of General John B. Turchin,
who had been court-martialed and sentenced to dismissal from service because his brigade pillaged Athens, Alabama, in May, 1862. He remained in
service until October 4, 1864.

To Ginery Twichell[1]

Executive Mansion
My Dear Sir   Washington September 5. 1862
I have the honor to acknowledge the receipt from you of a large
amount of Hospital Stores, contributed for the use of the wounded
soldiers of the United States Army, by patriotic citizens of Brook-
line, Brighton, Newton, Watertown and Roxbury.
    Have the kindness, Sir, to accept my cordial thanks for your own
courtesy in the matter, and convey to the generous donors the assurance of my grateful appreciation of their efforts for the health

and comfort of those brave men, to whom we are all so deeply indebted. I have the honor to be Very respectfully Your Obt Servt A. LINCOLN

G. Twichell Esq
&c   &c   &c

[1] Copy, Office of Town Clerk, Watertown, Massachusetts. The original letter has not been found, but there seems to be little reason to question the copy preserved in the Town Clerk's office. Ginery Twichell was president of the Boston and Worcester Railroad and U.S. representative from Massachusetts 1867-1873.

To Henry W. Halleck[1]

Gen. Halleck, please see Gen. Burnside, and exercise his free discretion, on the subject Gen. B. will speak of.

Sep. 6. 1862. A. LINCOLN

[1] ALS, owned by Carlton J. Corliss, Washington, D.C. Burnside's "subject" was probably the assignment of Major General Reno to McDowell's command. AGO *Special Orders No. 224*, September 6, 1862, relieved McDowell "at his own request" from command of the Third Army Corps, and assigned Reno to replace him. (OR, I, XIX, II, 197). See Lincoln to McClellan, *infra*.

To George B. McClellan[1]

With entire respect, I must repeat that Gen. Halleck must control these questions. A. LINCOLN

Sep. 6. 1862.

[1] AES, DLC-McClellan Papers. Lincoln's endorsement is written on a "confidential" letter from McClellan, September 6, 1862, which referred to "a note I have just written to Genl Halleck asking that Genl Hooker may be assigned to the command of M'Dowell's Corps instead of Genl Reno. I ask this altho' an intimate friend & an admirer of Genl. Reno. Hooker has more experience with troops . . . to take Reno now is to break up Burnside's Corps the temporary command of which will fall to Reno the moment I have placed Burnside *in command of a wing*. I also asked that the order removing Porter[,] Franklin & Griffin from their commands may be suspended until I can get through with the present crisis. . . ." McClellan's *Special Orders No. 3*, September 6, 1862, assigned Hooker to the command instead of Reno (OR, I, XIX, II, 198). McDowell had asked for a court of inquiry as a result of criticism of his action at the Second Battle of Bull Run. Chase's *Diary* (pp. 66-67) quotes McDowell as saying on September 6, "I did not ask to be relieved —I only asked for a court."

Memorandum: Appointment of John Love[1]

Executive Mansion, Washington, Sep. 6, 1862.
To-day, Judge Hughes for Gov. Morton, recommends John Love, (West Pointer) for Brigadier Genl.

¹ AD, IHi. Judge James Hughes of Bloomington, Indiana, had resigned from the U.S. Court of Claims to practice law in Washington. Major John Love, inspector general of Indiana Volunteers and major general of the Indiana Legion, was not appointed brigadier general.

To Edwin D. Morgan¹

September 6, 1862

I hereby relieve Frederick Van Tine, from the effect of the discharged [*sic*] mentioned, so far as to authorize the Governor of New-York to give him a Military appointment if he sees fit.

Sep. 6. 1862. A. LINCOLN.

¹ AES, RPB. Lincoln's endorsement is written on a letter from Thurlow Weed, August 30, 1862, "Mr. Van tine, a soldier who has been doing his whole duty during the war, was dismissed for leaving his Regiment with a wound. Gov. Morgan desires to avail himself of the services of a good Officer but can not till he is relieved from the effect of his Discharge." Second Lieutenant Frederick Van Tine, Fifth New York Infantry, dishonorably discharged July 28, 1862, served as captain Company I, One Hundred Thirty-first New York Infantry, September 25, 1862 to July 26, 1865.

To Edwin M. Stanton¹

September 6, 1862

The indiscriminate dismissal of all the officers of Col. Mason's regiment, who surrendered Clarks'ville Tenn. may be wrong. Will the Sec. of War please see and hear Capt. Houck?

Sep. 6. 1862. A. LINCOLN.

¹ AES, DNA WR RG 94, Adjutant General Letters Received, P 872. Lincoln's endorsement is written on an envelope containing a letter from Samuel S. Cox to Lincoln, Columbus, Ohio, August 30, 1862, in behalf of Captain Solomon J. Houck, Seventy-first Ohio Volunteers, cashiered along with eleven fellow officers for having published a card stating that they had advised Colonel Rodney Mason to surrender Clarksville, Tennessee, on August 18, 1862. Lincoln's endorsement on Cox's letter, "Submitted to the Sec. of War," is also dated September 6. Stanton referred the case to Halleck, who on September 17 endorsed as follows: "It being shown that Capt S. J. Houck did *not* advise the surrender of Clarksville & that he signed the card justifying the surrender under a misapprehension of its contents, I respectfully recommend that the order of his dismissal be revoked." AGO *General Orders No. 133*, September 18, 1862, revoked "so much of General Orders, No. 120," as cashiered Houck.

To Jeremiah T. Boyle¹

Gen. Boyle: Washington City, D.C.
Louisville, Ky. Sep. 7 1862

Where is Gen. Bragg? What do you know on the subject?

A. LINCOLN

¹ ALS, RPB. General Boyle's reply received at 9 P.M. reported, "I do not know . . . but believe he is in Tennessee threatening Genl Buell. . . ." A second telegram received at 10:40 P.M. confirmed the first and conjectured that General Braxton Bragg would cross the Cumberland River above Nashville, and "as Buell crosses at that place he will move into Ky at Burkesville or Tompkinsville." (DLC-RTL). On September 8 at 11:30 A.M. Boyle telegraphed further that "Intelligent persons who left Nashville on Sixth Inst say that nothing is known of Bragg's army in Tennessee. There is some conjecture that Bragg may have joined the forces near Washington. My view of their plans is likely all wrong." (*Ibid.*).

To Don. C. Buell¹

Major Genl. Buell
Nashville, Tenn.

Washington City, D.C.
Sep. 7 1862 [7:20 P.M.]

What degree of certainty have you, that Bragg, with his command, is not now in the valley of the Shenandoah, Virginia?

A. LINCOLN

¹ ALS, RPB. This telegram is misdated September 8, 1862, in the *Complete Works* (VIII, 22). Buell replied September 10, 12 M., "Bragg is certainly this side of the Cumberland Mountains with his whole force, except what is in Kentucky under [E. Kirby] Smith. His movements will probably depend on mine. I expect that for the want of supplies I can neither follow him nor remain here. Think I must withdraw from Tennessee. I shall not abandon Tennessee while it is possible to hold on. Cut off effectually from supplies, it is impossible for me to operate in force where I am; but I shall endeavor to hold Nashville, and at the same time drive Smith out of Kentucky and hold my communications." (OR, I, XVI, II, 500).

To John E. Wool¹

Major General Wool
Baltimore–

Washington City, D.C.
Sep. 7, 1862

What about Harper's Ferry? Do you know any thing about it? How certain is your information about Bragg being in the valley of the Shenandoah?

A. LINCOLN

¹ ALS, RPB. At 7:30 A.M. Wool had telegraphed Halleck, "Colonel [George R.] Dennis, at Gettysburg, communicates the following . . . from undoubted authority: 'Brig. Gen. B. [T.] Johnson, with 5,000 infantry, came into Frederick about 12 m. yesterday. . . . Jackson followed with 25,000 at 2.30 p.m. . . . Johnson's brigade encamped a mile north of the city. . . . He said he would be there only one day; then for Pennsylvania or Baltimore. General Bragg was advancing up the Shenandoah Valley for Pennsylvania, with 40,000 troops. . . .'" (OR, I, XIX, II, 205). He replied to Lincoln's telegram at 8:05 P.M., "Your dispatch rec'd Genl Hill is menacing Harper's Ferry but with what force is not stated I think Harpers Ferry will be defended. Bragg is reported to be advancing through Valley of Shenandoah with forty thousand. . . . More than thirty thousand . . . were reported in & near Frederick yesterday with three . . . Batteries & more coming. Number of Cavalry not started [*sic*] & not included in above Estimate Rebels proclaimed that [*sic*] were going Either to Philadelphia or Baltimore All my information is second hand. . . ." (DLC-RTL).

To Horatio G. Wright[1]

Gen. Wright   Washington City, D.C.
Cincinnati, O.   Sep. 7 1862
Do you know, to any certainty, where Gen. Bragg is? May he
not be in Virginia?   A. LINCOLN

[1] ALS, RPB. Wright replied at 5:30 P.M., "Nothing reliable about Bragg all
rumors agree that he has crossed river above Chattanooga & a gentleman late
from Nashville reported his advance at Sparta Tenn. All intelligence coming
to me from the southward is very unreliable" (DLC-RTL).

To George B. McClellan[1]

Major General McClellan   Washington, D.C.,
Rockville, Md.   Sep. 8. 1862.
            How does it look now?   A. LINCOLN

[1] ALS, owned by Charles W. Olsen, Chicago, Illinois. McClellan replied at
5:30 P.M., "In reply to your dispatch of 5 o'clock this p.m., I have the honor
to state that General [Alfred] Pleasonton, at 4.20 p.m., reports from Dawson-
ville that his advance, within 3 miles of Poolesville [Copy, DLC-RTL, has
"Barnesville"], was fired on by artillery, the shells passing over them; also,
that infantry were moving out of the woods in force at that point. He also
heard the command under Colonel [John F.] Farnsworth, near Poolesville,
was fired on by artillery, but heard no report from Colonel Farnsworth. I do
not think, from the tenor of General Pleasonton's dispatches, that any great
force was seen, but he guards every approach carefully, and will keep me
fully advised. I will inform you of everything of importance that occurs. Burnside will be at Mechanicsville to-night. While I am writing, another dispatch
from General Pleasonton, dated 5.15 p.m., says Colonel Farnsworth has occupied Poolesville after a skirmish, in which the rebels brought up one gun.
Ours soon silenced it, and they retreated toward Barnesville, where there is
some force—not over 800. Six prisoners were taken, and some others wounded.
Two squadrons are in pursuit toward Barnesville, and have killed some of the
rebels. Our loss only 2 or 3 wounded." (OR, I, XIX, II, 210).

To Edwin M. Stanton[1]

If a Commissary is needed in the place indicated, let the appointment be made.   A. LINCOLN
Sep. 8. 1862.

[1] AES, IHi. Lincoln's endorsement is written on a letter from Rufus F.
Andrews, surveyor of customs at New York City, August 29, 1862, introducing
Reverend A. D. Gillette and recommending his son Lieutenant James Gillette
of the Third Maryland Infantry "now acting as Brigade Quartermaster of
Gen. [Henry] Prince's Brigade. A strong petition has been presented . . . to
have him appointed to the position which he is now temporarily filling. . . ."
Gillette was appointed commissary with rank of captain September 10, 1862.

To Edwin M. Stanton[1]

Sec. of War, please respond to this?   A. LINCOLN
Sep. 8. 1862.

[1] AES, NHi. Lincoln's endorsement is written on a telegram from Governor Hamilton R. Gamble, September 7, 1862, 10:15 P.M., asking authority for Colonel Clinton B. Fisk of the Thirty-third Missouri Infantry to "raise a Brigade to be commanded by himself." No reply has been found, but Fisk was appointed brigadier general of Volunteers on November 24, 1862.

To Edwin M. Stanton[1]

Hon. Sec. of War.   Executive Mansion,
Sir.   Washington, Sep. 9. 1862.
    Father O'Hara, of Syracuse, New-York, coming to me well recommended by Hon. Daniel S. Dickinson, & others, as working earnestly & efficiently for our cause, with the people of his county & church, asks that his brother, Daniel O.Hara, who also has spent much time and money in the cause, may be made, a Brigadier Quarter Master, or Commissary. If such an officer is needed, I should be glad for Mr. O.Hara to be appointed. Yours truly
                                          A. LINCOLN

[1] ALS, IHi. On the bottom of the second page of the letter Secretary Seward endorsed, "This is the very appointment that I desire most." Reverend James A. O'Hara was granted his request with the appointment of Daniel O'Hara on September 9 as captain and assistant quartermaster of Volunteers.

To Edwin M. Stanton[1]

Secretary of War, please respond to this; and do as well as possible in the premises.   A. LINCOLN
Sep. 9. 1862.

[1] AES, NHi. Lincoln's endorsement is written on a telegram from Henry T. Moore, president of the St. Louis Union Merchants Exchange, to Edward Bates, September 8, 1862, recommending Colonel Clinton B. Fisk for appointment as brigadier general. Concerning Fisk, see Lincoln to Stanton, September 8, *supra*.

To Thomas Webster[1]

Thomas Webster   Washington,
Philadelphia.   Sep. 9. 1862
    Your despatch received & referred to Gen. Halleck, who must control the questions presented. While I am not surprized at your

anxiety, I do not think you are in any danger. If half our troops were in Philadelphia, the enemy could take it, because he would not fear to leave the other half in his rear; but with the whole of them here, he dares not to leave them in his rear. A. LINCOLN

[1] ALS, RPB, Vice-chairman Thomas Webster of the Citizens Bounty Fund Committee of Philadelphia, telegraphed Lincoln on September 9, 1862, concerning "the exposed condition" of Philadelphia, and transmitting resolutions adopted by the committee. (OR, I, XIX, II, 230-31).

To George B. McClellan[1]

Major Genl. McClellan.   Washington City,
Rockville, Md.   Sep. 10. 10/15 A.M. 1862.
        How does it look now?   A. LINCOLN

[1] ALS, owned by Foreman M. Lebold, Chicago, Illinois. McClellan's telegram received at 1:40 P.M. is as follows: "In reply to your dispatch of the morning I have the honor to state that Genl Pleasanton at Barnesville reports that a movement of the Enemy last night is said to have been made across the Potomac from this side to the other Side. We shall know the truth of this rumor soon. Pleasanton is watching all the fords as high as Conrad's ferry & has pickets out to the mouth of the Monocacy He has sent out this morning to occupy Sugar Loaf Mountain from which a large extent of country can be seen in all directions.
"Genl Burnside had his scouts out last night to Ridgeville & within 3 miles of New Market No Enemy seen with the exception of a few pickets They were told that Stuart's Cavalry 5000 in number occupied New Market & that the main Rebel force under Jackson was still at Frederick. Burnside has sent a strong reconnaissance today to the mountain pass at Ridgeville I propose if the information I have rec'd proves reliable regarding the natural strength of this position to occupy it with a sufficient force to resist an advance of the Enemy in that direction. I have scouts & spies pushed forward in every direction shall soon be in possession of reliable & definite information The statements I get regarding the Enemy's forces that have crossed to this side range from 80 to 150,000. I am perfectly certain that none of the Enemy's troops have crossed the Potomac within the last 24 hours below the mouth of the Monocacy. I was informed last night by Genl Pleasanton that his information rendered it probable that Jackson's forces had advanced to New Market with Stuart's Cavalry at Urbana. In view of this I ordered the army forward this morning to the line along the high ridge from Ridgeville through Damascus[,] Clarksburg &c but the information subsequently obtained from Genl Burnside's Scouts that the mass of the Enemy was still at Frederick induced me to suspend the movement of the right wing until I could verify the truth of the reports by means of Burnside's reconnaissance in force today. My extreme left advances to Poolesville this morning. The work of reorganization & re-fitting is progressing very satisfactorily with the new heads of staff Dept's. Dispatch this instant rec'd from Genl Pleasanton dated Barnesville 10.30 a. m. says 'My Scouts occupy the ferry at the mouth of the Monocacy They found no Enemy except a few pickets on the other side of the Monocacy at Licksville. About 3 miles from that Stream it was reported there was a force of 6,000 men.' " (DLC-RTL).

To John A. McClernand[1]

Executive Mansion, Washington.

Major Genl. John A. McClernand,   Sep. 10. 1862.

Hon. W. J. Allen may be discharged if you advise it, on such terms as you may advise. Yours truly   A. LINCOLN

[1] ALS, IHi. On the inside pages of Lincoln's letter Allen wrote the following:

"Dear Genl   Washington Sept 10 1862
"I wrote you yesterday but was so feeble as to be scarcely able to write at all. On the first page of this sheet you will find a note from President Lincoln which he was kind enough to send me a few minutes since. He is so very busy that he cannot pay attention to Illinois matters
"I rely on you entirely and whatever you say will be observed by me to the death, my health is improving slightly though I am still confined to my room. Hoping to hear from you soon and regretting most deeply the trouble I am giving you I am as ever, Very Truly   WILLIAM J. ALLEN
"Maj Genl John A McClernand
"Springfield Ill
"P.S. If not taxing you too much and your decision is favorable to me, may I ask you to telegraph. Prest Lincoln says he will act upon a telegraph.
                        "WJA"

Allen had been elected to fill the vacancy in congress caused by John A. Logan's resignation, but, openly advocating the division of Illinois so that "Egypt" might secede and join the Confederacy, he was arrested and held prisoner first at Cairo and later in the "Old Capitol Prison" in Washington, where he was at this time. See Lincoln's authorization for Allen September 16, *infra.*

To Edwin M. Stanton[1]

Hon. Sec. of War.   Executive Mansion,
Sir.   Washington, Sep. 10. 1862.

Gen. Casey's report of arrival of troops is different from that of the Railroad agent. The agent reports to me this morning as follows, for yesterday.

133	N.Y.	950
11	Vt.	991
139.	N.Y.	1017
119.	Do	800
	Recruits for old Regs.	254
		4012

You see the difference   A. LINCOLN

[1] ALS, RPB. General Casey was in charge of recruiting and encamping new troops upon arrival at Washington. George S. Koontz, agent of the Baltimore

[413]

and Ohio Railroad, reported on arrival of new troops beginning on August 20 and continuing through September 13. Lincoln's figures are taken from Koontz's report of September 10 (DLC-RTL).

Approval of Contract
with Ambrose W. Thompson[1]

Executive Mansion, Washington, September 11, 1862.

The within contract is approved, and the Secretary of the Interior is directed to execute the same.   A. LINCOLN.

[1] Forty-seventh Congress, First Session, *House of Representatives Executive Document No. 46*, p. 136. The provisional contract between Ambrose W. Thompson for the Chiriqui Improvement Company and Caleb B. Smith for the United States, September 12, 1862, provided for colonization of land owned by Thompson in Chiriqui, designated Senator Pomeroy as special agent of the president, and contracted for purchase of coal to be produced by the colony for the use of the Navy. See note to Lincoln's Address on Colonization, August 14, *supra*.

To Andrew G. Curtin[1]

His Excellency Andrew G. Curtin,   War Department,
Governor of Pennsylvania,   Washington, D.C.,
Harrisburg, Pa.:   September 11, 1862.

Sir: The application made to me by your adjutant-general for authority to call out the militia of the State of Pennsylvania has received careful consideration. It is my anxious desire to afford, as far as possible, the means and powers of the Federal Government to protect the State of Pennsylvania from invasion by the rebel forces, and since, in your judgment, the militia of the State are required, and have been called upon by you, to organize for home defense and protection, I sanction the call that you have made, and will receive them into the service and pay of the United States to the extent that they can be armed, equipped, and usefully employed. The arms and equipments now belonging to the General Government will be needed for the troops called out for the national armies, so that arms can only be furnished for the quota of militia furnished by the draft of nine-months' men, heretofore ordered. But as arms may be supplied by the militia under your call, these, with the 30,000 in your arsenal, will probably be sufficient for the purpose contemplated by your call. You will be authorized to provide such equipments as may be required, according to the regulations of the United States service, which, upon being turned over to the United States Quartermaster's Department, will be paid for at regulation prices, or the rates allowed by the department for such articles. Railroad transportation will also be paid for, as in other cases. Such general officers will be supplied as the exigencies of the service will permit. Yours, truly, A. LINCOLN.

¹ OR, III, II, 538-39. Alexander L. Russell was adjutant general of Pennsylvania. No further correspondence concerning this matter has been found.

To Andrew G. Curtin¹

Hon. A. G. Curtin Washington, D.C.,
Harrisburg, Penn Sep. 11. 12.M. 1862.

Please tell me at once, what is your latest news from, or towards Hagerstown, or of the enemies movements in any direction.

A. LINCOLN

¹ ALS, RPB. Curtin replied at 3:30 P.M., "Your dispatch of 12 m. reached me at 2 p.m. At 9 o'clock this morning the rebel cavalry occupied Hagerstown. At 12 their pickets were within half a mile of the Pennsylvania line at Greencastle. It is the advance cavalry of Jackson's column. . . . From indications the people of Greencastle expect a dash on that place this afternoon. . . ." (OR, I, XIX, II, 268).

To George B. McClellan¹

Executive Mansion, Washington,
Major Gen. McClellan Sep. 11. 6.P.M. 1862.

This is explanatory. If Porter, Heintzelman, and Sigel were sent you, it would sweep everything from the other side of the river; because the new troops have have [sic] been distributed among them, as I understand. Porter reports himself twenty one thousand strong, which can only be by the addition of new troops. He is ordered to-night to join you as quick as possible. I am for sending you all that can be spared, & I hope others can follow Porter very soon. A. LINCOLN

¹ ALS, NN. At 3:45 P.M. McClellan telegraphed Halleck for "all the troops you can spare from Washington, particularly Porter's, Heintzelman's, Sigel's, and all the other old troops." (OR, I, XIX, II, 253).

To Caleb B. Smith¹

I will see Mr. Ross at 9 A.M. to-morrow, if he calls.

Sep. 11, 1862 A. LINCOLN.

¹ Thomas A. Madigan, A Catalogue of Lincolniana (1929), No. 37. According to the catalog description this endorsement is on Secretary Smith's letter asking Lincoln to see Ross. John Ross, chief of the Cherokees, brought a letter

of introduction from Mark W. Delahay, August 21, 1862 (DLC-RTL). Loyal to the Union, the Cherokees sought protection in Kansas when other tribes were stirred up by Confederate agents. See further Lincoln's letter to Ross September 25, *infra*.

To Edwin M. Stanton[1]

Hon. Secretary of War   Executive Mansion
My dear Sir   Sept. 11, 1862

I have two long letters from Mr. Belmont, and the above extract is the only part in either, which can be construed to alude to you. I will show you the letters if you wish. Yours as ever

                                         A. LINCOLN

[1] ALS, NHi. August Belmont's twelve-page letter of September 4, 1862, communicating views of influential parties in England and concerned with the danger of foreign recognition of the Confederacy following military defeat, is in the Nicolay Papers (DLC). The extract from it which Lincoln enclosed to Stanton (not in Lincoln's handwriting) reads as follows:

"I think that new vigor and energy would be infused into our military operations, and the exhausted ranks of our army would be speedily filled, if you would place General Halleck at the head of the Department as Secretary of War, and appoint General McClellan Commander-in-Cheif of the United States forces east of the Allegheny mountains, which would place the operations in Virginia, Washington and Maryland, under his sole control."

To Jeremiah T. Boyle[1]

Gen. Boyle–   Washington,
Louisville, Ky.   Sep. 12. 1862

Your despatch of last evening received. Where is the enemy which you dread in Louisville? How near to you? What is Gen. Gilbert's opinion? With all possible respect for you, I must think Gen. Wright's military opinion is the better. He is as much responsible for Louisville, as for Cincinnati. Gen. Halleck telegraphed him on this very subject yesterday; and I telegraph him now; but for us here, to control him there on the ground would be a Babel of confusion which would be utterly ruinous. Where do you understand Buell to be? and what is he doing?   A. LINCOLN

[1] ALS, RPB. General Boyle telegraphed on September 11, 9:15 P.M. that "Genl Wrights withdrawing the troops from this place and sending to Cincinnati is creating a panic and will ruin the State." (DLC-RTL). Major General Charles C. Gilbert telegraphed Lincoln on September 12 at 10:30 A.M., "The Enemy must destroy Buells army . . . before attempting the capture of Cincinnati If we secure Buells line of communication with this place an attack on Cincinnati in force is an impossibility unless by the way of the Kanawha and Western Va. . . ." (DLC-RTL). Boyle replied to Lincoln's telegram at 10 P.M., "I expect no Enemy here soon. If Bragg is in the State when [E.

Kirby] Smith and he unites they may move on Louisville. Genl Gilberts opinion may be inferred from dispatch he sent you. I believe he concurs with me   I have no idea there is any considerable force of the Enemy near Cincinnati. Bragg is reported already in the State with large force on the lines I indicated some days ago. I do not believe it. There is some force but it is not large   Bragg may enter soon   Buell is at Nashville. Part of his Army are at Bowling Green. [Alexander M.] McCooks Division which was on this side the Cumberland, now is reported to have recrossed to the Nashville side. I have heard nothing from Buell   My information is from Col Bruce at Bowling Green   I concur with you that Genl Wrights military opinion is better than I ever thought mine to be but I can know facts as well as the ablest military man   There are many reports   Deserters from Buckner report him with ten thousand 10000 men near Tompkinsville. Bragg reported at Burkesville and Columbia advancing into the centre of the State. I do not believe any of the reports of an early attack at any point. They can and I hope will be driven out before they attack." (DLC-RTL). See Lincoln to Wright, *infra*.

To Andrew G. Curtin[1]

Hon. A. G. Curtin   Washington, D.C.,
Harrisburg, Penn.   Sep. 12. 10/35 [A.M.] 1862.

Your despatch asking for eighty thousand disciplined troops to be sent to Pennsylvania is received. Please consider. We have not to exceed eighty thousand disciplined troops, properly so called, this side of the mountains, and most of them, with many of the new regiments, are now close in the rear of the enemy supposed to be invading Pennsylvania. Start half of them to Harrisburg, and the enemy will turn upon and beat the remaining half, and then reach Harrisburg before the part going there, and beat it too when it comes. The best possible security for Pennsylvania is putting the strongest force possible into the enemies rear.   A LINCOLN

[1] ALS, RPB. Governor Curtin's telegram of September 11, 8 P.M., asked for 80,000 troops and estimated enemy forces as not less than 120,000. His reply to Lincoln's telegram was received at 4:15 P.M., "Your message received   Reasons for not sending force entirely satisfactory. We are doing all that is possible to throw forces into the Valley to check any movement the Rebels may attempt in this direction. I have advices that Jackson is crossing Potomac at Williamsport & probably the whole Rebel army will be drawn from Maryland" (DLC-RTL).

To Alexander Henry[1]

Hon. Alexr. Henry   Washington City, D.C.
Philadelphia.   Sep. 12. 1862

Yours of to-day received. Gen. Halleck has made the best provision he can for Generals in Pennsylvania. Please do not be offended when I assure you that, in my confident belief, Philadelphia is in no danger. Gov. Curtin has just telegraphed me   "I have advices that Jackson is crossing the Potomac at Williamsport & probably

[417]

the whole rebel Army will be drawn from Maryland." At all events Philadelphia is more than a hundred and fifty miles from Hagerstown, and could not be reached by the rebel Army in ten days, if no hinderance was interposed. A LINCOLN

1 ALS, RPB. Henry telegraphed from Philadelphia at 4 P.M. on September 12 that "The Emergency demands the assignment of a compe[te]nt Genl to take command in this City." (DLC-RTL).

To George B. McClellan[1]

Major General McClellan Washington City, D.C.
Clarksburg, Md. Sep. 12. 4.A.M. 1862
How does it look now? A. LINCOLN

1 ALS, DLC. No reply to this telegram has been found.

To George B. McClellan[1]

Washington City, D.C., September 12, 1862– 5:45 P.M.

Major-General McClellan: Governor Curtin telegraphs me:

"I have advices that Jackson is crossing the Potomac at Williamsport, and probably the whole rebel army will be drawn from Maryland."

Receiving nothing from Harper's Ferry or Martinsburg to-day, and positive information from Wheeling that the line is cut, corroborates the idea that the enemy is recrossing the Potomac. Please do not let him get off without being hurt. A. LINCOLN.

1 OR, I, XIX, II, 270; copy, DLC-McClellan Papers. The received copy is dated 6 P.M. instead of 5:45. McClellan had telegraphed Halleck at 10 A.M., 5:30 P.M., and 6 P.M. (ibid., 270-72). He replied to Lincoln at 9 P.M. as follows: "You will have learned by my telegrams to Genl Halleck that we hold Frederick & the line of the Monocacy. I have taken all possible means to communicate with Harper's Ferry so that I may send to its relief if necessary. Cavalry are in pursuit of the Westminster party with orders to catch them at all hazards   The main body of my cavalry & horse arty are ordered after the enemys main column with orders to check its march as much as possible that I may overtake it. If Harpers Ferry is still in our possession I think I can save the garrison if they fight at all. If the Rebels are really marching into Penna. I shall soon be up with them. My apprehension is that they may make for Williamsport & get across the River before I can catch them." (DLC-RTL). McClellan's mention of "the Westminster party" refers to a Confederate cavalry raid on that place, September 11.

To Caleb B. Smith[1]

Executive Mansion, September 12, 1862.

The Department of the Interior is charged, under the direction of the President, with the execution of the 11th section of the act

[418]

for the release of certain persons held to service or labor in the District of Columbia, approved April 16, 1862; and that portion of section 1 of the act making supplemental appropriations for sundry civil expenses, approved July 16, 1862, which appropriates $500,-000 for the colonization of certain persons of African descent.

ABRAHAM LINCOLN.

[1] Thirty-ninth Congress, First Session, *Senate Executive Document No. 55*, p. 12. See Lincoln's Approval of Contract, September 11, *supra*.

To Horatio G. Wright[1]

Major Gen. Wright   Washington,
Cincinnati, O.   Sep. 12. 1862

I am being appealed [to] from Louisville against your withdrawing troops from that place. While I can not pretend to judge of the propriety of what you are doing, you would much oblige me by furnishing me a rational answer to make to the Governor and others at Louisville.   A. LINCOLN

[1] ALS, RPB. In addition to General Boyle's protest (*supra*), Lincoln had received communications from Governor Robinson and numerous other influential Kentuckians. General Wright replied on September 13, 10 P.M., "Your dispatch of yesterday by some mistake was not laid before me. I see it now for the first time. I have no intention of abandoning Louisville or of leaving it without adequate protection. Two regiments only were withdrawn, and that at a time when Cincinnati was seriously threatened, leaving at Louisville about thirty regiments and more than thirty guns. . . . Louisville has not been threatened at all, while Kirby Smith's forces did approach to within 8 miles of Cincinnati. He is now retreating from before the force hastily collected." (OR, I, XVI, II, 513).

Reply to Emancipation Memorial Presented by Chicago Christians of All Denominations[1]

September 13, 1862

"The subject presented in the memorial is one upon which I have thought much for weeks past, and I may even say for months. I am approached with the most opposite opinions and advice, and that

[1] Chicago *Tribune*, September 23, and *National Intelligencer*, September 26, 1862. Reverend William W. Patton and Reverend John Dempster composed the delegation which presented the president with a memorial in favor of national emancipation adopted by a public meeting of Christians of all denominations held in Bryan Hall, Chicago, on September 7. The delegation also presented a similar memorial in German signed by German citizens of Chicago. On September 20 following their visit to Washington, the delegates reported to a meeting in Bryan Hall. This report dated September 21, and signed by Patton and Dempster provides the present text, which includes all of Lincoln's remarks as quoted.

by religious men, who are equally certain that they represent the Divine will. I am sure that either the one or the other class is mistaken in that belief, and perhaps in some respects both. I hope it will not be irreverent for me to say that if it is probable that God would reveal his will to others, on a point so connected with my duty, it might be supposed he would reveal it directly to me; for, unless I am more deceived in myself than I often am, it is my earnest desire to know the will of Providence in this matter. *And if I can learn what it is I will do it!* These are not, however, the days of miracles, and I suppose it will be granted that I am not to expect a direct revelation. I must study the plain physical facts of the case, ascertain what is possible and learn what appears to be wise and right. The subject is difficult, and good men do not agree. For instance, the other day four gentlemen of standing and intelligence (naming one or two of the number) from New York called, as a delegation, on business connected with the war; but, before leaving, two of them earnestly beset me to proclaim general emancipation, upon which the other two at once attacked them! You know, also, that the last session of Congress had a decided majority of anti-slavery men, yet they could not unite on this policy. And the same is true of the religious people. Why, the rebel soldiers are praying with a great deal more earnestness, I fear, than our own troops, and expecting God to favor their side; for one of our soldiers, who had been taken prisoner, told Senator Wilson, a few days since, that he met with nothing so discouraging as the evident sincerity of those he was among in their prayers. But we will talk over the merits of the case.

"What *good* would a proclamation of emancipation from me do, especially as we are now situated? I do not want to issue a document that the whole world will see must necessarily be inoperative, like the Pope's bull against the comet! Would *my word* free the slaves, when I cannot even enforce the Constitution in the rebel States? Is there a single court, or magistrate, or individual that would be influenced by it there? And what reason is there to think it would have any greater effect upon the slaves than the late law of Congress, which I approved, and which offers protection and freedom to the slaves of rebel masters who come within our lines? Yet I cannot learn that that law has caused a single slave to come over to us. And suppose they could be induced by a proclamation of freedom from me to throw themselves upon us, *what should we do with them?* How can we feed and care for such a multitude? Gen. Butler wrote me a few days since that he was issuing more rations to the slaves who have rushed to him than to all the white troops under his command. They *eat*, and that is all, though it is true Gen. Butler is feeding the whites also by the thousand; for it nearly amounts to a famine there. If, now, the pressure of the war should call off our forces from New Orleans to defend some other point, what is to prevent the masters from reducing the blacks to slavery again; for I am told that whenever the rebels take any black prisoners, free or slave, they immediately auction them off! They did so with those they took from a boat that was aground in the Tennessee river a few days ago. And then *I am very ungenerously attacked for it*! For instance, when, after the late battles at and near Bull Run, an expedition went out from Washington under a flag of truce to bury the dead and bring in the wounded, and the rebels seized the blacks who went along to help and sent them into slavery, Horace Greeley said in his paper that the Government would probably do nothing about it. What *could* I do? [Here your delegation suggested that this was a gross outrage on a flag of truce, which covers and protects all over which it waves, and that whatever he could do if *white* men had been similarly detained he *could* do in this case.]

"Now, then, tell me, if you please, what possible result of good would follow the issuing of such a proclamation as you desire? Understand, I raise no objections against it on legal or constitutional grounds; for, as commander-in-chief of the army and navy, in time of war, I suppose I have a right to take any measure which may best subdue the enemy. Nor do I urge objections of a moral nature, in view of possible consequences of insurrection and massacre at the South. I view the matter as a practical war measure, to be decided upon according to the advantages or disadvantages it may offer to the suppression of the rebellion."

Thus invited, your delegation very willingly made reply to the following effect; it being understood that a portion of the remarks were intermingled by the way of conversation with those of the President just given.

We observed (taking up the President's ideas in order) that good men indeed differed in their opinions on this subject; nevertheless *the truth was somewhere,* and it was a matter of solemn moment for him to ascertain it; that we had not been so wanting in respect, alike to ourselves and to him, as to come a thousand miles to bring merely *our opinion* to be set over against the *opinion* of other parties; that the memorial contained facts, principles, and arguments which appealed to the intelligence of the President and to his faith in Divine Providence; that he could not deny that the Bible denounced oppression as one of the highest of crimes, and

[421]

threatened Divine judgments against nations that practice it; that our country had been exceedingly guilty in this respect, both at the North and South; that our just punishment has come by a slave-holder's rebellion; that the virus of secession is found wherever the virus of slavery extends, and no farther; so that there is the amplest reason for expecting to avert Divine judgments by putting away the sin, and for hoping to remedy the national troubles by striking at their cause.

We observed, further, that we freely admitted the probability, and even the certainty, that God would reveal the path of duty to the President as well as to others, provided he sought to learn it in the appointed way; but, as according to his own remark, Providence wrought by means and not miraculously, it might be, God would use the suggestions and arguments of other minds to secure that result. We felt the deepest personal interest in the matter as of national concern, and would fain aid the thoughts of our President by communicating the convictions of the Christian community from which we came, with the ground upon which they were based.

That it was true he could not now enforce the Constitution at the South; but we could see in that fact no reason whatever for not proclaiming emancipation, but rather the contrary. The two appealed to different classes; the latter would aid, and in truth was necessary to re-establish the former; and the two could be made operative together as fast as our armies fought their way southward; while we had yet to hear that he proposed to abandon the Constitution because of the present difficulty of enforcing it.

As to the inability of Congress to agree on this policy at the late session, it was quite possible, in view of subsequent events, there might be more unanimity at another meeting. The members have met their constituents and learned of marvellous conversions to the wisdom of emancipation, especially since late reverses have awakened thought as to the extreme peril of the nation, and made bad men as well as good men realize that we have to deal with God in this matter. Men of the most opposite previous views were now uniting in calling for this measure.

That to proclaim emancipation would secure the sympathy of Europe and the whole civilized world, which now saw no other reason for the strife than national pride and ambition, an unwillingness to abridge our domain and power. No other step would be so potent to prevent foreign intervention.

Furthermore, it would send a thrill through the entire North, firing every patriotic heart, giving the people a glorious principle for which to suffer and to fight, and assuring them that the work was to be so thoroughly done as to leave our country free forever from danger and disgrace in this quarter.

We added, that when the proclamation should become widely known (as the law of Congress has *not* been) it would withdraw the slaves from the rebels, leaving them without laborers, and giving us *both laborers and soldiers.* That the difficulty experienced by Gen. Butler and other Generals arose from the fact that *half-way measures could never avail.* It is the inherent vice of half-way measures that they create as many difficulties as they remove. It is folly merely to receive and feed the slaves. They should be welcomed and fed, and then, according to Paul's doctrine, that they who eat must work, be made to labor and to fight for their liberty and ours. With such a policy the blacks would be no incumbrance and their rations no waste. In this respect we should follow the ancient maxim, and learn of the enemy. What the rebels most fear is what we should be most prompt to do; and what they most fear is evident from the hot haste with which, on the first day of the present session of the Rebel Congress, bills were introduced threatening terrible vengeance if we used the blacks in the war.

The President rejoined from time to time in about these terms:

"I admit that slavery is the root of the rebellion, or at least its *sine qua non.* The ambition of politicians may have instigated them to act, but they would have been impotent without slavery as their instrument. I will also concede that emancipation would help us in Europe, and convince them that we are incited by something more than ambition. I grant further that it would help *somewhat* at the North, though not so much, I fear, as you and those you represent imagine. Still, some additional strength would be added in that way to the war. And then unquestionably it would weaken the rebels by drawing off their laborers, which is of great importance. But I am not so sure we could do much with the blacks. If we were to arm them, I fear that in a few weeks the arms would be in the hands of the rebels; and indeed thus far we have not had arms enough to equip our white troops. I will mention another thing, though it meet only your scorn and contempt: There are fifty thousand bayonets in the Union armies from the Border Slave States. It would be a serious matter if, in consequence of a proclamation such as you desire, they should go over to the rebels. I do not think they all would—not so many indeed as a year ago, or as six months ago—not so many to-day as yesterday. Every day increases their Union feeling. They are also getting their pride enlisted, and want to beat the rebels. Let me say one thing more: I

think you should admit that we already have an important principle to rally and unite the people in the fact that constitutional
government is at stake. This is a fundamental idea, going down
about as deep as any thing."

We answered that, being fresh from the people, we were naturally more hopeful than himself as to the necessity and probable
effect of such a proclamation. The value of constitutional government is indeed a grand idea for which to contend; but the people
know that *nothing else has put constitutional government in danger but slavery;* that the toleration of that aristocratic and despotic
element among our free institutions was the inconsistency that had
nearly wrought our ruin and caused free government to appear a
failure before the world, and therefore the people demand emancipation to preserve and perpetuate constitutional government. Our
idea would thus be found to go deeper than this, and to be armed
with corresponding power. ("Yes," interrupted Mr. Lincoln, "that
is the true ground of our difficulties.") That a proclamation of
general emancipation, "giving Liberty and Union" as the national
watch-word, would rouse the people and rally them to his support
beyond any thing yet witnessed—appealing alike to conscience,
sentiment, and hope. He must remember, too, that present mani-
festations are no idex of what would then take place. If the leader
will but utter a trumpet call the nation will respond with patriotic
ardor. No one can tell the power of the right word from the right
man to develop the latent fire and enthusiasm of the masses. ("I
know it," exclaimed Mr. Lincoln.) That good sense must of course
be exercised in drilling, arming, and using black as well as white
troops to make them efficient; and that in a scarcity of arms it was
at least worthy of inquiry whether it were not wise to place a portion of them in the hands of those nearest to the seat of the rebellion and able to strike the deadliest blow.

That in case of a proclamation of emancipation we had no fear
of serious injury from the desertion of Border State troops. The
danger was greatly diminished, as the President had admitted. But
let the desertions be what they might, the increased spirit of the
North would replace them two to one. One State alone, if necessary, would compensate the loss, were the whole 50,000 to join the
enemy. The struggle has gone too far, and cost too much treasure
and blood, to allow of a partial settlement. Let the line be drawn
at the same time between freedom and slavery, and between loyalty and treason. The sooner we know who are our enemies the
better.

In bringing our interview to a close, after an hour of earnest and frank discussion, of which the foregoing is a specimen, Mr. Lincoln remarked: "Do not misunderstand me, because I have mentioned these objections. They indicate the difficulties that have thus far prevented my action in some such way as you desire. I have not decided against a proclamation of liberty to the slaves, but hold the matter under advisement. And I can assure you that the subject is on my mind, by day and night, more than any other. Whatever shall appear to be God's will I will do. I trust that, in the freedom with which I have canvassed your views, I have not in any respect injured your feelings."

To Cassius M. Clay[1]

Executive Mansion, Washington,

Major-General C. M. Clay—   Sept. 14, 1862.

Dear Sir:—You need not proceed to New Orleans until you hear from me again. I have an understanding with the Secretary of War and General Halleck on this subject. Yours truly,   A. LINCOLN.

[1] *The Life of Cassius Marcellus Clay* (1886) I, 315. Clay wrote Lincoln on September 9, 1862, "As the emergencies of the country are pressing, I have concluded to go at once into the field. In doing so, I *don't mean to waive* my right to avail myself of your kind promise to allow me—should Mr. Cameron resign or be recalled—to return to St. Petersburg . . . as your minister." (DLC-RTL). On September 12, AGO *Special Orders No. 235* assigned him to duty at New Orleans, but when Clay took the order to Lincoln on September 14, Lincoln, according to Clay's report, "immediately sat down and wrote the following counter order [as above]"

To Horatio G. Wright[1]

"Cypher"

Gen. Wright   Washington, D.C.,
Cincinnati, O.   Sep. 14. 1862.

Thanks for your despatch. Can you not pursue the retreating enemy, and relieve Cumberland Gap?   A. LINCOLN

[1] ALS, RPB. See Lincoln to Wright, September 12, *supra.* Wright's telegram of September 13 was received at Washington on September 14, 1:50 A.M.

To Jesse K. Dubois[1]

Hon. J. K. Dubois   Washington, D.C.,
Springfield, Ills.   Sep. 15. 3. PM 1862.

I now consider it safe to say that Gen. McClellan has gained a great victory over the great rebel army in Maryland between

[425]

Fredericktown and Hagerstown. He is now pursuing the flying foe.   A. LINCOLN

[1] ALS, RPB. Governor Richard Yates replied at midnight: "Your despatch to Col Dubois has filled our people with the wildest joy. Salutes are being fired & our citizens are relieved from a fearful state of suspense. We thank you for the welcome news." (DLC-RTL).

To George B. McClellan[1]

Washington, D.C.,
Major General McClellan.   Sep. 15, 2/45 1862.
Your despatches of to-day received. God bless you, and all with you. Destroy the rebel army, if possible.   A. LINCOLN

[1] ALS, IHi. McClellan's ebullient dispatches to Halleck at 8 A.M. reported "the Enemy . . . in a perfect panic & Gen Lee last night stated publicly that he must admit they had been shockingly whipped," (DLC-RTL); and at 10 A.M. reported General Lee wounded and "It is stated that Lee gives his loss as 15000." (*Ibid.*). The prelude to Antietam was somewhat exaggerated. The battles at South Mountain and Crampton's Gap, Maryland, were, however, definite Union victories.

To Edwin M. Stanton[1]

September 15, 1862
I wish Capt. E. G. Beckwith, to be a Paymaster in the Army, this taking date, as of July 4 1862—the day on which I recommended & which recommendation is lost.   A. LINCOLN
Sep. 15. 1862

[1] AES, RPB. Lincoln's endorsement is written on a letter from Senator James W. Nesmith, July 1, 1862, recommending that "Capt Edward G. Beckwith, of the 3rd. Artillery . . . who has served with great distinction on the staff of Maj. Genl. Banks" be promoted to major and made a paymaster. Further endorsements indicate that the appointment was made out November 29, 1862, and "sent to the Secretary but not signed." Beckwith's appointment dating from February 8, 1864, finally reached the Senate on May 4 and was confirmed on May 18, 1864.

To Edwin M. Stanton[1]

Secretary of War please respond to these.   A. LINCOLN
Sep. 15, 1862.

[1] AES, NHi. Lincoln's endorsement is written on a telegram from Governor James F. Robinson, Louisville, September 15, 10 A.M., complaining of "irregular & changing system of Military arrests" and suggesting that "it should all be

subordinate to the Executive of the State." A similar telegram from Joshua F. Speed was sent at the same time. On the same day Stanton ordered General Jeremiah T. Boyle to "abstain from making any more arrests except upon the order of the Governor of Kentucky." (OR, I, XVI, II, 519).

Authorization for William J. Allen[1]

September 16, 1862

Hon. William J. Allen is hereby authorized to report himself to Major General John A. McClernand at Springfield, Illinois, or wherever else he may be found, and to be subject to his, the General's, direction.   A. LINCOLN

Sept. 16. 1862.

[1] AES, IHi. See Lincoln to McClernand, September 10, *supra*. Lincoln's endorsement is written on a letter from McClernand, Springfield, September 12, 1862, as follows:

"I feel it to be my duty to enclose you the accompanying communication.

"Old associations emphasise the appeal and prompt me to urge Mr. Allen's discharge.

"I will vouch for him under the circumstances, and pledge his best endeavors both as a citizen and Representative of the People, in behalf of the Government and Union, and will accordingly so advise him."

To Andrew G. Curtin[1]

Gov. Curtin   Washington, D.C.,
Harrisburg: Pa.   Sep. 16. 12.M. 1862.

What do you hear from Gen. McClellan's army? We have nothing from him to-day.   A. LINCOLN

[1] ALS, RPB. Curtin replied, "We have no definite news. Our telegraph operator at Hagerstown reports that a battle is progressing near the Potomac, between Sharpsburg and Williamsport. What success did McClellan meet with yesterday? We have not heard, and should know, in order to use our forces that are now being pushed into Maryland." (OR, I, XIX, II, 310).

To Andrew G. Curtin[1]

Gov. Curtin   Executive Mansion, Washington,
Harrisburg   Sep. 16. 2/25 P.M. 1862.

Since telegraphing you, despatch came from Gen. McClellan, dated, 7 o'clock this morning. Nothing of importance happened with him yesterday. This morning he was up with the enemy at Sharpsburg, and was waiting for heavy fog to rise.   A. LINCOLN

[427]

[1] ALS, RPB. In addition to the information relayed by Lincoln's telegram to Curtin, McClellan's telegram to Halleck promised an attack "as soon as situation of Enemy is developed." (DLC-RTL).

To Oliver P. Morton[1]

Gov. O. P. Morton,   Washington, D.C.
Indianapolis, Ia.   Sep. 17, 1862.

I have received your despatch in regard to recommendations of Gen. Wright. I have received no such despatch from him—at least, not that I can remember.

I refer yours for Gen. Halleck's consideration.

A. LINCOLN

[1] ALS, RPB. Neither Governor Morton's dispatch nor the dispatch from General Wright has been found.

To Edwin M. Stanton[1]

September 17, 1862

The writer of this, is a personal acquaintance of mine who has been on duty at New-Orleans as a Quarter Master. I have thought it not improper that the Sec. of War should see his suggestions.

Sep. 17. 1862.   A. LINCOLN

[1] AES, RPB. Lincoln's endorsement is written on a letter from John W. Shaffer, as follows:

"His Excellency   New York
"A Lincoln   Sept 14 1862

"Dear Sir. I endeavoured to see Mr Stanton yesterday but he was out and I was compelled to leave without seeing him

"I will return in a few days from the west and see you before starting to New Orleans. I write you this letter for the reason that I feel deeply impressed with the knowledge that this negro question has and will continue to cause you great trouble

"As I told you yesterday the great question of what disposition is to be made of them and w[h]ether they can be made self supporting must be decided in the Department of the Gulf and I believe Butler is more likely to succeed than any man I know.

"It is reported in New York that Genl Clay goes to New Orleans. Allow me to make a suggestion in that connection. Genl Butler is not much of a soldier, and needs to be surrounded with good officers. And at present with the exception of Lieut Weitzell (who I hope has or will be made a Brigadier) he has not near him an officer who is competent to advise him in Military Matters, Arnold being at Pensacola.

"You know Mr Lincoln that whatever good qualities Genl Clay may possess he has not the elements of a *prudent* and skilfull General. Genl Butler listens much to those around him (who have had experience on proper Military education) on Military Matters and I earnestly hope for the success of the department that none but army officers of known ability will be sent him, he then can trust his army in the field to them and he take charge of the rebels & Negroes

"Did I not feel deeply the importance to the country and to you of what I yesterday said to you and what I now write I would not trouble you with this letter

"I Remain most respectfully Your Friend and Obt Servt
                                                    "J Wilson Shaffer"

To William A. Hammond[1]

Executive Mansion, Washington,
Surgeon General.   Sep. 18. 1862.

Please ascertain for me whether Isaac Schneider, of the 100th. New-York Regiment, and now at the Douglas hospital is likely soon, or ever to be fit for duty again. He was wounded at Fair Oaks, as I understand; is but sixteen years old, and I am appealed to to [sic] discharge him.   A. LINCOLN

[1] ALS-P, ISLA. Hammond endorsed as follows: "Respectfully referred to Assist. Surg. Webster U.S.A for immediate report." No further record has been found.

To Edwin M. Stanton[1]

Executive Mansion, Washington,
Honorable Secretary of War.   September 18, 1862.

Sir: The attached paper is said to contain a list of civilians imprisoned at Salisbury, N.C. Please preserve it. Yours, truly,
                                                    A. LINCOLN.

[1] OR, II, IV, 528. The accompanying paper lists fifty-six names.

To Caleb B. Smith[1]

To the Honorable Caleb Smith   Washington City,
    Secretary of the Interior   September 19th 1862.

It being reported to me by the Secretary of War that the building now occupied as the United States Penitentiary, in the District of Columbia, is absolutely necessary to be used for military purposes as an Arsenal, you are hereby authorized and directed to turn it over, as speedily as possible, to the War Department with its premises and appurtenances.

The prisoners confined therein, you will cause to be transported securely, with suitable escort, to such place or places within the

United States, as you may be able to provide for their maintenance and imprisonment during the period of their sentences, and until discharged by its expiration. And for so doing this shall be your warrant.   ABRAHAM LINCOLN

[1] Copy, DNA WR RG 156, Office of Chief of Ordnance, WD 1637 (see Z). The prisoners were transferred to the old county jail at Albany, New York (*National Intelligencer*, September 23, 1862).

To Edwin M. Stanton[1]

Hon. Sec. of War   Executive Mansion, Washington,
Dear Sir   Sep. 19. 1862.

Mr. Henry G. Ward, accredited Agent for the government of China, represents to me that he purchased three hundred and thirty six barrels of powder at New-York, which he is prevented from shipping by your order. The preventing of the shipping of powder may be a military necessity with us at this time, and if so, it can be no just ground of offence to any other government, as I suppose. But should we not, in such case, tender the purchase money to the agent so that he can use it elsewhere? Yours truly

A LINCOLN

[1] ALS, NHi. No reply from Stanton or further record has been found.

To Edwin M. Stanton[1]

If another Commissary is needed, let the within appointment be made   A. LINCOLN
    Sep. 19, 1862

[1] AES, IHi. Lincoln's endorsement is written on a letter of Edwin Henry, Flushing, New York, to Stanton, September 19, 1862, calling attention to his application for a commission as commissary of subsistence. See Lincoln's previous endorsement to Stanton concerning Henry, July 19, *supra*.

To William S. Ketchum[1]

Gen. Ketchum,   Executive Mansion,
Springfield, Ills.   Washington, Sep. 20, 1862.

How many regiments are there in Illinois, ready for service, but for the want of arms? How many arms have you there ready for distribution?   A. LINCOLN

¹ ALS, RPB. Inspector General William S. Ketchum, who had been sent to Illinois to expedite the forwarding of new troops, replied the same day, "Six regiments under orders; nine armed, but want pay; ten mustered, but not filled or paid; eighteen organizing. Governor insists on ordering regiments off, but not ordered until paid, and delayed for want of money. Not been able to see Governor for several days, but have had eight regiments ordered within last three days. Arms for distribution 16,429, but no accouterments." (OR, III, II, 575).

To William Sprague¹

His Excellency Gov. William Sprague—   Executive Mansion,
My dear Sir   Washington, Sep. 20. 1862.

I am sure you can not be ignorant of my strong desire to oblige you, so far as in my own judgment, I consistently can; but I can not now so do, that, the procuring of which, seems to be the mission of your friend, J. A. Perry. Yours truly   A. LINCOLN

¹ ALS, CSmH. John A. Perry, captain and chaplain of the First Rhode Island Light Artillery, was possibly Governor Sprague's emissary. A letter from Thomas A. Jenckes of Providence, September 11, 1862, with envelope indicating its delivery to the president by "Capt Perry," reads as follows: "Our Governor desires that I shall join him in the request that his 6th (colored) regiment shall be received into the service of the United States. I do so with the greatest pleasure. . . ." (DLC-RTL). On September 26 Sprague replied to Lincoln's letter, "Your recent Proclamation changes somewhat the policy of the war. I had that policy only in mind in calling the negros to arms. . . ." (Ibid.).

To Edwin M. Stanton¹

[c. September 20, 1862]

Col. Berdan's Sharp shooters, are an irregular (in a sense, an illegal) organization. It's field and staff officers have had no commissions. It is a good deal reduced by skirmishes, battles, and other hard service. So far as I know, there are no jealousies against it, and it is universally appreciated. I therefore propose that the Sec. of War, with the assistance of the Adjutant General, and Col. Berdan, put the corps into the most effective form, regardless of existing regulations; and I will recommend to Congress to ratify it, giving Commissions, pay &c from the time individuals respectively entered the service.   A. LINCOLN

¹ AES, NHi. Lincoln's endorsement is written on a letter from Colonel Hiram Berdan of the First U.S. Sharpshooters, September 18, 1862, asking that he be authorized to recruit additional battalions or regiments of sharpshooters and that his officers be given commissions by the government. Authorized by a non-extant note to Governor Edwin D. Morgan in July, 1861 (see Berdan to Lincoln, July 21, 1861, DLC-RTL), the Sharpshooters had neither state nor federal authority, and hence were serving without official status or pay.

To Edwin M. Stanton[1]

Hon. Sec. of War   Executive Mansion,
Dear Sir.   Washington, Sep. 20, 1862.

I know it is your purpose to send the paroled prisoners to the seat of the Indian difficulties; and I write this only to urge that this be done with all possible despatch. Gen. Wool telegraphs that including those from Harper's Ferry, there are now twenty thousand at Anapolis, requiring four good unparoled regiments to guard them. This should not be endured beyond the earliest moment possible to change it. Arm them and send them away just as fast as the Railroads will carry them. Each regiment arriving on the frontier will relieve a new regiment to come forward. Yours truly   A. LINCOLN

[1]ALS, NHi. On August 22, 1862, Governor Alexander Ramsey notified Stanton, "The Third Regiment of Minnesota Volunteers is on parole at Benton Barracks, Saint Louis. We need a well-drilled force . . . to resist the overwhelming force of Indians now attacking our frontier settlements. Cannot you order the Third Regiment to report at once to me . . . . ? This service would not be a violation of their parole. . . ." (OR, II, IV, 417).

On September 9, Governor David Tod pursued the question further, "If the Indian troubles in Minnesota are serious and the paroled Union prisoners are not soon to be exchanged would it not be well to send them to Minnesota? It is with great difficulty we can preserve order among them at Camp Chase." (OR, II, IV, 499).

Stanton replied the same day, "Your suggestion as to the paroled prisoners being sent to the Indian borders is excellent and will be immediately acted upon." (*Ibid.*).

On October 14, Lorenzo Thomas gave his opinion that employment of paroled troops "against Indians would seem to be contrary to the fourth article of the cartel." (*Ibid.*, p. 621). The terms of parole specified that paroled Union troops were to be kept in Union camps as non-combatants until they were exchanged for Confederate prisoners. Insubordination and mutiny among parolees at both Camp Chase and Camp Douglas, as well as the need for troops in Minnesota, prompted the project, but no reference has been found to the actual service of any of the paroled regiments in Minnesota, excepting a portion of the Third Minnesota, as first requested by Governor Ramsey. See also Lincoln to Halleck, October 3, *infra.*

To Edwin M. Stanton[1]

Sec. of War, please read & return these letters to me.
Sep. 21. 1862.   A. LINCOLN

[1] AES, NHi. Lincoln's endorsement is written on a letter from Seward, September 20, 1862, enclosing two letters from Governor Stephen S. Harding of Utah and suggesting the advisability of sending "some of the paroled troops to that Territory." An endorsement by Assistant Secretary of War Peter H. Watson, September 22, referred the papers to Halleck, but no further action is of record.

Preliminary Emancipation Proclamation[1]

September 22, 1862

By the President of the
United States of America
A Proclamation.

I, Abraham Lincoln, President of the United States of America, and Commander-in-chief of the Army and Navy thereof, do hereby proclaim and declare that hereafter, as heretofore, the war will be prossecuted for the object of practically restoring the constitutional relation between the United States, and each of the

[1] ADS, N; DS, DNA FS RG 11, Proclamations. The autograph proclamation in the New York State Library was presented by Lincoln to the Albany Army Relief Bazaar held in February and March, 1864, where it was purchased by Gerrit Smith for $1,100 and given to the U.S. Sanitary Commission, whence it was purchased again for $1,000 in April, 1865, by the State of New York for the State Library. A letter of transmittal from Frederick W. Seward to Mrs. Emily W. Barnes, January 4, 1864, correctly describes the body of the document as being in Lincoln's "own handwriting, the pencilled additions in the hand of the Secretary of State, and the formal beginning and ending, in the hand of the chief clerk." Seward's emendations as well as other peculiarities of the document are indicated in succeeding footnotes.

From Lincoln's original the engrossed copy in the National Archives was made and an official printing was issued by the State Department accompanied by a Circular from Secretary Seward to Diplomatic and Consular officers. A copy of this Circular printing is preserved in the Lincoln Papers bearing Lincoln's endorsement "Preliminary Proclamation from which a scrap was cut to paste onto the final one." The "scrap" cut away comprised paragraphs three and four of the Preliminary Proclamation, incorporated as paragraphs two and three of the Final Proclamation January 1, 1863, *infra*.

The purported facsimile of the original document which appears in Whitney, *Life on the Circuit with Lincoln*, and which has been referred to as a forgery (Charles Eberstadt, "Lincoln's Emancipation Proclamation," *The New Colophon*, 1950, pp. 312-56), is not reliable in detail, but appears to have been made from the original by a tracing process rather than by photography, and presents the passages which appear in the original as clippings from the official printings of the acts referred to, in type face and line length which do not correspond to the clippings themselves.

The history of the original document, prior to the cabinet meeting on September 22 at which Lincoln presented it, is somewhat obscure, except for the notation in Hay's *Diary* on September 23 that "The President rewrote the Proclamation on Sunday morning carefully." This may be interpreted to mean that Lincoln rewrote directly from the draft of July 22 (*supra*), or that he rewrote from an intervening draft in more or less complete form. If the latter possibility is the case, the intervening draft has not been found. Later accounts of the writing of the Preliminary Proclamation are reminiscent and unreliable in detail (see George S. Boutwell, *The Lawyer, the Statesman, and the Soldier*, 1887, pp. 116-17). The full reports of the cabinet meeting on September 22 as recorded in the diaries of Chase and Welles are too long for reproduction here, but should be consulted by anyone interested in the reaction of the several members to Lincoln's announcement that he had made up his mind to issue the Proclamation forthwith.

states, and the people thereof, in which states that relation is, or may be suspended, or disturbed.

That it is my purpose, upon the next meeting of Congress to again recommend the adoption of a practical measure tendering pecuniary aid to the free acceptance or rejection of all slave-states, so called, the people whereof may not then be in rebellion against the United States, and which states,[2] may then have voluntarily adopted, or thereafter may voluntarily adopt, immediate, or gradual abolishment of slavery within their respective limits; and that the effort to colonize persons of African descent, with[3] their consent, upon this continent, or elsewhere, with[4] the previously obtained consent of the Governments existing there, will be continued.

That on the first day of January in the year of our Lord, one thousand eight hundred and sixty-three, all persons held as slaves within any state, or designated part of a state, the people whereof shall then be in rebellion against the United States shall be then, thenceforward, and forever free; and the executive government of the United States, including the military and naval authority thereof, will[5] recognize and maintain the freedom of such persons, and will do no act or acts to repress such persons, or any of them, in any efforts they may make for their actual freedom.

That the executive will, on the first day of January aforesaid, by proclamation, designate the States, and parts of states, if any, in which the people thereof respectively, shall then be in rebellion against the United States; and the fact that any state, or the people thereof shall, on that day be, in good faith represented in the Congress of the United States, by members chosen thereto, at elections wherein a majority of the qualified voters of such state shall have participated, shall, in the absence of strong countervailing testimony, be deemed conclusive evidence that such state and the people thereof, are not then in rebellion against the United States.

That attention is hereby called to an act of Congress entitled "An act to make an additional Article of War" approved March 13, 1862, and which act is in the words and figure following:[6]

2 "And" inserted and deleted at this point not in Lincoln's handwriting.
3 "With their consent" inserted by Seward.
4 "With the previously obtained consent of the Governments existing there" inserted by Seward.
5 At this point, following a suggestion of Seward concurred in by Chase and other members at the cabinet meeting, Lincoln deleted and revised his original phrasing, which read as follows: "will, during the continuance in office of the present incumbent, recognize such persons, as being free, and will" etc.
6 A clipping from the official printing of the act is pasted on the page of Lincoln's autograph document.

*Be it enacted by the Senate and House of Representatives of the
United States of America in Congress assembled,* That hereafter the
following shall be promulgated as an additional article of war for
the government of the army of the United States, and shall be obeyed
and observed as such:

Article—. All officers or persons in the military or naval service of
the United States are prohibited from employing any of the forces
under their respective commands for the purpose of returning fugitives from service or labor, who may have escaped from any persons
to whom such service or labor is claimed to be due, and any officer
who shall be found guilty by a court-martial of violating this article
shall be dismissed from the service.

SEC. 2. *And be it further enacted,* That this act shall take effect
from and after its passage.

Also to the ninth and tenth sections of an act entitled "An Act
to suppress Insurrection, to punish Treason and Rebellion, to seize
and confiscate property of rebels, and for other purposes," approved July 17, 1862, and which sections are in the words and
figures following:[7]

SEC. 9. *And be it further enacted,* That all slaves of persons who
shall hereafter be engaged in rebellion against the government of the
United States, or who shall in any way give aid or comfort thereto,
escaping from such persons and taking refuge within the lines of the
army; and all slaves captured from such persons or deserted by them
and coming under the control of the government of the United States;
and all slaves of such persons found *on* (or) being within any place
occupied by rebel forces and afterwards occupied by the forces of the
United States, shall be deemed captives of war, and shall be forever
free of their servitude and not again held as slaves.

SEC. 10. *And be it further enacted,* That no slave escaping into any
State, Territory, or the District of Columbia, from any other State,
shall be delivered up, or in any way impeded or hindered of his liberty, except for crime, or some offence against the laws, unless the
person claiming said fugitive shall first make oath that the person to
whom the labor or service of such fugitive is alleged to be due is his
lawful owner, and has not borne arms against the United States in the
present rebellion, nor in any way given aid and comfort thereto; and
no person engaged in the military or naval service of the United States
shall, under any pretence whatever, assume to decide on the validity
of the claim of any person to the service or labor of any other person,
or surrender up any such person to the claimant, on pain of being
dismissed from the service.

And I do hereby enjoin upon and order all persons engaged in
the military and naval service of the United States to observe,
obey, and enforce, within their respective spheres of service, the
act, and sections above recited.

[7] This quotation is also in the form of a clipping from the official printing.

And the executive will in due time[8] recommend that all citizens of the United States who shall have remained loyal thereto throughout the rebellion, shall (upon the restoration of the constitutional relation between the United States, and their respective states, and people, if that relation shall have been suspended or disturbed) be compensated for all losses by acts of the United States, including the loss of slaves.

In[9] witness whereof, I have hereunto set my hand, and caused the seal of the United States to be affixed.

L.S.   Done at the City of Washington, this twenty second day of September, in the year of our Lord, one thousand eight hundred and sixty two, and of the Independence of the United States, the eighty seventh.

By the President: ABRAHAM LINCOLN

WILLIAM H. SEWARD, Secretary of State.

[8] "In due time" is inserted in handwriting not Lincoln's, to replace "at the next session of Congress," which had been inserted by the chief clerk at this point.   [9] The remainder, including signatures, is in the hand of the clerk.

Testimonial for Isachar Zacharie[1]

Dr. Zacharie has operated on my feet with great success, and considerable addition to my comfort.   A. LINCOLN

Sep. 22. 1862.

[1] ADS, ORB. For an account of Isachar Zacharie's activities, see Bertram W. Korn, *American Jewry and the Civil War* (1951), pp. 194-202. Zacharie's testimonials from Lincoln and members of the cabinet were so well publicized by the chiropodist that they provoked a humorous article in the New York *Herald*, October 3, 1862, which began by observing that "It is a true but trite maxim that great events are determined by insignificant causes. . . . The fact may be a singular one; but from evidence before us we are inclined to believe that many of the haps and mishaps of the nation, during this war, may be traced to a matter no greater than the corns and bunions which have afflicted the feet of our leaders. . . ." The writer further pointed out that "The President has been greatly blamed for not resisting the demands of the radicals; but how could the President put his foot down firmly when he was troubled with corns?"

Proclamation Suspending the Writ of Habeas Corpus[1]

September 24 1862

By the President of the United States of America:

A Proclamation.

Whereas, it has become necessary to call into service not only volunteers but also portions of the militia of the States by draft in order to suppress the insurrection existing in the United States, and disloyal persons are not adequately restrained by the ordinary processes of law from hindering this measure and from giving aid and comfort in various ways to the insurrection;

Now, therefore, be it ordered, first, that during the existing insurrection and as a necessary measure for suppressing the same, all Rebels and Insurgents, their aiders and abettors within the United States, and all persons discouraging volunteer enlistments, resisting militia drafts, or guilty of any disloyal practice, affording aid and comfort to Rebels against the authority of the United States, shall be subject to martial law and liable to trial and punishment by Courts Martial or Military Commission:

Second. That the Writ of Habeas Corpus is suspended in respect to all persons arrested, or who are now, or hereafter during the rebellion shall be, imprisoned in any fort, camp, arsenal, military prison, or other place of confinement by any military authority or by the sentence of any Court Martial or Military Commission.

In witness whereof, I have hereunto set my hand, and caused the seal of the United States to be affixed.

Done at the City of Washington this twenty fourth day of September, in the year of our Lord one [L.S.] thousand eight hundred and sixty-two, and of the Independence of the United States the 87th.

By the President: ABRAHAM LINCOLN.

WILLIAM H. SEWARD, Secretary of State.

[1] DS, DNA FS RG 11, Proclamations.

To Edwin M. Stanton[1]

September 24, 1862

The within recommendations are most ample;—in fact, not often equalled. I respectfully submit the case to the Secretary of War, or, to any Head of a Department or Bureau, with a sincere wish that Mr. Grandin may find a place   A. LINCOLN

Sep. 24. 1862.

[1] AES, DLC-RTL. Lincoln's endorsement is written on the cover of a sheaf of recommendations in favor of appointment of William G. Grandin of New York. Stanton endorsed, "There is no position in the War Department *at present* vacant."

To Whom It May Concern[1]

Executive Mansion   Washington
Whom it may concern   September 24th 1862

Hon Edward Everett goes to Europe shortly. His reputation & the present condition of our country are such, that his visit there is sure to attract notice and may be misconstrued. I therefore think fit to say, that he bears no mission from this government, and yet no gentleman is better able to correct misunderstandings in the minds of foreigners, in regard to American affairs.

While I commend him to the consideration of those, whom he may meet, I am quite conscious that he could better introduce me than I him, in Europe. ABRAHAM LINCOLN.

¹ Copy, DLC-RTL. The copy in Everett's handwriting is enclosed with a letter from Everett, September 25, 1862, "In compliance with your request, I enclose a copy of the paper, which you were good enough to hand me, this morning." (DLC-RTL).

Reply to Serenade
in Honor of Emancipation Proclamation¹

September 24, 1862

FELLOW-CITIZENS: I appear before you to do little more than acknowledge the courtesy you pay me, and to thank you for it. I have not been distinctly informed why it is this occasion you appear to do me this honor, though I suppose [interruptions] it is because of the proclamation. [Cries of "Good," and applause.] I was about to say, I suppose I understand it. [Laughter—Voices: "That you do," "You thoroughly understand it."] What I did, I did after very full deliberation, and under a very heavy and solemn sense of responsibility. [Cries of "Good," "Good," "Bless you," and applause.]

I can only trust in God I have made no mistake. [Cries "No mistake—all right; you've made no mistakes yet. Go ahead, you're right."] I shall make no attempt on this occasion to sustain what I have done or said by any comment. [Voices—"That's unnecessary; we understand it."] It is now for the country and the world to pass judgment on it, and, may be, take action upon it. I will say no more upon this subject. In my position I am environed with difficulties. [A voice—"That's so."]

Yet they are scarcely so great as the difficulties of those who, upon the battle field, are endeavoring to purchase with their blood and their lives the future happiness and prosperity of this country. [Applause, long and continued.] Let us never forget them. On the 14th and 17th days of the present month there have been battles bravely, skillfully and successfully fought. [Applause.] We do not yet know the particulars. Let us be sure that in giving praise to particular individuals, we do no injustice to others. I only ask you, at the conclusion of these few remarks, to give three hearty cheers to all good and brave officers and men who fought those successful battles.

[1] New York *Tribune*, September 25, 1862; *National Intelligencer*, September 26, 1862. The *National Intelligencer* has basically the same text as the *Tribune* but with less extensive interruptions from the crowd. Brackets are in the source. Following Lincoln's speech, the crowd paraded to the residence of Secretary Chase, where they heard speeches from Chase and Cassius M. Clay, and thence to the residence of Attorney General Bates, who also made a speech.

To John Ross[1]

John Ross   Executive Mansion,
Principal Chief of the   Washington,
Cherokee Nation   Sept. 25, 1862.

Sir: Your letter of the 16th. Inst. was received two days ago. In the multitude of cares claiming my constant attention I have been unable to examine and determine the exact treaty relations between the United States and the Cherokee Nation. Neither have I been able to investigate and determine the exact state of facts claimed by you as constituting a failure of treaty obligation on our part, excusing the Cherokee Nation for making a treaty with a portion of the people of the United States in open rebellion against the government thereof. This letter therefore, must not be understood to decide anything upon these questions. I shall, however, cause a careful investigation of them to be made. Meanwhile the Cherokee people remaining practically loyal to the federal Union will receive all the protection which can be given them consistently with the duty of the government to the whole country.[2] I sincerely hope the Cherokee country may not again be over-run by the enemy; and I shall do all I consistently can to prevent it. Your Obt. Servt.   A. LINCOLN.

[1] ALS-F, ISLA; ADfS, DLC-RTL. See Lincoln to Smith, September 11, *supra.* John Ross' letter to Lincoln, September 16, 1862, reads in part as follows:

"During the interview which I had the honor to have with your Excellency the 12th instant, you requested that the objects of my visit should be communicated in writing. I therefore beg leave very respectfully to represent—

"1st That the relations which the Cherokee Nation sustained towards the United States, have been defined by Treaties . . . extending through a long series of years.

"2d Those Treaties were Treaties of Friendship and Alliance—The Cherokee Nation . . . placing itself under the protection of the United States . . . and the United States solemnly promising that Protection.

"3rd . . . . in consequence of the want of that protection . . . The Cherokees were forced for the preservation of their country and their existence to negotiate a Treaty with the 'Confederate States.'

". . . . The advance of the Indian Expedition gave the Cherokee People an opportunity to manifest their views by taking . . . a prompt and decided stand in favor of their relations with the U States Government. The withdrawal of that expedition and the reabandonment of that people and country to the forces of the Confederate States leaves them in a position fraught with distress, danger and ruin. What the Cherokee People now desire is ample military protection . . . and a recognition by the Government of the obligations of existing Treaties. . . .

"For the satisfaction and encouragement of my own People and of the Indian Nations who live near them, I beg leave very respectfully to suggest that you will issue a Proclamation to them, if deemed proper, in accordance with the views which you entertain on this subject and which will enable me to make assurances in behalf of the Government in which they can confide. . . ." (DLC-RTL).

2 "No more than this can safely be promised, even to the loyal white people of Missouri, or other border states" has been deleted at this point in Lincoln's draft.

To Alexander II[1]

September 26, 1862

Abraham Lincoln,
President of the United States of America,

To His Imperial Majesty Alexander II,
Emperor and Autocrat of all the Russias,
&c.   &c.   &c.

Great and Good Friend: I have received the letter which Your Majesty address[ed] to me on the 6th. of July last, informing me that on the 1st. of that month, Her Imperial Highness the Grand Duchess Alexandra Joseephowna, spouse of Your Majesty's well-beloved Brother, His Imperial Highness, the Grand Duke Constantin Nicolaewitsch, was happily delivered of a son, who has received the name of Viatcheslaw.

Your Majesty does but justice to my sentiments in the conviction you have been pleased to express that I will take in an event so satisfactory to your Imperial House the same interest which Your Majesty takes in all that concerns the prosperity of the United States; and I beg Your Majesty to accept my sincere congratulations upon the occasion: and so I recommend Your Majesty and Your Majesty's Imperial Family to the protection of the Almighty. Your Good Friend,   ABRAHAM LINCOLN

Washington, 26th. Septr., 1862.

By the President:
William H. Seward, Secretary of State.

1 Copy, DNA FS RG 59, Communications to Foreign Sovereigns and States, III.

Reply to Delegation of Loyal Governors[1]

September 26, 1862

The President's reply was brief, and consisted of thanks to the Governors for all they had done and for all they had promised to do to help the General Government in this great crisis. As to the proclamation, he said no fact had assured him so thoroughly of the justice of the conclusion at which he had arrived as that the Executives of the loyal States gave it their hearty approbation. As to the suggestions which they had made in the address just read, he was grateful for them all, but at that moment he would not answer them specifically, although he could say that he would give them his most favorable consideration, and believed he should carry most if not all of them out, so far as possible.

[1] New York *Tribune*, September 29, 1862. Following the conference of governors at Altoona, Pennsylvania, a group of eleven or twelve governors repaired to Washington for an interview with the president. An address prepared by Governor John A. Andrew and concurred in by the other governors is summarized by the *National Intelligencer*, September 27, 1862, as follows:

"The address expresses, first, a cordial personal and official respect for the President.

"Second, a determination, under all circumstances, to support and maintain his constitutional authority, speaking for themselves and people of their respective States.

"Third, pledges their aid in all measures to bring the war to an early termination, and that it should be prosecuted to ultimate victory, unless all rebels voluntarily return to their constitutional duty and obedience.

"Fourth, congratulates the President upon his proclamation, believing it will do good as a measure of justice and sound policy.

"Fifth, concludes with a reference to those who have fought our battles."

After the formal proceedings, "an informal conversation followed, lasting for two or three hours, running over a great many topics, in which the greatest harmony prevailed among all those in attendance" (*Tribune*, September 29, 1862).

To Edwin M. Stanton[1]

September 26, 1862

There could scarcely be a stronger case made for an appointment than this.

If another Brigade Quarter Master can be used profitably, let Asa D. Baker, named within, be appointed.   A. LINCOLN

Sep. 26. 1862

[1] AES, IHi. Lincoln's endorsement is written on a petition signed by officers of the Army of the South West, asking appointment of Asa D. Baker as assistant commissary of subsistence or assistant quartermaster for the Second Brigade, Third Division. Baker had been acting without pay since December, 1861. He was appointed commissary as of November 18, 1862.

Record of Dismissal of John J. Key[1]

September 26-27, 1862

We have reason to believe that the following is an exact copy of the record upon which Major John J. Key was dismissed from the military service of the United States.

Executive Mansion

Major John J. Key   Washington, Sept. 26. 1862.

Sir: I am informed that in answer to the question "Why was not the rebel army bagged immediately after the battle near Sharpsburg?" propounded to you by Major Levi C. Turner, Judge Advocate &c. you answered "That is not the game" "The object is that neither army shall get much advantage of the other; that both shall be kept in the field till they are exhausted, when we will make a compromise and save slavery."

I shall be very happy if you will, within twentyfour hours from the receipt of this, prove to me by Major Turner, that you did not, either litterally, or in substance, make the answer stated. Yours,

A. LINCOLN

(Indorsed as follows)

"Copy delivered to Major Key at 10.25 A.M. September 27th. 1862.

JOHN HAY."

At about 11 o'clock, A.M. Sept. 27. 1862, Major Key and Major Turner appear before me. Major Turner says: "As I remember it, the conversation was, I asked the question why we did not bag them after the battle at Sharpsburg? Major Key's reply was that was not the game, that we should tire the rebels out, and ourselves, that that was the only way the Union could be preserved, we come together fraternally, and slavery be saved"

On cross-examination, Major Turner says he has frequently heard Major Key converse in regard to the present troubles, and never heard him utter a a [sic] sentiment unfavorable to the maintainance of the Union. He has never uttered anything which he Major T. would call disloyalty. The particular conversation detailed was a private one   A. LINCOLN.

(Indorsed on the above)

In my view it is wholly inadmissable for any gentleman holding a military commission from the United States to utter such sentiments as Major Key is within proved to have done. Therefore

[442]

let Major John J. Key be forthwith dismissed from the Military service of the United States.   A LINCOLN.

The foregoing is the whole record, except the simple order of dismissal at the War Department. At the interview of Major Key and Major Turner with the President, Major Key did not attempt to controvert the statement of Major Turner; but simply insisted, and sought to prove, that he was true to the Union. The substance of the President's reply was that if there was a "game" ever among Union men, to have our army not take an advantage of the enemy when it could, it was his object to break up that game.

[1] AD, DLC-RTL. Although written down later (c. October 14), this document entirely in Lincoln's handwriting preserves not only Lincoln's letter of September 26 to Major Key but also the record of subsequent events. The original letter of September 26 and the other original documents copied by Lincoln have not been found. On September 27, Major Key wrote Lincoln an explanation as follows:

". . . I have never uttered a word that might not have been addressed to you without giving offence The conversation held with Major Turner was in his own room and with him as a friend—and although I have no recollection of the expression, as reported—I have no doubt Major Turner so understood me.

"I have often remarked, that the Rebels would never let this contest be decided, if they could help it—by a decided battle between us, but would protract this war—as they hoped to make a compromise in the end & that they were fighting with that end in view.

"In conclusion I solemnly aver—that if this war terminates in the entire destruction of the South—they have brought it on themselves." (DLC-RTL). See Lincoln's letter to Key, November 24, infra.

To Edwin M. Stanton[1]

Will the Secretary of War please consider this, and give me the benefit of his opinion?   A. LINCOLN

Sep. 27. 1862.

[1] AES, owned by Richard Lufkin, West Medford, Massachusetts. Lincoln's endorsement is preserved on the back of a fragment of the last page of a letter, the only remaining portion of which gives no clue to the author or the substance. An endorsement by Stanton immediately following that of Lincoln suggests the possibility that the letter concerned the advisability of evacuating the Capitol, which had been requisitioned by the War Department. Stanton's endorsement is as follows: "The Secretary of War respectfully reports etc. that the great number of wounded soldiers in the battles on the Rappahannock[,] Manassas & Centreville made the occupation of the Capitol an absolute necessity and it was taken on the requisition of the Surgeon General for temporary purposes. Orders have been given to the Surgeon General to evacuate the Capitol as speedily as possible. [See Lincoln's order of October 14, infra.]

"2. Directions were given about two months ago to remove the bakeries which has been partially accomplished. The sudden increase of troops has occasioned delay in removing all the ovens but it is in process of execution."

To Hannibal Hamlin[1]

(Strictly private.)

Executive Mansion,
Washington, September 28, 1862.

My Dear Sir: Your kind letter of the 25th is just received. It is known to some that while I hope something from the proclamation, my expectations are not as sanguine as are those of some friends. The time for its effect southward has not come; but northward the effect should be instantaneous.

It is six days old, and while commendation in newspapers and by distinguished individuals is all that a vain man could wish, the stocks have declined, and troops come forward more slowly than ever. This, looked soberly in the face, is not very satisfactory. We have fewer troops in the field at the end of six days than we had at the beginning—the attrition among the old outnumbering the addition by the new. The North responds to the proclamation sufficiently in breath; but breath alone kills no rebels.

I wish I could write more cheerfully; nor do I thank you the less for the kindness of your letter. Yours very truly,

A. LINCOLN.

[1] NH, VIII, 49-50. Hamlin's letter of September 25, written from Bangor, Maine, expressed "sincere thanks for your Emancipation Proclamation. It will stand as the great act of the age. It will prove to be wise in statesmanship as it is patriotic. It will be enthusiastically approved and sustained, and future generations will, as I do, say God bless you for this great and noble act." (DLC-Nicolay Papers).

To William A. Hammond[1]

Will the Surgeon General please al[l]ow Dr. Fo[r]sha to try the case named within?   A. LINCOLN

Sep. 29. 1862.

[1] AES, DLC-RTL. Lincoln's endorsement is written on a letter from Salmon P. Chase, September 28, asking that a ward in the Capitol Hospital be assigned to Dr. S. W. Forsha to treat wounded soldiers with his "Balm." Dr. Forsha had been denied access to a wounded soldier who wished to try his remedy. Apparently the surgeon general did not act, for on December 17, Attorney General Bates endorsed a note from Forsha with the comment that "it is evident that *Dr. Forsha* is not much of a scholar. But he certainly has great *curative* powers; and really works wonders in relieving pain and healing wounds." Forsha's letter reads as follows: "If the President will give me the charge of a hospital or a ward in one to use my owne medisen in and up on the wounded Soldiers for three Months I will insure ninety percent of all the flesh wounds to be well and the Soldiers to be in a healthy condition and fit for duty within thirty days from the time I take them if I can have them within 8 or 10 days from

the time they are wounded and I will only ask the same assistance that the other Surgeons are allowed   The Soldiers will not suffer the twentieth part as much as they do in the other hospitals and their general health shall not be impared from the Effects of the wounds." (DLC-RTL). A letter from Hammond to Lincoln, February 13, 1863, in reply to a communication from the president which has not been located, specified that "I have met with Dr. Forsha before, and am satisfied that he is an ignorant quack." (*Ibid.*).

To Edward Stanly[1]

Hon. Edward Stanley   Executive Mansion,
My dear Sir.   Washington, Sep. 29, 1862.

Your note informing me that you will leave for North Carolina soon, is received. Your conduct as Military Governor of that State, as reported to me by Gen. Burnside, and as I have heard it personally from yourself, has my entire approbation; and it is with great satisfaction that I learn you are now to return in the same capacity, with the approbation of the War Department.

I shall be much gratified if you can find it practicable to have congressional elections held in that State before January. It is my sincere wish that North Carolina may again govern herself conformably to the constitution of the United States. Yours very truly

A. LINCOLN

[1] ADfS, DLC-RTL. Governor Stanly wrote Lincoln on September 29, 1862, "I have completed my business with the War Department, and shall very soon be ready to start for North Carolina. . . . Allow me to express my deep gratification, on learning from your own lips, after a full and free conference, that my conduct as Military Governor . . . , which had been misrepresented and misunderstood, had met your approbation, as well as that of the Secretary of War. . . . If you have any further suggestions to make, I will call at any hour you may designate" (DLC-RTL). See Lincoln's communication to the House of Representatives concerning Stanly, June 4, *supra*.

To Edwin M. Stanton[1]

September 29, 1862

It seems by the within that there is danger of the different religious denominations having some collision in their ministering among the colored people about Port-Royal, and perhaps elsewhere. I should think each church should minister according to it's own rules, without interference by others differing from them; and if there still be difficulties about *places* of worship, a real christian charity, and forbearance on the part of all might obviate it. With these views, I submit the subject to the Secretary of War.

Sep. 29. 1862.   A. LINCOLN

¹ AES, owned by Perc S. Brown, Newark, New Jersey. Lincoln's endorsement is written on a memorial from S. Peck of the Baptist Home Mission Society, September 26, 1862, asking that "the beneficent labors" of ministers assigned by the Society to work with freedmen in and near Port Royal, South Carolina, "be suffered to proceed without unnecessary interference; that no religious test or question will be applied *ab extra* to such persons, as *conditional* to their admission to or continuance on the islands;—that the churches & congregations spoken of will be allowed to assemble & worship as heretofore in their respective meetinghouses without 'let or hindrance,' except as the use of the said houses shall be imperatively required by military exigencies;—especially, that no measure, designedly or unwittingly, will be suffered to infringe on the internal economy of the churches, but the rights of conscience, in matters of purely religious faith & practice, be held inviolate. . . ." No reply from Stanton has been found.

To Edwin M. Stanton¹

Ought not something to be done for Gen. Casey? What says the Secretary of War?   A. LINCOLN

Sep. 29. 1862.

¹ AES, owned by Herman Blum, Blumhaven Library, Philadelphia. Lincoln's endorsement is written on a letter from General Silas Casey protesting that he had not been promoted for his services in the Peninsular Campaign. On January 16, 1863, Lincoln nominated Casey brigadier general by brevet in the Regular Army for "meritorious conduct at the battle of Fair Oaks," to date from May 31, 1862, and appointed him major general of Volunteers to rank from May 31, 1862. The appointment as major general was returned to the president by the Senate on February 12, 1863. Lincoln renominated Casey as major general on March 6, and the appointment was confirmed by the Senate on March 9, 1863.

To Edwin M. Stanton¹

If the within would not violate the rules let it be done.

Sep. 29. 1862.   A. LINCOLN

¹ AES, owned by R. E. Burdick, New York City. Lincoln's endorsement is written on a letter from Major General Franz Sigel, September 27, 1862, asking that Captain Ulric Dahlgren of his staff be appointed major so that he may be "chief of my artillery." No record of the appointment has been found.

To S. Yorke At Lee¹

Executive Mansion,
My Dear Sir   Washington, September 30, 1862.

Will you have the kindness to give William Johnson two days leave of absence, if not inconvenient, and oblige. Yours truly

A. LINCOLN

[1] LS, OClWHi. S. Yorke At Lee was a clerk in the Treasury Department where William H. Johnson worked. See Lincoln's recommendation for Johnson March 7, 1861.

To Henry W. Halleck[1]

September 30, 1862

This letter is written by Nathaniel P. Talmadge, long time ago, U.S. Senator for New-York, and afterwards Territorial Governor of Wisconsin.

I personally know nothing of Col. Bragg; and I submit the case to Gen. Halleck.   A. LINCOLN

Sep. 30. 1862.

[1] AES, IHi. Lincoln's endorsement is written on a letter from former Senator Nathaniel P. Tallmadge of New York (1833-1844) to Secretary Seward, Fond du Lac, Wisconsin, September 27, 1862, recommending Lieutenant Colonel Edward S. Bragg of the Sixth Wisconsin Infantry for brigadier general. Bragg was not appointed brigadier general of Volunteers until June 25, 1864.

To Gideon Welles[1]

September 30, 1862

Col. Harding desires a position in the Navy. I know not that it can be given him; but as the within letters are written by excellent men personally known to me, I refer the case to the Secretary of the Navy, asking respectful attention to it.   A. LINCOLN

Sep. 30. 1862.

[1] AES, THaroL. The endorsement is no longer with the papers concerned, and the editors have not been able to identify the case involved, but it is possible that Colonel Abner C. Harding of the Eighty-third Illinois Volunteers was the man seeking a Navy appointment. He was nominated brigadier general of Volunteers and confirmed by the Senate on March 13, 1863.

To John E. Wool[1]

Majr. Gen. Wool.   Executive Mansion
Sir—   Washington, Sep. 30. 1862

Thomas Stackpole, bearer of this, I have known rather intimately since my coming to the White-House; and I believe him to be a worthy and competent business man. Yours truly

A LINCOLN

[1] ALS, The Rosenbach Company, Philadelphia and New York. Accompanying Lincoln's letter is a note from Mrs. Lincoln recommending Stackpole for a "Sutler's place." Thomas Stackpole is listed in the *U.S. Official Register*, 1861, as watchman at the White House. No record of his appointment as sutler has been found, and the *Official Register* continued to list him in 1863 as watchman.

Memorandum on Troops at Antietam[1]

October 1-3, 1862

Head-Quarters Army of the Potomac, 1862.

Sumner	24.130
Burnside	14.000
Porter	16.479
Hooker	8.136
Franklin—	17.000
Cavalry—	4.000
	83.745
	2.190
	85.935
	2 160
	88.095

[Endorsement]

Men Memoranda obtained Oct. 1,2,& 3, 1862

[1] AD, DLC-RTL. Lincoln visited McClellan's headquarters October 1-3, 1862, for a military conference.

To William I[1]

October 1, 1862

Abraham Lincoln,
President of the United States of America.

To His Majesty William I,
  King of Prussia,
  &c.,   &c.

Great and Good Friend: I have received the letter which Your Majesty was pleased to address to me on the 15th. of August, last, announcing that Her Royal Highness the Princess Victoria Adelaide Mary Louisa, spouse of the Prince Royal of Prussia, Your Majesty's well-beloved daughter-in-law, had on the preceding day safely given birth to a Prince.

I participate in the satisfaction which this happy event has afforded to Your Majesty and to Your Majesty's Royal Family, and offer my sincere congratulations upon the occasion.

[448]

May God have Your Majesty always in His safe and holy keeping! Your Good Friend, ABRAHAM LINCOLN.
Washington, October 1, 1862.
By the President:
WILLIAM H. SEWARD, Secretary of State.

¹ Copy, DNA FS RG 59, Communications to Foreign Sovereigns and States, III, 193.

Concerning Mrs. Disney[1]

I would be very glad to oblige Mrs. Disney but I can do no more than I have done, refer her to the Surgeon General.
October 3, 1862   A. LINCOLN

¹ Copy, ISLA. The autograph dealer who transcribed this item described it as "a six lines A.L.S." No further information is available, and Mrs. Disney has not been identified.

To Henry W. Halleck[1]

Major General Halleck.   Head-Quarters Army of the Potomac,
Washington, D.C.   October 3d. 1862. 8. A.M

General Stuart of the Rebel Army, has sent in a few of our prisoners under a flag of truce, paroled with terms to prevent their fighting the Indians, and evidently seeking to commit us to their right to parole our prisoners in that way. My inclination is to send the prisoners back with a distinct notice that we will recognize no parole given to our prisoners by the rebels, as extending beyond a prohibition against fighting them. Yet I wish your opinion upon it, based upon the general law and our cartel. I wish to avoid violations of law and bad faith. Answer as quick as possible, as the thing, if done at all, should be done at once.   A. LINCOLN

¹ Copy, DLC-McClellan Papers. Concerning the Union troops paroled by Confederate General James E. B. Stuart, Halleck at first replied that he thought there was "nothing against" Lincoln's proposal (OR, II, IV, 593), but later on the same day he replied, "When I telegraphed you this morning I had only heard the cartel read by the Secretary of War. I have since examined the original document and withdraw my opinion. I am disposed to think the parole is made by the cartel to include all military duty." (*Ibid.*, 593-94). On October 4, he concluded, "After full consultation with the Secretary of War and Colonel Holt it is concluded that the parole under the cartel does not prohibit doing service against the Indians." (*Ibid.*, 598). But Attorney General Bates on October 18 gave his opinion that "The terms of the contract are . . . explicit . . . beyond a doubt. . . . It is the plainly declared purpose of the Cartel to prevent the use of prisoners paroled . . . in the discharge of any of the duties of a soldier. . . ." (DLC-RTL). See also the note to Lincoln's letter to Stanton, September 20, *supra.*

Speech at Frederick, Maryland[1]

October 4, 1862

In my present position it is hardly proper for me to make speeches. Every word is so closely noted that it will not do to make trivial ones, and I cannot be expected to be prepared to make a matured one just now. If I were as I have been most of my life, I might perhaps, talk amusing to you for half an hour, and it wouldn't hurt anybody; but as it is, I can only return my sincere thanks for the compliment paid our cause and our common country.

[1] New York *Tribune*, October 6, 1862. Lincoln's brief remarks were made to a group of citizens at "Mrs. Ramsey's house" where he called to visit wounded Brigadier General George L. Hartsuff.

Second Speech at Frederick, Maryland[1]

October 4, 1862

FELLOW-CITIZENS: I see myself surrounded by soldiers, and a little further off I note the citizens of this good city of Frederick, anxious to hear something from me. I can only say, as I did five minutes ago, it is not proper for me to make speeches in my present position. I return thanks to our soldiers for the good service they have rendered, for the energies they have shown, the hardships they have endured, and the blood they have so nobly shed for this dear Union of ours; and I also return thanks not only to the soldiers, but to the good citizens of Maryland, and to all the good men and women in this land, for their devotion to our glorious cause. I say this without any malice in my heart to those who have done otherwise. May our children and our children's children to a thousand generations, continue to enjoy the benefits conferred upon us by a united country, and have cause yet to rejoice under those glorious institutions bequeathed us by Washington and his compeers. Now, my friends, soldiers and citizens, I can only say once more, farewell.

[1] New York *Tribune*, October 6, 1862. Lincoln spoke to a crowd gathered at the railway station before the departure of his train.

To Salmon P. Chase[1]

If the Sec. of the Treasury can tell what this means it is more than I can.   A. LINCOLN

Oct. 6. 1862

[1] AES, MH-Nolen Collection. Lincoln's endorsement has been removed from the accompanying papers, and there is no clue to its reference.

Memorandum[1]

[c. October 6, 1862]

Mr. Walker tells me verbally that Mr. Crittenden, Mr. Cushing[,] Mr. Bates, have severally given opinions adverse to his within, the latter of which was given since this, without the knowledge of this, as Mr. W. understands; and the two former, were unknown to Mr. W. when he prepared this.   A.L.

[1] AES, DLC. Lincoln's memorandum is written on a pamphlet *Argument of [Robert J.] Walker & [Frederick P.] Stanton as to the Conclusive Character of the Decision of the Accounting Officers of the Treasury, under the Act of 1789, and Especially of the Third Auditor under the Act of Third of March, 1849, Submitted in the Case of J. & R. H. Porter*, Washington, 1862. Nathan Sargent, Office of Commissioner of Customs, wrote Lincoln on October 20, 1862, concerning this pamphlet "left with you some two weeks ago." The case involved "a *war* account, and a *war* expenditure, and inasmuch as Congress had given to the Secretary of War . . . the power to prescribe in *advance* the rules and regulations under which the Auditor should adjudicate these accounts . . . it is perfectly clear that the duty of the Secretary of the Treasury is purely *ministerial*, involving no discretion or responsibility on his part. . . ." (*Argument*, p. 32).

To William H. Seward[1]

Respectfully submitted to the Secretary of State, with the remark that for some time I have desired to find a place for Mr. Kerr.

Oct. 6. 1862   A LINCOLN

[1] AES, DNA FS RG 59, Appointments, Box 322. Lincoln's endorsement is written on a letter from Edward Stanly, September 30, 1862, recommending John B. Kerr of Maryland for appointment to Chile or "some other Spanish American Government." Kerr had served as chargé d'affaires to Nicaragua 1850-1854. No record of his appointment to foreign service by Lincoln has been found, but on January 15, 1864, Lincoln nominated him deputy solicitor of the Court of Claims, and the Senate confirmed the nomination on February 2.

To Joseph R. Smith[1]

October 6, 1862

Assistant Surgeon General please see Dr. Stipp. He says he is ordered to Gen. Mc.Clellan's camp while his preparations—tools, so to speak—are at Corinth, Miss. Not intending to interfere by an order, I still would be glad if he could be sent to Corinth.

Oct. 6. 1862.   A. LINCOLN

[1] ALS, InU. See Lincoln to Lorenzo Thomas, August 4, *supra*, and Lincoln to Townsend, June 24, 1863, *infra*.

[451]

To George B. McClellan[1]

Major General McClellan   Executive Mansion,
Hd. Qrs. A.P.   Washington, Oct. 7. 1862.

You wish to see your family, and I wish to oblige you. It might be left to your own discretion—certainly so, if Mrs. M. could meet you here at Washington.   A. LINCOLN

[1] ALS, owned by S. H. McVitty, Salem, Virginia. No communication from McClellan bearing on this letter has been found. On October 6, 1862, General Halleck had communicated the following to McClellan:

"I am instructed to telegraph you as follows: The President directs that you cross the Potomac and give battle to the enemy or drive him south. Your army must move now while the roads are good. If you cross the river between the enemy and Washington, and cover the latter by your operation, you can be re-enforced with 30,000 men. If you move up the Valley of the Shenandoah, not more than 12,000 or 15,000 can be sent to you. The President advises the interior line between Washington and the enemy, but does not order it. He is very desirous that your army move as soon as possible. You will immediately report what line you adopt and when you intend to cross the river; also to what point the re-enforcements are to be sent. It is necessary that the plan of your operations be positively determined on before orders are given for building bridges and repairing railroads.

"I am directed to add that the Secretary of War and the General-in-Chief fully concur with the President in these instructions." (OR, I, XIX, I, 72).

To Thomas H. Clay[1]

Thomas H. Clay.   Washington, D.C.,
Cincinnati O.   Oct. 8 1862.

You *can not* have reflected seriously when you ask that I shall order Gen. Morgan's command to Kentucky as a favor, because they have marched from Cumberland Gap. The precedent established by it would instantly break up the whole army. Buell's old troops now in pursuit of Bragg, have done more hard marching recently. And, in fact, if you include marching and fighting, there are scarcely any old troops East or West of the mountains that have not done as hard service.

I sincerely wish war was an easier and pleasanter business than it is; but it does not admit of holy-days. On Morgan's command, where it is now sent, as I understand, depends the question whether the enemy will get to the Ohio River in another place.

         A. LINCOLN

[1] ALS, RPB. Thomas H. Clay, Henry Clay's son whom Lincoln appointed minister to Nicaragua on October 21, 1862, telegraphed Lincoln from Cincinnati on October 8, as follows:

"I have been waited on this morning by a committee of loyal Kentuckians now here, refugees, to request that Your Excellency will order the division under command of General G. W. Morgan to Kentucky. They think this division has done so much and suffered so much in their late march from Cumberland Gap to Greenupsburg that they are entitled to this favor at the hands of Your Excellency; and it is believed to be the wish of every loyal Kentuckian that this should be done." (OR, I, XVI, II, 589).

To Ulysses S. Grant[1]

Major Genl. Grant   Washington, D.C.,
Jackson, Tenn.   Oct. 8. 1862.

I congratulate you and all concerned on your recent battles and victories. How does it all sum up?

I especially regret the death of Gen. Hackelman; and am very anxious to know the condition of Gen. Oglesby, who is an intimate personal friend.   A. LINCOLN

[1] ALS, RPB. Brigadier General Pleasant A. Hackleman of Indiana was killed and Brigadier General Richard J. Oglesby of Illinois wounded at the Battle of Corinth, Mississippi, on October 3, 1862. On October 10, Grant replied from Jackson, Tennessee, as follows: "Your dispatch recd. I cannot answer it as fully as I would wish Paroled now eight-thirteen 813 Enlisted Men & forty three (43) Commissioned Officers in good health seven hundred Confederate wounded already to Iuka. Paroled three fifty (350) wounded paroled still at Corinth Cannot tell the number of dead yet. About Eight hundred Rebels already buried. Their loss in Killed about Nine to one of ours. The ground is not yet cleared of their unburied dead Prisoners yet arriving by Every wagon Road & train This does not include Casu[a]lties where [Edward O. C.] Ord attacked in the rear. He has three fifty (350) well prisoners besides the batteries & small arms in large numbers. Our loss there was between four & five hundred (500) Rebel loss about the same Genl Oglesby is shot through the breast & ball lodged in the spine. Hopes for his recovery. Our killed & wounded at Corinth will not Exceed Nine hundred (900) Many of them slightly." (DLC-RTL).

To Henry W. Halleck[1]

Gen Banks says he is a good man. Submitted to Gen. Halleck
Oct. 8. 1862.   A. LINCOLN

[1] AES, owned by Irvin F. Westheimer, Cincinnati, Ohio. Lincoln's endorsement is written on a printed envelope from the "Custom House, Baltimore."

To Edwin M. Stanton[1]

Sec. of War, may, at his discretion, allow this.   A. LINCOLN
Oct. 8. 1862.

[1] AES, NHi. Lincoln's endorsement is written on a letter from John M. Johnston of the Highland County Union Central Committee, Hillsborough, Ohio, asking that paroled soldiers of the Sixtieth Ohio Volunteers, captured at Harper's

Ferry, be allowed to return home and vote in order to counteract the secession strength in the Sixth District. The Sixtieth Ohio, a one-year regiment enlisted about a year before, was ordered discharged on October 10, 1862. Representative Chilton A. White, Democrat and a strong opponent of administration policy, was returned to congress in the Sixth District.

To Morton McMichael[1]

Morton McMichael   Executive Mansion,
Office "North American"   Washington,
Philadelphia Pa   October 9, 1862.
The letter alluded to in your despatch of yesterday has not been received.   A. LINCOLN.

    Operator
    Please send above and oblige   A. L.

[1] Telegram, RPB. The telegram is in John Hay's handwriting. The telegram from Morton McMichael and John W. Forney, Philadelphia, October 8, notified Lincoln that "A communication from the city executive committee goes to you by this nights mail It is important that you should see it." (DLC-RTL). No such communication is in the Lincoln Papers, however, and efforts to locate it elsewhere have failed. Morton McMichael, editor of the *North American*, was one of the founders of the Union League.

To Montgomery C. Meigs[1]

Quarter-Master General   Executive Mansion,
My dear Sir,   Washington, Oct. 9, 1862
The bearer of this, Elbridge Meconkey, was on Gen. Mc.Call's staff, and was wounded at Gaines' Mill. He now wishes to be a Quarter-Master; and I would like to appoint him, if another Q.M. is now needed.
Please answer. Yours truly   A. LINCOLN

Let Elbridge Meconkey be appointed at once.   A. LINCOLN
Oct. 10, 1862.

[1] ALS, owned by Mrs. K. J. T. Ekblaw, Eustis, Florida. Meigs endorsed Lincoln's letter on October 10, as follows:
"Respectfully returned to the President of the United States.
"This Department has now calls for details of Quarter-Masters of Volunteers which it cannot supply, & the Quarter Master General will gladly avail of the services of any efficient officer who may be appointed & directed to report to him for duty."
Lincoln's endorsement of October 10 follows that of Meigs. No further record of Elbridge Meconkey has been found, but his recommendation from Lincoln and perhaps other papers are listed as missing from the Quartermaster General's files (DNA WR RG 92, P 100).

To Edwin M. Stanton[1]

October 9, 1862

Submitted to the Secretary of War, with the remark that I know little of Senator Rice except that he has been a very faithful friend to the Govt. in the present troubles.   A. LINCOLN
Oct. 9. 1862.

P. S. It might be well to see Mr. Dole, the Com. of Indian Affairs, who has recently returned from that scene of action.   A.L.

[1] AES,. IHi. Lincoln's endorsement appears on a letter from Benjamin F. Wade, September 30, 1862: "I have just returned from a six weeks residence about the head of Lake Superior. I have taken pains, to make myself acquainted with our relations with the Indians in that region and from all I can learn I fear that there is danger of trouble with the Chippeways as well as the Sioux. I know that the people there live under the greatest apprehension of an outbreak, and have no doubt that measures should be immediately taken to prevent it. What those measures should be, Mr [Henry B.] Whipple will be able to inform you, but my principal object in writing to you . . . is, to induce you, if possible to appoint Hon. Henry M. Rice, Major Genl. with full command of the Department now under command of Genl. Pope. And this I do without any disparagement of Genl. Pope, who I regard as one of our very best officers, but he has no acquaintance with the Indian character, or experience of their mode of warfare, without which, no man is competent to command against them. Now for God's sake, let us not in this Sioux war, repeat the blunders of Genl. Braddock in the French war, or of our Administration in the conduct of the Florida War. What we want is, a man thoroughly acquainted with the Indian character, who is acquainted with their method of warfare and who can speak their language. A man, who the Indians both fear and respect. Such a man is Henry M. Rice of Minnesota, he is also well acquainted with military affairs, having spent a large portion of his active life with the army, as well as among the Indians. From what I have seen, I know the Chippeway tribe have the fullest confidence in him, and the Sioux before the war had like confidence in him. From all I can learn the people who are exposed to Indian depredations, have more confidence in his ability to protect them than in any other man. Mr. Rice is brave, sagacious and vigilant and persevering beyond any man I know. I hope therefore you will appoint him at once and I will answer with my head for the result. Genl. Pope might in the meantime be assigned to a field more in accordance with his wishes and better adapted to his knowledge of the profession. . . ."

To Edwin M. Stanton[1]

Hon. Sec. of War   Executive Mansion,
Sir   Washington, Oct. 9, 1862.

Gen. Wool, now present, requests that DeWitt Clinton, now a Lieut. be made an aid-de-camp, with the rank of Captain, to serve with the 8th. Army, corps, commanded by Gen. Wool.

Let the General be obliged in this, if it can be done according to law. Yours truly   A. LINCOLN

1 ALS, DNA WR RG 94, Adjutant General, Letters Received, P 926, P 62, filed with 2514-ACP-1872. Lieutenant DeWitt Clinton's appointment as captain and aide-de-camp on October 9, 1862, was confirmed by the Senate on March 11, 1863.

To Samuel R. Curtis[1]

Major General Curtis   Executive Mansion,
St. Louis, Mo.   Washington, Oct. 10. 1862.

I believe some Cherokee Indian Regiments, with some white forces operating with them, now at or near *Fort-Scott*, are within your Department, & under your command. John Ross, principal Chief of the Cherokees, is now here, an exile; and he wishes to know, and so do I, whether the force above mentioned, could not occupy the Cherokee country, consistently with the public service. Please consider and answer.   A. LINCOLN

1 ALS, RPB. See Lincoln to John Ross, September 25, *supra*. General Curtis replied on October 10, "My forces have driven the enemy to Pineville, near the Indian line. I yesterday ordered an advance, driving them into the Territory and beyond. I doubt the expediency of occupying ground so remote from supplies, but I expect to make rebels very scarce in that quarter pretty soon." (OR, I, XIII, 723).

To Edwin M. Stanton[1]

October 10, 1862

The organization attempted by Mr. Boswell, makes a place for people in that region inclined our way, to go; and, in that respect is important. While it is proper that a corps of Northern men should not be raised, & be called Mississippians, still I see no objection to Alabamian's, and even persons from other Southern states, found in Missi[ssi]ppi, joining in the organization. Suppose the Sec. of War modifies his order so as to admit of this; and also providing that when enough for a regiment are obtained they shall go into the service at once, not waiting for the completion of a Brigade—nevertheless Mr. Boswell proceeding to get the materials for a Brigade, if practicable. One man there is worth two here in this, that it adds one to us, and takes one from the enemy; and for which advantage we can afford to endure a little extra extra [*sic*] trouble and perplexity.   A. LINCOLN
Oct. 10. 1862.

1 AES, NHi. Lincoln's endorsement is written on both sides of an envelope which presumably contained at one time papers referring to the proposal made. Stanton endorsed at the end of Lincoln's note, "Boswells Case. Oct 11. The Secretary of War refuses to extend Boswells authority." Daniel K. Boswell of Cor-

inth, Mississippi, was recommended by Representative Aaron Harding and other members of the Kentucky delegation in congress for appointment as brigadier general in February, 1862 (DLC-RTL). Senator Orville H. Browning recommended him on March 4, "to return to Mississippi, and raise troops for the service of the Government." (*Ibid.*). The New York *Tribune*, August 14, 1862, reported Boswell's departure for Corinth, "authorized by the President to raise a Brigade of Union Volunteers in Northern Mississippi." But no further record of Boswell's appointment has been found.

To Jeremiah T. Boyle[1]

Gen. Boyle,   Washington City, D.C.
Louisville, Ky.   Oct. 11– 4.PM 1862
  Please send any news you have from Gen. Buell to-day.
                                               A. LINCOLN.

[1] ALS, RPB. Boyle telegraphed Halleck at 2 P.M. on October 10 that "Men from Tennessee report [John C.] Breckinridge moving northward. Some believe his purpose is to attack Nashville; others believe he is coming up to re-enforce Bragg. . . . Terrible battle yesterday near Perryville. Buell drove Bragg 8 miles, with great slaughter on both sides. . . ." (OR, I, XVI, II, 602). For Boyle's reply to Lincoln's request, see note to Lincoln's telegram to Boyle, October 12, *infra*.

To Henry W. Halleck[1]

                                               October 11, 1862
The writer of the within is a most reliable gentleman—father-in-law, to Gen. Wallace[2] killed at Shiloh. I do not personally know Col. Ransom; but refer the case to Gen. Halleck   A. LINCOLN
Oct. 11. 1862.

[1] AES, IHi. Lincoln's endorsement is written on a letter from Colonel T. Lyle Dickey of the Fourth Illinois Cavalry, Jackson, Tennessee, June 21, 1862, praising the leadership of Lieutenant Colonel Thomas E. G. Ransom of the Eleventh Illinois Infantry and recommending his appointment as brigadier general. The letter bears also a concurring endorsement by John A. McClernand. Ransom was appointed brigadier general to rank from November 29, 1862.
[2] Brigadier General William H. L. Wallace.

Memorandum:
Reappointment of George A. Rowley[1]

This, as I remember, is one of the cases submitted to Gen. McClellan; & from whom I have not yet heard.   A. LINCOLN
Oct. 11, 1862.

[1] AES, DLC-RTL. See Lincoln to John F. Lee, August 8, and to McClellan August 12, *supra*. Lincoln's endorsement is written on a letter from Rowley, October 8, 1862, summarizing the failure of his efforts to get a further hearing, "On application at the War Dept., on my return here 2d. inst., I found the

original papers had been recd. & were forwarded to Gen. Halleck. On inquiry at
his H'd Q'rs, all the information I could get, was, in the words of Col. Kelton,
A.A.G., that 'Gen. Halleck does not approve of the action of the President &
Gen. McClellan, & has ordered the papers to be filed in his office'; by which ac-
tion, I understand the matter is *quashed*." Lincoln reappointed Rowley as of
January 31, 1863.

To Edwin M. Stanton[1]

If consistent, let the appointment be made.   A. LINCOLN
Oct. 11. 1862.

[1] Copy, ISLA. Lincoln's endorsement appears on the back of a letter from
George W. Dunlap, Louisville, Kentucky, September 8, 1862, recommending
appointment of Green Clay as major of Volunteers. Green Clay became major
in the Third Kentucky Cavalry.

To Edwin M. Stanton[1]

Submitted to the Secretary of War asking "what are the facts of
this case."?   A LINCOLN
October 11. 1862

[1] AES, DLC-RTL. Lincoln's endorsement is written on a copy of a letter from
Hannibal Hamlin, September 26, 1862, forwarded with a concurring note by
Senator Lot M. Morrill, requesting investigation of the case of Captain Charles
Weston, military storekeeper at the Watertown (Massachusetts) Arsenal, who
had been summarily dismissed without a hearing. On October 21, Assistant Secretary of War Peter H. Watson sent Lincoln "all the papers in the case" and
stated that "An investigation of Weston's accounts, since his dismissal, discloses
the fact that they were not only in arrears, but in great confusion, demonstrating
conclusively his unfitness for the office." (DLC-RTL). On August 8, 1863, Weston wrote Lincoln thanking him for having revoked the order of dismissal:
"Through all these weary months, I never doubted, if you examined the case,
you would do me justice." (*Ibid.*).

To Jeremiah T. Boyle[1]

Gen. Boyle   Washington City, D.C.
Louisville, Ky   Oct. 12. 4/10 PM 1862
We are very anxious to hear from Gen. Buell's Army. We have
had nothing since day-before yesterday. Have you any-thing?
A. LINCOLN

[1] ALS, RPB. Boyle replied, "Your dispatches received. Have no reliable information since 10th instant. Battle was fought on Wednesday by two divisions
of McCook's corps, and most of rebel force, under [William J.] Hardee and
[Leonidas] Polk, [Braxton] Bragg commanding the whole. We lost Generals
[James S.] Jackson and [William R.] Terrill, Colonel [George] Webster,
Lieutenant-Colonel [George P.] Jouett, Major [William P.] Campbell. . . . Our
loss estimated at 1,500 to 2,000 killed and wounded. The enemy's loss as great, and

believed to be greater. . . . My understanding is that Buell is pressing the enemy. Heavy fighting reported at Harrodsburg. Expect to receive news by courier to night. Will send it to you." (OR, I, XVI, II, 609).

To Samuel R. Curtis[1]

Major General Curtis   Washington D.C.
St. Louis, Mo.   Oct. 12, 1862

Would the completion of the railroad some distance further in the direction of Springfield, Mo, be of any military advantage to you? Please answer.   A. LINCOLN

[1] ALS, RPB. This telegram is misdated August 12, 1862, in the *Official Records* (I, XIII, 560; also NH, VII, 308). No answer from Curtis has been found. See also Lincoln's order extending the Pacific Railroad, July 11, *supra.* On September 11, Attorney General Bates wrote Lincoln urging the completion of the railroad "at all events to Little Piney—without delay. If that is not done, we put to fearful hazard, the success of the campaign in that region. . . ." (DLC-RTL). On September 19, Bates wrote again about Missouri matters in general and the railroad in particular, and on September 23 addressed Lincoln "earnestly to entreat you to grant . . . an order for the continuation of the . . . S. W. Branch of the Pacific Railroad, from Rolla to Lebanon, through the Ozark Mountains. [a draft of an order for that purpose, is herewith presented.]" (*Ibid.*). Brackets are in the source.

If the order of July 11 was actually issued on that date, Bates' letters of September 11, 19, and 23 are hardly comprehensible. It seems barely possible that the "draft of an order" enclosed by Bates on September 23 may have been the order signed by Lincoln on July 11, but in this case it is difficult to conjecture why Bates dated it "June 27" and later changed the date to "July 11." It is also possible that the "draft of an order" enclosed by Bates on September 23 was an undated draft of a letter which is preserved in the Lincoln Papers (No. 18528) immediately following Bates' letter of September 19 rather than following the letter of September 23. If so, there is no evidence that the letter was ever sent by Lincoln. The text of the draft of the letter is as follows:

"To Major General Curtis
"Commanding Department of Missouri
    "General Many persons, including several Major Generals who have commanded in Missouri, have urged me to order the completion of the South West Branch of the Pacific Railroad to Lebanon. Nevertheless the burdens of the National Treasury are so enormous that I hesitate to make this order, and have concluded to refer the subject to you with the following instructions.
    "You will investigate the matter thoroughly, and in doing so, you will exclude all considerations of a local character and confine yourself to the point whether the completion of this road will decrease instead of increasing the national expenditures in the prosecution of the war and the maintainance of the supremacy of the Government in that section of the country.
    "Should you be well satisfied upon this point you will order the work to be done and the materials to be provided as expeditiously and as economically as possible, and for this purpose you are hereby authorized to appoint a Superintendant of the same; and to make such contracts as may be requisite therefor, and to make the proper requisitions upon the Quartermaster at St. Louis for payment thereof.
    "You will be especially careful to undertake no work beyond Little Piney unless you are thoroughly satisfied that you are acting within these instructions,

[459]

and you will also be careful to guard the Government against imposition as to the price or quality of the work and materials."

See further Lincoln's letter to Samuel T. Glover, January 20, 1863, *infra*.

To George B. McClellan[1]

Major General McClellan   Executive Mansion,
My dear Sir   Washington, Oct. 13, 1862.

You remember my speaking to you of what I called your over-cautiousness. Are you not over-cautious when you assume that you can not do what the enemy is constantly doing? Should you not claim to be at least his equal in prowess, and act upon the claim?

As I understand, you telegraph Gen. Halleck that you can not subsist your army at Winchester unless the Railroad from Harper's Ferry to that point be put in working order. But the enemy does now subsist his army at Winchester at a distance nearly twice as great from railroad transportation as you would have to do without the railroad last named. He now wagons from Culpepper C.H. which is just about twice as far as you would have to do from Harper's Ferry. He is certainly not more than half as well provided with wagons as you are. I certainly should be pleased for you to have the advantage of the Railroad from Harper's Ferry to Winchester, but it wastes all the remainder of autumn to give it to you; and, in fact ignores the question of *time*, which can not, and must not be ignored.

Again, one of the standard maxims of war, as you know, is "to operate upon the enemy's communications as much as possible without exposing your own." You seem to act as if this applies *against* you, but can not apply in your *favor*. Change positions with the enemy, and think you not he would break your communication with Richmond within the next twentyfour hours? You dread his going into Pennsylvania. But if he does so in full force, he gives up his communications to you absolutely, and you have nothing to do but to follow, and ruin him; if he does so with less than full force, fall upon, and beat what is left behind all the easier.

Exclusive of the water line, you are now nearer Richmond than the enemy is by the route that you *can*, and he *must* take. Why can you not reach there before him, unless you admit that he is more than your equal on a march. His route is the arc of a circle, while yours is the chord. The roads are as good on yours as on his.

You know I desired, but did not order, you to cross the Potomac below, instead of above the Shenandoah and Blue Ridge. My idea was that this would at once menace the enemies' communications, which I would seize if he would permit. If he should move Northward I would follow him closely, holding his communications. If he should prevent our seizing his communications, and move towards Richmond, I would press closely to him, fight him if a favorable opportunity should present, and, at least, try to beat him to Richmond on the inside track. I say "try"; if we never try, we shall never succeed. If he make a stand at Winchester, moving neither North or South, I would fight him there, on the idea that if we can not beat him when he bears the wastage of coming to us, we never can when we bear the wastage of going to him. This proposition is a simple truth, and is too important to be lost sight of for a moment. In coming to us, he tenders us an advantage which we should not waive. We should not so operate as to merely drive him away. As we must beat him somewhere, or fail finally, we can do it, if at all, easier near to us, than far away. If we can not beat the enemy where he now is, we never can, he again being within the entrenchments of Richmond.

Recurring to the idea of going to Richmond on the inside track, the facility of supplying from the side away from the enemy is remarkable—as it were, by the different spokes of a wheel extending from the hub towards the rim—and this whether you move directly by the chord, or on the inside arc, hugging the Blue Ridge more closely. The chord-line, as you see, carries you by Aldie, Hay-Market, and Fredericksburg; and you see how turn-pikes, rail-roads, and finally, the Potomac by Acquia Creek, meet you at all points from Washington. The same, only the lines lengthened a little, if you press closer to the Blue Ridge part of the way. The gaps through the Blue Ridge I understand to be about the following distances from Harper's Ferry, towit: Vestal's five miles; Gregorie's, thirteen, Snicker's eighteen, Ashby's, twenty-eight, Mannassas, thirty-eight, Chester fortyfive, and Thornton's fifty-three. I should think it preferable to take the route nearest the enemy, disabling him to make an important move without your knowledge, and compelling him to keep his forces together, for dread of you. The gaps would enable you to attack if you should wish. For a great part of the way, you would be practically between the enemy and both Washington and Richmond, enabling us to spare you the greatest number of troops from here. When at length, running for Richmond ahead of him enables him to move this way; if he does so, turn and attack him in rear. But I think he should be engaged long before such point is reached. It is all easy if our troops march as well as the enemy; and it is unmanly to say they can not do it.

This letter is in no sense an order. Yours truly   A. LINCOLN.

¹ ADfS, DLC-RTL. On October 16, 8:30 A.M., McClellan acknowledged Lincoln's letter "just received from Colonel [Delavan D.] Perkins. . . . I go to the front. . . . This may delay my reply." (OR, I, XIX, I, 16). On October 17, McClellan replied as follows:

"Your letter of the 13th . . . reached me yesterday morning by the hands of Colonel Perkins.

"I had sent out strong reconnaissances . . . and as sharp artillery fire was heard, I felt it incumbent to go to the front. I did not leave Charlestown until dark, so that I have been unable to give Your Excellency's letter that full and respectful consideration which it merits at my hands.

"I do not wish to detain Colonel Perkins beyond this morning's train; I therefore think it best to send him back with this simple acknowledgment of the receipt of Your Excellency's letter. . . . I promise you that I will give to your views the fullest and most unprejudiced consideration, and that it is my intention to advance the moment my men are shod and my cavalry are sufficiently renovated to be available. . . ." (*Ibid.*).

No further reply has been found, but McClellan continued to delay and sought changes in the order of October 6 (see note, Lincoln to McClellan, October 7, *supra*). On October 21, Halleck telegraphed McClellan that the president "directs me to say that he has no change to make in his order of the 6th instant. If you have not been and are not now in condition to obey it, you will be able to show such want of ability. The President does not expect impossibilities, but he is very anxious that all this good weather should not be wasted in inactivity. Telegraph when you will move, and on what lines you propose to march." (OR, I, XIX, I, 81).

To Benjamin F. Butler, George F. Shepley and Others[1]

(Copy).

Executive Mansion,
Washington, October 14. 1862

Major General Butler, Governor Shepley, & and [*sic*] all having military and naval authority under the United States within the S[t]ate of Louisiana.

The bearer of this, Hon. John E. Bouligny, a citizen of Louisiana, goes to that State seeking to have such of the people thereof as desire to avoid the unsatisfactory prospect before them, and to have peace again upon the old terms under the constitution of the United States, to manifest such desire by elections of members to the Congress of the United States particularly, and perhaps a legislature, State officers, and United States Senators friendly to their object. I shall be glad for you and each of you, to aid him and all others acting for this object, as much as possible. In all available ways give the people a chance to express their wishes at these elections. Follow forms of law as far as convenient, but at all events get the expression of the largest number of the people possible. All see how such action will connect with, and affect the proclamation of September 22nd. Of course the men elected should be gentlemen of character, willing to swear support to the constitution, as of old, and known to be above reasonable suspicion of duplicity. Yours very Respectfully   A. LINCOLN

[Endorsement]²

Similar letter to Gen. Grant, Gov. Johnson & others in Tenn. dated Oct. 21. 1862.
And to, Steele, Phelps & others in Arkansas.
Nov. 18. 1862

¹ ALS copy, DLC-RTL.
² Lincoln's endorsement is written on the back of the second page of the letter. See the letters referred to, *infra*.

To John A. Dahlgren¹

Capt. Dahlgren may let "Tad" have a little gun that he can not hurt himself with.   A. LINCOLN
    Oct. 14, 1862.

¹ ALS, IHi. The miniature brass cannon, a model of Dahlgren's Boat How-itzer, is preserved with Lincoln's note in the Illinois State Historical Library.

Order to Remove Bakeries from the Capitol¹

Executive Mansion
Washington, Oct 14, 1862.

Whereas by a provision of the civil appropriation act approved July 11, 1862, which provision is in the words following towit:

"For the purpose of enabling the commissioner of public build-ings and grounds to remove the army bakery from the basement floor of the Capitol, and to repair the damage caused by said bak-ery, the sum of eight thousand dollars, or so much thereof as may be necessary," is appropriated, and the intention of congress is manifested, that said commissioner shall remove said bakery and repair said damage; and whereas said commissioner represents to me that he apprehends some collision or difficulty with the military authorities in attempting to execute his duty in this respect,

It is therefore ordered that the military authorities, and all other United States authorities in any way connected with the matter, forbear to hinder, and give all reasonable co-operation to the said commissioner, in the performance of said duty.   A. LINCOLN

¹ Copy, DLC-RTL. See Lincoln to Stanton, September 27, *supra*.

To Edward Bates[1]

Let the appointment be made as recommended by Judge Ballard.
Oct. 15. 1862   A. LINCOLN

[1] AES, DNA RG 60, Papers of Attorney General, Appointments, Box 479. Lincoln's endorsement is written on a letter from Judge Bland Ballard, Louisville, Kentucky, October 9, 1862, recommending removal of U.S. Marshal Alexander H. Sneed for failure to render accounts, pay witnesses and jurors, and generally to perform his duties. Ballard also recommended Henry C. McDowell of Louisville to succeed Sneed. McDowell is listed as marshal in the *Official Register* for 1863.

Memorandum[1]

Thinks there is a vacancy at Ebenezer Church, Navy Yard here, & applies for it.   A LINCOLN
Oct. 15. 1862

[1] AES, MnHi. Lincoln's endorsement is on a scrap torn from an unidentified document.

To Lorenzo Thomas[1]

October 15, 1862

The within letter of Gen. McClellan is in answer to one from me in regard to Lieut. John S. Knapp of 17th Regular Infantry, being detailed on recruiting service. Adjt. General, please fix it up. Mr. Nicolay goes to you with the father, and please hear them as to where the Lieut. is to go.   A. LINCOLN
Oct. 15, 1862

[1] Thomas F. Madigan, *A Catalogue of Lincolniana* (1929), p. 23. According to the catalog description Lincoln's endorsement is written on the back of a letter from McClellan suggesting that the president direct his request to the adjutant general. Lincoln's letter to McClellan has not been found and there is no further record of the case.

Memorandum:
Appointment of William H. Channing[1]

Executive Mansion,
Washington, Oct. 16. 1862.

To-day, Mr. Goodloe calls with Rev. Mr. Channing of the Unitarian Church here, (now used as a hospital) to be Chaplain there, or elsewhere here. I believe him entirely worthy, but I have not now an appointment to make.   A. LINCOLN

1 ADS, RPB. Daniel R. Goodloe was chairman of the Commission for Emancipation of Slaves in the District of Columbia. Reverend William H. Channing was appointed hospital chaplain on November 8, 1862, and served as chaplain of Stanton Hospital until July 19, 1865.

To Francis H. Peirpoint[1]

Gov. Pierpoint   Washington City, D.C.
Wheeling, Va.   Oct. 16, 1862

Your despatch of to-day received. I am very sorry to have offended you. I appointed the Collector, as I thought, on your written recommendation; and the Assessor also with your testimony of worthiness, although I knew you preferred a different man. I will examine to-morrow whether I am mistaken in this.

A. LINCOLN.

1 ALS, RPB. Governor Peirpoint telegraphed on October 16, 1862, "I am totally at a loss to understand the influences brought to bear on your mind in the appointment of collector & assessor of this district Union men must sink in despair if all their counsels are unheeded" (DLC-RTL). The New York *Tribune*, October 18, 1862, announced the appointment of James C. Orr of Wheeling as collector and John Parkinson of Marshall as assessor for the First District of Virginia. See further Lincoln to Peirpoint, October 23, *infra*.

To Lorenzo Thomas[1]

Let the resignation mentioned, be not accepted.   A. LINCOLN
Oct. 16. 1862

1 AES, RPB. Lincoln's endorsement is written on a telegram from George C. Bates, Chicago, Illinois, October 15, 1862, "My only son Lt Kinsie Bates 1st US Infantry resigns because I foolishly published a letter of his from Corinth The fault was all mine, not his. Do not let it be accepted Pity a Fathers weakness." Lieutenant Kinzie Bates was brevetted captain as of October 4, 1862, for services at Corinth, Mississippi.

To Edward Bates[1]

Hon. Attorney General   Executive Mansion,
Dear Sir   Washington, October 17, 1862.

Please make out and send me a commission for David Davis of Illinois, as an Associate Justice of the Supreme Court of the United States, for the eighth judicial circuit. Yours truly   A. LINCOLN

1 ALS, IHi. Bates wrote Lincoln on October 15, 1862, "I have examined the matter which you mentioned yesterday, touching your power to fill a vacancy on the bench of the Supreme Court, now, in the recess of the Senate. . . . I give it as my opinion that you have lawful power, now, in the recess of the Senate, to

fill up a vacancy . . . which . . . existed during the last session of the Senate, 'by granting a commission which shall expire at the end of their next session.' . . . ." (DLC-RTL). See Lincoln to David Davis, *infra*.

To John F. Callan[1]

Executive Mansion, Washington,
My Dear Sir   October 17, 1862.
    I have this day received the copy of your "Military Laws," which you had the goodness to send me.
    Pray accept my cordial thanks for your thoughtful courtesy and believe me   Very truly   Your Obt. Servt   A. LINCOLN
    J. F. Callan Esq
        &c   &c

[1] LS, RPB. The letter is in John Hay's handwriting. John F. Callan, who served as clerk of the Senate committee on military affairs, published several editions of his *The Military Laws of the United States. . . .* 1858, 1863, 1864.

To David Davis[1]

Judge David Davis   Executive Mansion.
Lincoln Illinois.   Washington DC.
Dear Davis,   Oct. [17?], 1862
    I send you the enclosed commission which I hope you will accept. I would like to see you on private business this fall.
                                          A. LINCOLN

[1] Copy, IHi-Davis Papers. The copy does not have a day date, but see Lincoln to Bates, *supra*. Davis replied on October 30, "The commission with your note are rec'd. . . . I intended going to Washington some time in Nov'r. The tenor of your note will hasten my departure." (DLC-RTL).

To Edwin M. Stanton[1]

Executive Mansion, Washington, Oct. 17, 1862.
To-day Gen. Michael Corcoran, calls and asks that Morgan Doheny, now a Lieuten[an]t in the 42nd. New-York vols, may be a Lieutenant in the regular Army. There are special reasons for this, and perhaps the rule might be departed from in so low a place as a 2nd. Lieut. I wish to oblige Gen. Corcoran; the Sec. of War will oblige me if he will find a way to do it. Yours truly   A. LINCOLN

[1] ALS, owned by Charles W. Olsen, Chicago, Illinois. Lieutenant Morgan Doheny was discharged November 21, 1862, but enrolled again as first Lieutenant in Company K of the Forty-second New York Volunteers. There is no record of his appointment to the Regular Army.

To William A. Hammond[1]

Surgeon General.   Executive Mansion,
Sir.   Washington, Oct. 18. 1862.

A Baltimore Committee call on me this morning saying that City is full of straggling soldiers half sick, half well, who profess to have been turned from the hospitals with no definite directions where to go. Is this true? Are men turned from the hospitals without knowing where to go. Yours truly   A. LINCOLN

[1] ALS, DLC-RTL. Hammond replied on the same day:

"I am sure there is no blame to be attached to the Military Authorities in Baltimore. I have however referred your communication to Surg Simpson the Medical Director for report.

"The orders of this Bureau are that all soldiers fit for duty shall be turned over to the Military Authorities and I have heard of no instances in which this has not been done.

"The fault lies probably with the men themselves who neglected to obey their orders." (DLC-RTL).

On October 22, 1862, Lincoln's letter was "Respectfully returned, with the accompanying Report" by Surgeon Josiah Simpson: "In reply, I would state that the allegation made by the Committee of Baltimore Citizens is entirely without foundation. . . ." (DLC-RTL).

To William H. Seward[1]

Sec. of State please send me a Commission for the appointment of Elwood Evans, according to the within recommendation.

Oct. 18. 1862.   A. LINCOLN

[1] AES, DNA FS RG 59, Appointments, Box 281. Lincoln's endorsement is written on a note from William H. Wallace, ex-governor of Washington Territory, Executive Mansion, October 18, 1862, advising removal of the incumbent secretary of that territory, Leander J. S. Turney, and appointment of Elwood Evans of Olympia. Evans' appointment was confirmed by the Senate on February 18, 1863.

Executive Order Establishing
A Provisional Court in Louisiana[1]

Executive Mansion, Washington City, D.C. October 20, 1862.

The insurrection which has for some time prevailed in several of the States of this Union, including Louisiana, having temporarily subverted and swept away the civil institutions of that State, including the judiciary and the judicial authorities of the Union, so that it has become necessary to hold the State in military occupation, and it being indispensably necessary that there shall be some judicial tribunal existing there capable of administering justice, I have therefore thought it proper to appoint, and I do hereby constitute, a provisional court, which shall be a court of record, for the State of Louisiana, and I do hereby appoint Charles A. Peabody, of New York, to be a provisional judge to hold said court, with authority to hear, try, and determine all causes, civil and criminal, including causes in law, equity, revenue, and admiralty, and particularly all such powers and jurisdiction as belong to the district and circuit courts of the United States, conforming his proceedings so far as possible to the course of proceedings and practice which has been customary in the courts of the United States and Louisiana, his judgment to be final and conclusive. And I do hereby authorize and empower the said judge to make and establish such rules and regulations as may be necessary for the exercise of his jurisdiction, and empower the said judge to appoint a prosecuting attorney, marshal, and clerk of the said court, who shall perform the functions of attorney, marshal, and clerk according to such proceedings and practice as before-mentioned and such rules and regulations as may be made and established by said judge. These appointments are to continue during the pleasure of the President, not extending beyond the military occupation of the city of New Orleans or the restoration of the civil authority in that city and in the State of Louisiana. These officers shall be paid out of the contingent fund of the War Department compensation as follows: The judge, at the rate of $3500 per annum; the prosecuting attorney, including the fees, at the rate of $3000 per annum; the marshal, including the fees, at the rate of $3000 per annum, and the clerk, including the fees, at the rate of $2500 per annum; such compensations to be certified by the Secretary of War. A copy of this order, certified by the Secretary of War and delivered to such judge, shall be deemed and held to be a sufficient commission. ABRAHAM LINCOLN,

President of the United States.

[1] OR, I, XV, 581-82; copy, DNA WR RG 94, Adjutant General, Letters Received, P 1328, and printed executive order, PHi, both omit several phrases which appear in the *Official Records.*

To John A. McClernand[1]

October 20, 1862

This order, though marked confidential, may be shown by Gen. McClernand, to Governors, and even others, when, in his discretion, he believes so doing to be indispensable to the progress of the expedition. I add that I feel deep interest in the success of the expedition, and desire it to be pushed forward with all possible despatch, consistently with the other parts of the military service.

Oct. 20. 1862.   A. LINCOLN

1 AES, IHi. Lincoln's endorsement is written on the following order:

"*Confidential*   War Department   Washington City,
October 21st 1862

"Ordered. That Major General McClernand be, and he is directed to proceed to the States of Indiana, Illinois and Iowa, to organize the troops remaining in those States and to be raised by volunteering or draft, and forward them with all despatch to Memphis, Cairo, or such other points as may hereafter be designated by the General-in-Chief—to the end, that when a sufficient force, not required by the operations of General Grant's command, shall be raised, an expedition may be organized under General McClernand's command against Vicksburg and to clear the Mississippi river and open navigation to New Orleans.

"The forces so organized will remain subject to the designation of the General-in-Chief, and be employed according to such exigencies as the service, in his judgment, may require.   EDWIN M STANTON
"Secretary of War"

Memorandum on Army of the Potomac[1]

War Department
Washington City, D. C.

[October 20] 1862

A report of the A.P. Oct. 20, 1862, shows,

Grand total	231,997–	Of them
Fit for duty	144,662	
Ab. with leave,	66,808.	Remainder of Grand total, pres. sick. pres in arrest & Ab. without leave
Defence of W.	90,613.	
	60,426	
	17,173	

1 AD, DLC-RTL.

Memorandum on Confederate Army[1]

[October 20, 1862]

Va.	21,580	S. C.	12,850
Ala.	8,205	Ark	500
La.	6,263	Florida	1 650
N C.	14,189	Texas	1 250
Ga.	16,725	Miss	3 951
Tenn.	2,400		

89,563

¹ AD, DLC-RTL. The memorandum is attached to a letter from General Nathaniel P. Banks of October 20, 1862, enclosing a "general description and estimate of the Rebel Army . . . . compiled by Colonel Jno. S Clark of my Staff. . . ."

Notice to Aliens¹

Executive Mansion, Washington, October 20, 1862.

It is hereby ordered that all persons who may have actually been drafted into the militia [military]² service of the United States and who may claim exemption on account of alienage, will make application therefor directly to the Department of State or through their respective ministers or consuls.   ABRAHAM LINCOLN.

By the President:

WILLIAM H. SEWARD, Secretary of State.

¹ OR, III, II, 960; New York *Tribune*, October 22, 1862.
² The version in the *Official Records* has "military service," but the draft was actually made for the militia by the various states. See Lincoln's calls of June 30 and July 1, *supra*.

To Edwin M. Stanton¹

Let the appointment within recommended, be made.

Oct. 20. 1862.   A. LINCOLN

¹ AES, IHi. Lincoln's endorsement appears on a letter from Senator James Harlan, September 25, 1862, recommending William P. Clark of Iowa City, Iowa, for appointment as paymaster. Clark was appointed additional paymaster of Volunteers as of January 22, 1863.

To Ulysses S. Grant, Andrew Johnson and Others¹

Executive Mansion, Washington, Oct. 21. 1862.

Major General Grant, Governor Johnson, & all having military, naval, and civil authority under the United States within the State of Tennessee.

The bearer of this, Thomas R. Smith, a citizen of Tennessee, goes to that state, seeking to have such of the people thereof as desire to avoid the unsatisfactory prospect before them, and to have peace again upon the old terms under the constitution of the United States, to manifest such desire by elections of members to the Congress of the United States particularly, and perhaps a legislature, State officers, and a United States' Senator, friendly to their object.

[470]

I shall be glad for you and each of you to aid him, & all others acting for this object, as much as possible. In all available ways give the people a chance to express their wishes at these elections. Follow law, and forms of law as far as convenient; but at all events get the expression of the largest number of the people possible. All see how such action will connect with, and affect the proclamation of Sept. 22nd. Of course the men elected should be gentlemen of character, willing to swear support to the constitution as of old, & known to be above reasonable suspicion of duplicity. Yours very Respectfully   A. LINCOLN.

[1] ALS, NNP. See Lincoln to Butler and Shepley, October 14, *supra.*

To Charles D. Jameson[1]

Gen. Jameson.   Executive Mansion,
Upper Stillwater   Washington,
Maine.   Oct. 21. 1862.

How is your health now? Do you or not wish Lieut. R. P. Crawford to be restored to his office?   A. LINCOLN

[1] ALS, RPB. Brigadier General Charles D. Jameson of Maine contracted fever after the Battle of Fair Oaks and died November 6, 1862. No reply to Lincoln's telegram has been found, but AGO *General Orders No. 175,* October 31, 1862, revoked "So much of 'General Orders' No. 125, as dismisses Lieutenant R. P. Crawford, Aide-de-Camp . . . ." who had been dismissed for being absent without proper leave. First Lieutenant Robert P. Crawford is listed with the Fifty-seventh Pennsylvania Infantry from February 10, 1862, and was appointed captain and assistant adjutant general of Volunteers on September 4, 1863.

To Edwin M. Stanton[1]

October 21, 1862

I wish the Secretary of War would see Mr. Wilson, and, in view of what he has suffered in the country's cause, find him a place, if possible.   A. LINCOLN
Oct. 21. 1862.

[1] AES, owned by Carl E. Wahlstrom, Worcester, Massachusetts. Lincoln's endorsement is written on an envelope containing a letter from Major John P. Post of the Eighth Illinois Infantry, October 16, 1862, bearing concurring endorsements by Major General John A. McClernand and Brigadier General Benjamin M. Prentiss in favor of First Lieutenant Joseph F. Wilson's appointment as paymaster or assistant commissary. Joseph F. Wilson, a lawyer of Peoria, Illinois, had been seriously wounded at Fort Donelson in such a way as to affect his power of speech. He was appointed captain and commissary of subsistence November 26, 1862.

To Edwin M. Stanton[1]

Please let this appointment be made at once.   A. LINCOLN
Oct. 21, 1862.

[1] AES, IHi. Lincoln's endorsement appears on a letter from John H. Wickizer, lawyer and former member of the Illinois legislature from Bloomington, Illinois, to Ward H. Lamon, September 28, 1862, reminding him that Wickizer's appointment as quartermaster had not been made. Wickizer was nominated assistant quartermaster of Volunteers as of November 4, 1862, and the appointment was confirmed by the Senate on February 19, 1863.

To Edwin M. Stanton[1]

October 22, 1862

In this case I can say no more than that individuals should not be allowed to impose terms on purchasers of Cotten, beyond those contained in the rules established by the Government. If individuals are doing this, it should be stopped. Will the Sec. of War please look to it.   A. LINCOLN

Oct. 22. 1862

[1] AES, DLC-Stanton Papers. Lincoln's endorsement is written on the back of a series of documents submitted by Frederick Ziegler in a complaint of the course he was compelled to take by Moses Bates, financial agent of the Louisiana State Penitentiary at Baton Rouge, in order to get cotton from New Orleans. Ziegler had been required to sign an agreement not to purchase above the maximum price fixed for purchases of cotton to operate the penitentiary factory (*Private and Official Correspondence of General Benjamin F. Butler*, II, 580).

To Salmon P. Chase[1]

October 23, 1862

I shall be very glad if the Secretary of the Treasury, or any Head of a Department, or Bureau can, and will find employment for Miss. Sommers.   A. LINCOLN

Oct. 23. 1862.

[1] ALS, CSmH. Miss A. E. Sommers is listed in the *U.S. Official Register*, 1863, as an employee in the Treasury whose duties were counting notes and currency preparatory to burning.

To Ben Field[1]

Executive Mansion, Washington,
Ben. Field, Esq., Astor House: October 23, 1862.
Your letter of 20th received. Think your request cannot safely be granted.   A. LINCOLN.

[1] Tarbell (Appendix), p. 352. Ben Field of Albion, New York, secretary of the Union State Central Committee, wrote Lincoln on October 20, 1862, "I am directed by this committee to represent to you that it is important that Genl Sigel

should visit this state and address one or more meetings in behalf of Wadsworth and Tremain. It is believed that this would influence favorably the result. He should come on as Early as the forepart of next week" (DLC-RTL). James S. Wadsworth was the Union candidate for governor and Lyman Tremain the candidate for lieutenant governor.

To William A. Hammond[1]

Surgeon General   Oct. 23, 1862

Sir   Is a hospital chaplain needed at Ebenezer Church & Odd Fellows Hall, Navy Yard, Washington? Please answer on the sheet below. Yours truly   A. LINCOLN

[1] Stan. V. Henkels Catalog 1373, March 19, 1925, No. 86. According to the catalog description this is an autograph letter signed. Hammond's reply is not given.

To Francis H. Peirpoint[1]

Hon. F. H. Pierpoint,   Executive Mansion,
Wheeling, Va.:   Washington, October 23, 1862.

Your letter of the 17th just received. When you come to Washington, I shall be pleased to show you the record upon which we acted. Nevertheless answer this, distinctly saying you wish Ross and Ritcher, or any other two you do really want, and they shall be appointed.   A. LINCOLN.

[1] Tarbell (Appendix), p. 352. The date of this letter may be October 25 rather than October 23 as given by Tarbell (also NH, VIII, 67). The letter has been advertised for sale in a dealer's catalog and given the date of October 25, but efforts to obtain a photostat have not availed. Further difficulty is encountered by reason of the fact that Governor Peirpoint's letter of October 17, to which Lincoln replied, is not in the Lincoln Papers or referred to elsewhere. The men "Ross and Ritcher" have not been identified. Peirpoint's telegram of October 18, however, is as follows: "Suspend your examination of papers. I will write today. There is a great misunderstanding some place.   Not offended but worried." (DLC-RTL). Lincoln's original appointments of James C. Orr as collector and John Parkinson as assessor for the First District of Virginia were allowed to stand, and were confirmed by the Senate—Parkinson on February 3 and Orr on February 27, 1863.

Memorandum:
Appointment of George T. Harris[1]

Executive Mansion, Washington, Oct. 24, 1862.

Bishop McIlvaine calls and asks that George T. Harris, son of G. W. Harris Philada. (Peabody & Co.) be sent to West-Point. I promise to try to do this   A.L

[1] ADS, DNA WR RG 94, U.S. Military Academy, 1862, No. 117, Box 80. Charles P. McIlvaine was Episcopal Bishop of Ohio. There is no record of George T. Harris' appointment.

Memorandum: Appointment of J. H. Hawes[1]

On the strength of this paper I have made the appointment requested
                                    A. LINCOLN
Oct. 24. 1862

[1] AES, DLC-RTL. Lincoln's endorsement is written on the back of a letter from James M. Edmunds, General Land Office, October 23, 1862, recommending appointment of J. H. Hawes principal clerk of surveys to replace S. J. Dallas.

Recommendation for William H. Johnson[1]

The bearer of this, William Johnson (colored), came with me from Illinois; and is a worthy man, as I believe.   A. LINCOLN
Oct. 24. 1862

[1] ADS, IHi.

To George B. McClellan[1]

                                 Washington City, D.C.
Majr. Genl. McClellan   Oct. 24 [25]. 1862

I have just read your despatch about sore tongued and fatiegued horses. Will you pardon me for asking what the horses of your army have done since the battle of Antietam that fatigue anything?   A. LINCOLN

[1] ALS, IHi. Lincoln obviously misdated this telegram, since McClellan's despatch to Halleck transmitting a report of Colonel Robert Williams of the First Massachusetts Cavalry was not received at the War Department until 12 M., October 25. Williams reported as follows:

"I have in camp 267 horses . . . of these, 128 are positively and absolutely unable to leave the camp, from the following causes, viz, sore-tongue, grease, and consequent lameness, and sore backs. . . . The horses, which are still sound, are absolutely broken down from fatigue and want of flesh. . . ." (OR, I, XIX, II, 485-86).

McClellan replied to Lincoln at 6 P.M. October 25, as follows:

"In reply to your telegram of this date, I have the honor to state, from the time this army left Washington, on the 7th of September, my cavalry has been constantly employed in making reconnaissances, scouting, and picketing. Since the battle of Antietam, six regiments have made a trip of 200 miles, marching 55 miles in one day, while endeavoring to reach Stuart's cavalry.

"General Pleasonton, in his official report, states that he, with the remainder of our available cavalry, while on Stuart's track, marched 78 miles in twenty-four hours.

"Besides these two remarkable expeditions, our cavalry has been engaged in picketing and scouting 150 miles of river front ever since the battle of Antietam, and has made repeated reconnaissances since that time, engaging the enemy on every occasion, and, indeed, it has performed harder service since the battle than before. I beg that you will also consider that this same cavalry was brought from the Peninsula, where it encountered most laborious service, and was, at the com-

[474]

mencement of this campaign, in low condition, and from that time to the present has had no time to recruit.

"If any instance can be found where overworked cavalry has performed more labor than mine since the battle of Antietam, I am not conscious of it." (OR, I, XIX, II, 485).

To Edwin M. Stanton[1]

Hon. Sec. of War.   Executive Mansion,
Sir   Washington, Oct. 24, 1862.

Colfax is very anxious for the appointment of Elihu Griffin, of Ia. as an Additional Pay-Master. If at all consistent, let it be done. Yours truly   A. LINCOLN

[1] ALS, PHi. Elihu Griffin of Indiana was appointed additional paymaster of Volunteers as of November 13, 1862.

Order Disapproving Death Sentence of José Maria Rivas[1]

October 25, 1862.

Waiving the question of jurisdiction in the case, the sentence is not approved, because the accused is not shown to have been within our lines in disguise, or by false pretense, except by hearsay testimony; and because in his admission that he was a "Spy," he may not have understood the technical term, and may have meant no more than that he was a scout of the enemy. He clearly is a prisoner of war.   A. LINCOLN.

[1] AGO General Orders No. 174; OR, II, IV, 669. José Maria Rivas was sentenced by a military commission in Sante Fé, New Mexico, on charges of acting as a spy.

Order Mitigating Death Sentence of Sely Lewis[1]

October 25, 1862

So far as the sentence in the case relates to the accused as a Spy, it is disapproved, the Commission not having jurisdiction of the offense. The sentence of death is mitigated to imprisonment for the term of six months, commencing this day—October 25, 1862.

A. LINCOLN.

[1] AGO General Orders No. 170; OR, II, IV, 662. Sely Lewis was found guilty by a military commission in Memphis, Tennessee, July 28, 1862, on charges of smuggling goods through the lines and violation of the fifty-seventh Article of War. The commission further expressed conviction that Lewis was a spy and recommended that he be hanged.

Order Mitigating Death Sentence
of Conrad Zachringer[1]

October 25, 1862.

The prisoners' offense in this case, being to some extent the result of sudden passion, and not of premeditation, the sentence of death is mitigated to imprisonment for one year, commencing on this day, and to be dishonorably discharged the service, with loss of pay and emoluments. A. LINCOLN.

[1] AGO *General Orders No. 173*, October 29, 1862. Private Conrad Zachringer of Company A, Twelfth Missouri Volunteers, charged with violation of the seventh Article of War ("caused and excited mutiny by taking hold of First Lieutenant Mittman, then Officer of the Day, by the throat. . . .") and of the ninth Article of War (". . . did strike First Lieutenant Engelmann, and throwed him on the ground. . . .), and of the twenty-seventh Article of War (". . . did refuse to obey . . . . did resist and strike. . . ."), was found guilty by a court-martial at Helena, Arkansas, on all charges and sentenced to be shot. Zachringer pleaded "That he was drunk, and knew nothing of them."

To William H. Seward[1]

October 25, 1862

Write Canissius that in view of our own aspirants we can not find a place for a Military officer of high rank from abroad.

Better send the account of the explosive material to Capt. Dahlgren. A L.

Oct. 25. 1862

[1] ALS, NAuE. On October 25, Secretary Seward forwarded a letter from Theodore Canisius, consul at Vienna, October 4, 1862, as follows:

"General Baron Lenk, the *best* and most prominent artillery officer of the Austrian army desires to enter into our army, and he, therefore, requested me to offer to you his services.

"I have referred to Gen. Lenk in my dispatch of this day to the Secretary of State. . . . Men like the general we ought not to refuse. . . ." (DLC-RTL).

To John A. Dix[1]

"Private & confidential"

Major General Dix   Executive Mansion,
Fort-Monroe, Va.   Washington, Oct. 26. 1862.

Your despatch to Mr. Stanton, of which the inclosed is a copy has been handed me by him. It would be dangerous for me now to begin construing, and making specific applications of, the Proclamation. It is obvious to all that I therein intended to give time, and opportunity. Also it is seen I left my self at liberty to exempt *parts* of states. Without saying more, I shall be very glad if any Congressional District will, in good faith, do as your despatch contemplates.

Could you not give me the facts which prompted you to telegraph? Yours very truly   A. LINCOLN.

¹ ALS, IHi. The copy of Dix's telegram to Stanton of October 23, 1862, reads as follows: "Will a congress District being in an Insurgent State and represented on the 1st. of January next in the congress of the United States by a member chosen at an election wherein a majority of the qualified Voters of the District shall have participated be considered not in rebellion & exempt from the penalty announced in the Presidents Proclamation of the 22nd. of September?" (*Ibid.*). Dix replied to Lincoln's letter on October 28, "I have just received your private and confidential letter of the 26th inst. My despatch to the Secretary of War was dictated by an earnest desire, not without hope, to induce the people of the Congress District, of which Norfolk is a part, to return to their allegiance and send a loyal member to the House. . . . I am about to call on them, through their Military Governor, to take the oath of allegiance, and I wish to give them the assurance, if I can, that, by complying with the conditions of your Proclamation of the 22nd of Sept. they will avoid the penalties of disloyalty. . . ." (DLC-RTL).

To George B. McClellan¹

Executive Mansion, Washington,
Maj. Gen. McClellan   Oct. 26. 1862. [11:30 A.M.]

Yours in reply to mine about horses received. Of course you know the facts better than I, still two considerations remain. Stuart's cavalry outmarched ours, having certainly done more marked service on the Peninsula, and everywhere since. Secondly, will not a movement of our army be a relief to the cavalry, compelling the enemy to concentrate, instead of "foraging" in squads everywhere?

But I am so rejoiced to learn from your despatch to Gen. Halleck, that you begin crossing the river this morning.   A. LINCOLN

¹ ALS copy, DLC-RTL. McClellan replied at 9 P.M., "I have the honor to acknowledge the receipt of your telegram of this morning. You will pardon me for most respectfully differing with you in regard to the expression in your dispatch 'Stuart's cavalry has done more marked service on the Peninsula and everywhere since.' I cannot resist the strength of my own conviction that some one has conveyed to your mind an erroneous impression in regard to the service of our cavalry, for I know you would not intentionally do injustice to the excellent officers and men of which it is composed. . . .

"With the exception of the two raids by Stuart, I am unconscious of a single instance where the rebel cavalry has exhibited any superiority over ours. The fact that Stuart outmarched Pleasonton in his last raid is easily accounted for. It is said that he received a relay of fresh horses when he crossed the river at McCoy's Ferry. From that point he had extra lead horses to take the places of those that gave out on the road, besides which he stole some 1,000 horses in Pennsylvania, which contributed toward giving him another relay. Notwithstanding all this, he dropped a great many broken-down horses along the road. Pleasonton made his entire trip without a change of horses.

"After this statement of facts has been placed before you, I feel confident you will concur with me that our cavalry is equally as efficient as that of the rebels." (OR, I, XIX, II, 490-91).

[477]

Reply to Eliza P. Gurney[1]

October 26, 1862

I am glad of this interview, and glad to know that I have your sympathy and prayers. We are indeed going through a great trial —a fiery trial. In the very responsible position in which I happen to be placed, being a humble instrument in the hands of our Heavenly Father, as I am, and as we all are, to work out his great purposes, I have desired that all my works and acts may be according to his will, and that it might be so, I have sought his aid—but if after endeavoring to do my best in the light which he affords me, I find my efforts fail, I must believe that for some purpose unknown to me, He wills it otherwise   If I had had my way, this war would never have been commenced; If I had been allowed my way this war would have been ended before this, but we find it still continues; and we must believe that He permits it for some wise purpose of his own, mysterious and unknown to us; and though with our limited understandings we may not be able to comprehend it, yet we cannot but believe, that he who made the world still governs it.

[1] Copy, DLC-RTL. The copy of the interview preserved in the Lincoln Papers is in an unknown handwriting and bears the date 1862, "Sept (28?)" having been inserted in a different handwriting. Under this date Lincoln's reply is printed in the *Complete Works* (VIII, 50-51). The New York *Tribune*, October 28, 1862, however, gives an account of the interview as occurring on October 27, but Lincoln's letter to Mrs. Gurney, September 4, 1864, *infra*, specifies Sunday, September 26. Mrs. Gurney was the widow and third wife of Joseph J. Gurney, English Quaker, philanthropist and religious writer. Her address to the president as reproduced in the copy of the interview in the Lincoln Papers is in effect a sermon, at the conclusion of which Mrs. Gurney knelt "and uttered a short but most beautiful, eloquent, and comprehensive prayer that light and wisdom might be shed down from on high, to guide our President. . . . After a brief pause the President replied." No newspaper which gives a verbatim report similar to the copy in the Lincoln Papers has been found.

To Edwin M. Stanton[1]

October 26, 1862

This, to my annoyance, shows that at half past two P.M. yesterday, Gen. Rosecrans was still at Corinth!

Let him have the Staff officer he asks.　　　　A. LINCOLN

Oct. 26. 1862.

[1] AES, owned by Frank L. Pleadwell, Honolulu, Hawaii. The endorsement is removed from the document referred to, and efforts to locate an appropriate communication from Rosecrans have been unsuccessful.

To George B. McClellan[1]

Executive Mansion, Washington,
Majr. Gen. McClellan.   Oct. 27. 1862
Yours of yesterday received. Most certainly I intend no injustice
to any; and if I have done any, I deeply regret it. To be told after
more than five weeks total inaction of the Army, and during which
period we had sent to that Army every fresh horse we possibly
could, amounting in the whole to 7918 that the cavalry horses
were too much fatiegued to move, presented a very cheerless, almost hopeless, prospect for the future; and it may have forced
something of impatience into my despatches. If not recruited, and
rested then, when could they ever be? I suppose the river is rising,
and I am glad to believe you are crossing.   A. LINCOLN

[1] ALS, IHi.

To George B. McClellan[1]

Executive Mansion, Washington,
October 27, 1862. [3:25 P.M.]
Major-General McClellan: Your dispatch of 3 p.m. to-day, in
regard to filling up old regiments with drafted men, is received,
and the request therein shall be complied with as far as practicable.

And now I ask a distinct answer to the question, Is it your purpose not to go into action again until the men now being drafted
in the States are incorporated into the old regiments?

A. LINCOLN.

[1] OR, I, XIX, II, 497; copy, DLC-McClellan Papers. McClellan's telegram of
3 P.M. reads as follows:
"Your Excellency is aware of the very great reduction of numbers that has
taken place in most of the old regiments of this command, and how necessary it
is to fill up these skeletons before taking them again into action. I have the honor,
therefore, to request that the order to fill up the old regiments with drafted men
may at once be issued." (OR, I, XIX, II, 496).
At 7:15 P.M. McClellan replied to Lincoln's query:
"I have the honor to acknowledge the receipt of your dispatch of . . . to-day
. . . . deeply impressed with the importance of filling up the old regiments. . . .
I . . . called an aide, and . . . directed him to write for me a dispatch asking
Your Excellency to have the necessary order given. I regret to say that this officer,
after writing the dispatch, finding me still engaged, sent it to the telegraph office
without first submitting it to me, under the impression that he had communicated
my views. He, however, unfortunately added 'before taking them into action
again.' This phrase was not authorized or intended by me. It has conveyed altogether an erroneous impression as to my plans and intentions. To Your Excellency's question I answer distinctly that I have not had any idea of postponing the
advance until the old regiments are filled by drafted men. I commenced crossing
the army into Virginia yesterday, and shall push forward as rapidly as possible to
endeavor to meet the enemy. . . ." (Ibid., 497).

[479]

To Edwin M. Stanton and Henry W. Halleck[1]

Sec. of War & Gen. Halleck, please consider within; and if they approve, I am ready to concur.   A. LINCOLN
Oct. 27. 1862.

[1] AES, MHi. Lincoln's endorsement has been removed from the document to which it refers.

To Gideon Welles[1]

[c. October 27, 1862]

Mr. Rogers wishes to be an Asst. Paymaster in the Navy. I know not whether there is a vacancy. The within shows that my son "Bob" has a high opinion of him.   A. LINCOLN

[1] Henry M. Rogers, *Memories of Ninety Years* (1928), p. 70. Henry M. Rogers was a student at Harvard who brought a letter of introduction from his friend Robert T. Lincoln. He was appointed acting assistant paymaster in the Navy, November 6, 1862.

To Henry W. Halleck[1]

October 28, 1862

Submitted to Majr. Gen. Halleck asking an examination of the record of Col. Alfred T. A. Torbert, to be a Brigadier General, to command the Brigade left without a commander by the death of Gen. Geo. W. Taylor, and in which he Col. Torbert is senior Colonel.   A. LINCOLN.
Oct. 28. 1862.

[1] AES-P, ISLA. Colonel Alfred T. A. Torbert of the First New Jersey Volunteers was appointed brigadier general to rank from November 29, 1862. The appointment, rejected by the Senate on February 12, 1863, and again on March 12, was confirmed by the Senate on March 13, 1863. Colonel Torbert was on sick leave January to June, 1863.

Allotment of Supreme Court Judges to Circuits[1]

Executive Mansion, Washington, October 29, 1862.

Two associate justices of the Supreme Court of the United States having been appointed since the last adjournment of said court, and consequently no allotment of the members of said court to the several circuits having been made by them, according to the fifth section of the act of Congress entitled "An act to amend the judicial system of the United States," approved April 29, 1802, I, Abraham Lincoln, President of the United States, in virtue of said section, do make an allotment of the justices of said court to the circuits now existing by law, as follows:

For the first circuit: Nathan Clifford, associate justice.
For the second circuit: Samuel Nelson, associate justice.
For the third circuit: Robert C. Grier, associate justice.
For the fourth circuit: Roger B. Taney, Chief Justice.
For the fifth circuit: James M. Wayne, associate justice.
For the sixth circuit: John Catron, associate justice.
For the seventh circuit: Noah H. Swayne, associate justice.
For the eighth circuit: David Davis, associate justice.
For the ninth circuit: Samuel F. Miller, associate justice.

ABRAHAM LINCOLN.

[1] James D. Richardson, *A Compilation of the Messages and Papers of the Presidents*, VI, 123. Samuel F. Miller of Iowa was appointed on July 16, 1862, and David Davis on October 17, 1862.

To George B. McClellan[1]

Executive Mansion,
Major Genl. McClellan.   Washington, Oct. 29. 1862

Your despatches of night before last, yesterday, & last night, all received. I am much pleased with the movement of the Army. When you get entirely across the river let me know.

What do you know of the enemy?   A. LINCOLN

[1] ALS, owned by Perc S. Brown, Newark, New Jersey. McClellan's telegram of October 27 has been given in the note to Lincoln's telegram to McClellan on that date, *supra*. On October 28, McClellan telegraphed at 5 P.M., "Headquarters are now at Berlin. All of Franklin's troops are over, and most of his train. General Stoneman has probably crossed at White's Ford by this time. Reynolds' corps is massed here, and will, I hope, complete his supplies of clothing to-day and early to-morrow. Franklin will move for here in the morning if nothing unusual occurs. Everything is moving as rapidly as circumstances will permit. I go to Lovettsville in a few minutes, to return to-night. We need more carbines and muskets. I shall not wait for them, but ought to be supplied at once." (OR, I, XIX, II, 501).

At 1:23 A.M. on October 29, he telegraphed "We occupy Leesburgh." (DLC-RTL).

At 5:30 P.M. on the same day he answered Lincoln as follows: "In reply to your dispatch of this morning I have the honor to state that the accounts . . . of the enemys position & movements are conflicting   A dispatch I have just recd. . . . says . . . Generals [Ambrose P.] Hill, Jackson & [Wade] Hampton are encamped near . . . Ridgesville. Gen Pleasonton reports . . . Hill . . . at Upperville. . . . Gen Porter reports last night that . . . R E Lee is not far distant from him & that Stuart is within an hours march. . . . In the meantime I am pushing forward troops & supplies as rapidly as possible. . . ." (*Ibid.*).

At 9:45 A.M. on November 1, he telegraphed that "all the corps of this Army have crossed the Potomac except Franklins" (*ibid.*), and on November 5 reported at 11:20 P.M. that Franklin "finished crossing the Potomac at Berlin on Monday the third inst. . . . (*ibid.*)."

[481]

To Andrew G. Curtin[1]

Gov. Curtin   Executive Mansion,
Harrisburg.   Washington, Oct. 30, 1862.

By some means I have not seen your despatch of the 27th. about order No. 154, till this moment. I now learn, what I knew nothing of before, that the history of the order is as follows, towit. Gen. McClellan telegraphed asking Gen. Halleck to have the order made. Gen. Halleck went to the Sec. of War with it, stating his approval of the plan, the Secretary assented, and Gen. Halleck wrote the order. It was a military question which the Secretary supposed the Generals understood better than he. I wish I could see Gov. Curtin   A LINCOLN

[1] ALS, RPB. On October 27, 1862, Governor Curtin telegraphed Lincoln his protest against AGO *General Orders No. 154*, October 9, 1862, "as unjust to the people of the States, and calculated to demoralize and destroy volunteer organizations. . . ." (OR, I, XIX, II, 500). Order No. 154, issued on McClellan's recommendation, instructed that, "The commanding officer of each regiment, battalion, and battery of the Regular Army in the field, will appoint one or more recruiting officers, who are hereby authorized to enlist, with their own consent, the requisite number of efficient volunteers to fill the ranks of their command to the legal standard. . . ." Lincoln referred Curtin's telegram to the Secretary of War, and Stanton returned it on October 30 with his endorsement, "Order No 154 referred to within was made at the special request of Major General McClellan approved by General Halleck. . . . The protest of Governor Curtin is ill advised, revolutionary and tends to excite discontent and mutiny in the army and in my judgment should be severely rebuked by the President." (DLC-RTL). On October 31, Halleck authorized McClellan, "if you deem best, to revoke all enlistments from the volunteer artillery under your command, and to return them to their batteries." (OR, I, XIX, II, 516).

To Frederic, Grand Duke of Baden[1]

October 30, 1862

Abraham Lincoln,
President of the United States of America.

To His Royal Highness Frederic,
Grand Duke of Baden.

Great and Good Friend: I have received the letter which Your Royal Highness was pleased to address to me on the 27th. of last month, announcing the marriage of Her Grand Ducal Highness the Princess Leopoldine of Baden, with His Most Serene Highness the Prince Hermann of Hohenloe Langenburg.

I participate in the satisfaction afforded by this happy event, and pray Your Royal Highness to accept my sincere congratula-

tions upon the occasion, together with the assurances of my highest consideration. Your Good Friend, ABRAHAM LINCOLN.
Washington, October 30, 1862.
By the President:
WILLIAM H. SEWARD, Secretary of State.

[1] Copy, DNA FS RG 59, Communications to Foreign Sovereigns and States, III, 193-94.

To Edwin M. Stanton[1]

October 30, 1862

Except an outside word now and then recently I know nothing of this recruiting for the regulars, from the volunteer regiments. How is this? I have heard a good deal of dissatisfaction about it before seeing this letter. A. LINCOLN

Oct. 30, 1862

[1] Ritter-Hopson Galleries Catalog 37, March 9, 1933, No. 125. According to the catalog description, this endorsement is written on a letter from Colonel George C. Burling of the Sixth New Jersey Volunteers complaining of *General Orders No. 154.* See also Lincoln to Curtin, *supra.*

To Edwin M. Stanton[1]

I am entirely willing to accept the Regiment proposed, if the Sec. of War & Gov: of New-York concur. A. LINCOLN

Oct. 30. 1862

[1] AES, NHi. Lincoln's endorsement is written on a letter from Representative Elijah Ward of New York, October 28, 1862, recommending acceptance by the government of a regiment recruited in New York City under the name of the "Federal Guard" by Captain Henry E. Gotlieb formerly of the Fortieth New York Infantry. Stanton endorsed below Lincoln's endorsement, "Referred to Governor Morgan. The Department will accept the regiment if sanctioned by him." Gotlieb was given authority to recruit and appointed colonel on November 19, 1862, but the order was revoked on January 24, 1863, and Gotlieb was not commissioned or transferred with the troops to the One Hundred Seventy-eighth New York Infantry.

To Andrew Johnson[1]

Gov. Andrew Johnson
Nashville, Tenn. via Louisville, Ky   Oct. 31. 1862

Yours of the 29th. received. I shall take it to Gen. Halleck; but I already know it will be very inconvenient to take Gen. Morgan's command from where it now is. I am glad to hear you speak hopefully for Tennessee. I sincerely hope Rosecrans may find it possible to do something for her.

"David Nelson" son of the M.C. of your state, regrets his father's final defection, and asks me for a situation. Do you know him? Could he be of service to you, or to Tennessee, in any capacity in which I could send him?[2]   A. LINCOLN

[1] ALS, RPB. Governor Johnson's telegram of 8 A.M. October 29, reads as follows: "General [George W.] Morgan's entire command ought to be sent to Tennessee, and if not, all the Tennessee regiments should be sent. They are the troops we need here. Press the importance of sending these regiments to Tennessee upon General Halleck. I know if his attention is called to it he will not hesitate one moment. Let them come and we will redeem East Tennessee before Christmas. East Tennessee must be redeemed. I have much to say upon this subject at the proper time. Let sufficient forces be sent to Nashville. It must and can be held. I will communicate fully all that has transpired as soon as mail facilities are restored." (OR, I, XVI, II, 651).

[2] David Nelson wrote Lincoln on October 22, "I have just arrived from the south where I have been imprisoned for the last six months. I reside in Jonesboro East Tennessee . . . my father is the Hon T. A R Nelson. At the time of the secession . . . I commanded a company of uniformed militia. . . . In July last I got together some seventy . . . of my old company and attempted to escape to Cumberland Gap . . . . we were intercepted and made prisoners. . . . I wish to enter the service of the Federal Government & will serve it faithfully My father you are probably aware has at last given up all hope & gone over body & soul to Jeff Davis. This is very mortifying to me. . . ." (DLC-RTL).

Memorandum on Furloughs[1]

Nov., 1862.

The Army is constantly depleted by company officers who give their men leave of absence in the very face of the enemy, and on the eve of an engagement, which is almost as bad as desertion. At this very moment there are between seventy and one hundred thousand men absent on furlough from the Army of the Potomac. The army, like the nation, has become demoralized by the idea that the war is to be ended, the nation united, and peace restored, by *strategy*, and not by hard desperate fighting. Why, then, should not the soldiers have furloughs?

[1] Hertz, II, 888. No further reference has been found concerning this memorandum.

To Whom It May Concern[1]

Executive Mansion,
Whom it may concern   Washington, Nov. 1, 1862
Capt. Derrickson, with his company, has been, for some time keeping guard at my residence, now at the Soldiers' Retreat. He,

and his Company are very agreeable to me; and while it is deemed proper for any guard to remain, none would be more satisfactory to me than Capt. D. and his company.

A. LINCOLN

[1] ALS-P, ISLA, Captain David V. Derickson of Company K, One Hundred Fiftieth Pennsylvania Volunteers continued to act as presidential bodyguard until he was appointed provost marshal for the Nineteenth District of Pennsylvania on April 27, 1863. His company remained as presidential guard until mustered out in June, 1865.

To William P. Dole[1]

November 3, 1862

Commissioner of Indian Affairs, please see the bearer of this, Mr. Pierce, who is well vouched to me, and talk with him and ascertain if there is any service in the Indian department, to which you can put him, with advantage to the public.   A. LINCOLN

Nov. 3, 1862

[1] ALS, ORB. Pierce has not been identified, but may have been John Pierce of Colorado, nominated surveyor general of Colorado and Utah on March 10 and confirmed by the Senate on March 13, 1863.

To Henry W. Halleck[1]

Executive Mansion, Washington, [November 5, 1862].

"By direction of the President, it is ordered that Major General McClellan be relieved from the command of the Army of the Potomac; and that Major General Burnside take the command of that Army.

Also, that Major General Hunter take command of the Corps in said Army, which is now commanded by General Burnside.

That Major General Fitz-John Porter be relieved from the command of the corps he now commands in said Army; and that Major General Hooker take command of said corps."

The General-in-Chief, is authorized, in discretion, to issue an order substantially as the above, forthwith, or so soon as he may deem proper.   A. LINCOLN

[1] ALS, IHi. Halleck issued the first paragraph of Lincoln's order relieving McClellan and appointing Burnside as AGO *General Orders No. 182*, November 5, 1862. The second paragraph concerning Hunter was not issued, but "no revocation of the order is of record." (OR, I, XIX, II, 545 n.). The Ninth Corps which had been commanded by Burnside was under command of Brigadier General Orlando B. Willcox as of November 10, 1862 (OR, I, XIX, II, 569). The third paragraph appointing Hooker to the Fifth Corps was issued as AGO *Special Orders No. 337*, November 10, 1862. Burnside assumed command on November 9.

Lincoln's order of removal had been long delayed in spite of tremendous pressure from many political figures and private citizens, as well as the majority of his cabinet. On August 30, Secretary Chase had drawn up a letter to the president which Secretaries Stanton and Smith joined him in signing, recommending "the immediate removal of George B. McClellan." (ORB). On September 2, a similar document was drafted by Secretary Bates "declaring to you our deliberate opinion that, at this time, it is not safe to entrust to Major General McClellan the command of any of the armies of the United States." (DLC-Stanton Papers). Stanton, Chase, Smith, and Bates signed this document, a copy of which is in the Nicolay Papers bearing the following note in Bates' handwriting:

"Note. M. Blair p.m.g. declined to sign (no reason given that I heard, but preserving a cautious reticence)

Gideon Welles, Secy Navy, declined to sign, for some reasons of etiquette, but openly declared in Council, his entire want of confidence in the general

W.H. Seward, Sec of State, *absent*

The Prest. was in deep distress. He had already, with, apparently, Gen Halleck's approbation, assigned Genl McClellan to the command of the forts in & around Washington & entrusted him with the defence of the City. At the opening of the Council, he seemed wrung by the bitterest anguish—said he felt almost ready to hang himself—in ansr to something said by Mr. Chase, he sd. he was far from doubting our sincerity, but that he was so distressed, precisely because he knew we were earnestly sincere.

"He was, manifestly alarmed for the safety of the City. He had been talking with Gen Halleck (who, I think is cowed) & had gotten the idea that Pope's army was utterly demoralized—saying that "if Pope's army came within the lines (of the forts) as *a mob*, the City wd be overrun by the enemy in 48 hours!!"

"*I* said that if Halleck doubted his ability to defend the City, he ought to be instantly, broke. 50,000 men were enough to defend it against all the power of the enemy. If the City fell, it would be by treachery in our leaders, & not by lack of power to defend. The shame was that we were reduced to the defensive, instead of the aggressive policy &c. That all the army was not needed to defend the City, & now was the time, above all others, to strike the enemy behind & at a distance &c"

To William R. Morrison[1]

Col. William R. Morrison   Executive Mansion,
Waterloo, Ills.[2]   Washington, Nov. 5. 1862

Your letter of Sept. 23rd. is this moment received. While your words of kindness are very grateful, your suspicions that I intend you injustice are very painful to me. I assure you such suspicions are groundless. I can not even conjecture what juniors of yours, you suppose I contemplate promoting over you. True, seniority has not been my rule, in this connection; but in considering military merit, it seems to me the world has abundant evidence that I discard politics.   A. LINCOLN

1 ALS, RPB. Colonel William R. Morrison of the Forty-ninth Illinois Volunteers, who had been severely wounded at Fort Donelson and who was elected to congress as a Democrat on November 4, 1862, wrote Lincoln from Bethel, Tennessee, on September 23, 1862:

"After the battle of Ft. Donelson you promoted numerous Ill. Cols. to be Brig. Genls. for 'Gallant Conduct. . . .' One of the Cols. promoted for 'Gallantry' was denounced by his maj. as a coward, the maj. was made a Col., the Col . . . a General. Another Col. made a General . . . was not in the fight, but he had a brother-in-law in Congress. And &c &c &c. . . . All these promotions were made from my Seniors, in command, *placed upon that ground* they are unobjectionable.

"I am told that now you have promoted or are about to promote one or more Cols. my Juniors in Command. Having been always opposed to you politically, of course I could not ask any especial political favor, but it seems to me that there are good reasons why you should not wrong me in this behalf. . . . I protest against it as an insult to my manhood, a most wicked injustice. I have not deserved this of you" (DLC-RTL).

2 A telegraph operator in the War Department added to the address as given by Lincoln, "mail St. Louis."

To Moses F. Odell[1]

Hon. M. F. Odell,   Executive Mansion,
Brooklyn, N. Y.   Washington, Nov. 5. 1862.
    You are re-elected. I wish to see you at once. Will you come? Please answer.   A. LINCOLN

1 ALS, RPB. Representative Odell answered Lincoln's telegram on the same day, "Will leave tonight at Eleven (11)." (DLC-RTL).

To Benjamin F. Butler[1]

       Executive Mansion, Washington,
Maj. Genl. Butler,   Nov. 6th '62.
    My dear Sir: This morning the Secretary of the Treasury read to me a letter of yours to him. He read to me at the same time one from Mr. Denison[2] (I think), at New Orleans. I was much interested by the information in one of them that some of the planters were making arrangements with their negroes to pay them wages. Please write to me to what extent, so far as you know, this is being done. Also what, if anything, is being done by Mr. Bouligny, or others, about electing members of Congress. I am anxious to hear on both these points. Yours truly,   A. LINCOLN.

1 *Private and Official Correspondence of General Benjamin F. Butler*, edited by Jessie A. Marshall (1917), II, 447. Butler replied on November 28 that Colonel John W. Shaffer "has had put up to be forwarded to you a Bbl. of the first sugar ever made by *free black labor* in Louisiana. . . . The planters seem to have been struck with a sort of judicial blindness, and some of them so deluded have abandoned their crops rather than work them with free labor." Concerning the elections to be held on November 12, Butler added, "I found Dr. [Thomas E. H.] Cottman to be one of the candidates . . . but he had voluntarily signed the Ordi-

[487]

nance of Secession . . . and as the Doctor had never by any public act testified his abnegation of that act . . . I thought it would be best that the Government should not be put to the scandal of having a person so situated elected, although the Doctor may be a good Union man now. . . . I fear . . . we shall lose Mr. Bouligny. He was imprudent enough to run for the office of Justice of Peace under the Secessionists . . . and although . . . a good Union man . . . that fact tells against him. However, Mr. [Benjamin F.] Flanders will be elected in his District and a more reliable or better Union man can not be found. . . ." (*Ibid.*, pp. 447-50).

2 George S. Denison, a lawyer formerly of Pensacola, Florida, and San Antonio, Texas, who served as agent of the Treasury under Chase.

To Henry W. Halleck[1]

The within just handed to me, with such account of it's source as to induce me to believe it is reliable.   A. LINCOLN

Nov. 6. 1862.

1 AES, MH. Lincoln's endorsement is written on the following unsigned document:

"Four days since there were no other rebel soldiers at Culpepper Court House than a Provost guard under a captain.

"For the previous week it was said among the citizens there, that portions of the army were passing back that way from the valley. My informant, a young lady (Union) saw herself but about a single regiment marching near Culpepper C.H. in that direction, as most of them were understood to be going by the Amisville and other roads than the direct road through Culpepper C.H. I shall learn more of their movements in that direction this evening."

Unaddressed Note[1]

[c. November 6, 1862?]

I am informed as a certainty, that a lady coming from Culpeper C.H. to Warrenton, met Walker's[2] Division going south, who said they were going to Petersburg.   A. LINCOLN

1 Tracy, p. 236. Printed in the source without date, this note seems obviously related to Lincoln's endorsement to Halleck of this date, *supra*.

2 General John G. Walker, CSA.

To Edwin M. Stanton[1]

If consistent with the public service I shall be glad for Mr. Edwards to be obliged as he asks within.   A. LINCOLN

Nov. 6. 1862

1 AES, DLC-Stanton Papers. Lincoln's endorsement is written on a letter from Captain Ninian W. Edwards applying for leave of absence for ten days and urging payment of a claim of Cairo, Illinois, on the government.

To Gideon Welles[1]

Executive Mansion, Washington, [November 6], 186[2]

First idea

Purchase one of those now being constructed for our enemies—or some other of not let [sic] less speed or power, deliverable at a given point fully equipped. Then take possession.

Second idea

Charter for twelve months with the previlege of purchasing and taking possession at any point for a certain sum within that period. Then advertise for some Port in the vicinity of the intended cruising ground. Charter also another on the same conditions, dispatch her with fuel, stores and the armament to an unfrequented harbor, under the direction of a reliable man, there to await orders. After getting information as we can with the first named steamer join the tender and arm the cruiser, Pursue the enemy, exhibit your authority only when absolute necessity requires it

[Endorsement]

I was asked to inquire what the Govt. would pay, on delivery, for the Capture of a "Secesh vessel" I could not answer & so refer the question to the Sec. of the Navy.   A. Lincoln

Nov. 6. 1862.

[1] AD-P and AES-P, ISLA. No further reference has been found to the matter proposed in Lincoln's memorandum and endorsement.

To Salmon P. Chase[1]

Executive Mansion,
Dear Sir: Washington, November 7, 1862.

Please send me the latest "Picayune" and "True Delta" you can lay your hands upon. Yours truly,   A. Lincoln.

[1] NH, VIII, 73. Lincoln probably wanted the New Orleans newspapers for news of the approaching election. See his letter to Butler, November 6, *supra*.

To William W. Lowe[1]

Col. W. W. Lowe   Executive Mansion,
Fort-Henry, Tenn.   Washington, Nov. 7, 1862.

Yours of yesterday received. Gov. Johnson, Mr. Ethridge[2] & others are looking after the very thing you telegraph about.

A. Lincoln.

[1] ALS, RPB. Colonel William W. Lowe of the Fifth Iowa Cavalry telegraphed at 3 P.M. on November 6, "The people of the 9th Congressional district express a desire to be represented in the next congress. I cannot communicate with Gov Johnson and ask you if an order can be issued for an election? Answer" (DLC-RTL). [2] Emerson Etheridge.

Order to Alfred W. Ellet[1]

Executive Mansion
Ordered.   Nov. 7. 1862.

That Brigadier General Ellett report to Rear Admiral Porter for instructions, and act under his direction until otherwise ordered by the War Department.   ABRAHAM LINCOLN

[1] Copy, DNA WR NB RG 45, Executive Letters, No. 20. Alfred W. Ellet was a brother of Charles Ellet, inventor of the steam rams operating with Union forces on the Mississippi, who died June 21, of wounds received in a naval engagement off Memphis, Tennessee, on June 6, 1862. At a White House conference attended by Welles, Stanton, and Halleck on November 7, the question of the disposition of the fleet of rams was decided by Lincoln in accordance with a congressional order. Welles' *Diary* summarizes the situation prior to the conference as follows: "Congress wisely ordered a transfer of all war vessels on the Mississippi to the Navy. . . . It has . . . greatly disturbed Stanton, who, supported by Halleck and Ellet, opposes a transfer of the ram fleet as not strictly within the letter . . . of the law. That Ellet should wish a distinct command is not surprising. It is characteristic. He is full of zeal to overflowing; is not, however, a naval man, but is, very naturally, delighted with an independent naval command in this adventurous ram service. . . ." (*Diary of Gideon Welles*, November 4, 1862, I, 180).

To Salmon P. Chase[1]

Executive Mansion,
Hon. Sec. of Treasury   Washington, Nov. 8, 1862.

My dear Sir: I now understand that a Commission has been sent to some gentleman as Collector for the 13th District of New York, in place of Mr. Masten whom I appointed at the request of Hon. Mr. Steele. If I have signed a Commission superseding him I have done it inadvertently, not remembering having done so at all, and not having known any just reason for doing so.

Having appointed Mr. Masten deliberately, I do not wish to revoke such appointment without a sufficient reason; and, of course, I do not wish to be made to appear as having prevaricated. If Mr. Masten has tendered a sufficient bond, I wish him to have the office. Yours truly,   A. LINCOLN.

[1] Tracy, pp. 212-13. See Lincoln's memorandum concerning the appointment of William Masten, August 19, *supra*, and his further memorandum concerning the appointment of Eli D. Terwilliger, *infra*.

Memorandum:
Appointment of Eli D. Terwilliger[1]

[c. November 8, 1862]

This note confounds me utterly. I am sure I have never been conscious that I was superseding Mr. Steele's man.

[1] AE, DLC-RTL. Lincoln's endorsement is written on a letter from Secretary Chase, November 8, 1862, in reply to Lincoln's letter to Chase, *supra*. Chase wrote that "A Committee from the 13th District called on you to ask for the appointment of Mr. Terwilliger, in place of Mr. Masten. . . . I consulted Secretary Seward, who thought the change should be made, and I accordingly referred the matter to you. Mr. Seward was present when you received my note accompanying the new papers, &, as he informed me, told you, in answer perhaps to some inquiry from you, that it was all right. . . . Mr. Terwilligers commission has been sent. . . . If it is to be recalled it will be necessary to notify him . . . & to reappoint Mr. Masten. . . . Mr. Steele, I presume, supported Mr. Seymour against Gen. Wadsworth; and Mr. Masten I doubt not contributed his full share to the defeat of the Republican nominee for Congress, if not to that of the State Ticket." (*Ibid.*).

Order Concerning James W. Walters[1]

[c. November 8, 1862]

I suppose the case within was, at least technically, a desertion. In consideration of his after conduct, let the boy, James W. Walters, be pardoned.   A. LINCOLN

[1] AES, IHi. Lincoln's undated endorsement is written on a letter from Jesse K. Dubois, November 1, 1862, asking pardon for the son of Lincoln's old friend Green Berry Walters, wounded at Donelson and discharged for disability:
"But it seems before this he was a regular soldier under [Nathaniel] Lyon and left and joined the volunteer service under Col. [Isaac C.] Pugh. Now we have all signed and you have all the papers before you, and the olny [*sic*] object of this letter is to call your attention to the fact. [Shelby M.] Cullom called your attention to it   The boys Name on the Regular Army roll is James W. Walters." The date of the endorsement is supplied on the basis of an endorsement on the letter "Recd. AGO Nov. 8, 1862."

Recommendation for Mr. Calvert[1]

November 8, 1862

I can very cheerfully say that Mr. Calvert has for some time been employed at the White-House, and has appeared to be a very faithful, worthy and gentlemanly young man.   A. LINCOLN
Nov. 8. 1862.

[1] ADS, IHi. Calvert has not been identified.

To William H. Seward[1]

Will be glad to see Col. Hamilton, & his friend, whenever it may be convenient for them   A. LINCOLN

Nov. 8. 1862

[1] AES, DLC-Nicolay Papers. Lincoln's endorsement is written on a note from Secretary Seward, "Will you see Col. [Andrew J.] Hamilton of Texas with Col. Rogers of the same state, a moment." Colonel Rogers has not been identified.

To Mary Todd Lincoln[1]

Mrs. A. Lincoln   Washington,
Boston, Mass.   Nov. 9. 1862

Mrs. Cuthbert & Aunt Mary want to move to the White House, because it has grown so cold at Soldiers Home. Shall they?

A. LINCOLN

[1] ALS, CSmH. This note sent by telegraph bears the operator's time notation "10.10 am." Mary Ann Cuthbert was seamstress, and later "stewardess" at the White House; "Aunt Mary" Dines was a colored nurse employed by the Lincolns.

To Edward Bates[1]

Hon. Attorney General   Executive Mansion
Dear Sir   Washington, D.C. Nov. 10. 1862

I am not quite ready to appoint a Judge for the District of Indiana; and, therefore I will thank you to take proper measures for having court held by a neighboring Judge. Yours truly

A. LINCOLN

[1] ALS, DLC. Judge Elisha M. Huntington died on October 26, 1862. On October 30 Governor Oliver P. Morton telegraphed Lincoln to "please defer appointment" of his successor "until you can have an expression from the State." (DLC-RTL). On November 11, Bates replied to Lincoln's note as follows: "Yesterday, I received (by the hand of the Hon. Mr. White of Indiana) your note . . . referring to the vacancy in the District Judgeship in Indiana, and directing me 'to take proper measures for having court held by a neighboring Judge.' . . . I do not see how I can legally take any measures for the accomplishment of the end proposed, nor indeed, that the subject matter lies within the Executive competency . . . . all the provisions referred to require *Judicial* and not *Executive* action. . . ." (*Ibid.*).

On November 12, Secretary Caleb B. Smith asked that for reasons of health he be relieved from his post and given the vacant judgeship. Smith's appointment to the judgeship was confirmed by the Senate on December 22, and John P. Usher's appointment to the Department of Interior was confirmed on January 8, 1863.

To John Pope[1]

Major General Pope   Executive Mansion,
St. Paul, Minnesota   Washington, Nov. 10. 1862.

Your despatch giving the names of three hundred Indians condemned to death, is received. Please forward, as soon as possible, the full and complete record of these convictions. And if the record does not fully indicate the more guilty and influential, of the culprits, please have a careful statement made on these points and forwarded to me. Send all by mail.   A. LINCOLN.

[1] ALS, owned by Dale Carnegie, New York City. Pope's telegram of November 7, listing the names of Indians condemned by the military commission at the Lower Sioux Agency, was received at 7:40 P.M., November 8. Governor Alexander Ramsey telegraphed Lincoln on November 10, "I hope the execution of every Sioux Indian condemned by the military court will be at once ordered. It would be wrong upon principle and policy to refuse this. Private revenge would on all this border take the place of official judgment on these Indians." (OR, I, XIII, 787). On November 11 Lincoln endorsed Ramsey's telegram "Respectfully referred to Secretary of War."

On November 11 Pope replied to Lincoln's message of November 10 as follows: "Your dispatch of yesterday received. Will comply with your wishes immediately. I desire to represent . . . that the only distinction between the culprits is as to which of them murdered most people or violated most young girls. All of them are guilty of these things in more or less degree. The people . . . are exasperated . . . and if the guilty are not all executed I think it nearly impossible to prevent the indiscriminate massacre of all the Indians—old men, women, and children. . . ." (*Ibid.*, 788).

Succeeding telegrams from Pope on November 24 and Ramsey on November 28 (DLC-RTL) insisted on the necessity for speedy execution, but on November 28 in conference with Senator Morton S. Wilkinson and Representative Cyrus Aldrich, who pressed for immediate execution, Lincoln "promised to . . . make a final determination upon it after completing his [Annual] Message." (New York *Tribune*, November 29, 1862). See further Lincoln to Joseph Holt, December 1, *infra*.

To Carl Schurz[1]

"Private & confidential"

Gen. Schurz.   Executive Mansion,
My dear Sir   Washington, Nov. 10. 1862.

Yours of the 8th. was, to-day, read to me by Mrs. S[churz]. We have lost the elections; and it is natural that each of us will believe, and say, it has been because his peculiar views was not made sufficiently prominent. I think I know what it was, but I may be

[1] ALS, DLC-Schurz Papers. Schurz's letter dated at headquarters of the Third Division of the Eleventh Corps at New Baltimore, Virginia, November 8, 1862, is in the Lincoln Papers, but Lincoln's letter so adequately summarizes as well as answers the general's political opinions that further quotation seems superfluous.

mistaken. Three main causes told the whole story. 1. The demo-crats were left in a majority by our friends going to the war. 2. The democrats observed this & determined to re-instate them-selves in power, and 3. Our newspaper's, by vilifying and disparag-ing the administration, furnished them all the weapons to do it with. Certainly, the ill-success of the war had much to do with this.

You give a different set of reasons. If you had not made the following statements, I should not have suspected them to be true. "The defeat of the administration is the administrations own fault." (opinion) "It admitted its professed opponents to its coun-sels" (Asserted as a fact) "It placed the Army, now a great power in this Republic, into the hands of its' enemies" (Asserted as a fact) "In all personal questions, to be hostile to the party of the Government, seemed, to be a title to consideration." (As-serted as a fact) "If to forget the great rule, that if you are true to your friends, your friends will be true to you, and that you make your enemies stronger by placing them upon an equality with your friends." "Is it surprising that the opponents of the ad-ministration should have got into their hands the government of the principal states, after they have had for a long time the prin-cipal management of the war, the great business of the national government."

I can not dispute about the matter of opinion. On the the [sic] three matters (stated as facts) I shall be glad to have your evi-dence upon them when I shall meet you. The plain facts, as they appear to me, are these. The administration came into power, very largely in a minority of the popular vote. Notwithstanding this, it distributed to it's party friends as nearly all the civil patronage as any administration ever did. The war came. The administra-tion could not even start in this, without assistance outside of it's party. It was mere nonsense to suppose a minority could put down a majority in rebellion. Mr. Schurz (now Gen. Schurz) was about here then & I do not recollect that he then considered all who were not republicans, were enemies of the government, and that none of them must be appointed to to [sic] military positions. He will correct me if I am mistaken. It so happened that very few of our friends had a military education or were of the profession of arms. It would have been a question whether the war should be conducted on military knowledge, or on political affinity, only that our own friends (I think Mr. Schurz included) seemed to think that such a question was inadmissable. Accordingly I have scarcely appointed a democrat to a command, who was not urged by many republicans and opposed by none. It was so as to McClellan. He was first brought forward by the Republican Governor of Ohio, & claimed, and contended for at the same time by the Republican Governor of Pennsylvania. I received recommendations from the republican delegations in congress, and I believe every one of them recommended a majority of democrats. But, after all many Republicans were appointed; and I mean no disparagement to them when I say I do not see that their superiority of success has been so marked as to throw great suspicion on the good faith of those who are not Republicans. Yours truly,   A. LINCOLN

To David G. Farragut[1]

Comodore Farragut:

Executive Mansion,
Washington, Nov. 11, 1862.

Dear Sir: This will introduce Major General Banks. He is in command of a considerable land-force for operating in the South; and I shall be glad for you to co-operate with him, and give him such assistance as you can consistently with your orders from the Navy Department. Your Obt. Servt.   A. LINCOLN

[1] ALS, DeHi. Nathaniel P. Banks was assigned to command of the Department of the Gulf, AGO *General Orders No. 184*, November 9, 1862, and he took over command on December 17.

To Henry W. Halleck[1]

Submitted to Gen. Halleck, asking as favorable consideration as may be consistent   A. LINCOLN
Nov. 12. 1862.

[1] AES, IHi. Lincoln's endorsement is written on the back of a note from Ozias M. Hatch and William Butler, Springfield, October 27, 1862, "We most cordially unite in the within request. Colonel [Thomas W.] Harris is in command of the 54th. Regiment, Infantry, Illinois Volunteers." The enclosed request is no longer with the note.

Order Concerning Blockade[1]

Ordered:

Executive Mansion
Washington Nov. 12th, 1862

1st. That clearances issued by the Treasury Department for vessels or merchandize bound for the port of Norfolk for the military necessities of the Department, certified by the military Commandant of Fort Monroe, shall be allowed to enter said port.

2nd. That vessels and domestic produce from Norfolk permitted by the military Commandant at Fort Monroe for the military

[495]

purpose of his command, shall on his permit be allowed to pass from said port to its destination to any port not blockaded by the United States   ABRAHAM LINCOLN

¹ Copy, DNA WR NB RG 45, Executive Letters, No. 39.

Order Concerning the Confiscation Act¹

Ordered by the President

Executive Mansion,
November 13. 1862.

That the Attorney General be charged with the superintendence & direction of all proceedings to be had under the Act of Congress of the 17th of July 1862 entitled "an Act to suppress Insurrection, to punish Treason and Rebellion, to seize and confiscate the property of Rebels, and for other purposes," in so far as may concern the seizure, prosecution and condemnation of the estate, property and effects of Rebels and Traitors as mentioned and provided for in the fifth, sixth and seventh sections of the said Act of Congress.

And the Attorney General is authorised and required to give to the Attornies and Marshals of the United States, such instructions and directions as he may find needful and convenient touching all such seizures, prosecutions and condemnations. And moreover, to authorise all such Attornies and Marshals, whenever there may be reasonable ground to fear any forcible resistance to them, in the discharge of their respective duties, in this behalf, to call upon any military officer, in command of the forces of the United States, to give to them such aid, protection and support as may be necessary to enable them safely and efficiently to discharge their respective duties.

And all such commanding officers are required, promptly, to obey such call, and to render the necessary service, as far as may be in their power consistently with their other duties.

ABRAHAM LINCOLN

¹ Copy, DLC-Nicolay Papers; OR, III, II, 765-66. The copy bears the following endorsement in the handwriting of Attorney General Bates: "March 1864 Atty General to the Secy of War. About *military* confiscation. 'The Prests orders to the Atty Genl &c[.']"

To Francis P. Blair, Jr.¹

Hon. F. P. Blair, Jr.
St. Louis, Mo.

Washington City, D.C.
Nov. 14. 1862

Please telegraph me the result of the election in Missouri, on Congress and Legislature.   A. LINCOLN

1 ALS, RPB. Blair replied at 7:30 P.M., "We have elected 5 Republicans one Emancipationist Democrat 2 Unconditional Union & 2 proslavery Dem's to Congress. The Legislature is emancipation in both Branches on your plan & Secures two Senators to Support the administration My Election is certain. I think the army vote yet to come in will not change the result." (DLC-RTL).

To Andrew Johnson[1]

Gov. Andrew Johnson   Washington City, D.C.
Nashville, Tenn.   Nov. 14th. 1862

Your despatch of the 4th. about returning troops from Western Virginia to Tennessee, is just received, and I have been to Gen. Halleck with it. He says an order has already been made by which those troops have already moved, or soon will move, to Tennessee.

A. LINCOLN.

1 ALS, RPB. Governor Johnson's dispatch of November 4 is not in the Lincoln Papers. On November 15, Halleck instructed General Horatio G. Wright that General Jacob D. Cox in command of the District of Western Virginia "should be directed to leave sufficient troops to hold the access to the Kanawha Valley, and move immediately with the remainder . . . to the defense of the railroad at Grafton. . . . The Tennessee troops should be sent to General Rosecrans." (OR, I, XIX, II, 586).

To Hamilton R. Gamble[1]

I have not yet been able to get the document, but have the Sec. of War hunting for it.   A. LINCOLN
Nov. 15, 1862

1 ADS, RPB. On the basis of Governor Gamble's letter to Lincoln of November 17, it may be inferred that the "document" in question was Lincoln's order of November 6, 1861, *supra*. See further Lincoln's letter to Bates, November 29, 1862, *infra*.

Order for Sabbath Observance[1]

Executive Mansion, Washington, November 15, 1862.

The President, Commander-in-Chief of the Army and Navy, desires and enjoins the orderly observance of the Sabbath by the officers and men in the military and naval service. The importance for man and beast of the prescribed weekly rest, the sacred rights of Christian soldiers and sailors, a becoming deference to the best sentiment of a Christian people, and a due regard for the Divine will, demand that Sunday labor in the Army and Navy be reduced to the measure of strict necessity.

The discipline and character of the national forces should not suffer, nor the cause they defend be imperiled, by the profanation of the day or name of the Most High. "At this time of public distress"—adopting the words of Washington in 1776—"men may find enough to do in the service of God and their country without abandoning themselves to vice and immorality." The first General Order issued by the Father of his Country after the Declaration of Independence,[2] indicates the spirit in which our institutions were founded and should ever be defended: *"The General hopes and trusts that every officer and man will endeavor to live and act as becomes a Christian soldier defending the dearest rights and liberties of his country."* ABRAHAM LINCOLN.

[1] AGO *General Orders* (not numbered), November 15, 1862; Navy *General Orders No. 5*, February 10, 1863. The original is missing from the file of Adjutant General Letters Received (DNA WR RG 94) but a typewritten copy (P-1070 with 5706 AGO 1884) has been preserved. An account dated November 13 in the New York *Tribune*, November 14, 1862, records that "Messrs. Fred. Winston, David Hoodley, Foster, Booth, and another gentleman, representing religious bodies in New-York City, called upon the President and heads of departments to-day to urge upon him the propriety of enforcing a better observance of the Sabbath in the army. The interviews are represented as agreeable and satisfactory." [2] July 9, 1776.

To Gideon Welles[1]

November 15, 1862

The Vanderbilt is at sea. If we could get one, two or three more, heavy, swift steamers out, on something like the same plan, I think it would be a good thing. Sec. of Navy, please see Mr. Halstead.

A. LINCOLN.

[1] Stan. V. Henkels Catalog 1342, January 4, 1924, No. 48. According to the catalog description, Lincoln's note is written on both sides of a small card. "Mr. Halstead" has not been positively identified, but may have been Oliver S. Halsted, Jr., of Newark, New Jersey, who wrote Lincoln on August 27, 1861, concerning government purchase of steamers (DLC-Nicolay Papers).

To Francis P. Blair, Jr.[1]

"Cypher"   Executive Mansion
Hon. F. P. Blair, Jr.   Washington, Nov. 17. 1862

Your brother says you are solicitous to be ordered to join Gen. McClernand. I suppose you are ordered to St. Helena. This means that you are to form part of McClernand's expedition, as it moves down the river; and he—McC.—is so informed.

I will see Gen. Halleck as to whether the additional forces you mention can go with you. A. LINCOLN.

[1] ALS, RPB. Stanton telegraphed General McClernand at 1:40 P.M., November 15, "General Frank Blair will be attached to your expedition, and ordered to Helena, that being designated as one point of concentration. The troops sent to Helena are not to be withdrawn from your command, but are only sent there temporarily for organization. . . ." (OR, I, XVII, 348-49).

To John D. Defrees[1]

Will Mr. Defrees please call and see me? A. LINCOLN
Nov. 17. 1862

[1] ALS, owned by Dale Carnegie, New York City. Probably Lincoln wished to see Defrees about the printing of his Annual Message to Congress, December 1, *infra.*

To Robert A. Maxwell[1]

Robert A. Maxwell   Washington, D.C.,
Philadelphia, Pa.   Nov. 17. 1862.
Your despatch of to-day received. I do not at all understand it.
A. LINCOLN

[1] ALS, RPB. Robert A. Maxwell's despatch of November 17 has not been found, but Anson Stager of the Military Telegraph wrote an undated note which seems to refer to it: "I translate Maxwell's message as follows—'The Richmond campaign with General Franklin remaining is a foregone disaster. Persevere in the sanctification of your material aims.' " (DLC-RTL). Maxwell answered Lincoln's telegram the next day, "Your telegraph is answered by our mail of this evening." (*Ibid.*). The letter has not been found. Maxwell was a resident of Philadelphia, several of whose somewhat incoherent letters are in the Lincoln Papers.

To John A. Dix[1]

"Cypher"
Major Gen. Dix   Washington, DC.
Fort-Monroe, Va.   Nov. 18 1862
Please give me your best opinion, as to the number of the enemy now at Richmond, and also at Petersburg. A. LINCOLN

[1] ALS, RPB. General Dix telegraphed at 2 P.M., "My only reliable information . . . comes from a man who has not been here for four weeks. It was then 11,000 on and near the Blackwater . . . at Petersburg, 700; at Richmond, 7,000; between the James and Chickahominy, 7,000; and near White House, 1,500; total, 27,200. This is my latest information. . . . I place little reliance on reports . . . by deserters, stragglers, and negroes. . . . The moment I can get any reliable information as to the force in Richmond and Petersburg I will forward it. . . ." (OR, I, XVIII, 458-59).

To Caleb B. Smith[1]

Let the appointment be made, as within recommend[ed].
Nov. 18. 1862.   A. LINCOLN

[1] AES, DNA NR RG 48, Applications, Registers and Receivers, General Land
Office, California, Box 1276. Lincoln's endorsement is written on a letter from
Aaron A. Sargent, November 18, 1862, recommending that Charles A. Murdock
be appointed register of the Land Office at Humboldt, California, in place of
Alvan Flanders, "who has failed to qualify." Murdock's appointment was con-
firmed by the Senate on December 23, 1862.

To Frederick Steele, John S. Phelps and Others[1]

Executive Mansion, Washington, Nov. 18. 1862.
Gen. Steele, Governor Phelps, and all having military and Naval
authority, under the United States, within the State of Arkansas.

Mr. William M. McPherson goes to Arkansas, seeking to have
such of the people thereof as desire to avoid the unsatisfactory
prospect before them, and to have peace again upon the old terms
under the Constitution of the United States, to manifest such desire by elections of members to the Congress of the United States
particularly, and perhaps a legislature, State officers, and United
States Senators friendly to their object. I shall be glad for you and
each of you to aid him and all others acting for this object, as much
as possible. In all available ways give the people a chance to express their wishes at these elections. Follow law & forms of law as
far as convenient, but at all events get the expression of the largest
number of the people possible. All see how such action will connect
with and affect the proclamation of September 22d. Of course the
men elected should be gentlemen of character, willing to swear
support to the Constitution, as of old, and known to be above reasonable suspicion of duplicity. Yours very Respectfully

A. LINCOLN

[1] LS, CSmH. The body of the letter is not in Lincoln's handwriting, but the
date, persons addressed, the words "Mr. William M. McPherson" and "Arkansas," in the first sentence, and "law &" in the fourth sentence, as well as the
close and signature were added by Lincoln. See the similar letters to Butler and
others, October 14 and to Grant and others, October 21, *supra.* Letters from
William McPherson in the Lincoln Papers are dated at St. Louis, Missouri. Efforts
to trace his activities in Arkansas have been of no avail.

To Edward Bates[1]

Let a pardon be made out in this case for Gov. Gamble to take to
Missouri with him.   A. LINCOLN
Nov. 19. 1862

[500]

1 AES, DNA RG 204, U.S. Pardon Attorney, A 449. Lincoln's endorsement is written on a letter from Governor Hamilton R. Gamble, November 18, 1862, asking a pardon for Confederate General Edwin R. Price, son of Confederate General Sterling Price. Edwin R. Price had been captured by Union forces, paroled, and later exchanged for General Benjamin S. Prentiss. Upon returning to the South, he resigned his commission and went home. Gamble concluded his letter, "I venture to suggest that this is a case in which it will be expedient to grant a pardon . . . to this young man, who will as I believe be of service in keeping down the spirit of rebellion."

To Edwin M. Stanton[1]

Sec. of War, please make such response to this as may seem proper.

Nov. 19. 1862   A. LINCOLN

1 AES, NHi. Lincoln's endorsement is written on a telegram from Governor Andrew Johnson, 8:30 P.M., November 18, 1862, "I hope my telegram of 8th sent by Courier in regard to ordering Tennessee Regiments here & requesting the appointment of Col Alvan C. Gillem of the army Commanding 1st. Middle Tenn Infy as Br Genl has been rec'd & favorably acted upon." Johnson also recommended that Brigadier General William B. Carter not be made a major general, and expressed hope that "things will go well in a few days as we have a man at the head of this army who will fight." On October 30, General William S. Rosecrans had assumed command of the Department of the Cumberland and the Fourteenth Corps, which had been under General Don C. Buell. Colonel Alvan C. Gillem was not made a brigadier general until August 17, 1863. No reply by Stanton has been found. See Lincoln to Johnson, August 17, 1863, *infra*.

To Samuel Treat[1]

PRIVATE

Judge S. Treat   Executive Mansion,
St. Louis, Mo.   Washington, Nov. 19, 1862.

My dear Sir   Your very patriotic and judicious letter, addressed to Judge Davis, in relation to the Mississippi, has been left with me by him for perusal. You do not estimate the value of the object you press, more highly than it is estimated here. It is now the object of particular attention. It has not been neglected, as you seem to think, because the West was divided into different military Departments. The cause is much deeper. The country will not allow us to send our whole Western force down the Mississippi, while the enemy sacks Louisville and Cincinnati. Possibly it would be better if the country would allow this, but it will not. I confidently believed, last September that we could end the war by allowing the enemy to go to Harrisburg and Philadelphia, only that we could not keep down mutiny, and utter demoralization among the Pennsylvanians. And this, though very unhandy sometimes, is not at all strange. I presume if an army was starting to-day for New-

Orleans, and you confidently believed that St. Louis would be sacked in consequence, you would be in favor of stopping such army.

We are compelled to watch all these things. With great respect Your Obt. Servt A. LINCOLN

1 ALS, MoSHi. Although Judge Treat's letter to Judge David Davis has not been located, its contents may be inferred from Lincoln's reply.

To John A. Dix[1]

November 20, 1862

Your letter of the 17th in relation to the Eastern Shore of Virginia. Omitting to class that part of the country, in the proclamation of July, as being loyal, was a mere oversight. . . .

1 Thomas F. Madigan, *The Autograph Album*, June, 1928. This fragment of text is all that is available. General Dix wrote Lincoln on November 17, "I feel a strong Sympathy in behalf of the people of the Eastern Shore of Virginia—Accomac and Northampton Counties . . . . they have united themselves to Western Virginia: they have had two elections: and they have sent strong Union men to the Legislature and Congress. . . . When you issued your Proclamation in July last designating the States and parts of States that were to be deemed loyal & omitting these two Counties, I thought to write to you begging that they should be added to the number thus designated I write now to make the request, in order that they may be relieved from the penalties of disloyalty. . . ."(DLC-RTL). On November 24 Dix acknowledged receipt of Lincoln's letter and expressed gratification "to learn . . . that there is no objection to recognition of their loyal condition. . . ." (*Ibid.*).

To George Robertson[1]

PRIVATE

Hon. George Robertson   Executive Mansion,
My dear Sir.   Washington, Nov. 20. 1862.

Your despatch of yesterday is just received. I believe you are acquainted with the American Classics, (if there be such) and probably remember a speech of Patrick Henry, in which he represented a certain character in the, revolutionary times, as totally disregarding all questions of country, and "hoarsely bawling, beef! beef!! beef!!!"[2]

Do you not know that I may as well surrender this contest, directly, as to make any order, the obvious purpose of which would be to return fugitive slaves? Yours very truly A. LINCOLN

1 ALS, DLC-RTL. This letter seems never to have been sent. See Lincoln to Robertson, November 26, *infra*. Robertson had telegraphed Lincoln on November 19, "The Conduct of a few of the officers of the army in forcibly detaining the

Slaves of Union Kentuckians may provoke a conflict between Citizens & Soldiers; . . . we desire you to say as we believe you will that military force will not be permitted for the detention any more than for the restoration of such property & especially in resistance & contempt of the loyal process of a Civil tribunal." (DLC-RTL).

2 In the *Life of Patrick Henry* (1841), William Wirt narrates Henry's defense in court, after the Revolution, of an army commissary named Venable, who had been sued by a suspected Tory, John Hook, for two steers commandeered by Venable to furnish beef for his troops. After magnificently depicting the scene of triumph following the surrender of the British at Yorktown, Henry concluded, "But hark! what notes of discord are these which disturb the general joy, and silence the acclamations of victory—they are the notes of *John Hook*, hoarsely bawling through the American camp, *beef! beef! beef!*" (pp. 389-90).

Order Prohibiting Export of Arms and Munitions[1]

Executive Mansion, Washington City, D.C.,

Ordered,   November 21, 1862.

That no arms, ammunition, or munitions of war be cleared or allowed to be exported from the United States until further order.

That any clearances for arms, ammunition, or munitions of war issued heretofore by the Treasury Department be vacated, if the articles have not passed without the United States, and the articles stopped.

That the Secretary of War hold possession of the arms, &c., recently seized by his order at Rouse's Point, bound for Canada.

ABRAHAM LINCOLN.

1 Copy, DLC-RTL; copy, DNA WR RG 107, Secretary of War, Letters Received, P 224.

Remarks to Union Kentuckians[1]

November 21, 1862

On Friday President Lincoln, in the course of an interview with unconditional Union Kentuckians, discussed at length the question of Emancipation. He said that he would rather die than take back a word of the Proclamation of Freedom, and he dwelt upon the advantages to the Border States of his scheme for the gradual abolishment of Slavery, which he urged them to bring fairly before their people.

They assured him that it should be done. They propose to start two Emancipation journals in Kentucky to counteract the influence of the Louisville papers, and when the proper time comes, Congressman Casey, Judge Williams, and perhaps Joseph Holt also

[503]

will canvass the State. They are confident of achieving a success equal to that of the Missouri Emancipationists after they have once fairly got the question before the people.

Mr. Lincoln also expressed his determination to enforce vigorous measures to rid the State of Rebel sympathizers, and for that purpose a new Provost-Marshal General who has his heart in the work will be appointed.

1 New York *Tribune,* November 24, 1862.

To George F. Shepley[1]

Hon. G. F. Shepley   Executive Mansion,
Dear Sir.   Washington, Nov. 21. 1862.

Dr. Kennedy, bearer of this, has some apprehension that Federal officers, not citizens of Louisiana, may be set up as candidates for Congress in that State. In my view, there could be no possible object in such an election. We do not particularly need members of congress from there to enable us to get along with legislation here. What we do want is the conclusive evidence that respectable citizens of Louisiana, are willing to be members of congress & to swear support to the constitution; and that other respectable citizens there are willing to vote for them and send them. To send a parcel of Northern men here, as representatives, elected as would be understood, (and perhaps really so,) at the point of the bayonet, would be disgusting and outrageous; and were I a member of congress here I would vote against admitting any such man to a seat. Yours very truly   A. LINCOLN

1 ADfS, DLC-RTL. Dr. Hugh Kennedy, brother-in-law of Cuthbert Bullitt, was a pharmacist and one-time editor who served one term as mayor of New Orleans in 1864. Governor Shepley had this letter printed as a poster under date of November 27.

To George F. Shepley[1]

Hon. G. F. Shepley   Executive Mansion,
My dear Sir   Washington, Nov. 21. 1862.

Your letter of the 6th. Inst. to the Secretary of War has been placed in my hands; and I am annoyed to learn from it that, at it's date, nothing had been done about congressional elections. On the 14th. of October I addressed a letter to Gen. Butler, yourself and others upon this very subject, sending it by Hon. Mr. Bouligny. I now regret the necessity of inferring that you had not seen this letter up to the 6th. Inst. I inclose you a copy of it, and also a copy of another addressed to yourself this morning, upon the same general subject, and placed in the hands of Dr. Kennedy. I ask attention to both.

I wish elections for Congressmen to take place in Louisiana; but I wish it to be a movement of the people of the Districts, and not a movement of our military and quasi-military, authorities there. I merely wish our authorities to give the people a chance—to protect them against secession interference. Of course the election can not be according to strict law—by state law, there is, I suppose, no election day, before January; and the regular election officers will not act, in many cases, if in any. These knots must be cut, the main object being to get an expression of the people. If they would fix a day and a way, for themselves, all the better; but if they stand idle not seeming to know what to do, do you fix these things for them by proclamation. And do not waste a day about it; but, fix the election day early enough that we can hear the result here by the first of January. Fix a day for an election in all the Districts, and have it held in as many places as you can. Yours very truly   A. LINCOLN

[1] ADfS, DLC-RTL. Governor Shepley's letter to Stanton of November 6 has not been found. His letter of November 15 to Lincoln had apparently not yet reached Washington. In it he acknowledged receipt of the letter of October 14 (*supra*) carried by John E. Bouligny, and added,

"In accordance with the views expressed by you I have issued a proclamation for an election in the first and second Congressional Districts.

"I entertain no doubt that these elections will result in the choice of two representatives of unquestioned loyalty to the Government. . . ." (DLC-RTL).

The election took place on December 3 and resulted in the election of Benjamin F. Flanders in the First District and Michael Hahn in the Second District.

To Nathaniel P. Banks[1]

My dear General Banks

Executive Mansion,
Washington, Nov. 22, 1862.

Early last week you left me in high hope with your assurance that you would be off with your expedition at the end of that week, or early in this. It is now the end of this, and I have just been overwhelmed and confounded with the sight of a requisition made by you, which, I am assured, can not be filled, and got off within an hour short of two months! I inclose you a copy of the requisition, in some hope that it is not genuine—that you have never seen it.

My dear General, this expanding, and piling up of *impedimenta*, has been, so far, almost our ruin, and will be our final ruin if it is not abandoned. If you had the articles of this requisition upon the wharf, with the necessary animals to make them of any use, and forage for the animals, you could not get vessels together in two weeks to carry the whole, to say nothing of your twenty thousand men; and, having the vessels, you could not put the cargoes aboard in two weeks more. And, after all, where you are going, you have no use for them. When you parted with me, you had no such idea in your mind. I know you had not, or you could not have expected to be off so soon as you said. You must get back to something like the plan you had then, or your expedition is a failure before you start. You must be off before Congress meets. You would be better off any where, and especially where you are going, for not having a thousand wagons, doing nothing but hauling forage to feed the animals that draw them, and taking at least two thousand men to care for the wagons and animals, who otherwise might be two thousand good soldiers.

Now dear General, do not think this is an ill-natured letter—it is the very reverse. The simple publication of this requisition would ruin you. Very truly your friend   A. LINCOLN

¹ ADfS, DLC-RTL. General Banks answered on November 24, "Your letter of the 22d instant with inclosures received this morning. I never contemplated waiting supplies referred to in requisition No. 40 one moment. It was drawn up by an officer who did not fully comprehend my instructions, and inadvertently approved by me without sufficient examination and proper explanation. My purpose has not been changed since I left Washington, and I have waited nothing not absolutely necessary. . . . I have explained by letter to Secretary of War." (OR, III, II, 865). Banks' despatch to Stanton of the same date specified that his requisition was for supplies which would be needed "for ultimate operations some weeks hence. I deeply regret that my purpose was not more clearly explained. I have waited only vessels, men, commissary stores and ordnance stores. . . ." (*Ibid.*).

To Edwin M. Stanton¹

November 22, 1862

I know not whether the within is admissable. If it is, I would, both on account of Gen. Banks and Col. Ullmann, be glad for it to be done. Will the Sec. of War, and Gen. Halleck please consider it.

Nov. 22. 1862   A. LINCOLN

¹ AES, DNA WR RG 108, HQA, B-1102, Box 57. Lincoln's endorsement is written on a letter from Nathaniel P. Banks, November 19, 1862, requesting that Colonel Daniel Ullmann of the Seventy-eighth New York Regiment "with such Regiments as you may place under his command" be assigned to Banks' expedition bound for Louisiana. No record has been found of Ullmann's transfer at this time, but on March 25, 1863, Stanton notified Banks that Ullmann, who had been made a brigadier general as of January 13, had been "intrusted with authority" to raise "a large military force from the colored population of Louisiana . . . and directed to report to you. . . ." (OR, III, III, 101-102).

To William L. Vance[1]

Mr. W. L. Vance   Executive Mansion,
Sir: Washington, Nov. 22, 1862.

You tell me you have in your hands some two hundred and seventy thousand dollars of "Confederate Scrip" which was forced upon Union men of Kentucky, in exchange for supplies, by the rebels during their late raid into that State; and you wish government authority for you to take this Scrip into the Cotten-States, exchange it for cotten if found practicable, and to bring the cotten out.

While I have felt great anxiety to oblige you, and your friends, in this matter, I feel constrained to decline it. It would come to something, or it would come to nothing—that is, you would get cotten for the Scrip, or you would not. If you should get none, the effort would have been a useless failure. If you should get *any*, to precisely that extent, this government would have aided in giving currency to this Scrip—that is, men seeing that the Scrip would bring cotten, would gladly give produce for the scrip; and hence a scramble for it, as for gold would ensue. If your two hundred and seventy thousand dollars, was to be the sole instance, I would gladly risk it. But it would not be the beginning, or, at most, only the beginning. Having begun, I could not stop. What I had done for some, I must do for others. All that sort of Scrip now in Kentucky, and much not yet in Kentucky, would find it's way into Union-hands and be presented under the rule. We all know how easily oaths are furnished, when required, in transactions of this sort. And the thing would become even broader yet. Men who have been robbed out-right by the rebels, without even receiving scrip would appeal, (and with quite as equitable a case) to be permitted a means of indemnity, by leave to go in and bring out cotten. This would run till at length I should have to abandon all restraint, or put a stop to what it is now much easier to not begin.

[1] ADf, DLC-RTL. A William L. Vance was a resident of Woodford County, Kentucky, but that he was the person addressed is not certain.

To George S. Boutwell[1]

Comr. of Internal Revenue   Executive Mansion,
Sir: Washington, Nov. 24, 1862.

It was by mere over-sight that the Eastern Shore counties of Virginia, and some other counties of Hon. Mr. Segar's District, were not classed as loyal in the proclamation of July. I intend to set this right the first convenient opportunity. Meantime, please consult with Mr. Segar, and act with his District, in regard to the Revenue, as with a loyal District. Yours truly   A. LINCOLN

1 ALS-F, ISLA. See Lincoln to John A. Dix, November 20, *supra.* Joseph E. Segar was representative from Eastern Virginia March 15, 1862–March 3, 1863.

To Salmon P. Chase[1]

If Secretary of Treasury has written his part of message, please send over.   A. LINCOLN.
November 24, 1862.

1 Warden, *Life of Chase*, p. 507. Lincoln referred to the Annual Message to Congress, December 1, 1862, *infra.*

To John J. Key[1]

Major John J. Key   Executive Mansion,
Dear Sir: Washington, Nov. 24, 1862

A bundle of letters including one from yourself, was, early last week, handed me by Gen. Halleck, as I understood, at your request. I sincerely sympathise with you in the death of your brave and noble son.[2]

In regard to my dismissal of yourself from the military service, it seems to me you misunderstand me. I did not charge, or intend to charge you with disloyalty. I had been brought to fear that there was a class of officers in the army, not very inconsiderable in numbers, who were playing a game to not beat the enemy when they could, on some peculiar notion as to the proper way of saving the Union; and when you were proved to me, in your own presence, to have avowed yourself in favor of that "game," and did not attempt to controvert the proof, I dismissed you as an example and a warning to that supposed class. I bear you no ill will; and I regret that I could not have the example without wounding you personally. But can I now, in view of the public interest, restore you to the service, by which the army would understand that I indorse and approve that game myself? If there was any doubt of your having made the avowal, the case would be different. But when it was proved to me, in your presence, you did not deny or attempt to deny it, but confirmed it in my mind, by attempting to sustain the position by argument.

I am really sorry for the pain the case gives you, but I do not see how, consistently with duty, I can change it. Yours, &c.
     A. LINCOLN

1 LS (copy?), DLC-RTL. See also Lincoln's record of dismissal of Key, September 26-27, *supra*, and endorsement of December 27, *infra*, which was written on the envelope containing this letter. The "bundle of letters" to which Lincoln refers have not been located.

2 Captain James (Joseph?) Rudd Key, Company I, Fiftieth Ohio Volunteers, died November 11, 1862, of wounds received at the battle near Perryville, Kentucky. There is some question as to his first name, both "Joseph" and "James" being given in the *Official Roster of the Soldiers of the State of Ohio* (IV, 577, 797), but the census of 1860, Cannelton, Indiana, lists James R. Key, age 16, as the son of John J. Key.

To David D. Porter[1]

Admiral Porter   Executive Mansion,
Dear Sir.   Washington, Nov. 24, 1862.

Allow me to introduce my friend, Hon. Samuel Galloway, of Ohio. Any attention or kindness you can give him, without interference with the public interest, will be appreciated by me. Yours very truly   A. LINCOLN

1 ALS-F, Watertown, New York, *Times*, April 17, 1948. No further reference has been found to Galloway's business with Commander Porter.

To Carl Schurz[1]

Gen. Carl Schurz   Executive Mansion,
My dear Sir   Washington, Nov. 24. 1862.

I have just received, and read, your letter of the 20th. The purport of it is that we lost the late elections, and the administration is failing, because the war is unsuccessful; and that I must not flatter myself that I am not justly to blame for it. I certainly know that if the war fails, the administration fails, and that I *will* be blamed for it, whether I deserve it or not. And I ought to be blamed, if I could do better. You think I could do better; therefore you blame me already. I think I could not do better; therefore I blame you for blaming me. I understand you *now* to be willing to accept the help of men, who are not republicans, provided they have "heart in it." Agreed. I want no others. But who is to be the judge of hearts, or of "heart in it"? If I must discard my own judgment, and take yours, I must also take that of others; and by the time I should reject all I should be advised to reject, I should have none left, republicans, or others—not even yourself. For, be assured, my dear sir, there are men who have "heart in it" that think you are performing your part as poorly as you think I am performing mine. I certainly have been dissatisfied with the slowness of Buell and McClellan; but before I relieved them I had great fears I should not find successors to them, who would do better; and I am sorry to add, that I have seen little since to relieve those fears. I do not clearly see the prospect of any more rapid movements. I fear we shall at last find out that the difficulty is in our case, rather than in particular generals. I wish to disparage no one—certainly not those who sympathize with me; but I must say I need success more than I need sympathy, and that I have not seen the so much greater evidence of getting success from my sympathizers, than from those who are denounced as the contrary. It does seem to me that in the field the two classes have been very much alike, in what they have done, and what they have failed to do. In sealing their faith with their blood, Baker, an[d] Lyon, and Bohlen, and Richardson, republicans, did all that men could do; but did they any more than Kearney, and Stevens, and Reno, and Mansfield, none of whom were republicans, and some, at least of whom, have been bitterly, and repeatedly, denounced to me as secession sympathizers?[2] I will not perform the ungrateful task of comparing cases of failure.

In answer to your question "Has it not been publicly stated in the newspapers, and apparantly proved as a fact, that from the commencement of the war, the enemy was continually supplied with information by some of the confidential subordinates of as important an officer as Adjutant General Thomas?" I must say "no" so far as my knowledge extends. And I add that if you can give any tangible evidence upon that subject, I will thank you to come to the City and do so. Very truly Your friend   A. LINCOLN

1 ALS, DLC-Schurz Papers. On November 20, Schurz replied to Lincoln's communication of November 10, *supra*, in part as follows:

"I fear you entertain too favorable a view of the causes of our defeat in the elections. . . .

"Whatever proportion of Republicans may have entered the army—if the administration had succeeded in preserving its hold upon the masses, your majorities would . . . have put the majorities of 1860 into the shade. . . . But the general confidence and enthusiasm yielded to general disappointment, and . . . too many Republicans . . . either voted against you or withheld their votes. I *know* this to be a fact. . . . That some of our newspapers disparaged and vilified the administration may be true. . . . But however that may be, I ask you . . . what power would there have been in newspaper-talk . . . had the administration been able to set up against it the evidence of great successes? . . . .

"I am far from presuming to blame you for having placed old democrats into high military positions. . . . But it was unfortunate that you sustained them . . . after they had been found failing;—failing not only in a political but also in a military sense. Was I really wrong in saying that the principal management of the war had been in the hands of your opponents? Or will perhaps anybody assert, that such men as McClellan and Buell and Halleck have the least sympathy with you or your views and principles?—or that their efficiency as military leaders has offered a compensation for their deficiency of sympathy, since the first has in 18 months succeeded in effecting literally nothing except the consumption of our resources with the largest and best appointed army this country ever saw;—since the second by his criminal tardiness and laxity endangered even the safety of Cincinnati; and since the appearance of the third on the battlefield of Shiloh served suddenly to arrest the operations of our victorious troops. . . . Has it not been publicly stated in the newspapers and apparently proved as a fact, that from the commencement of the war the enemy has [been] continually supplied with information by some of the confidential subordinates of so important an officer as Adjutant General Thomas? . . . . I am far from being inclined to impeach the loyalty and good faith of any man; but the coincidence of circumstances is such, that if the case were placed before a popular jury, I would find it much easier to act on the prosecution than on the defence. . . . You say that our Republican generals did no better. . . . I ask . . . what Republican General has ever had a fair chance . . . ?

"No, sir, let us indulge in no delusions as to the true causes of our defeat in the elections. . . . The people had sown confidence and reaped disaster and disappointment. They wanted a change, and . . . they sought it in the wrong direction. I entreat you, do not attribute to small incidents . . . what is a great historical event. It is best that you . . . should see the fact in its true light and appreciate its significance: *the result of the elections was a most serious and severe reproof administered to the administration.* . . ." (DLC-RTL).

Upon receipt of Lincoln's answer Schurz wrote on December 2 asking for a private and confidential interview (DLC-Nicolay Papers).

2 Edward D. Baker, killed at Ball's Bluff, October 21, 1861; Nathaniel Lyon, killed at Wilson's Creek, August 10, 1861; Henry Bohlen, killed at Freeman's Ford, August 22, 1862; Israel B. Richardson, died November 3, 1862, of wounds received September 17, 1862, at Antietam; Philip Kearney, killed September 1, 1862, at Chantilly; Isaac I. Stevens, also killed September 1, 1862, at Chantilly; Jesse L. Reno, killed September 14, 1862, at South Mountain; Joseph K. F. Mansfield, died September 18, 1862, of wounds received September 17 at Antietam.

To Ambrose E. Burnside[1]

Major General Burnside. Executive Mansion, Washington,
Falmouth, Va. Nov. 25. 1862. [11:30 A.M.]

If I should be in a Boat off Aquia-Creek, at dark to-morrow (wednesday) evening, could you, without inconvenience, meet me & pass an hour or two with me? A. LINCOLN

1 ALS, owned by Foreman M. Lebold, Chicago, Illinois. Burnside's reply was received at 2:45 P.M., "I will meet you, as you request, to-morrow evening. Please inform me what boat you will be on." (OR, I, XXI, 798).

To Salmon P. Chase[1]

Executive Mansion, Washington, November 25, 1862.

Dear Sir: Please remember to confer with the Secretary of the Interior, so as to clear the discrepancy as to amounts derived from sale of public lands. Yours truly, A. LINCOLN.

1 NH, VIII, 87. Secretary Chase replied on November 26: "Secretary Smiths amount is probably right—the amount given by me certainly is.

"The discrepancy arises from the fact that the Treasury Statement is of moneys *actually paid* into the Treasury, and may *include* moneys received by officers of the Interior Department in the fiscal year 1861 & *exclude* moneys received in the fiscal year 1862, while the Interior Statement, is of moneys received by these

Officers in the fiscal year 1862 only, *excluding* nothing received in that year & *including* nothing received in the preceding year" (DLC-RTL).

The figures referred to were in the reports of the Treasury and Department of Interior for the Annual Message to Congress, December 1, *infra.*

To Mrs. Abraham H. Hoge[1]

Mrs. A. H. Hoge   Executive Mansion,
Dear Madam   Washington, Nov. 25. 1862.

Your note of this morning is just received. If I can learn that your son has a commission from the Governor, enabling me to give him a staff appointment, and then any Brigadier General entitled to another staff officer, will ask to have your son for the place, I will appoint him. Without the first condition, it is not lawful for me to appoint him; and without the second, it would obviously be improper. Preserve this note & send it to me with any papers you may send, as evidence on the points named. Yours &c.

A. LINCOLN

1 ALS, DLC-RTL. Mrs. Hoge's note is not in the Lincoln Papers. Both she and her husband were active in organizing the Chicago Sanitary Fair of 1863. Her son Holmes Hoge enlisted as a private in the Chicago Mercantile Battery on August 17, 1862, and his appointment as captain and assistant quartermaster was confirmed on March 13, 1863. Another son, Captain George Blaikie Hoge of the Twenty-fifth Missouri Infantry, was appointed colonel of the One Hundred Thirteenth Illinois on October 1, 1862, and brevetted brigadier general of Volunteers as of March 13, 1865. Mrs. Hoge's maiden name was Blaikie. See further Lincoln's letter to Mrs. Hoge January 6, and Lincoln's endorsement to Stanton, February 8, 1863, *infra.*

To George Robertson[1]

Private   Executive Mansion,
Hon. George Robertson,   Washington, Nov. 26, 1862.

My dear Sir: A few days since I had a despatch from you which I did not answer. If I were to be wounded personally, I think I would not shun it. But it is the life of the nation. I now understand the trouble is with Col. Utley; that he has five slaves in his camp, four of whom belong to rebels, and one belonging to you. If this be true, convey yours to Col. Utley, so that he can make him free, and I will pay you any sum not exceeding five hundred dollars. Yours, &c.   A. LINCOLN

1 Copy, DLC-RTL. See Lincoln's first letter of November 20, *supra,* in reply to Robertson's dispatch of November 19, 1862. On November 17, Colonel William L. Utley of the Twenty-second Wisconsin Volunteers wrote Lincoln from Nicholasville, Kentucky, as follows:

"Permit me respectfully to appeal to you. . . . For a long time . . . enduring hardships and privasions of military life and of army marches . . . we penetrated the state of Kentucky, the devastating hords of rebels fleeing before us. . . .

"As a compensation for these sacrifices, hardships and exposures . . . I now find myself indited for *man-stealing*, by a Kentucky court, and hunted by her officers as a fellon for her penitentiary.

"The facts in the case are few, simple, and easily understood. . . . On Friday last, Judge Robinson of Lexington, representing himself as a Union man of whose counsels . . . you have seen fit to avail yourself, came into my lines, and claimed and demanded as his property, a Negro boy found in the regiment. How, when, where, or by what means the boy came into the lines, or by whom he was claimed as property, I had previously no knowledge. . . . I refused to recognize his claims, to lead the boy, as he requested, beyond my lines, or to forbid the soldiers from interfereing should he attempt to do so. He was not, however, forbidden to take him. . . . The boy refused to go with him and *claimed* protection from the power of one whose cruel treatment, as he asserted, had already made him a *dwarf* instead of a man. . . . To you, I now appeal for . . . protection . . . for simply standing by the Constitution, obeying the laws of Congress and honoring the Proclamation . . . issued on the 23d day of September last. . . . Judge Robinson declared the President's proclamation of the 23d of Sept, to be unconstitutional, to have no bearing on Kentucky and that the state would never submit to it. . . ." (DLC-RTL).

On the same day Colonel Utley penned another classic to his friend Alexander W. Randall, recently returned from his post as minister to Rome, who transmitted it to the president. Although too long to reproduce in full, the pertinent portions read as follows: "I am in a devil of a scrape, and appeal to you for assistance. . . . I am ahead yet, but they have taken a new dodge on me, they have got me indicted at Lexington under the Laws of Kentucky. The Warrant is in the hands of the Sherriff of this county he finds the same difficulty that the rats did in getting the bell on the cat, it would be a good thing to have done, but a bad thing to do. they find it so in arresting me. they can never do it while there is a man left in the 22d Regiment. the Brig. Genl. in whose Brigade we now are, Refuses to assist in arresting me. Now what I want, is to have you use your influence with the President to have him retained in command of this Brigade. for he certainly will be removed . . . unless measures are taken to prevent, or we shall again be placed under some pro Slavary *Jcass* (?) as we have been . . . untill we were placed under him. You know how we was hurried off without blankets, tents or anything. . . . Kentucky was howling like a set of d—d Hyenas (as they are) for help. the men left their grain standing . . . we all throwed down our impliments and . . . came directly to Kentucky. . . . We have been Brigaded under five or six different Genls all just alike all chosen for their adherence to the Kentuckey policy. We have had to submit to the most degrading orders. . . . We have laid in the dirt five nights on an old Rebel ex Congressmans farm (with a large straw stack roting down within 40 Rods of us). . . . When we left there two or three of his nigers got in the Regt and claimed protection. I refused to be made a niger ketcher, as you have no doubt seen by the papers. . . . I have tryed to avoid trouble on the niger question, but I could not escape it, but I am just the boy to meet it when it comes. . . . There is no such thing as unionism in Kentuckey. . . . I wish Abraham Lincoln could hear what the professed union men call him. I told the Governor (Robinson) that all Kentuckeyans were either d—d trators or cowards, that there was no loyalty in the state, that you might put it all in to one end of the scales, and a niger baby in the other end, and Loyalty and unionism would go up with a rush I have given them hell, and now they intend to give me h—l. . . . What I want is . . . to be kept under Generals that acknowledge the power of the president, or be taken out of the state. there is a general understanding among the genl officers commanding in Kentucky to ignore the proclimation. . . . I am the first man that has attempted to carry it out, and now I am indicted by *Loud mouthed Union men*. . . ." (DLC-RTL).

On December 1, Judge Robertson replied to Lincoln's letter, "In my late telegram to you I did not allude to either my boy Adam, or to Col. Utley, or to his case. Divining your information, as you must have done, from some other source, you have been misinformed, and . . . misconceived the motive of my dispatch. . . . I had put Col. Utley in the position which I preferred, and I neither intended nor disired to seek any . . . intervention in . . . my own case. . . . The citation in my civil suit against him having been served, I can certainly obtain a judgement for $1000, and perhaps more. . . . My object in that suit was far from mercenary—it was solely to try the question whether the civil or the military power is Constitutionally supreme in Kentucky. . . ." (DLC-RTL).

Whatever his intentions were at this time, Robertson pressed his suit in the courts and on October 6, 1871, eventually obtained judgment against Utley in the U.S. Circuit Court for the Eastern District of Wisconsin, in the amount of $908.06 plus costs of $26.40. By an act approved February 14, 1873, congress directed the Secretary of the Treasury to pay the amount "together with interest from the date of recovery" for the relief of William L. Utley.

To George Robertson[1]

Hon. George Robertson   Executive Mansion,
Lexington, Ky.   Washington, Nov. 26. 1862.

I mail you a short letter *to-day*.   A. LINCOLN

[1] ALS, RPB. See Lincoln's letter, *supra*.

To Henry W. Halleck[1]

Steamer Baltimore
Major General Halleck   Off Acquia Creek, Va
Sir: Nov. 27. 1862

I have just had a long conference with Gen. Burnside. He believes that Gen. Lees whole army, or nearly the whole of it is in front of him, at and near Fredericksburg. Gen. B. says he could take into battle now any day, about, one hundred and ten thousand men, that his army is in good spirit, good condition, good moral, and that in all respects he is satisfied with officers and men; that he does not want more men with him, because he could not handle them to advantage; that he thinks he can cross the river in face of the enemy and drive him away, but that, to use his own expression, it is somewhat risky. I wish the case to stand more favorable than this in two respects. First, I wish his crossing of the river to be nearly free from risk; and secondly, I wish the enemy to be prevented from falling back, accumulating strength as he goes, into his intrenchments at Richmond. I therefore propose that Gen. B. shall not move immediately; that we accumulate a force on the South bank of the Rappahanock—at, say, Port-Royal, under protection of one or two gun-boats, as nearly up to twentyfive thousand strong as we can. At the same time another force of about the same strength as high up the Pamunkey, as can be protected by gunboats. These being ready, let all three forces move simultaneously, Gen. B.'s force in it's attempt to cross the river, the Rappahanock force moving directly up the South side of the river to his assistance, and ready, if found admissable, to deflect off to the turnpike brigdge over the Mattapony in the direction of Richmond. The Pamunkey force to move as rapidly as possible up the North side of the Pamunkey, holding all the bridges, and especially the turnpike bridge immediately North of Hanover C.H; hurry North, and seize and hold the Mattapony bridge before mentioned, and also, if possible, press higher up the streams and destroy the railroad bridges. Then, if Gen. B. succeeds in driving the enemy from Fredericksburg, he the enemy no longer has the road to Richmond, but we have it and can march into the city. Or, possibly, having forced the enemy from his line, we could move upon, and destroy his army. Gen. B.'s main army would have the same line of supply and retreat as he has now provided; the Rappahanock force would have that river for supply, and gun-boats to fall back upon; and the Pamunkey force would have that river for supply, and a line between the two rivers—Pamunkey & Mattapony—along which to fall back upon it's gun-boats. I think the plan promises the best results, with the least hazzard, of any now conceiveable.

Note— The above plan, proposed by me, was rejected by Gen. Halleck & Gen. Burnside, on the ground that we could not raise and put in position, the Pamunkey force without too much waste of time   A. L.

[1] ADfS, DLC-RTL. A dispatch from Washington dated November 29 in the New York *Herald*, November 30, 1862, reported that "Major General Burnside arrived here last night, and spent this forenoon principally in consultation with President Lincoln and General Halleck. He has already returned to his headquarters." Lincoln's note at the end of the draft was presumably added after this conference.

To Edward Bates[1]

Executive Mansion, Washington,
Hon. Attorney General   Nov. 29, 1862.

My dear Sir: Few things perplex me more than this question between Gov. Gamble, and the War Department, as to whether the peculiar force organized by the former in Missouri are "State troops," or "United States troops." Now, this is either an immaterial, or a mischievous question. First, if no more is desired than to have it settled what name the forces is to be called by, it is immaterial. Secondly, if it is desired for more than the fixing a name, it can only be to get a position from which to draw practical inferences, then it is mischievous. Instead of settling one dispute by deciding the question, I should merely furnish a nest full of eggs for hatching new disputes. I believe the force is not strictly either "State troops" or "United States troops." It is of mixed character. I therefore think it is safer when a practical question arises, to decide that question directly, and not indirectly, by deciding a general abstraction supposed to include it, and also including a great deal more. Without dispute, Gov. Gamble appoints the officers of this force, and fills vacancies when they occur. The question now practically in dispute is "Can Gov. Gamble make a vacancy, by removing an officer, or accepting a resignation? Now, while it is proper that this question shall be settled, I do not perceive why either Gov. Gamble, or the government here, should care which way it is settled. I am perplexed with it only because there seems to be pertinacity about it. It seems to me that it might be either way without injury to the service; or that the offer of the Secretary of War to let Gov. Gamble make vacancies, and he, the Secretary, to ratify the making of them, ought to be satisfactory.

[1] ADf, DLC-RTL. On November 17, Governor Gamble, who was in Washington, wrote Lincoln concerning Lincoln's order of November 6, 1861, "You accepted the proposal . . . with the condition, that I should appoint the Major Genl. of . . . the Department, the Major General of the force thus to be raised. . . . I proceeded to raise the force and put it in the field, where it has rendered eminent service. . . .

"A question has now arisen between the War Department and myself—Whether the force thus raised is a state force or a United States force. . . . I have acted with perfectly good faith on the clear conviction that I was dealing with a state force.

"The question now pending . . . involves the construction of the instrument in which my offer to raise this force is accepted by you. . . ." (DLC-RTL).

See further Lincoln's order to Stanton, December 2, *infra*.

To Henry S. Lane and Joseph A. Wright[1]

[c. November 29, 1862]

Will Senators Lane and Wright, of Indiana, please report to me on this case   A. LINCOLN

[1] AES, DLC-RTL. Lincoln's endorsement is written on a letter for publication signed "Union," written by J. W. Bailey of Aurora, Indiana, November 28, 1862, to the editor of the Cincinnati *Gazette* denouncing the appointment of George W. Lane as superintendent of the Denver Mint on grounds of his disloyalty. The editor of the *Gazette*, Richard Smith, forwarded the letter to Lincoln on November 29. Both Senator Lane and Governor Wright replied on December 15, 1862, confirming their recommendation and conviction of George W. Lane's loyalty. (DLC-RTL).

To Samuel R. Curtis[1]

"Cypher"

Major General Curtis   Washington,
St. Louis, Mo.   Nov. 30. 1862

Frank Blair wants Manter's 32nd. Curley's 27th. Boyd's 24th. and the 9th. & 10th. Cavalry, to go with him down the river. I understand it is with you to decide whether he shall have them; and if so, and if also it is consistent with the public service, you will oblige me a good deal by letting him have them.

A. LINCOLN

[1] ALS, RPB. Concerning the regiments commanded by Francis H. Manter, Thomas Curly, and Sempronius H. Boyd, Curtis telegraphed at 10 P.M. on the same day, "Only one of the Regiments named full will try to organize immediately by urging Gov to consolidate & come as near to the request as law will permit." (DLC-RTL).

Memorandum Concerning J. Wesley Greene[1]

[December, 1862?]

After inquiry, I believe it is true that a man calling himself J. Wesley Greene, and professing to reside at Pittsburg, Pa., called on the President some time in November, and stated to him that he, Greene, had had two interviews with Jeff. Davis, at Richmond, Va., on the last day of October; and also related certain statements which he said Davis had made to him upon the occasion. The President became satisfied that Greene had not seen Davis at all, and that the whole thing was a very shallow attempt at humbuggery. Jeff. Davis can redeem Greene's character if he will, by verifying his statement.

[1] Hertz, II, 961. As printed by Hertz this item is described as "a manuscript memo." But Hertz's date, February, 1865, probably taken from the American Art Association Anderson Galleries Catalog, October 20, 1930, would seem to be incorrect. The New York *Tribune* for December 11, 1862, prints a similar statement at the end of a news item reprinted from the Chicago *Times*, Wednesday, December 10, 1862, which gives an account of J. Wesley Greene's visits to Jefferson Davis and to President Lincoln. The *Tribune* does not, however, credit the statement as Lincoln's, although implying that Lincoln is the source of information, and it seems possible that Lincoln may have written the memorandum in answer to a query from the press on the reliability of Greene's narrative. A letter from Greene to Lincoln, November 11, 1862, reads in part as follows:

"An entire stranger to fame, and almost unknown . . . but at the same time an ardent lover of the country which for nearly fifty years has encompassed me with its protection, I presume to introduce myself to your notice in reference to the . . . termination of the Rebellion and the restoration of the Union.

"One week has but just elapsed since I returned to my home in this city, fresh from two interviews with the controlling man of the rebellious states. I not only found him depressed in spirit, beyond my conception of him, in view of the terrible circumstances in which he is placed and the condition of the Confederacy, but I found him anxious for an end of hostilities and a return to the Union. In the last interview he cautiously intimated the terms on which the desired end might be accomplished. They are of a nature which forbids me to commit them to writing from this distance. This much I can say that, while he now deprecates foreign intervention or foreign mediation, the terms are such as may be secretly negotiated, and can in no way reflect upon the Government of which you are the head should they in any future period become known.

"I am no visionary, . . . no speculator, no party demagogue. I am but a plain business man, who in other days became incidentally acquainted with Mr. Davis, an acquaintance which secured his friendship. . . .

"I sincerely and daily pray for the peace and unity and prosperity of my beloved country, again. I honestly believe they can be brought about at an early day, honorably to the North without the continuance of bloodshed and devastation. If, therefore, Your Excellency desires an interview with me on this subject such an order as will convey me to Washington will be promptly complied with.

"Permit me to add, Sir, that I have never intimated this matter to any human being; and desire that it may, at least for the present, be treated confidentially." (DLC-RTL).

Annual Message to Congress[1]

December 1, 1862

Fellow-citizens of the Senate and House of Representatives:

Since your last annual assembling another year of health and bountiful harvests has passed. And while it has not pleased the Almighty to bless us with a return of peace, we can but press on, guided by the best light He gives us, trusting that in His own good time, and wise way, all will yet be well.

The correspondence touching foreign affairs which has taken place during the last year is herewith submitted, in virtual compliance with a request to that effect, made by the House of Representatives near the close of the last session of Congress.[2]

If the condition of our relations with other nations is less gratifying than it has usually been at former periods, it is certainly more satisfactory than a nation so unhappily distracted as we are, might reasonably have apprehended. In the month of June last there were some grounds to expect that the maritime powers which, at the beginning of our domestic difficulties, so unwisely and unnecessarily, as we think, recognized the insurgents as a belligerent, would soon recede from that position,[3] which has proved only less injurious to themselves, than to our own country. But the temporary

[1] DS, DNA RG 46, Senate 37A F1. The first two pages of the official copy are missing. For that portion of the text we have followed the printing in Thirty-seventh Congress, Third Session, *House of Representatives Executive Document No. 1*, where also may be found the reports of the several cabinet members.
[2] See Lincoln's communication of July 12, *supra.*
[3] The text to this point follows *Executive Document No. 1*. The remainder follows the manuscript document signed by Lincoln.

reverses which afterwards befell the national arms, and which were exaggerated by our own disloyal citizens abroad have hitherto delayed that act of simple justice.[4]

The civil war, which has so radically changed for the moment, the occupations and habits of the American people, has necessarily disturbed the social condition, and affected very deeply the prosperity of the nations with which we have carried on a commerce that has been steadily increasing throughout a period of half a century. It has, at the same time, excited political ambitions and apprehensions which have produced a profound agitation throughout the civilized world. In this unusual agitation we have forborne from taking part in any controversy between foreign states, and between parties or factions in such states. We have attempted no propagandism, and acknowledged no revolution. But we have left to every nation the exclusive conduct and management of its own affairs. Our struggle has been, of course, contemplated by foreign nations with reference less to its own merits, than to its supposed, and often exaggerated effects and consequences resulting to those nations themselves. Nevertheless, complaint on the part of this government, even if it were just, would certainly be unwise.

The treaty with Great Britain for the suppression of the slave trade has been put into operation with a good prospect of complete success. It is an occasion of special pleasure to acknowledge that the execution of it, on the part of Her Majesty's government, has been marked with a jealous respect for the authority of the United States, and the rights of their moral and loyal citizens.

The convention with Hanover for the abolition of the stade dues has been carried into full effect, under the act of Congress for that purpose.

A blockade of three thousand miles of sea-coast could not be established, and vigorously enforced, in a season of great commercial activity like the present, without committing occasional mistakes, and inflicting unintentional injuries upon foreign nations and their subjects.

A civil war occurring in a country where foreigners reside and carry on trade under treaty stipulations, is necessarily fruitful of complaints of the violation of neutral rights. All such collisions tend to excite misapprehensions, and possibly to produce mutual reclamations between nations which have a common interest in preserving peace and friendship. In clear cases of these kinds I have,

4 In spite of persistent efforts by the Department of State, the recognition extended to the Confederacy by England and France was not withdrawn and continued until the end of the war.

so far as possible, heard and redressed complaints which have been presented by friendly powers. There is still, however, a large and an augmenting number of doubtful cases upon which the government is unable to agree with the governments whose protection is demanded by the claimants. There are, moreover, many cases in which the United States, or their citizens, suffer wrongs from the naval or military authorities of foreign nations, which the governments of those states are not at once prepared to redress. I have proposed to some of the foreign states, thus interested, mutual conventions to examine and adjust such complaints. This proposition has been made especially to Great Britain, to France, to Spain, and to Prussia. In each case it has been kindly received, but has not yet been formally adopted.

I deem it my duty to recommend an appropriation in behalf of the owners of the Norwegian bark Admiral P. Tordenskiold, which vessel was, in May, 1861, prevented by the commander of the blockading force off Charleston from leaving that port with cargo, notwithstanding a similar privilege had, shortly before, been granted to an English vessel. I have directed the Secretary of State to cause the papers in the case to be communicated to the proper committees.[5]

Applications have been made to me by many free Americans of African descent to favor their emigration, with a view to such colonization as was contemplated in recent acts of Congress. Other parties, at home and abroad—some from interested motives, others upon patriotic considerations, and still others influenced by philanthropic sentiments—have suggested similar measures; while, on the other hand, several of the Spanish-American republics have protested against the sending of such colonies to their respective territories. Under these circumstances, I have declined to move any such colony to any state, without first obtaining the consent of its government, with an agreement on its part to receive and protect such emigrants in all the rights of freemen; and I have, at the same time, offered to the several states situated within the tropics, or having colonies there, to negotiate with them, subject to the advice and consent of the Senate, to favor the voluntary emigration of persons of that class to their respective territories, upon conditions which shall be equal, just, and humane. Liberia and Hayti are, as yet, the only countries to which colonists of African descent from here, could go with certainty of being received and adopted as citizens; and I regret to say such persons, contemplating coloniza-

[5] An act approved February 14, 1863, compensated the owners of the *Admiral P. Tordenskiold* in the amount of $14,309.13.

tion, do not seem so willing to migrate to those countries, as to some others, nor so willing as I think their interest demands. I believe, however, opinion among them, in this respect, is improving; and that, ere long, there will be an augmented, and considerable migration to both these countries, from the United States.

The new commercial treaty between the United States and the Sultan of Turkey has been carried into execution.

A commercial and consular treaty has been negotiated, subject to the Senate's consent, with Liberia; and a similar negotiation is now pending with the republic of Hayti. A considerable improvement of the national commerce is expected to result from these measures.

Our relations with Great Britain, France, Spain, Portugal, Russia, Prussia, Denmark, Sweden, Austria, the Netherlands, Italy, Rome, and the other European states, remain undisturbed. Very favorable relations also continue to be maintained with Turkey, Morocco, China and Japan.

During the last year there has not only been no change of our previous relations with the independent states of our own continent, but, more friendly sentiments than have heretofore existed, are believed to be entertained by these neighbors, whose safety and progress, are so intimately connected with our own. This statement especially applies to Mexico, Nicaragua, Costa Rica, Honduras, Peru, and Chile.

The commission under the convention with the republic of New Granada closed its session, without having audited and passed upon, all the claims which were submitted to it. A proposition is pending to revive the convention, that it may be able to do more complete justice. The joint commission between the United States and the republic of Costa Rica has completed its labors and submitted its report.

I have favored the project for connecting the United States with Europe by an Atlantic telegraph, and a similar project to extend the telegraph from San Francisco, to connect by a Pacific telegraph with the line which is being extended across the Russian empire.

The Territories of the United States, with unimportant exceptions, have remained undisturbed by the civil war, and they are exhibiting such evidence of prosperity as justifies an expectation that some of them will soon be in a condition to be organized as States, and be constitutionally admitted into the federal Union.

The immense mineral resources of some of those Territories ought to be developed as rapidly as possible. Every step in that direction would have a tendency to improve the revenues of the government, and diminish the burdens of the people. It is worthy of your serious consideration whether some extraordinary measures to promote that end cannot be adopted. The means which suggests itself as most likely to be effective, is a scientific exploration of the mineral regions in those Territories, with a view to the publication of its results at home and in foreign countries—results which cannot fail to be auspicious.

The condition of the finances will claim your most diligent consideration. The vast expenditures incident to the military and naval operations required for the suppression of the rebellion, have hitherto been met with a promptitude, and certainty, unusual in similar circumstances, and the public credit has been fully maintained. The continuance of the war, however, and the increased disbursements made necessary by the augmented forces now in the field, demand your best reflections as to the best modes of providing the necessary revenue, without injury to business and with the least possible burdens upon labor.

The suspension of specie payments by the banks, soon after the commencement of your last session, made large issues of United States notes unavoidable. In no other way could the payment of the troops, and the satisfaction of other just demands, be so economically, or so well provided for. The judicious legislation of Congress, securing the receivability of these notes for loans and internal duties, and making them a legal tender for other debts, has made them an universal currency; and has satisfied, partially, at least, and for the time, the long felt want of an uniform circulating medium, saving thereby to the people, immense sums in discounts and exchanges.

A return to specie payments, however, at the earliest period compatible with due regard to all interests concerned, should ever be kept in view. Fluctuations in the value of currency are always injurious, and to reduce these fluctuations to the lowest possible point will always be a leading purpose in wise legislation. Convertibility, prompt and certain convertibility into coin, is generally acknowledged to be the best and surest safeguard against them; and it is extremely doubtful whether a circulation of United States notes, payable in coin, and sufficiently large for the wants of the people, can be permanently, usefully and safely maintained.

Is there, then, any other mode in which the necessary provision for the public wants can be made, and the great advantages of a safe and uniform currency secured?

I know of none which promises so certain results, and is, at the same time, so unobjectionable, as the organization of banking associations, under a general act of Congress, well guarded in its provisions. To such associations the government might furnish circulating notes, on the security of United States bonds deposited in the treasury. These notes, prepared under the supervision of proper officers, being uniform in appearance and security, and convertible always into coin, would at once protect labor against the evils of a vicious currency, and facilitate commerce by cheap and safe exchanges.

A moderate reservation from the interest on the bonds would compensate the United States for the preparation and distribution of the notes and a general supervision of the system, and would lighten the burden of that part of the public debt employed as securities. The public credit, moreover, would be greatly improved, and the negotiation of new loans greatly facilitated by the steady market demand for government bonds which the adoption of the proposed system would create.

It is an additional recommendation of the measure, of considerable weight, in my judgment, that it would reconcile, as far as possible, all existing interests, by the opportunity offered to existing institutions to reorganize under the act, substituting only the secured uniform national circulation for the local and various circulation, secured and unsecured, now issued by them.

The receipts into the treasury from all sources, including loans and balance from the preceding year, for the fiscal year ending on the 30th June, 1862, were $583,885,247 06, of which sum $49,056,397 62 were derived from customs; $1,795,331,73 from the direct tax; from public lands $152,203,77; from miscellaneous sources, $931,787 64; from loans in all forms, $529,692,460 50. The remainder, $2,257,065 80, was the balance from last year.

The disbursements during the same period were for congressional, executive, and judicial purposes, $5,939,009 29; for foreign intercourse, $1,339,710,35; for miscellaneous expenses, including the mints, loans, post office deficiencies, collection of revenue, and other like charges, $14,129,771 50; for expenses under the Interior Department, $3,102,985 52; under the War Department, $394,368,-407,36; under the Navy Department, $42,674,569 69; for interest on public debt, $13,190,324 45; and for payment of public debt, including reimbursement of temporary loan, and redemptions, $96,096,922 09; making an aggregate of $570,841,700 25; and leaving a balance in the treasury on the first day of July, 1862, of $13,043,546,81.

It should be observed that the sum of $96,096,922 09, expended for reimbursements and redemption of public debt, being included also in the loans made, may be properly deducted, both from receipts and expenditures, leaving the actual receipts for the year $487,788,324 97; and the expenditures, $474,744,778 16.

Other information on the subject of the finances will be found in the report of the Secretary of the Treasury, to whose statements and views I invite your most candid and considerate attention.

The reports of the Secretaries of War, and of the Navy, are herewith transmitted. These reports, though lengthy, are scarcely more than brief abstracts of the very numerous and extensive transactions and operations conducted through those departments. Nor could I give a summary of them here, upon any principle, which would admit of its being much shorter than the reports themselves. I therefore content myself with laying the reports before you, and asking your attention to them.

It gives me pleasure to report a decided improvement in the financial condition of the Post Office Department, as compared with several preceding years. The receipts for the fiscal year 1861 amounted to $8,349,296 40, which embraced the revenue from all the States of the Union for three quarters of that year. Notwithstanding the cessation of revenue from the so-called seceded States during the last fiscal year, the increase of the correspondence of the loyal States has been sufficient to produce a revenue during the same year of $8,299,820 90, being only $50,000 less than was derived from all the States of the Union during the previous year. The expenditures show a still more favorable result. The amount expended in 1861 was $13,606,759 11. For the last year the amount has been reduced to $11,125,364 13, showing a decrease of about $2,481,000 in the expenditures as compared with the preceding year and about $3,750,000 as compared with the fiscal year 1860. The deficiency in the department for the previous year was $4,551,-966.98. For the last fiscal year it was reduced to $2,112,814.57. These favorable results are in part owing to the cessation of mail service in the insurrectionary States, and in part to a careful review of all expenditures in that department in the interest of economy. The efficiency of the postal service, it is believed, has also been much improved. The Postmaster General has also opened a correspondence, through the Department of State, with foreign governments, proposing a convention of postal representatives for the purpose of simplifying the rates of foreign postage, and to expedite the foreign mails. This proposition, equally important to our adopted citizens, and to the commercial interests of this country, has been favorably entertained, and agreed to, by all the governments from whom replies have been received.

I ask the attention of Congress to the suggestions of the Postmaster General in his report respecting the further legislation required, in his opinion, for the benefit of the postal service.

The Secretary of the Interior reports as follows in regard to the public lands:

"The public lands have ceased to be a source of revenue. From the 1st July, 1861, to the 30th September, 1862, the entire cash receipts from the sale of lands were $137,476 26—a sum much less than the expenses of our land system during the same period. The homestead law, which will take effect on the 1st of January next, offers such inducements to settlers, that sales for cash cannot be expected, to an extent sufficient to meet the expenses of the General Land Office, and the cost of surveying and bringing the land into market"

The discrepancy between the sum here stated as arising from the sales of the public lands, and the sum derived from the same source as reported from the Treasury Department arises, as I understand, from the fact that the periods of time, though apparently, were not really, coincident at the beginning point—the Treasury report including a considerable sum now, which had previously been reported from the Interior—sufficiently large to greatly overreach the sum derived from the three months now reported upon by the Interior, and not by the Treasury.

The Indian tribes upon our frontiers have, during the past year, manifested a spirit of insubordination, and, at several points, have engaged in open hostilities against the white settlements in their vicinity. The tribes occupying the Indian country south of Kansas, renounced their allegiance to the United States, and entered into treaties with the insurgents. Those who remained loyal to the United States were driven from the country. The chief of the Cherokees has visited this city for the purpose of restoring the former relations of the tribe with the United States. He alleges that they were constrained, by superior force, to enter into treaties with the insurgents, and that the United States neglected to furnish the protection which their treaty stipulations required.

In the month of August last the Sioux Indians, in Minnesota, attacked the settlements in their vicinity with extreme ferocity, killing, indiscriminately, men, women, and children. This attack was wholly unexpected, and, therefore, no means of defence had been provided. It is estimated that not less than eight hundred persons were killed by the Indians, and a large amount of property was destroyed. How this outbreak was induced is not definitely known, and suspicions, which may be unjust, need not to be stated. Information was received by the Indian bureau, from different sources, about the time hostilities were commenced, that a simultaneous attack was to be made upon the white settlements by all the tribes between the Mississippi river and the Rocky mountains. The State of Minnesota has suffered great injury from this Indian war. A large portion of her territory has been depopulated, and a severe loss has been sustained by the destruction of property. The people of that State manifest much anxiety for the removal of the tribes beyond the limits of the State as a guarantee against future hostilities. The Commissioner of Indian Affairs will furnish full details. I submit for your especial consideration whether our Indian system shall not be remodelled. Many wise and good men have impressed me with the belief that this can be profitably done.

I submit a statement of the proceedings of commissioners, which shows the progress that has been made in the enterprise of constructing the Pacific railroad. And this suggests the earliest completion of this road, and also the favorable action of Congress upon the projects now pending before them for enlarging the capacities of the great canals in New York and Illinois, as being of vital, and rapidly increasing importance to the whole nation, and especially to the vast interior region hereinafter to be noticed at some greater length. I purpose having prepared and laid before you at an early day some interesting and valuable statistical information upon this subject. The military and commercial importance of enlarging the Illinois and Michigan canal, and improving the Illinois river, is presented in the report of Colonel Webster to the Secretary of War, and now transmitted to Congress. I respectfully ask attention to it.

To carry out the provisions of the act of Congress of the 15th of May last, I have caused the Department of Agriculture of the United States to be organized.

The Commissioner informs me that within the period of a few months this department has established an extensive system of correspondence and exchanges, both at home and abroad, which promises to effect highly beneficial results in the development of a correct knowledge of recent improvements in agriculture, in the introduction of new products, and in the collection of the agricultural statistics of the different States.

Also that it will soon be prepared to distribute largely seeds, cereals, plants and cuttings, and has already published, and liberally diffused, much valuable information in anticipation of a more elaborate report, which will in due time be furnished, embracing some valuable tests in chemical science now in progress in the laboratory.

The creation of this department was for the more immediate

benefit of a large class of our most valuable citizens; and I trust that the liberal basis upon which it has been organized will not only meet your approbation, but that it will realize, at no distant day, all the fondest anticipations of its most sanguine friends, and become the fruitful source of advantage to all our people.

On the twenty-second day of September last a proclamation was issued by the Executive, a copy of which is herewith submitted.

In accordance with the purpose expressed in the second paragraph of that paper, I now respectfully recall your attention to what may be called "compensated emancipation."

A nation may be said to consist of its territory, its people, and its laws. The territory is the only part which is of certain durability. "One generation passeth away, and another generation cometh, but the earth abideth forever." It is of the first importance to duly consider, and estimate, this ever-enduring part. That portion of the earth's surface which is owned and inhabited by the people of the United States, is well adapted to be the home of one national family; and it is not well adapted for two, or more. Its vast extent, and its variety of climate and productions, are of advantage, in this age, for one people, whatever they might have been in former ages. Steam, telegraphs, and intelligence, have brought these, to be an advantageous combination, for one united people.

In the inaugural address I briefly pointed out the total inadequacy of disunion, as a remedy for the differences between the people of the two sections. I did so in language which I cannot improve, and which, therefore, I beg to repeat:

"One section of our country believes slavery is *right*, and ought to be extended, while the other believes it is *wrong*, and ought not to be extended. This is the only substantial dispute. The fugitive slave clause of the Constitution, and the law for the suppression of the foreign slave trade, are each as well enforced, perhaps, as any law can ever be in a community where the moral sense of the people imperfectly supports the law itself. The great body of the people abide by the dry legal obligation in both cases, and a few break over in each. This, I think, cannot be perfectly cured; and it would be worse in both cases *after* the separation of the sections, than before. The foreign slave trade, now imperfectly suppressed, would be ultimately revived without restriction in one section; while fugitive slaves, now only partially surrendered, would not be surrendered at all by the other.

"Physically speaking, we cannot separate. We cannot remove our respective sections from each other, nor build an impassable wall between them. A husband and wife may be divorced, and go out of the presence, and beyond the reach of each other; but the different parts of our country cannot do this. They cannot but remain face to face; and intercourse, either amicable or hostile, must continue between them. Is it possible, then, to make that intercourse more advantageous, or more satisfactory, *after* separation than *before*? Can aliens make treaties, easier than friends can make laws? Can treaties be more faithfully enforced between aliens, than laws can among friends? Suppose you go to war, you cannot fight always; and when, after much loss on both sides, and no gain on either, you cease fighting, the identical old questions, as to terms of intercourse, are again upon you."

There is no line, straight or crooked, suitable for a national boundary, upon which to divide. Trace through, from east to west, upon the line between the free and slave country, and we shall find a little more than one-third of its length are rivers, easy to be crossed, and populated, or soon to be populated, thickly upon both sides; while nearly all its remaining length, are merely surveyor's lines, over which people may walk back and forth without any consciousness of their presence. No part of this line can be made any more difficult to pass, by writing it down on paper, or parchment, as a national boundary. The fact of separation, if it comes, gives up, on the part of the seceding section, the fugitive slave clause, along with all other constitutional obligations upon the section seceded from, while I should expect no treaty stipulation would ever be made to take its place.

But there is another difficulty. The great interior region, bounded east by the Alleghanies, north by the British dominions, west by the Rocky mountains, and south by the line along which the culture of corn and cotton meets, and which includes part of Virginia, part of Tennessee, all of Kentucky, Ohio, Indiana, Michigan, Wisconsin, Illinois, Missouri, Kansas, Iowa, Minnesota and the Territories of Dakota, Nebraska, and part of Colorado, already has above ten millions of people, and will have fifty millions within fifty years, if not prevented by any political folly or mistake. It contains more than one-third of the country owned by the United States—certainly more than one million of square miles. Once half as populous as Massachusetts already is, it would have more than seventy-five millions of people. A glance at the map shows that, territorially speaking, it is the great body of the republic. The other parts are but marginal borders to it, the magnificent region sloping west from the rocky mountains to the Pacific, being the deepest, and also the richest, in undeveloped resources. In the production of provisions, grains, grasses, and all which proceed from them, this great interior region is naturally one of the most important in the world. Ascertain from the statistics the small proportion of the region which has, as yet, been brought into cultivation, and also the large and rapidly increasing amount of its products, and we shall be overwhelmed with the magnitude of the prospect presented. An[d] yet this region has no sea-coast, touches no ocean anywhere. As part of one nation, its people now find, and may forever find, their way to Europe by New York, to South America and Africa by New Orleans, and to Asia by San Francisco. But separate our common country into two nations, as designed by the present rebellion, and every man of this great interior region is thereby cut off from some one or more of these outlets, not, perhaps, by a physical barrier, but by embarrassing and onerous trade regulations.

And this is true, *wherever* a dividing, or boundary line, may be fixed. Place it between the now free and slave country, or place it south of Kentucky, or north of Ohio, and still the truth remains, that none south of it, can trade to any port or place north of it, and none north of it, can trade to any port or place south of it, except upon terms dictated by a government foreign to them. These outlets, east, west, and south, are indispensable to the well-being of the people inhabiting, and to inhabit, this vast interior region. *Which* of the three may be the best, is no proper question. All, are better than either, and all, of right, belong to that people, and to their successors forever. True to themselves, they will not ask *where* a line of separation shall be, but will vow, rather, that there shall be no such line. Nor are the marginal regions less interested in these communications to, and through them, to the great outside world. They too, and each of them, must have access to this Egypt of the West, without paying toll at the crossing of any national boundary.

Our national strife springs not from our permanent part; not from the land we inhabit; not from our national homestead. There is no possible severing of this, but would multiply, and not mitigate, evils among us. In all its adaptations and aptitudes, it demands union, and abhors separation. In fact, it would, ere long, force reunion, however much of blood and treasure the separation might have cost.

Our strife pertains to ourselves—to the passing generations of men; and it can, without convulsion, be hushed forever with the passing of one generation.

In this view, I recommend the adoption of the following resolution and articles amendatory to the Constitution of the United States:

"Resolved by the Senate and House of Representatives of the United States of America in Congress assembled, (two thirds of both houses concurring,) That the following articles be proposed to the legislatures (or conventions) of the several States as amendments to the Constitution of the United States, all or any of which articles when ratified by three-fourths of the said legislatures (or conventions) to be valid as part or parts of the said Constitution, viz:

"Article ——.

"Every State, wherein slavery now exists, which shall abolish the same therein, at any time, or times, before the first day of January, in the year of our Lord one thousand and nine hundred, shall receive compensation from the United States as follows, to wit:

"The President of the United States shall deliver to every such State, bonds of the United States, bearing interest at the rate of —— per cent, per annum, to an amount equal to the aggregate sum of   for each slave shown to have been therein, by the eig[h]th census of the United States, said bonds to be delivered to such State by instalments, or in one parcel, at the completion of the abolishment, accordingly as the same shall have been gradual, or at one time, within such State; and interest shall begin to run upon any such bond, only from the proper time of its delivery as aforesaid. Any State having received bonds as aforesaid, and afterwards reintroducing or tolerating slavery therein, shall refund to the United States the bonds so received, or the value thereof, and all interest paid thereon.

"Article ——.

"All slaves who shall have enjoyed actual freedom by the chances of the war, at any time before the end of the rebellion, shall be forever free; but all owners of such, who shall not have been disloyal, shall be compensated for them, at the same rates as is provided for States adopting abolishment of slavery, but in such way, that no slave shall be twice accounted for.

"Article ——.

"Congress may appropriate money, and otherwise provide, for colonizing free colored persons, with their own consent, at any place or places without the United States."

I beg indulgence to discuss these proposed articles at some length. Without slavery the rebellion could never have existed; without slavery it could not continue.

Among the friends of the Union there is great diversity, of sentiment, and of policy, in regard to slavery, and the African race amongst us. Some would perpetuate slavery; some would abolish it suddenly, and without compensation; some would abolish it gradually, and with compensation; some would remove the freed people from us, and some would retain them with us; and there are yet other minor diversities. Because of these diversities, we waste much strength in struggles among ourselves. By mutual concession we should harmonize, and act together. This would be compromise; but it would be compromise among the friends, and not with the enemies of the Union. These articles are intended to embody a plan of such mutual concessions. If the plan shall be adopted, it is assumed that emancipation will follow, at least, in several of the States.

As to the first article, the main points are: first, the emancipation; secondly, the length of time for consummating it—thirty-seven years; and thirdly, the compensation.

The emancipation will be unsatisfactory to the advocates of perpetual slavery; but the length of time should greatly mitigate their dissatisfaction. The time spares both races from the evils of sudden derangement—in fact, from the necessity of any derangement—while most of those whose habitual course of thought will be disturbed by the measure will have passed away before its consummation. They will never see it. Another class will hail the prospect of emancipation, but will deprecate the length of time. They will feel that it gives too little to the now living slaves. But it really gives them much. It saves them from the vagrant destitution which must largely attend immediate emancipation in localities where their numbers are very great; and it gives the inspiring assurance that their posterity shall be free forever. The plan leaves to each State, choosing to act under it, to abolish slavery now, or at the end of the century, or at any intermediate time, or by degrees, extending over the whole or any part of the period; and it obliges no two states to proceed alike. It also provides for compensation, and generally the mode of making it. This, it would seem, must further mitigate the dissatisfaction of those who favor perpetual slavery, and especially of those who are to receive the compensation. Doubtless some of those who are to pay, and not to receive will object. Yet the measure is both just and economical. In a certain sense the liberation of slaves is the destruction of property—property acquired by descent, or by purchase, the same as any other property. It is no less true for having been often said, that the people of the south are not more responsible for the original introduction of this property, than are the people of the north; and when it is remembered how unhesitatingly we all use cotton and sugar, and share the profits of dealing in them, it may not be quite safe to say, that the south has been more responsible than the north for its continuance. If then, for a common object, this property is to be sacrificed is it not just that it be done at a common charge?

And if, with less money, or money more easily paid, we can preserve the benefits of the Union by this means, than we can by the war alone, is it not also economical to do it? Let us consider it then. Let us ascertain the sum we have expended in the war since compensated emancipation was proposed last March, and consider whether, if that measure had been promptly accepted, by even some of the slave States, the same sum would not have done more to close the war, than has been otherwise done. If so the measure would save money, and, in that view, would be a prudent and economical measure. Certainly it is not so easy to pay *something* as it is to pay *nothing;* but it is easier to pay a *large* sum than it is to pay a larger one. And it is easier to pay any sum *when* we are able, than it is to pay it *before* we are able. The war requires large sums, and requires them at once. The aggregate sum necessary for compensated emancipation, of course, would be large. But it would require no ready cash; nor the bonds even, any faster than the emancipation progresses. This might not, and probably would not, close before the end of the thirty-seven years. At that time we shall probably have a hundred millions of people to share the burden, instead of thirty one millions, as now. And not only so, but the increase of our population may be expected to continue for a long time after that period, as rapidly as before; because our territory will not have become full. I do not state this inconsiderately. At the same ratio of increase which we have maintained, on an average, from our first national census, in 1790, until that of 1860, we should, in 1900, have a population of 103,208,415. And why may we not continue that ratio far beyond that period? Our abundant room—our broad national homestead—is our ample resource. Were our territory as limited as are the British Isles, very certainly our population could not expand as stated. Instead of receiving the foreign born, as now, we should be compelled to send part of the native born away. But such is not our condition. We have two millions nine hundred and sixty-three thousand square miles. Europe has three millions and eight hundred thousand, with a population averaging seventy-three and one-third persons to the square mile. Why may not our country, at some time, average as many? Is it less fertile? Has it more waste surface, by mountains, rivers, lakes, deserts, or other causes? Is it inferior to Europe in any natural advantage? If, then, we are, at some time, to be as populous as Europe, how soon? As to when this *may* be, we can judge by the past and the present; as to when it *will* be, if ever, depends much on whether we maintain the Union. Several of our States are already above the average of Europe—seventy three and a third to the square mile. Massachusetts has 157; Rhode Island, 133; Connecticut, 99; New York and New Jersey, each, 80; also two other great States, Pennsylvania and Ohio, are not far below, the former having 63, and the latter 59. The States already above the European average, except New York, have increased in as rapid a ratio, since passing that point, as ever before; while no one of them is equal to some other parts of our country, in natural capacity for sustaining a dense population.

Taking the nation in the aggregate, and we find its population and ratio of increase, for the several decennial periods, to be as follows:—

1790	3,929,827		
1800	5,305,937	35.02 per cent.	ratio of increase
1810	7,239,814	36.45	"
1820	9,638,131	33.13	"
1830	12,866,020	33.49	"
1840	17,069,453	32.67	"
1850	23,191,876	35.87	"
1860	31,443,790	35.58	"

This shows an average decennial increase of 34.60 per cent. in population through the seventy years from our first, to our last census yet taken. It is seen that the ratio of increase, at no one of these seven periods, is either two per cent. below, or two per cent. above, the average; thus showing how inflexible, and, consequently, how reliable, the law of increase, in our case, is. Assuming that it will continue, gives the following results:—

1870	42,323,341	1910	138,918,526
1880	56,967,216	1920	186,984,335
1890	76,677,872	1930	251,680,914
1900	103,208,415		

These figures show that our country *may* be as populous as Europe now is, at some point between 1920 and 1930—say about 1925—our territory, at seventy-three and a third persons to the square mile, being of capacity to contain 217,186,000.

And we *will* reach this, too, if we do not ourselves relinquish the chance, by the folly and evils of disunion, or by long and exhausting war springing from the only great element of national discord among us. While it cannot be foreseen exactly how much one huge example of secession, breeding lesser ones indefinitely, would retard population, civilization, and prosperity, no one can doubt that the extent of it would be very great and injurious.

The proposed emancipation would shorten the war, perpetuate peace, insure this increase of population, and proportionately the wealth of the country. With these, we should pay all the emancipation would cost, together with our other debt, easier than we should pay our other debt, without it. If we had allowed our old national debt to run at six per cent. per annum, simple interest, from the end of our revolutionary struggle until to day, without paying anything on either principal or interest, each man of us would owe less upon that debt now, than each man owed upon it then; and this because our increase of men, through the whole period, has been greater than six per cent.; has run faster than the interest upon the debt. Thus, time alone relieves a debtor nation, so long as its population increases faster than unpaid interest accumulates on its debt.

This fact would be no excuse for delaying payment of what is justly due; but it shows the great importance of time in this connexion—the great advantage of a policy by which we shall not have to pay until we number a hundred millions, what, by a different policy, we would have to pay now, when we number but thirty one millions. In a word, it shows that a dollar will be much harder to pay for the war, than will be a dollar for emancipation on the proposed plan. And then the latter will cost no blood, no precious life. It will be a saving of both.

As to the second article, I think it would be impracticable to return to bondage the class of persons therein contemplated. Some of them, doubtless, in the property sense, belong to loyal owners; and hence, provision is made in this article for compensating such.

The third article relates to the future of the freed people. It does not oblige, but merely authorizes, Congress to aid in colonizing such as may consent. This ought not to be regarded as objectionable, on the one hand, or on the other, in so much as it comes to nothing, unless by the mutual consent of the people to be deported, and the American voters, through their representatives in Congress.

I cannot make it better known than it already is, that I strongly favor colonization. And yet I wish to say there is an objection urged against free colored persons remaining in the country, which is largely imaginary, if not sometimes malicious.

It is insisted that their presence would injure, and displace white labor and white laborers. If there ever could be a proper time for mere catch arguments, that time surely is not now. In times like the present, men should utter nothing for which they would not willingly be responsible through time and in eternity. Is it true, then, that colored people can displace any more white labor, by being free, than by remaining slaves? If they stay in their old places, they jostle no white laborers; if they leave their old places, they leave them open to white laborers. Logically, there is neither more nor less of it. Emancipation, even without deportation, would probably enhance the wages of white labor, and, very surely, would not reduce them. Thus, the customary amount of labor would still have to be performed; the freed people would surely not do more than their old proportion of it, and very probably, for a time, would do less, leaving an increased part to white laborers, bringing their labor into greater demand, and, consequently, enhancing the wages of it. With deportation, even to a limited extent, enhanced wages to white labor is mathematically certain. Labor is like any other commodity in the market—increase the demand for it, and you increase the price of it. Reduce the supply of black labor, by colonizing the black laborer out of the country, and, by precisely so much, you increase the demand for, and wages of, white labor.

But it is dreaded that the freed people will swarm forth, and cover the whole land? Are they not already in the land? Will liberation make them any more numerous? Equally distributed among the whites of the whole country, and there would be but one colored to seven whites. Could the one, in any way, greatly disturb the seven? There are many communities now, having more than one free colored person, to seven whites; and this, without any apparent consciousness of evil from it. The District of Columbia, and the States of Maryland and Delaware, are all in this condition. The District has more than one free colored to six whites; and yet, in its frequent petitions to Congress, I believe it has never presented the presence of free colored persons as one of its grievances. But why should emancipation south, send the free people north? People, of any color, seldom run, unless there be something to run from. *Heretofore* colored people, to some extent, have fled north from bondage; and *now*, perhaps, from both bondage and destitution. But if gradual emancipation and deportation be adopted, they will have neither to flee from. Their old masters will give them wages at least until new laborers can be procured; and the freed men, in turn, will gladly give their labor for the wages, till new homes can be found for them, in congenial climes, and with people of their own blood and race. This proposition can be trusted on the mutual interests involved. And, in any event, cannot the north decide for itself, whether to receive them?

Again, as practice proves more than theory, in any case, has there been any irruption of colored people northward, because of the abolishment of slavery in this District last spring?

What I have said of the proportion of free colored persons to the whites, in the District, is from the census of 1860, having no reference to persons called contrabands, nor to those made free by the act of Congress abolishing slavery here.

The plan consisting of these articles is recommended, not but that a restoration of the national authority would be accepted without its adoption.

Nor will the war, nor proceedings under the proclamation of September 22, 1862, be stayed because of the *recommendation* of this plan. Its timely *adoption*, I doubt not, would bring restoration and thereby stay both.

And, notwithstanding this plan, the recommendation that Congress provide by law for compensating any State which may adopt emancipation, before this plan shall have been acted upon, is hereby earnestly renewed. Such would be only an advance part of the plan, and the same arguments apply to both.

This plan is recommended as a means, not in exclusion of, but additional to, all others for restoring and preserving the national authority throughout the Union. The subject is presented exclusively in its economical aspect. The plan would, I am confident, secure peace more speedily, and maintain it more permanently, than can be done by force alone; while all it would cost, considering amounts, and manner of payment, and times of payment, would be easier paid than will be the additional cost of the war, if we rely solely upon force. It is much—very much—that it would cost no blood at all.

The plan is proposed as permanent constitutional law. It cannot become such without the concurrence of, first, two-thirds of Congress, and, afterwards, three-fourths of the States. The requisite three-fourths of the States will necessarily include seven of the Slave states. Their concurrence, if obtained, will give assurance of their severally adopting emancipation, at no very distant day, upon the new constitutional terms. This assurance would end the struggle now, and save the Union forever.

I do not forget the gravity which should characterize a paper addressed to the Congress of the nation by the Chief Magistrate of the nation. Nor do I forget that some of you are my seniors, nor that many of you have more experience than I, in the conduct of public affairs. Yet I trust that in view of the great responsibility resting upon me, you will perceive no want of respect to yourselves, in any undue earnestness I may seem to display.

Is it doubted, then, that the plan I propose, if adopted, would shorten the war, and thus lessen its expenditure of money and of blood? Is it doubted that it would restore the national authority and national prosperity, and perpetuate both indefinitely? Is it doubted that we here—Congress and Executive—can secure its adoption? Will not the good people respond to a united, and earnest appeal from us? Can we, can they, by any other means, so certainly, or so speedily, assure these vital objects? We can succeed only by concert. It is not "can *any* of us *imagine* better?" but "can we *all* do better?" Object whatsoever is possible, still the question recurs "can we do better?" The dogmas of the quiet past, are inadequate to the stormy present. The occasion is piled high with difficulty, and we must rise with the occasion. As our case is new, so we must think anew, and act anew. We must disenthrall our selves, and then we shall save our country.

Fellow-citizens, *we* cannot escape history. We of this Congress and this administration, will be remembered in spite of ourselves. No personal significance, or insignificance, can spare one or another of us. The fiery trial through which we pass, will light us down, in honor or dishonor, to the latest generation. We *say* we are for the Union. The world will not forget that we say this. We know how to save the Union. The world knows we do know how to save it. We—even *we here*—hold the power, and bear the responsibility. In *giving* freedom to the *slave*, we *assure* freedom to the *free*—honorable alike in what we give, and what we preserve. We shall nobly save, or meanly lose, the last best, hope of earth. Other means may succeed; this could not fail. The way is plain, peaceful, generous, just—a way which, if followed, the world will forever applaud, and God must forever bless.

December 1, 1862. ABRAHAM LINCOLN

To Joseph Holt[1]

Executive Mansion, Washington,

Judge Advocate General Dec. 1. 1862.

Sir: Three hundred Indians have been sentenced to death in Minnesota by a Military Commission, and execution only awaits my action. I wish your legal opinion whether if I should conclude to execute only a part of them, I must myself designate which, or could I leave the designation to some officer on the ground? Yours very truly   A. LINCOLN

1 ALS-P, ISLA. See Lincoln's communication to John Pope, November 10, *supra.* Joseph Holt, who had been appointed judge advocate general as of September 3, 1862, replied to Lincoln's letter on December 1:

"I do not understand the precise form in which the question, referred to in your note of this morning, presents itself. If it be on an application to pardon the indians condemned, or a part of them, I am quite sure that the power cannot be delegated, and that the designation of the individuals, which its exercise involves, must necessarily be made by yourself. The designation of those upon whom the sentence is to be executed, is but the exercise of the same power, being merely an approval of the sentences and a refusal to pardon. I am not aware of any instance in which the delegation of this delicate and responsible trust, has been attempted.

"In view of the large amount of human life involved in these proceedings, would it not be well—if this step has not already been taken—to submit them to the Attorney General for the purpose of more satisfactorily determining the question of their regularity?" (DLC-RTL).

See further Lincoln letter to Henry H. Sibley, December 6, *infra.*

To Edwin M. Stanton[1]

December 2, 1862

Ordered that all officers of the peculiar military force organized in Missouri by Governor Gamble[2] . . . may be, by said Governor, in his discretion, removed from office; and he may accept resignations tendered by them, or any of them, he notifying this Department in each case, wherein his action in such cases will be confirmed.

1 Parke-Bernet Catalog 841, February 25, 1947, No. 168. According to the catalog description this item is a one-page autograph letter signed. On December 28, AGO *Special Orders No. 417* transmitted Lincoln's order substantially as given in our source.

2 The ellipsis is in the source. A parenthetical exception which appears in *Special Orders No. 417* may substantially represent the omitted text as follows: "(except the major-general, in regard to whom special provision is already made)." (OR, III, II, 955).

To Edwin M. Stanton[1]

December 2, 1862.

On authority of this report I direct that Capt. Benjamin P. Walker be restored if practicable without detriment by the dismissal.   A. LINCOLN.

1 OR, II, V, 5. Lincoln's endorsement is on a letter from Joseph Holt, December 1, 1862, stating that "could the testimony now on file be submitted to the consideration of a court-martial I believe that Captain Walker would be unhesitatingly acquitted of all the charges made against him, and so believing I cannot but

recommend his restoration to the service." A second endorsement by Stanton ordered Walker's restoration. Captain Benjamin P. Walker, assistant commissary of subsistence at Camp Chase, Ohio, had been dismissed by AGO *General Orders No. 136,* September 22, 1862, for "habitual absence from his post and wilful neglect of duty."

To the Senate and House of Representatives[1]

December 3, 1862

To the Senate and House of Representatives.

On the third of November, 1861, a collision took place off the coast of Cuba between the United States War Steamer 'San Jacinto' and the French Brig 'Jules et Marie,' resulting in serious damage to the latter. The obligation of this government to make amends therefor, could not be questioned if the injury resulted from any fault on the part of the 'San Jacinto.' With a view to ascertain this, the subject was referred to a Commission of the United States and French naval officers at New York, with a naval officer of Italy as an arbiter. The conclusion arrived at was, that the collision was occasioned by the failure of the 'San Jacinto' seasonably to reverse her engine. It then became necessary to ascertain the amount of indemnification due to the injured party. The United States Consul General at Havana was consequently instructed to confer with the Consul of France on this point, and they have determined that the sum of nine thousand five hundred dollars is an equitable allowance under the circumstances.

I recommend an appropriation of this sum for the benefit of the owners of the 'Jules et Marie.'

A copy of the letter of Mr. Shufeldt, the Consul General of the United States at Havana, to the Secretary of State on the subject is herewith transmitted.   ABRAHAM LINCOLN

Washington—December 3, 1862.

1 DS, DNA RG 46, Senate 37A F2; DS, DNA RG 233, House Executive Document No. 4. Robert W. Shufeldt's letter to Secretary Seward, November 14, 1862, recommended settlement as proposed by Lincoln. An act approved December 15, 1862, awarded $9,500 to the owners of the *Jules et Marie.*

To Edwin M. Stanton[1]

Hon. Sec. of War   Executive Mansion,
My dear Sir,   Washington, Dec. 3. 1862.

I wish Edmund Gifford of Ills. appointed an Additional Paymaster at once. I am under some obligation to Col. Farnsworth[2] in this matter. Yours truly   A. LINCOLN

1 ALS, IHi. Edmund Gifford, attorney of Elgin, Illinois, was appointed additional paymaster of Volunteers on February 19, 1863.
2 Colonel John F. Farnsworth of the Eighth Illinois Cavalry.

To Edwin M. Stanton[1]

I personally know the writer of this to be a good man.

Dec. 4. 1862   A. LINCOLN

1 AES, IHi. Lincoln's endorsement appears on a letter of John W. True to William P. Dole, Union City, Tennessee, November 25, 1862: "I am & have been for the past year Adjutant of the 54th Regt Ill Vol. being in turn at Cairo Ill Columbus Ky & for the past five months guarding the Mobile & O. RR. and am tired of this country, around Union City, besides (I tell you in confidence) that I do not admire some of our Field officers.
"I would like to get a paymasters place. . . ." See further, Lincoln to Stanton, February 9, 1863, infra.

To Salmon P. Chase[1]

Hon. Sec. of the Treasury   Executive Mansion,
My dear Sir   Washington, Dec. 5. 1862.

With my understanding of the present condition of Missouri, and especially that part of it, North of the Missouri River, I think the attached resolutions are reasonable. Have you any thing to do with it, or does it belong exclusively to the Secretary of War? Please answer me, returning this note & resolution[s] to me. Yours truly   A. LINCOLN

1 ALS, DLC-RTL. The "attached resolutions" are in the form of a clipping from the Quincy, Illinois, Whig Republican of November 22, 1862, protesting against and asking repeal of regulations restraining trade with Northern Missouri. Chase's reply of December 7, 1862, pointed out that the restrictions were "those of general application . . . concerning Internal and Coastwise Commercial Intercourse . . . under Acts of Congress approved July 13, 1861, and May 20, 1862," for the purpose of preventing articles of commerce from passing into areas in a state of insurrection. "I am not aware, that there has ever been . . . any local regulation which would affect the business interests of Quincy more injuriously in any respect than those of her sister cities located on the Ohio and Mississippi rivers. . . . I have, however, this day transmitted a copy of your letter and enclosure to the Special Agent . . . in the district embracing Quincy. . . ." (DLC-RTL).

To Caleb B. Smith[1]

Hon. Sec. of Interior   Executive Mansion,
Sir: Washington, Dec. 5. 1862.

Please have the Commissioner of Indian Affairs make out and send me as complete an answer to the enclosed Resolution of the

Senate, as the means for so, doing, can be found in his Office. Yours very truly   A. LINCOLN

¹ ALS, MnHi. The resolution adopted by the Senate on December 5 requested the president to furnish "all information in his possession touching the late Indian barbarities in the State of Minnesota. . . ." See Lincoln's communication to the Senate, December 11, *infra*.

To Edwin M. Stanton¹

December 5, 1862

I would be glad for the leave of absence to be granted if it can consistently be done.

¹ Copy, DNA WR RG 107, Secretary of War, Register of Letters Received, P 5, Irregular Book 5. A copy of Lincoln's endorsement is preserved in the Register notation of his referral of a letter from Governor Richard Yates of Illinois, asking leave of absence for Colonel Alonzo W. Mack of the Seventy-sixth Illinois Volunteers, who resigned on January 7, 1863. Yates' letter with Lincoln's endorsement is missing from the file.

To Cyrus Aldrich¹

Hon. Cyrus Aldrich   Executive Mansion,
My dear Sir: Washington, Dec. 6. 1862.

In answer to your inquiries I can only say, at this distance of time, that I remember the Land-officers at Vandalia, Palestine, Danville and Dixon, in the State of Illinois, who went in under the administration of President Taylor, afterwards made a claim in connection with the location of Land-Warrants in the respective offices, which claim was disallowed by the accounting officers at Washington; that the claim, and consequently the question in all the cases was the same, and that the officers, of whom you were one, determined to test the legality of the claim in a suit against one of them, which might be brought by the government; & I think the District Attorney also agreed to it, so far as to sue one only— Daniel Clapp, of Danville & Judge Logan and myself were engaged to defend; and while I, do not now remember the exact question, I do remember that I *expected the defence would succeed, and I am sure there was nothing in the claim, to cast any imputation upon the parties making it.* My recollection is that the defendants or rather, *the single defendant,* constantly sought to bring the suit to trial, *that the District Attorney was never ready,* and that the case lingered many years, and, as I think *was still on the docket when I came on here.* Yours very truly   A. LINCOLN

1 ALS, owned by Mrs. B. E. Buckmaster, Tacoma, Washington. Representative Cyrus Aldrich of Minneapolis, Minnesota, had been receiver of the Land Office at Dixon, Illinois, in 1851, and had moved to Minnesota in 1854. No letters from Aldrich have been located which deal with the matter alluded to in Lincoln's letter.

To Henry H. Sibley[1]

Brigadier General H. H. Sibley
St. Paul
Minnesota.

Executive Mansion,
Washington,
December 6th. 1862.

Ordered that of the Indians and Half-breeds sentenced to be hanged by the Military Commission, composed of Colonel Crooks, Lt. Colonel Marshall, Captain Grant, Captain Bailey, and Lieutenant Olin,[2] and lately sitting in Minnesota, you cause to be executed on Friday the nineteenth day of December, instant, the following named, towit

"Te-he-hdo-ne-cha."	No. 2. by the record.
"Tazoo" alias "Plan-doo-ta."	No. 4. by the record.
"Wy-a-tah-to-wah"	No. 5 by the record.
"Hin-han-shoon-ko-yag."	No. 6 by the record
"Muz-za-bom-a-du."	No. 10. by the record.
"Wah-pay-du-ta."	No. 11. by the record
"Wa-he-hud."	No. 12. by the record
"Sna-ma-ni."	No. 14. by the record.
"Ta-te-mi-na."	No. 15. by the record.
"Rda-in-yan-kna."	No. 19. by the record.
"Do-wan-sa."	No. 22. by the record.
"Ha-pan."	No. 24. by the record.
"Shoon-ka-ska." (White Dog).	No. 35. by the record.
"Toon-kan-e-chah-tay-mane."	No. 67. by the record.
"E-tay-hoo-tay."	No. 68. by the record.
"Am-da-cha."	No. 69. by the record.
"Hay-pee-don—or, Wamne-omne-ho-ta."	No. 70. by the record.
"Mahpe-o-ke-na-ji."	No. 96. by the record.
"Henry Milord"—a Half-breed.	No. 115. by the record.
"Chaskay-don"—or Chaskay-etay."	No. 121. by the record.
"Baptiste Campbell" a Half-breed.	No. 138. by the record.
"Tah-ta-kay-gay."	No. 155. by the record.
"Ha-pink-pa."	No. 170 by the record.

"Hypolite Ange" a Half-breed.   No. 175 by the record.
"Na-pay-Shue."   No. 178. by the record.
"Wa-kan-tan-ka."   No. 210. by the record.
"Toon-kan-ka-yag-e-na-jin."   No. 225. by the record.
"Ma-kat-e-na-jin."   No. 254. by the record
"Pa-zee-koo-tay-ma-ne."   No. 264. by the record.
"Ta-tay-hde-don."   No. 279. by the record.
"Wa-She-choon," or "Toon-
kan-shkan-shkan-mene-hay."   No. 318. by the record.
"A-e-cha-ga."   No. 327. by the record.
"Ha-tan-in-koo."   No. 333. by the record.
"Chay-ton-hoon-ka."   No. 342. by the record.
"Chan-ka-hda."   No. 359. by the record.
"Hda-hin-hday."   No. 373. by the record.
"O-ya-tay-a-koo."   No. 377. by the record.
"May-hoo-way-wa."   No. 382. by the record.
"Wa-kin-yan-na."   No. 383 by the record

The other condemned prisoners you will hold subject to further orders, taking care that they neither escape, nor are subjected to any unlawful violence.   ABRAHAM LINCOLN,
President of the United States.

[1] ALS, MnHi. First governor of Minnesota, Henry H. Sibley had been appointed brigadier general on September 29 and placed in command of the District of Minnesota on November 23, 1862. For his reply to this letter see the note to Lincoln's telegram to Sibley, December 16, *infra.*
[2] Members of the commission were: Colonel William Crooks of the Sixth Minnesota Volunteers, Lieutenant Colonel William R. Marshall of the Seventh Minnesota Volunteers, Captain Hiram P. Grant and Captain Hiram S. Bailey of the Sixth Minnesota, and Captain Rollin C. Olin, assistant adjutant general on Sibley's staff.

To Edwin M. Stanton[1]

Hon. Sec. of War.   Executive Mansion,
Sir: Washington, Dec. 6. 1862.
This morning Senator Henderson Hon. T. L. Price of Mo both of Missouri, call and ask that Rufus K. Sanders be appointed an Additional Paymaster. It is believed that papers in his favor are already on file. I would like for these gentlemen to be obliged so soon as it can consistently be done. Yours truly

A. LINCOLN

[1] ALS, Herman Blum, Blumhaven Library, Philadelphia. There is no record of the appointment of Rufus K. Sanders as recommended by Senator John B. Henderson and Representative Thomas L. Price.

To B. Gratz Brown[1]

Hon. B. Gratz Brown　　　　　　　　Executive Mansion,
St. Louis Mo.　　　　　　　　Washington, Dec. 7, 1862.

Yours of the 3rd. received yesterday. Have already done what
I can in the premises.　　　　　　　　　A. LINCOLN.

[1] ALS, RPB. Brigadier General Benjamin Gratz Brown, editor of the *Missouri
Democrat* who was elected to the U.S. Senate in 1863, wrote Lincoln on December 3, 1862, "Hearing incidentally that you have under consideration the subject of ordering an Election for Congress in Arkansas, or such districts as are
held by our troops I would . . . call your attention to the fact that on the South
west our advance post is and has for some time been at Elkhorn. Genl [James G.]
Blunt is some 60 miles from the state line and intends holding his position. With
him are considerable numbers of loyal Arkansas citizens. . . . With an Election
ordered we can by legal voting send to Congress a Union administration Emancipation member of Congress. . . . It seems to me that under this state of things,
it would be unwise in the government, if it has embarked upon the policy of
ordering Elections held in the rebel territories occupied by our armies, to loose
this opportunity to secure a support from the state of Arkansas while it can when
it can be done legally and without opposition. . . ." (DLC-RTL).

To Charles P. Kirkland[1]

Charles P. Kirkland, Esq　　　　　　　Executive Mansion,
New-York.　　　　　　　　Washington, Dec. 7, 1862.

I have just received, and hastily read your published letter to
the Hon. Benjamin R. Curtis. Under the circumstances I may not
be the most competent judge, but it appears to me to be a paper of
great ability, and for the country's sake, more than my own, I
thank you for it. Yours very truly　　　　　　　A. LINCOLN

[1] ALS, IHi. This letter is misdated December 7, 1863 in Tarbell (Appendix), p.
403, and in Nicolay and Hay, IX, 217. On December 5, 1862, Kirkland mailed
the president a copy of his pamphlet *A Letter to the Hon. Benjamin P. Curtis.*
. . . (New York, Latimer Brothers and Seymour, 1862) with a note expressing
his hope that "the President may find a moment's leisure, amid his pressing
duties, to read Mr. K's paper . . . . in answer to the pamphlet of Judge Curtis
(late of the U.S. Sup. Ct) charging the President with 'usurpation,' exercise of
'arbitrary powers' in the proclamation of Sept. 22d & Sept. 24th." (DLC-RTL).
Judge Curtis' pamphlet *Executive Power* was published by Little, Brown and
Company, Boston, 1862.

To Henry J. Raymond[1]

Hon. H. J. Raymond　　　　　　　　Executive Mansion,
Times Office　　　　　　　　Washington,
New-York.　　　　　　　　Dec. 7, 1862.

Yours of Nov. 25. reached me only yesterday. Thank you for it.
I shall consider and remember your suggestions.

　　　　　　　　　　　　A. LINCOLN

¹ ALS, RPB. On November 25, 1862, Raymond wrote Lincoln as follows:
"I beg permission 'just once' to intrude upon your time . . . in order to make a suggestion concerning the best *mode* of carrying into practical effect the policy of your Proclamation.

"1. I think it clear that any attempt to make this war *subservient to* the sweeping abolition of Slavery, will revolt the Border States, divide the North and West, invigorate and make triumphant the opposition party, and thus defeat *itself* as well as destroy the Union.

"2. I think it equally clear that an effort to use emancipation, within the limitations of law, against rebels as a *military weapon* purely & exclusively, will be sustained by the whole loyal country, Border States and all.

"3. I suggest, then, that the Proclamation to be issued in January, *take the form of a* MILITARY ORDER,—commanding the Generals of the Army, within every designated state and part of a state in rebellion, *to deprive the rebel forces of the aid direct & indirect derived from their slaves, by setting them free and protecting them in their freedom.*

". . . The only drawback I can think of is, that such a mode of reaching a result will not suit those who deem the *mode* of more importance than the result itself." (DLC-RTL).

To John A. Dahlgren¹

Will Capt. Dahlgren please call and see me at once?

Dec. 8. 1862.   A. LINCOLN

¹ ALS, THaroL.

To Henry W. Halleck¹

Executive Mansion, Washington,

Maj Genl. Halleck.   Dec 8th. 1862.

I find on maps here that Huntsville [Hartsville, Tennessee] is on the North bank of Cumberland river, sixteen miles directly east of Gallatin, and apparently on a turnpike road leading towards East Tennessee generally. What on earth an isolated Brigade was doing there I can not concieve

The road is not a line between any two places in our possession.

Yours truly,   A. LINCOLN.

¹ Copy, DNA WR RG 108, HQA, Letters Received, L 1243. On December 9, 1862, Halleck directed Rosecrans to "immediately report why an isolated brigade was at Hartsville, and by whose command; and also by whose fault it was surprised and captured." (OR, I, XX, I, 42). Rosecrans replied at 11 P.M. on December 9:

"In reply to your telegram, inquiring why the brigade was stationed at Hartsville, I respectfully state that it was necessary to cover the crossing of the Cumberland River against rebel cavalry, who would essay to attack our road and capture our trains. We have, for all our immense line of front communications, picket, and couriers, less than 4,000 cavalry, and the enemy not less than 10,000, who are much relieved by guerrilla scouts, and can concentrate for mischief with almost perfect secrecy and impunity. The subjoined copy of General Thomas' report shows that it was a pretty full brigade, posted strongly, with a cavalry regiment for picket duty on the north side of the river, in a commanding position; that it was strongly supported within 9 miles, and, but for being surprised and making feeble resistance, it would have been succored, and the enemy badly whipped. That outpost was stronger and better supported than our outpost at Rienzi, 7 miles below Corinth, last summer. The difference was in the superiority and number of rebel cavalry:

" 'Hartsville was garrisoned by the Thirty-ninth Brigade, Twelfth Division (Dumont's), for duty, and was commanded by Col. A. B. Moore, One hundred and fourth Illinois. There was also a regiment of cavalry posted there, the Second Indiana, sent there by your order. The effective force not known. The troops were posted so as to guard the ford and the approaches from the direction of Lebanon, and the cavalry for picket duty and scouting. Col. J. M. Harlan, Second Brigade, First Division, was posted at Castalian Springs. This brigade reports 2,725 men present for duty. Colonel [Abram O.] Miller, commanding the Fortieth Brigade, was also posted at Castalian Springs, sent there to relieve Colonel Harlan. This brigade reports 2,274 men present for duty. The last two brigades were nine miles distant from Hartsville when the attack was made. As soon as cannonading was heard, Colonel Harlan ordered Colonel Miller to march with his command in the direction of Hartsville, and, with a portion of his brigade, followed Colonel Miller, and orders were given to the cavalry from these headquarters to be vigilant and scour the country, so that no enemy could approach without giving timely notice to the garrison. Colonel Harlan, upon being relieved by Colonel [Joseph R.] Scott at Hartsville, informed me that the position was strong and defensible; added to the information received from my officers, led to the belief that the officer in command allowed himself to be surprised, which resulted in the capture of nearly his whole force. The attack was sudden, and so quickly decided that it was impossible to reach Hartsville in time to take part in the action, and the enemy have been defeated and probably cut off before crossing the river.' " (*Ibid.*, p. 43).

On February 13, 1863, Halleck recommended that Colonel Absalom B. Moore be dismissed for neglect of duty. Moore was not dismissed, however, but resigned on account of disability, his resignation taking effect on September 9, 1863, (*ibid.*, p. 45, note). See also Lincoln to Stanton, December 26, *infra*.

To Andrew Johnson[1]

Gov. Andrew Johnson   Executive Mansion,
Nashville, Tennessee–   Washington, Dec. 8. 1862.

Jesse H. Strickland is here asking authority to raise a Regiment of Tennesseans.

Would you advise that the authority be given him?

A. LINCOLN

[1] ALS, RPB. Governor Johnson telegraphed his reply at 1:30 P.M., "I know strickland well   unless he is greatly improved he is no manner (of) account there are more persons here desiring to raise regiments who are known to the People than it is prudent to authorize at this Time. If strickland is in the service let him stay where he is. . . ." (DLC-RTL). Jesse H. Strickland recruited and became Colonel of the Fifth East Tennessee Cavalry and later of the Eighth Tennessee Cavalry. Scattered references in the *Official Records* suggest that his recruiting was irregular, if not unauthorized.

To the Senate and House of Representatives[1]

December 8, 1862

To the Senate and House of Representatives:

In conformity to the Law of 16 July 1862, I most cordially recommend that Commander John L. Worden, U.S. Navy, receive a vote of thanks of Congress for the eminent skill and gallantry, exhibited by him in the late remarkable battle between the U.S. Iron clad steamer Monitor, under his command, and the Rebel Iron clad Steamer Merrimack, in March last.

The thanks of Congress for his services on the occasion referred to, were tendered by a Resolution approved 11 July 1862, but the recommendation is now specially made in order to comply with the requirements of the 9th. Section of the Act of 16 July 1862, which is in the following words, viz:—

"That any line Officer of the Navy or Marine Corps may be advanced one grade, if, upon recommendation of the President by name, he receives the thanks of Congress for highly distinguished conduct in conflict with the enemy, or for extraordinary heroism in the line of his profession."   ABRAHAM LINCOLN

Washington, D.C.

8 December 1862.

[1] DS, DNA RG 46, Senate, 37A F2; DS, DNA RG 233, House Executive Document, No. 8. The resolution of thanks to Commander John L. Worden was approved February 3, 1863.

To Henry W. Halleck[1]

Gen. Halleck please examine the within, with reference to appointing a Brig Genl.   A. LINCOLN

Dec. 9, 1862

[1] AES IHI. This endorsement has been clipped from accompanying papers.

To the Senate[1]

To, The Senate of the United States.   December 9, 1862

In compliance with the Resolution of the Senate of the United States of the 13th of March last, requesting a copy of the correspondence relative to the attempted seizure of Mr. Fauchet, by the Commander of the "Africa," within the waters of the United States, I transmit a report from the Secretary of State, and the documents by which it was accompanied.

Washington, December, 9th, 1862.   ABRAHAM LINCOLN

[1] DS, DNA RG 46, Senate 37A F3. Secretary Seward's report to Lincoln, December 9, 1862, included a lengthy correspondence concerning the attempt to

seize Joseph Fauchet, minister from France, on August 1, 1795, on board the American packet ship *Peggy* bound from New York to Newport, Rhode Island. The report is printed in full in Thirty-seventh Congress, Third Session, *Senate Executive Document No. 4.*

To Samuel R. Curtis[1]

Major General Curtis   Executive Mansion, Washington,
St. Louis, Mo.   Dec. 10, 1862. [10:25 A.M.]

Please suspend, until further order, all proceedings on the order made by Gen. Schofield on the 28th. day of August last, for assessing and collecting from Secessionists and Southern sympathizers the sum of Five hundred thousand dollars &c and, in the meantime make out and send me a statement of facts pertinent to the question, together with your opinion upon it.   A. LINCOLN

[1] ADfS, DLC-RTL; LS, RPB. Major General Curtis, who had been placed in command of the Department of the Missouri on September 19, 1862, telegraphed a brief acknowledgment at 12:30 P.M., "Dispatch rec'd. Proceedings suspended." (DLC-RTL). On December 12 he replied at length as follows:

"Your telegraphic dispatch of the 10th inst. suspending proceedings in the order made by General Schofield for collecting half a million from Secessionists and southern sympathizers, . . . was duly received, and proceedings immediately suspended. . . . I had supposed and so held, that Gen. Schofield issued the order in his capacity of Brigadier General of Enrolled Missouri Militia, and I only stood ready to support the State in the execution of her affairs. But the Governor and Genl. Schofield send me papers . . . which try to place the United States in the front rank. Before taking that place myself, I had referred the matters to my Commanding General, presenting some legal doubts such as these:—

"1st. The words defining the persons to be assessed . . . are too indefinite.

"2d. . . . . Is it competent for the United States to make assessments for State purposes, and if we do it for one State, will we not open a wide door. . . .

"3d. If there was a *military necessity* . . . which would justify an assessment, as a *military* duty, I cannot say it now exists. . . .

"4th. If it is a *tax*, it conflicts with the Constitution of the United States. . . .

"5th. It conflicts with the direct tax prescribed by the revenue laws of Congress. . . .

"6th. It conflicts with the Confiscation act . . . by taking for State purposes, that which should be confiscated for the United States.

"In my judgement, some of these objections are insurmountable. Besides, I consider the sum exorbitant for one County. . . .

"To 'suspend' is better than to relinquish or annul, as it acts as a restraint on disloyal persons who fear its execution. Let the matter rest till the rebels all come in and swear their fidelity to our cause. . . ." (DLC-RTL).

To Jesse K. Dubois[1]

Hon. J. K. Dubois   Executive Mansion,
My dear Sir   Washington, Dec. 10. 1862.

In the summer of 1859 when Mr. Freeman visited Springfield, Illinois, in relation to the McCallister & Stebbins bonds I promised him that, upon certain conditions, I would ask the members of the

Legislature to give him a full and fair hearing of his case. I do not now remember, nor have I time to recall exactly what the conditions were, nor whether they were completely performed; but there can be, in no case, any harm his having a full and fair hearing, and I sincerely wish it may be given him. Yours truly

A. LINCOLN

[1] ALS, ICHi. "Mr. Freeman" has not been identified.

To the House of Representatives[1]

To the House of Representatives: December 10, 1862

In answer to the resolution of the House of Representatives of the 17th of July last, requesting the communication of correspondence relating to the arrest of a part of the crew of the brig Sumter, at Tangier, Morocco, I herewith transmit a report from the Secretary of State.   ABRAHAM LINCOLN.

Washington, December 10, 1862

[1] Thirty-seventh Congress, Third Session, *House of Representatives Executive Document No. 10.* Seward's report of December 10 transmitted by Lincoln, called attention to the fact that the correspondence requested "will be found . . . among the documents from the Department of State communicated to Congress with the President's message at the opening of the present session." Henry Myers of Georgia, an ex-paymaster in the Navy and acting as lieutenant on the *Sumter,* and Thomas T. Tunstall of Alabama, ex-consul at Cadiz, landed at Tangier from the French vessel *Ville de Malaga.* On their way to Cadiz to buy coal they were arrested, February 19, 1862, by James DeLong, U.S. consul at Tangier, and shipped back to the U.S. to be confined at Fort Warren.

Memorandum:
Appointment of Thomas M. Wilmot[1]

Executive Mansion, Washington, Dec. 10, 1862.

To-day Hon. David Wilmot calls and asks that his son Thomas M. Wilmot be appointed a cadet at West-Point. Will be, 18. years of age Aug. 4, 1863. Not particular whether appointed this year or next. I wish to appoint him before I leave here.

A. LINCOLN

[1] ADS, DNA WR RG 94, U.S. Military Academy, 1864, No. 460, Box 83. There is no record of the appointment.

To the Senate and House of Representatives[1]

December 10, 1862

To the Senate and House of Representatives:

In conformity to the Law of 16 July 1862, I most cordially recommend that Lieutenant Commander George U. Morris, U.S.

Navy, receive a vote of thanks of Congress, for the determined valor and heroism displayed in his defence of the U.S. Sloop of War Cumberland, temporarily under his command, in the Naval engagement at Hampton Roads, on the 8 March 1862, with the Rebel iron-clad Steam Frigate Merrimack.

Washington, D.C.   ABRAHAM LINCOLN
10 December 1862.

1 DS, DNA RG 46, Senate 37A F2; DS, DNA RG 233, House Executive Document No. 9. The resolution of thanks to Lieutenant Commander George U. Morris passed the House on December 19, 1862, but failed to pass in the Senate.

To the Senate[1]

To the Senate of the United States   December 11, 1862
I transmit to the Senate for its consideration with a view to ratification, a Treaty between the United States and the Republic of Liberia, signed at London by the Plenipotentiaries of the parties, on the twenty-first of October, last.   ABRAHAM LINCOLN
Washington,
11th. December, 1862.

1 DS, DNA RG 46, Senate 37B B9. The Senate ratified the treaty on January 9, 1863.

To the Senate[1]

To the Senate of the United States: December 11, 1862
In compliance with your resolution of December 5th, 1862, requesting the President "to furnish the Senate with all information in his possession touching the late Indian barbarities in the State of Minnesota, and also the evidence in his possession upon which some of the principal actors and head men were tried and condemned to death," I have the honor to state, that on receipt of said resolution I transmitted the same to the Secretary of the Interior, accompanied by a note, a copy of which is herewith inclosed, marked "A.," and in response to which I received, through that Department, a letter of the Commissioner of Indian Affairs, a copy of which is herewith inclosed, marked "B."
I further state, that on the 8th. day of November last I received a long telegraphic dispatch from Major General Pope, at St. Paul, Minnesota, simply announcing the names of the persons sentenced

to be hanged. I immediately telegraphed to have transcripts of the records in all the cases forwarded to me, which transcripts, however, did not reach me until two or three days before the present meeting of Congress. Meantime I received, through telegraphic dispatches and otherwise, appeals in behalf of the condemned, appeals for their execution, and expressions of opinion as to proper policy in regard to them, and to the Indians generally in that vicinity, none of which, as I understand, falls within the scope of your inquiry. After the arrival of the transcripts of records, but before I had sufficient opportunity to examine them, I received a joint letter from one of the Senators and two of the Representatives from Minnesota, which contains some statements of fact not found in the records of the trials, and for which reason I herewith transmit a copy, marked "C." I also, for the same reason, inclose a printed memorial of the citizens of St Paul, addressed to me, and forwarded with the letter aforesaid.

Anxious to not act with so much clemency as to encourage another outbreak on the one hand, nor with so much severity as to be real cruelty on the other, I caused a careful examination of the records of trials to be made, in view of first ordering the execution of such as had been proved guilty of violating females. Contrary to my expectations, only two of this class were found. I then directed a further examination, and a classification of all who were proven to have participated in *massacres*, as distinguished from participation in *battles*. This class numbered forty, and included the two convicted of female violation. One of the number is strongly recommended by the Commission which tried them, for commutation to ten years' imprisonment.[2] I have ordered the other thirty-nine to be executed on Friday, the 19th. instant. The order was dispatched from here on Monday, the 8th. instant, by a messenger to General Sibley; and a copy of which order is herewith transmitted, marked "D."

An abstract of the evidence as to the forty is herewith enclosed, marked "E."

To avoid the immense amount of copying, I lay before the Senate the original transcripts of the records of trials, as received by me.

This is as full and complete a response to the resolution as it is in my power to make. ABRAHAM LINCOLN

1 DS, DNA RG 46, Senate 37A F2. Printed as *Senate Executive Document No. 7*, this communication is accompanied by the enclosures which Lincoln names.
2 O-Ta-kla, alias Godfrey, a Negro, recommended for ten years' imprisonment on the basis of the fact that he supplied information.

To Edwin M. Stanton[1]

John Speed named within, is a son of a particular friend of mine.
Dec. 11. 1862.   A. LINCOLN

[1] AES, owned by Foreman M. Lebold, Chicago, Illinois. Lincoln's endorsement is written on a letter from Brigadier General Charles C. Gilbert, commanding the Tenth Division, Army of the Ohio, and troops on the Louisville and Nashville Railroad, December 4, 1862, asking appointment of Second Lieutenant John Speed (son of James Speed) of the Ninth Kentucky Cavalry, as a captain in the Adjutant General's Department. The appointment was made as of March 11, 1863.

To Ambrose E. Burnside[1]

Maj. Gen. Burnside.   Executive Mansion,
My dear Sir   Washington, Dec. 12, 1862.
The bearer, Mr. J. G. Nicolay, is, as you know, my private Secretary. Please treat him kindly, while I am sure he will avoid giving you trouble   Yours truly   A. LINCOLN

[1] ALS, DLC-Nicolay Papers. Nicolay found a battle impending at Fredericksburg on December 13 and later wrote to his fiancée that he "only stayed long enough to ride through two or three of the principal streets and get off and drink a cup of coffee with some of the officers who were lunching in one of the houses." (Helen Nicolay, *Lincoln's Secretary*, p. 158).

To the Senate and House of Representatives[1]

December 12, 1862

Fellow-citizens of the Senate and House of Representatives:

I have in my possession three valuable swords, formerly the property of Gen. David E. Twiggs, which I now place at the disposal of Congress. They were forwarded to me from New Orleans by Major General Benjamin F. Butler. If they, or any of them, shall be by Congress disposed of in reward or compliment of military service, I think General Butler is entitled to the first consideration. A copy of the General's letter to me, accompanying the swords, is herewith transmitted.   ABRAHAM LINCOLN
December 12, 1862.

[1] DS, DNA RG 46, Senate 37A F2; DS, DNA RG 233, House Executive Document No. 11. Butler's letter forwarding the swords—one of which had been presented to the hero of Monterey by Congress, one by the State of Georgia, and one by his native city of Augusta—is printed in *House Executive Document No. 11*. Upon fleeing from New Orleans, Twiggs presented the swords to Miss Rowena Florence, "but as she had neglected to inform her father of this singular donation,

causa fugae, and as the girl's mother caused them to be given to a negro, to be sent back to General Twiggs' house, I ventured to interfere. . . ." Butler suggested that the congressional sword be presented to "some officer as a token of appreciation of loyalty," that the State of Georgia sword be placed in the library at West Point "as a perpetual memento . . . how worse than useless are all education and military training . . . if heartfelt patriotism and undying fealty to the Constitution and the flag is wanting," and that the Augusta sword be placed in the Patent Office "as a warning against the folly and uselessness of such an invention as 'secession.' " A resolution (S. 116) introduced on January 7, 1863, disposing of the swords as Butler had suggested and following Lincoln's recommendation that Butler receive the congressional sword, was pigeonholed. Butler deposited the swords in the Treasury, and after the war they were returned to Twiggs' daughter (*Butler's Book*, p. 568 note).

To Fernando Wood[1]

Executive Mansion, Washington,
Hon. Fernando Wood   December 12, 1862.

My dear Sir Your letter of the 8th. with the accompanying note of same date, was received yesterday. The most important paragraph in the letter, as I consider, is in these words: "On the 25th. November last I was advised by an authority which I deemed likely to be well informed, as well as reliable and truthful, that the Southern States would send representatives to the next congress, provided that a full and general amnesty should permit them to do so. No guarranties or terms were asked for other than the amnesty referred to."

I strongly suspect your information will prove to be groundless; nevertheless I thank you for communicating it to me.

Understanding the phrase in the paragraph above quoted "the Southern States would send representatives to the next congress" to be substantially the same as that "the people of the Southern States would cease resistance, and would re-inaugerate, submit to, and maintain the national authority, within the limits of such states under the Constitution of the United States," I say, that in such case, the war would cease on the part of the United States; and that, if within a reasonable time "a full and general amnesty" were necessary to such end, it would not be withheld.

I do not think it would be proper now for me to communicate this, formally or informally, to the people of the Southern States. My belief is that they already know it; and when they choose, if ever, they can communicate with me unequivocally. Nor do I think it proper now to suspend military operations to try any experiment of negotiation.

I should, nevertheless, receive with great pleasure the exact information you now have, and also such other as you may in any way obtain. Such information[2] might be more valuable before the first of January than afterwards.

While there is nothing in this letter which I shall dread to see in history, it is, perhaps, better for the present, that it's existence should not become public.

I therefore have to request that you will regard it as confidential.

Your Obt. Servt   A. LINCOLN

[1] ADfS, DLC-RTL. Fernando Wood's letter of December 8, 1862, reads in part as follows:

"On the 25th November last I was advised by an authority which I deemed likely to be well informed, as well as reliable and truthful that the southern states would send representatives to the next congress, provided that a full and general amnesty should permit them to do so No guarantees or terms were asked for other than the amnesty referred to. Deeming this information of great value . . . I communicated it . . . to . . . George Opdyke . . . whom I knew to hold confidential relations to members of your administration, and proposing through him that if the government would permit the correspondence, under its own inspection I would undertake to procure something definite & positive from persons connected with the so called Confederate authorities. Mr. Opdyke in reply stated that several senators from New England . . . were then in this city . . . to whom he would at once communicate the proposition and advise me of the answer . . . supposing that they would immediately confer with you. . . .

"I now learn . . . from Mr. Opdyke this day that he failed to see these Senators. . . . Therefore the object of this letter.

"As an humble, but loyal citizen . . . I ask your immediate attention to this subject. . . . I suggest that gentlemen whose former social & political relations with the leaders of the southern revolt may be allowed to hold unofficial correspondence with them on this subject. . . . Your Inaugural address . . . pointed out with prophetic vision . . . . that after a bloody and terrible struggle 'the still small voice of reason' would intervene and settle the controversy. . . . Has not the time arrived when to quote your own language we should 'cease fighting'— at least long enough to ascertain whether the 'identical questions' about which we began the fight may not be amicably & honorably adjusted, and 'the terms of intercourse' be once more established? It is to this end that I address you. . . ." (DLC-RTL).

On December 17, Wood replied to Lincoln's letter, "Your letter of the 12th inst. was handed to me on the afternoon of the 15th inst. by Mr. Wakeman, the Postmaster of this city;—Pardon me Mr. President when I say that your reply has filled me with profound regret. It declines what I had conceived to be an innocent effort to ascertain the foundation for information in my possession of a desire in the South to return to the Union. . . . In compliance with your request, that your letter shall not for the present become public I shall withhold its publication at this time." (DLC-RTL).

[2] This paragraph was revised; Lincoln had first written: "Any information you may in your own way, obtain upon this subject, I shall be glad to receive, if you please. Any such information. . . ."

Date Due
